Oracle Press™

Oracle Enterprise Manager 101

ORACLE®

Oracle Press™

Oracle Enterprise Manager 101

Lars Bo Vanting
Dirk Schepanek

McGraw-Hill/Osborne

New York Chicago San Francisco
Lisbon London Madrid Mexico City Milan
New Delhi San Juan Seoul Singapore Sydney Toronto

McGraw-Hill/Osborne
2600 Tenth Street
Berkeley, California 94710
U.S.A.

To arrange bulk purchase discounts for sales promotions, premiums, or fund-raisers, please contact **McGraw-Hill**/Osborne at the above address. For information on translations or book distributors outside the U.S.A., please see the International Contact Information page immediately following the index of this book.

Oracle Enterprise Manager 101

1234567890 CUS CUS 0198765432

ISBN 0-07-222307-3

Publisher
Brandon A. Nordin

Vice President & Associate Publisher
Scott Rogers

Acquisitions Editor
Jeremy Judson

Project Editor
Julie M. Smith

Acquisitions Coordinator
Athena Honore

Technical Editor
Robert McCormick

Copy Editor
Brian MacDonald

Proofreader
Susie Elkind

Indexer
Jack Lewis

Computer Designers
Tabitha M. Cagan, Lucie Ericksen, Elizabeth Jang

Illustrators
Michael Mueller, Lyssa Wald

Series Design
Jani Beckwith

This book was composed with Corel VENTURA™ Publisher.

To my wife Barbara, patiently walking the path with me while walking her own, her brothers' families and mom, who also became part of my family, especially 94 year old grandma, who enjoys living with us, and to my daughter Rebecca, more than 90 years younger, who is holding the future in her hands

Dirk Schepanek

To my wife and children for their love and for being a great family
To my parents for providing me a good childhood and youth, and for supporting me in my different choices throughout my life

Lars Bo Vanting

About the Authors

Dirk Schepanek

Dirk Schepanek works in Product Management of Enterprise Manager at Oracle Corporation. His academic qualifications include masters of mechanical engineering and industrial engineering. Besides system management and administration, his career spans various roles including sales consulting, project management and technical marketing. In his job at Oracle he is working on numerous global projects around Oracle Enterprise Manager and is a frequent speaker on international tradeshows. Dirk can be contacted at Dirk.Schepanek@gmx.net.

Lars Bo Vanting

Lars Bo Vanting has been working with database related issues since 1989 and has worked with Oracle RDBMS and PL/SQL development since 1992 including Oracle versions 6 to 9i. He has successfully implemented Oracle Enterprise Manager at a larger customer having 150+ monitored target nodes, which completely is relying on EM for administering and monitoring purposes. Lars Bo is Danish, but currently living with his family in southern Germany, working as a consultant for *Forum Informatik AG* (http://www.forum-informatik.ch) in Switzerland. He can be contacted at lbv@vanting.com and maintains his own website at http://www.vanting.com

Contents at a Glance

PART IV

Other Useful Information

Contents

PART II
Looking at the EM Console Components

PART III

Using EM

PART IV

Other Useful Information

Preface

The book you hold in your hands is like a great travel book, complete with the history and culture of terrific places to visit, helpful pictures and maps, and informative listings of things to do. Written for the new or experienced database administrator (DBA), *Oracle Enterprise Manager 101* provides an invaluable guide to the premiere tool for managing an Oracle environment. Knowledge of how best to use the capabilities of Oracle Enterprise Manager, together with a strong conceptual understanding of the operations of the Oracle9*i* database and application servers, are the keys to efficient and effective use of your Oracle-based systems for maximum business benefit.

This book covers everything from the architecture, installation and configuration of the Enterprise Manager framework to operational guidance on how to set up and use its powerful capabilities to monitor and manage an Oracle-based infrastructure, including the Oracle9i database, application server and Oracle-based applications. Read this book to learn how Enterprise Manager discovers Oracle-based services available on your company's network and how to set up events and jobs so you can monitor status and performance, and automate administrative tasks. You'll also learn how to use the Enterprise Manager console to perform routine tasks and employ wizards and advisors to be guided through procedures that will help you ensure the security, reliability and performance of your Oracle environment. In short, this book is your travel guide and roadmap to success as an Oracle DBA, using Oracle Enterprise Manager.

It goes without saying that databases (and the application servers that are increasingly being used to deploy the applications that access them) are at the heart of the information systems that keep our enterprises functioning. Whether they are used for transaction processing or business intelligence, or as a repository of textual or multi-media data, database applications are critical to most business operations. If they are not available, are not secure, or are slow and unresponsive, the effect is often felt on the bottom line. In the modern on-line world of e-business, where employees, customers and suppliers must have (authorized) access to information around the clock from around the world, systems that don't run optimally can cause serious financial losses, thwart the very success of an enterprise or even put public safety at risk.

The database administrator's job is an important one, and the typical DBA faces growing challenges. The DBA is responsible for the optimal performance of the database system, and for its efficient use of computer resources like storage, memory and processing cycles. Systems must not only perform efficiently, but often must do so 24 hours a day, so the DBA has to establish high-availability strategies, policies and procedures. DBAs must also define and maintain procedures that protect information from unauthorized access and from hardware and software failures, including complete data center failures. Terabyte-scale databases have become common, and DBAs must know how to efficiently allocate, tune and protect the storage they comprise. DBAs often are called upon to do capacity planning, and to diagnose and correct performance problems, identifying bottlenecks and making configuration changes required for acceptable performance. In the face of changes in business requirements, application demands and hardware configurations, the DBA must ensure that information is available and that systems respond predictably and quickly to user requests.

DBAs face another challenge: to keep up with the pace of change in technology. Computing platforms are changing, with some key trends including the growing use of new operating systems like Linux, adoption of storage area networks, and deployment of clustered hardware just to name a few. Even the experienced Oracle DBA must learn about a flurry of new capabilities in Oracle9i, the latest version of the database software. The advent of Oracle9i Real Application Clusters makes it attractive to construct large configurations from a number of lower-cost commodity computers, and DBAs should understand how to deploy and exploit this technology. Effective DBAs will want to be familiar with other new and enhanced database capabilities like Oracle Data Guard for standby databases, materialized views, new indexing and storage management schemes, new integrated business intelligence features and enhanced security functionality.

A truly successful Oracle DBA, one who is most valuable to his enterprise, will learn not only how to use Oracle Enterprise Manager and the technology of the database system itself, but will apply that knowledge for business benefit. Since personnel costs are a significant part of the total cost of ownership, the wise DBA thinks in terms of his contribution to the bottom line, not solely about the bits and bytes of technology. To that end, a database administrator must use the tools at his disposal to be both "scalable" and "strategic."

Just as the computer hardware and software systems must scale to meet growing requirements, today's DBAs are being asked to do more with less. In many organizations, DBAs must manage ever-growing databases with increasing numbers of users and more demanding performance and availability requirements. And, the DBA has a role to play in managing application servers and distributed application components. The industry trends of globalization, server consolidation and applications hosting (where multiple client organizations are supported on shared facilities) mean that more users depend on fewer DBAs to ensure that their systems are up, their data is available, and their applications responding as expected. Effective DBAs will learn new tools and techniques to scale their capabilities to meet these demands.

Equally important as "managing more" is "managing more strategically." By this we mean making technical decisions in light of the business impact of those decisions. Of course the DBA always seeks good or excellent performance, but for which operations? How does the DBA balance trade-offs between conflicting performance requirements? Can the DBA anticipate the effect of a configuration change on the end-user experience before the change is implemented? The DBA with maximum value to his organization will focus on the needs of the business user as well as the technology he manages. It's important to measure and monitor the actual availability and performance of the application as seen by that user, rather than solely looking at metrics and statistics that describe the internal operations of the database system itself. To obtain that strategic view, the DBA must be able to manage the entire stack, end–to-end, from the application through the network to the application server and then to the database and back.

Oracle Corporation has invested heavily for several years in an effort to "make the complex simple", focusing on reducing the costs of database administration. Our intent is to help database administrators do more with less, and to scale their capabilities so they can manage more strategically, thereby allowing organizations meet their IT and business goals at lower cost. Thus, in addition to providing the required scalability, reliability and security features needed for server consolidation, each new version of Oracle includes enhancements designed to make it easier to manage. Oracle's goals are to eliminate, automate, and simplify the most time-consuming, common and important database administration tasks.

For example, Oracle9i completely eliminates the need for the database administrator to manage rollback segments, which are used to support undoing incomplete transactions for recovery as well as Oracle's read consistent concurrency model. The DBA can rely on the system to allocate, free and utilize undo storage instead of making tedious decisions about the number, placement, size and usage of rollback segments. As a result, the DBA is free to do other things, and the system will operate more effectively. The DBA can set "undo quotas" to prevent a single transaction from using too much space, and can establish an "undo retention period" so that the system will preserve as much undo information as needed to resolve long-running queries.

Similarly, Oracle9i has automated the task of memory allocation for decision support queries. No longer must the DBA determine (or guess) the memory requirements for sorts and joins, and manually adjust system parameters in an attempt to provide sufficient memory for these operations when important queries are presented. Instead, Oracle9i will dynamically and automatically allocate memory for these operations as needed, with the result that the DBA has less work to do, and the entire query workload will run more efficiently.

As another example, Oracle9i implements simple new storage management capabilities that free the DBA from the tedious and error-prone task of setting a variety of storage parameters. No longer does the DBA need to consider low-level storage issues like managing extents and lists of free blocks. Oracle9i, through its bit-mapped segment space management capabilities, ensures that storage for data is located efficiently, and that fragmentation of storage space is kept to a minimum.

In addition to the improvements in database manageability, each release of Oracle Enterprise Manager has been designed to make the DBA's job easier. In addition to a flexible alert system that can notify DBAs when monitored events warrant, Enterprise Manager for Oracle9i now includes new features such as powerful and flexible HTML-based reporting capabilities, so the DBA can see at a glance the entire status of the computing environment. Through the Database Overview Chart, Enterprise Manager makes the DBA aware of database and operating system metrics that are out of balance, so he can identify problems and use the provided methodology for correcting them. Enterprise Manager supports precision monitoring of performance as experienced at the end-user level, so that DBAs can manage the configuration for best business results. Among other enhancements, Enterprise Manager also includes predictive tuning wizards, so that the DBA can determine, for example, the benefit of adding an index to a table before taking the time and space to do so. In the form of "guided diagnostics", Enterprise Manager builds in the intelligence of experts (developers, consultants and support engineers) so that DBAs can quickly identify and correct the causes of anomalous behavior.

As you can see, database administrators have an important job, with many challenges. Fortunately, Oracle Corporation has been making it easier for the DBA to be more efficient and more effective, so he can deliver greater benefit to the bottom line of the business. With a sound understanding of the workings of the Oracle9i database, and a thorough knowledge of how to exploit the many capabilities of Oracle Enterprise Manager, you can run a better Oracle environment for better business advantage. Oracle Enterprise Manager 101 deserves a prominent place among the other "travel guides" on the DBA's bookshelf.

Best wishes for successful operations of your database environment. As I say in closing my Dr. DBA show on the Oracle E-Business Network,

Good Data, and Good Day!

—Ken Jacobs
(aka Dr. DBA)
VP Product Strategy
Server Technologies
Oracle Corporation

Acknowledgments

I would like to thank my wife Barbara who provided endless moral support and understanding for the months during which this book was written; especially tough during the weekends. I thank my two and a half year old daughter Rebecca, whose daddy will now spend more time with her. Someday she will be able to read this.

My parents who provided the foundation for what I am today.

Lars Bo Vanting, who is fun to work with and who mastered all spoiled weekends with the professionalism that I hopefully showed too.

All members of System Management Products at Oracle who supported this book especially by patiently answering even the oddest types of questions.

Ken "Dr. DBA" Jacobs for lending his name and experience by contributing the foreword.

Athena, Julie, Jeremy, and Brian at McGraw-Hill for creating and maintaining a pleasant working atmosphere.

Matthias Weiss, who initially hired me like many other "starters" at Oracle. It is his own fault that he now reads his name in a book like this.

Marija Celebicanin for giving feedback, encouragement and advice on language and style questions I had in the early phases of writing this book.

And very importantly: Martin Pena and Bob McCormick not only for tech reviewing this book, but also for patient coaching over the last years and above all, for continuously providing me with advice, encouragement, and opportunities to be successful.

—Dirk Schepanek

First of all I'd thank my wife Lene for constantly providing me with moral support, even when she needed me to participate in the family life duties. Also I'd like to thank my two boys, Nicolai and Oliver, for accepting the fact that their father had to sit in his office all the time and work at his computer, rather than play with them.

Dirk for being a great co-author throughout this project, for his dedication to EM issues, and for keeping up the spirit. Thank you for your constant research, including passing my questions on to the EM development team.

My colleague Sten Vesterli (author of *Oracle Web Applications 101*) for encouraging me to begin this project at all, and for helping me out with issues on writing as well as Java and web-related technical issues.

The project team at McGraw Hill, including Athena, Julie, Jeremy, and Brian for their professionalism during the development of this book.

Bob McCormick for his constructive and very appreciated technical reviews, nothing slipped his eyes and his thorough tests.

Thanks to Henrik Pedersen for being helpful with technical issues and for always having the latest software releases downloaded. Thanks to Susanne Ritter for always entertaining my two boys in her home, so I could concentrate on writing. Also thanks to my friends and neighbors for their interest and participation in this book.

—Lars Bo Vanting

Introduction

We are very proud to present the first book about the Oracle Enterprise Manager, a product which has been available for quite some years now. We wanted the first book to be a beginner's guide to the installation, configuration, and usage of EM. The goal of this book is to *explain* what EM really is—its architecture and available features—and to get you *started* using EM, and get the most that you can out of it. It is not a complete reference guide to all EM features, but it will take you by the hand and lead you through basic issues concerning installation of EM software and repository, first-time configuration. Additionally it will provide an overview of all the available EM components and bring you examples of core EM features, such as events, jobs, database applications and wizards.

Intended Audience

Enterprise Manager is not only for DBAs; it's a tool for many developers working with Oracle, either for the more traditional client/server development, or Java and web-related. The EM tool suite is very broad and goes from the standalone EM Console to the full-featured Management Server version of EM providing advanced mechanisms for proactively monitoring and managing your whole Oracle environment. The strategy of Oracle Corporation with EM clearly is to provide a single- point-of-control for all Oracle products. This ranges from the RDBMS and its different features (Replication, Text, OLAP, JVM), Real Application Clusters (RAC), DataGuard configurations and Oracle Appliance over Forms, web/application servers to Oracle eBusiness Suite. This book is intended for all, who intend to use EM to manage and assist them in their work with these Oracle products, be it DBAs, developers or end-users.

How to Read This Book

We have divided the book into four major parts (with some bonus material to be found on the web):

- Part I: Introduction to EM as well as software and repository installation issues
- Part II: Description of all EM components, including the optional packs
- Part III: Configuring your EM environment and beginning to use the different core components within EM console. Examples are provided along the way and best practices are discussed for utilizing EM in the most productive way
- Part IV: Other useful information, including command-line interfaces, troubleshooting as well as sources for EM related information in the Internet
- Web Bonus: On the web at http://www.oraclepress.com, you will find additional materials, including configuration files and parameters, EM Websites and other resources, as well as a Rapid Deployment Checklist

Chapter 1 is an introduction to EM, the history of EM and a description of the architecture.

Chapter 2 covers issues such as requirements to run EM, installation of EM software, creating the EM repository and configuring the Management Server and Intelligent Agent components.

Chapter 3 describes the EM Console and its various features including the concepts behind these features.

Chapter 4 describes jobs and events system, as well as the group concepts and the reporting available with EM9i.

Chapter 5 describes all functionality of the console, which relates to administering the EM framework and internals.

Chapter 6 will focus on the database management features and wizards included I the console.

Chapter 7 will provide an overview of the optional Management Packs available to extend EM.

Chapter 8 covers the actions performed in order to discover your target nodes and the different targets to be monitored and managed by EM.

Chapter 9 will discuss first-time configuration issues as well as the configuration in general, which you do within EM.

Chapter 10 takes a look at the special group feature, which is available with EM, by which you can group your targets into logical groups to provide an overview and to ease management.

Chapter 11 will show you how one of the key features of EM, the job system is working, including creating normal and fixit jobs and monitoring their progress and status.

Chapter 12 covers another key feature, namely the EM event system, which is used for proactively monitoring your environment. Also the Event Handler will be discussed and examples of its configuration and usage shown.

Chapter 13 covers the EM reporting framework and provides examples of how to create and publish your own EM reports.

Chapter 14 covers all the features available in the EM Navigator for database management and provides some examples for most of these.

Chapter 15 provides examples for most of the database applications and wizards, which are available in the EM Console Tools menu. This includes applications such as LogMiner Viewer, Data Guard Manager, Text Manager and SQL+Plus Worksheet as well as the Data Manager, Backup Management, Summary Management and Analyze wizards.

Chapter 16 and 17 will put focus on management of other services than those directly related to Oracle RDBMS. These include Net Manager, Oracle Internet Directory Manager and the Nodes, Listeners, HTTP Servers, and Real Application Clusters target types.

Chapter 18 concentrates on showing you how to configure and use the EM thin client, which enables you to run the EM Console through a web browser.

Chapter 19 covers the most important command-line utilities available for managing the different EM components, including the Management Server and Intelligent Agent.

Chapter 20 provides information that will hopefully assist you in troubleshooting your EM environment. Not all possible error situations will be covered, but the typical ones, which we have experienced ourselves in our work with EM.

How will you get the most out of this book?

It is possible to read this book to gain knowledge about how EM works and which features are available, without doing any hands-on. But we recommend you get hold of a PC, this being Linux or Windows NT/2000, and follow up with your own practical exercises as you read the book. Chapter 2 will provide information about the HW and SW requirements for such a machine. Also it is a good idea for you to have the Oracle documentation ready when you read this book and do your experiments.

The examples provided are simple to follow and after you manage these, you'll be able to exploit other more complex features in EM. We choose to use Windows 2000 as the basis for our practical work related to this book, although EM server and client components are available on Unix and Linux platforms as well. We have been deploying EM9i on Solaris and Linux ourselves, but choose Windows, because this platform (still) seems to be the most commonly used platform, especially as client. Besides some differences in how to start the EM Console between Windows and Unix, the EM Console interface is working in the same way. So this shouldn't make a big difference to Unix/Linux users who read this book.

PART I

Introduction to Oracle Enterprise Manager

CHAPTER 1

What is Enterprise Manager?

his chapter defines what Enterprise Manager is, provides a brief history of the product, and explains the multi-tier architecture behind it and what the benefits are. This will help you choose how to install, which we will cover in the next chapter after reviewing the hardware and software requirements.

Getting to Know Enterprise Manager

Oracle Enterprise Manager (EM) is a software product offered by Oracle as an add-on to the database to make administration of Oracle software much easier. EM is not only a database management tool, it is a management framework designed to manage the complete Oracle environment. With EM, administrators can manage more Oracle systems and a larger variety of systems in less time with less cost, making them more efficient.

Not long ago, few people thought about management tools. Today there is a multi-billion-dollar market that revolves around managing all kinds of systems, including Oracle databases, with graphical user interface (GUI)-based tools. Version 9i of Enterprise Manager does much more than simply manage the Oracle database. Oracle's overall strategy states that all systems should be easy to manage and maintain, which they achieve with two major focused activities. One is making the database itself easier to manage by eliminating, simplifying, or automating administrative tasks; the other is enhancing these database features through Enterprise Manager. You need a management framework, not just a tool, to manage the Oracle environment, because Oracle's product offerings consist of much more than just the database. Oracle has added a fully capable Internet Application Server (*i*AS) and a complete set of standard applications to its product portfolio called the E-Business Suite. In addition, Oracle's development tools have been revamped and are offered as the 9iDevelopment Suite. Enterprise Manager monitors the underlying operating systems of all these components as well, because healthy systems can be affected by an unhealthy operating system.

Oracle foresees that Enterprise Manager will manage all these components with version 9i. EM has come a long way from its early versions, and is today a state of the art management framework for anyone who deals with administering any Oracle software product.

History

By the mid-1990s, the Oracle database had been established as a de facto database standard. Most large- or mid-sized companies had at least one Oracle database installed and running. According to many market research analysts, Oracle already offered the best database product on the market, leading the pack ahead of Informix, Sybase, IBM, and Microsoft. The Oracle database had the image of being capable and solid, but it was also said to be difficult to administer and maintain. Microsoft, on the other hand, has long had a reputation for making even complex software products more user-friendly. Microsoft's Windows 3.11 and Windows NT 3.51 operating systems, and Windows 95 and Windows NT 4.0 afterwards, with their GUI-based and wizard-driven technology, were considered a series of breakthroughs in user friendliness. The public increasingly demanded more of this kind of user friendliness from all fields of software and the ease-of-use factor was established as a standard criteria to evaluate the quality of all kinds of software.

At the same time, the system management market was also gaining speed. Companies realized that the Internet was here to stay, creating an explosive growth in the amount of text and digitized content to be stored, and with it the number of servers, networks, databases, and other systems that needed to be managed and maintained. The upcoming IT skill shortage added more demand for GUI-based administration tools, especially for database administrators (DBAs) and system administrators.

At the same time, a new discussion started, which is still active today: the command-line interface (CLI) versus the graphics user interface (GUI). GUI tools generally make things easier for the user because of their built-in intelligence. The user does not have to know all the commands and syntax options for each command, nor where to find the particular information needed to perform the task. The wizards would know, freeing the time of overloaded DBAs because DBAs could do some tasks much faster with the help of such wizards. Command-line utilities are considered more difficult to learn, and require the DBA to understand lots of background information, not to mention a number of commands and syntaxes. On the other hand, the CLI supporters argue jokingly that "a fool with a tool is still a fool, maybe a faster fool." A certain amount of background knowledge is required to effectively use any tool, which is the reason that tools are sometimes considered a dangerous power in the hands of inexperienced users.

The solution to this discussion seems to be one that can be applied in many similar situations—as little as possible, as much as needed. GUI tools speed up problem solving, but totally relying on them without any technical background at all leads to difficulties when you do not understand basic concepts of the problem solution. A total commitment to CLI is inappropriate in the modern IT landscape, however. It takes too much time to efficiently solve problems solely based on commands entered at a command prompt. A balanced mix between both approaches is a good solution, in most cases; every DBA has to find out for himself or herself which relation GUI vs. CLI is best for having optimal administrative performance.

The Enterprise Manager Journey

The first mention of the Enterprise Manager product was in the documentation available with the database version 7.3.2 for Windows NT 3.51, in April of 1996.

It was briefly mentioned that components called 32-bit Database Administration Tools would cease to exist, and that from that time on a product called Oracle Enterprise Manager would ship instead. Enterprise Manager version 1.1 shipped with database release 7.3.2 and was only available for the Windows NT 3.51 operating system. It could manage version 7.3 of the database, and could also manage version 7.2, with some restrictions. The Oracle documentation of the database 7.3.2 on Windows NT 3.51 dated April 1996 mentions Enterprise Manager as follows: "Oracle Enterprise Manager is Oracle Corporation's newest generation of system management tools. Enterprise Manager combines a single point-of-control management console, intelligent agents, and common services in an integrated, comprehensive systems management platform." This strategy has been pursued with every version of EM.

Early users will remember the "Dude," which was the internal nickname for the splash-screen for EM shown to users during startup (Figure 1-1). The user community and also Oracle initially called it OEM, for Oracle Enterprise Manager, which was and still is constantly confused with OEM for Original Equipment Manufacturer. Oracle has attempted to get away from "OEM" and head towards the use of "EM" instead, but this has not been fully adopted, perhaps because the distinction is largely irrelevant. In this book, we will use the abbreviation EM.

Many concepts formed in this initial release of Enterprise Manager are still valid today with regard to managing the Oracle database. EM today has the task of managing all of the Oracle environment, which the initial version did not do to a great extent. Version 1.1 mostly concentrated on the database. The goal was to have one central console (Figure 1-2) from which the DBA could administer Oracle databases. Version 1.1 also featured the Intelligent Agent, which was designed to discover services, run jobs, and monitor for events, and is still part of version 9i's functionality. The plan was to have a central console running on GUI-based operating systems like Windows, and an agent on each node that hosted the Oracle database, regardless of the individual

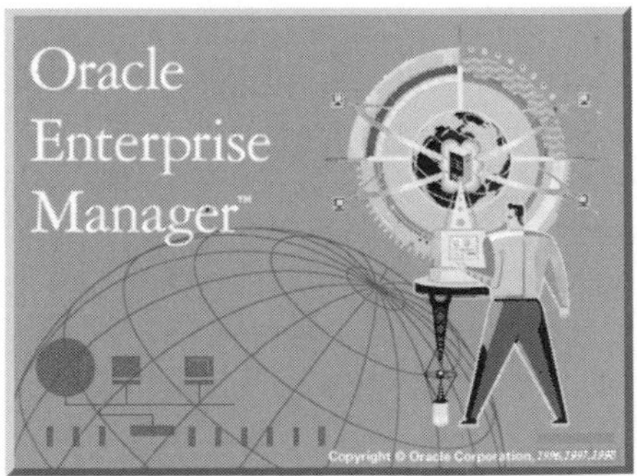

FIGURE 1-1. *Enterprise Manager startup graphic from version 1.x*

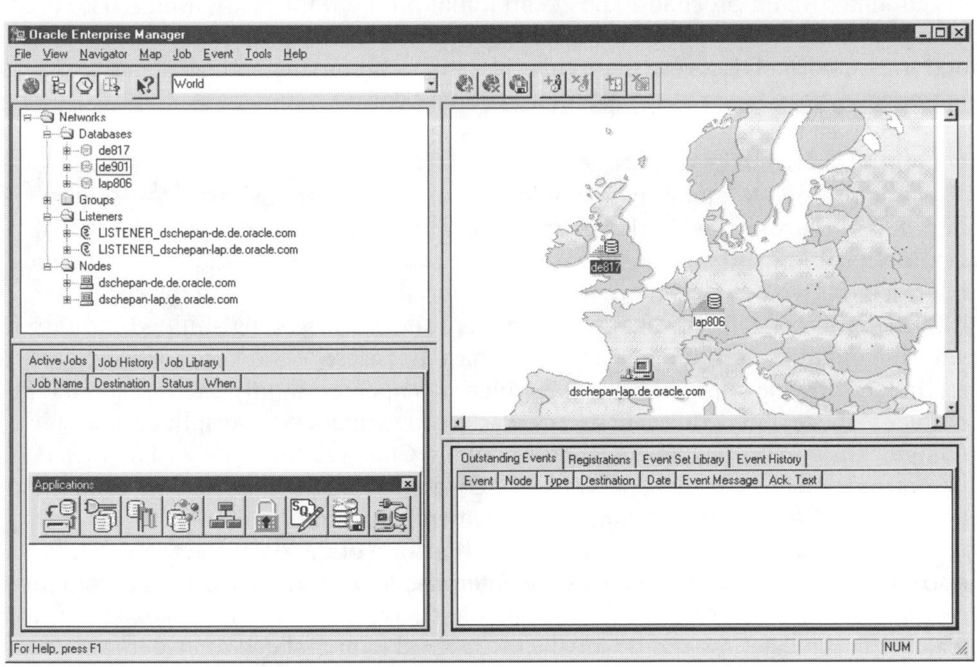

FIGURE 1-2. *Enterprise Manager console in version 1.x*

operating system. That required agents to be developed or ported with identical functionality, but on different platforms. That didn't appear to be too big a challenge since Oracle had been successfully supporting multiple platforms for years with the database itself.

With EM version 1.1 there was already a *repository*, which contained all kinds of information DBAs needed to do their jobs. The repository enabled the DBA to store various types of information so they could continue administering from where they left off last time. Although the repository could not be shared among DBAs, and would not be for several future releases, it helped a great deal to perform administrative tasks more efficiently. EM included tools that could be started from within the console specializing in certain areas, such as Schema Manager, Security Manager, or Storage Manager.

A downside of the first releases was the amount of time and effort required to set up Enterprise Manager itself. It required users to run several scripts and perform certain steps manually to create the repository, which was needed before you could successfully start the console. This complexity, in conjunction with a poorly documented setup procedure, posed an initial problem for many users. Also, the reliability and stability of the Intelligent Agent varied greatly depending on the version and the platform. Discovery of services was not as automatic and complete as it was intended to be, which caused lots of additional confusion in releases to come. Once users got past the difficult installation process, most of them were grateful with the benefits EM provided.

In addition to the tools available in the console, other advanced tools were bundled in the so-called Performance Pack which later evolved into the current version's Tuning and Diagnostics Packs. The tools in the Performance Pack were intended to give the DBA more features for monitoring and tuning the database. Although the console, the agent, and the repository were being shipped for free with the database, customers had to purchase licenses for the Performance Pack separately. Starting with version 1.5.5, which was released shortly after version 8.0.5 of the database, the Performance Pack was greatly enhanced and split up into the Diagnostics and Tuning Packs. In addition, the Change Management Pack was introduced, which helped to deal with differences in databases and changes in schema definitions. We address the Oracle Management Packs in Chapter 7.

Oracle's strategy intended that with each release of the database there would also be a new and enhanced release of Enterprise Manager. This followed from the requirements that the Oracle database should become easier to manage, and new features in the database should ideally be covered in the related management tool. Therefore, the product development team dealing with Enterprise Manager had to solve a difficult problem. With each of the frequent database releases, the team had to come up with a new release of EM that would be able to manage the latest features of that database. In addition, they had to develop, implement, and test all these features at a time when the database itself was still under development. This paradox posed lots of problems in the beginning and is now solved with credit to Oracle's development, by setting up and deploying new development workflows. By solving this development paradox, Oracle can offer supporting tools simultaneously with the release of a new database version. This is something no other tool vendor can currently do.

Java and Three Tiers

One principle was directly set into place with the initial release of EM: A close communication was to be established with Oracle's customers using EM. After a number of releases of EM, some conceptual problems surfaced, two of which are outlined here.

The first problem was that customers and Oracle wanted EM to be available on all platforms and operating systems the database offered. The majority of Oracle databases were running on UNIX-based operating systems, and the UNIX community had a split opinion about the quality and reliability of Windows NT as a server operating system in general. Oracle wanted to satisfy the large UNIX community, which frequently asked for EM to be made available for UNIX platforms. However, EM was developed in C++, a rather CPU-oriented development language. In contrast to a non-hardware-specific development language with an interpreter included, slowing down performance significantly, EM would have needed to be ported to other flavors of C++ designed for the other individual platforms. Although this was happening with the database anyway, Oracle decided to switch EM to the emerging Java development language. Java promised an ideal solution because it was portable and still very close to the hardware at the same time.

The second conceptual discussion emerged from Oracle's goal of offering increased manageability to its most important customers, specifically the large- and mid-sized companies with thousands of databases scattered across the globe, with each node connected through worldwide company internal networks. This multitude of databases had to be managed not only by one DBA, but by multiple teams of DBAs also scattered across the globe. EM's repository offered many advantages, but didn't offer any sharing between multiple DBAs or teams of DBAs in version 1.x. Once a DBA started the console and connected to the repository, no other DBA could connect to it, which resulted in each individual DBA having a private repository. The information inside could not be shared among the DBAs. This problem was solved by switching from the two-tier architecture (consisting of the console and the agents) to the current three-tier architecture, which added a new component between console and agents: the Oracle Management Server (OMS). Starting with release 2.0 of EM, the console connects to the OMS, which provides indirect access to the repository. That way, many DBAs can connect to an OMS simultaneously and share the information the repository contains. The OMS also talks to the agents on behalf of the console.

It turned out that switching to Java was more daring than expected, considering the general lack of experience with it. Java also had fewer development tools compared to C++, and those that did exist were quite immature, just like the language itself. In short, Java could not initially provide everything consumers were hoping for. Users were disappointed with the slow performance of the first couple of Java applications, including EM version 2.0. This and the addition of another layer in the EM architecture, the OMS, created heavy demands for performance improvement. Java did provide the desired portability effects, however. Besides appearing on Windows-based platforms, EM was made available on Solaris, which today is Oracle's primary development platform. The console could also run as a Java applet in a browser on Windows-based platforms. At the same time, the graphic interface of EM was changed to the visually enhanced and more intuitive style, as shown in Figure 1-3. This style spread towards all other areas of Oracle's software products over time.

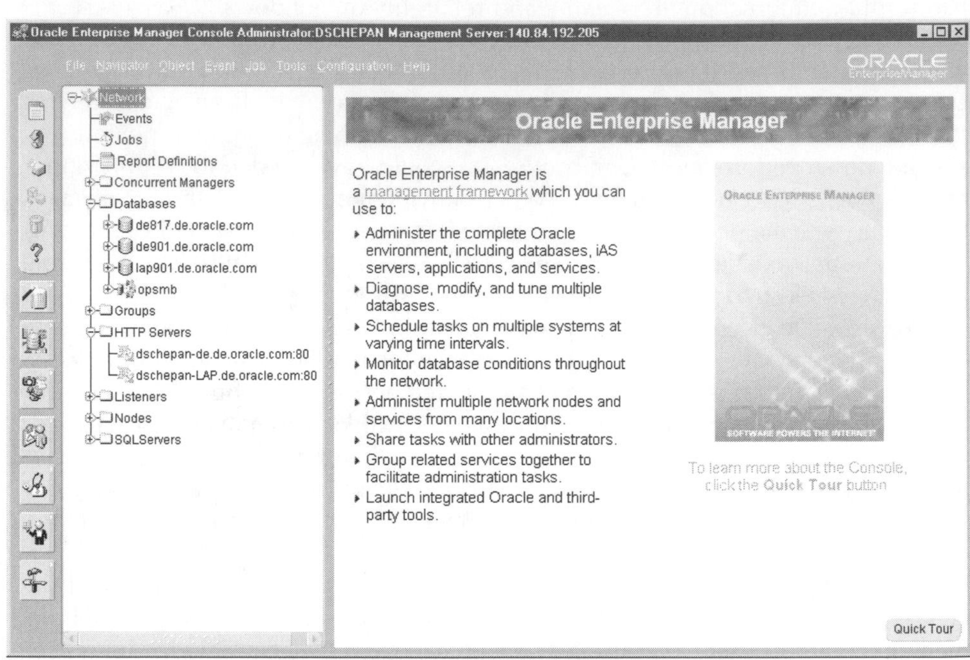

FIGURE 1-3. *Enterprise Manager 9i console*

Today most Java-related performance issues have been resolved with great success, because Oracle's development members have also become Java experts and were extremely successful in making Java applications run almost as fast as those developed in C++.

As EM began to manage all kinds of Oracle systems, the developers sometimes found it easy to find a way to administer systems, and sometimes not, depending on the design of the systems. EM's development team had to work closely with other development teams to suggest modification of the structure or features of software to make administration easier, or possible at all. This collaboration often included features of the database. One of Oracle's key messages for the 9i database is *manageability*. EM is a huge part of this strategy, but lots of features that help make the database easier to manage are built into today's 9i database directly. These are automatic rollback management, mean time to recovery, resource management, and automated database configuration, just to name a few. These are features that Enterprise Manager uses or complements for the benefit of Oracle DBAs.

Another very simple change which helps users a lot is changing EM's version to just the same as the database: EM9i ships with 9i of the database. No more confusion like "With which database version did EM 2.1 actually ship?" Table 1.1 lists all the releases of EM, their release dates, the database versions they shipped with, and the date that Oracle stopped supporting them.

Licensing

Some Enterprise Manager components were always shipped to customers as part of the database license, free of charge. These free components, the console, OMS, repository, and Intelligent Agent, are referred to as *Base EM.* Many potential customers still do not know that EM exists at all, or that several parts ship for free with the database license. Customers frequently buy management tools from third-party vendors for a big part of their IT budget, not knowing that EM performs the same tasks, and, in some cases, does so more efficiently. Other customers know that EM exists, but have not really looked at the most recent releases and underestimate the

EM Release	Release Date	Released with	Desupport Date
9i NT	September 2001	9.0.1 NT	
9i HP, SUN, Linux	June 2001	9.0.1 HP, SUN, Linux	
2.2 NT	November 2000	8.1.7 NT	December 2003
2.2 SUN	October 2000	8.1.7 SUN	December 2003
2.1 NT	March 2000	8.1.6 NT	October 2001
2.1 SUN	December 1999	8.1.6 SUN	October 2001
2.0.4	March 1999	8.1.5	December 2001
1.6.5	March 2000	8.0.6	September 2001
1.6.0	July 1998	8.0.5	June 2001
1.5.5	August 1998		March 2001
1.5.0	December 1997	8.0.4	March 2000
1.4.0	June 1997	8.0.3	March 1999
1.3.6	October 1997	7.3.4	December 2000
1.3.5	March 1997	7.3.3	December 1998
1.2.2	September 1996		January 1998
1.2.0	August 1996	7.3.2	January 1998

TABLE 1-1. *EM Release Dates and Related Release Information*

wealth of functionality that has been added to recent releases. Others fall into the psychological trap of thinking that "what costs nothing can't be worth much," for which EM is the perfect counter-example.

Although Base EM has a lot of functionality, some sophisticated features, especially around monitoring and tuning, have to be purchased separately. As mentioned earlier, Oracle is releasing the Oracle Management Packs, which offer help with specific tasks a DBA has to perform frequently. These Management Packs are explained in more detail in Chapter 7.

Components and Architecture

The following is a list of components found in version 9i of the EM architecture. We will compare them with parts of the human body to clarify their role in the framework, and describe how they are connected in Figure 1-4.

- **Console — The senses** The console is the user interface for the DBA, and can be run as a fat client install or via the Web. Both versions look the same.
- **Intelligent Agents — The muscles** Intelligent Agents run on the node with managed targets, and are responsible for target discovery, event monitoring, job execution, and collection and maintenance of historical data.
- **The Oracle Management Server (OMS) — The heart** The OMS contains EM's back-end application logic; therefore, its tasks are very important for the framework to function. The OMS talks to all consoles and all agents to achieve this.
- **The Repository — The brain** The repository contains all information available about the management framework, its targets, nodes, jobs, events, DBAs, and much more.

The Console

Some DBAs still expect a database tool to have a client/server architecture. This concept was widely spread in early stages of the system management market, and is still common today, although client/server is no longer sufficient to support managing numerous heavy-duty systems simultaneously. It is still useful for certain tasks, but has serious downsides considering the administrative IT requirements of a corporation in today's competitive markets. As mentioned previously, early versions of EM used the client/server concept, the EM console can still be run in that mode optionally, but EM is primarily designed to be used as a three-tier management framework. To get the most out of EM, DBAs have to understand the framework concept and the role of each individual component. Only after it is clear what each component

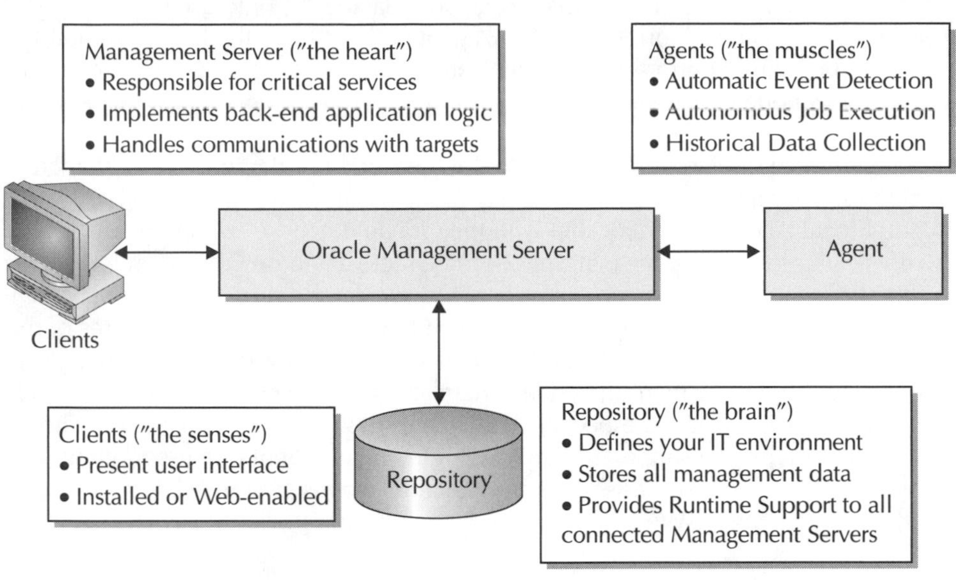

FIGURE 1-4. *The Enterprise Manager framework components*

does, why it is needed, and how it works together with the other components, can you fully understand and use the benefit that EM provides. The console will not be discussed in greater detail in this chapter; it will be fully explained in Part II.

Intelligent Agent

The Intelligent Agent is part of the muscles in the framework and is required to be run on each node that needs to be managed, or contains targets that need to be managed. An agent is a process that is started separately on the node and comes as a standard component of the default database installation. Because of the architectural design, there can only be one agent per machine, but that one agent is sufficient to take over all tasks that need to be performed. We recommend using the latest version of the agent, 9i, because it offers the most features and functionality. Each agent can manage databases of the same release or lower. That means that an 8.1.5 agent is able to manage databases of the same version (8.1.5) or lower, which could be 8.0.6 or 7.3.4. Note that release 7.3.4 of the database and also release 7.3.4 of the agent ran out of support at the end of 2000, but a large number of customers are still running this version for various reasons.

For example, assume that you have a node running an 8.0.6 and an 8.1.7 database. You have the choice to install the 9i agent using the custom install option into a new separate Oracle Home and use it to manage both databases, or to use the 8.1.7 agent if you cannot install version 9i. The 8.1.7 agent will not have the latest 9i features available, but can perform most tasks for both databases depending on your specific needs for this node and its services. The rest of the EM framework (console and OMS) is also designed to work with agents of previous releases, so DBAs can upgrade agents gradually. We will clarify in Chapter 2 which versions of databases the 9i agent officially supports.

Intelligent Agents generally ship with the Oracle database, which means it is usually available on the same platforms as the Oracle database. The agent is designed to offer the same functionality no matter on which platform it runs. Certain functionality might be adjusted to offer best performance and address the specific features of the individual type of platform. If required standards do not exist for individual platforms, functionality might also be restricted in certain areas. It may be a good idea to check if all functionality is available, especially if the platform you are using is not commonly used or is not typically supported by Oracle. Having an agent process running on the nodes to be managed has some important advantages that go far beyond normal database management. We will make them clear during the book.

Controlling the Agent

Version 9i of the Intelligent Agent is controlled with a new command called `AGENTCTL`. This has evolved from previous versions in which control over the agent process was included with the listener control utility `LSNRCTL`. You start the agent process with the `AGENTCTL START` command or from the processes window on Windows-based platforms.

Target Discovery

When the 9i Agent process is started for the first time on the node to be managed, it starts discovering its environment. It looks for any known types of targets that are installed, such as databases, database listeners, Web listeners, or the node itself, to mention a few. Once the targets have been discovered, it writes information about these targets into three files called `SERVICES.ORA`, `SNMP_RO.ORA`, and `SNMP_RW.ORA`, and by default places them into the `$ORACLE_HOME/NETWORK/ADMIN` directory of the agent. When the node is later added to the management framework, the agent will be contacted and asked for this information, which will then be ready for delivery. After this is done, the agent basically does nothing; it awaits contact and instructions to perform specific tasks such as event monitoring, job execution, or collection and management of historical data.

Monitoring Events

Certain pre defined conditions can cause problems for targets, from decreasing the performance of a database or the node as a whole, to rendering a database instance completely unavailable. In EM, these pre defined conditions are called *events,* and can be defined for any type of target. The goal is to prevent performance problems and above all, a complete unavailability of a database. The results for the business can range from slight inconvenience to heavy revenue loss. As businesses tend to rely more and more on databases and other systems because of their increasing effects on speed and efficiency, the ultimate goal is to keep databases available at all times. The DBA's task is to prevent total unavailability at any time, but also to keep the databases performing well, even under the strain of enormous workloads. Availability of a database depends on many things. It would require quite a number of people to do nothing but checking to see if certain metrics pose a danger to performance or availability. Having such close monitoring done by human DBAs is unrealistic. Metrics that are crucial for the health of a database slowly get worse without being noticed, and cause serious trouble if not taken care of.

For example, a database can be operated in archive log mode, but it can only write archive logs if there is enough disk space available. If there is no disk space left and no archive log information can be written, the database stops operating, because it can not secure the data. For another example, a database only performs well if the percentage of sorts done in memory is as high as possible. Both conditions should be frequently checked by an automated mechanism.

At least one third of professional DBAs admit they frequently experience complete database standstills because the database is unable to write archive logs to disk as a result of insufficient free disk space. The Intelligent Agent can frequently check the status of disk space consumption on behalf of the DBA. Checking the health of the node is also important, according to the rule that a healthy database can only exist on a healthy node. That means that the agent has an interface to check metrics of the node that both the agent and the database run on. Regarding the example of in-memory sorts, the agent can log on to the database and query its data dictionary. Depending on how the agent was instructed, it will warn the DBA that in-memory sorts have dropped below an acceptable level, or that there is only five percent disk space left. The effect is that upcoming trouble spots or bottlenecks can be monitored automatically by the agent, and the DBA can deal with the problem before performance or availability are affected. This frees the DBA from doing the mundane monitoring himself.

Running Jobs

Most DBAs have a number of scripts that need to be run frequently or on demand. The Intelligent Agent can take over these tasks completely. EM comes with a fully functional job scheduling system, which enables the DBA to schedule jobs to be run at predefined dates and times or at intervals. A job can also be run only once at a future specified time. The job can be a database script to be run or an ordinary batch job executed on the node the agent runs on. Be aware that this poses no security risk, because the agent will need to log on to any database or any operating system with valid credentials, which have to be provided by the DBA. If the agent is meant to run jobs frequently, it simply replaces the human DBA. It still needs all information the human DBA would need, specifically, login information.

Combining the job system with the event system provides even more benefit. Assume the database listener process seems unstable and frequently crashes, which prevents users or applications from connecting to the database. You could instruct the agent to monitor whether the listener process is still alive, and notify the DBA if there is a problem. The DBA would then simply restart the listener process. This task can be done by the agent as well; a so-called fixit job. If the countermeasure to a problem is known, the agent can be instructed to execute the countermeasure as a job to respond to a detected problem. This way, the agent can not only divert tedious monitoring tasks away from the DBA, but also solve the actual problem. The DBA will receive a notification that problem *X* occurred, countermeasure *Y* has been taken, and the problem has ideally been eliminated. We explain specifics of the job system in Chapter 4 and include details about fixit jobs in Chapters 11 and 12.

Collecting Historical Data

DBAs often need to know how key metrics of services are behaving at present or how they have changed over time; for example, how fast the disk space is being consumed, how CPU-usage of the node is increasing, or how the number of concurrent database sessions develops. These and related questions are dealt with in the Oracle Diagnostics Pack. Performance Manager and Capacity Planner are applications in the Diagnostics Pack that use the Agent to collect information on key metrics. In previous versions of EM, this was done by another separate process called the Data Gatherer. This process has completely vanished with 9i, because the agent's architecture has been redesigned and can now take over the Data Gatherer's tasks. We discuss the Diagnostics Pack in Chapter 7.

Oracle Management Server and Repository

The Oracle Management Server (OMS) is considered the heart of EM's management framework. It has several important tasks to perform, and therefore contains all important background logic. This includes management of the event and job systems, notifications, and the reporting framework. The OMS communicates with all Intelligent Agents and all consoles and stores all information in the repository. It sometimes seems that the word *repository* intimidates some users, but it is actually nothing more than a schema in any existing database which is created and populated through the Enterprise Manager Configuration Assistant (EMCA). EMCA is usually started during the installation process, and guides the user through the configuration steps from the start. The structure of the repository schema and ways to retrieve information are discussed in Appendix C of the "Oracle Enterprise Manager Administrator's Guide" of the EM Documentation. We will explore in detail installation and configuration issues in Chapter 2.

Controlling the OMS

The OMS process can be controlled with its own command-line utility called `OEMCTL`, which has emerged from `OEMCTRL` in previous versions for standardization purposes. See Chapter 19 for a detailed description. The OMS can be started with `OEMCTL START OMS` or on Windows platforms through the service control window. A common problem is that users try to start the OMS before actually directing it to a repository. When started, the OMS first tries to find its repository to both retrieve and store information. If the repository is not available, or this information has not been provided, there is no real value in having an OMS running and it will exit with an error message. This is especially confusing for first-time users who try to start the OMS on Windows platforms in the services dialog box, which results in a vague message communicating an "NT-internal error number 2140." The solution is to configure a proper repository with EMCA prior to starting the OMS. We will provide more information during the setup section in Chapter 2 and within the troubleshooting section in Chapter 20.

Performance Considerations

Because the OMS is an essential part of the management infrastructure, you should consider certain factors. The OMS needs to be able to operate at maximum performance, and therefore needs to have enough memory and CPU available. Most customers choose to have one dedicated node that runs the OMS and a database that holds only the repository. Because the OMS will have lots of network connections to both DBAs and targets in your environment, you should make sure that the node running the OMS has a favorable location in terms of network bandwidth to all other communication partners. If you have some remote targets that are only accessible through a low-bandwidth connection or are outside a firewall, consider establishing Management Regions. Management Regions specify that a number of Agents in a remote environment will exclusively talk to a certain OMS, which is located near them in terms of network performance. We discuss how to define Management Regions in Chapter 9. Also note that an OMS cannot support an endless number of targets. Oracle recommends having one OMS to manage up to 70 nodes, which in total contain up to 400 targets.

Failover Considerations

You should also consider installing at least two OMSes in your network on separate machines. This is important if you reach the limits mentioned in the previous section regarding the number of nodes or targets, so the second OMS can take over tasks through its built-in load-balancing feature. Also, the second OMS provides automatic failover mechanisms, which keep the framework operable should the primary OMS become unavailable. How to install an additional Management Server is described in Chapter 2.

Event Handler

The Event Handler is a new feature of the OMS version 9i. Whenever the agent communicates an event to the OMS, the Event Handler can be instructed to write related information to a log file or to execute external commands. Event-related information can be passed along with the command execution, enabling a very powerful method of integrating with other management frameworks such as Computer Associates' Unicenter, HP OpenView, or Tivoli. This is addressed in Chapter 12.

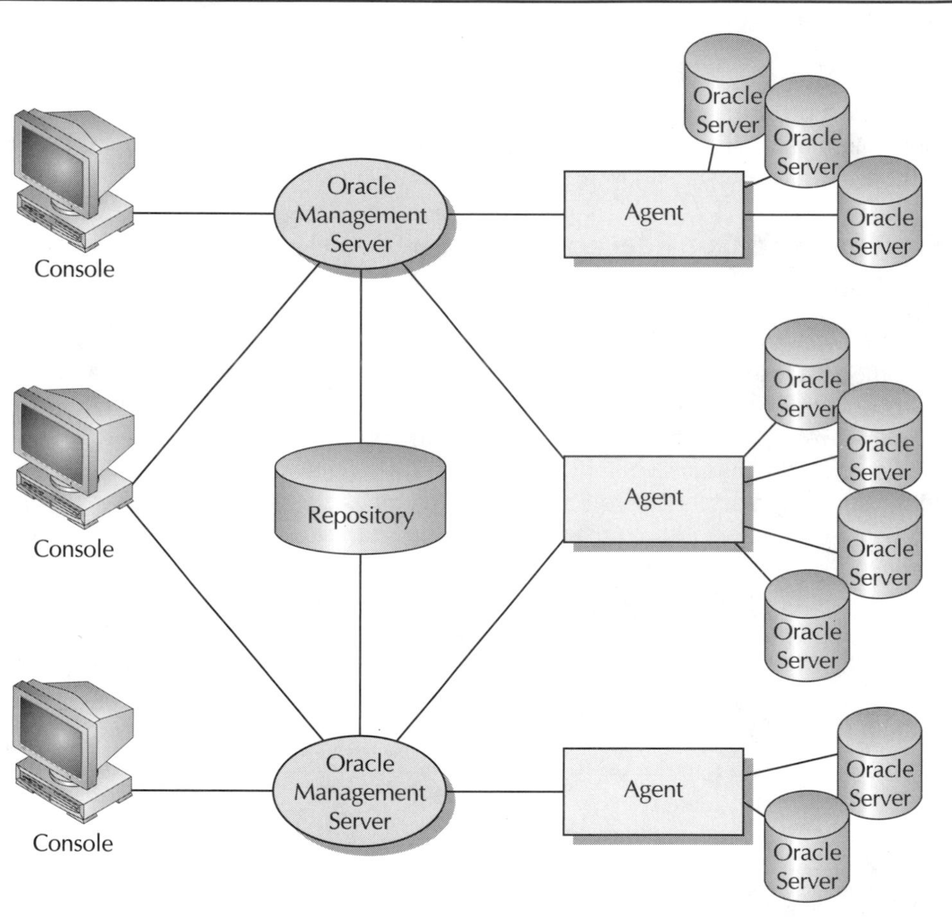

FIGURE 1-5. *The Enterprise Manager9i architecture*

Why and When to Use EM

With Oracle9i, manageability of the Oracle environment has achieved significant attention from Oracle's Chairman and CEO Larry Ellison. Ellison shows a lot more interest in what is happening around Enterprise Manager. He also takes special care to ensure that his visions are really fulfilled regarding manageability of all Oracle products. The best evidence of this concern is that Ellison and other Oracle executives frequently feature live demos of EM during keynotes at Oracle's OpenWorld tradeshows. In addition Oracle's marketing campaign, "Making the Complex Simple," focuses on better manageability of all Oracle software.

Oracle's strategy is perfectly clear: manageability is now fundamental. The sooner DBAs realize this, the more efficient they will be in doing their jobs. EM is powerful already and will be enhanced in future releases. Today many companies use IT systems as essential parts of their business, their success relies on the availability and performance of their systems. This applies especially to businesses that rely heavily on revenue made by using the Internet. Companies realize the importance of managing IT for their business success even if they do not totally derive their business from the Internet, like Amazon or eBay. Most companies have already introduced the role of a CIO, the Chief Information Officer, who reports directly to the CEO. Some companies still have IT as one of many general administration departments, which in many cases doesn't reflect its importance.

Business requirements are broken down into tasks for DBAs, such as maintaining many databases, networks, nodes, and application servers with maximum uptime and performance, and with a minimum number of people. This forces DBAs to rely heavily on new administration frameworks and system management strategies. EM offers the most complete set of features to achieve exactly what the Oracle DBA needs today. EM was designed to be versatile. We already talked about multi-billion-dollar companies with thousands of databases and DBA teams spread across the globe. The following sections describe some typical characteristics for each type of company in terms of size. There are no strict limits between classifications; all of the characteristics can occur in any of the bigger corporations, too.

Small Corporations or Teams

In small companies, there may be only one or two DBAs who try to keep a comparably small number of systems running. They have more difficulties attracting experienced staff, and get help by hiring external contractors on a case-by-case basis. They tend to struggle with solving a variety of different tasks, as they require extensive knowledge and experience. They cannot specialize as much as their colleagues in big corporations, and need more assistance to keep up-to-date. EM offers support with its integrated help systems and educational features like quick tours, wizards, advice functionality, and more. Small corporations are usually a bit undecided about whether to set up a management framework or not. They often stick to client/server usage of EM.

Medium-sized Companies

Medium-sized companies may have a higher number of DBAs available, but may also be using external help on a case-by-case basis. They also may not be able to attract or pay for the type of staff they would like to have. EM helps these DBAs manage the existing system landscape as professionally as global corporations do. Furthermore, DBAs can manage their whole Oracle environment through the use of a single console. They often use the management framework as it offers many features to support teams of DBAs. They also find the event and job system very helpful, because the number of databases to be managed allows for a standardized set of events or jobs. The customizable console or the reporting framework come into play when external contractors need access to systems.

Global Corporations

EM is designed to manage the whole Oracle environment. A company with vast amounts of Oracle software installed will find the ultimate benefit in EM. It is designed to ease the administrative burden not only for Oracle databases, but also for Oracle's Application Server (9iAS), as well as Oracle's set of standard applications, the E-Business Suite. EM's event, notification, and job system with its extreme flexibility and extensibility, offers the host to global corporations with a huge variety of requirements. The new Event Handler enables seamless integration of event notifications into already deployed management frameworks such as the ones from CA, HP, or Tivoli. These systems cover a wide variety of targets, but may lack management depth regarding Oracle systems. Enterprise Manager offers in-depth management functionality and can optionally communicate events to the frameworks mentioned above. Other requirements of huge corporations, such as diagnostics or tuning, can be easily added to Enterprise Manager through the Management Packs. They are covered in Chapter 7. Global corporations usually have multiple teams of DBAs located around the world. They can take advantage of the powerful DBA- management features of EM, including its notification system or its customizable console, and the extensible reporting framework. The console is addressed in Chapter 3, and the Reporting Framework in Chapters 4 and 13.

Summary

In this chapter, after defining and reflecting on the history of EM, we explained all of the components of EM's three-tier architecture, including the console, the management server with its repository, and the Intelligent Agent. We outlined the importance of making Oracle software easy to manage, Oracle's strategy to achieve this goal, and EM's vital part in that strategy. Finally, we outlined how organizations of varying sizes can benefit from using EM. In the next chapter, we'll explain hardware and software requirements and guide you through the installation process.

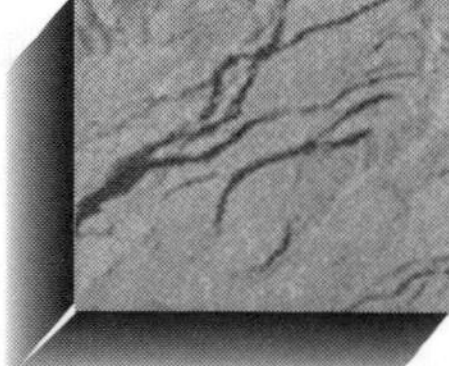

CHAPTER 2

Installing the Components of EM

This chapter will show you how to install the Oracle9i database and EM9i components on a Windows 2000 Professional machine. You should have such a machine available, and you should make sure that your account has been assigned administrator rights, or that you know the password for the local administrator account.

NOTE
You can also install the software on a UNIX or Linux machine, for example, Solaris 8 or SUSE 7.2. Oracle9i Relational Database Management System (RDBMS), Management Server, and EM Client all run on both UNIX and Linux, and the installation is similar. Windows 2000 was chosen for the examples in this book because most people are more likely to be using Windows NT4 or Windows 2000 rather than UNIX or Linux, especially as a desktop computer.

What You Need to Get Started

There are certain requirements to install and run EM9i as with any software. Before looking at the actual installation, we will discuss the currently supported platforms and operating systems as well as the software requirements. With EM9i, more components of the framework are available on more platforms. In the following section, we will outline which component is now available on which platform, including the respective requirements per component.

Supported Platforms and Operating Systems

After looking at the components of the EM architecture in Chapter 1, you learned that each component of the framework is available on a variety of platforms. This gives you a number of options regarding which component you want to install on which platform. It gives you some restrictions as well, in terms of which release of the operating system is on the list of officially supported ones for EM9i components. A list of supported operating systems or configurations does not necessarily mean that other configurations will not run or function at all. *Supported* means that Oracle has tested these configurations and guarantees to help through its support service. You may try out configurations other than ones listed in this chapter, but we strongly discourage you from doing that in production systems, especially because there is a higher chance of failure with unsupported versions of operating systems than with unsupported combinations of framework components, such as OMS/Agent combinations.

Table 2-1 gives an overview of the operating-system-based software requirements with the available platforms for each component. Note that Windows 95 is no longer supported by EM9i, and that the Intelligent Agent exists on more platforms than mentioned in this table, theoretically on all platforms of the database.

To efficiently run a component of EM, your system needs to meet certain hardware requirements in addition to the operating system restrictions mentioned in Table 2-1. These are usually certain CPU performance and available disk space and memory. Oracle tested EM9i with configurations of its primary development platforms Sun Solaris and Windows NT, and came up with a minimal configuration and a recommended configuration. Remember that these are guidelines, and does not mean that EM will not run at all with less resources. However, undesired effects may range from inappropriate performance to intermittent errors as with any software that runs on less than the recommended resources. Because the framework consists of multiple components, designed to be run separately on designated nodes in the network, there are different hardware requirements for a machine running the console or a machine running the OMS, as explained in the following sections.

Platform	**Console**	**OMS**	**Intelligent Agent**
Windows NT 4.0 with Service Pack6a	√	√	√
Windows 2000 with Service Pack2	√	√	√
Windows 98	√		
Windows 95			
Sun SPARC Solaris 2.6, 2.7, 2.8	√	√	√
Intel Solaris	√	√	√
HP-UX 64bit 11.0	√	√	√
IBM AIX 64bit 4.3.3	√	√	√
Compaq Tru64 5.0a, 5.1	√	√	√
Intel Linux 32bit SuSe 7.1, Kernel 2.4, glib 2.2	√	√	√

TABLE 2-1. *Supported Platforms for EM Components*

Client Requirements

Table 2-2 contains information about CPU and memory requirements for Sun or Windows NT machines running the EM console. This applies also to machines that are intended to run the thin-client EM console in a Web browser. The disk space required for a fat client installation on both operating systems amounts to 625MB, which also includes installation of the Management Packs.

OMS Requirements

Table 2-3 contains information about CPU and memory requirements for Sun or Windows NT machines running the EM Management Server (OMS) in addition to the EM client. The disk space required amounts to 730MB. This does not include disk space consumed or hardware required for the repository or the database holding the repository.

Software Requirements

The first thing you need to obtain is the media that contains the Oracle9i software. There are various ways to retrieve it. You can obtain it throughOracle's update service or download it from Oracle Technology Network (OTN) at http://technet.oracle.com. In previous versions, EM came on a separate CD-ROM. The additional Management Packs also came on separate media, totaling quite a number of CD-ROMs to obtain in order to completely install EM. With version 9i, the installation and setup procedures have been simplified, beginning with the number of products you need to obtain. With version 9i you get all of EM included with the database installation. Oracle's strategy is to make install and setup of its software as easy and integrated as possible, so EM and the Management Packs are now being part of the database installation. The downside is that the 9i database on Windows NT presently ships with three CD-ROMs, although everything can be installed, including all parts of Enterprise Manager.

At this point, you need to be aware of the version behind 9i, which is 9.0.1. The marketing name 9i is a continuation of the Internet-branding that began with Oracle 8.1.5, which was called 8i. The databases 8.1.6 and 8.1.7 were named

OS	Minimal Equipment	Recommended Equipment
Windows NT	Pentium 166 MHz, 64MB RAM	Pentium 266 MHz, 128MB RAM
Sun Solaris	Sparc 20, 128MB RAM	Sparc Ultra 1, 256MB RAM

TABLE 2-2. *Hardware Requirements for Running EM Client Software*

OS	Minimal Equipment	Recommended Equipment
Windows NT	Pentium III 866 MHz, 128 MB RAM	Pentium III 1GHz, 256 MB RAM
Sun Solaris	SPARC Ultra 1 266 MHz, 256 MB RAM	SPARC Ultra 1 3000 MHz, 512 MB RAM

TABLE 2-3. *Hardware Requirements for Running EM9i Management Server*

"8i Release 2" and "8i Release 3" respectively. The release after 9.0.1 will be named 9i Release 2.2, because Oracle is changing version rules as a result of the introduced Application Server Rel2 product. The goal is to have an integrated version for both products.

Supported Configurations and Platforms

You have already seen the EM architecture in Chapter 1, which gives you a number of options regarding which component we can use in which version. Keep in mind that a list of supported operating systems or configurations does not necessarily mean that other configurations will not run or function at all. You may try out configurations other than those on the lists in this chapter, but we strongly discourage you from doing this as certain functionality may not be working. Oracle support cannot be expected to help in such a case.

Console/Database Supported Configurations

The EM console can either connect to a Management Server or directly to databases in conventional client/server mode. One rule that gives DBAs no choice is the combination of console and OMS. These two components are tightly connected and must be the same version. This rule applies to all versions of EM. Therefore, a console of EM9i can only be connected to an OMS version 9i. In terms of database versions supported with each release of the console or console/OMS combination, the console or console/OMS combination can manage databases of the same release or lower. Please keep in mind that some database versions have run out of support. Table 2-4 gives an overview.

OMS/Repository Supported Configurations

You have learned that the OMS always needs a connection to a repository in order to store and retrieve information regarding the environment to be managed. This repository can be put in any existing database in the network. In order to allow access to the data in this repository as efficiently as possible, the OMS attempts to use the latest database technology. This results in some restrictions regarding which database version can be a container for an EM repository. Table 2-5 lists the supported combinations.

Console Version	Supported Database Versions
9.0.1	9.0.1, 8.1.7, 8.1.6, 8.0.6
2.2.*x*	8.1.7, 8.1.6, 8.1.5, 8.0.6, 7.3.4
2.1.*x*	8.1.6, 8.1.5, 8.0.*x*, 7.3.4.*x*
2.0.*x*	8.1.5, 8.0.*x*, 7.3.*x*
1.6.5.*x*	8.0.6, 8.0.5, 8.0.4, 8.0.3, 7.3.*x*

TABLE 2-4. *Supported Databases for Each Version of EM*

OMS/Intelligent Agent Supported Configurations

The OMS is the only component of Base EM that talks to the Intelligent Agents. Because the agents have been improved and developed further, certain restrictions regarding functionality apply, depending on the version of the agent. In addition, each OMS can communicate to a number of various agents, which are listed in Table 2-6.

Intelligent Agent/Database Supported Configurations

We mentioned in Chapter 1 that the Intelligent Agent is designed to work with databases of the same version or lower. However, it is also limited to currently supported database versions. That means you do not have to upgrade to the latest

OMS Version	Supported Database Versions as container for repository
9.0.1	9.0.1, 8.1.7, 8.1.6, 8.0.6
2.2.*x*	8.1.7, 8.1.6, 8.0.6, 7.3.4
2.1.*x*	8.1.6, 8.1.5, 8.0.6, 8.0.5, 8.0.4, 7.3.4.*x*
2.0.*x*	8.1.5, 8.0.5.*x*, 8.0.4.*x*, 7.3.*x*
1.6.5.*x*	8.0.6.*x*, 8.0.5.*x*, 7.3.4.*x*

TABLE 2-5. *Databases Supported as Repository Containers for Each Version of EM*

OMS Version	Supported Agent Versions
9.0.1	9.0.1, 8.1.7, 8.1.6, 8.0.6
2.2.*x*	8.1.7, 8.1.6, 8.1.5, 8.0.6, 7.3.4
2.1.x	8.1.6, 8.1.5, 8.0.*x*, 7.3.4.*x*
2.0.*x*	8.1.5, 8.0.6.*x*, 8.0.5.*x*, 7.3.4.*x*
1.6.5.*x*	8.0.6.*x*, 8.0.5.*x*, 7.3.4.*x*

TABLE 2-6. *Supported Intelligent Agents for Each Version of OMS*

version of the Agent if the installed version offers sufficient functionality. Furthermore, the node should not contain any database of a higher release. Table 2-7 lists the database versions the agents can officially manage.

Preparing and Planning the Installation

Before you install the EM software, you should consider how you want to configure your EM environment. How you plan to use EM has influence on how you configure it, how many components you install, and where you install them. To perform a proper EM configuration that suits your needs, consider the following:

- Do you need an EM repository or will you only be using EM in standalone mode, also known as the *Client/Server Deployment* option? This is discussed in "Log in or not Log in: Using EM Without Management Server" in Chapter 3.

Agent Version	Supported Database Versions
9.0.1	9.0.1, 8.1.7, 8.1.6, 8.0.6
8.1.7	8.1.7, 8.1.6, 8.1.5, 8.0.6, 7.3.4
8.1.6	8.1.6, 8.1.5, 8.0.*x*, 7.3.4.*x*
8.1.5	8.1.5, 8.0.*x*, 7.3.*x*
8.0.6	8.0.6, 8.0.5, 8.0.4, 8.0.3, 7.3.*x*

TABLE 2-7. *Supported Database Versions for Each Version of the Intelligent Agent*

- If you want an EM repository, and go for the full configuration, the *Three-Tier Deployment* option, do you already have a database available for this purpose or do you need to create a new database to hold the EM repository?
- If you want an EM repository, do you want this to reside on a separate server or together with the Management Server?
- If you want an EM repository, where do you want your Oracle Management Server component to be installed and how many Management Servers do you need?
- Are the Intelligent Agents already in place, perhaps in a previous version, or do you have to plan installation of this component on the target nodes as well?
- Where will you install the EM client part (EM Console), and will you take advantage of the Web-enabled EM Console?

Choosing Installation Options

In the rest of this chapter, different descriptions of how to install EM components are presented, each to be used according to your choice of EM installation and configuration.

- The "Installing the Database and Management Server" section assumes that you want to configure the Three-Tier Deployment option and take full advantage of EM, including database software, Management Server, and Intelligent Agent, and assumes that you are creating a new database and EM repository. This is the option to choose if you are starting completely from scratch.
- The "Installing the Management Server Only" section describes how to install only the Management Server component. Use this option when you already have a database available for the EM repository, and you only need to install the Management Server, EM repository, and EM Client components. This option is also used when you are adding a Management Server for load balancing or availability reasons.
- The "Creating the EM Repository" section describes how to create the EM repository in an existing database.
- The "Installing the EM Client" section describes the steps required to install the EM client (EM Console) software only.
- Finally, the "Installing the Intelligent Agent" part shows how to install the Intelligent Agent component, which is required on target nodes for monitoring and job scheduling purposes.

Reading the Release Notes and Installation Guide

Remember to read the Release Notes and the Installation Guide before proceeding. You'll frequently find a lot of important information here, such as operating-system–dependent information, system requirements, restrictions, and so on.

To read the Release Notes, place the first CD of the Oracle9i software distribution set in your CD-ROM drive. When you close the drive, it should automatically start and show the Oracle9i Server - Autorun screen, which is shown in Figure 2-1. Click Browse Documentation to get to the Oracle9i Server documentation screen.

If the Autorun screen does not appear automatically, go to the root of the CD (or to the "Disk 1" directory, if you copied the software to a staging area), and double-click the file welcome.htm. The Oracle9i Server documentation screen should appear. From this screen, click Release Notes. Browse through this file to check if it contains information that you need.

To read the Installation Guide, go back to the Oracle9i Server documentation screen and click Documentation. Here you'll find the Database Installation Guide, as well as the EM Configuration Guide in HTML and PDF formats. The PDF format

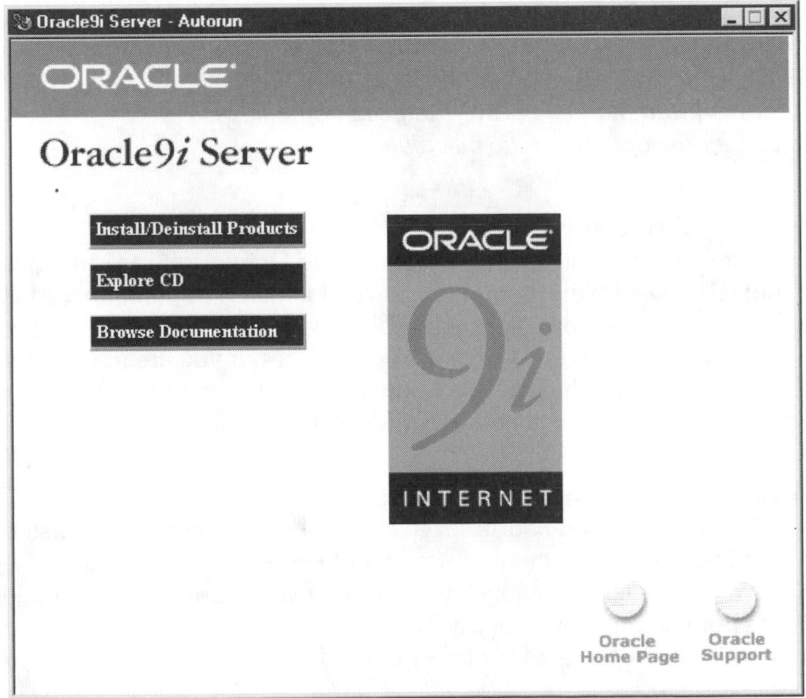

FIGURE 2-1. *The Oracle9i Server Autorun Screen*

is useful if you want to print it on paper. An Enterprise Edition Installation Instructions Quick Tour is also available.

Preparing Your Hardware

You should keep your Oracle software, and especially your database files, separate from the operating system, which on Windows systems is normally on your C: drive. If you need to reinstall Windows and the C: drive is reformatted, you will still have your database after the reinstallation; you will only need to install the Oracle software again.

We will now go through the preparation steps of logging onto the machine, checking the network connections, and securing that enough space is available for the installation.

Logging on to Your Machine

Remember to log on to your machine as the local administrator or use an account that is a member of the Administrators group.

NOTE
If the machine is part of a Windows NT or 2000 domain, you normally log on to the domain in order to access network resources. In order to install software, however, you must log on to the machine as an administrator. If there is a "Domain" drop-down list in the login dialog, you can normally select either the domain or the machine.

Setting up a Drive for Oracle

You should create a dedicated disk partition for the Oracle software and database. For the Three-Tier Deployment option, you should make this partition 2 to 3GB in size. If your disk is already partitioned, you need a third-party tool like Partition Magic from PowerQuest to change your partition sizes. If you are not comfortable with this, just install everything on the C: drive. For the examples in this chapter, assume that you have this extra partition, and its drive letter is F:.

Securing Enough Temporary Space

You need 400MB of temporary disk space to install the Oracle9i Enterprise Edition 400MB. The installer checks this and stops if not enough free temporary space is available. Ensure that there is enough free space in your current temporary location, or set this to point to another directory by setting the environment variable TEMP. On Windows 2000, click Start | Settings | Control Panel | System | Advanced |

Environment Variables, select TEMP, and click Edit. On Windows NT4, click Start | Settings | Control Panel | System | Environment, highlight the environment variable, and modify its value.

Network Configuration Issues

Oracle does not support assigning a dynamic IP address via DHCP (Dynamic Host Configuration Protocol) on nodes running the Management Server or Intelligent Agent. You can get it working for a test installation, but you should use fixed IP addresses for these nodes in a productive environment. DHCP is supported only on EM clients, which are also capable of using a dial-up network connection to connect to the Management Server. If using a dial-up connection between the EM Client and Management Server, the connection speed should be at least 56K.

Firewall Issues If you have a firewall between your EM Client and Management Server components, the following ports must be opened in order for the client to communicate with the OMS:

7771, 7773, 7776:	Communication between the EM Console and OMS
7774:	Communication between OMS and the Oracle Applications Manager
7775, 7777:	Communication between OMS and Paging Server

If there is a firewall between the OMS and the Intelligent Agent on the monitored nodes, the following port numbers must be opened.

1748, 1754:	Used for discovering new targets
7772:	Communication between OMS and Intelligent Agent
7773:	Communication between OMS and Intelligent Agent via SSL

The OMS and Intelligent Agent cannot be separated by a firewall using the NAT (Network Address Translation) feature, which masks the true IP address into another IP address. Because the OMS and Intelligent Agent communication includes the host address information in the data packet, rather than in the IP header, NAT is not allowed.

Additionally, if the EM Console is running in a Web browser, the firewall needs to allow HTTP traffic on port number 3339 (default) between the EM Website Web server and the browser clients.

Installing the Database and Management Server

This section describes how to install the Three-Tier Deployment option, which includes the Oracle9i database software as well as the Management Server and the EM Client software. The creation of a new database to hold the EM repository is also included in this description.

1. Place the first CD of the Oracle9i software distribution set in your CD-ROM drive. When you close the drive, the CD should automatically start and show the Oracle9i Server - Autorun screen (see Figure 2-1). Click Install/Deinstall Products, and the Oracle Universal Installer Welcome screen appears. If the autorun screen is not shown automatically, go to the root of the CD (or to the Disk 1 directory, if you copied the software to a staging area) and double-click the file setup.exe; the Welcome screen should appear. Click Next in the Welcome screen to continue with the installation.
2. Next, the File Locations screen appears, which is shown in Figure 2-2. Here you must enter a name for the Oracle Home for the database and management server software (such as "OraHome90" or "OraNT9i"), and choose a directory. If you are installing to your F: drive, you can choose F:\oracle\oraNT9i. The Oracle home name and the directory name do not have to match, but it is a good idea to use the same name. Writing this in upper or lower case makes no difference on the Windows platform. When you have entered all the information, click Next.

NOTE
Even though you chose drive F: for the Oracle software, the Oracle Universal Installer (OUI) installs its inventory and installation logs on the C: drive in the C:\Program Files\Oracle\Inventory\logs directory. The file installActions.log file contains the most recent installation log; any previous logs will be renamed with a timestamp. On the Summary screen (shown in Figure 2-9), you will be able to see exactly how much space is required on each drive.

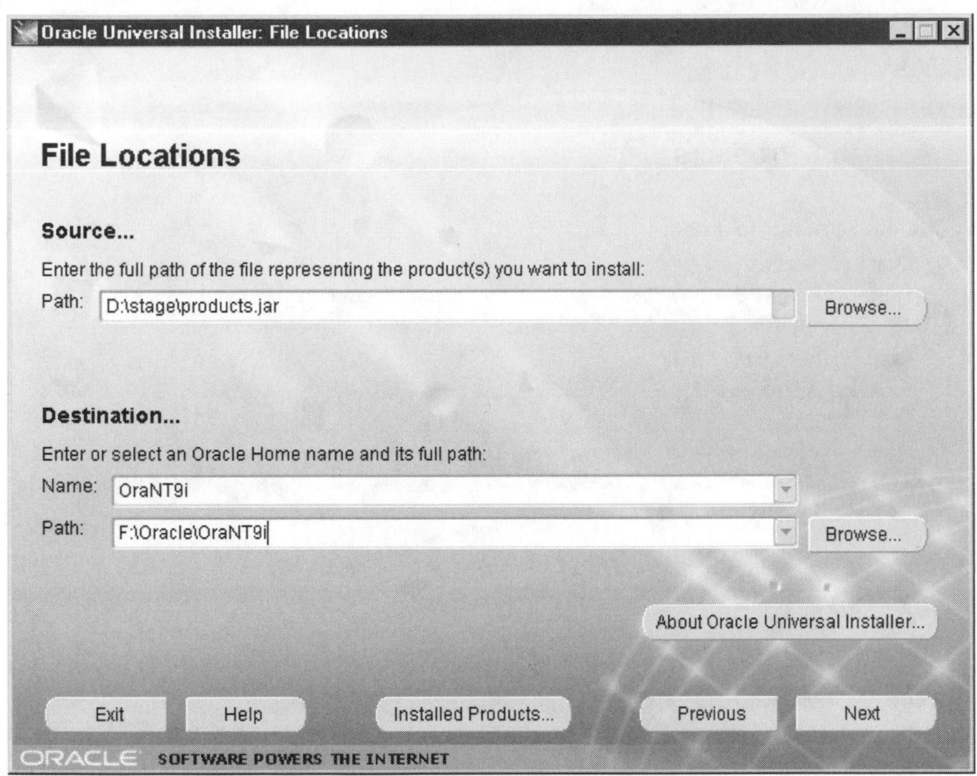

FIGURE 2-2. *Selecting a Home name and path for installation*

3. After a little while, the Available Products screen appears, as shown in Figure 2-3. You want to install database and management server software, so choose Oracle 9i Database 9.0.1.1.1 and click Next.

NOTE
If you want to install the Oracle software in a language other than English, click Product Languages and choose the language you want on the Language Selection screen. Click OK to return to the Oracle Universal Installer.

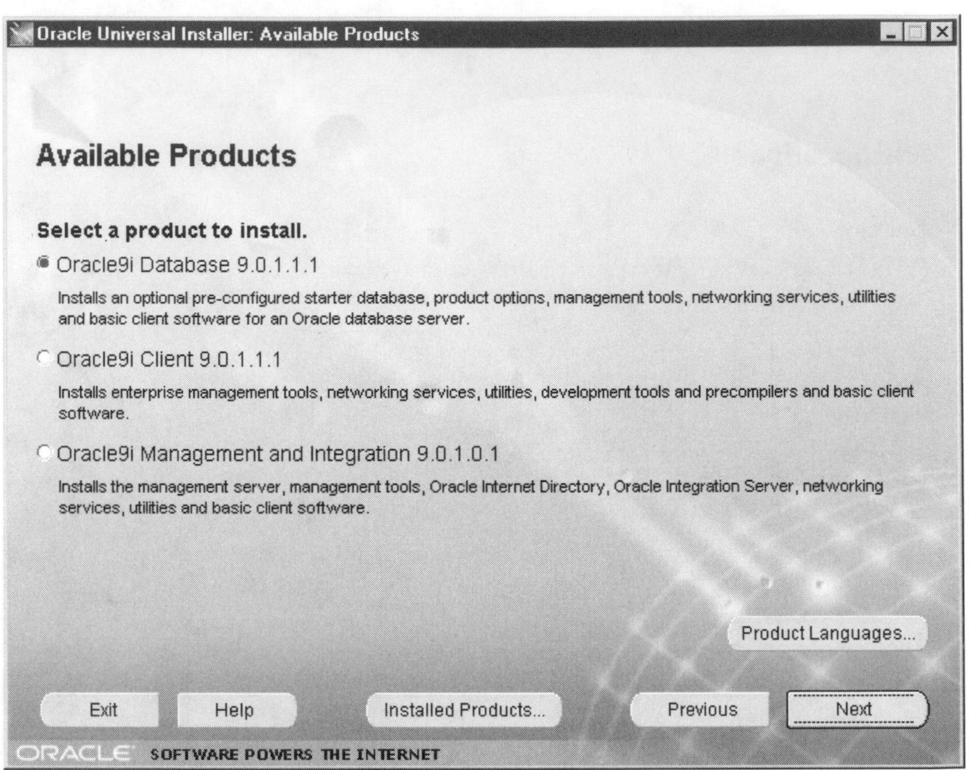

FIGURE 2-3. *Selecting the product to install*

4. The Installation Types screen appears, as shown in Figure 2-4. Choose "Enterprise Edition" and click Next.
5. Next, the Database Configuration screen appears (see Figure 2-5). Here you decide what type of database you want to install. The General Purpose database configuration will work fine as EM repository. Select General Purpose, and then click Next.

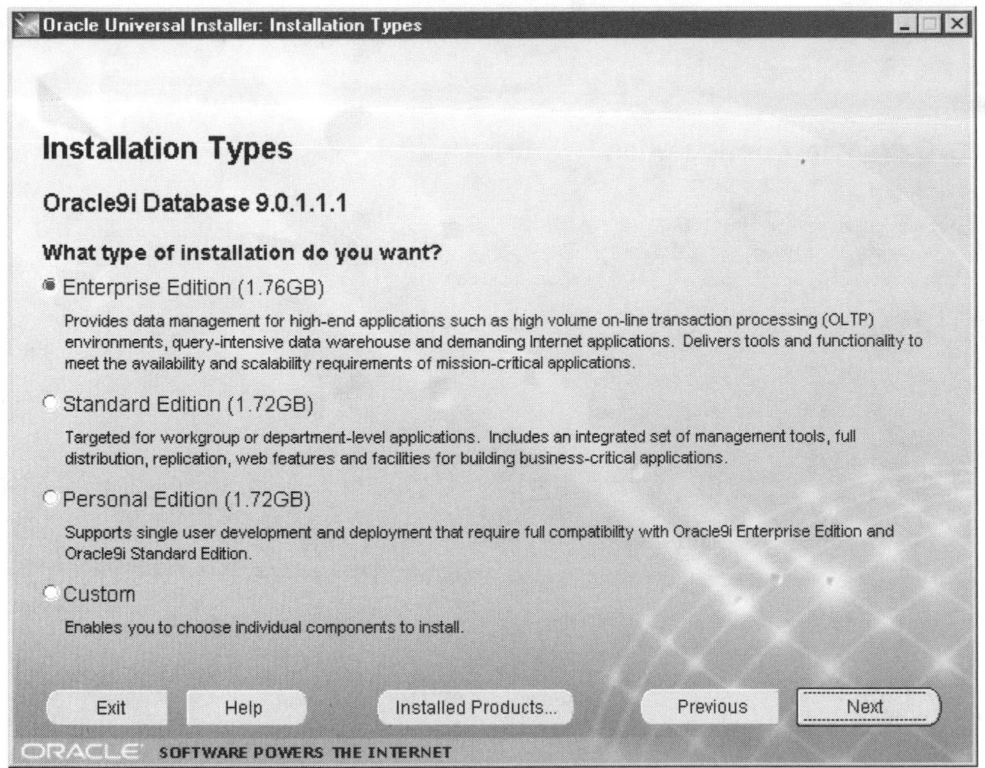

FIGURE 2-4. *Selecting the type of installation*

NOTE

With Oracle9i, you can define your own template for a database creation, store it, and use it for future database creations. For productive use of an EM repository, you might not want to use the predefined database templates because they contain a considerable amount of demo and example data. You can customize your own EM repository database by selecting Customized on the Database Configuration screen.

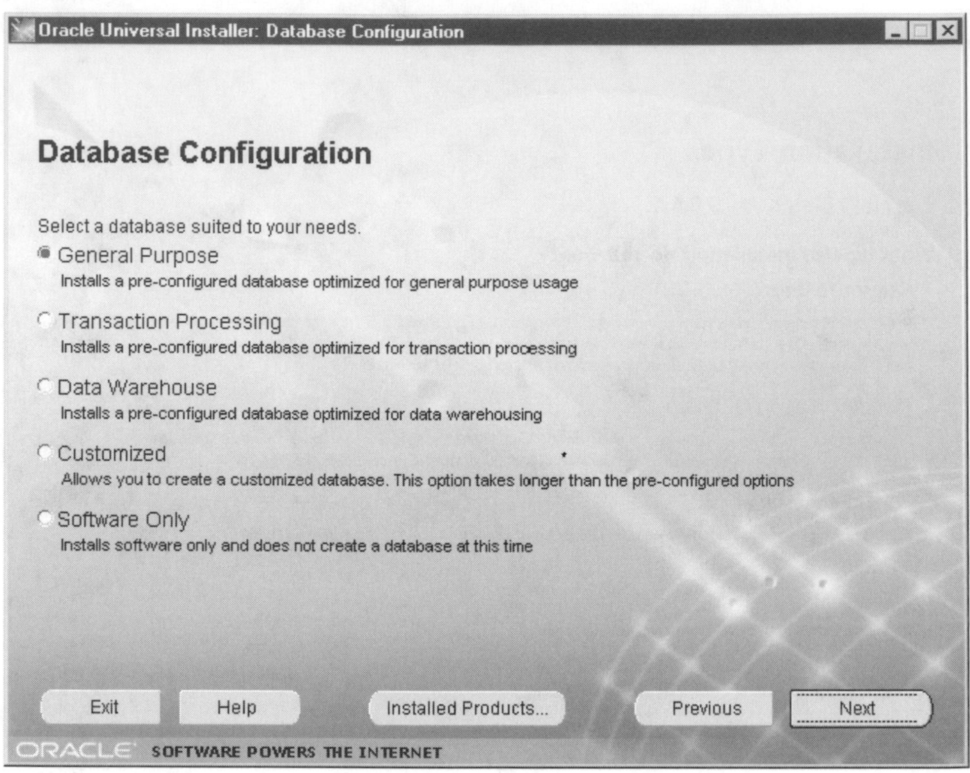

FIGURE 2-5. *Selecting the database configuration*

6. The Database Identification screen appears, as shown in Figure 2-6. Enter a Global Database Name and a System Identifier (SID). For example, you can use OEMREP for both. Then click Next.

NOTE
You do not need to include "WORLD" as part of the global database name, but if you are using a domain different from the default "WORLD" as part of your global database name, you should include this, for example, OEMREP.YOURDOMAIN.

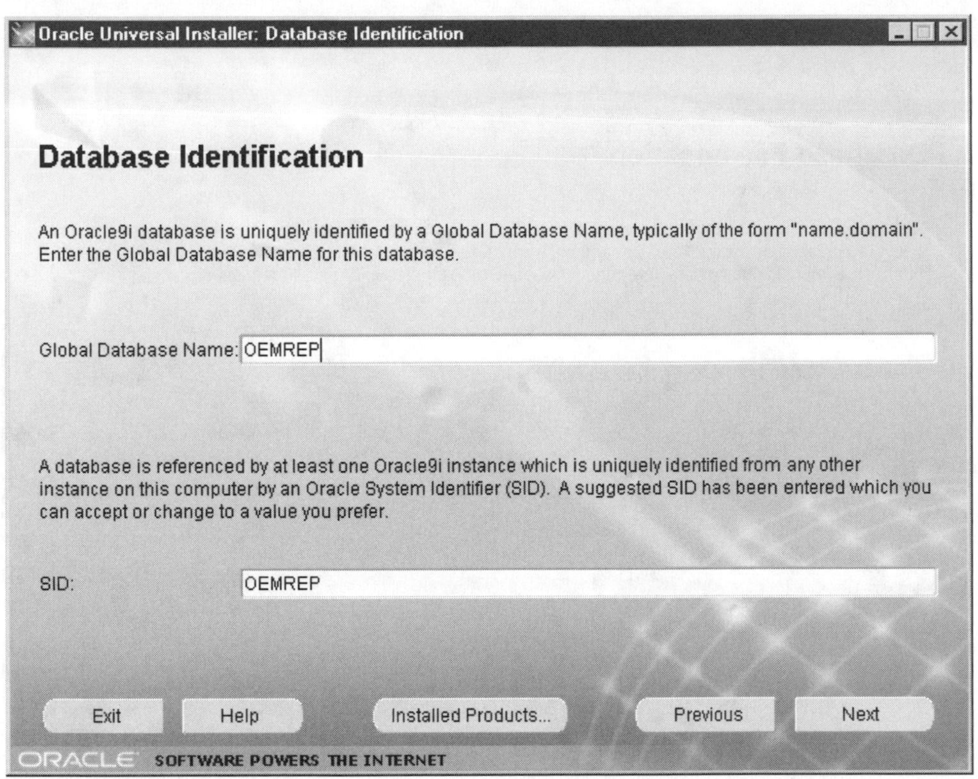

FIGURE 2-6. *Selecting a database name and SID*

7. The Database File Location screen appears, as shown in Figure 2-7. Enter the path for the directory holding your Oracle database files, such as F:\Oracle\Oradata. The database files will then be placed here in a directory with the same name as the SID. Click Next.

8. The Database Character Set screen is shown in Figure 2-8. Where, you choose the database character set used in your database. You are not required to use the Unicode (UTF8) character set for EM repository, so you can choose the default value, which is based on your Windows settings. Choose Use the default character set and click Next.

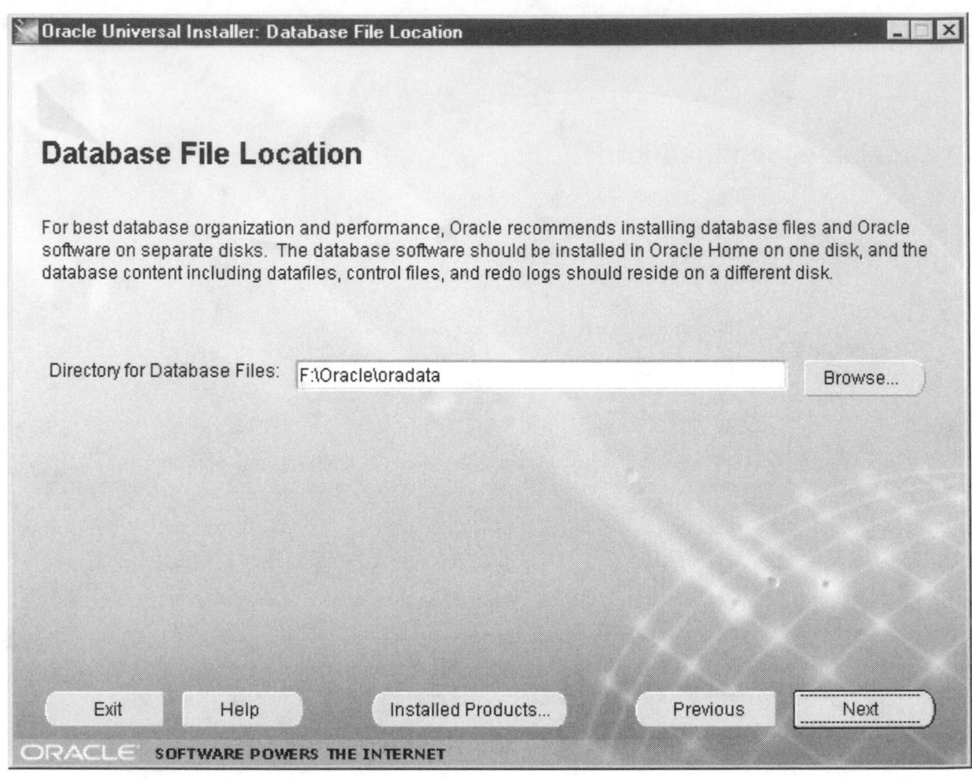

FIGURE 2-7. *Specifying a location for the database file*

9. Finally, a Summary of the installation is shown, where you can scroll through the list of products being installed. As you can see from Figure 2-9, about 13MB is installed on the C: drive (the OUI Inventory, installation logs, and Java Runtime,) and approximately 1.5GB are installed in the new Oracle Home OraNT9i on the F: drive. Continue with the installation by clicking Install.

NOTE
Depending on the performance of your machine, it will take quite a while for the installation to complete (plan for at least one hour). You do not have to watch the computer while it works, but at some point you will be prompted to insert Disk 2 and Disk 3 of the 9i installation set if you are installing from a CD.

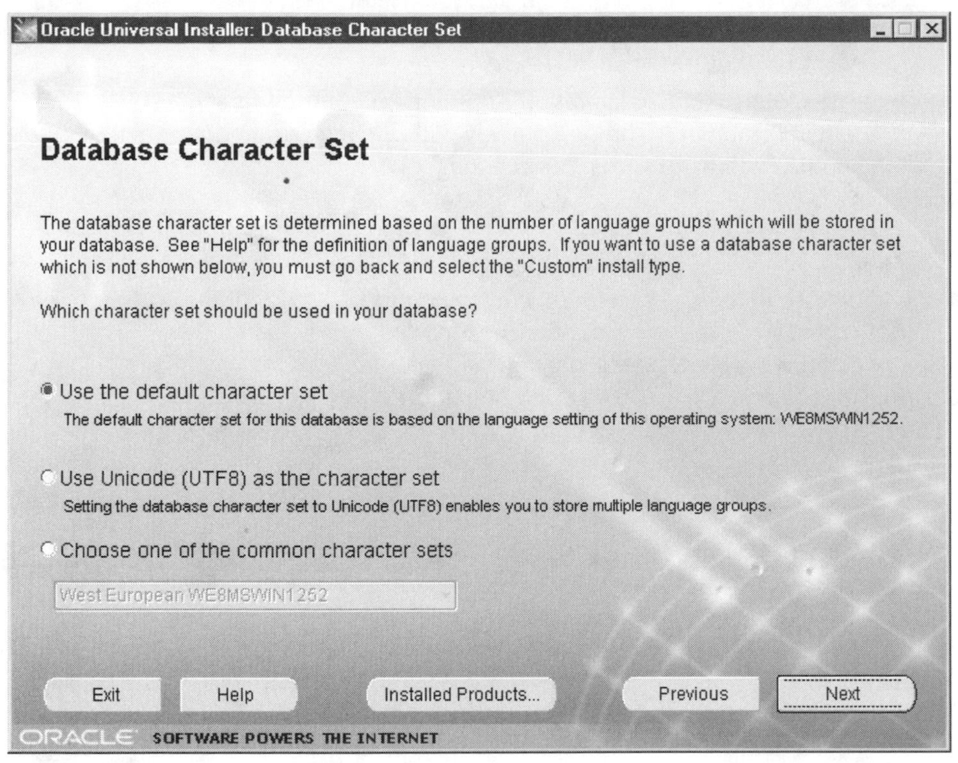

FIGURE 2-8. *Choosing the database character set*

10. After the installation has been running for a while (approximately 44% through), you will be prompted for Disk 2, if you are installing from a CD. Insert the second CD-ROM or browse to the directory where it is located, if you are using a staging area and the installer cannot locate it itself. Then click OK to continue the installation.
11. The installer now copies the starter database files and will stay at 44 percent for a short while, so be patient. When the installer is approximately 88 percent through, you will be prompted for Disk 3. Insert the third CD-ROM or browse to the directory where it is located, and click OK.
12. Now the installation will be running quite a while again, even after announcing that it is 100 percent done. When the installation of the software is complete, the Configuration Tools screen appears, as shown in Figure 2-10 where four different operations are performed automatically:
    - Oracle Net Configuration Assistant
    - Starting Oracle HTTP service

- Oracle Database Configuration Assistant
- Oracle Intelligent Agent

The Oracle Net Configuration Assistant and Starting Oracle HTTP service parts normally run through quickly without any required user action, and should both have status "Succeeded."

NOTE
If any of these configurations fail, or for some reason you choose to interrupt them (by clicking on the tool you want to stop and clicking the Stop button), you can always start them separately at a later time from the Oracle Configuration and Migration Tools and HTTP-Server program groups.

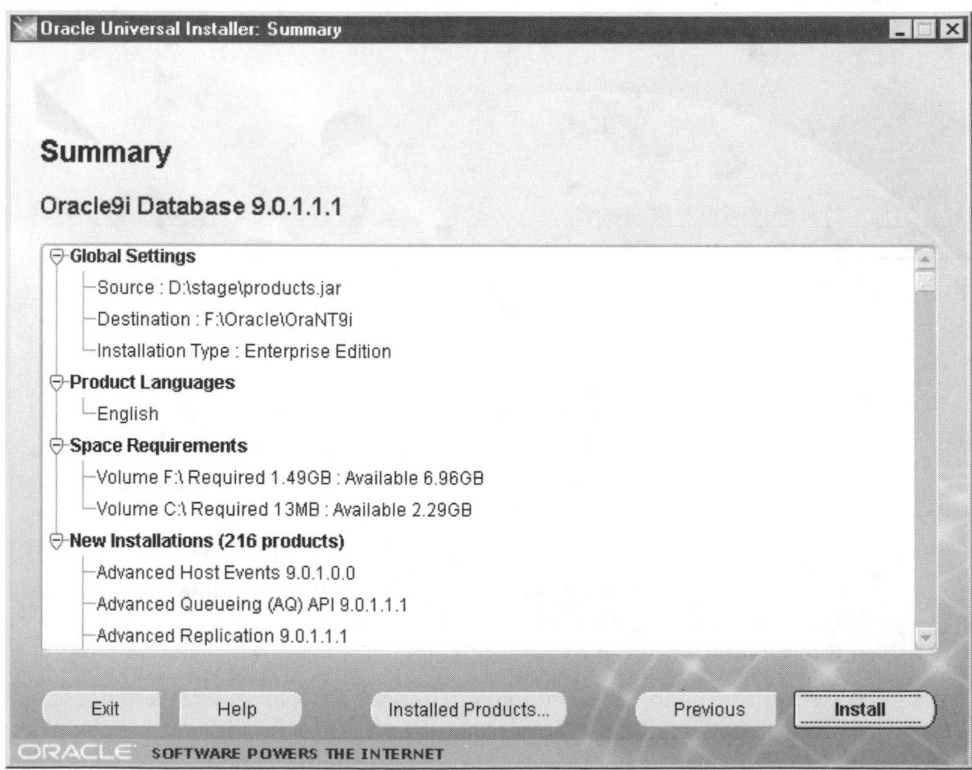

FIGURE 2-9. *Viewing the installation summary*

13. The Oracle Database Configuration Assistant creates the database as specified earlier, again without any required user action. After the database creation, which takes approximately 20 minutes (database files are copied, and the database is initialized according to the database template chosen), a summary is shown.

14. If you want to change the passwords for the administrator accounts SYS and SYSTEM (recommended), or unlock other accounts, you can do this now by clicking Password Management. The Password Management screen is displayed, and you can perform the password change. Otherwise, click Exit to proceed to the last step, which is to configure and start the Oracle Intelligent Agent service.

15. Now the software installation and database creation is finished and the End of Installation screen is displayed. Click Exit to exit the Oracle Universal Installer and OK to confirm when prompted.

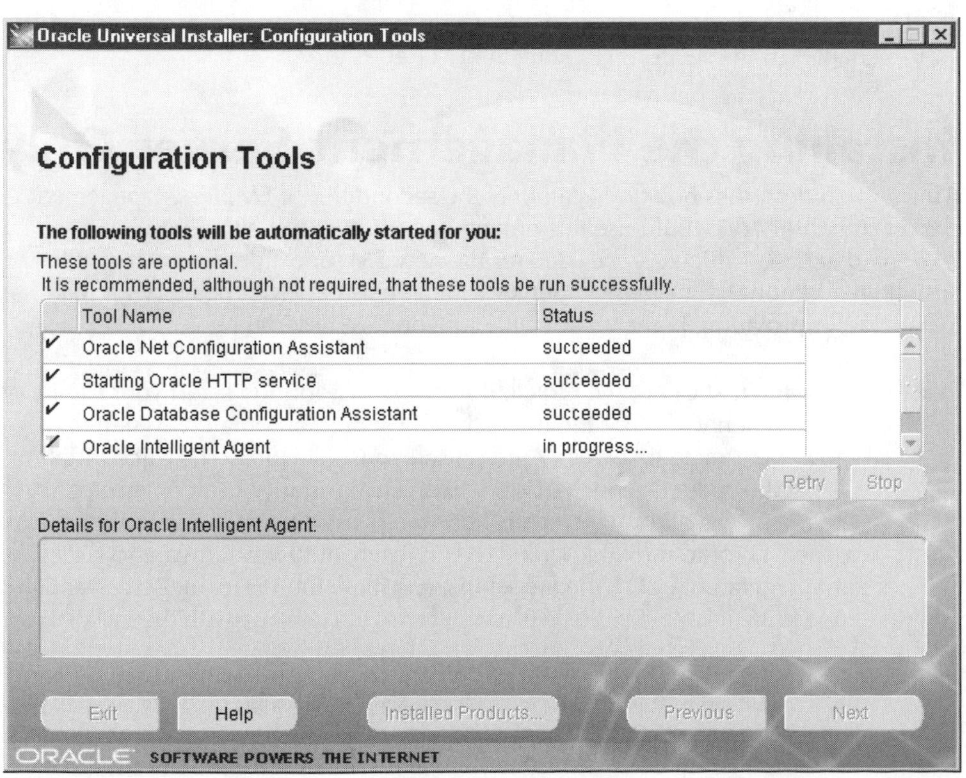

FIGURE 2-10. *Running the configuration tools*

At this point, you have installed all necessary software components for your Oracle database and Management Server. Several Windows NT/2000 services have been created, and your database is ready for EM repository creation (test that a connection is possible as user SYSTEM using SQL*Plus). Do not worry that there is no Management Server NT service created yet, this is done when you create the EM repository and configure the Management Server to use it.

NOTE
The NT services with a startup mode of Automatic should be started now. If not all services are started, and you cannot start them (typically HTTP Server), reboot your server, which normally solves the problem. When the server has come up again, check that the services are started and that the database is open for connections.

Now you need to create the EM repository in the database just created. Creating the EM repository and configuring the Management Server to use it is described later in this chapter in the section "Creating the EM Repository."

Installing the Management Server Only

This section describes how to install only the second tier of EM, the Management Server software. You would use this procedure in two cases: either you have an existing database, which can be used for the new EM repository, or you want to install an additional Management Server with an existing EM repository for load balancing or providing higher availability for your EM environment.

1. Place the first CD of the Oracle9i software distribution set in your CD-ROM drive. When you close the drive, the CD should automatically start and show the Oracle9i Server - Autorun screen (see Figure 2-1). Click Install/Deinstall Products, and the Oracle Universal Installer Welcome screen appears. If the autorun screen is not shown automatically, go to the root of the CD (or to the Disk 1 directory if you copied the software to a staging area) and double-click the file setup.exe, where the Welcome screen should appears. Click Next in the Welcome screen to continue with the installation.
2. Next, the File Locations screen shown in Figure 2-2 appears. Here you must enter a name for the Oracle Home for the Management Server software (such as "OraEM9i") and choose a directory. If you already have an Oracle9i home, you can also install the Management Server software into this (recommended). Then click Next.

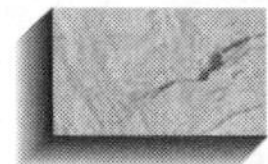

NOTE
When installing the Oracle Management Server Infrastructure in the same home as the Oracle9i database software, it is also possible for the Enterprise Manager Configuration Assistant to create a new database for the repository. If you do not install the Management server in the same home as the database software, you can use the Database Configuration Assistant to create the database instead.

3. After a little while, the Available Products screen appears, as shown in Figure 2-3. Choose Oracle 9i Management and Integration 9.0.1.0.1 and click Next.

NOTE
If you want to install the Oracle software in a language other than English, click Product Languages and choose the language you want on the Language Selection screen. Click OK to return to the Oracle Universal Installer.

4. The Installation Types screen now appears as shown in Figure 2-11. Choose Oracle Management Server and click Next.
5. After a little while, the Oracle Management Server Repository screen appears, as shown in Figure 2-12. Here you decide whether you will be using an existing EM repository or want to create a new one. If you want to create a new EM repository, continue with the following section. If you don't want to create a new EM repository, skip to the section "Installing Management Server with an Existing EM Repository."

Installing Management Server and Creating a New EM Repository

In this section, you will create a new EM repository in an existing database.

1. Choose "The Management Server will require a new repository," as shown in Figure 2-12, and click Next.
2. Next, a summary of the installation is shown, where you can scroll through the list of products being installed. Continue with the installation by clicking Install.

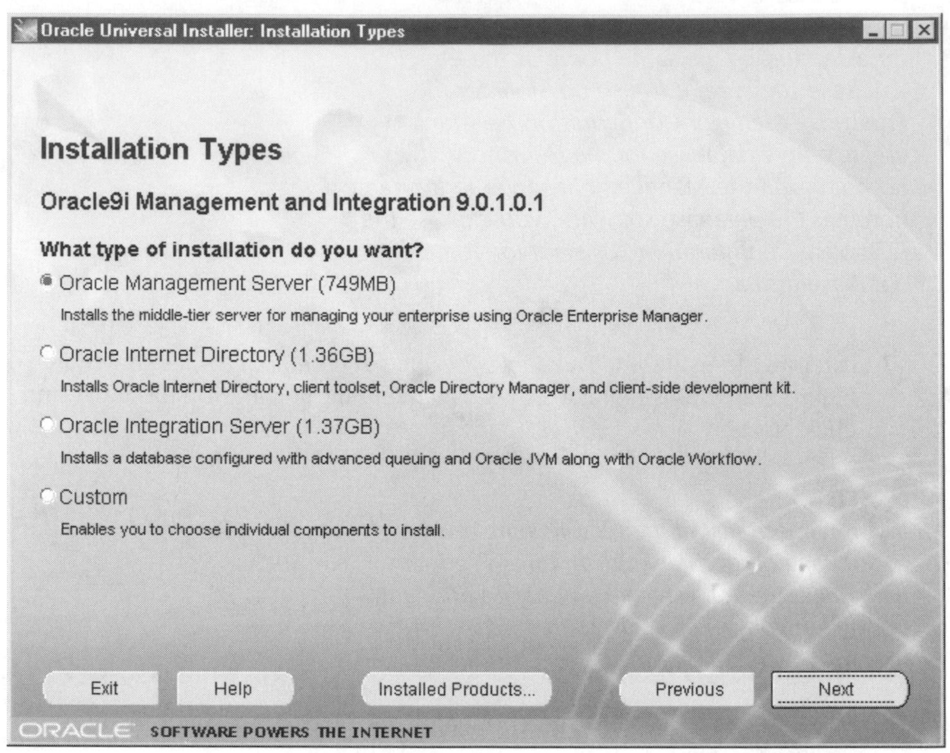

FIGURE 2-11. *Selecting the type of installation*

3. The software installation begins. After the installation has been running for a while (approximately 92 percent through), you will be prompted for Disk 2. Insert the second CD-ROM, or browse to the directory where it is located if you are using a staging area and the installer cannot locate it (normally, it will). Then click OK.
4. After a short while (when the installer is approximately 97 percent through), you will be prompted for Disk 3. Insert the third CD-ROM or browse to the directory where it is located, if you are using a staging area, and click OK to continue.
5. When the installation of the software is complete, a screen will appear, as shown in Figure 2-13, where three different operations are performed:
   - Oracle Net Configuration Assistant
   - Start HTTP Listener
   - Oracle Enterprise Manager Configuration Assistant

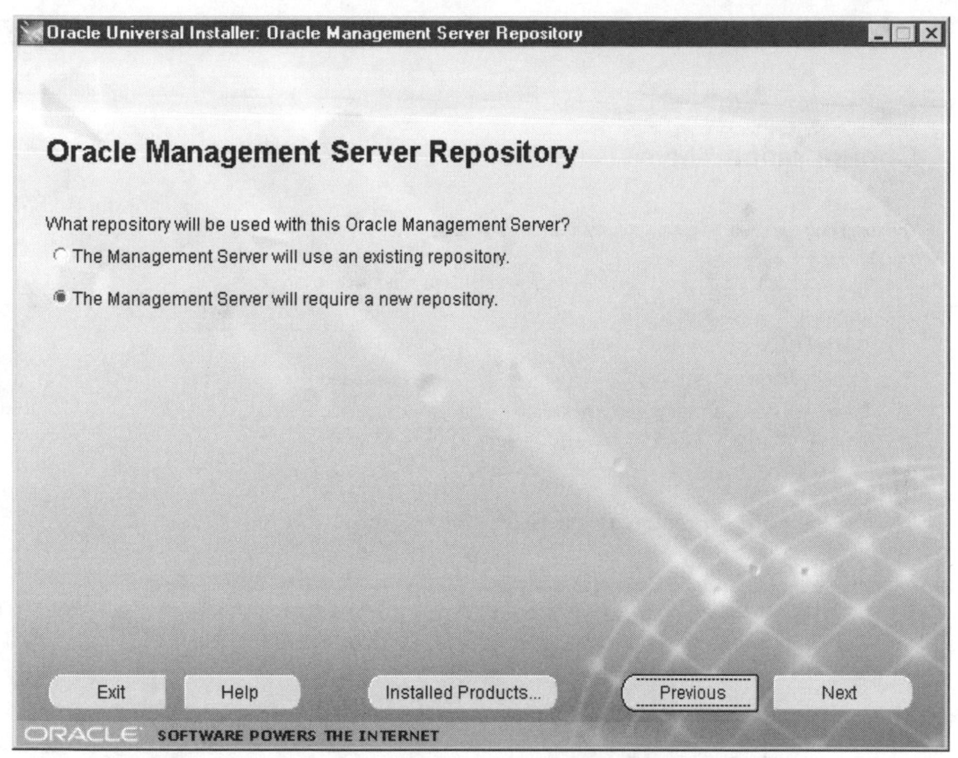

FIGURE 2-12. *Choosing between creating a new repository and using an existing one*

6. The Oracle Enterprise Manager Configuration Assistant (EMCA) starts and walks you through five steps to create a new repository in an existing database. The first screen is a Welcome screen explaining what the EMCA is doing. Click Next to continue.
7. The second step of the EMCA is to provide information about the database where the EM repository is to be installed. The database can be entered either using a TNS alias such as OEMREP.WORLD (or without WORLD if this is your default domain) or by using the *<host>*:*<port>*:*<SID>* syntax, for example CHBSLLAVA:1521:OEMREP. Then click Next.
8. The third step of the EMCA is to define the user name in which the EM Repository will be created. For example, enter OEMREP_CHBSLLAVA as the EM repository owner, when CHBSLLAVA is the host name. The user name you use for an EM Repository must be *unique* across your whole Oracle environment. Therefore, it is a good idea to include the host name in the EM repository schema name. As a reminder, a popup is shown. Be sure that the user name is unique and click Yes to continue.

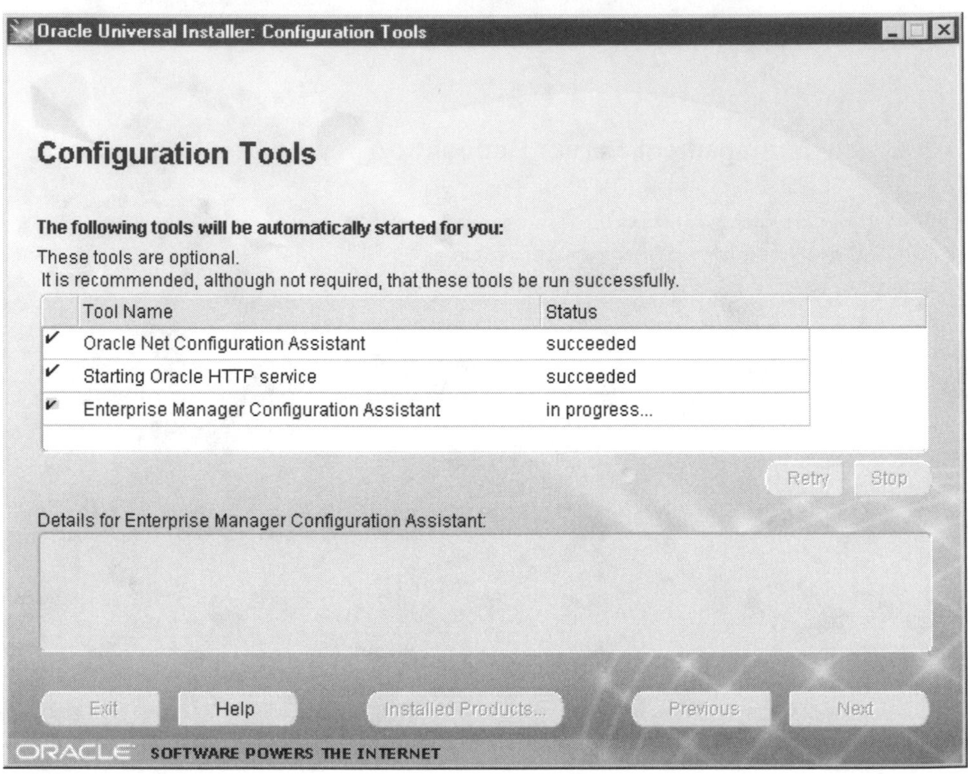

FIGURE 2-13. *Running the configuration tools*

9. The fourth step of the EMCA is to provide information about the default tablespace (used for storing the EM repository) and the temporary tablespace (for sort operations) for the EM user. The default is the OEM_REPOSITORY and TEMP tablespace, respectively. Click Next to continue.

NOTE
The EM9i repository requires between 30 and 40MB when it is created. Ensure that enough free space is available in the tablespace chosen to hold the EM repository. 50MB is a good starting point.

10. The last step is just a summary of what is going to be created; click Finish to continue.

11. The EMCA begins the EM repository creation. The progress will be shown. When all three steps have finished, click Close to continue.

Now the EM repository is created and ready for use by the Management Server, and you should have a running Management Server. Check to see if you have an NT service called OracleOraNT9iManagementServer (where OraNT9i is your Oracle Home). If you do not, this indicates a problem with your installation, which you should analyze. The Management Server NT service can be created by running EMCA again or by using the OMSNTSRV.EXE command-line utility, which is also used by the NT service. See Chapter 20 for more details about this utility.

Installing Management Server with an Existing EM Repository

This section describes how to install the Management Server software only. You may want to do this when installing additional Management Servers to your EM Repository in order to improve the availability and load balancing of your EM environment.

1. Choose "The Management Server will use an existing repository" on the screen, as shown in Figure 2-12, and click Next.
2. Next, a summary of the installation is shown, where you can scroll through the list of products being installed. Continue with the installation by clicking Install.
3. The software installation begins. After the installation has been running for a while (approximately 92 percent through), you will be prompted for Disk 2. Insert the second CD-ROM, or browse to the directory where it is located, and click OK.
4. After a short while (when the installer is approximately 97 percent through), you will be prompted for Disk 3. Insert the third CD-ROM, or browse to the directory where it is located, and click OK to continue.
5. The installation will run for quite a while, even after having reached 100 percent. When the installation of the software is complete, the Oracle Enterprise Manager Configuration Assistant (EMCA) launches and walks you through four steps in order to use an existing EM repository. The first screen is a Welcome screen explaining what the EMCA is doing. Click Next to continue.
6. The next step of the EMCA is to provide information about the existing EM Repository, which must be running and open for connections. Enter the user name and password, as well as the database name where the EM repository is located, and then click Next. As shown in Figure 2-14, the database service name is OEMREP.WORLD (if WORLD is your default domain, you can leave this out) and the user name is OEMREP_CHBSLLAVA.

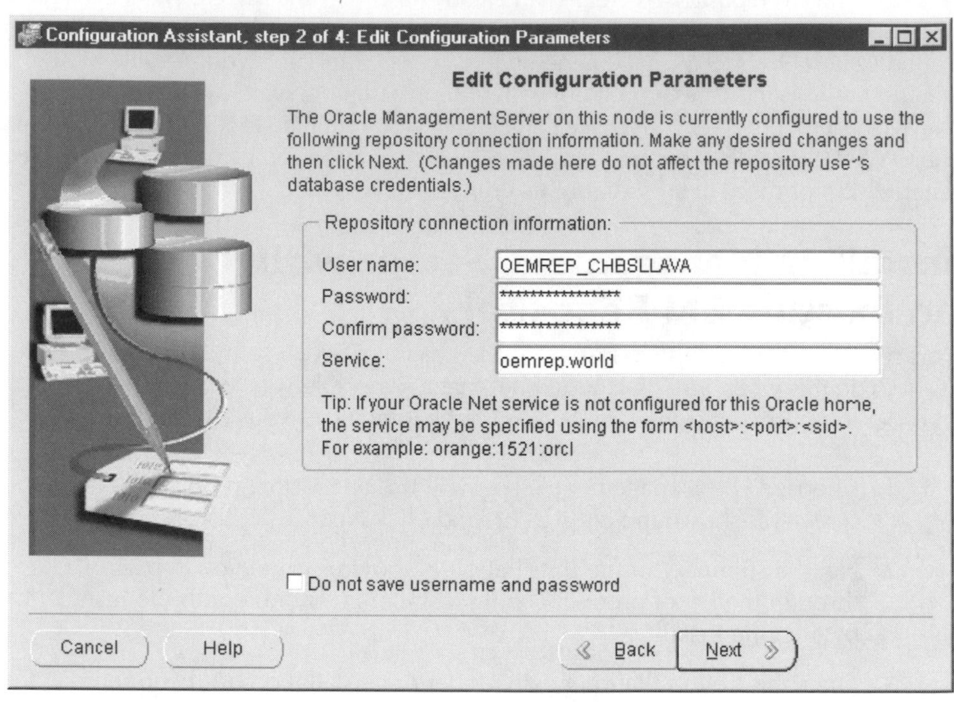

FIGURE 2-14. *Entering the user name and password for the existing repository*

NOTE
*In order to connect to the existing EM repository, you must ensure that the repository is running and that you have a functioning SQL*Net connection to the database. You can either use TNSPING or SQLPLUS for this test. If you cannot connect, you will probably receive an ORA-12154: could not resolve service name error. Add the database name to your TNSNAMES.ORA file, for example, by using the Net Configuration Assistant, and repeat the connection test until it succeeds. You can also try to connect using the <hostname>:<listener port>:<Oracle SID> connection qualifier. In this example, you would enter* ***CHBSLLAVA:1521:OEMREP*** *in the Service field.*

7. Now you must select the Management Region in which the EM Repository will be created. Accept the DEFAULT region and click Next to continue.

NOTE
If you want to use a Management Region other than the DEFAULT, you must create this region first. You can do this from this screen by entering the name in the field "a new region you create." Management Regions are discussed in more detail in Chapters 5 and 9.

8. The final step of the EMCA shows a summary of the configuration. Click Finish to continue.
9. The EMCA configures the Management Server to use the EM repository as specified. The progress will be shown. When this has finished (within a few seconds), click Close to continue.

Now the Management Server is installed and configured to use the existing EM Repository, and your Management Server should be running. Check to see if you have an NT service called OracleOraNT9iManagementServer (where OraNT9i is your Oracle Home). If you do not, this indicates a problem with your installation, which you should analyze. The Management Server NT service can be created by running EMCA again or by using the OMSNTSRV.EXE command-line utility, which is also used by the NT service. See Chapter 20 for more details about this utility.

Creating the EM Repository

This section describes how you install the EM repository in an existing database, for example, the one you created in the "Installing the Database and Management Server" section at the beginning of this chapter. You must create an EM repository before you can configure the Management Server. The EM repository is simply a database schema containing database objects (tables, indexes, and so on) used to store the information maintained by the Management Server and by the administrators through the EM Console. If you created your EM repository in the previous section, "Installing the Management Server Only," you do not need to create the repository. The rest of this section describes the Enterprise Manager Configuration Assistant (EMCA), which you can use to modify the Management Server configuration.

The Enterprise Manager Configuration Assistant (EMCA) is used for creating a new EM repository, performing maintenance or upgrade operations on an existing EM repository, or dropping a repository. With the EMCA, it is even possible to create a new database to hold the EM repository, if you want to. To use the EMCA for creating a new EM repository, follow these steps:

1. To invoke the Enterprise Manager Configuration Assistant, click Start | Programs | Oracle – OraNT9i | Configuration and Migration Tools |

Enterprise Manager Configuration Assistant. Notice that the "OraNT9i" will be whatever you called your Oracle Home. The EMCA Welcome screen appears; click Next to continue.

2. Next, you need to provide information about which kind of repository operation you are performing. Because you are creating a new EM repository, choose "Configure local Oracle Management Server" (see Figure 2-15), and click Next.

NOTE
If you already have configured the Management Server to use an EM repository, you will be notified through a dialog box. Click Edit to modify the existing configuration or Create to create a new one.

3. The Configure Oracle Management Server screen appears. You must choose whether to create a new repository or configure the management server to use an existing one (used for adding management servers to an existing EM repository). If you want to create a new EM repository, choose "Create a new repository," as shown in Figure 2-16, and click Next.

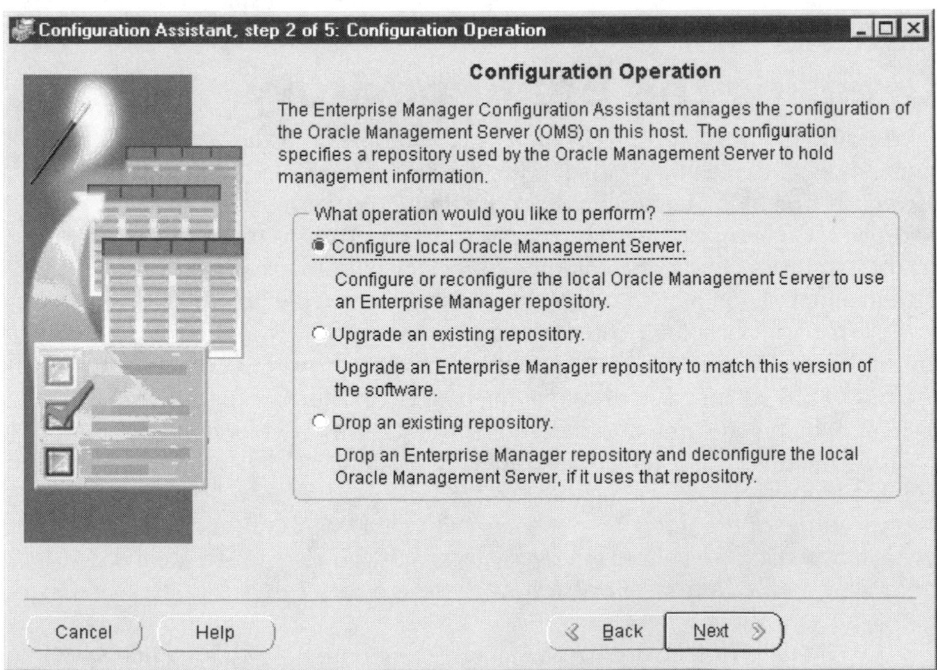

FIGURE 2-15. *Selecting the configuration operation*

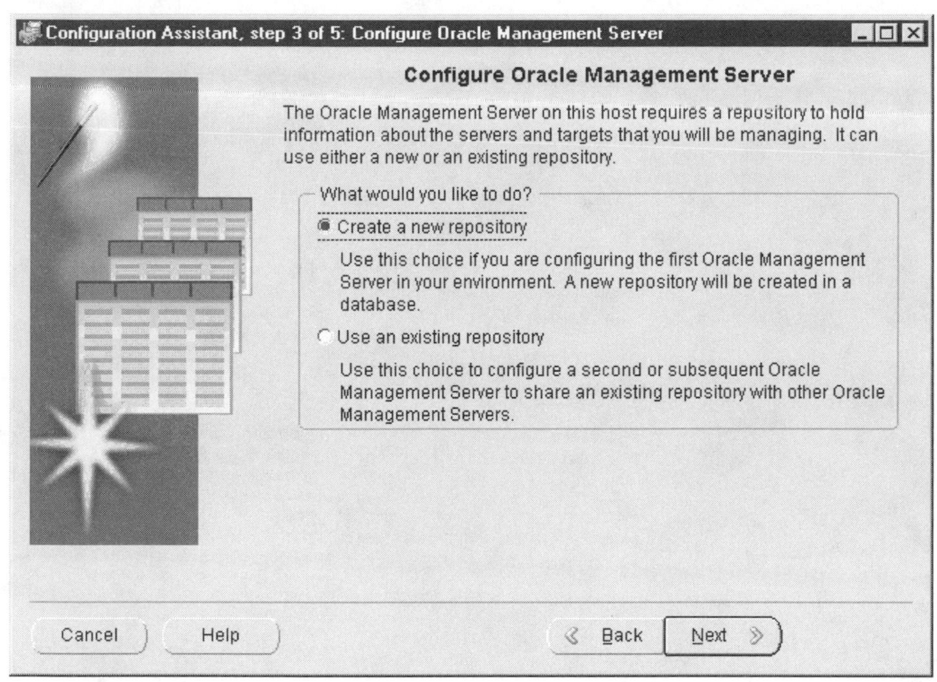

FIGURE 2-16. *Creating a new repository*

4. The Create New Repository Options screen appears. Now you must decide if you want to use the typical settings for the new repository, or use your own custom settings. Choose Custom, as shown in Figure 2-17, and click Next.

5. The Select Database Location screen appears. Here, you specify whether you will use an existing database for your new EM repository or whether you want to create a completely new database. Choose "In another existing database," as shown in Figure 2-18, and click Next.

6. The Select Database for Repository screen appears. Here, you must provide information about the database (the field with the label Service), where the EM repository is to be created, as well as the user name and password of a user with DBA privileges. The user defaults to SYS with SYSDBA privileges. In Oracle9i (or Oracle8i for that matter), a database connection as SYS must be either as SYSOPER or SYSDBA, if the initialization parameter O7_DICTIONARY_ACCESSIBILITY is set to FALSE, which is the default

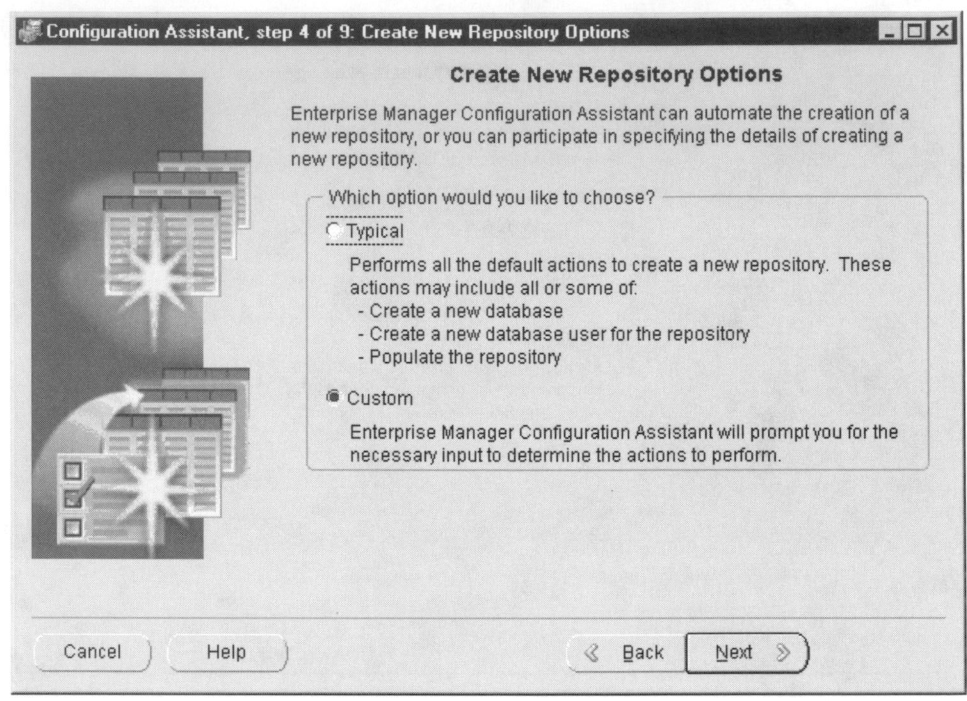

FIGURE 2-17. *Selecting a custom repository*

and recommended value. In this case, the database service name is called OEMREP, and the user with DBA privileges is SYSTEM, using the NORMAL mode (see Figure 2-19). Enter the information and click Next.

7. The Repository Login Information screen appears. You must specify the schema and username in which the EM repository will be created (see Figure 2-20). OEMREP_CHBSLLAVA is chosen as the EM repository owner (because CHBSLLAVA is the host name), and a password is entered for this Oracle user. You can use the "Do not save username and password" check the box to explicitly tell the Management Server not to store the username and password in encrypted format in the omsconfig.properties file, located in the ORACLE_HOME\sysman\config directory. This file is used by the Management Server at startup; in Chapter 19, we will look at this configuration file in more detail. If the repository credentials are stored in the file, the Management Server uses them to log in to the repository. If not, you will be prompted for the EM repository user name and password. This is known as the *Secure Management Server* mode. Click Next to continue.

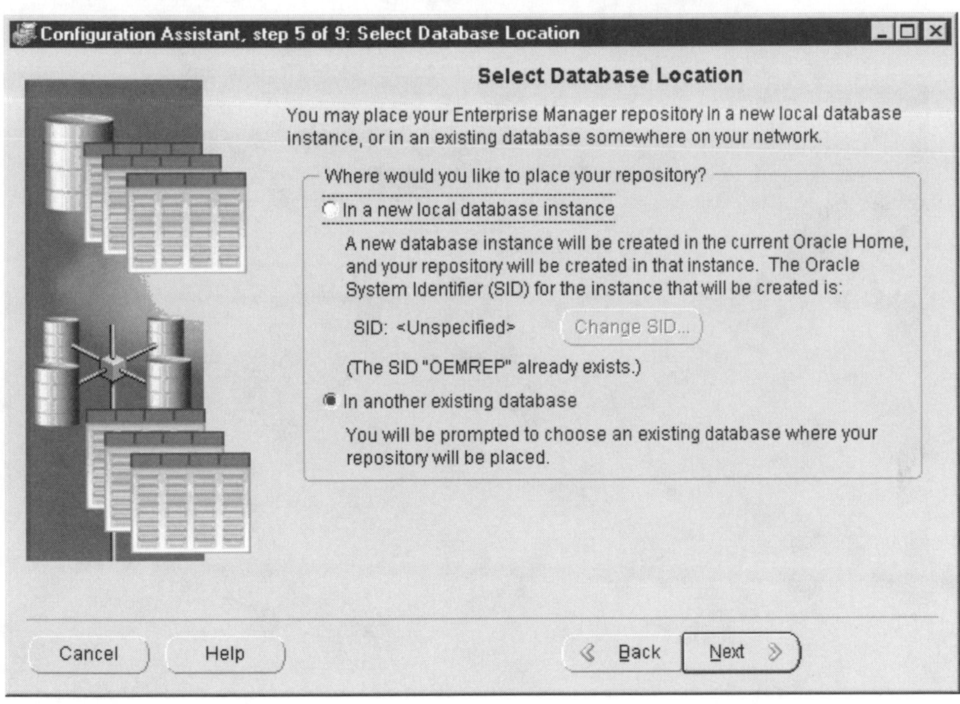

FIGURE 2-18. *Selecting a database location*

NOTE
With the EM9i architecture, the schema name used for an EM Repository must be unique across your whole Oracle environment. Therefore, it is a good idea to include the host name in the EM repository schema name.

8. Next, you must provide information about the default tablespace (used for storing the EM repository objects) and the temporary tablespace (for sort operations) for the EM repository owner, then click Next to continue. Per default, the OEM_REPOSITORY tablespace is selected for storing the EM repository and TEMP is selected as the temporary tablespace.

NOTE
The EM9i repository requires between 30 and 40MB when it is created. Ensure that enough free space is available in the tablespace chosen for the EM repository. 50MB is a good starting point.

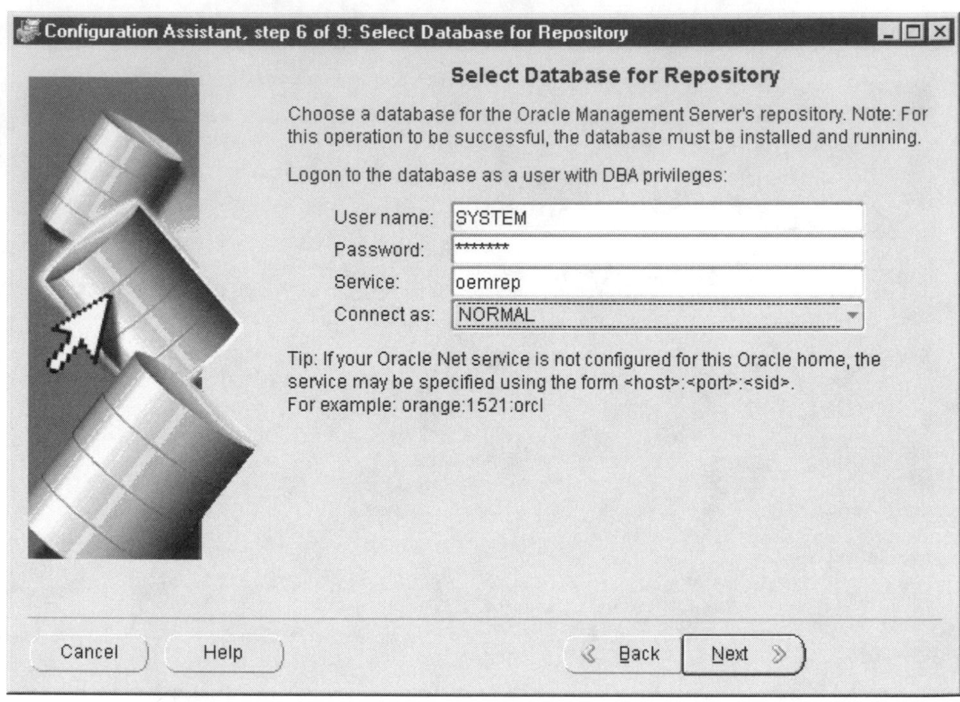

FIGURE 2-19. *Selecting a database to hold the repository*

9. The last step is just a summary of what is going to be created; click Finish to continue. The EMCA begins the EM repository creation, and the progress will be shown. When all three steps have finished, click Close to continue.

Now the EM Repository is created and ready for use by the Management Server.

Installing the EM Client

This section describes how you install only the EM client (EM Console) software. This is typically done when you have installed the database and management server on a separate server and you want to access the EM repository from your own client PC.

1. Place the first CD of the Oracle9i software distribution set in your CD-ROM drive. When you close the drive, the CD should automatically start and show the Oracle9i Server - Autorun screen (see Figure 2-1). Click Install/Deinstall Products, and the Oracle Universal Installer Welcome screen

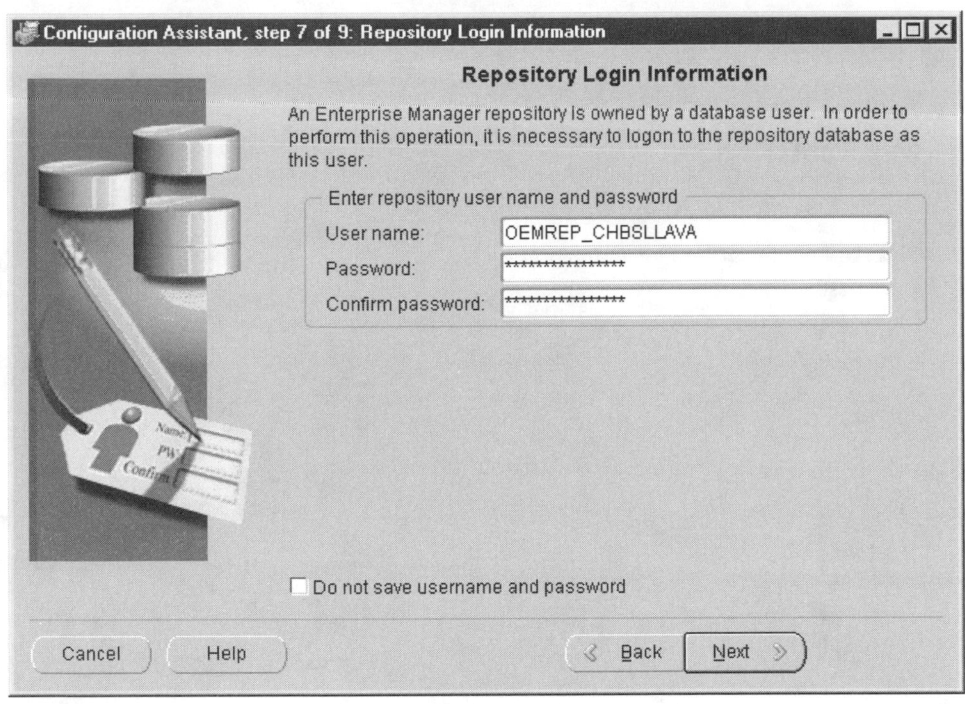

FIGURE 2-20. *Entering the repository user name and password*

appears. If the autorun screen is not shown automatically, go to the root of the CD (or to the "Disk 1" directory if you copied the software to a staging area) and double-click the file setup.exe; the Oracle Universal Installer Welcome screen should appear. Click Next in the Welcome screen to continue with the installation.

2. Next, the File Locations screen shown in Figure 2-2 appears. Here you must enter a name for the Oracle Home for the EM Client software and choose a directory. Then click Next.

NOTE
If you already have an older Oracle version installed, you must install the EM client software into a new Oracle Home.

3. The Available Products screen appears, as shown in Figure 2-3. Select Oracle9i Client 9.0.1.1.1 and click Next.

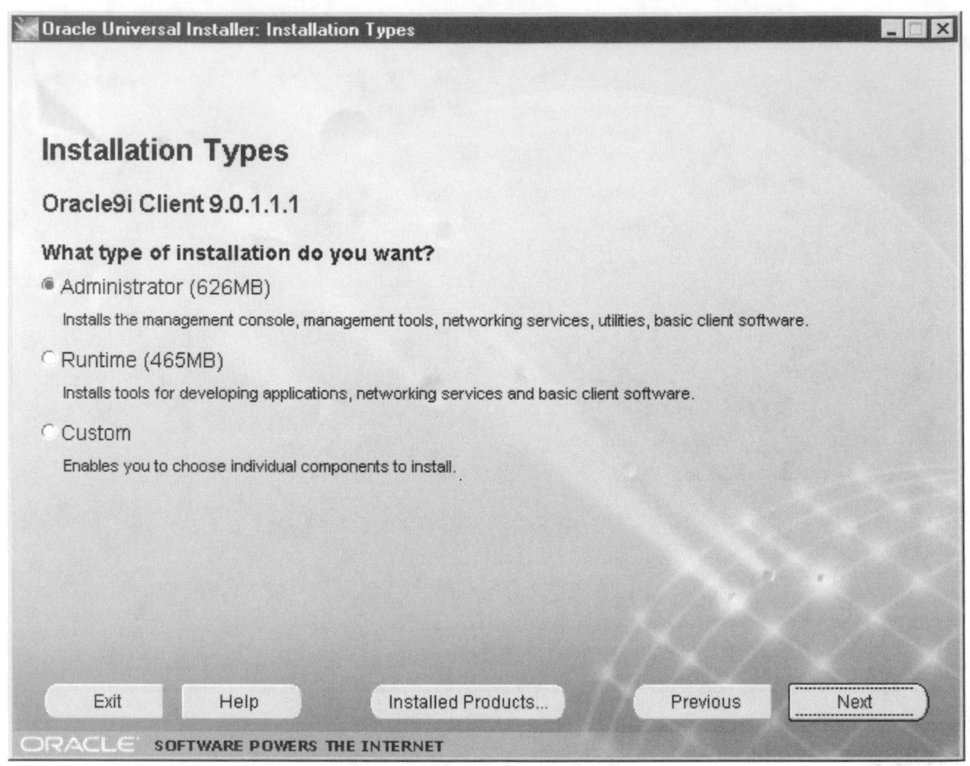

FIGURE 2-21. *Selecting the Administrator installation type*

4. The Installation Types screen appears (see Figure 2-21). Choose Administrator and click Next. The summary screen appears; click Install to begin the software installation.
5. After the installation has been running for a while, you will be prompted for Disk 2. Insert the second CD-ROM, or browse to the directory where it is located. Then click OK to continue the installation.
6. You will be prompted for Disk 3, when the installation has been running for a while. Insert the third CD-ROM, or browse to the directory where it is located. Then click OK to continue the installation.
7. Eventually, the EM client software installation will finish, and the End Installation screen is shown. Click Exit to end the installation.

Now the EM Client has been installed on your machine and can be launched from the Windows NT/2000 Oracle9i program group (**Start** | Programs | Oracle - <Oracle Home Name> | Enterprise Manager Console).

Installing the Intelligent Agent

This section describes how to install the Oracle Intelligent Agent software on the target nodes, that is, the machines you want to monitor and administer through EM. Normally, the Intelligent Agent is always installed together with the Oracle database or Management Server software, but there might not be an Intelligent Agent installed, or you may want to install the latest version to take advantage of the latest functionalities.

Using the Oracle Universal Installer, you can select the Intelligent Agent for installation from two different locations: the Enterprise Manager tree list or the database server tree list (this installs both the database and the Intelligent Agent). The following steps describe how to install just the OIA component in a new Oracle Home.

1. Place the first CD of the Oracle9i software distribution set in your CD-ROM drive. When you close the drive, the CD should automatically start and show the Oracle9i Server - Autorun screen (see Figure 2-1). Click Install/Deinstall Products and the Oracle Universal Installer Welcome screen appears. If the autorun screen is not shown automatically, go to the root of the CD (or to the Disk 1 directory if you copied the software to a staging area) and double-click the file setup.exe; the Oracle Universal Installer Welcome screen appears. Click Next in the Welcome screen to continue with the installation.

2. The File Locations screen appears, as shown in Figure 2-2. Here you must enter a name for the Oracle Home for the Intelligent Agent software, and choose a directory. Then click Next to continue the installation.

NOTE
If you already have an older Oracle version installed, you must install the Intelligent Agent into a new Oracle Home.

3. The Available Products screen appears, as shown in Figure 2-3. Choose Oracle 9i Management and Integration 9.0.1.0.1 and click Next.

4. When the Installation Types screen appears (see Figure 2-22, choose Custom and click Next.

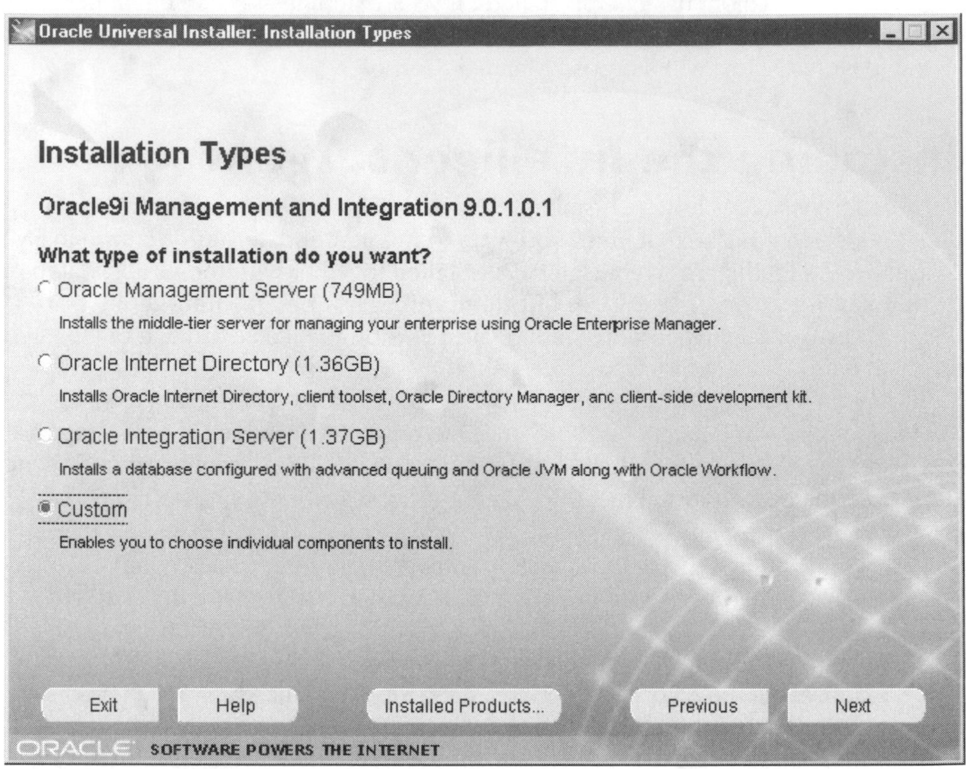

FIGURE 2-22. *Selecting the Custom installation type*

5. The Available Product Components screen appears. Because you only want to install the Intelligent Agent, deselect all other products, leaving only Oracle Intelligent Agent 9.0.1.0.1 and Oracle Enterprise Manager Products 9.0.1.0.1 selected (see Figure 2-23). When you deselect components, begin from the bottom; otherwise, the installer keeps track of dependencies and will not allow you to deselect them. Click Next to continue.
6. Next, the Component Locations screen appears, as shown in Figure 2-24. For components that do not need to be copied to the ORACLE_HOME, you can specify another location. In this case, you can choose to copy the Java Runtime Environment (JRE) version 1.1.8 to a specific directory. The default location is C:\Program Files\Oracle\jre\1.1.8. Click Next to continue.
7. After the installation has been running for a while, you will be prompted for Disk 2. Insert the second CD-ROM, or browse to the directory where it is located. Then click OK to continue the installation.

8. When the installation of the software is complete, the Configuration Tools screen will appear and the Oracle Net Configuration Assistant is launched. Wait for this to finish and then click Next.

At this point in the installation, all required software components are installed, only the configuration is being done. If the Net Configuration Assistant fails, or for some reason you choose to interrupt it (by clicking on the tool line and pressing Stop), it can be started separately at a later time from the Oracle Configuration and Migration Tools program group.

Verify that the Intelligent Agent is running by opening the Windows NT/2000 Services panel. The service is named "Oracle<Home name>Agent", for example "OracleOraNT9iAgent". If the service has been started, the Intelligent Agent has already performed discovery of the available targets on the node (databases, listeners, and so on). These targets have been registered in the SERVICES.ORA file in the ORACLE_HOME\network\agent directory and the SNMP_RO.ORA and

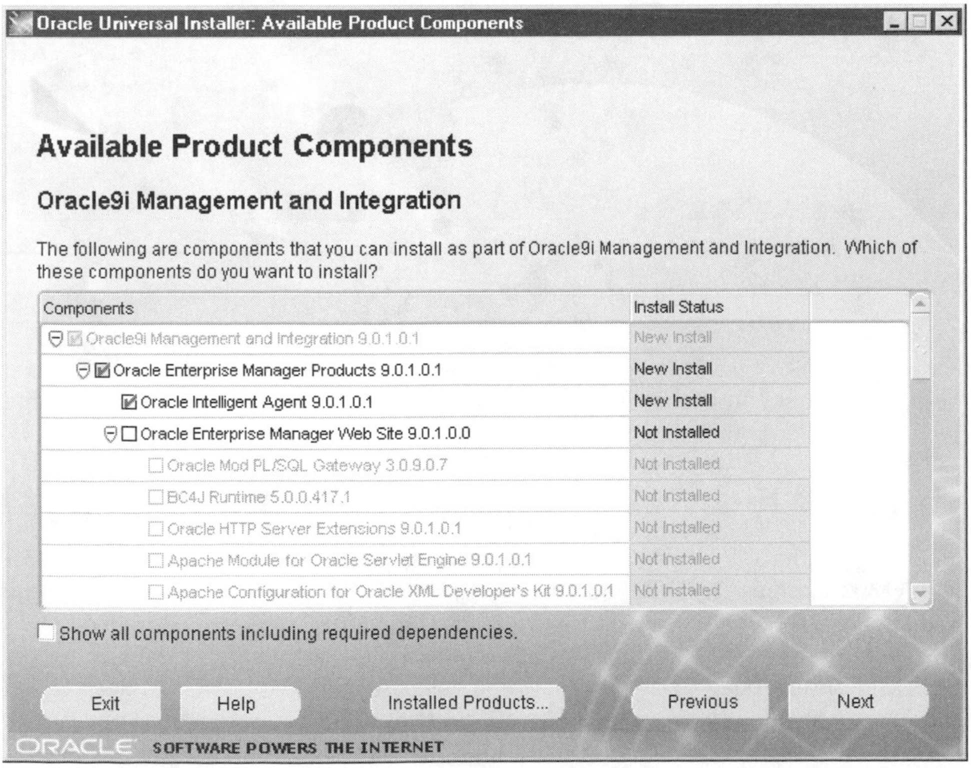

FIGURE 2-23. *Selecting just the Intelligent Agent and Enterprise Manager*

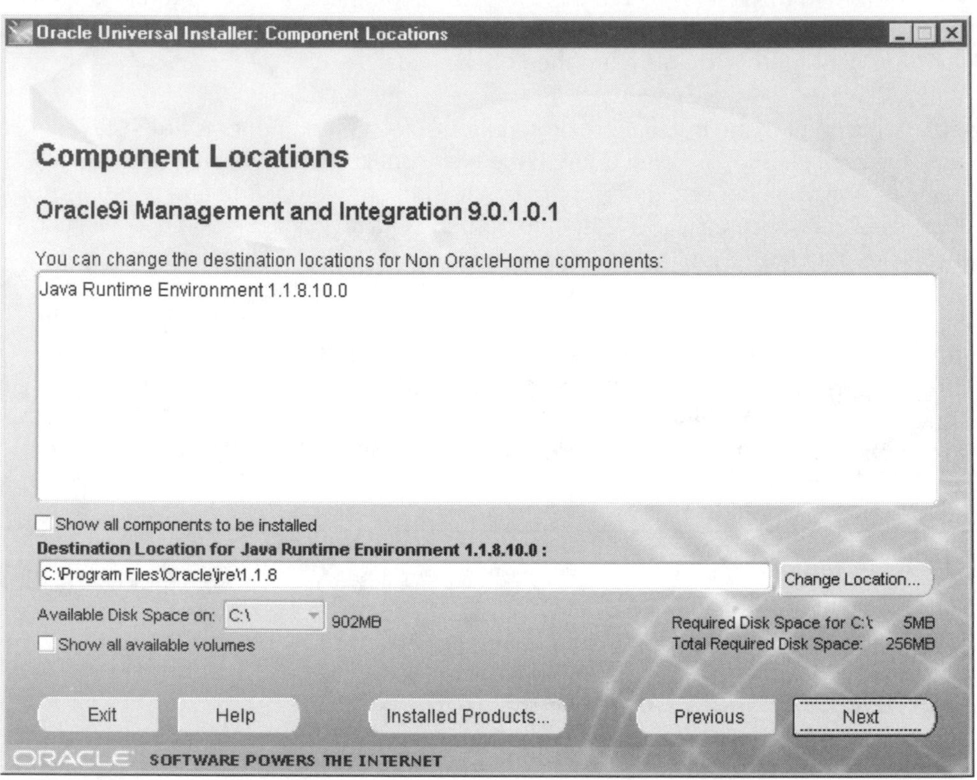

FIGURE 2-24. *Selecting the locations for components*

SNMP_RW.ORA files in ORACLE_HOME\network\admin. Now you are ready to discover the node from the EM Console. Refer to Chapter 8 for more details about how to discover your target nodes and services.

Summary

Now that you have learned what is required to install the different components within your EM environment (RDBMS for the EM repository, Management Server, EM Client and Intelligent Agent) you are able to install the individual software components. You also learned how to create the EM repository in a (new or existing) database. At this point you, should have an EM repository in a database used by a running Management Server, and also the Intelligent Agent should be installed and started on your target node(s). You can now launch the EM Console, either in standalone mode or connected to the Management Server, and begin your quest through the EM framework. In the next chapter, we will take a closer look at the EM Console, how it is organized, and the different components available.

PART II

Looking at the EM Console Components

CHAPTER 3

Introducing the Console

EM is designed to have all functionality and integrated tools available from one common starting point: The Enterprise Manager Console. The console is very versatile and can be used in a number of different circumstances. You have already learned about the EM framework that you can access through the console. The console can also be started in standalone mode, in which case it serves as a common client/server tool for database management only. This chapter introduces the console's functionality and the concepts behind it. We discuss these features in more detail in Part III.

Oracle's strategy is to have as many products as possible managed through EM. We cannot provide a complete list of all the available tools here, because the list is quite extensive and changes frequently. There might be an integrated management application shipping with the Oracle product you are using, but which is not mentioned in this book. For example, you might encounter a target of the type Directory Servers, or you may be able to manage the Oracle Internet File System (iFS) through a tool that integrates seamlessly with EM. Read the documentation of your specific Oracle product to see if there is an integrated application available for EM.

Log in or not Log in: Using EM Without Management Server

When you start the console, you are given the choice starting in standalone mode or connecting to an Oracle Management Server (OMS). If you choose standalone, you will not be able to use any of the features associated with the management framework. That means that the console does not recognize the management server, repository, or agents. No access to a management server means the console will not acknowledge any information stored in the repository. Not knowing the agent means no access to jobs, events, or the discovery mechanisms. If started standalone, the console runs as a simple local program (as shown in Figure 3-1) and connects to Oracle databases as a client to a server. You need to provide information about databases to connect to, such as the hostname or IP address, the valid ports, and the SID of the database. In addition, you require valid login information—you need everything as if connecting to a database using SQL*Plus. Although this sounds restricting, the console still offers many benefits, even in standalone mode. You should understand that the console can be started and used immediately after the installation process without any configuration at all. Try it right away by selecting the console from the start menu, or typing `oemapp console` at a command prompt. You will see a login window asking for the type of mode you would like to run the console in.

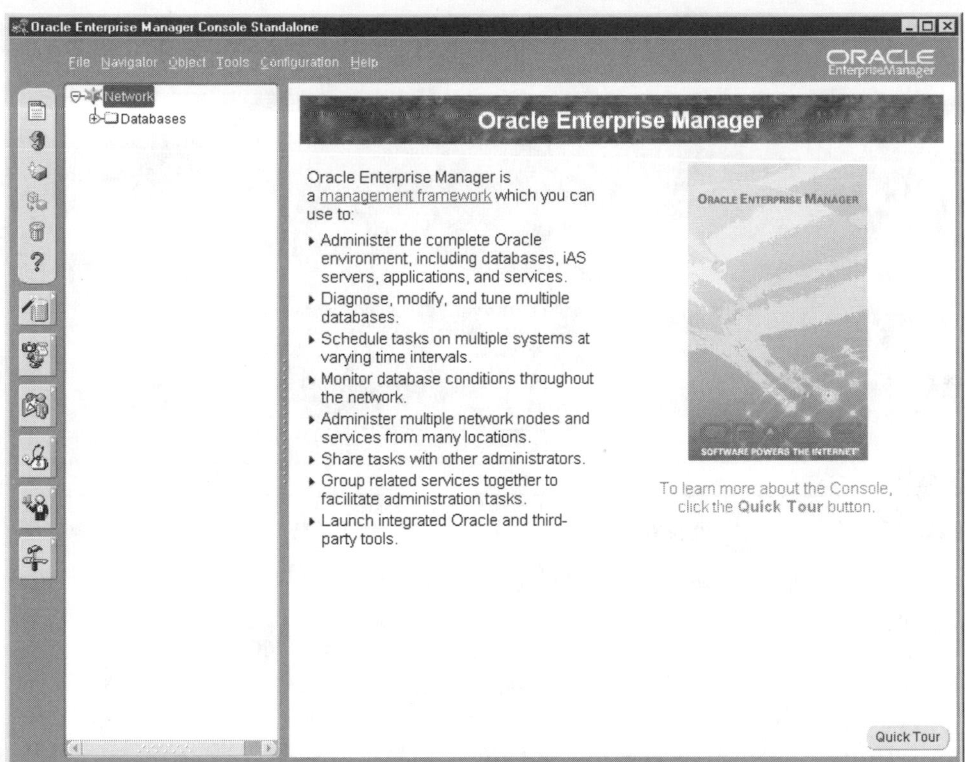

FIGURE 3-1. *Running the console in standalone mode*

If you decide to connect to an existing management framework, you can select the other option Login to Management Server. The window will change the moment you select this option, and will ask you for more information, as shown in Figure 3-2. It asks for the name of the machine running the OMS, and for valid login credentials. Any database administrator (DBA) needs to have an account created in the framework to be able to log on. If you try to log in for the first time after the installation, there will be a Super DBA account called SYSMAN with the initial password OEM_TEMP. If you want to connect to an OMS on a different machine, add the name of that node through the management server dialog box, or simply type in the machine name with the DBA credentials.

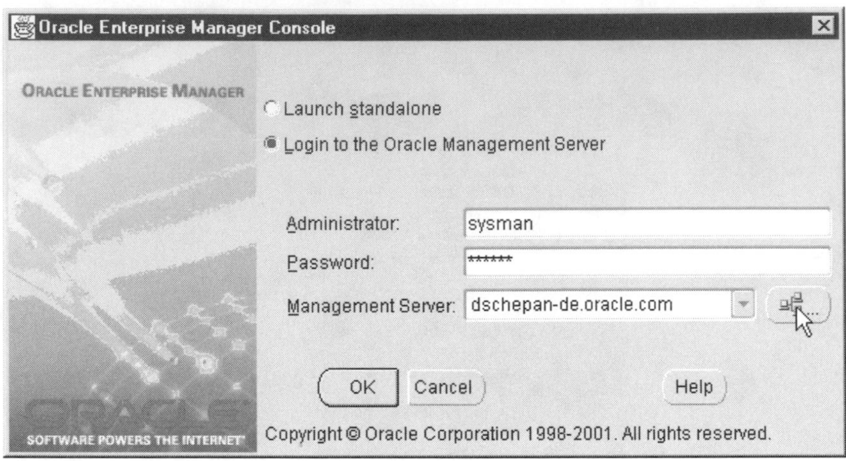

FIGURE 3-2. *Entering credentials to connect to an OMS*

NOTE
The account to access the framework is different from an account to access targets like databases. Access to the framework does not automatically provide access to databases or other targets. You still need to provide a database user name and password once you are logged into an OMS.

The following sections describe the console functionality when connected to an OMS, which is broader than in standalone mode. Instead of discussing each service in detail at this point, we will focus on briefly describing each service and explaining whether they are available in standalone mode. At the end of Part II, you will have a good overview of what you can expect from using the console in both standalone and connected modes.

Discovery

Before you can start to administer your databases or other targets, you have to *discover* them so that they appear as objects in the navigator tree. As explained in Chapter 1, the Intelligent Agent collects information about known targets when it is started, and waits until it is contacted by an OMS. That means you should first have an agent running on a node that contains targets to be managed. This process is described in more detail in Chapter 8. You now have to instruct the EM framework to transmit information about these targets from the agents to the repository. They can then appear in the console's navigator tree, and can also be made visible to other administrators. The discovery process is automated if you have an agent running on the target nodes.

If you do not have an agent running on the node to be discovered, but you know information about a database on that node, you can also discover these targets manually. You have to enter all the information needed to reach these databases, like the SID, port, and hostname. Bear in mind that with manual discovery, no agent-related functionality like jobs or events will be available. If you install or start an agent on a node after you have discovered targets manually, you need to delete the node and all targets from the EM framework to start automatic discovery for this node and the targets related to it. In Part III, we discuss in detail the prerequisites for automatic discovery, how to start the discovery process from the console, and how to manually populate the navigator tree if necessary. For now, you need to know that each time the agent is started, it writes information concerning automatically discovered targets to the SERVICES.ORA file in the $ORACLE_HOME/network/agent/ folder on the agent node. This information is transferred to the management framework during the discovery process that is initiated from the console.

Types of Targets

Because the current version of EM was designed to be able to manage all existing Oracle products and related targets, the EM console version 9i supports the widest range of possible targets, compared to previous versions. The following types of targets are the most common.

Databases

Although EM can manage many different kinds of targets, the database is probably the most important type. This is reflected in the number of tasks you can perform on a database from EM. To discover database information, the agent uses information from the ORATAB file in Unix, or the registry from Windows operating systems. Information from the LISTENER.ORA and TNSNAMES.ORA configuration files on the host is also used. The agent uses a specific algorithm (outlined in the Intelligent Agents Users Guide) to discover which databases actually exist on the node. Also note that the 9i database clusters called Real Application Clusters (RAC) are displayed in this category.

Database Listeners

When a client on the network requests a connection to a database, the database listener has the task of establishing the connection. If the database listener is not functioning properly, no remote client can connect to the database. A listener can be configured to serve multiple databases, and can be restricted to only listen to specified types of requests based on port numbers, protocols, and other standards. When selecting a listener icon in the navigator tree, you can see the databases the listener is responsible for, as well as the corresponding TNS addresses. You can also issue a ping to the listener process.

Hosts

The agent also discovers the host it runs on. Other targets, like databases and their listeners, live on these hosts, and if the host is removed from the framework, the corresponding targets are also removed. Starting with version 8.1.7, the agent is able to determine operating system information, such as type and version. With version 9i it even displays information about the Oracle Homes installed on the machine. A functioning agent is required to enable access to host information and functionality. For this reason, the status of the agent on the selected node is displayed in addition to the time when the agent was last pinged. You can also initiate a random ping from within this dialog box.

HTTP Servers

Oracle HTTP Servers (OHS), or Web listeners, are a part of the standard installation of an Oracle environment. EM uses this Apache-based Web listener for its own Website, enabling EM to run in a browser, or to enable users to access EM's reporting framework. You can start, stop, and ping the HTTP Server process from within the console, and view the following properties of the server:

- Server name
- Port
- Version
- Server's root directory
- Server's config file location
- URL to request the server's status via HTTP

Concurrent Managers

Concurrent Managers are part of Oracle's e-business suite, and schedule processing requests on Oracle Applications databases. Initially, you can view configuration information in this object's detail pane. These services are not discovered automatically, as the databases are. You must manually enter services into a file called OAPPS.ORA located in the $ORACLE_HOME/network/agent/config folder. The agent reads this file during each startup and discovers these types of services semi-automatically.

SAP R/3 systems

EM was extended to also monitor SAP R/3 middle tiers using one of SAP's monitoring API's, because approximately 75 percent of all SAP installations run on an Oracle database. To discover this type of service, you need to edit a file called SAP.CONF in the folder $ORACLE_HOME/network/agent/config with service information, which is read with each startup of the agent. Note that SAP-related functionality does not belong to the standard equipment of the agents and usually requires installation of agent extensions.

SQL Server

Many customers wanted EM's monitoring capabilities extended to cover Microsoft SQL Server. In addition to the event system, the monitoring aspect is mostly covered in the Diagnostics Pack, which is why the offered SQL Server functionality in the console is limited compared to an Oracle database.

Groups

Groups are not real targets in the sense of the others mentioned in this section. They are virtual targets designed to make certain tasks easier. Groups always contain other targets and combine them logically. By choosing a group as a target, you are actually selecting the applicable group members as targets of your action. The group concept is discussed in more detail in the next chapter.

Use the Console

This section describes how to use the console when it is connected to an OMS. Configuring the framework and discovering the targets are explained starting with Chapter 8. This section provides an overview of the functionality without going into too much detail about the setup. Start by examining the EM9i console connected to an OMS, as shown in Figure 3-3.

Master-Detail View

The EM9i console uses the *master-detail* concept. The interface shows a list of targets in the navigator tree on the left side of the window, and a more detailed description of the selected target on the right side. Depending on the type of object you select in the navigator tree, the detail view on the right side will change. Just after startup,

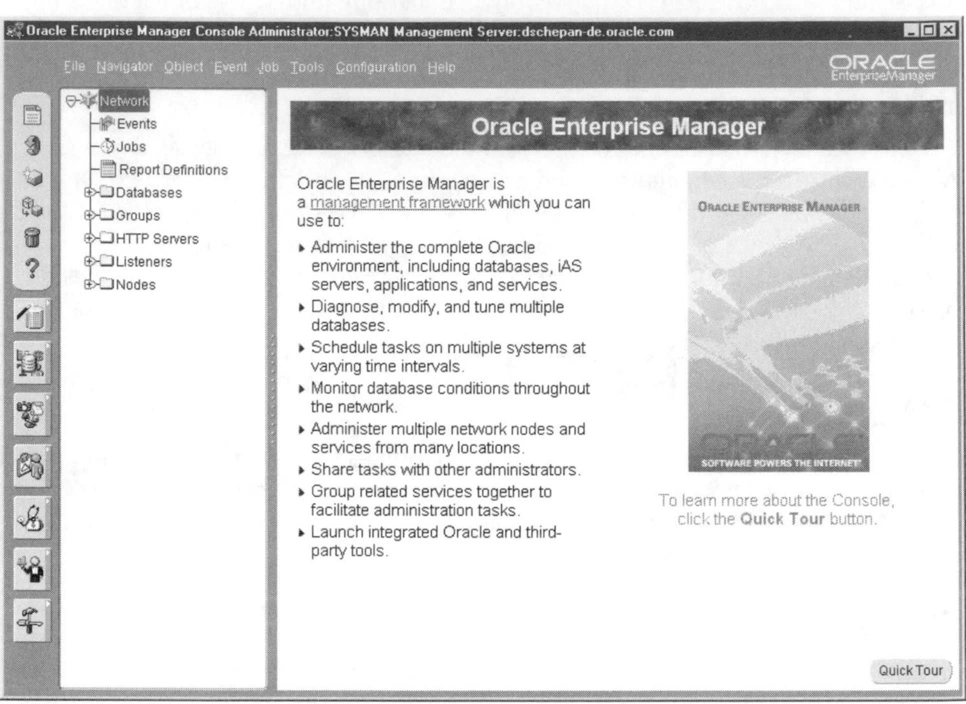

FIGURE 3-3. *Console connected to an Oracle Management Server*

when the Network object is selected, the detail view offers some general information. Click some other folders in the navigator tree and see how the detail window changes.

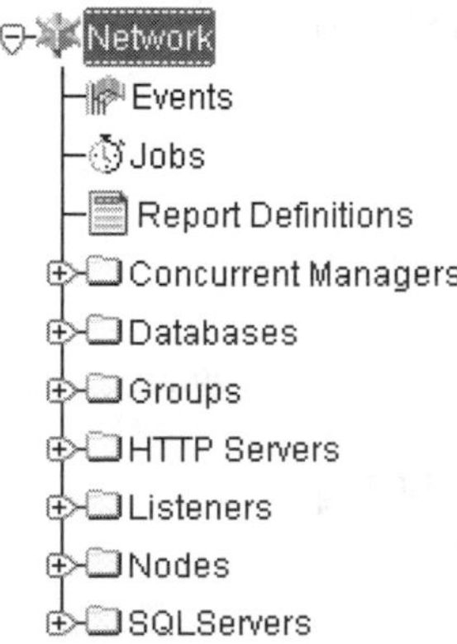

Quick Tours

Note the Quick Tour button in the lower right corner of most of the detail sections. This button is offered in many windows when a more general item like *databases* or *schema management* is selected. Clicking the button opens a new window with explanatory information about the selected object or area (see Figure 3-4). Quick Tours offer brief and graphically enhanced information about many topics such as architecture, new features, or general functionality of EM. Quick Tours let you learn or recall specific information during the actual use of the product.

Pull-Down Menus and Context-Sensitive Menus

The top of the console window contains a number of pull-down menus that offer various kinds of functionality. We will talk more about each of the functions accessible through the pull-down menus in the course of this chapter. The File menu enables you to close the application; the Navigator menu offers functionality for dealing with targets in the console. The Object menu is special, because it is one of several

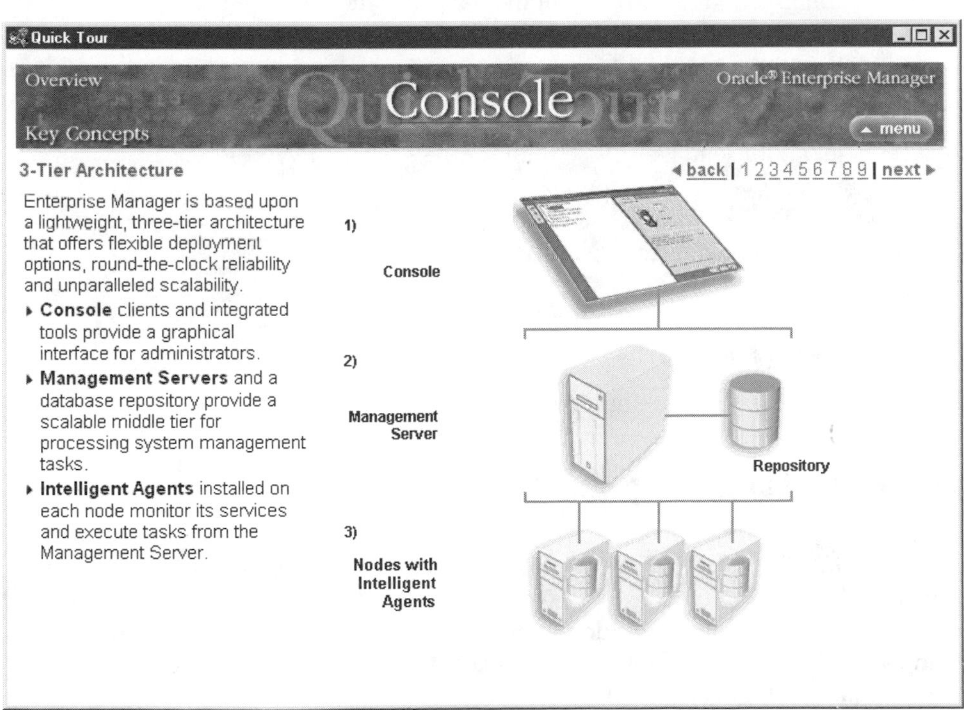

FIGURE 3-4. *Learning about EM with Quick Tours*

context-sensitive menus. That means that the commands available may change in context with the type of object selected in the navigator tree. Possible effects may be that commands are simply grayed out if not available or the commands presented may be different in wording. This applies especially to the object menu because it changes in context with the object selected. In most cases, right-clicking on objects in the navigator tree offers the same choice of commands as the Object menu. The list of commands displayed in such a case are only those that make sense for the selected type of object, hence they are called context-sensitive menus.

We will explore the other menus in detail within their respective chapters: the Event and Job menus are covered in Chapter 4, as well as the reports available. The Tools menu contains applications that are part of the free portion of EM, and some others which are part of the Management Packs. These have to be licensed separately, although they are installed per default with the 9i database. The Configuration menu contains useful commands that configure various attributes of the EM framework.

Toolbar

The toolbar is on the upper-left side of the console. It allows you to access several basic manipulation functions for objects in the navigator tree and the console in general. The toolbar is context sensitive, like some of the pull-down menus. As a consequence, some functionality is unavailable depending on which object is selected in the navigator tree. Possible object functionality includes (top to bottom):

- View published Enterprise Manager reports via a Web server
- Refresh Navigator views
- Create a new object
- Create a new object based on an existing object
- Delete an object
- Display the master contents page of the help system

Integrated Applications

There are a variety of tools called *integrated applications* available with EM, but they are found in different places. We will provide an overview at this point and briefly explain where they are and what they do. First, you learn about the tool drawers on the left side of the console window below the toolbar. These and some others are also available in the Tools menu at the top of the console window, which we will explain after that. Finally, you will see more tools available by accessing the Start menu of your Windows desktop, none of which appear in the console.

Tool Drawers

The tool drawers offer quick access to a range of functionality. You can pull these drawers out by clicking them once. Figure 3-5 shows all the drawers pulled out simultaneously. If you hover the cursor over a drawer or a component inside a drawer, the application's name is displayed. All these tools are also accessible from the Tools menu.

Database Wizards Drawer

The Database Wizards Drawer, the top drawer, contains some of the wizards available for various areas of database management. It has wizards to manage backups, exports, and imports and also a wizard for analyzing database objects should you need to update statistics for certain objects. The last wizard in this drawer is the Summary Advisor Wizard, which guides you through the process of generating materialized views inside the database. Because the backup, export, and import wizards require the agent to run the specific application on the target node, they are only available when connected to an OMS.

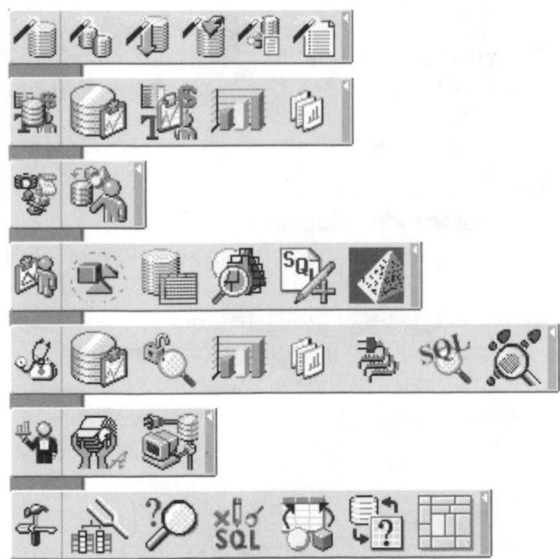

FIGURE 3-5. *The tool drawers fully expanded to show all the available tools*

Application Management Drawer

The Application Management Drawer contains tools that help with monitoring Oracle Applications components. This drawer is not visible if the console is launched in standalone mode. Performance Manager monitors concurrent managers in real time, whereas Capacity Planner sets up monitoring in the background and enables historical data analysis. The Concurrent Processing Tuning Assistant (CPTA) connects to the foundation tables of an Applications schema and analyzes the data for performance bottlenecks. Performance Overview is a shortcut to one of the charts available in Performance Manager that displays specific Application-related information.

Change Management Pack Drawer

The Change Management Pack Drawer provides access to the separately licensed Change Management Pack, which consists of only one application: the Change Manager. It provides access to six more modules that deal with managing changes in schema definitions: DB Capture, DB Diff, DB Search, DB Quick Change, DB Alter, and DB Propagate. In previous versions, the Change Management Pack was not as integrated as it is today and offered all the components separately. Customer feedback was the impetus for integrating all these components into the one Change Manager interface for ease of use. The Change Management Pack is discussed in Chapter 7.

Database Applications Drawer

The Database Applications Drawer contains various tools that offer some special database features.

Data Guard Manager Oracle9i Data Guard is the new name for what was previously called Oracle8i Standby Database. As the former name suggests, it works with standby databases to protect data against errors or failures. It basically automates the creation, management, and monitoring of a standby database. Data Guard can be managed through two interfaces of the Data Guard Broker: one is a command-line interface, the other is Data Guard Manager, which is integrated in the Enterprise Manager framework. Data Guard Manager allows you to create, change, and monitor Data Guard-specific configurations. It is not available in a console running in standalone mode.

LogMiner Viewer LogMiner is a new feature of the database introduced with version 9i. It enables you to access Oracle's redo log mechanisms via relational methods. The chain of redo information, often called the *redo stream*, contains a lot of important information: the history of changes made to the database, the type and time of the change, the affected table and schema name, and the user causing the change. It also includes the SQL behind these changes as well as the SQL to undo the change. The LogMiner Viewer provides a GUI interface to access that database functionality. It enables you to specify all the query criteria, to filter data from redo log files, and view the results, including SQL redo and undo statements. LogMiner Viewer is not visible in a console running in standalone mode.

Spatial Index Advisor Spatial Index Advisor is a tool that helps you tune and analyze spatial indexes. If you are using spatial data in the database, and you have spatial indexes defined with this data, you can use this application to analyze the effectiveness of your indexes. You can easily find out if the indexes are defined properly to achieve best performance results. In addition, the tool visually explains the distribution of the data. You can envision a spatial index as a set of tiles of the database. With Spatial Index Advisor, the administrator can define the number and size of these tiles. This is important because the impact of the index on query performance depends on the geometric coverage of these tiles. You can inspect the relation of tiles with their geometric coverage in addition to the performance of queries against the current definitions.

SQL*Plus Worksheet You can use SQL*Plus Worksheet when administering databases with SQL, SQL*Plus, or PL/SQL commands. This tool enables you to enter SQL and PL/SQL code or commands and run them dynamically. You can also load, develop, and run scripts in this interface. One convenient feature is that you can see the output of your commands or scripts in a special output area of the window. SQL*Plus Worksheet also maintains a history of the last 50 commands issued.

Text Manager Oracle9i Text is a feature of the database that helps to manage and search for text or any other type of data inside the database. This feature, known as interMedia and Context in previous versions, can be utilized more easily with Text Manager, which is integrated into the EM console. It helps to use the full-scale document management features of the database with various functions. For instance, you can create and manage Text indexes, which speed up queries searching for specific strings or types of text.

Diagnostics Pack Drawer

The Diagnostics Pack is a separately licensed toolset that includes components that help to monitor systems. It enables you to take certain actions that lead to greater overall availability. It contains Performance Manager for real-time monitoring, drilldown, and advice functionality. Capacity Planner assists you to set up monitoring in the background and enables historical data analysis. Both Performance Manager and Capacity Planner can perform their tasks for a variety of targets other than the database. Capacity Planner is not available in standalone mode, because it requires the Agent to collect information in the background. In addition, some shortcuts to specialized real-time charts are offered: Lock Monitor, Performance Overview, Top Sessions, and Top SQL are frequently used charts of Performance Manager. The Top Sessions and Lock Monitor functionality had been implemented as separate applications in previous versions, and after integrating their functionality into

Performance Manager, some customers wondered where these tools had vanished to. For this reason, shortcuts to the related information within Performance Manager still have their separate icons within the Diagnostics Pack folder. The last component in this drawer is the Oracle Trace Data Viewer, intended to format trace data previously collected by Oracle's trace mechanisms for better viewing. In previous versions, a component called Trace Manager was supplied, which helped to set up the trace collection. It has been discontinued in version 9i. One more component of the Diagnostics Pack is the Advanced Events. They extend the range of events you can instruct the Agent to watch for. Because they are visible in the event definition dialog box, they have no separate icon here. We address the event system and the events available in Chapter 4.

Service Management Drawer

The Service Management Drawer contains a variety of tools managing other services than the Oracle database, e.g., the Oracle Internet Directory or Net components.

Directory Manager Oracle Internet Directory (OID) is a Lightweight Directory Access Protocol (LDAP)-based product designed for enterprise-wide service naming and service access conventions. Oracle intends for customers to use it with Oracle Names, Net8, and the remainder of the Oracle product stack, particularly because Oracle Names will be discontinued after release 9i. Directory Manager is EM's tool for managing the OID server. Directory Manager offers enough functionality to solve most of the necessary tasks: connecting to directory servers; managing configuration parameters; adding, modifying, and deleting entries, attributes, and object classes; setting up access control policies; configuring security; and viewing and modifying replication agreements. Some other tools are offered with EM to manage information inside the directory server, which will be explained later. Apart from OID, there are several other LDAP-compliant directory products available in the market today, such as Microsoft Active Directory, Novell Directory Service (NDS), and Netscape Directory Server. Directory Manager is not available when the console is running in standalone mode.

Net Manager Oracle Net Manager enables you to define network communication services within the Oracle world. It can define names as services based on a local tnsnames.ora definition, a centralized LDAP-compliant directory server, or an Oracle Names server. It also defines the naming methods, that is, the way in which the connect descriptors are resolved, as well as profiles and listeners. In the case of Oracle Names servers, Net Manager can also start, stop, tune, or collect statistics for servers.

Tuning Pack Drawer

The Tuning Pack belongs to the group of EM extensions which have to be licensed separately. All the components in this toolset have the goal of helping administrators improve database performance. This can be achieved through a variety of methods, depending on the individual configurations and circumstances. Tuning pack tries to approach the most common methods through a number of specialized components. Components in this Management Pack are addressed in more detail in Chapter 7. For now, this section provides a brief definition of each of the components.

Expert Oracle Expert attempts to tune the performance of the Oracle database comprehensively. It collects information on areas to be tuned and evaluates the collected performance data with its implemented rule-based tuning knowledge engine. It generates recommendations based on its observations and provides recommendations on which actions to take in order to improve performance, which it also explains in detail. Expert can also generate scripts to make the implementation of the tuning recommendations easier. You can compare Expert with a real human expert or consultant who has the task of looking at a specific database and improving performance.

Index Tuning Wizard Index Tuning Wizard helps to find tables with inefficient indexes and recommends how to improve performance when accessing these tables. It generates recommendations, explains them, and offers scripts to run for easier implementation. Index Tuning Wizard is designed to be used for the cost-based optimizer only. It is not available in standalone mode.

SQL Analyze SQL Analyze finds, evaluates, and tunes inefficient SQL statements in your database. Because SQL is very flexible, statements can be written in various ways and achieve the same results. These SQL statements might have different performance impacts on the database. Performance of individual statements is also affected by the settings of the target database and the schema definitions inside. SQL Analyze tries to find inefficient SQL, analyzes it, and suggests ways to rewrite it for better performance. This application includes the newly introduced 9i Virtual Index Wizard, which enables you to test the usefulness and performance impact of a new index without actually creating it.

Tablespace Map Tablespace Map graphically displays space consumption and allocation of segments inside a tablespace. It can analyze specific tablespaces to pinpoint existing or upcoming storage problems, and explain why it thinks there might be a problem with certain segments.

Reorg Wizard Reorg Wizard is intended for correcting detected storage problems inside tablespaces, such as row chaining or migration, index stagnation, or tablespace fragmentation. It can be invoked from Tablespace Map, and can be run for the whole tablespace or for selected segments. Reorg Wizard generates scripts and impact reports depending on the version of the database that contains the objects to be reorganized. This enables the tool to use the features of the respective database version that are most suitable to perform the desired activity. A reorganization is scheduled as job through the agent, which means that Reorg Wizard is not available if the console is started in standalone mode.

Outline Management A new feature of the Oracle9i database is the *plan stability* feature. It neutralizes the impact of database environment changes on the performance of applications. Because applications issue SQL statements to the database, their performance is affected by the execution plan or explain plan the database generates. The methods of explain plan generation are affected by database parameters, meaning that a certain statement can perform much worse from one minute to the next if certain database parameters like optimizer mode, statistics, or memory settings are changed. The 9i database allows the storage of outlines, which are fixed explain plans for specific SQL statements. You can manage these stored outlines with the Outline Management tool found in EM. This tool includes another utility called Outline Editor, which actually creates these outlines by editing and changing individual steps in the execution of the targeted SQL statement.

Additional Tools in the Tools Menu

The Tools Menu contains some important functionality regarding data management. It contains a number of wizards to help you backup your data or export and import it. You can also find a wizard to load unformatted data into your database.

Backup Management

The Backup Management menu offers features that are only partially offered through the tool drawers. Specifically, we mean the important Recovery Wizard, which guides you through the process of recovering a database. You can create various backup configurations by selecting the respective wizard and storing them for later use or administration in two different places. You can store a backup locally in a configuration library, or in a backup catalog, which requires a database connection. For both choices, an individual tool enables you to change the configurations. Both are accessible from this menu by selecting Backup Configuration Library or Catalog Maintenance, as shown in the following illustration:

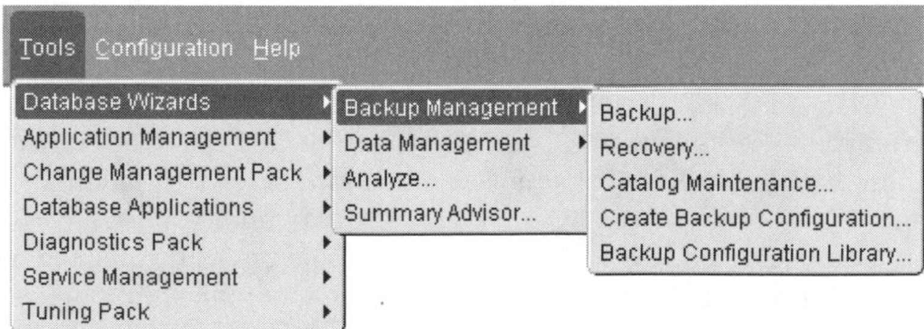

Data Management

The additional feature found in the Tools menu, but not in the tool drawers, is the Load command (Tools | Database Wizards | Database Management | Load), as shown in the following illustration. It assists you in loading data from any external file into the database by specifying the actual control file used for the load task. The wizard guides you through the process of defining what you want to load and submits the generated control file to the EM job system. This option is not available if the console is started in standalone mode.

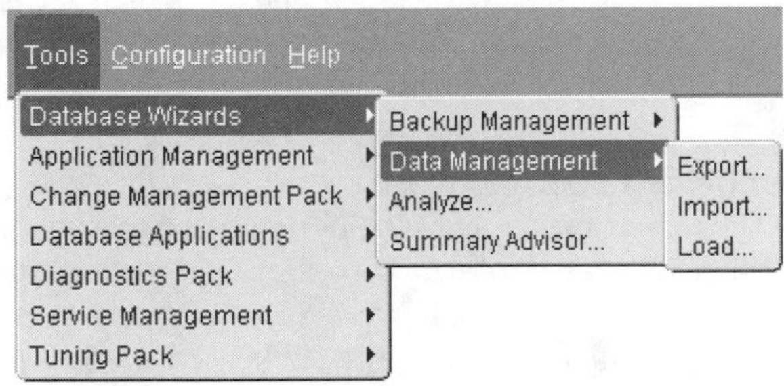

Security Tools in the Windows Start Menu

The tools described in this section ship with the standard database installation and mainly cover security features. All of them are designed to run standalone. They are all accessed through the Windows Start menu (Start | Programs | Oracle | Integrated Management Tools), as shown in the following illustration:

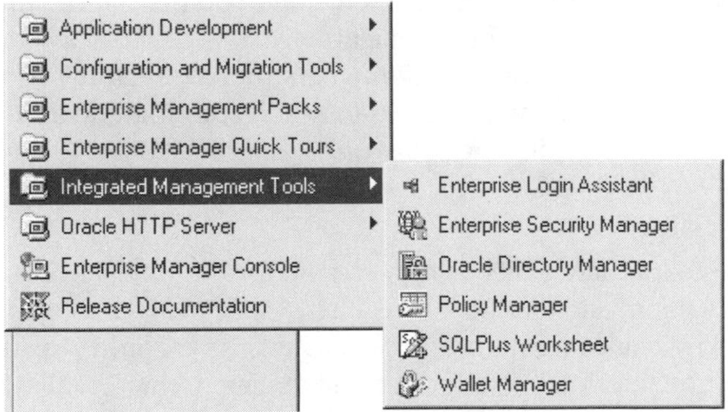

All these tools are intended for the enterprise user, who maintains multiple accounts on different databases or other systems. This requires dealing with a huge number of passwords, making it difficult to keep track of all login information. It generally leads to too many passwords for users to remember, and too many accounts for DBAs to manage effectively. Such an environment creates a lot of problems in various types of situations, which include users writing down their passwords, or DBAs not having enough time to disable or change accounts when employees leave the company. Enterprise Security tries to address all these issues by centralizing user-related information in an LDAP-compliant directory. The following sections briefly explain the tools available with EM9i, without going into too much detail about the security concept itself. The company maintains a central Directory, which contains all security related information. The product Oracle offers is called Oracle Internet Directory, which is a service like a database that needs to be managed. You administer this service through Directory Manager, which we have talked about earlier in the "Tool Drawers" section. In addition, the user information inside this directory needs to be managed, which you can do with Enterprise Security Manager.

Enterprise Security Manager

Oracle Enterprise Security Manager (ESM) helps you manage Enterprise User Security by administering enterprise-level role authorization. Enterprise Users are created and centrally managed in an Oracle Directory Server, which is an LDAP-compliant directory. It uses digital certificates and Secure Sockets Layer (SSL) to achieve a single sign-on functionality to multiple databases. When authenticating an Enterprise User, Oracle9i searches for its Enterprise Role authorizations in the LDAP Directory. Such roles enable authorization to access a variety of targets.

Enterprise Login Assistant

The Login Assistant simplifies the process of authentication when using Enterprise User Security, and masks the complexity behind it. To avoid numerous or permanent connections to the Directory Server, authentication/authorization information can be stored locally and encrypted on the client in what is called a *wallet*. The Enterprise Login Assistant helps you download information from a directory server to your local wallet or vice versa. It also enables or disables the auto-login feature associated with the wallet and lets you change the password.

Wallet Manager

Security administrators and wallet owners can use Oracle Wallet Manager to administer and edit security information inside their wallets. Tasks involved range from generating public/private key pairs and managing certificates to synchronizing information in the wallet with the information in a directory service. Oracle Wallet Manager lets you store wallets in the user profile area of the Windows registry or in a flat file.

Policy Manager

Oracle Policy Manager is used to administer various features of Oracle label security. Label security manages access to rows and tables in a database based on a label contained in the row and the label and privilege associated with each user session.

That means that the same select statement can return different results for different users, based on their privileges to access the data. Label security is built on the virtual private database (VPD) technology of Oracle9i, which uses policies to decide on a row level if a certain user may access specific data or not. These policies can be managed with Oracle Policy Manager. It lists policies together with their labels, authorizations, and protected objects, and above all helps to create a virtual private database concept.

Summary

In this chapter, we described the various tools available in the various menus of the EM console. We looked at all pull-down menus, tool drawers, and the functionality of the toolbar. We also mentioned which of the components would be available in standalone mode. The next chapter will discuss the navigator tree features of the console.

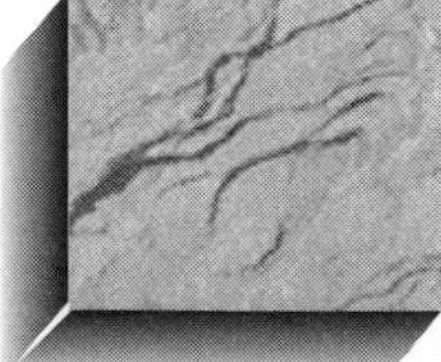

CHAPTER 4

Jobs, Events, Groups, and Reporting Concepts

hapter 3 covered many of the items in the Navigator except Jobs, Events, Groups, and Reports, which are explained in this chapter. Remember that all of these features require that you have the console connected to the Management Server (OMS).

Job System

Almost any DBA needs to run certain jobs frequently, performing a large variety of tasks. *Jobs* are predefined tasks that are executed from time to time. Jobs can start or stop other processes, run certain SQL scripts against databases, or gather statistics. They can be run only once, immediately or in the future, or frequently at certain intervals or as response to certain conditions. Jobs can contain multiple tasks to be performed in a specific order, or depending on the outcome of previous tasks. Jobs can do almost anything on the DBA's behalf, and most DBAs maintain a number of scripts developed to relieve them of repetitive tasks and automate standard processes. Enterprise Manager includes a fully scalable job system through the Intelligent Agent for this purpose, which fulfills all the requirements mentioned and more. EM can optionally notify you when a job has started, completed, failed, or been deleted. The job system can be accessed through the Jobs pull-down menu of the console, which is shown in the following illustration. Remember that this menu is context-sensitive, which means that certain functionality might be grayed out depending on the currently selected object in the console.

Creating a Job

You can tell the console that you would like to create a new job in three different ways: You can select Jobs | Create Job, right-click the Jobs item in the navigator tree, or click the Create icon in the toolbar on the upper left side of the console. The last option opens a generic window asking which type of object you would like to create. Whichever selection you make, you will always get to the same dialog box to create a new job, as shown in Figure 4-1.

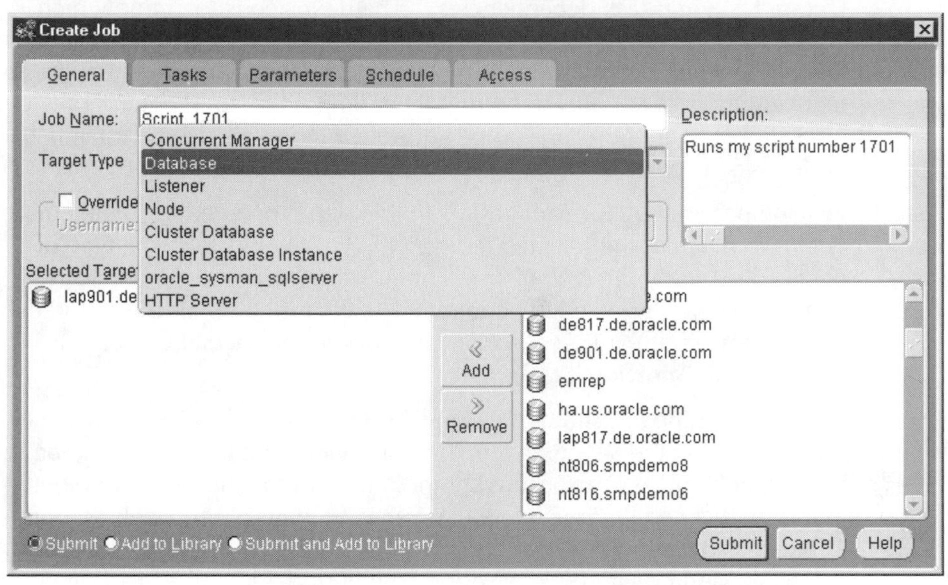

FIGURE 4-1. *Creating a new job*

Since the job system is flexible and powerful, it offers a large range of options for the user. At this point, we will explain the concept of dealing with jobs and provide an example with a more detailed walkthrough in Chapter 11. The workflow of creating a job can be described as follows, according to the tabs in Figure 4-1.

1. **Name the job and define the type and target.** The first thing you have to do is give the job a name that you, other DBAs, the repository, and the agent will recognize, on the General tab. You also have to select which type of target you want to run the job against. This will determine the type of job, such as running a SQL script, execute one specific command on a host, or a series of commands in a batch job. After selecting the target type, EM will offer you a list of actual targets of the selected type available which make sense in your current management environment. You can select one or multiple targets.

NOTE
You cannot select a database job as a type if you have not discovered any databases yet. Remember that you need to discover targets automatically, because you will need an agent for running jobs. Manually discovered targets will not be available in this dialog box.

2. **Define tasks and task dependencies.** The next step is to define which actual tasks the job consists of, on the Tasks tab. Again EM offers available tasks depending on your previously selected choices. You can also specify that certain tasks are only to be run depending on the outcome of previous tasks. Regardless of the target type you select, you will also be offered node tasks by default.
3. **Provide parameters for each task.** In this step, you need to specify more details for each of the selected tasks on the Parameters tab. The type of details depend on the type of task. For example, you need to enter the command if you selected OS-command as the task type, or the script text if you selected run SQL script. You can also define special credentials to be used for individual tasks.
4. **Define when the job should be run.** You need to tell the agent when to run this job, on the Schedule tab. You can select that the job should be run immediately, once at a specified point in time in the future, or frequently—that is, with a certain time interval, on specific days of the week or month. You can also determine when these settings should be activated, for example, run a job Mondays and Fridays during the period September 1 through September 31. Alternatively, you can specify that this job is a fixit job, which has no predefined schedule but will be run in response to a fired event. The fixit job is explained more in the next section of this chapter.
5. **Define access privileges for this job.** If you create a new job, you are the owner of this job and can determine which other DBAs will have access to it, on the Access tab. Super administrators always have access, but for other non-super administrators, you can define whether they have either full access, may only view or modify, or have no access at all. For both types of DBAs, you can define whether they are notified on certain conditions of jobs.
6. **Submit or save.** The last step is to either submit the job to the specified agents, save it to the Job Library, or both. The Job Library is maintained in the repository, enabling you to complete, change, or submit the job later, or share it with other DBAs. If you submit the job to the agents, you can view the progress of the job execution in the console. Click the jobs node in the navigator tree and see the active jobs in the detail window. Once jobs are finished or no longer active, the console moves them to the history page.

Prerequisites for Using Jobs

To successfully run jobs, you need to make sure that certain prerequisites are met:

- Targets must be discovered automatically. When you add targets to your management framework, you must use automatic discovery. Automatic discovery makes sure that the agent is available and can get to the targets in order to run the jobs. If a target becomes unavailable later on, the agent will notify you.

- **An agent must be available.** After submitting the job, the Management Server tries to contact the agent on the respective node. If the agent does not respond, the submission will eventually fail.
- **Preferred Credentials for the host and targets must be set.** When the agent runs jobs, it needs valid credentials, specifically a valid username and password for the host, and also the database user and password for database jobs. By default, the agent will be automatically provided with the preferred credentials defined for your DBA account in the EM framework. You have the option to override these default values for the job as a whole or sometimes for specific tasks during the job definition procedure.
- **You must provide an OS account.** Make sure the OS account allows the execution of jobs. Windows NT/2000 requires the account to have a special privilege called "logon as batch job" to successfully authorize the agent for the operating system.

TIP

Remember that the agent runs the job on your behalf. If the agent encounters authentication problems performing tasks, check if you have all the required privileges to perform them yourself.

- **You must use the correct version of the agent.** The choice of available jobs depends on the version of the agent you are using. We recommend you use the 9i agent to get the greatest capability. If you use a pre-9i agent, expect that certain behavior may be different. For example, the capability to run a job only once at a future time was added with the 9i agent. Submitting this type of job to an earlier agent version will cause an error.

Managing Jobs

In the following sections, we describe how to submit a job and track its progress. We will also talk about the role of TCL and blackouts.

Submitting Jobs

Once you have clicked Submit in the console, the job will be registered in the repository and transferred to the agent by the OMS. That means it is stored in two places, which are automatically always kept in sync. The agent encrypts and stores the job definition and all related information locally in the $OH\network\agent folder in files with the extension .q. This enables the agent to run the jobs even if the network breaks down directly after submitting the job.

NOTE
Never delete these .q-files; only use the console to delete jobs. If you delete the .q files, the agent does not know about these jobs anymore, but they are still registered in the repository, causing the repository and agent information to be out of sync.

Job Failure Protection Mechanisms

If the agent process is stopped while it has jobs scheduled, it will not be able to execute those jobs. The next time the agent starts, it will look for the .q files and continue where it left off. If it realizes that scheduled jobs were skipped because the agent was down, the target was not available, or if the job was still running from the previous execution time, it will notify you. If the agent cannot contact any Management Server, it queues up the messages and sends them as soon as an OMS is available.

Tracking and Canceling Jobs

Once you have submitted a job, you can track its progress in the details window of the console. You can access the command options edit, create like, copy to library, and remove by either selecting a job and clicking the Job menu, or by right-clicking one of the jobs. Removing deletes the job, which means it will be removed from the repository and from the agent's directory. Be careful when canceling a job that is running and composed of multiple tasks with complex dependencies. It may be difficult to determine which tasks of the larger job have been completed successfully. You can edit a submitted job and add more targets or change the access privileges. You can also copy an existing job to the library or create a new job like the existing one. EM also keeps track of all jobs in the job history. You can delete individual jobs from the history or clear the whole history. EM maintains a lot of statistics about jobs in the repository, such as how often each job has run and how long it took. You can access this information via the reporting features of EM, which are discussed later in this chapter.

TCL: Tool Command Language

The agent runs different kinds of jobs and events based on the Tool Command Language (Tcl, often pronounced "tickle") which was first developed by Dr. John Osterhout of the University of California at Berkeley. It has been extended by Oracle with certain verbs (OraTcl) to enable database commands, for example. You can look at the Intelligent Agent User's Guide for a complete list and description of these extensions. Tcl was chosen because it exists on many platforms, is extensible, and is free. According to the Scriptics Web site, "Tcl is available freely in source form at the Tcl Developer Xchange. You can do anything you want with it, such as modifying it to suit your needs or incorporating it into commercial products." If you have written your own Tcl scripts, you can implement them by using the Run TCL Script job task type. The agent's job definition files written in Tcl are located in the $OH\network\agent\jobs directory.

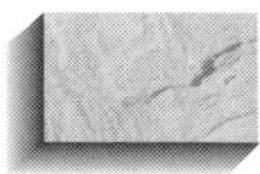

NOTE
The Internet offers a wealth of information on TCL; two good starting points are stage.caldera.com/Technology/tcl/Tcl.html or http://www.scriptics.com.

Blackouts

There may be situations when you would like to temporarily suspend the agent's job activities, such as when you need to shut down the database for an offline backup. These periods are called *blackout periods*, and you can manage them in a number of ways. To better understand the options for establishing blackouts, you need to be clear about the path a notification takes to the DBA. A notification is triggered by the agent, which raises an alarm because of a status change for a job or an event. The agent sends a message to the OMS to notify the DBA on duty. The first option you have is via commands in the console to activate a blackout on OMS-level. The agent keeps doing its regular job, recognizes status changes, probably runs associated fixit jobs, and keeps communicating trouble to the OMS, but the OMS suspends notification on a per-target basis for recurring predefined times. You can also set a total blackout, which means that all notifications will be immediately suspended with indefinite duration until the total blackout is revoked, regardless of any OMS-based scheduled blackouts. We show how to use these OMS-based blackout options in Chapters 5 and 9. The other option is to create a blackout period on the agent level using the AGENTCTL command directly on the machine the agent resides on. Blackouts can also be defined per target, which means that not only jobs, but also events and data collections are suspended. If a job is not run because a blackout is activated, you are notified later on. Refer to Chapter 19 for a description of the AGENTCTL command.

Migrating Jobs to a 9i Agent

As we mentioned earlier, the higher an agent's version number, the more functionality it has. Depending on your requirements, you could also be fine with a pre-9i agent, if for some reason you cannot install the latest version of the agent on your node. If you decide to install the latest agent, and we encourage this, you can install only the agent component into a new Oracle Home. After that, you have the option to use a command-line tool called NMUMIGR8 to convert pre-9i .q files to the 9i format. This is easier than switching to the new agent manually, which results in one-by-one deregistration and resubmission of all jobs and other tasks. This tool works for

.q files of agents with versions 8.0.6, 8.1.6 and 8.1.7. For other versions, you need to migrate manually. The NMUMIGR8 utility is explained more in Chapter 19.

Event System

In addition to running jobs, the Intelligent Agent can also take over the task of monitoring targets. The agent can be configured to frequently check the values of certain metrics 24 hours a day, and trigger activities if the values exceed predefined thresholds. Such an activity can be a notification of certain problems or conditions. The agent can also automatically run a fixit job as a predefined response for an anticipated problem. The event notification system of EM9i can optionally be configured to feed event information into other systems like Tivoli, CA Unicenter, HP OpenView, or others through the Event Handler, which is part of the OMS. When you use the agent to monitor tasks, you can monitor an almost unlimited number of databases, nodes, or other targets more effectively. We will guide you through the event system, starting with creating an event. The following illustration shows the Events menu, listing the available commands. We will explain each of them in context when we address managing events.

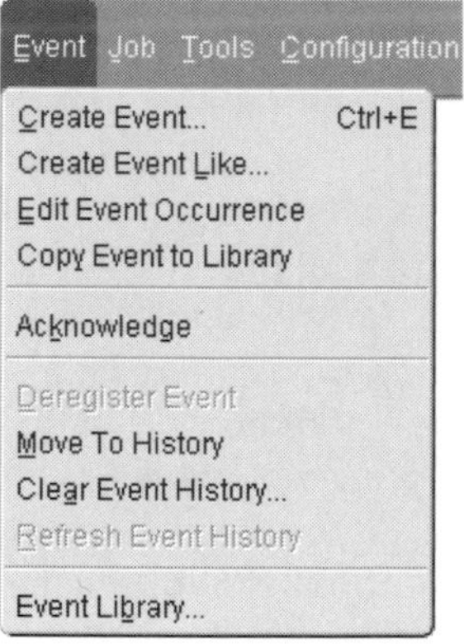

Creating an Event

Because events are handled much the same as jobs, the procedure of creating an event is almost identical. Events can be shared among DBAs by saving them to the event library, which is located in the repository. The event system depends on the agent, which means that most of the requirements valid for jobs apply to events as well. The event system of EM9i offers even more options than the job system. We will briefly talk about them while explaining the workflow of setting up an event. To create a new event, select Event | Create Event, right-click the events item in the navigator tree, or click the generic create icon in the toolbar. All of these options bring up the Event creation dialog box, shown in Figure 4-2.

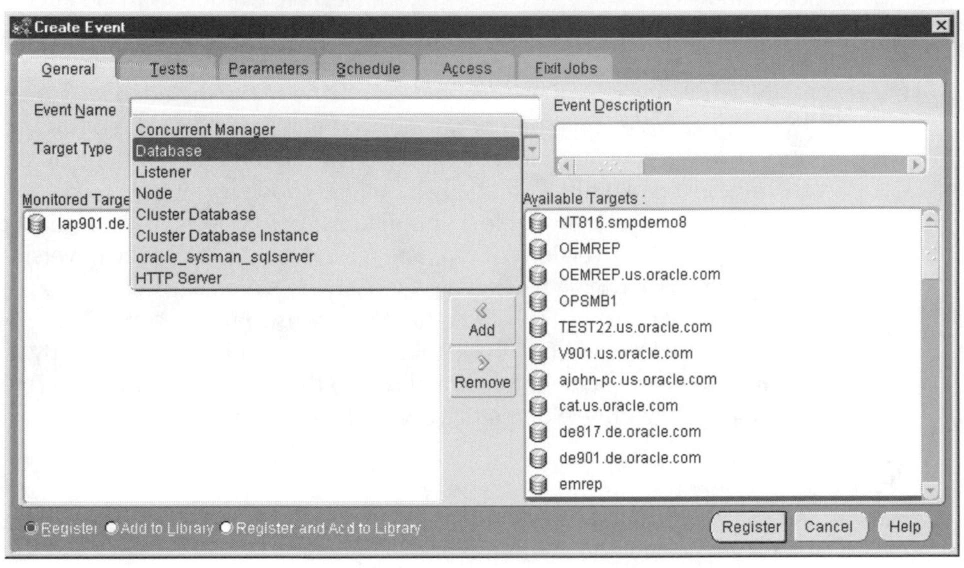

FIGURE 4-2. *Creating a new event*

Follow these steps to set up a new event:

1. **Name the event and define type and target.** As when you create a job, you need to label the event by giving it a name, on the General tab. You must specify which type of target the event will be created for, and for which actual targets you will register the event. As with jobs, EM will offer you a list of valid types and targets.

NOTE

If you select the target type Node, you will be able to choose specialized node events for specific operating systems. For example, if you pick Solaris as the operating system in this tab, you will have a far larger choice of Solaris-specific metrics available as event tests in the next step. This applies to all displayed operating systems. You need to have an 8.1.7 or 9.0.1 agent running to use this feature.

2. **Select event tests.** An event consists of one or more event tests, which define the actual metric you would like to monitor. You can select event tests from a list of predefined tests on the Tests tab. If you select multiple tests in a single event, the whole event will be triggered if any one of the included tests is positive; for example, if the number of sessions is greater than 500 or the memory sorts percentage is less than 80 percent. No matter which type of target you select, you will additionally be offered node event tests by default. The choice of event tests available in this dialog box has been vastly expanded compared to previous versions of EM. The reason is that starting with version 9i, the agent takes over the tasks of a previously delivered separate process called the Data Gatherer. This Data Gatherer was mainly used in the Diagnostics Pack for charting, historical monitoring, and data analysis. By combining the Data Gatherer functionality into the Intelligent Agent, you have a much larger choice of metrics available for event tests.

NOTE
Most of the events you see in this dialog box are called Advanced Events, and are part of the Diagnostics Pack, which is licensed separately. The free version of the EM framework contains limited choices with basic up-or-down monitoring capabilities. In previous versions of EM, you had to obtain separate media to install the Diagnostics Pack and with it the Advanced Events, making it easier to distinguish what was free and what had to be licensed separately. With version 9i of the database, EM and all packs are integrated in the database install for easier setup, making it more difficult for the user to tell what is part of the free portion.

Apart from the predefined events you see in this dialog, you can define your own events, called *user-defined events*. We will explain these and a feature called Unsolicited Events later in this chapter.

3. **Provide parameters for each event test.** The next step is to specify more details for each of the tests you selected, by using the Parameters tab. As with other jobs, the details depend on the type of tests selected. Most tests will ask you for the two threshold values where you would like the event to trigger: the warning threshold and the alert threshold. The warning threshold should fire before the alert threshold, letting you know that the metric is moving

towards a range you consider unsafe, but not bad enough that immediate action is necessary. Note that the alert threshold is not necessarily higher than the warning threshold. It depends on the selected metric if the ideal value is high or low. For example, for a tablespace fillgrade, the worst value is 100 percent. You might consider setting the warning threshold to 80 percent and the alert threshold to 90 percent. However when testing the buffer cache hit ratio the worst value is 0 percent. Because this metric's value should be as high as possible, you might want to consider setting the warning threshold to 90 percent and the alert threshold to 80 percent.

NOTE
Some events offer the option of not firing the first time a certain threshold is crossed, but only after it has been crossed a number of times. This way you are not notified in case a metric has a temporary spike, but only if the problem is more persistent. You can enter the number of threshold violations after which you want the agent to fire.

For some event tests you might need to enter more parameters, such as the tablespace name or the disk drive, if you want to check for space consumption. Database event tests typically offer to override the default credentials when testing this event. This might be of interest to you, if single tests should be performed under a different database login than your preferred credentials for the selected targets.

4. **Specify the schedule for testing this event.** This step requires you to define when and how frequently the agent should test the event, by using the Schedule tab. You can specify that the agent should test on a certain day of the month, a certain day of the week, or at a certain time interval. You can instruct the agent to start testing right away or at a later time.

5. **Define access privileges for this event.** As you have already learned from jobs, you own the events you create. With the Access tab, you can determine which other DBAs should have access to them. Super administrators will always have access, but for other administrators you can define whether they have either full access, view access, modify rights, or no access at all. You can also manipulate notification settings and view the current notification schedule for all DBAs.

NOTE
On the Access tab, all timeslots that are covered by any of the selected DBAs show up green. White slots are not covered at all by any of the selected DBAs. Right-clicking on one of the white timeslots displays the option to add another DBA for notification. It will offer only those DBAs who have any notification set up during the selected timeslot in their preferences. If no DBA is offered, that means no DBA has set up notification preferences for that timeslot.

In addition, you can specify if the agent should be able to send SNMP traps to external systems in case the event fires. These are messages based on the Simple Network Management Protocol (SNMP). More information about SNMP is available in the SNMP Support Reference Manual.

6. **Optionally define a fixit job.** We have already mentioned that you can define a corrective action in the form of a job for anticipated problems, such as cleaning up temporary folders in case of a disk space shortage, or restarting the database listener process if it goes down. You can activate this functionality by checking the box on top of the Fixit Jobs tab. These fixit jobs need to be defined and submitted to the agent before you can select them in this dialog box. In previous versions of EM, you had to cancel out at this point and go back to the job creation process if you had not already defined a suitable fixit job. With EM9i you can now create a fixit job right away, and you do not need to switch back to the job creation workflow.

7. **Register or save.** You can save the event definition to the library in the repository, register it with the agent, or both. After registering, you can see the registration process in the details window of the console after clicking the Events icon in the navigator tree. If the event remains in the status registration pending, you might want to check if the agent process is up and running.

Prerequisites for Using Events

The prerequisites mentioned in the jobs section also apply for events. You need to have an agent available, and the targets involved must be discovered using the automatic discovery mechanisms. We again recommend that you use the highest agent version to take advantage of the latest features in the event system.

Credentials of the OEM_MONITOR Role

You need to make sure that preferred credentials are set in the console before you register the event because they will be sent to the agent along with the event definition. These credentials must be equipped with sufficient privileges to access the monitored objects. In most cases, you do not need to provide full DBA privileges for monitoring events; in fact, most customers refrain from giving DBA privileges to every DBA. You can use the OEM_MONITOR role instead, which was created for this purpose. It is generated with the database creation scripts since database version 8.0.6. You can also create this role manually as outlined in the Enterprise Manager Administrator's Guide.

Monitoring Strategy

A question which typically arises when talking about monitoring relates to how much workload the monitoring itself generates in the database, commonly referred to as *overhead*. This is a valid question and requires some consideration. The first thing you need to be aware of is that you never get any monitoring information for free. That is, monitoring always requires putting in configuration effort or generating at least some overhead by the monitoring activity. There will always be a mechanism you need to install and to set up if you want the mechanism to perform according to your individual needs. The mechanism always consumes some database capacity, CPU/memory capacity, or disk I/O to collect information for you. That's why it is essential to develop a monitoring strategy regarding which metrics you need to monitor and how often you need samples of these metrics in order to evaluate them properly. You will agree that it does not make much sense to check for free disk space every five seconds, or to check for the buffer cache hit ratio only once per day. Having an idea about your preferences and documenting them before you start monitoring enables you to use EM's event system best. This also applies to any other monitoring mechanism.

Managing Events

Once you click the Register button in the creation dialog, the agent is contacted and all event-related information is transferred. The agent will store that information in encrypted .q files just as it does with job related information. The NMUMIGR8 tool mentioned earlier in the chapter also migrates event definition files from previous versions of the agent to the format the 9i agent uses.

Tracking and Canceling Events

Once the event is registered and the agent starts monitoring for threshold violations, you can check the status of the event in the console's detail page by selecting Events in the navigator tree. You will see three tabs labeled Alerts, Registered, and History.

Alerts Tab The Alerts page displays all event notifications. The ideal situation is when this page is empty. If one of the event test thresholds defined in the event has been crossed, or if a problem with the event has occurred, the console displays that information here. The color of the flag indicates the severity of the event. A yellow flag means that the warning threshold has been crossed, whereas a red flag means that both the warning and alert thresholds have been crossed. A green flag signals that everything is back in order after there was a yellow or a red flag. These flags change in color according to the state of the event. That means you might see an event changing flag colors frequently if the status changes often.

In addition, the Alerts page notifies you if there is a problem with the proper operation of an event. A grey flag means that the OMS cannot communicate with the agent, setting the status to unknown. There are a variety of possible reasons for this: the network connection may be interrupted, the machine may be unreachable, or the agent may be down or does not respond. This does not necessarily mean that the affected target database is in trouble, only that the monitoring functionality is interrupted and the system cannot check if everything is fine. You might also encounter an Error notification—an exclamation mark in a yellow circle. This means that the agent cannot evaluate the event as instructed. There may be a variety of reasons for this circumstance, such as specifying to test an object that does not exist by providing an invalid tablespace name or disk drive. Invalid credentials are also a common cause for such an error notification.

If you see the notification icon accompanied by an icon that looks like a pair of glasses, no DBA has acknowledged this notification so far. Double-click the notification to investigate it by starting the Event Viewer. Here you can view the log and the notification history, assign a DBA, or access real-time charts or the advice system that comes with Performance Manager. You can move the event to the History tab or edit the event occurrence.

Changing event parameters dynamically—while the event is still registered with the agent—may not be possible with all events, because this is a feature introduced with the 9i agent. The General tab of the edit event dialog box will tell you if there are restrictions and why. Also note that editing may be restricted if you are not the owner of the event and have no privileges to modify it.

Registered Tab The Registered page displays which events are registered with the agents. You can display more columns in this window by checking the Show targets check box at the bottom of this window. Right-clicking an event enables you to either copy the event definition to the library, create a new event like the existing one, deregister the event, or edit it.

TIP

You can dynamically edit some event parameters while they are registered starting with version 9i of the agent. For earlier versions of the agent, you might consider using the following procedure: Copy the event definition to the library, deregister the event, choose to create an event like the one you just copied, change the parameters as desired, and re-register.

History Tab All notifications have to be moved to the history page before they can be deleted. You can select single events for deletion or completely clear the event history from the pull-down menu.

Blackouts

The previous section regarding blackouts for jobs also applies to blackouts for events. That means you have the option to schedule a blackout or activate an immediate total blackout on OMS-level. You can also use the AGENTCTL command to suspend notification activities on agent-level. Refer to Chapter 19 for a description of the AGENTCTL command.

Special Features

In the following, we talk about the options you have to define your own events and how to set up communication with other management frameworks or systems using the Event Handler and Unsolicited Events.

User-Defined SQL-Based Events

The choice of predefined events available is huge, and has been expanded further with version 9i of the agent. However, if you need to monitor a value not offered by EM, you can define the event test yourself. You need to provide the select statement that returns the value that you want to evaluate. You need to select User Defined SQLTest as the event to test, and instruct the agent how to evaluate the number your statement returns. It is your responsibility to make sure the returned values make sense. This way, you have total flexibility to test any value in the database using standard SQL.

User-Defined OS-Based Events

Starting with version 9i of EM, you also have the option to implement your own OS-based events. This works much like SQL-based events, but on the OS level. That means you can implement your own OS-based events using the User-Defined Event test to run scripts in any language which can be run on the agent's node, such as Perl scripts. The value the script returns will be checked against the thresholds you define in the event test parameters. Instead of typing, copying, or loading a script here, you can specify the path to the script to be run. This path must be accessible and identical for all agents you register the event against. You can also run a self-written program here, as long as you follow the documented rules to return a metric that can be evaluated by the agent. A sample script is provided with $OH/sysman/admin/udeload.pl. This feature gives you almost unlimited flexibility in defining new events on the OS level if you want to monitor a metric that is not offered through the predefined node events. Both the user-defined SQL-based and OS-based events are part of the Advanced Events implemented in the Diagnostics Pack.

Unsolicited Events

If you have some other monitoring mechanism installed on the same node as the agent, you can feed messages from this mechanism through the Intelligent Agent into EM's event system. From the EM point of view, such an event is called an *unsolicited event*. The actual event testing and evaluation is done by an outside mechanism and the agent is just told to fire. To use this feature, you first need to enable the agent to receive such events by defining the Unsolicited Event Filters test, which can be found under the node tests when creating a new event. Defining an unsolicited event allows you to filter events, and requires you to follow a special syntax, which is outlined in the Enterprise Manager Administrator's Guide. To raise such an event in EM, the external mechanism can either use the OS-command OEMEVENT or the OraTcl verb ORAREPORTEVENT from within a Tcl script. Starting with the 9i agent, you can also register a fixit job as a response to an unsolicited event notification.

Event Handler

As described in the previous section, other mechanisms can feed events into EM's event system. To do this, these frameworks need to be able to trigger an external command, which causes the event to be raised in EM. In return, EM can also feed messages to other monitoring systems, which is done by a component of the Management Server called the Event Handler. The Event Handler has been part of EM since version 2.2, and has been enhanced further in version 9i. It consists of two components called the Event Logger and Command Executor. As the names suggest, the Event Logger can write event messages to a designated log file, and the Command Executor can execute an OS-based command as a response to an event. You can specify either or both of these components as response to events. You can also define filters to trigger actions depending on the event parameters. Note that the Event Handler is disabled by default in a newly configured OMS, and must be enabled manually.

The difference between the Command Executor and a fixit job is that the fixit job needs to be defined explicitly as response to a specific event, which will be run by the involved agent on the affected node. The Command Executor can run an OS command based on all event notifications coming in from all existing agents. It is well suited to trigger actions that needs to be taken for more than one event, such as communicating certain events to another third-party framework.

Configuring the Event Handler is done by editing a configuration file, which needs to be imported into the Management Server. Use the following procedure with the oemctl command from a super administrator account:

1. Stop the OMS: OEMCTL STOP OMS *<username>*/*<password>*
2. Enable the Event Handler: OEMCTL ENABLE EVENTHANDLER

3. Export the configuration file: OEMCTL EXPORT EVENTHANDLER <*filename*>
4. Edit the configuration file. Exact syntaxes can be found in Chapter 6 of the *EM Administrator's Guide*.
5. Import the file: OEMCTL IMPORT EVENTHANDLER <*filename*>
6. Start the OMS: OEMCTL START OMS

Groups System

The groups system lets you organize targets into logical categories. These categories can be defined according to your individual preferences like versions, function, location, or others. Using groups enables you to manage a larger number of targets more efficiently, because you can submit jobs and register events to all valid group members with less effort. Groups do not have their own pull-down menu like jobs and events, but are displayed as folders in the navigator tree like other services. This makes more sense, because groups are used as virtual target types and targets for jobs and events.

Creating a Group

When you initially set up the EM framework, the Groups folder is empty, because no groups have been created yet. Creating groups always requires that targets are available to be assigned to the group. This means you must successfully discover targets before creating groups. You can create a group by right-clicking the Groups folder in the navigator tree and selecting create, or through the generic create button in the toolbar. Either way, you will see a dialog box with three pages called View, General, and Access, as shown in Figure 4-3.

You first have to define a name for the group object you are about to create and then you can add targets to this group. You can add targets of the same type, generating a homogeneous group, or mix target types, generating a heterogeneous group. You can add a description of the group and implement a background image. Some geographical maps are provided by default, and can be selected via pull-down menu. We will explain how to add your own images when we walk you through the group creation process in more detail in Chapter 10. The Access page lets you provide privileges for other DBAs to access this object. Remember that no other DBA except the super administrators have access to an object you create if you don't provide privileges. The View page lets you view the group in a separate window, once you have finished defining it. It is the same view you get in the detail window of the console when selecting the group in the navigator tree. Click the Create button to save the group to the repository.

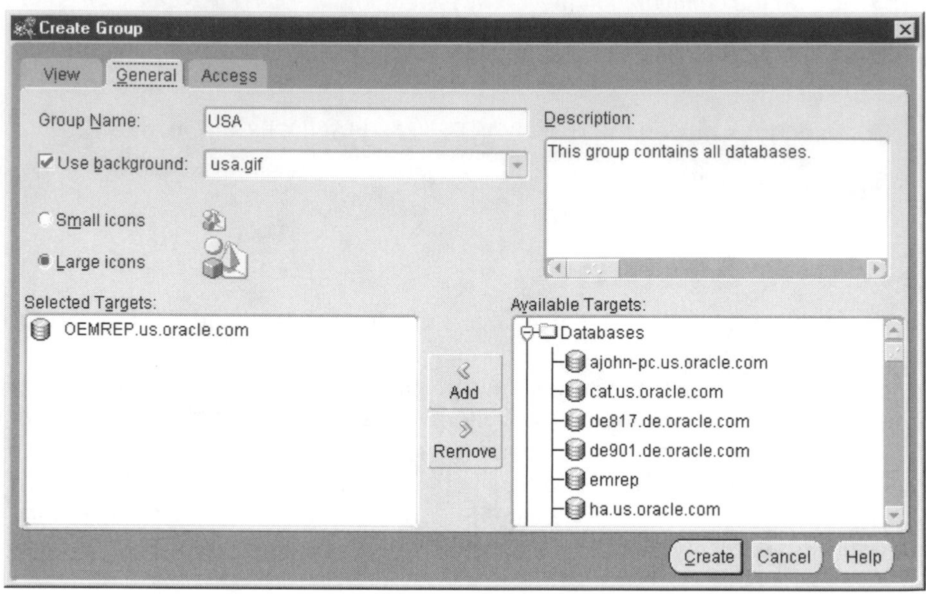

FIGURE 4-3. *Creating a new group*

Managing Groups

Once created, the group will appear in the navigator tree and can be opened to display all group members. You can edit a group at any time by adding more targets or removing existing targets, or you can remove the whole group. You can create a group like an existing one, or create subgroups inside an existing group by right-clicking an existing group instead of the overall groups folder and selecting Create. A subgroup can also be created by simply dragging and dropping a group onto another group in the navigator tree.

Using Groups with Jobs and Events

Because groups are virtual targets, they also appear in the list of valid targets during the creation process for jobs and events. When you submit a job or an event, EM sends it to all applicable targets in the group. For example, a job to run a SQL script will be submitted to all databases in the group selected. If you add a database after submitting the job, EM will not retroactively submit the job to the newly added target; you have to submit the job for that target separately. Also, you cannot cancel jobs or deregister events for groups. Groups do not exist from the agent's point of view, that's why you never see groups as target types in the jobs and events status pages. This means that you have to deregister an event separately, although you were able to register it for a group. You also must be aware that a group can contain manually discovered targets, but because an agent is needed to run jobs or events, they will not be submitted against manually discovered targets in the group. When an event triggers for one of the targets inside a group, the group icon displays the most severe status as event notification. That means if one group member has an alert warning (a red flag) associated with it, the whole group will inherit this status from that member.

Reports

Reporting is a very important feature of EM; it enables you to access any information in the EM framework from a browser. In version 2.2, you could access the Enterprise Reports, which were a set of HTML pages generated frequently through a job submitted to the agent. With EM9i, this concept has been modified and developed much further, and now offers many more features. There are various kinds of reports available in EM, all of which are accessed from various different places. The following section describes where they can be found and what they can do for you.

Reporting Website

The Reporting Website is the most important reporting feature and new with EM9i. You can access it from anywhere in your network, and it contains pure HTML. The information you can access here can be generated on demand, which means it always contains the latest changes. You can access the Reporting Website through EM's general Web site, which is also used to start EM through a browser.

Accessing EM via a Browser

The standard install of EM9i also installs the Apache WebServer, which is used to access EM via the Web. Directly after installation, you should be able to access the general EM Web site by using the URL of the machine name and the default port 3339, like this: http://<*machine-name*>:3339. In the upper part of the page, you will have the option to start the EM console in a browser and connect to a Management Server. The browser then downloads and starts the console as a Java applet, which enables you to run most components of EM with an identical look and feel, without actually installing it on your client. There are certain restrictions and requirements if you choose this option, which we will clarify in Chapter 18. In the lower part of the EM Web site, you can access the Reporting Home Page (Figure 4-4). You must configure the Home Page before you can use it, as explained in the following section. You will also be taken to this page if you click the View published Reports button of the toolbar in the upper left corner of the console.

You can see in one page how many services you have in your repository, how many are monitored, and what the monitoring status for each of them is. From here

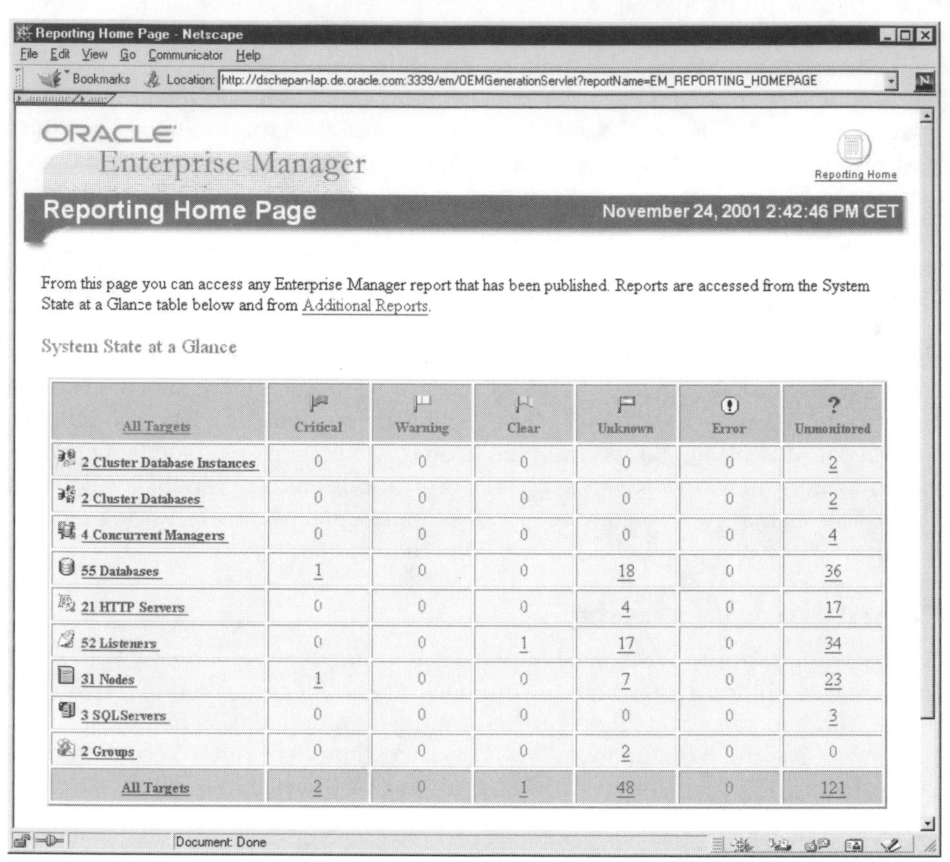

FIGURE 4-4. *Using the Reporting Home Page*

you start your investigation by clicking the offered links and drill down into individual targets, or you can even access current information inside any database. The Reporting Website is very convenient if you receive a paging message while away from your desk and you would like to get more details before you decide what to do. You can use any machine with a browser to access the Reporting Website, drill down to any event notification, and read the details from anywhere in your network. You can even access real-time or historical monitoring information, which is part of the Diagnostics Pack. If you want additional information displayed here, you can easily add your own reports.

Configuring the Reporting Website

The Reporting Website gives you access to information that is in your repository. That means that the Web server needs to have access to a Management Server, because this is the only way to access information inside the repository. The Web server process logs into the management framework using an account called REPORTS_USER, which is the other super administrator account created during startup besides SYSMAN. You just need to tell the Web server which OMS to log into, with which password, and prepare the OMS for which Web server will access it. That is done through use of oemctl configure `RWS`, which asks for a couple of configuration parameters. What you need to do before logging in is change the password for REPORTS_USER to something other than OEM_TEMP, which will not be accepted as a valid password during configuration. You do this by logging into the OMS as SYSMAN, and then change the password of the REPORTS_USER by editing its credentials. We will explain how to do this in further detail in Chapters 5 and 9.

If the REPORTS_USER account does not have any credentials set for specific databases, then it will not be able to obtain information from that database for you. For example, suppose you access the reporting Web site and want to see the instance parameter configuration for a specific database. To obtain this information, the REPORTS_USER has to connect to the database and query the data dictionary. This is not possible if you don't provide valid credentials to the REPORTS_USER account in the EM framework.

You can always check for which Web server the OMS you are connected to is configured by selecting Configuration | View Reporting Website Configuration in the console. We provide a detailed example on how to configure the Reporting Website in Chapter 13.

Reports in the Console

Behind each page you see when accessing the Reporting Website stands a report definition. These report definitions are stored in the repository, and are provided with EM by default. You can see all available report definitions in the console's detail page if you click the Reports icon. Whether or not you have set up and configured the reporting framework, you can always trigger the console to generate any report you are interested in. Since reports are stored in the repository, they can also be shared among DBAs. You can modify existing reports or create new reports like existing ones. You also have the option to publish your own report to the Reporting Website. For each report, you can determine if the content is generated dynamically each time a user accesses it, or if you use the 9i agent job system to frequently generate a HTML file. You have huge flexibility when designing your report. EM offers you the opportunity to not only determine which data is displayed by letting you specify the SQL statement

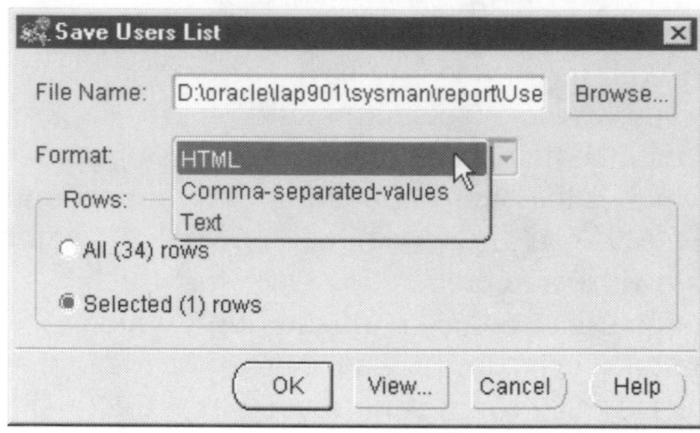

FIGURE 4-5. *Saving a list or object report information to a file*

for selecting the data, but also the look and feel of the graphical items on the Web page. This allows you to create your own corporate reporting Web site. We guide you through setting up some custom reports in Chapter 13.

Object Reports

When you are administering the targets displayed in the navigator tree, and you right-click on objects or categories of objects, you will very often find the command Save List. This command assists you in generating instant reports containing the information that is currently displayed.

You get a dialog box (see Figure 4-5) in which you can specify the file name, path, and type of report. You can simply save it, or view it right away for further processing. In addition, you can fill the report with all rows available or just the selected subset. This functionality is available for most lists throughout all console functionality.

In version 9i of EM, you should expect to see lots of options for saving and printing lists, printing screens, or generating reports on all kinds of screens and dialogs. Although you could search for printing or reporting functionality in vain in earlier versions of EM, you can now print almost anything in EM9i. Most of the lists or object reports are also available when the console is running in standalone mode.

Summary

This chapter introduced the jobs and event systems with related agent background information, the group concept, and the reporting features available in EM9i. The next chapter will explain which features the console offers to configure the EM framework.

CHAPTER 5

Configuration Options in the Console

In this chapter, we will explain the various functions in the console that help you to configure your management environment. We will walk through the Configuration and Navigator menus of the console, as they appear when connected to an OMS using a super administrator account. Some features might also be available in stand-alone mode with slightly modified functionality. We will explain these features where necessary.

The Configuration Menu

Figure 5-1 shows the Configuration menu in a console connected to an OMS. Bear in mind that some of the commands might not be available if you connected using a regular DBA account. This section outlines the options available from this menu.

Preferences

When you are logged into the OMS, you can define the preferences of your own account. There are a number of preferences you can define, and therefore a number of tabs to walk through. Figure 5-2 shows the dialog box you use to modify all these preferences. Modifications are on a per-account basis, which means that the repository maintains one set of preferences per DBA account. This command is also available when the console runs in stand-alone mode, but the only definable preferences are the username and password combination for each database. The following sections describe the settings on each tab.

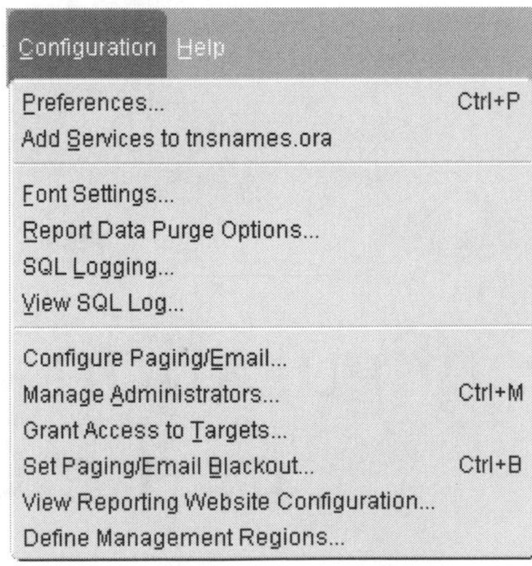

FIGURE 5-1. *The Configuration menu of the console*

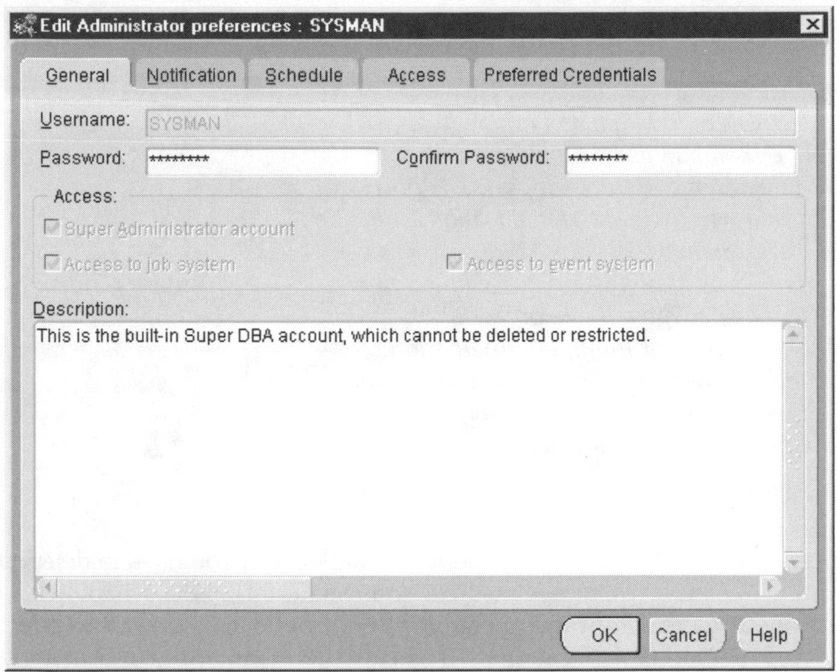

FIGURE 5-2. *The Administrator preferences dialog box*

General

The General tab enables you to change your own password to access the EM framework, and the descriptive text for the account. Note that you cannot change your own privileges regarding access to job or event system and your classification as a regular or super administrator.

Notification

The Notification tab allows you to customize the console's behavior regarding your own paging or e-mail notifications. That means you can control when you would like to be notified and by which medium. For example, you may want to be notified via pager when an event alert is triggered, via e-mail when the event is cleared, and not at all when a job is completed. For e-mail notification, you must specify your e-mail address. You can further customize the contents of the subject line and the body text of the message, depending on how verbose you would like the message to be. Similar options exist for setting up the paging message; examples for both options are provided in Chapter 9. You can also have notifications sent to your mobile or cell phone via SMS (Short Message Service). You will need to determine your phone's e-mail address and gateway from your mobile phone provider.

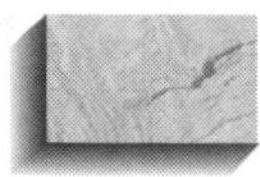

NOTE
Often DBAs would like to get notified via two different e-mail addresses simultaneously, a feature that EM does not currently support. The only workaround was to have the notification sent to an e-mail list containing all your addresses. This can be simplified by applying a patch with number EM_901_1847262, available on Metalink, after which you can enter multiple e-mail addresses separated by commas. Metalink is the official support website of Oracle Corporation that can be accessed via Internet at http://metalink.oracle.com.

Schedule

After setting up the conditions and methods for notification, you have to determine during which times you want to be notified. You can do this in the schedule tab by clicking on one or more of the boxes representing one hour of a day, and then selecting your preferred method of notification. You can also paint randomly over multiple boxes or select whole days (rows) and hours (columns) in this sheet. You can decide to be notified via e-mail, paging, or not at all for every individual hour of the week.

Access

In the discussion of jobs, events, and groups in the previous chapter, you learned that every time you create one of these objects, you are automatically its owner. During the creation process, you can determine which privileges other DBAs have in relation to the object you just created. On the Access tab, you can set up default privileges for other DBAs, which remain valid for all future objects you create. Remember that all super administrator accounts are grayed out at this point because they have general access to all objects by default, regardless of who the owner is.

Preferred Credentials

The credentials you normally use are referred to as *preferred credentials* in EM. One of the great advantages of EM and the repository is that it remembers the logon information you use, so you don't have to enter them over and over each time you open a database. The same applies to other target types where appropriate. EM adjusts the required fields you have to fill out depending on the selected target type. You can manage all your preferred credentials from the Preferred Credentials tab; you can enter all the username and password combinations, or change them if you need to.

If you are using a standardized account with the same password on most of the databases you administer, you can specify this in the <DEFAULT> line for each target type. EM will use this default password if you connect to a database and there is no specific logon information provided for this individual database. If you provide other credentials for individual targets, then EM always uses these first, and then looks for default settings. If you are submitting jobs or events through EM, you must enter the host information on this tab for the agent to use before you can successfully submit a job or event. The agent must have valid logon credentials to take any kind of action on the remote node.

Add Services to tnsnames.ora

Choosing the Add Services to tnsnames.ora command allows you to write information about the services you have access to through the console to the local tnsnames.ora file. It will write the information to the \network\admin folder of the Oracle Home from which the console was started. If you already have an existing tnsnames.ora file in this folder, new services will be appended and the previous file will be backed up by copying and renaming it with the extension .001 or higher numbers, if necessary. Updating the local tnsnames.ora file with information about databases in the EM framework is especially useful when you are working with other tools. SQL*PLUS, for example, has no access to the OMS or repository information and requires an entry in the local tnsnames.ora file.

Font Settings

You can customize the look and feel of the console and related EM tools by adjusting the font and font size that the console and all other tools use to display information. You can choose among different fonts and enlarge the size up to 18 points. You can optionally switch to bold or italics styles. This feature was introduced in earlier versions of EM because it was a frequent enhancement request from a range of customers. Many customers consider this a less important feature, but it was very easy to implement. It is especially beneficial for educational events and demos, where people sitting in the back of the room may have trouble reading the text displayed in the small default font size. This enhanced feature is also available when the console runs in stand-alone mode.

Report Data Purge Options

The reporting framework, described in Chapter 4, offers a wealth of information. Included is historical data which is collected over time, for example, to offer you a historical view of various service levels. EM collects and stores this information and related historical data in the repository. To prevent this amount of data endlessly growing, old data needs to be purged frequently. EM offers an automatic way to perform this purge, which can be configured through the Report Data Purge Options command. You can specify how long the historical data should be kept, or after what period of time the data should be deleted. This directly influences the size of the repository.

SQL Logging

When you are actively managing databases and objects inside databases using EM, you interact with a graphical user interface. Because the database is only able to understand SQL statements, EM constructs these statements based on what you click in the console and sends them to the database. During database management you often have the option to display the SQL statement which is sent. Look for a button labeled Show SQL in database management dialogs. By activating SQL Logging, as shown in Figure 5-3, you can now start to log all such SQL sent to the databases when using EM. The framework collects all statements for all DBAs to a table in the repository, which you can query comfortably later on. You can log either Data Manipulation Language (DML), Data Definition Language (DDL), or both. You can further restrict the amount of data to be collected by specifying a maximum number of statements to be stored. The mechanism will always keep the latest statements and purge the oldest. This option is not available for non super administrators.

When you are running EM in standalone mode, you can activate this option for your own session. In such a case, the console will write the information to a file, for which you need to specify a name and location. You can restrict the amount of data to be collected by specifying the maximum file size, and optionally instruct EM to copy the file when it reaches the specified maximum size and oldest data is about to be purged.

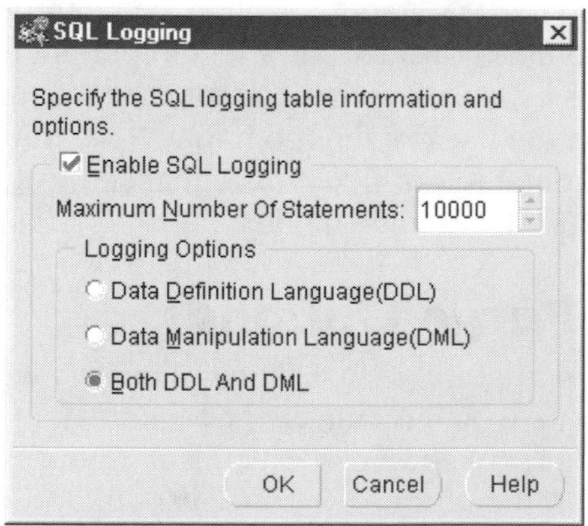

FIGURE 5-3. *Setting up SQL logging*

View SQL Log

The View SQL Log option lets you view the SQL logs which have been created by using the mechanism described in the previous section, as shown in Figure 5-4. If you do not have SQL logging activated, this option is grayed out. You will be able to discover which administrator issued which SQL statements, at what time, and to which database. The information also includes the database account used for each transaction. There are numerous filtering options, and you can produce a report to save or print the data as well as purge the log. This option is not available in stand-alone mode, you have to access the specified log file directly with a suitable editor.

Configure Paging/Email

Every DBA in the EM framework can specify when they want to be notified and by what means, either paging or e-mail. The DBA sets up the e-mail address, but that is not enough for EM to actually send a message. The Configure Email/Paging option lets you specify which e-mail gateway and sender account should be used to actually send the notifications. You need to enter this information before EM can send out any e-mail. Make sure you test the settings through the Test Email button when entering individual addresses for DBAs in the notification tab of their preferences. You similarly have to specify which paging server to use for sending out all paging notifications. Because notification is not available in stand-alone mode, this option is only available when connected to an OMS.

Manage Administrators

The Manage Administrators option is one of the more important configuration options when connected to the framework, and is only available for super administrators. This option opens the dialog box shown in Figure 5-5. It enables you to create, edit, and delete the accounts other DBAs use to access the EM framework, which is important because the only two accounts created by the setup scripts are SYSMAN

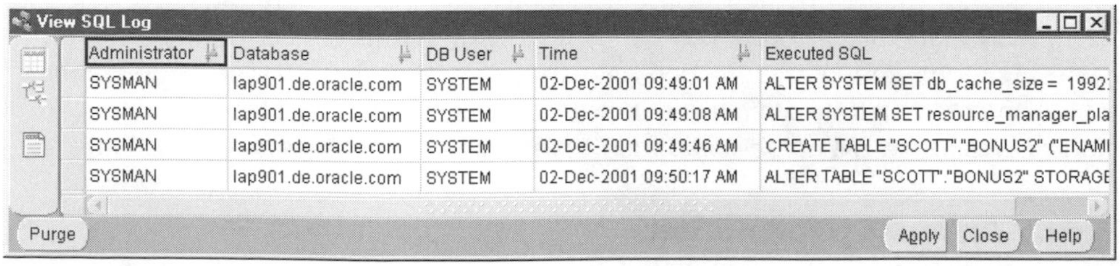

View SQL Log

Administrator	Database	DB User	Time	Executed SQL
SYSMAN	lap901.de.oracle.com	SYSTEM	02-Dec-2001 09:49:01 AM	ALTER SYSTEM SET db_cache_size = 1992
SYSMAN	lap901.de.oracle.com	SYSTEM	02-Dec-2001 09:49:08 AM	ALTER SYSTEM SET resource_manager_pla
SYSMAN	lap901.de.oracle.com	SYSTEM	02-Dec-2001 09:49:46 AM	CREATE TABLE "SCOTT"."BONUS2" ("ENAMI
SYSMAN	lap901.de.oracle.com	SYSTEM	02-Dec-2001 09:50:17 AM	ALTER TABLE "SCOTT"."BONUS2" STORAGE

Purge Apply Close Help

FIGURE 5-4. *Viewing the SQL log*

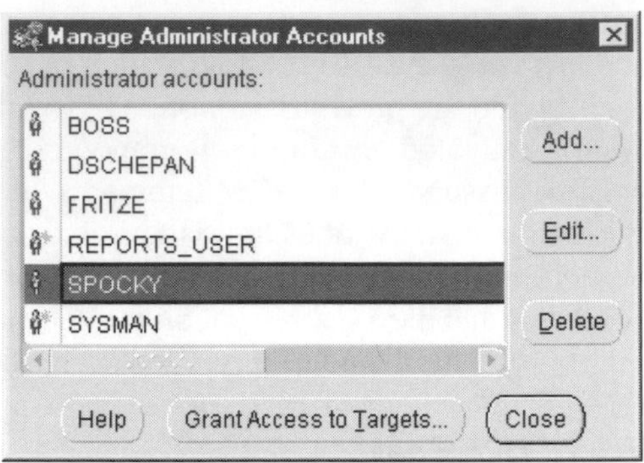

FIGURE 5-5. *Managing administrator accounts*

and REPORTS_USER. Neither should be used for common DBA activities, especially the REPORTS_USER account, which should be used by the reporting framework only. The process of creating other DBA accounts can be split into three steps: creating an account, editing the account information, and granting access to targets for the account. This process is described in detail in the following sections.

NOTE
Although the initial password for both accounts is OEM_TEMP, you cannot connect using the REPORTS_USER account, which has been purposely disabled for security reasons. You need to change the password before this account can be used in any way, especially for the reporting framework.

Creating a DBA account

When you create a DBA account, you can determine the account name and initial password, and whether the new account will be a super administrator account. In case of a normal DBA account, you can generally disable access to the job or event system. Accounts cannot be renamed once they are created. You need to delete the account and create it from scratch with a new name. Remember that this account only grants access to the EM framework, and not to individual databases.

Editing Account Information

The Editing Account Information dialog box is the same as when editing your own preferences, as outlined earlier in this chapter, except that this information will be applied to the selected account. That means you can specify notification details and schedules as well as object access privileges. Most importantly, you can also specify the preferred credentials the DBA will be using. This can be convenient if you want to grant individual DBAs access to databases without disclosing the actual account password to them.

Grant Access to Targets

New in version 9i of EM is the ability to customize the choice of visible targets for each DBA individually. In the Access to Targets dialog box (shown in Figure 5-6), you can specify which services will be displayed in the console for the DBA when he or she logs into the OMS, regardless of the type of service. You can only grant access to targets if you also grant access to the underlying node. For example, if you grant access to a database, you also need to grant access to the underlying node. This dialog box automatically checks the mark to grant access to the node the database runs on. The same concept works in reverse: If you want to revoke access to a node as a whole, you need to manually revoke access to all services on that node beforehand. You can edit access information for multiple accounts simultaneously by selecting multiple accounts holding the Control or Shift key and selecting accounts. Super administrator accounts will not be displayed, because super administrators have a general access to all targets which cannot be restricted.

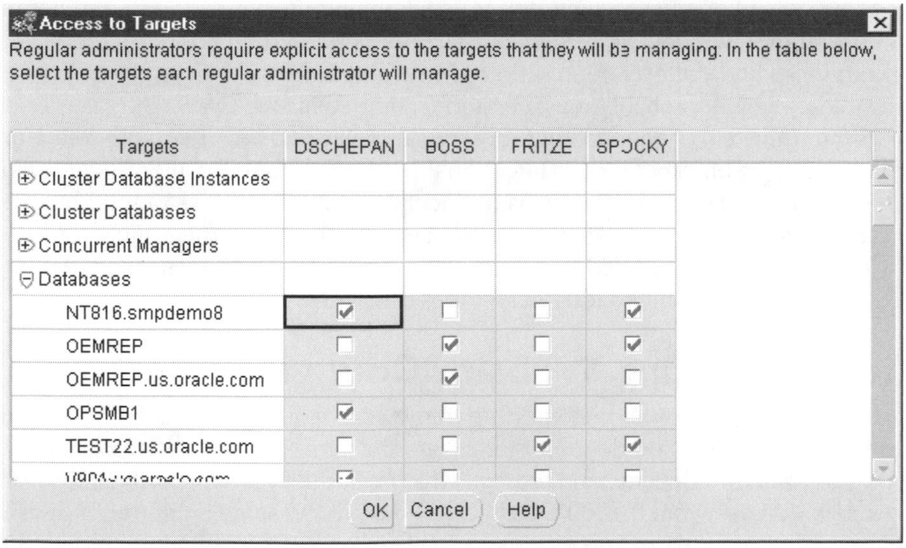

Access to Targets

Regular administrators require explicit access to the targets that they will be managing. In the table below, select the targets each regular administrator will manage.

Targets	DSCHEPAN	BOSS	FRITZE	SPOCKY
⊕ Cluster Database Instances				
⊕ Cluster Databases				
⊕ Concurrent Managers				
⊖ Databases				
NT816.smpdemo8	☑	☐	☐	☑
OEMREP	☐	☑	☐	☑
OEMREP.us.oracle.com	☐	☑	☐	☐
OPSMB1	☑	☐	☐	☐
TEST22.us.oracle.com	☐	☐	☑	☑

OK Cancel Help

FIGURE 5-6. *Granting access to targets*

Deleting Administrator Accounts

If a DBA leaves the company or changes jobs, you may need to delete a DBA account in the EM framework. Before deletion, EM checks whether the DBA owns any objects, and if so, forces you to assign new owners to each of them. This mechanism makes sure that there are no orphan jobs or events in the repository. A special dialog box appears displaying a list of objects for the DBA account to be deleted, and enables you to assign a new owner from a predefined list of the remaining DBA accounts.

Grant Access

You can explicitly jump to the Access to Targets dialog box by selecting the Grant Access command. The dialog box displays access information for all accounts that are not super administrator accounts. You can review and modify all access privileges for all targets and all non super administrator accounts.

Set E-mail/Paging Blackouts

You have already learned that you can instruct the agent to temporarily suspend any notification from jobs, events, or data collections (see Figure 5-7). This is done on a per-target basis directly on the node on which the agent resides, through use of the AGENTCTL command options. This agent-based blackout feature is new with EM9i and suspends notification at the source. Previous versions only had OMS-based blackout functionality, which is still available through this pull-down command. It works by way of instructing the OMS to block the notification process and defines a recurring time window as a frequent blackout period. That means that the agent still monitors and collects information as instructed, fires the event in case of a threshold violation, probably runs a fixit job, and notifies the OMS. The OMS does not communicate this notification further via e-mail or paging if you predefine an e-mail or paging blackout for this target on the OMS level. You will only see a yellow or red flag in the console window as notification. You can also set a total blackout on e-mail and paging notifications on a per-target basis, which means that regardless of any OMS-based scheduled blackouts, all notifications will be suspended with indefinite duration until the total blackout is revoked.

View Reporting Website Configuration

As discussed in Chapter 4, the reporting framework requires a certain configuration in order to function. You define this configuration through executing `oemctl configure rws` at a command prompt, which tells the Web server which OMS to use and which password the REPORTS_USER has. At the same time, the OMS is told which Web server to use. You can inspect the current OMS configuration with the View Reporting Website Configuration option (see Figure 5-8).

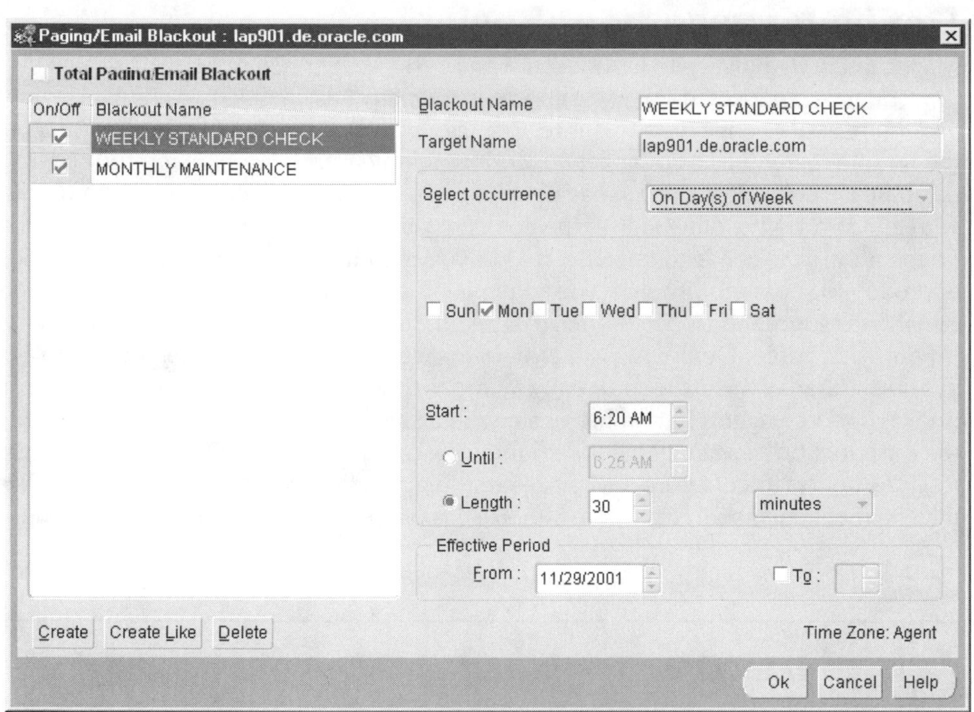

FIGURE 5-7. *Specifying blackouts at the OMS level*

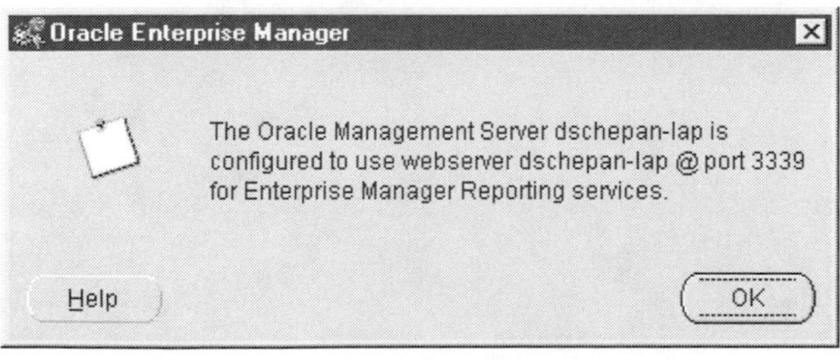

FIGURE 5-8. *Viewing the Reporting Website configuration*

Define Management Regions

Management Regions were introduced with EM9i to better reflect network topologies in worldwide deployments of EM. Suppose a company has an office in a remote region, and the network connection to this region has a very low bandwidth. Further, suppose the remote region has its own network with multiple nodes which each run several databases. Deploying agents on each of these nodes means that all agents communicate with an OMS on the other side of the bottleneck through the low-bandwidth network connection. This can lead to excessive network traffic and congestion. The common approach to solve this problem was to deploy a separate OMS in that remote region, which was supposed to communicate with all the remote agents and would bundle up network traffic. Deploying an OMS in that remote network region could not guarantee that all agents would really talk to that local OMS, however. There was no way to force agents to communicate with a specific OMS. This has changed with the introduction of Management Regions. You can now use the Define Management Regions option to configure a Management Region to reflect a network scenario like the one mentioned here (see Figure 5-9). First, you define a region and then add nodes

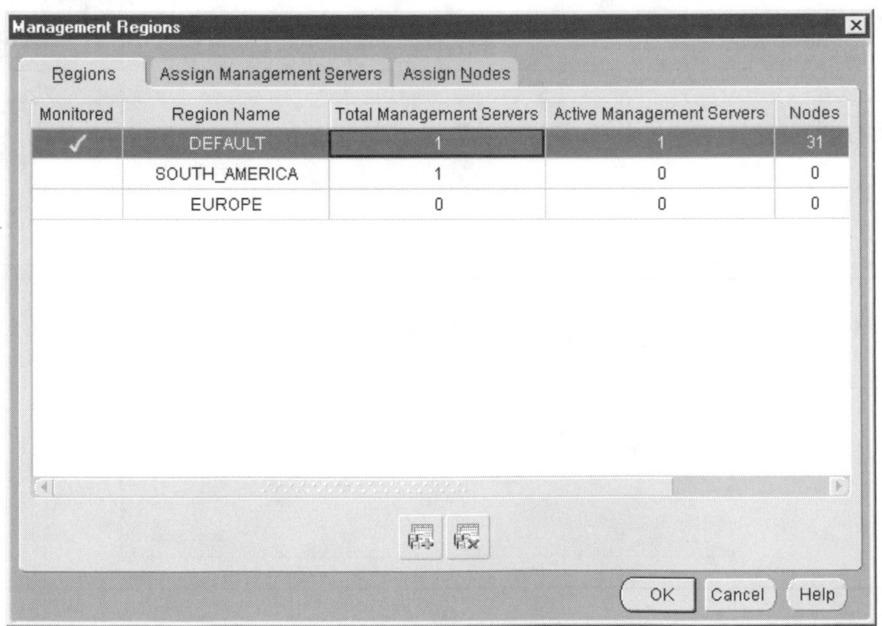

FIGURE 5-9. *Defining Management Regions*

and one or more OMSes to it, which causes the agents on these nodes to only talk to the OMS in the same region. Be aware that a node or an OMS can only belong to one region at a time.

The Navigator Menu

Figure 5-10 shows the Navigator menu in a console connected to an OMS. Note that some commands may not be available if you are connected via a regular DBA account. This section outlines the options available from this menu.

Refresh

The console is in frequent contact with the OMS and displays information received from it. In previous versions of EM, the OMS pushed information to the console whenever something new happened. This caused frequent network traffic and prevented the use of firewalls between OMS and console. In version 9i, the console contacts the OMS and asks for new information, such as events, jobs, or any changes in status, using a pull mechanism. If you are already using EM version 2.2, the 9i console might appear to display new information more slowly. The likely reason is The New Mechanism And The Default Refresh Rate Of 60 Seconds. With The Refresh command, you can force the console to connect to the OMS and refresh the display with new information, if any is available. You can also click the refresh icon in the console's toolbar located on the upper left side of the console.

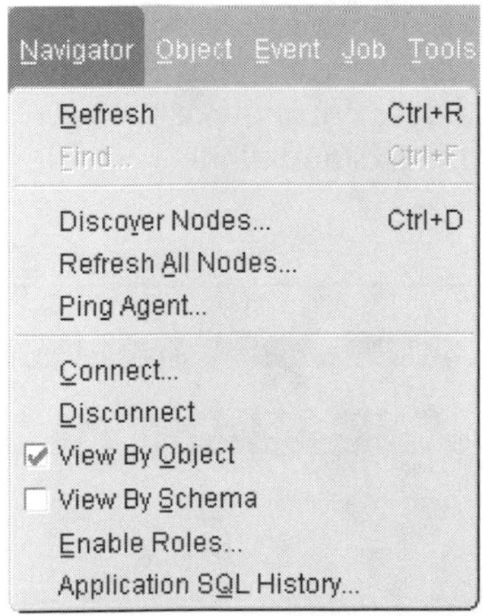

FIGURE 5-10. *The Navigator menu of the console*

Find

The Find command allows you to select certain database objects by name. It is useful when working in databases with a large number of objects. This option is grayed out until you select a category for which the console offers this feature (see Figure 5-11). It is also accessible from the pop-up menu on database object type folders, where you can also find a more generic Find Database Objects. This command offers you a more detailed dialog box specifying more parameters for the name and type of object you are looking for (see Figure 5-12). You can also restrict your search to certain schemas.

Discover Nodes

The Discover Nodes command launches the discovery dialog box, in which you can enter names of machines that you wish to add to the console. This process was initially described in Chapter 3, and will be explained in further detail in Chapter 8. When running in stand-alone mode, you will see the command Add Databases To Tree, which enables you to add more databases either from the local tnsnames.ora, or by specifying them directly. When running in stand-alone mode, you will find the Remove Databases From Tree command, which assists in removing targets, directly below the Add Databases To Tree command.

Refresh All Nodes

The Refresh All Nodes command contacts all agents on nodes currently in the console and retrieves updated information on targets (see Figure 5-13). With this command, you can easily get all information currently in the console updated and automatically synchronized with the agents' information. This can result in new services being added to the console, or nonexistent services being removed. You can select nodes to skip. Because the console does not know of any agents when running stand-alone, this command is not available in stand-alone mode.

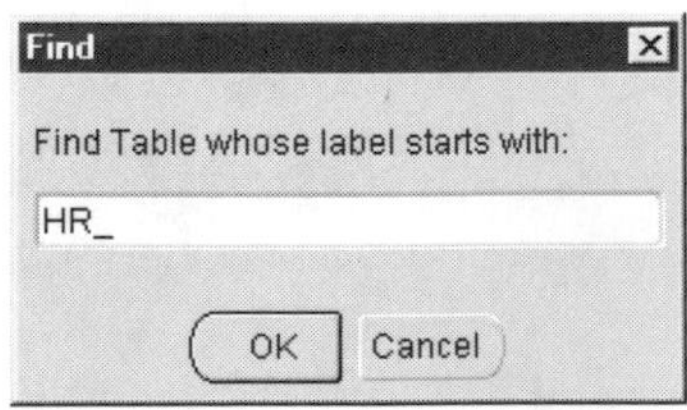

FIGURE 5-11. *Finding objects of the selected target type*

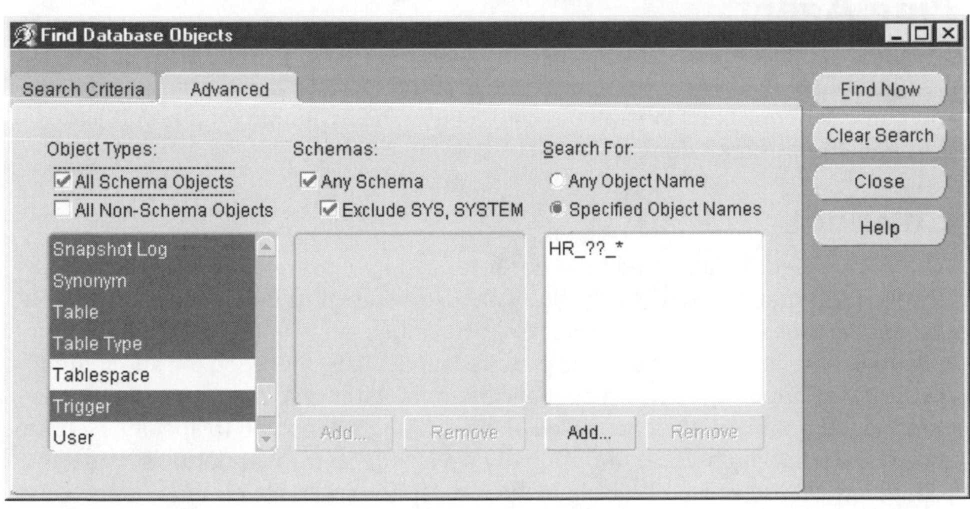

FIGURE 5-12. *Finding objects that match a specified pattern*

Refresh Wizard, step 1 of 3: Specify Nodes

Choose which nodes you want to refresh, skip, or manually configure.
Note: Refresh time increases as the number of nodes to refresh increases.

Node Name	Refresh	Skip	Manual
dlsun293.us.oracle.com	○	●	○
dlsun99.us.oracle.com	○	●	○
dsaggi-pc1.us.oracle.com	○	●	○
dschepan-de.oracle.com	○	○	○
dschepan-lap.de.oracle.com	●	○	○
kfrench-pc1.us.oracle.com	○	●	○
labsmpqa-pc13.us.oracle.com	○	●	○
labsmpqa-pc14.us.oracle.com	○	●	○

Cancel Help Back Next

FIGURE 5-13. *Refreshing agent information for selected targets*

Ping Agent

The Ping Agent command checks whether the agent running on the remote node is still responsive. If you encounter problems with features that require the agent, you can easily check whether the agent is still up and running. This command is not available in stand-alone mode.

Connect

When you select a database in the console, you can connect to it by using the Connect command. Alternatively, you can also connect to the database by simply clicking the plus sign next to the database icon in the navigator tree. When connecting to the database, the console uses the preferred credentials defined in the administrator account you are using. If no credentials and no default credentials are defined for the selected database, the console displays a dialog asking you to specify username and password, which you can optionally save as preferred credentials. When connected, the console will display which database account you are connected to, such as "system as sysdba". You can also use this command to change your active connection. For example, suppose you are connected as SCOTT, and you would like to change to SYSTEM. Choosing Connect either from the Navigator menu or the pop-up menu opens the dialog box to change the current logon credentials. This feature is also available in stand-alone mode.

Disconnect

The Disconnect command simply closes a currently active database connection. This function is needed because collapsing the database in the navigator tree closes the icon in the tree but does not disconnect from the database.

View By Object and View By Schema

When you are opening up a database in the navigator tree, and drill further down to schema management, you first need to specify which type of object and then the schema you would like to see. For example, first specify the SCOTT schema and then open the TABLE folder to display all tables in the SCOTT schema. Depending on the specific task, you may want to switch this procedure to first specify which objects you are interested in, and then in which schema. You can influence the navigator tree's display behavior regarding what to specify first when you open the schema management folder: View by Object or View by Schema. This feature is also available in stand-alone mode.

Enable Roles

The Enable Roles command opens a dialog allowing you to activate other roles available for this session (see Figure 5-14). This is convenient if you would like to change to a specific administrator role in mid-session.

View Application SQL History

The View Application SQL History command provides an overview of the SQL that has been recently issued by the console on the selected database (see Figure 5-15). It is meant to unravel exactly which SQL the console uses to obtain the displayed information, as opposed to logging DML and DDL. Logging DML and DDL is done by SQL logging, which is available in the Configuration menu, as discussed in the "SQL Logging" section earlier in this chapter. All information displayed in this window is lost when the console is closed. The main purpose of this feature is to show you how the console retrieves displayed information from the database. The Application SQL History stores the last 100 statements, even when running in stand-alone mode.

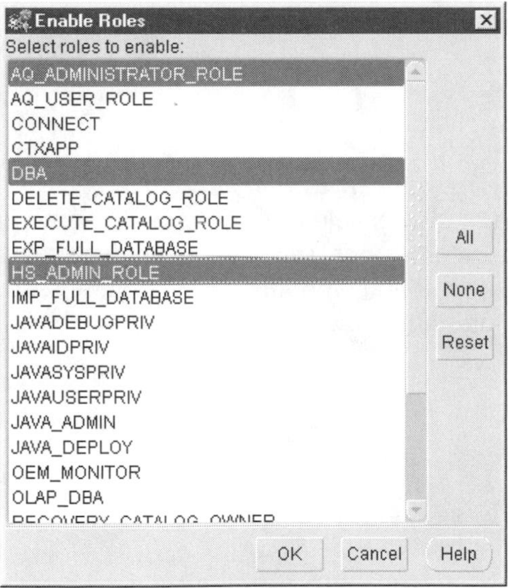

FIGURE 5-14. *Activating roles for this session*

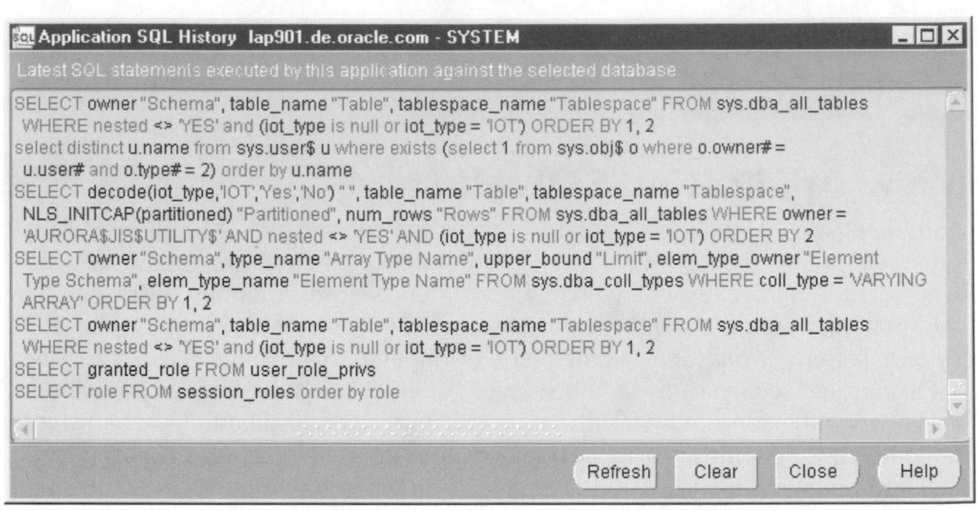

FIGURE 5-15. *Displaying recent SQL history*

Summary

In this chapter, we explained the configuration options in the console that help you to configure your management environment. We walked through the Configuration and Navigator menus of the console as they appear when connected to an OMS using a super administrator account. We also mentioned features that are available in stand-alone mode with slightly modified functionality. The next chapter will focus on console features and wizards available for database management.

CHAPTER 6

Database Management Features and Wizards

he Console offers a number of features to manage the Oracle database. This chapter provides an overview of the most important features of EM for managing databases. Some functions have wizards available, and we will mention those in their respective areas. We will go into more detail about some of these features in Chapters 14 and 15.

General Features

To manage a database, you need to expand its node in the navigator tree, which reveals several areas you can manage. You will see instance, security, schema, storage, replication, Java Virtual Machine (JVM), online analytical processing (OLAP), and Workspace topics, depending on your installed database options. If you select the database icon in the tree, you will see general information about this specific database in the details page of the console. Remember that you have Quick Tours available for each of the management topics. Click the topic node in the navigator tree to display the details page, from which you can access the Quick Tours. Whenever you select a folder in the tree, you see available multi-column lists. When you click objects in the navigator tree, you will see available property sheets. For most objects, you have a lot of relevant right-click commands available, which we discuss in the next sections. All EM functionality is fully aware of the version of the database you are managing, and only displays available objects and features.

Create Like

If you need to create a complex object similar to an existing one, you don't need to go through the process of defining each object tediously from scratch. You can select the Create Like command, which will prepopulate the properties for the new object and you just need to modify what you would like to be different. Imagine you have created a standard database user account with complex privileges. Now you need to create another similar one. Instead of creating this account totally new with defining every single privilege, you can simply create a new account like the existing one. You just need to choose "create like" and change the name and other parameters as necessary.

Show SQL

In many dialog boxes, you have the option to look at the SQL code generated by your modifications by clicking the Show SQL button. This feature is especially useful if you are a novice DBA and you want to look at the syntax and options involved, or if you want to copy the statement to paste it into scripts or other documents.

Show Dependencies

The Show Dependencies feature helps you to determine dependencies and dependents of objects, which is important to find out before you delete them. Objects in databases are often created with relationships to other objects. Tables, for example, have indexes, so the index depends on certain columns in the table. From the table's point of view, the index is a dependent, and the table itself may depend on some other objects, such as the schema or other tables, because a foreign key might be defined in this table. There are many such relationships between objects in a database, and sometimes it is not easy to find out which dependencies currently exist. When changing the architecture of objects slightly, such dependencies can be broken because the dependency was not clearly visible. With this feature, you can switch between dependencies and dependents for the object, generate a report, and modify affected objects directly from this dialog box.

Generate Object DDL

When you are looking at a database with existing objects and structures, you may find it useful to generate the SQL needed to create the object. The console offers this reverse engineering feature for all kinds of objects. Objects in databases are created through Data Definition Language (DDL). Because EM helps to create objects without requiring you to know the exact commands and syntax, you might never see the actual SQL behind the objects. If you need to implement `create` statements in a script, you can use the Generate Object DDL feature to automatically generate the DDL on a per-object basis. You may also want to know how to reverse-engineer multiple objects or a whole schema. This feature is also available in EM, but is part of the Change Management Pack, which is introduced in Chapter 7.

Instance

Instance Management helps you to manage database instances and database sessions. The General tab (shown in Figure 6-1) enables you to start up and shut down databases, view instance information, and edit instance parameters. When you are connected to an OMS, you can store the instance parameters in the repository and they will appear as objects in the Stored Configurations folder in the navigator tree. This feature also supports SPFILE-management introduced with version 9i of the database.

Instance Settings

The Memory tab lets you modify SGA settings, which can be done dynamically in 9i databases for some parameters. It also displays the settings for SORT_AREA_SIZE and PROCESSES. The 9i database also offers a Buffer Cache Advice feature to

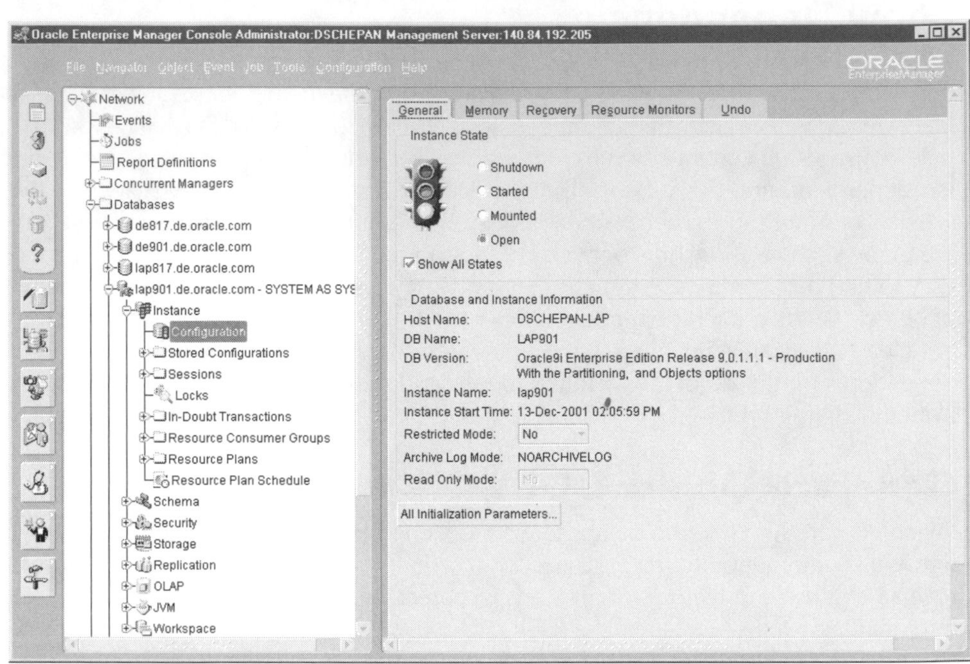

FIGURE 6-1. *The Instance Configuration tab*

give you an idea if it would help performance to increase the size of the database buffer cache. This feature must be enabled with the database, because it will have to collect information over time to have this data available. EM lets you view the data graphically for better interpretation.

The Recovery tab lets you modify settings regarding archive log mode, and also the MTTR-settings for 9i databases. MTTR stands for Mean Time To Recovery, and specifies the maximum time the database should need for recovery. The Resource Monitors tab is empty if you have not yet activated resource management in the database. We will explain this later in the chapter. The Undo tab helps you to manage the Undo feature of the 9i database. This feature allows you to undo data manipulations made through updates or deletes. The deleted or modified data will be kept in a designated undo tablespace for a certain time. You can modify how long this data will be kept available for undo, which dictates the amount of space you have to make available to store the data. The relationship between undo retention time and required space can be viewed graphically.

Resource Management

Resource Management was introduced with version 8i of the database. This feature helps you prioritize processing of specified sessions when the machine the database runs on has a CPU utilization of 100 percent. That means that you can influence which sessions will be processed faster, when resources are tight. For example, you may want to give your own session highest priority so you can find out what the reason for the bottleneck is. To do this, you can define Resource Consumer Groups by selecting the icon in the tree and adding users or roles to these groups in the detail pages. Bear in mind that users can switch to other consumer groups if they have the relevant privilege to do so. After setting up consumer groups, you have to set up a Resource Plan defining which of the groups have a higher priority, and also their level of parallelism. Above all, you need to activate a certain resource plan before any of your modifications become effective. Once you activate a plan, you will see statistics about your plan in the Resource Monitors page of the instance configuration. This page displays details about your current resource management settings, such as how much CPU was consumed in total by each group, or which group had to wait the longest to be processed. Depending on your needs, you many want to switch between various resource plans depending on the time of day. You can switch automatically by setting up a Resource Plan Schedule, and the database will automatically change priorities according to the individual resource plans.

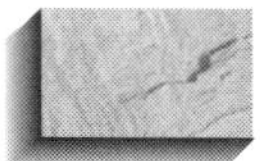

NOTE
The default behavior is that resource plans have to be activated manually each time the database is started. If you want a certain resource plan to be activated automatically when the database is started, you need to set the initialization parameter RESOURCE_MANAGER_PLAN to the name of the resource plan to be activated.

The Resource Plan Wizard helps you through the process of defining a new resource plan. Users have frequent problems in understanding the concept of Resource Management, and in setting up a valid resource plan that produces the effects they want. The wizard should make this process easier and less error-prone. You can access the wizard by right-clicking the Resource Plans folder, or any plan in this folder, and selecting Create using Wizard. In the wizard, you name the new resource plan, create resource consumer groups and assign database users to them, allocate resources of each resource consumer group, and optionally activate the plan. The wizard can be switched from basic to advanced mode, changing the steps from five to seven. The difference is that in advanced mode, you have more flexibility when defining the CPU percentages for the individual resource consumer groups, unused percentages are automatically moved to the groups in the next lower resource level, and you can manipulate the level of parallelism for sessions of a certain resource consumer group.

Session Management

The EM 9i console includes the capability to search for Top Sessions. If you select the Sessions folder in the navigator tree, you will see a list of all currently connected users in the details page. The sessions are sorted by CPU consumption by default, but you can sort by any other value by clicking the desired column header. In addition, you can display more session metrics by clicking the Customize button on the detail page. You can limit the total number of sessions displayed, and kill individual sessions from this dialog box. If you want to drill down into more session details, you can either click the Details button, which opens a new window, or open the sessions folder in the tree and select one of the displayed sessions. You can look at general session information, view the currently executed SQL statement including its explain plan, and even walk through it step by step. If you have the Tuning Pack installed, you can choose to see the explain plan displayed as graphical view in a customizable tree format. In addition, you can view session statistics, and determine if the session is responsible for creating a lock, which means that a session is actually blocking another session from proceeding. Locks can also be viewed on an overall level per database by selecting the Locks icon in the navigator tree. You can also view In-Doubt Transactions, which are distributed transactions that were interrupted before a commit was completed, for example, because of system or network failures.

The session management features also include support for long-running operations. The database can recognize certain sessions to be of a standard type, and can calculate the remaining time needed to complete the sessions's current activity based on the time the database needed to complete the session's current portion and the type of activity. The database stores information about such sessions in a view called v$session_longops, which EM uses to display related information. If you select a long running session in the navigator tree, which can be identified by its modified icon with a small clock, you see related information and a progress bar showing the remaining estimated running time.

Schema

The Schema Management category in the navigator tree allows you to create, alter, or drop most types of schema objects. Remember that you can modify the way you can drill down to the object you are targeting by toggling the settings in the Navigator menu between View By Schema and View By Object. To edit an object, you must select it in the navigator tree and view its properties in the details page. The details page enables you to modify the object. You can always click the View SQL button to view the SQL behind your modifications. As mentioned earlier, you need to be aware that a lot of functionality is available through the right-mouse menu for each object, as shown in Figure 6-2. You will have a lot more features at your fingertips than are visible in the rest of the GUI, of which the most important ones are mentioned in the following sections. Some of these commands are also available in context with other non schema objects, such as roles, users, or storage objects, but the commands are explained here as examples. The right-click menu also contains commands that point to functionality coming with the optional Management Packs. For example, Figure 6-2 contains the Reorganize command, which launches the Reorg Wizard, which is part of the Tuning Pack.

Table Data Editor

The Table Data Editor lets you view, filter, and edit table data. Upon startup, it first checks how many rows the table contains, and, if necessary, checks if you want to

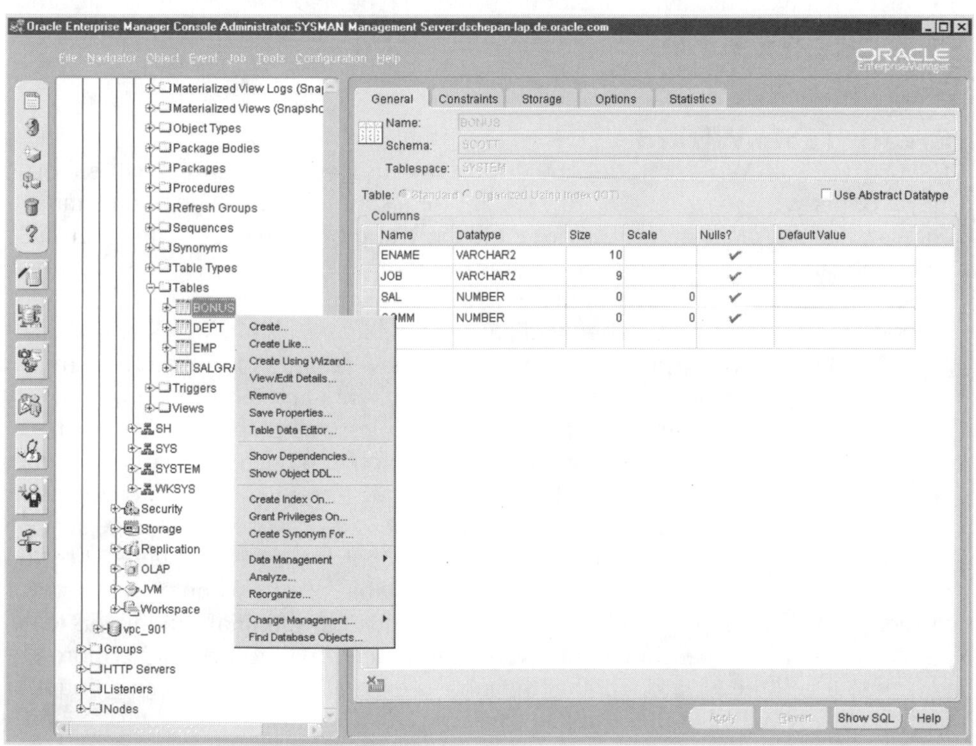

FIGURE 6-2. *The right-click menu in Schema Management*

restrict the initial query by applying a filter before retrieving the data. Once the data is displayed, you can change the values by overwriting them. You can sort the presented data by clicking any of the column headers and activating a filter per column. You can switch to the Graphical Select Mode to construct a select statement by pointing and clicking, or you can switch to the Show SQL display, which enables you to type or paste a SQL statement directly. The Table Data Eitor displays the result set of your SQL statement in the lower half of the window, which allows you to check the values your statement returns.

Schema Management Wizards

The Schema Management section offers a number of wizards which we will briefly introduce in the following sections: the Create Table Wizard, the Analyze Wizard, and the Create View Wizard. In general, there is an easy way to find out where a wizard is available for creating certain objects. Just click the generic create icon (the green cube) on the toolbar on the upper left side of the console window. In the window that opens, you will have to specify which type of object you want to create. If a wizard is available for the selected type of object, the "Use Wizard" check box at the bottom of this window will be available, and you can choose to create the selected object using a wizard.

Create Table Wizard

The Create Table Wizard guides you through the process of creating a table. You may wonder why you would need a wizard for a simple task like creating a table. That is true for simple tables, but does not apply to more complex tables, especially when the table includes complex features like partitions. You can access the wizard through the generic Create icon, or by right-clicking an existing table or the Tables folder in the navigator tree, when you have the navigator tree in View By Object mode. You first have to specify the name of the new table, and in which schema and tablespace the table should be placed. The schema and tablespace will be prepopulated with the name and the attributed tablespace of the schema you had selected when you started the wizard. After that, you can define the column names and types, default values, primary keys, null, unique, foreign, and check constraints. In the next step, you can specify whether you want to use the default storage attributes or if you want the wizard to calculate attributes according to the expected growth rates, transaction types, and data volume for this table. If you do not want to stick to the default attributes, you will have to specify the number of initial rows in this table, and how many rows per time period you expect the growth to be. Furthermore, you need to tell the wizard whether the table is expected to have a high amount of update activity, whether these updates will most likely increase the row size, and whether there will be a high amount of insert activity, optionally including deletes. Based on your specifications, the wizard will pick storage attributes mainly for

PCTFREE, PCTUSED, initial extent, and next extent to optimally accommodate this table. If the columns of your table definition are suitable for partitions, you can optionally define them in the subsequent steps. In the current release, this wizard supports the creation of range partitions only. It will ask you, based on which column the range partitions should be defined, for the smallest number in this column, the range of numbers per partition, the total number of partitions, and if you expect to add more partitions in the future. It will then create default names and show you the range and tablespace settings for each partition, which you can optionally modify. Because partitioned tables are very often created with indexes, the next steps help you to create a local prefixed partition index. Before the table is finally created, you can view the generated SQL statement, which you may also copy from this window and paste into a script.

Analyze Wizard

When you are using the cost-based optimizer, its behavior depends on the statistics the objects have. It is useful to update these statistics from time to time using the analyze command or the Analyze Wizard. This wizard helps you to manage the statistics for certain objects and can be invoked by selecting Analyze in the right-click menu of a table or an index. After an introductory page, you can specify default options for the wizard. You can delete, compute, or estimate statistics. In addition, you can use a package called dbms_stats, which was introduced with version 8.1.6 of the database. This package will compute statistics faster, more accurately, and more comprehensively. Refer to the *Oracle9i Database Performance Guide and Reference* and *Oracle9i Supplied PL/SQL Packages and Types Reference* for more information on dbms_stats. If you do not want to or cannot use this package, you need to specify if you want the objects' structure to be validated including indexes or not, or if you just want to know about migrated or continued rows, which are often also called *chained*. You also might need to disable the use of dbms_stats if you need to gather cluster statistics, which it does not support.

NOTE

Structure validation and analysis for chained or migrated rows require that the scripts utlvalid.sql and utlchain.sql are executed beforehand. These scripts create tables needed for the operations to be successful.

No matter how you invoked the wizard, in the next step you can add more tables and indexes to be analyzed, and also clusters if you disabled the use of the dbms_stats package. If you added more objects to the list, you can override the default options for individual objects. That means that the wizard uses the default options specified earlier for all objects except for objects, for which you specify other options. The only default option that applies to the whole process and can not be modified individually is the usage of the dbms_stats package. The analysis activities will then be fed as a job in EM's job system, which enables you to run this job at a certain time, or at recurring intervals, or to just save it to the job library for later processing. You can also add multiple targets to execute the job against. When you use this wizard and run the console in standalone mode, the generated SQL will be executed against the target database right away, because there is no access to the job system. You will also not be able to add more targets to submit the SQL against.

Create View Wizard

You can create a complex view using the Create View Wizard, which is accessible by right-clicking the Views folder, or any view inside this folder, and selecting Create Using Wizard. After naming the view, you will be able to determine the schema to create this view in, and select columns to be in this view from all available schemas. You can determine column aliases if you wish to display columns under a different name, and specify conditions for the view in order to display only filtered data when the view is used. Before the view is created, you can inspect the generated SQL, copy it from here, and paste it to other documents, or optionally modify the SQL statement directly. Make sure that you have sufficient privileges to access data of other schemas if your view includes other schemas' objects.

Security

Security Management helps you manage users, roles, and profiles in the database. You can create new users or create them like existing ones, but you can also manage account properties as well as roles and object privileges down to column level (as shown in Figure 6-3). You can manipulate the switch privilege of resource consumer groups, or define certain accounts to act as proxy for other users. You can also use the Show Dependencies feature, which shows you which objects the user account depends on, and which other objects in turn depend on it. Performing role operations are similar to profile management. You can easily find out who is granted a certain role by selecting the Show Grantee command in the right-click menu of a role. Security Management also includes extended password management, allowing you to lock certain accounts and manage password expiration, history, and complexity of passwords. If you are familiar with security management and want a quicker way of assigning privileges, you can right-click the Users or Roles items. You will find a dialog box that is quicker and very slim for assigning many privileges fast. There is also an equivalent dialog box available for assigning profiles to users, which can be accessed by right-clicking on Profiles or Users and selecting Assign Profiles to User(s).

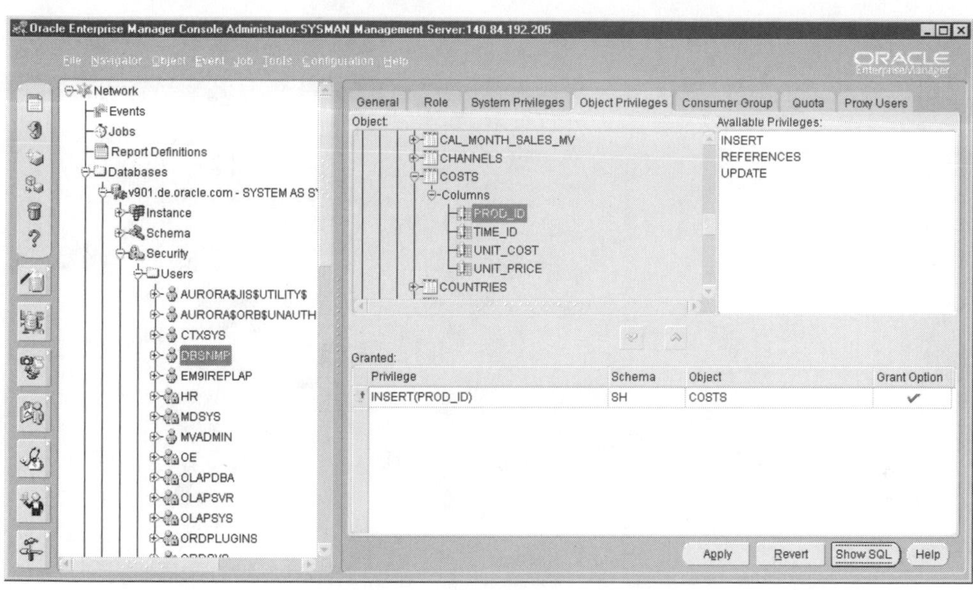

FIGURE 6-3. *Assigning column-level object privileges*

Storage

In Storage Management, you will find help for administering database components that relate to storage, such as tablespaces, datafiles, rollback segments, redo log groups, and archive logs. In addition, you can view control file information, such as the number of controlfiles created for this database, and associated statistics. Another typical task is to get an overview of the fillgrades of both tablespaces and datafiles, which can be achieved by selecting the respective folder in the navigator tree (see Figure 6-4). The list view that appears in the detail pane shows how much space is available for which objects, and which are set to autoextend. EM also supports defining multiple block sizes for tablespaces in databases. This is necessary to take advantage of transportable tablespaces, which can be plugged into other databases with a different blocksize setting. EM also supports management of undo tablespaces, which has been introduced with Oracle9i, and manages undo space more efficiently than rollback segments. If you use rollback segments, you can alter, create, shrink, or drop them with EM, as well as take them online or offline. Helpful commands available in the right-click menus for tablespaces are to view the tablespace map or reorganize it (with the Tuning Pack), add a datafile or rollback segment, make the tablespace read-only, or take it offline with the typical options of normal, temporary,

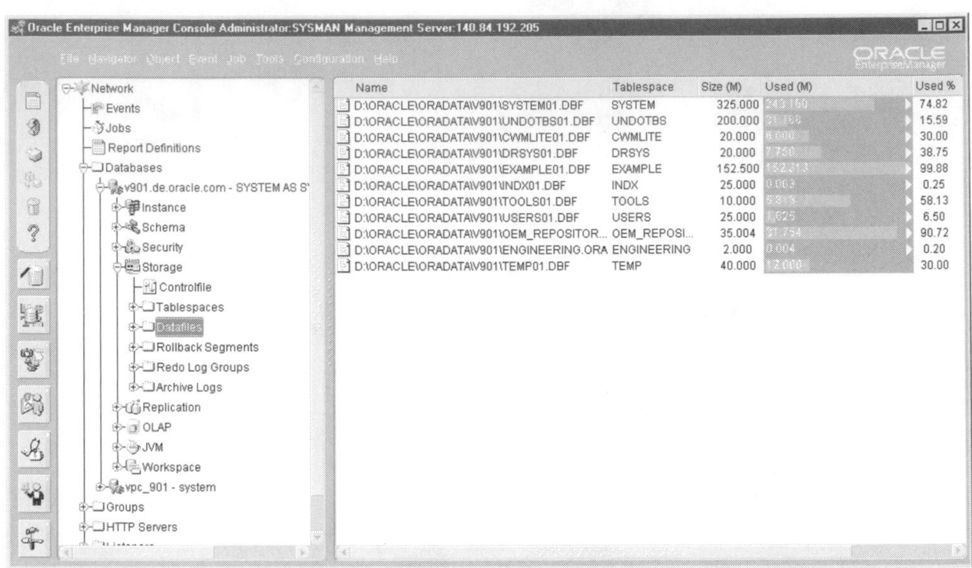

FIGURE 6-4. *Viewing tablespace fillgrades*

immediate or recover. Typical datafile operations are to create, clone, edit, and take it online or offline. For redo log groups, you can create, rename, or remove groups, or add members to a group. You can also switch to a different redo log group or trigger a checkpoint. A special feature is the Tablespace Conversion Wizard, which converts a tablespace from dictionary managed to locally managed.

The tablespace conversion wizard can be accessed by right-clicking a dictionary-managed tablespace and selecting Make Locally Managed. A locally managed tablespace administers its own extents through a bitmap in each datafile to keep track of the free or used blocks in that datafile. Locally managed tablespaces have several advantages over dictionary-managed tablespaces, which result in better performance and improved space management. In the first step of the wizard, you have to decide whether you would like to have Oracle manage the extent sizes automatically, or if you just want to use a uniform block size that you specify. Because all objects will be moved out of the tablespace, you need to specify which other tablespace has enough space left in order to temporarily store the objects. Because the affected storage parameters are defined during the creation of a tablespace, the old tablespace needs to be dropped and re-created with the new parameters, and locally managed. After that, the objects will be moved back to the new locally managed tablespace. Also, all objects in the tablespace are reorganized, because the tablespace will be created from scratch with new storage parameters. All this is done offline. You can then review an impact summary and the actual script. The whole process is submitted to the intelligent agent's job system, and can be scheduled to be executed at a later time. This also means that this wizard is not available when running the console in standalone mode.

Replication

Oracle Replication Manager enables you to set up, configure, and manage the replication functionality of the database. It supports managing replication environments of multiple master sites with master groups, and setting up replication of materialized views, which were formerly called snapshots. If replication is installed with the target database, the navigator offers one section for each replication type under the replication management node and also an Administration item, as you can see in the following illustration. Under Administration, you will find a number of property pages can be used to monitor and modify the replication setup. The topology of the currently active replication mechanism is displayed graphically in an easy-to- understand chart. The chart displays master and snapshot sites, and any errors that occurred during the replication process. These errors are displayed in different colors, and can be investigated by clicking the faulty connection. A separate window shows all erroneous replication communication and displays all necessary information available to resolve this issue.

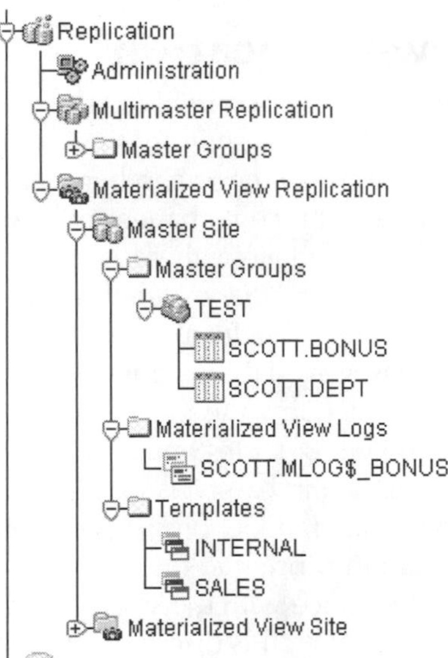

The actual setup should be done through wizards. Once replication is set up, more wizards help you to replicate schema objects using either multimaster replication, or a combination of multimaster and materialized view replication. If you are not familiar with replication technology, concepts, and terms, refer to the *Oracle9i Replication* section of the documentation. In EM, you can manage two kinds of replication, called *multimaster* and *materialized view* replication.

Multimaster Replication

In multimaster replication, you set up databases to be able to replicate data, and then define objects, such as tables, which are replicated among these sites. Any change in the data in any of these master sites is communicated to the objects in the other master sites. This can be done in real time, which is called *synchronous replication*, or only at frequent intervals, which is called *asynchronous replication*. Asynchronous replication has a risk of data conflicts, for example, when the same object is updated with different data and the changes have not been propagated to the other sites yet. You therefore need to provide rules to resolve such conflicts during replication. Before you can start replicating, you need to set up participating databases to be aware that they will be part of a replication environment. This is done through the Setup Master Sites Wizard. After that, you need to define which objects are replicated, which is done with help of the Create Master Group Wizard. Please refer to the "Setting up a Master Site" section in Chapter 14 for more information about how to use the wizards.

Materialized View Replication

A materialized view contains complete or partial data of a set of master data at a certain point in time, and was called *snapshots* in previous database versions. This materialized view can be taken from tables or another materialized view, and needs to be refreshed periodically to reflect recent changes in the data. If the materialized view is taken from another materialized view, these materialized view pairs are called the *master materialized view* and the *multitier materialized view*. The benefits of having materialized views are that you can have a local copy of data at a remote site, which improves response times, increases availability, and moves workload off the remote master site, because users can now query the local copy. Because the data does not need to be collected from a number of tables, materialized views are very attractive for data warehousing applications. In this case, it is very important to determine which materialized views should be created, depending on the space they consume in relation to the performance gain they bring to the users. To determine which views have the biggest effect on performance with the smallest impact on space, you can use the Summary Advisor Wizard, which is discussed in Chapter 15.

You can also increase the security of your data by replicating only a subset of the data. A materialized view can be read-only or updateable, causing changes to be propagated back to the master site. You can also set up a writeable materialized view in which users can update information, but which will not be propagated back to the master site, and will be lost when the next refresh takes place. Each of these configurations has certain characteristics providing benefits and restrictions depending on your needs. Please refer to the "Setting VP a Materialized View Site" section in Chapter 14 for more information.

OLAP

OLAP stands for Online Analytical Processing, and is used to perform complex statistical, mathematical, and financial analysis of data stored in a data warehouse, which is a special configuration of relational tables. It can be created using an ETL (Extraction, Transaction, and Loading) tool such as Oracle Warehouse Builder, and typically contains dimension tables and fact tables organized in a star schema. OLAP can be divided further into relational and multidimensional OLAP, depending on the method by which the data is managed and aggregated in the warehouse. Starting with Oracle9i, the database provides integrated data warehousing support regarding relational OLAP via OLAP services and OLAP metadata stored within the database. Refer to *Oracle9i Data Warehousing Guide* for more detailed information. You will see the OLAP icon in EM only when OLAP is also installed in the selected database. OLAP services can be described as child processes of a database instance responsible for OLAP-related functionality. These services can be managed through the OLAP Services Instance Manager, which you can access by right-clicking the OLAP icon in the navigator tree of the EM console. OLAP metadata is needed to describe data in a data warehouse. This metadata can be administered using OLAP management in EM, namely Cubes and Dimensions. Both are the mechanisms to build measures that are stored in the measures folder.

Cubes are purely logical schema objects, and contain only informational data. A cube is derived from a relational fact table or view that stores facts with the same dimensionality. Cubes are like dimensions; they are regular schema objects, which means that these objects can also be administered in the schema management of EM. The data inside a cube is categorized by *dimensions*. A dimension defines a parent-child relationship between two columns, which are called *levels*. These levels are used by the optimizer to perform query rewrites in order to use existing materialized views. They are also used by the Summary Advisor Wizard when recommending or testing materialized views.

Dimensions only contain metadata for informational purposes, just like cubes, and the dimension members (columns) remain in the source dimension tables. As an example, you might have two facts (such as sales and cost) that are both dimensioned by time, product, and region. All this information can be stored in a single fact table, which in return can serve as basis for a cube. From a cube, you can derive a measure or a number of measures with the same dimension. Measures can be organized in various folders for specific analysis types. The complete navigator tree structure and an example for a cube topology display is shown in Figure 6-5. EM offers two wizards in this area: the Create Cube Wizard and the Create Dimension Wizard.

Create Cube Wizard

You can access the Create Cube Wizard by right-clicking the Cubes folder, or any object in the folder, and selecting Create Using Wizard. The wizard lets you name the new cube and select a schema to accommodate it. You then need to choose a fact table and the dimensions the cube should reflect. For each dimension, you need to specify dimension properties, which consist of an optional alias name, a default hierarchy, and a join between the fact table and the dimension table. After that, you can specify the measures included in the cube, review the generated SQL

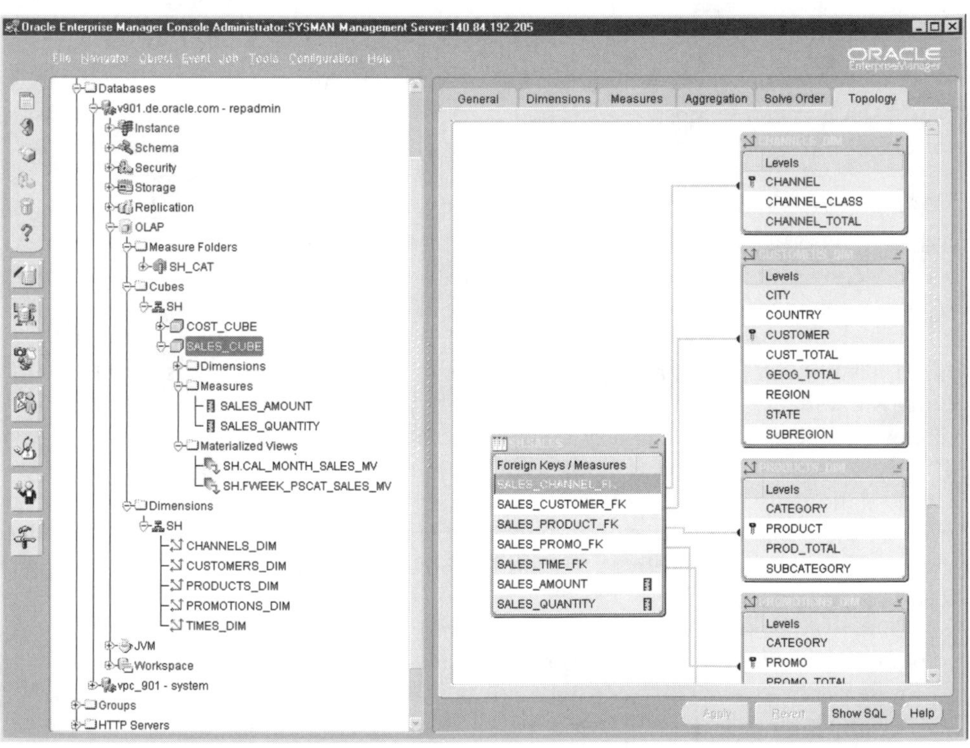

FIGURE 6-5. *Topology display of a cube in OLAP Management*

or a graphical view of the cube definition, and optionally start the Summary Advisor Wizard to optimize the cube's performance.

Create Dimension Wizard

You can access the Create Dimension Wizard from within the Create Cube Wizard or by right-clicking the Dimensions folder, or any object in the folder, and selecting Create Using Wizard. You first have to specify whether you would like to create a normal or time dimension, which targets time periods and requires units of time specified in the dimension tables. You then have to enter the name and schema for the new dimension, and define the levels, consisting of columns in the selected dimension table. The next steps are defining level attributes, level hierarchies, and sorting options before you can look at the summarized information page and create the dimension.

JVM

JVM stands for Java Virtual Machine, which is embedded in the Oracle database. It supports the storage and execution of CORBA and Enterprise Java Beans (EJB) components inside the database. EM supports managing the Java namespace, browsing all published CORBA and EJB components (as shown in the following illustration), changing access privileges for the components, executing the main() method in schema-resident Java classes, and examining their output.

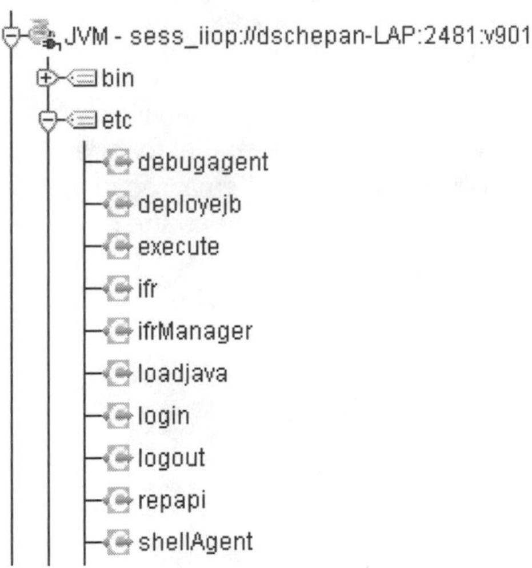

Workspace

Workspace Management has been introduced with version 9i of the database and EM, as shown in the following illustration, and allows you to maintain multiple versions of rows in tables regarding the data they contain. It allows you to manipulate table data while maintaining a copy of the old data. You can use workspaces to improve concurrent access and allow multiple what-if analyses to be run simultaneously against various versions of the same data. To use this feature you need to version-enable your tables first using workspace manager in the navigator tree, and you can then start to maintain various sets of data. A workspace is an environment that users can share to manipulate data. Workspaces also support hierarchies, which allow creation of child workspaces that a separate group of users can be given access to. These child workspaces can later be merged into the parent workspace when deleted, which might require you to set up conflict resolution rules. Workspaces also allow the use of savepoints, which mark points to which operations can be rolled back. Note that privileges for workspace management are separate from standard Oracle database privileges, as discussed in Chapter 14.

Summary

The chapter introduced selected features for database management that are included in the EM console. After explaining some general features available in most sections, we explained basic concepts of instance, schema, security, storage, replication, OLAP, JVM, and workspace management and outlined the benefits and use of most of the wizards available in the respective sections. The next chapter introduces the components of the optional Management Packs which expand EM's management capabilities to specialized areas.

CHAPTER 7

Management Packs

racle offers optional add-ons for Enterprise Manager called the *Management Packs,* some of which have to be licensed separately. These packs contain a number of additional tools that focus on certain problem areas corresponding to the name of the toolset. Diagnostics, Tuning, and Change Management are the most important of these packs. They are licensable with the Enterprise Edition of the database only, but there is no real technical reason why they are not available for the Standard Edition.

Oracle offers the Standard Management Pack free of charge for use with the Standard Edition of the database. It consists of a subset of tools of the Diagnostics, Tuning, and Change Management packs. The Management Packs are now included in the database installation CDs, which makes them easier to install, but also makes it more difficult for users to distinguish the free portion of EM from the extra-cost tools. The advantage is that you don't have to obtain any additional media, and you can take a peek at functionality in the packs. For customers running Oracle Applications or SAP R/3, Oracle offers the Management Pack for Oracle Applications (Apps Pack) and the Management Pack for SAP R/3 (SAP Pack) which extend EM's monitoring capabilities to cover services included in Oracle Applications and SAP R/3 environments. This chapter gives an overview of the tools offered with the Management Packs. Consult each individual component's documentation for in-depth information.

Diagnostics Pack

The tools in the Oracle Diagnostics Pack focus on monitoring, diagnosing, and capacity planning of Oracle environments. These components are the Advanced Events, Performance Manager, Capacity Planner, and Trace Data Viewer. You can access them from the Tools menu or the Diagnostics Pack drawer in the console. In addition, you can find shortcuts to charts in Performance Manager that contain lock and database health information.

Advanced Events

The Advanced Events extend the event system of the EM framework by adding a large number of event tests. Whereas the free portion of EM only contains a limited number of tests that are primarily basic up/down tests, DBAs need a more detailed set of tests to effectively monitor systems to prevent system failures.

The number of tests available with version 9i of the Diagnostics Pack has been increased, compared to version 2.2. This results from an architectural change of the background logic responsible for real-time and historical data collections. In previous versions of EM, real-time and historical monitoring required a process called the Data Gatherer, which was installed with the Intelligent Agent on each target node. Whereas the Data Gatherer had access to a huge number of performance metrics on any type of target and allowed extensive monitoring, the Agent had the task of monitoring events, which only covered a subset of the metrics the Data Gatherer had access to. This Data Gatherer process has been abandoned with version 9i because its functionality is taken over completely by the Agent. The Agent now does all monitoring, and has access to a much larger number of performance metrics, which it can also use for its event system. The following illustration shows the available event tests when creating a database event. The list now contains categories and sometimes even subcategories. You can also add your own events by defining a user-defined SQL-based event for databases, or user-defined events for operating systems. Using the new 9i Agent, you can now use EM's monitoring capabilities better by combining the reach of the Data Gatherer with the event system of the Agent. For a complete list of the advanced event tests, refer to the *Oracle Enterprise Manager Event Test Reference Manual.*

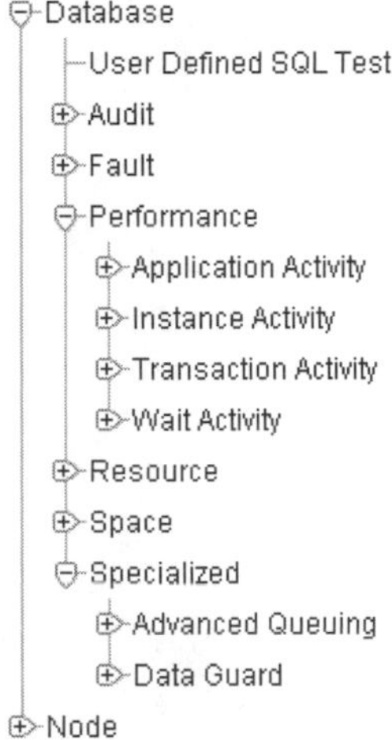

Performance Manager

Performance Manager is a real-time monitoring tool. It provides a system administrator with a number of graphical views of key metrics, ranging from overview charts to in-depth detail displays. Performance Manager, like many tools in EM, can be started in a number of ways both in the standalone and connected to an OMS console: through the Tools menu, the Diagnostics Pack drawer, or the pop-up menu of a target in the navigator tree. As with the console, you will encounter some restrictions when running Performance Manager standalone, which we will mention where appropriate. In the console, you will also find some direct links to charts within Performance Manager, such as Health Overview Chart, Top SQL, or Top Sessions, which are described in the following sections. First, take a look at the Performance Manager user interface, as shown in Figure 7-1.

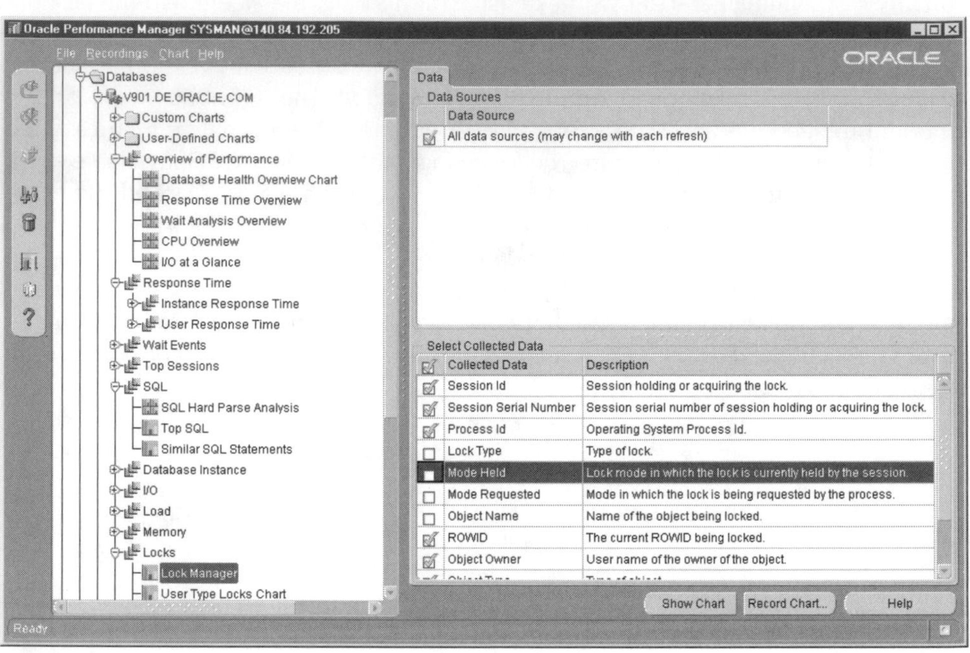

FIGURE 7-1. *The Performance Manager interface*

Performance Manager Interface

Performance Manager offers a huge number of charts for all types of targets discovered through the EM console. You can also add services manually that will be available only for your current monitoring session. You need to specify access information depending on which type of target you would like to add. In Figure 7-1, you can see a database tree opened up. You are offered a number of categories of metrics. Some contain overview charts like the Overview of Performance category; some contain subcategories with a mixture of overview charts and detail charts. You can always select the categories directly to get a comprehensive view of all charts in the respective category. Once you have selected a detail chart, you can also deselect certain metrics that you are not interested in. When you display the chart and modify it to your preferences, you can save these settings and the chart will appear under a new name in the Custom Charts folder. This feature is not available when running in standalone mode. If you would like to see a chart that is not offered by Performance Manager, you can add your own User-Defined Chart, which appears in the respective folder in the navigator tree. Using this option, you can enter a SQL statement that retrieves the information you need and displays it like all other charts. This also gives you the option to display any information in the database, not only performance-related or data-dictionary-based information. This feature is also available in standalone mode, but the charts can only be saved to the repository when you are running in OMS mode.

Some charts offer more functionality than the ones mentioned so far. In the Top SQL or Top Sessions charts, for example, you can find more filtering or sorting options. You may also find options for restricting available data sources displayed in the upper half of the detail page. When you select the Tablespace Default Chart in the Tablespace category of the Storage folder, you can select the displayed metrics per tablespace, but also for which data sources—here, that means tablespaces— the information should be displayed. Once you have selected a chart, you have the option to either view the chart or record the chart. Recording writes the data to a local file in the path with a name of your choice, and also registers it in the repository when you are running in OMS mode.

Chart Windows

The View Chart button opens a new window displaying the selected chart information in real time, using a default refresh rate. We will use the Database Health Overview Chart shown in Figure 7-2 as an example because it is not only new with EM9i, but it also combines several new features.

The top row of each chart contains a toolbar giving you access to a number of features. You can print the screen, generate reports on the displayed charts, modify the graphical display of the data to horizontal or vertical bars, pie graphs, or bar graphs, or just display the raw numbers. You can further modify the refresh rate of the chart, pause the refresh mechanism, or continue refreshing after pausing. The current refresh rate is displayed at the bottom of each chart window along with the timestamp when the last refresh occurred. You can also modify displayed data options for each chart, if available. This functionality corresponds to the data sources and selected charts options in Performance Manager and means that you can manipulate the displayed data sources and displayed information on them while running the chart, such as adding or removing a tablespace as data source in the tablespace chart. You can also switch to historical data on the selected chart. That requires that you have already collected historical information before, and you now just want to quickly view it in comparison with current values. This is very convenient when a certain metric seems out of the usual bounds and you want to compare it with past values. Managing the collection of historical data is done with Capacity Planner, which is discussed later in this chapter.

Database Health Overview Chart

The Database Health Overview chart was introduced with EM 9i, and is intended to be the all-in-one display for a number of key metrics of a database. You can

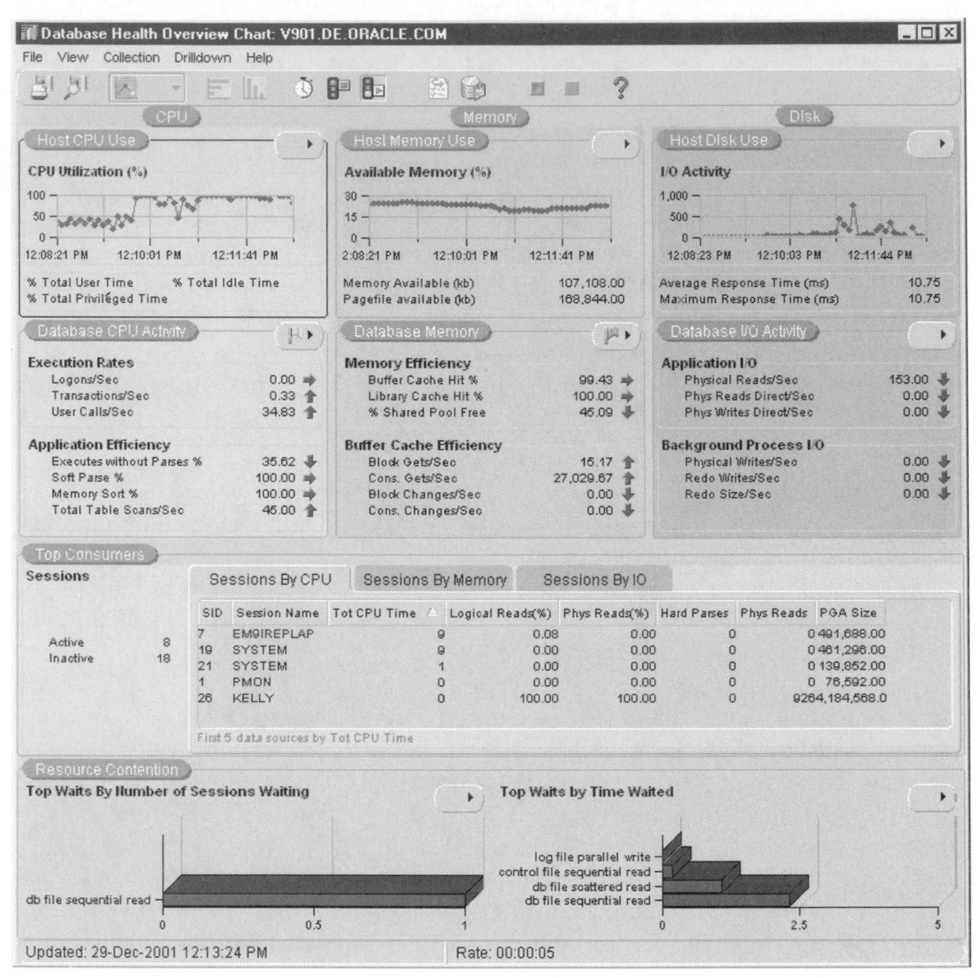

FIGURE 7-2. *Viewing the overall health of your database*

use it if the problem description is too vague to let you pinpoint the affected metric right away. It combines several important metrics of the database with those of the underlying operating system into logical blocks of metrics and subcharts. This enables you to determine quickly if the database inherits its problems from the node it runs on or if something in the database is causing performance bottlenecks. The top two rows in the chart display information on CPU, memory, and disk usage for both the host and the selected database. Whereas the host data section combines graphical displays with numbers, the database section complements the displayed metrics with trending information in the form of arrows, indicating the direction the displayed value has moved compared to the last refresh. Below the database section, the chart displays session information. It displays the number of active and inactive sessions, and lists the sessions causing the most CPU, memory, or disk usage. You can sort the sessions in each of these categories by the displayed columns. The last row contains information about resource contention, which occurs in the form of waits.

Depending on the individual block, each metric contains a number of options for you, like drilldowns or advice. Because many metrics are compound values, you can drill down into the individual components to investigate where your performance bottleneck comes from. You can also access the related historical data you have collected beforehand. In addition, you can get advice on each metric, which starts the integrated help system and explains what the metric does, where it comes from, how it is calculated, and how it can be influenced. You can also modify the behavior of the flags in this chart. They turn to yellow or red when a value in the respective block of metrics is unfavorable. You can customize when these flags signal a problem by modifying the thresholds behind each metric. With EM9i, Performance Manager charts are integrated with the event system. When you have an event registered to monitor a certain metric, the values defined in the event are used in this chart to determine the flags' colors. This also works the other way: You can define a new event directly from these charts. This integration between event system and real-time charts is available for database and node charts. The health overview chart is one good starting point to investigate general performance bottlenecks, and will lead you to other overview charts in the course of your investigation. There are some more overview charts you need to explore, like Session Details, Top Sessions, and Top SQL. Note that we only discuss the database charts in this chapter, but there are many more available for the other target types, especially for nodes.

Architectural Requirements and Options

The data displayed in the charts of Performance Manager takes a specific path from the source to your screen. The default path is that you have an Agent running on the node on which your targets reside. If you add a new node in Performance Manager to monitor its operating system metrics, Performance Manager tries to contact an Agent on that node. If you want to monitor a remote database, the Agent uses a database session to query the database for the information you request. In cases where you do not have an Agent running on the same node as the database, but you have an Agent elsewhere, you have two options: You can instruct Performance Manager to contact the database directly with no Agent involved, or specify an Agent on a different node. You can specify this by right-clicking the target database and selecting Set Connection Details, which brings up the dialog box displayed in the following illustration. You can choose to connect to the target database directly, or specify an Agent on a different host than your target database, which serves as a proxy Agent. That Agent then opens a session across the network, queries information, and routes it through to you. This requires that the proxy Agent is able to open a connection to the target database; in other words, there must be an entry for the service name used in the proxy Agent's tsnames.ora definition file. When you use the direct connection or a proxy Agent, no node information for the remote node will be available. This is because the Agent needs to be installed on the node directly to access node metrics. For example, if you open the Health Overview Chart mentioned in the previous section, the node information is not displayed. Also, remember that you must use the 9i Agent. Check the documentation for restrictions when using a pre-9i Agent.

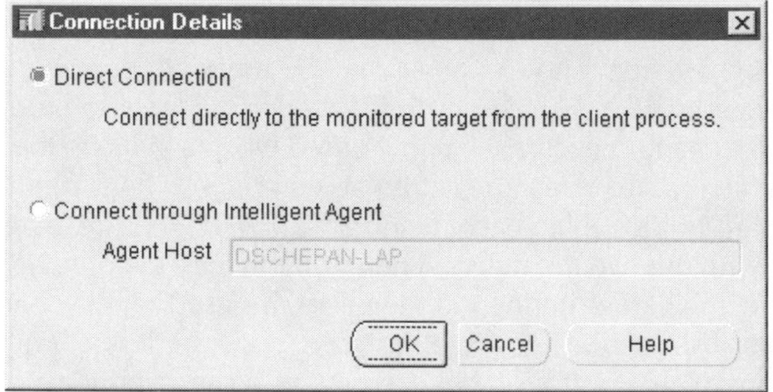

Capacity Planner

In the previous section, we mentioned that you can drill down to historical data that was collected beforehand. DBAs frequently need to know what happened with certain metrics in the past, or how resources have been consumed over time. You certainly do not have the time to look at real-time charts all day as a standard monitoring task. Information can be collected automatically in the background and accessed when needed. Capacity Planner is the tool in Diagnostics Pack that helps you to manage historical data collections. You can access it from the console in the same way as Performance Manager. The interface looks similar to Performance Manager, because the navigator tree is populated with the services of the console, and also the charts and categories of charts are similar. You can also add targets manually and set up collections, but you will have to reenter the target every time you start Capacity Planner. The functions of Capacity Planner can be categorized into collection and analysis. There are two tabs representing each of these two functions below the navigator tree, as shown in Figure 7-3.

Collecting Data

To collect data, you first need to determine some collection parameters on a per-target basis. Starting with version 9i, the Collection Options page gives you the choice to either collect a predefined comprehensive set of collection metrics, or

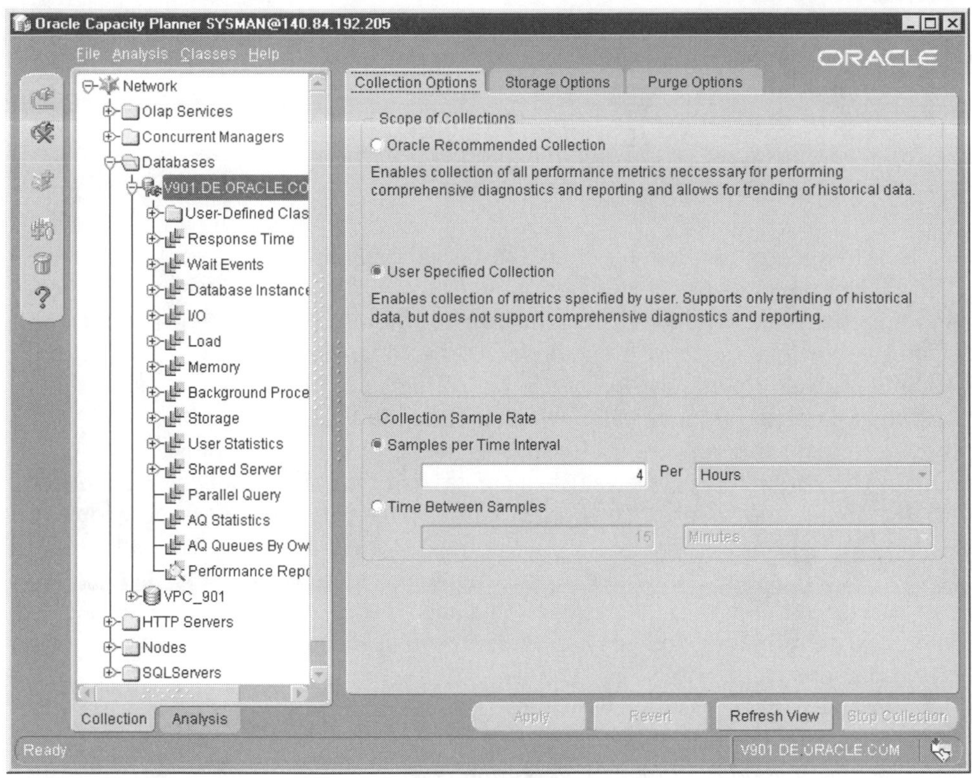

FIGURE 7-3. *Setting up collections with Capacity Planner*

to define your own. The Oracle-recommended options are only available with the 9i Agent, and are explained in Chapter 4 of *Getting Started with Oracle Diagnostics Pack*. You also need to specify the sampling rate. The Storage page lets you determine where to store the data. For your convenience, you can select the repository to be your historical database, but you can also specify any other existing database account in any database you already have. The term "Historical Database" may sound complicated, but there is really nothing you need to do about it except creating the account. All schema objects are automatically created and maintained by the Agent. Note that the service must be resolvable in the tsnames.ora file of the Agent doing the collection. When the Agent starts collecting, it stores the samples initially in local binary files, and uploads the data periodically to avoid a constant stream of data to your historical database. You can determine the interval for the Agent to load information. Note that information must be loaded to your historical database to be available for analysis.

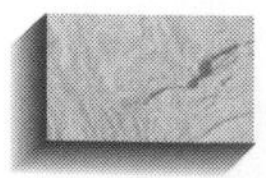

NOTE

If the historical database connection is not available when the Agent tries to load data, the Agent continues collecting samples and stores them locally. It frequently tries to reconnect to the historical database. If the monitored target becomes unavailable, the samples are marked as missing.

You might wonder how big such a historical database might grow over time. The answer depends on the number of metrics you monitor on how many targets and how long you keep the data. Some rules of thumb to calculate the expected size of a historical database are included in the Diagnostics Pack documentation. To limit endless growth, the Agent can be instructed to delete old data from the historical database automatically, which is set up in the Purge Options page. When the Agent loads the samples, it also creates averages. It creates hourly averages in addition to storing the sample values, it creates daily averages once there are enough hourly values, and so forth. The Purge Options pages let you specify how long you would like to keep each class of values in the historical database. The older the data is, the less interesting it might be to you, compared to daily or weekly averages. You can then go to the individual classes of data and select items to be collected. As with Performance Manager, you can create your own user-defined classes for databases based on SQL statements.

NOTE

The class called Performance Reporting Data is available with version 9i, and collects all performance related data. This data enables you to generate a comprehensive report called Diagnostics Report, which is accessible from the Reporting Website.

When you submit a collection to the Agent, a green dot appears in the navigator tree next to any class or category of data that is currently being collected. If you have a customized set of metrics, you can copy an existing collection to be applied to different databases in the same way. You also have the option to generate reports on your collections and cancel them. Like Performance Manager, you can specify a proxy Agent on an intermediate host with the same restrictions mentioned in the previous section.

Analyzing Historical Data

You can get to analysis mode in Capacity Planner by clicking the Analysis tab below the navigator tree. You have to connect to the historical database first, and you are asked to either select the repository or specify an alternative location. If you would like to use an analysis tool other than Capacity Planner, you can do so by accessing the tables holding the data directly. The schema structure is outlined in the "Understanding the Oracle Capacity Planner Historical Database" section of *Getting Started with the Oracle Diagnostics Pack.* Once you are connected, you can see what data is available for analysis. Remember that data that has already been collected but not transferred is not available for analysis. You can drill down into your collected data classes, items, and the aggregation level. If you have a previous chart still open, you can add the new chart to the existing display. This allows you to correlate heterogeneous data, such as database metrics against underlying host metrics, which is displayed in Figure 7-4 as an example.

You can see how the samples form a trend in the chart, and you can examine each value by hovering the mouse over the points or switching to the values pages. The top of the chart display window holds a number of options. You can print the screen, generate a report, or save the current chart to an analysis in the repository. You can add or remove items from the chart display and also extrapolate the data using the Trend Analysis Wizard. This wizard allows you to calculate how your

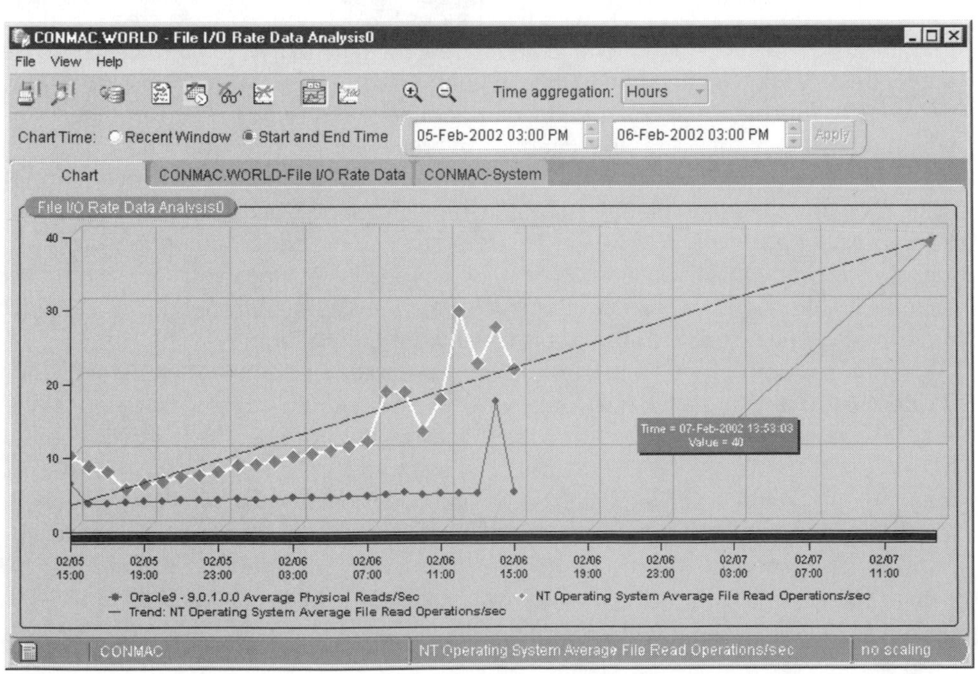

FIGURE 7-4. *Analyzing, comparing, and extrapolating host and database data*

trend will continue in the future, for example, how long until your disk space is used up, or when the buffer cache hit ratio falls under 40 percent. The wizard also adds a line to the display showing you the result of the extrapolation graphically. If you have specific sample points that are obviously distorting the extrapolation, they can be excluded. You can view all excluded points and re-include them. You can remove displayed lines, including the extrapolation line, switch the legend on and off, and also switch to auto-scaling. This can improve readability of charts when one displayed curve has very small numbers and the other has huge numbers, causing one curve to appear flat on the chart. You can switch to other time aggregates, and also modify the time window displayed in the chart. You can also adjust the displayed time window through a scrollbar at the bottom of the chart. You can zoom in by clicking and dragging a square over the graphs in the chart itself. Such an analysis is also available from the Reporting Website in a similar way.

Trace Data Viewer

The Oracle Trace Data Viewer helps you view and analyze data that has been collected using Oracle Trace. You need to have a schema ready that contains a previously collected and formatted trace data collection. You can create such a collection using the command OTRCCOL with the options START and STOP to create a trace file, and the FORMAT option to load and format the data to a schema in the database. This is the schema you need to connect to with Trace Data Viewer. Previous versions of EM's Diagnostics Pack contained a component called Oracle Trace Manager, which provided a graphical user interface to create a trace data collection. This has been discontinued with EM9i. You now have to create a trace data collection using the command line interface as outlined in Chapter 12 of the *Oracle9i Database Performance Guide and Reference.* This chapter also describes the options to use database tracing with init parameters or PL/SQL procedures. Once you have a formatted trace data collection, you can use the Trace Data Viewer to analyze and view it much more easily, because raw trace data is usually difficult to interpret.

When you start Trace Data Viewer, you have to enter complete credentials for your collected and formatted trace data, whether you start this tool from the standalone or OMS-connected console, or from the Windows Start menu. The account needs to have the `SELECT ANY DICTIONARY` privilege to access all dictionary data needed for computing statistics. If your database version does not have this privilege, you need to provide the `SELECT ANY TABLE` privilege. Once you are connected, the tool computes a number of statistics, and offers you a vast amount of predefined views, which also support sorting and drill-downs. Figure 7-5 shows an example analysis on SQL statements with the highest disk reads per execution ratio. The existing views can also be customized to your needs or you can create new views with the help of the integrated Data View Wizard.

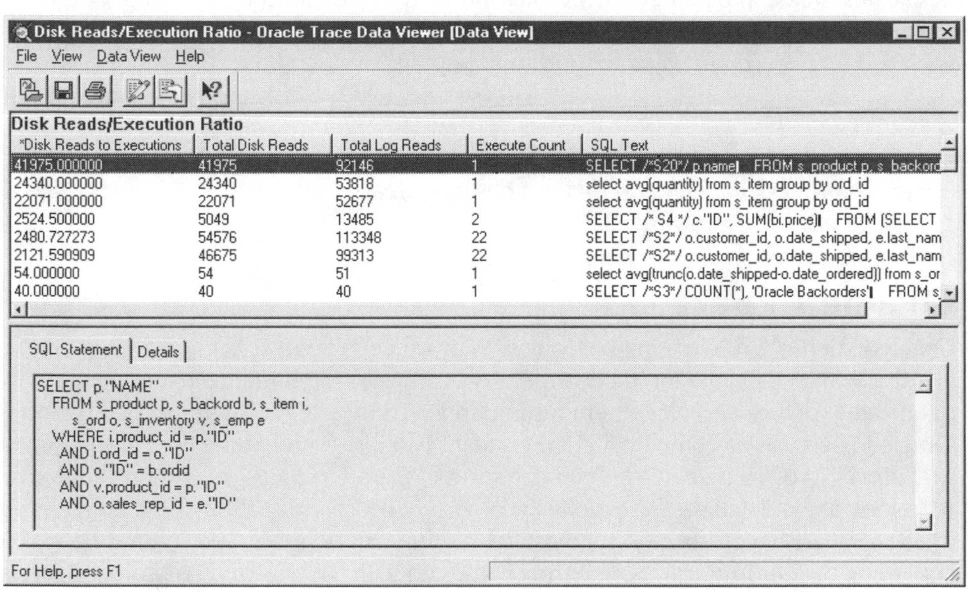

FIGURE 7-5. *A sample trace data analysis*

Tuning Pack

The tools found in the Oracle Tuning Pack focus on analysis and performance tuning of the database. These components are: Oracle Expert, for comprehensive tuning and analysis; Index Tuning Wizard, to create new or improve existing indexes; SQL Analyze and Virtual Index Wizard, for tuning of SQL statements; Tablespace Map, for tablespace analysis; Reorg Wizard, for reorganization of objects; and Outline Management tools, for manipulating and saving execution plans for SQL statements. You can access most of these tools from the Tools menu or the Tuning Pack drawer in the console.

Tuning is often considered to be very difficult, because it requires lots of detailed technical background knowledge and experience. Many tuning rules influence each other and depend on a number of components that are difficult to keep track of. Because of its complexity, your tuning process should follow a methodology, which allows you to develop a structure. Gaining experience is often the only way to efficiently solve performance problems, but what if you do not have enough experience or extensive background knowledge? Automated tools can help to check for the most common reasons for suboptimal performance. The scope of tools in the Tuning Pack is to offer fast and easy help to identify and solve common problems in various areas. In this section, we provide an overview of the functionality offered in the components of the Tuning Pack, but we recommend reading *Database Tuning with the Oracle Tuning Pack* for additional details.

NOTE
We recommend that you apply Patch 2012197, available on Oracle MetaLink, which was released especially for the Tuning Pack version 9i.

Oracle Expert

Oracle Expert is a rule-engine-based tool that you can use to collect, evaluate, verify, and implement database tuning changes. It covers areas like instance parameter tuning, database structure and placement tuning, index tuning, and SQL reuse evaluation. Oracle Expert can be compared to a consultant you hire for a limited time to investigate specific areas of your database. You can instruct Expert to focus on certain problems, or to look at the database as a whole. Expert first collects information and then analyzes the data in areas you specify. It investigates what can be improved in your database according to your instructions, and then comes up with findings and recommendations. It is up to you to decide what to do with these findings and if you want to implement Expert's recommendations or parts of them. Expert always explains why it recommends its activities, and generates reports and scripts to make implementations easier for you. It follows the methodology that you initially specify the scope of your tuning session, such as instance tuning only, or space management and instance tuning, or other options. Afterward, Expert collects data for a certain period of time, which you can view and edit.

Standalone Repository

When you start Expert from an OMS-connected console, you are automatically connected to the repository. Before version 9i of EM, this was the only way to run Oracle Expert. You can now run Expert version 9i without having an OMS available, but you need to provide logon credentials for a database schema in which Expert can store its data. This schema is called the Standalone Repository, and is automatically populated when you point one of the tools towards the account to be used. You can view and delete standalone repositories with the Enterprise Manager Configuration Assistant (EMCA).

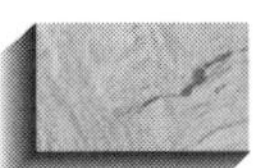

NOTE
The account to be used for a standalone repository needs to have the `EXECUTE ANY PROCEDURE`, `EXECUTE ANY TYPE`, `SELECT ANY TABLE` privileges, and the `SELECT_CATALOG_ROLE` role.

Collecting and Reviewing Information

After startup, Expert asks you whether you want to create a new tuning session, open an existing one, or load the sample tuning session. The sample tuning session is provided for demo purposes with the installation and helps you to get an idea of what to expect from Expert. You can analyze the sample data and generate recommendations from them without having to create your own collection first. After you make your selection, you see the Expert interface with the five tabs representing Expert's methodology.

As outlined in the previous section, you have to determine the scope of your tuning session. You have to specify whether Expert should watch for instance optimization, focus on SQL reuse opportunities, or both. These settings influence the amount of data to be collected. You can also specify your tuning session characteristics, because they influence the recommendations. The Collect page then gives you the option to influence what information Expert collects, and from which source. You can influence Expert's behavior on each of the displayed collection classes: System, Database, Instance, Schema, and Workload. These options range from entering characteristics of your machine to restricting the collection to certain schemas. Some information is collected once; some is collected periodically. Most data can also be retrieved from a previously collected session that was exported to an .XDL file. Workload data can also be retrieved from an account containing trace data or the SQL History. SQL History is a storage area in the EM repository containing SQL cache, Oracle Trace, or .XDL file data, which can be shared among various tuning tools. Once you have collected information, you can review it in the Review page. This is important because you can collect information from a variety of sources, and you want to make sure the correct data is used for the evaluation process. A second advantage is that you can later modify the collected values and repeat the evaluation process, allowing what-if scenarios.

Analyzing Tuning Sessions

The Recommendations page allows you to start the analysis and generate recommendations based on the applied rules, your specified scope, and the collected data (see Figure 7-6). You can view more detail for each of the recommendations, enabling you to understand exactly why Expert thinks that it has found room for improvement and what course of action it recommends to solve the problem. The Scripts page then points to files that contain the SQL needed to perform the suggested changes. Expert also creates a file with modified init.ora parameter settings and allows you to generate a number of reports on the collected data, the issued recommendations, and more.

Autotune

Expert provides a feature called Autotune, which monitors key database parameters automatically and writes recommendations to a file. This mechanism is designed to

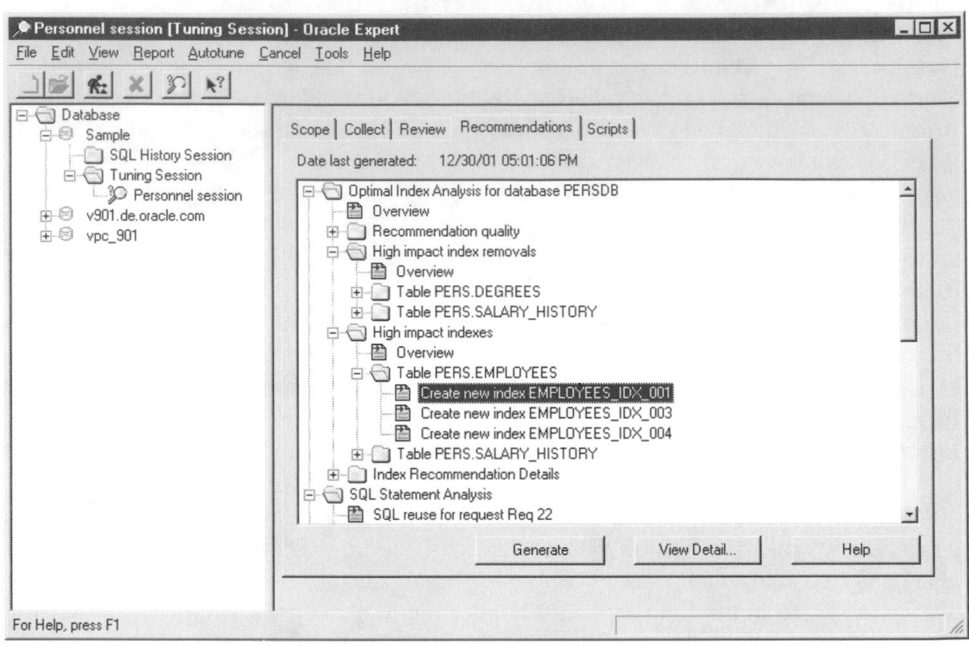

FIGURE 7-6. *Expert generates detailed recommendations*

be unobtrusive, and collects samples every 15 minutes, which are evaluated once a day. You can frequently review the recommendations and decide individually whether to implement them or not. Expert does not automatically change instance parameters, as the term Autotune might suggest. Autotune has to be started with an OMS connection.

Index Tuning Wizard

Oracle Expert's recommendations also include the creation of new indexes. However, this is part of a more comprehensive approach. The Tuning Pack also contains the Index Tuning Wizard to evaluate existing indexes or suggest creating new ones in a more focused way. It is available from the console and Oracle Expert when running with an OMS connection, and has to be launched in context with a selected database with valid credentials defined in the EM repository. You first have to specify what type of workload (OLAP, OLTP, or both) your selected database has, because this will influence index recommendations. You can then restrict the process to some specified schemas in your database to generate index recommendations. The wizard may recommend adding new indexes, changing existing ones, or changing the type of an existing index. You can view detailed descriptions for each of the recommendations, which are also available as reports for you to save or print. The wizard also generates the scripts needed to implement the recommended indexes. These scripts can be executed right away, saved to a script file, or the whole tuning session can be saved as an Oracle Expert Session for further analysis or manipulation.

SQL Analyze

When you are querying data with SQL statements, you can achieve the same result by taking different approaches. Although the different SQL statements may return the same result set, the performance can vary dramatically depending on a number of factors, like the way the statement is written, but also database environment, indexes, or the access paths chosen by the optimizer. SQL Analyze focuses on tuning individual SQL statements by retrieving the execution plan, analyzing and rewriting the statement, and comparing execution plans and statistics of alternative versions of the statement. It can also generate index recommendations to speed up the statement using built-in Index Tuning Wizard functionality, and test the impact of new indexes without actually creating them, using the Virtual Index Wizard.

Starting with version 9i of EM, SQL Analyze can also be used without OMS, but with a standalone repository in the same way as Oracle Expert. When you start SQL Analyze from an OMS-connected console, it automatically connects to the repository and populates its navigator tree with databases discovered through the console. You can also start SQL Analyze from Performance Manager of Diagnostics Pack by selecting the drill-down option Tune SQL Statement in the SQL Text window of the Session Details Overview chart. Performance Manager will automatically start SQL Analyze and populate the navigator tree with the currently monitored SQL statement.

There are a number of other ways to find tuning candidates. You can simply copy and paste a statement into SQL Analyze, retrieve it from the SQL History, or filter from the SQL Cache of your database, which contains all currently running or recently run SQL statements. You can also investigate the instance parameters of your database. Once you have selected a tuning candidate, it appears as node in the navigator tree, and the detail pages display the full SQL text and an execution plan (see Figure 7-7). You can walk through the individual steps of the execution plan, examine the steps and objects involved, view the execution statistics, and run the statement in different optimizer modes.

Graphical Explain Plan

With the Tuning Pack, you also get a graphical version of the explain plan, which converts the tabular view to a tree view. This enhanced display visually emphasizes high-volume operations as branches in the tree, and points out potential targets for tuning efforts, especially in large execution plans. The Graphical Explain Plan is available in the console's session display and in Performance Manager of Diagnostics Pack when viewing the SQL statement and execution plan of a current session. A simple example of the Graphical Explain Plan is shown in Figure 14-12 in Chapter 14.

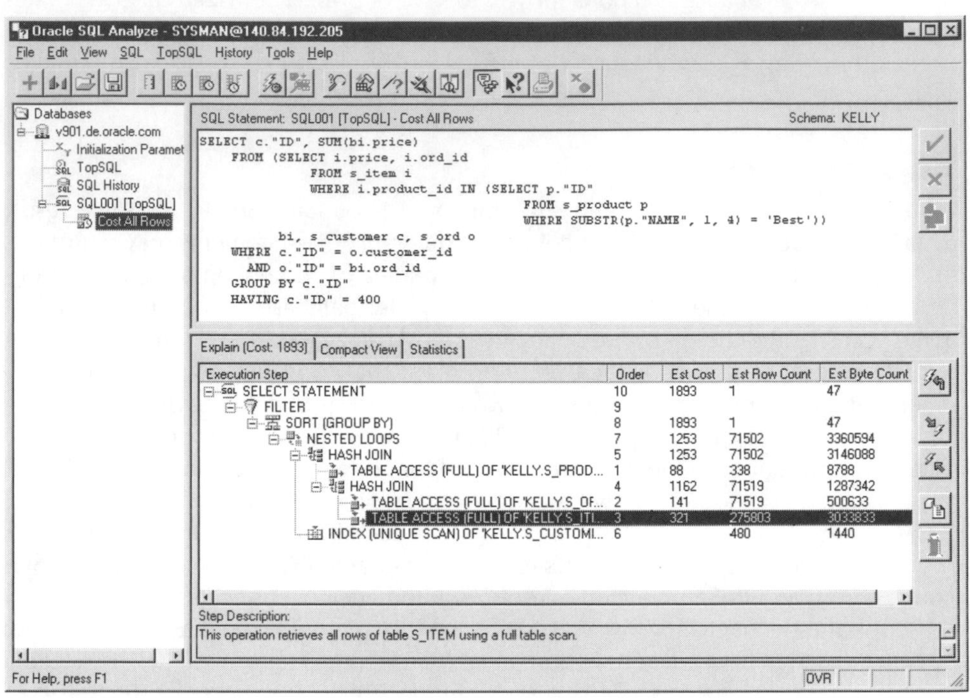

FIGURE 7-7. *SQL Analyze examining a heavy-impact SQL statement*

SQL Tuning Wizard

The SQL Tuning Wizard guides you through the process of tuning a statement for typical rule-of-thumb violations. When you start this wizard, it checks the statement currently selected in the navigator tree for inefficiencies by examining the statement itself, with no direct database involvement. When it discovers inefficiencies, it tries to project by which percentage the suggested changes will improve the statement's performance, based on available optimizer information. It then outlines which rule-of-thumb violations it has detected, suggests how to rewrite each section, and explains why this would improve performance. It then generates a new rewritten SQL statement, and retrieves the new explain plan, allowing you to check both versions of the explain plan. In addition, you can run both statements and compare their execution statistics. This enables you to gain quantifiable differences, such as how long each takes to run, how much CPU is consumed, or how many sorts are done and where (memory or disk).

Getting Index Recommendations

Rewriting a statement is one of the most promising steps you can take to improve a statement's performance, but in many cases this is not possible when you do not have access to the source code of the application that is issuing the statement. You can still try to speed up statements by adding appropriate indexes. SQL Analyze uses Index Tuning Wizard functionality to help you find such indexes, which improve performance of one specific statement currently in your tuning focus. You can right- click a statement in the navigator tree and select Get Index Recommendations. You can then have scripts generated that create the suggested indexes, or verify the recommendation. Verification shows you a new explain plan in comparison with the original one, and you can see if the optimizer would use any of the recommended indexes without actually creating them. This technology is borrowed from the Virtual Index Wizard described in the next section.

Virtual Index Wizard

Very often, administrators create new indexes to improve performance, and see in practice that this index is not used by the optimizer, or does not bring any significant improvement. The result is that the effort in defining, creating, and maintaining the index is lost. In addition, the index may require a lot of space and maintenance effort. The Virtual Index Wizard lets you define any index on any table, and gives you answers to these questions beforehand. It is available from within SQL Analyze and lets you define the index you would like to have tested. You can then force the optimizer to use the index or let it decide freely. It then applies the new index definition and the statement to the optimizer. This returns a new execution plan, allowing the wizard to estimate how much performance improvement to expect. You can compare the old with the new execution plan to see if the index is used at all and how it affects performance. You can then save your work as a new statement to the navigator tree.

Hint Wizard

The Hint Wizard helps you to detect and explain existing hints in a SQL statement. It allows you to delete existing hints, or add more hints, according to your specifications. It asks for necessary parameters regarding tables and indexes where appropriate, and rewrites the statement with the modified hints applied to it.

Tablespace Map

Tablespace Map gives you detailed information on objects in a tablespace. It can be started from the console in context with a specific tablespace. You not only see a sortable list of segments, but also a graphical representation of the segments and extents in the selected tablespace, as shown in Figure 7-8.

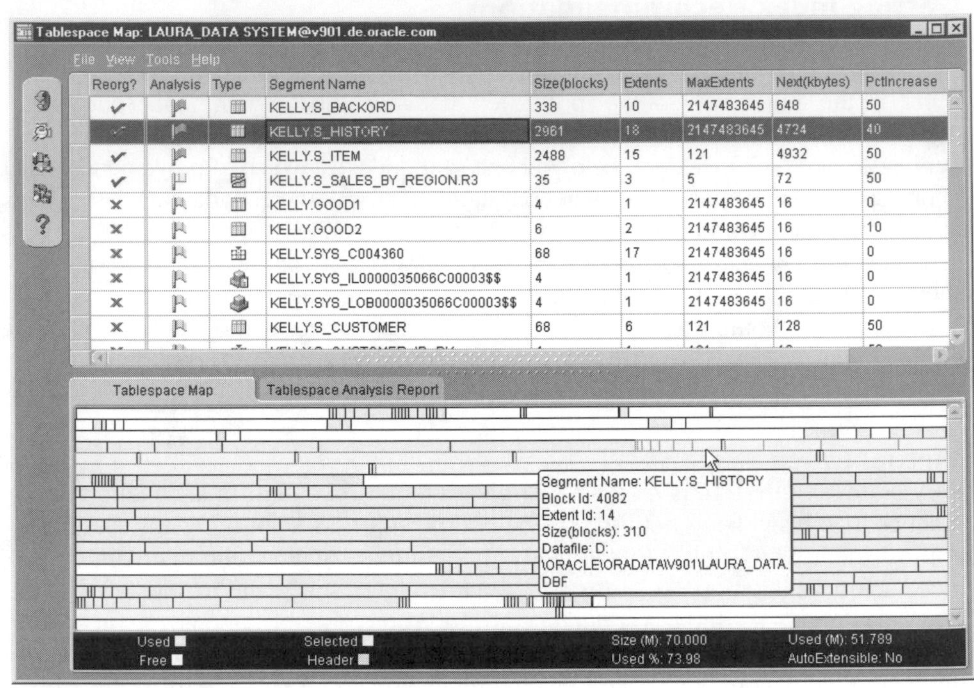

FIGURE 7-8. *Graphical representation of a tablespace*

When you select a segment in the list, the associated extents will be highlighted in the map, which can also be zoomed in or out for better viewing. You can also click on a graphical object in the map and see which segment it belongs to. Most importantly, you can see from the shape of the extents whether they have a uniform size or grow exponentially. Also, you can see if there is any unused space somewhere in the middle between used extents. You can run an analysis on the tablespace that points you towards potential trouble spots, and flags certain segments in the list as critical or warning. You can investigate details regarding the troublesome segments in the analysis report by clicking the Tablespace Analysis Report tab.

NOTE
The analysis uses existing statistics of the tablespace objects. Updating the statistics before doing a tablespace analysis improves accuracy of the analysis. You can update these statistics using the Analyze Wizard in the console.

The analysis preselects critical objects in the segment list as candidates for a reorganization. This can be done with the Reorg Wizard, which can be started in context from within Tablespace Map, and is described in the next section.

Reorg Wizard

The Reorg Wizard can be started from within Tablespace Map with specified parameters, or from the console when you are connected to an OMS. When you start Reorg Wizard from the Tuning Pack drawer or the Tools menu of the console, you can specify whether you would like to reorganize the whole tablespace, only certain objects, or repair migrated rows. When you select Reorganize in the pop-up menu of a tablespace, you also launch the Reorg Wizard, but only with the option to reorganize the entire tablespace.

Reorganizing Schema Objects

Choosing the option Reorganize Schema Objects allows you to select one or more table or other objects of various schemas to be reorganized. You also have the option to change some of each object's attributes. Starting with EM9i, you can choose whether the reorganization process should focus on speed while having the affected objects unavailable, or to focus on availability, which means that the process will be slower, but the objects will remain accessible to users. Choosing the availability option requires a database feature called Online Redefinition, which is introduced with version 9i. Redefining the tablespace for an object causes the object to be moved to the new tablespace, which has a reorganizing effect on the objects. If your database is from a pre-9i release, this option will not be available.

Because all affected objects need to be rebuilt during a reorganization, there will be a short period when they exist twice in your database, which requires enough temporary space. If the current tablespace has enough free space, the objects will be moved or re-created within the same tablespace. You can optionally specify a scratch tablespace with sufficient temporary free space to use. The wizard generates an impact report describing all activities and potential trouble spots for the upcoming reorganization process, and also shows you the script generated to perform the action. The generated script incorporates the best database functionality available for your database release. For example, if an `ALTER TABLE MOVE` command is not available with your database release, the wizard uses `CREATE TABLE AS SELECT`, which might be the best that can be done given the circumstances. That means that the wizard produces different scripts depending on your selections in previous wizard steps, the capabilities of your database release, and your available free space. You can print and save both the impact report and the generated script and submit it as job to EM's job system. Because many reorg operations are done offline, you can schedule this job to be run by the Agent at a more convenient time, using the job scheduling feature.

Reorganizing Entire Tablespaces

If you select the Reorganize Entire Tablespaces option, you can select one or more tablespaces and reorganize them. All objects are moved out of the selected tablespaces and back, which means you have to specify a scratch tablespace with sufficient free space. You do not have the option to change objects' storage parameters in this process. The wizard again generates an impact report and a script that contains the most efficient commands available for your database version. This script can also be scheduled as job to be run by the Agent.

Repair Migrated Rows

Migrated rows occur when an update statement increases the amount of space needed for this row beyond the amount of space available in a block. This causes the database to migrate the updated row to a block which has enough space available. Many migrated rows can be the cause of a performance problem, when the database has to access two blocks for each migrated row. Migrated rows are often mentioned in conjunction with chained rows, which are cut into pieces by the database because there is no single block with enough available space to host the entire row. The effect on performance is the same as with migrated rows. Index Tuning Wizard can repair the migrated row problem. It lets you select tables from various schemas, which are then checked for migrated rows. You again have to specify a tablespace with temporary free space, and the wizard generates an impact report and script. The rows are isolated and reinserted into the table.

Outline Management

The execution plan is a crucial factor when you are tuning a SQL statement to get best performance results. The execution plan is generated by the database optimizer, which evaluates a number of statistics, memory structures and database parameter settings to construct the best execution plan. Therefore, your tuning efforts stay only effective if these parameters are not changed so the optimizer can produce the same well-performing execution plan. Because statistics and other parameters usually can not be kept constant, the optimizer might produce different execution plans. Starting with version 9i, the database has a feature called Plan Stability that addresses this problem. This feature allows you to store outlines in the database, which guarantees that the optimizer will always produce the same execution plan for certain statements, preserving your tuning efforts. An outline is mainly a set of hints to influence the optimizer's behavior to produce the desired execution plan. When you create an outline, you actually store the data that will cause the optimizer to generate the "right" execution plan for the correlated statement.

You can access the Outline Management tool from the Tuning Pack drawer, the Tools menu, or the Graphical Explain Plan window in Performance Manager in the Diagnostics Pack. It allows you to view existing outlines and determine whether they have been used in the past. You can generate reports, delete, create, or edit outlines, and reset the Used flag to check for future usage of individual outlines. You can use the Outline Editor to change join orders, access methods, and other properties. Note that your changes may also result in invalid hints, which may be reverted by the optimizer. When you apply changes to outlines, they have to be validated and saved to be available to other users.

Change Management Pack

The tools in the Oracle Change Management Pack mainly focus on managing changes to schema object definitions inside one or more databases, and can be accessed through Change Manager. This is the only component in the Change Management Pack drawer of the EM console. Tools in Change Manager generally don't look at the data inside these objects, but only at the object definitions and attributes. You can start Change Manager from the console both in standalone mode or connected to an OMS. You can create a baseline to collect and store object definitions, or search and compare objects. When changing objects, everything evolves around change plans, which contain exemplars and directives, and describe changes that have not yet been executed.

An *exemplar* is the example of an object you want to reproduce. It is a complete object definition needed to reproduce either a totally new object, or the modification of an existing object definition of the same name and type. An exemplar demands "Reproduce this object definition." A *directive* can be considered as a set of changes for an existing object. A directive demands "Make these changes to this object definition."

There are a number of wizards to simplify creation of change plans for standardized change requests: DB Quick Change for changing single objects, DB Alter for executing complex changes, and DB Propagate to propagate multiple objects and changes to multiple databases. Like some components of the Tuning Pack, Change Manager needs to store information in a standalone repository when you start it in standalone mode. You see a navigator tree with containers for change plans, baselines, and comparisons. All these objects can be exported from the repository and imported to other repositories with the commands available in the Tools menu. The left side of the window contains a toolbar with icons providing access to the features.

Search Objects

Change Manager allows you to define a search pattern on the name, type, and hosting schema to find specific objects in a database. You can access this feature by choosing Tools | Find Database Objects, or by clicking on the icon with the magnifying glass in the toolbar. Similar functionality is available in the other tools when specifying objects.

Creating a Baseline

Change Manager enables you to capture current object definitions. Click the icon with the camera in the toolbar, and the Create Baseline Wizard starts up. It asks if you want to create a new baseline or a baseline like an existing one, and lets you select one of the available databases containing the objects you want to capture. You can then specify which data for which objects in which schema should be captured, and give your baseline a name. You can also reverse-engineer the objects you selected for this baseline. Change Manager then creates a script that creates the selected objects when executed. Using this feature, you can reverse-engineer entire schemas. The baseline definition appears in the navigator tree folder Baselines. Right-clicking it reveals several commands such as Recapture and View Versions. That means you can recapture the same baseline over and over, creating multiple versions over time. If you recapture a baseline frequently, you can keep track of changes made to objects. That can help you to track the progress in a development project, or in case of application failures in a production system, you can tell what has been changed to the schema definition since the last time the application ran without errors. You can perform this comparison with the wizard described in the following section. The baseline recapture process can be triggered from the Change Manager GUI, but also from a command-line interface using the `OCM` command, which is discussed in Chapter 19.

Compare Database Objects

You can start the Compare Database Objects wizard by clicking the scales icon in the toolbar. You can then specify what you would like to compare. You can choose to compare object definitions of two schemas that are both in one database or one baseline, or you can compare definitions of objects that are in two different databases, baselines, or both. For example, you can compare two schemas in different databases and find out the differences. You can find out what has been changed in a certain schema since the last time you took a baseline. You would then select that one schema in a database and the other in a baseline you took last week. You can then restrict the comparison to desired types of objects, such as tables and indexes. If the database and the baselines contain more than one schema, you can specify which ones you would like to compare and optionally restrict comparison to objects with a certain name pattern. You are presented with some more options regarding comparison of storage attributes, constraints, or objects' statistics. You can then decide if you want to do the comparison right away or later. The comparison definition and its results appear in the folder Comparisons of the navigator tree. Figure 7-9 shows an example of a comparison result that displays such differences. Several buttons allow you to restrict the view to only display the found differences, or the objects that don't exist on one side, for example. You

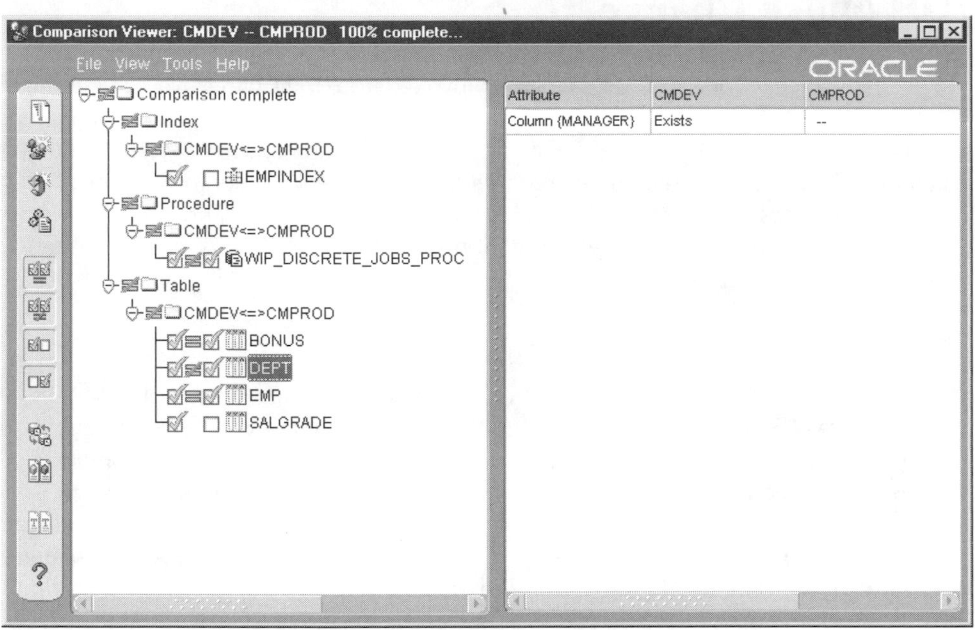

FIGURE 7-9. *The result of Comparing two schemas*

can also repeat the comparison or generate a report. The OCM command-line interface also allows you to trigger a repeat comparison process. To eliminate the found differences, you can launch the Synchronization Wizard by clicking the icon with the two databases in the toolbar of the Comparison Viewer window.

Synchronization Wizard

The Synchronization Wizard allows you to select the differences found with the Compare Database Objects feature, and generates a specific change plan. After you provide a name, the plan appears in the navigator tree under Plans. You can define options for synchronization regarding storage attributes, and enable a logical SQL compare or copy table data along with a table definition, for example. The wizard then generates an impact report that warns of potential trouble spots, and a script which you can both save or print. The script can be edited, executed right away, or submitted as job to the Agent for a later time. If you execute the script from within the wizard, you have the option to undo the changes by clicking the Undo button, which modifies the objects back to their original definitions. This is not entirely possible in some cases, and you will be informed about these situations in the impact report.

DB Quick Change

The DB Quick Change wizard helps you to define a change plan that makes changes to a single object in one database. It can be invoked from the Change Manager toolbar and the Tools menu. You have to select the database, the schema, and the object you would like to change attributes for. You can then edit parameters for the selected object as you would use the "create like" feature to create a new object in the console. The wizard generates an impact report and script that you can print and save. The script can be edited, executed right away, or submitted as a job to the Agent. The changes can also be rolled back when they are executed right away.

DB Alter

The DB Alter wizard helps you define a change plan that performs multiple changes on one or more objects in multiple databases. It allows you to start your change definitions from an existing change plan, or from scratch. You can then select all the objects you intend to change in this change plan, which can be a whole schema, meaning that all objects inside this schema are added to the list. In the next step, you can select each of these objects and add a change directive by changing attributes of the object. If you want to apply the directive to more objects, you can do so easily by editing the *scope* of the directive. You can then select the database to apply the changes to, and optionally map schema names if they are different in the source and target databases. The wizard again creates an impact report and script, which can be printed and saved, and offers to execute the script right away or submit it to the Agent. You also have the option to undo changes after script execution by clicking the Undo button.

DB Propagate

The DB Propagate wizard creates a change plan that copies objects from one database to another or from one schema to another within a database. You can decide to use a Quick Propagate, which quickly lets you select objects in a source database and a target database, and copies the objects "as-is," including data, to the destination database you selected. Note that the new object will overwrite an existing object of the same name in the target database. If you decide to use the Custom Propagate option, you have more flexibility. You can either create a new change plan or continue working with an existing plan. After you select the objects to be moved (exemplars), the propagation options can be customized. This includes whether table data should be copied, whether storage attributes should be ignored, or how to approach name differences, for example. Optionally, you can map schema names if they are different in the source and destination databases, or if you want to copy the objects to a different schema within the same database. You will then be offered the usual options: generate an impact report and script, print and save both; edit and execute the script right away, or through the Agent; and undo the changes if the script was executed without the Agent. You can access DB Propagate from the console when you drag and drop an object or schema to a new target, which is described in more detail in the "Copying a Database Object" section in chapter 14.

Plan Editor

All the tools described in the previous sections create and use change plans to define changes to be executed. Instead of creating change plans using these wizards, you can also generate a custom plan by selecting the Create Change Plan icon from the tool bar. It gives you the option to start the wizards, but also offers to let you create a plan manually. If you choose that option, you are taken to the Plan Editor. You can also access it by right-clicking an existing plan and selecting Edit Change Plan. The Plan Editor lets you modify existing directives, and remove or add new directives or exemplars. You can also add multiple target databases, generate individual impact reports, and create scripts with individual propagation options. This allows you to address the specifics of each individual target database. From here, you can run the scripts or submit them as jobs to the respective Agents.

Standard Management Pack

The Standard Management Pack is free of charge for customers who licensed the Standard Edition of the database. It contains a collection of tools from the Diagnostics, Tuning, and Change Management Packs. It can only be used with the Standard Edition of the database, whereas the Diagnostics, Tuning, and Change Management Packs can only be licensed and used with the Enterprise Edition of the database. There is no real technical reason for these restrictions. The components included in the Standard Management Pack are a subset from the other three packs: Performance Manager and the Top Sessions Chart from Diagnostics Pack, Index Tuning Wizard of the Tuning Pack, and Change Manager with the functionality of creating or viewing a baseline and the Synchronization Wizard.

Management Pack for Oracle Applications

The Management Pack for Oracle Applications (Apps Pack) makes EM's console and monitoring components available for Oracle Applications environments. It extends the Agent to discover and monitor Applications-specific services through specialized advanced events, makes Performance Manager and Capacity Planner available for Concurrent Managers, and provides the Concurrent Processing Tuning Assistant, which helps to analyze information in the foundation tables of the Applications System. Effective with the June 16, 2001 price list, customers who license the E-Business Suite are entitled to a free license of the Oracle Applications

Pack and the Oracle Diagnostics Pack. Customers who licensed the E-Business Suite prior to this price list are not entitled to these two packs until they have migrated their E-Business Suite licenses.

NOTE
You must apply some patches to the Oracle Applications instance for it to be managed by the Management Pack for Oracle Applications. Refer to Getting Started with the Oracle Management Pack for Oracle Applications.

Console and Agent Extensions

The agent discovers Services of the type Concurrent Manager, which are displayed by the console. As outlined in Chapter 3, you must manually enter services into a file called OAPPS.ORA located in the $ORACLE_HOME/network/agent/config folder. The agent reads this file during each startup. You also have access to special advanced events and jobs, which appear in the job and event creation dialog boxes when you select a target of the type Concurrent Manager.

Performance Manager Extensions

The Performance Manager available through the Diagnostics Pack is extended to monitor the performance statistics of concurrent managers. Once concurrent managers have been discovered, you can access new specialized classes of charts to monitor Applications systems the same way as databases and operating systems. A useful feature allows you to link an Applications database session back to the client across the Applications middle tier.

Capacity Planner Extensions

The Apps Pack also extends the Capacity Planner tool the same way it extends Performance Manager. You can use the extended Capacity Planner to instruct the Agent to also collect performance metrics on concurrent managers over time and store them in the historical database as it does with other collected data. The data is seamlessly integrated into the historical data collection, and is managed and maintained with the same interface.

Concurrent Processing Tuning Assistant

The Concurrent Processing Tuning Assistant (CPTA) analyzes information about concurrent managers, concurrent programs, and concurrent processing requests to improve throughput and performance. It can connect to the Concurrent Processing

Tuning Assistant repository, the Oracle Management Server, or the database schema containing the Oracle Application Object Library tables for the subsystems you want to tune. It includes Tuning Advisor to find performance bottlenecks of concurrent managers with the help of reports. You can then identify the time periods with the longest wait times, the requests that waited during these time periods, and periods with unused capacity. With CPTA you can store data from the FND tables of your Applications System to the EM repository to avoid the data getting lost through the routine purge mechanisms of the Applications System.

Oracle Applications Manager

The EM console can be extended by the Oracle Applications Manager (OAM) console, which is an Applications DBA-oriented subset of the current Oracle Applications System Administration functions and include administration of concurrent managers, processes, and requests. OAM is available for Releases 11.0 and 11i of Oracle Applications, and is provided in addition to the multiwindow Oracle Applications forms. OAM is not a component of the Apps Pack, but complements the monitoring capabilities of its tools. Oracle Applications Manager and the associated Oracle Applications Manager Server Extensions are released separately as a free download from Oracle MetaLink.

Management Pack for SAP R/3

Approximately 75 percent of all databases used in SAP R/3 deployments are Oracle databases. The Oracle Management Pack for SAP R/3 (SAP Pack) enables EM's console and monitoring components to be functional for SAP Application Servers. It extends the Agent to discover SAP middle tiers, and extends Performance Manager and Capacity Planner to monitor them. The SAP pack is available free of charge to qualifying customers. Contact your Oracle representative for more information.

Console and Agent Extensions

The agent discovers services of the type SAP R/3 Systems, which are displayed in the console. You also have special advanced events available, which will appear in the event creation dialog boxes when you select an SAP System as target. Similar to what was outlined for the Apps Pack, you need to edit a file called SAP.CONF in the folder $ORACLE_HOME/network/agent/config with SAP service information, which is read with each startup of the agent. You must use a Windows NT or 2000 Agent of release 8.1.5.0.1 or higher. Note that SAP-related functionality does not belong to the standard equipment of the agents and usually requires installation of agent extensions. In addition, you need to obtain the libraries librfc32.dll and msvcp60.dll from SAP's Website or media. Both are used by the Agent to connect to an SAP middle tier, and need to be available in the path of your Windows system. Refer to *Getting Started with Oracle Management Pack for SAP R/3* for more information.

NOTE
If you want to monitor an SAP middle tier running on an operating system other than Windows NT or 2000, you must use a proxy Agent on a Windows NT or 2000 node, edit its sap.conf file with the non-Windows NT or 2000 SAP System information, and discover the proxy node from the EM console.

Performance Manager Extensions

Performance Manager is extended to monitor the performance statistics of multiple SAP middle tiers. Once they have been discovered, you access new specialized classes of charts to monitor SAP-specific information the same way as databases and operating systems.

Capacity Planner Extensions

The Capacity Planner tool is extended like Performance Manager to be available for SAP systems. It can be used to instruct the Agent to also collect performance metrics on concurrent managers over time and store them in the historical database as it does with other collected data. You can use the same administrative mechanisms and correlate SAP middle tier data with other historical data.

Summary

This chapter described the optional Management Packs available to extend EM. The extra licensable packs are Diagnostics Pack, Tuning Pack, and Change Management Pack, which are available to manage Enterprise Edition databases. Also offered is the Standard Management Pack, with a subset of the components of the other three packs, which is free of charge to manage Standard Edition databases. In addition, customers can obtain the Management Pack for Oracle Applications and the Management Pack for SAP R/3—which extend EM's monitoring capabilities to also monitor services of the respective Systems. Starting with the next part of the book, we will provide you with hands-on examples on how to use EM. We will start in the next chapter with discovering your target nodes.

PART III

Using EM

CHAPTER 8

Discovering Your Oracle Environment

Before you can begin to work on your targets using EM Management Server, you must register the nodes in your EM repository, where the services you want to manage are located. A process known as *automatic discovery* was provided, beginning with EM version 1.3.5. With EM9i, this service is provided through the Discovery Wizard. This process enables administrators to add manageable Oracle Services to their EM Console, which must occur before you can run jobs and monitor which events on target nodes. Discovery of target nodes is only possible when the EM Console is connected to an EM Management Server, that is, not in standalone mode, where only database names are used.

Before you discover your target nodes, you should complete the basic configuration of your EM environment, including configuring paging and e-mail services, defining super and regular EM administrators and creating Management Regions if required. The reason for this is that you will be able to assign the discovered target nodes to management regions and EM administrators as they are discovered. Refer to Chapter 9 for more details about how to complete this configuration.

This chapter describes the different steps involved in registering your target nodes into your EM repository, as well as refreshing them in case of changes to the registered target nodes.

The Automatic Discovery Process

First, we will take a look at how the automatic discovery process takes place between the different Oracle components in your EM environment. The discovery process consists of two steps:

1. The Intelligent Agent must first determine if any services actually exist on its node that can be managed from the EM Console. This Intelligent Agent discovery process occurs each time the Intelligent Agent process is started. The information is stored on the target node in these files:

   - ORACLE_HOME\NETWORK\AGENT\SERVICES.ORA
   - ORACLE_HOME\NETWORK\ADMIN\SNMP_RO.ORA
   - ORACLE_HOME\NETWORK\ADMIN\SNMP_RW.ORA

   The output files SNMP_RO.ORA and SNMP_RW.ORA are written to the location specified by the environment variable TNS_ADMIN, or if the variable is not set, to the ORACLE_HOME\NETWORK\ADMIN directory.

Only the SNMP_RW.ORA file should be edited; the other two files are overwritten each time the Intelligent Agent starts up.

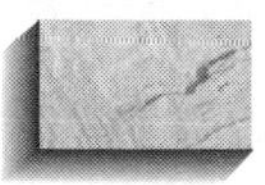

NOTE
For versions before 8i, the path includes `NET80` *instead of* `NETWORK` *on the Windows platform.*

2. When you initiate an automatic discovery via the EM Console by entering a hostname or IP address of a target node in the Discovery Wizard, that request is passed to the Management Server (OMS). The OMS then contacts the Intelligent Agent on the target node, which in turn sends the information about services located on that node back to the OMS. The OMS then stores the information in the EM Repository and updates the EM Console by displaying a view of the node and its manageable services.

Notice that without the Intelligent Agent discovery in the first step, there is no EM Console discovery. Both discoveries must be successful and must happen in the correct order for the services to appear in the EM Console.

NOTE
If you discover two or more targets with the exact same name, only one of the discovered targets appears in the navigator tree.

If no services appear, you should first check to make sure that everything is configured and running correctly on the Intelligent Agent side. For more about troubleshooting the Intelligent Agent, see Chapter 20.

Prerequisites for Automatic Discovery

The following are the prerequisites that must be fulfilled before the automatic discovery can occur:

- The Intelligent Agent must be installed and started on the target node.
- The target node, EM Client, and Management Server must have TCP/IP installed and configured with hostname resolution working correctly

from all three systems. There are two tests you can perform from the Management Server:

A. You can test that you can reach the target node from your Management Server by pinging the node using ping from a command prompt. Enter **ping <*node name*>**. The command should return Reply from <*IP address*>: Bytes 32..., which indicates that you can contact the node across the network. If you see Request timed out or Destination host unreachable, you have no network connection to the node and automatic discovery will fail.

B. You can test hostname resolution using nslookup from a Command Prompt. Enter **nslookup <*node name*>**. The command should return Name: <*target node name*> Address: <*target node IP address*>, which indicates that the target node name can be resolved correctly.

- If you are discovering databases, the LISTENER.ORA file must contain a SID_LIST containing a SID_DESC for each SID, known as *static* service configuration. Note that effective with Net8i, the SID_DESC is not required for making database connections, as the database registers itself with the Net Listener (known as *dynamic* service configuration). But the Intelligent Agent still requires the *static* configuration for discovery. Below you see an example of a *static* service configuration for the database instances LBV and OEMREP handled by the Net Listener "LISTENER":

```
SID_LIST_LISTENER =
  (SID_LIST =
    (SID_DESC =
      (GLOBAL_DBNAME = OEMREP)
      (ORACLE_HOME = F:\Oracle\OraNT9i)
      (SID_NAME = OEMREP)
    )
    (SID_DESC =
      (GLOBAL_DBNAME = LBV)
      (ORACLE_HOME = F:\Oracle\OraNT9i)
      (SID_NAME = LBV)
    )
  )
```

- Basic Oracle networking components must be configured. Database connections must be possible from the OMS system to the target node.

Allowing Discovery on a per-OMS Basis

You can configure the Intelligent Agent so that only OMSes on specific servers are allowed to discover this particular Intelligent Agent. This is accomplished by setting the validnode verification Net8 parameters on the Intelligent Agent side:

```
TCP.VALIDNODE_CHECKING = YES
TCP.INVITED_NODES = (hostname1, ...)
```

or

```
TCP.EXCLUDED_NODES = (hostname1, ...)
```

The `INVITED_NODES` parameter allow the listed hosts to discover the Intelligent Agent, and the `EXCLUDED_NODES` prevents discovery for the listed hosts. A discovery from an OMS on a node not invited or explicitly excluded through these parameters receives the VNI-4009 "Cannot contact agent on the node—agent may be down or network communication to the node has failed" error message. You can specify either hostname or IP address for the hosts. For an Oracle9i Intelligent Agent, you add these parameters to the `SQLNET.ORA` Net8 configuration file, for releases before Oracle9i, add them to the `PROTOCOL.ORA` file instead. After you have modified these parameters, restart the Intelligent Agent.

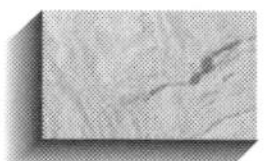

CAUTION
The parameters discussed here affect other Oracle components. For example, starting the TNS Listener with the same settings will restrict TCP connections to invited nodes or exclude connections from the excluded ones. Therefore, in such cases you should install the Intelligent Agent in a separate home using its own `SQLNET.ORA` or `PROTOCOL.ORA` file.

Discovering Target Nodes using the Discovery Wizard

This section assumes that you are logged into your EM Console using the Management Server and not the standalone mode. When you have logged on to the EM Management Server, you'll be able to discover the target nodes automatically using the Discovery Wizard.

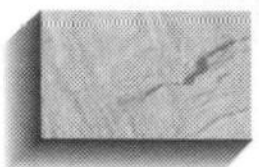

NOTE
If there are no discovered nodes at all in the EM repository when you enter the EM Console (which typically happens at the first logon), the Discovery Wizard starts automatically.

This section also assumes that the Intelligent Agent is running on your target nodes. This is the first requirement for nodes and their services to be discovered automatically. Nodes without an Intelligent Agent must be added manually to the EM Repository (see the section entitled "Manually Adding Nodes to the EM Repository" later in this chapter). You won't be able to submit EM events or EM jobs for these nodes.

In the following sections, two ways of discovering target nodes are described: you either enter all the names of nodes to be discovered or import these names from a text file.

Entering Node Names Manually

If you are dealing with a smaller number of target nodes, and are able to enter the node names yourself for automatic discovery, use the following steps:

1. Start the Discovery Wizard from EM Console by selecting Navigator | Discover Nodes, or by pressing CTRL-D. When the Discovery Wizard is started, the Introduction screen is displayed. Click Next.

2. The Specify Nodes screen is displayed (see Figure 8-1), in which you can enter node names or IP addresses for automatic discovery. You can separate the node names or IP addresses by a comma, space, tab, or new line. Enter all the targets to discover and click Next.

3. A Progress page appears, showing the status of the node discovery. When the discovery process is complete, a green check mark indicates that the node was discovered successfully, and a red X indicates that the discovery failed. If an error occurs, the error number and text explaining the reason for the error appears. When the discovery of all target nodes has finished, click Finish.

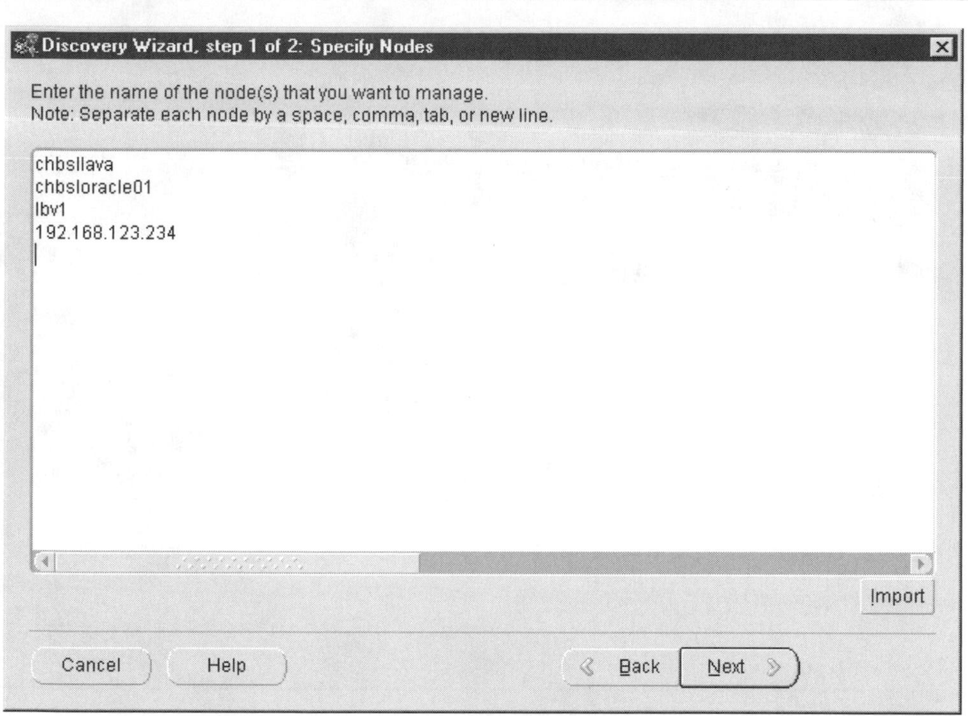

FIGURE 8-1. *The Discovery Wizard Specify Nodes screen*

4. Depending on whether there exist regular EM administrators (if administrators other than super administrators have been created), an Access to Targets page appears, allowing a super administrator to control what appears in the Navigator for these regular EM administrators. The first column shows all objects that appear in the Console Navigator. Click the plus + sign next to the target service objects to expand it. There is one column for each EM administrator defined by the super administrator. To allow a regular administrator to see a particular object within the Navigator, click the check box in the column belonging to that administrator. An example is shown in Figure 8-2, where the regular administrator ADMIN1 is granted access to the OEMREP database instance. Click Finish.

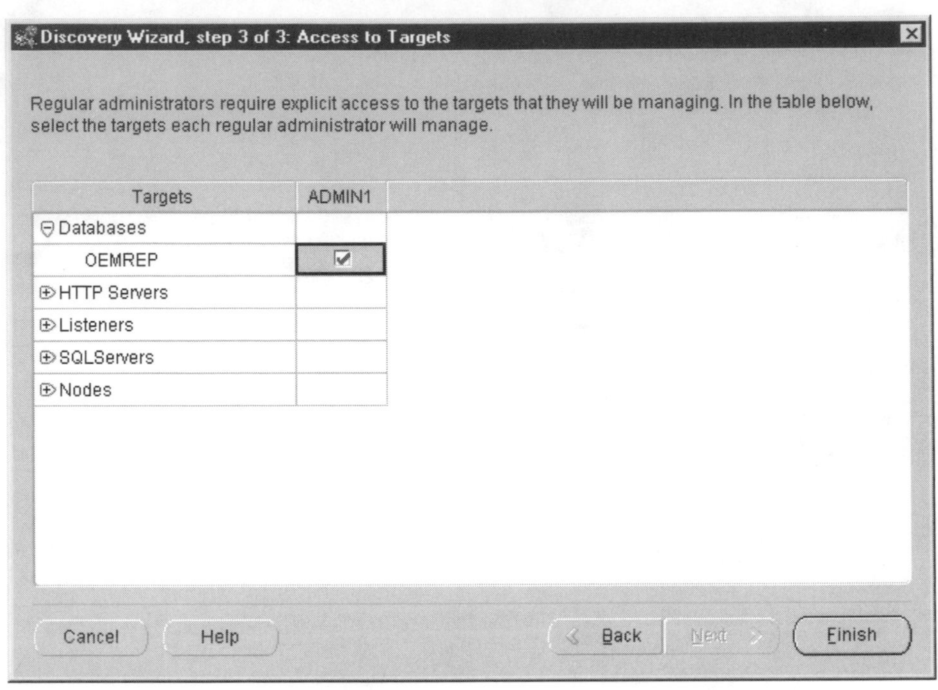

FIGURE 8-2. *The Discovery Wizard Access to Targets screen*

5. Finally, a summary of the discovery results are shown. Click OK to dismiss the dialog box and return to the EM Console.
6. In your Navigator tree, you will now find the discovered node. If expanding the tree (by clicking the Nodes entry), you'll see all the discovered services on the target node. The following is an example:

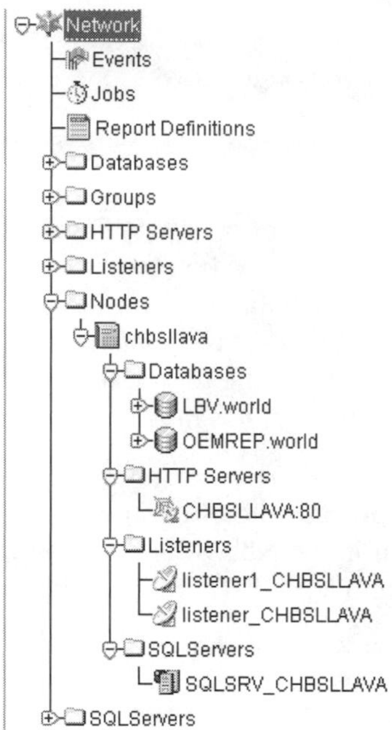

Now you are ready to manage these services from the EM Management Server.

Importing Nodes From a Text File

Instead of manually entering the names of all monitored node names (or IP addresses), you can import this information from a text file. This is useful in EM environments that have a large number of monitored nodes. To import node names, follow the steps listed below:

1. Create a text file containing all the target node names to be discovered. The names must be separated by a comma, space, tab, or new line. Store this file on a drive for later access from the Discovery Wizard.
2. Start the Discovery Wizard from EM Console by choosing the Navigator | Discover Nodes, or by pressing CTRL-D on your keyboard. The Discovery Wizard Introduction screen is shown. Click Next.

3. The Specify Nodes screen for entering node names or IP addresses is shown (see Figure 8-1). Click Import to browse for the file containing the node names.
4. Browse to the file, select it, and click Open to import it, as shown in Figure 8-3.
5. Click Next and the discovery begins. A Progress page appears, showing the status of the node discovery. When the discovery process is complete, a green check mark indicate that the node was discovered successfully and a red X indicates that the discovery has failed. If an error occurs, the error number and text explaining the reason for the error appears. When the discovery of all target nodes has finished, click Finish.
6. Depending on whether there are regular EM administrators, the Access to Targets screen appears, allowing super administrators to control which services will appear in the Navigator for the regular EM administrators. An example is shown in Figure 8-2. Enter this information and click Finish.
7. Finally, a dialog box with a summary of the discovery results is shown. Click OK to return to the EM Console.

In your Navigator tree, you'll now find the discovered nodes and their services.

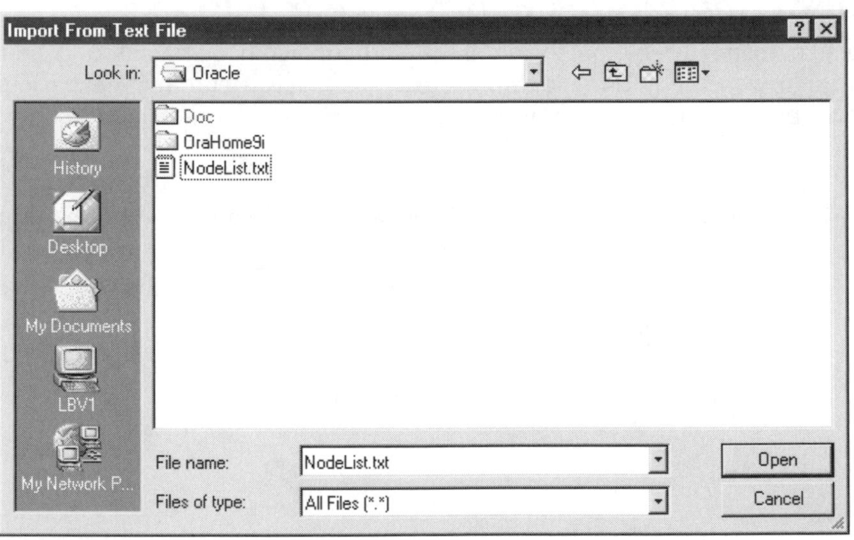

FIGURE 8-3. *Selecting the file to import*

Manually Adding Nodes to the EM Repository

As mentioned earlier in this chapter, you can add nodes and database names to the EM repository manually in case there is no Intelligent Agent available on the target node. When a node is manually discovered or added, no EM jobs can be scheduled, and no EM events can be registered against the node or the database service. To manually add node names, follow these steps:

1. Start the Discovery Wizard from EM Console by selecting Navigator | Discover Nodes, or by pressing CTRL-D. The Introduction screen is displayed. Click Next to continue.
2. The Specify Nodes screen is shown (see Figure 8-1). Enter the node name to be added manually. You can enter several node names separated by a comma, space, tab, or new line. Then click Next.
3. The Progress page appears, showing the status of the node discovery. Because the automatic discovery fails (which you expect it to), a dialog box is displayed. Click OK.
4. Now you are on the progress page, where a red X indicates the failure of the automatic discovery process. This is shown in Figure 8-4. Click Next.
5. The Discovery Wizard Errors page is shown. Because you want to add the node manually, select Manual for the node and click Finish.

NOTE
If you cannot select the Manual entry, this indicates that the specified host cannot be contacted at all. Adding a node manually requires that the Management Server can resolve the host name and contact it across the network.

6. The final step is to add database(s) for the manually added node, which you do in the Manual Configuration screen. Click on each manually added node, and enter the database name, Oracle Net Listener port number, and SID. Repeat this for each database present on the node and click Finish. Figure 8-5 shows adding one database with the name OEMREP and a SID of OEMREP on port number 1521.

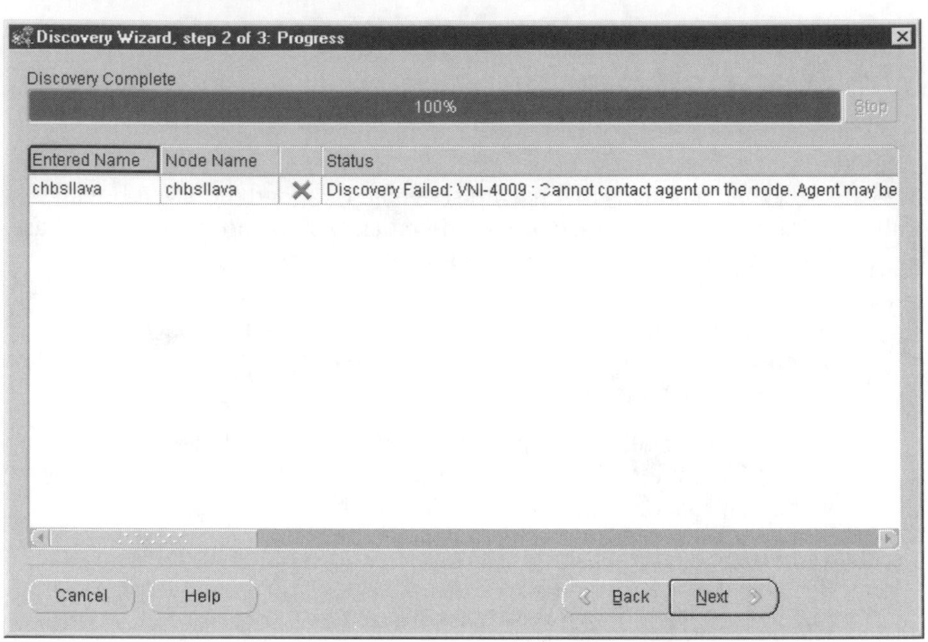

FIGURE 8-4. *Automatic discovery has failed*

7. In your Navigator tree, you'll now find the manually added node, and if you expand it, you'll see the database(s) as well. As you see in the following illustration, only the Databases service type is available for this node:

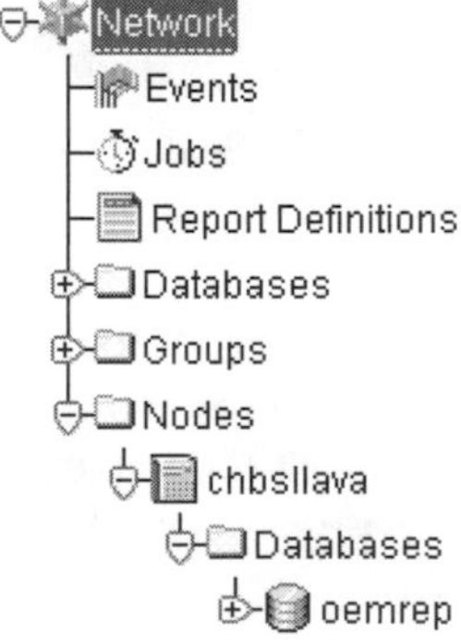

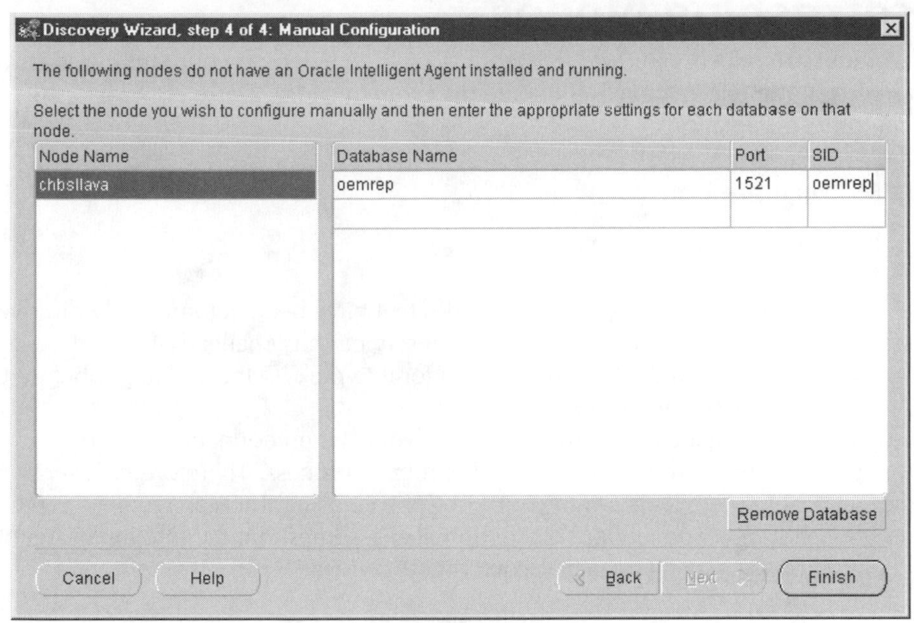

FIGURE 8-5. *Adding a database manually*

As the node has been manually added, no EM jobs can be scheduled and no EM events can be registered against the node or the database services. You can perform database administration against the database services located on that node, just like you would in the standalone mode of the EM console.

NOTE
You must drop manually discovered nodes from the Navigator tree before they can be automatically discovered. You will receive a "VD-4561: Node is manually configured, but an agent is now available for discovery" error if you are trying to discover such a node. Also, a node refresh performed on a manually added node will result in the same error, so you should drop and rediscover the node in this case, too. How to perform a node refresh is explained in the next section.

Refreshing Nodes

If services are added, removed, or in other ways changed on your target nodes, you can refresh the information and update the EM repository. There are two kinds of node refresh operations:

- For a single node
- For all discovered nodes

In both cases, you can only refresh nodes that have been automatically discovered using the Discovery Wizard. If the number of services has changed on a node, notice that you need to restart the Intelligent Agent for it to pick up these changes before the refresh process is started from EM.

Because automatic node discovery only works when connected to the Management Server, the same goes for the refresh process. Therefore, this section assumes that you are logged into your EM Console using the Management Server and not the standalone mode. This section also assumes that the Intelligent Agent is running on the target nodes that you want to refresh.

Refreshing a Single Node

To refresh the information about a single node, perform the following steps:

1. In the EM Console Navigator tree, expand the "Nodes" entry and click the node to be activated.
2. Start the Refresh Wizard from EM Console by right-clicking on the node to be refreshed and select the Refresh Node menu item. You can also invoke the refresh from the menu by selecting Navigator | Refresh Node.
3. The Refresh Wizard screen is shown and a progress bar appears.
4. When the refresh process has finished, the results are shown. A green check mark indicates that the node was refreshed successfully, and a red X indicates that the refresh failed. If an error occurs, the error number and text explaining the reason for the error appear. In Figure 8-6, you see a successful refresh operation of the node CHBSLLAVA. Click Finish.
5. Depending on whether there are any regular EM administrators, the Access to Targets page appears, as described in the Discovery section earlier in this chapter. This screen enables the super administrator to control which services will appear in the Navigator for the regular EM administrators. Check the check boxes for the services you want to grant access to for each regular administrator, and then click Finish.

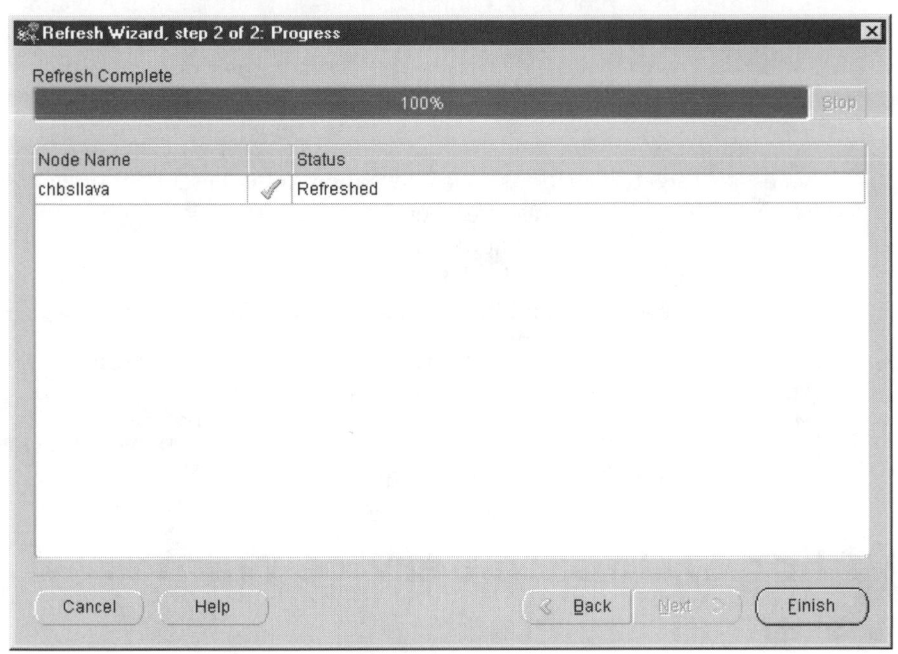

FIGURE 8-6. *After a successful refresh operation*

6. A dialog box with a summary of the refresh results is shown. Click OK to return to the EM Console.

In your Navigator tree, you'll now find the refreshed node and service information.

Refreshing all Discovered Nodes

To refresh the information about all discovered nodes existing in the EM repository, perform the following steps:

1. In the EM Console Navigator tree, do *not* click on a single node. Instead click Nodes, Network, or some other tree item.
2. Start the Refresh Wizard from the EM menu by choosing Navigator | Refresh All Nodes. If you selected the Nodes tree item, right-click and select the Refresh All Nodes menu item.
3. The Refresh Wizard screen is shown and a progress bar appears.

4. When the refresh process has finished, the results are shown. A green check mark indicates that the node was discovered successfully, and a red X indicates that the discovery has failed. If an error occurs, the error number and text explaining the reason for the error appear.

5. Depending on whether there are any regular EM administrators, the Access to Targets page appears, as described in the Discovery section earlier in this chapter. This screen enables the super administrator to control which services will appear in the Navigator for the regular EM administrators. Check the check boxes for the services you want to grant access to for each regular administrator, and then click Finish.

6. A dialog box with a summary of the refresh results is shown. Click OK to return to the EM Console.

7. In your Navigator tree, nodes and services will now be updated with the information from the refresh operation.

Adding Database Service Names in Standalone Mode

Until now, we have been talking about how to discover target nodes and their services automatically using the Discovery Wizard of the Management Server. When working with the EM Console in standalone mode, you can add database service names in two ways:

- Manually entering connection information for each database
- Importing selected TNS aliases from your TNSNAMES.ORA file

NOTE
When adding databases to your EM Navigator tree in standalone mode, the information is stored in encrypted format in a file locally on your machine on a per-user basis. For example, if you are logged into Windows NT as the user Administrator, the information is stored in the EM Oracle Home in the file `dbastudio-Administrator.crd` *in the* `ORACLE_HOME\sysman\config\pref` *directory. The great thing about this file is that it can be copied to another machine, so you do not have to enter the database information and username/password again.*

The following sections describe the two ways of adding database service names to the EM Console in standalone mode.

Manually Entering Database Connection Information

This section describes how to manually add a database to the EM Console Navigator tree in EM standalone mode:

1. Select Navigator | Add Database To Tree. The Add Database To Tree screen is displayed.
2. Choose the Add a database manually check box (which is checked by default).
3. Enter the hostname or IP address, TNS Listener port number, SID, and the database service name (TNS alias). Then click OK to store the information. An example is shown in Figure 8-7, where the LBV1.WORLD database service name is added on the host LBV1 with a SID of LBV1 and port number 1521.

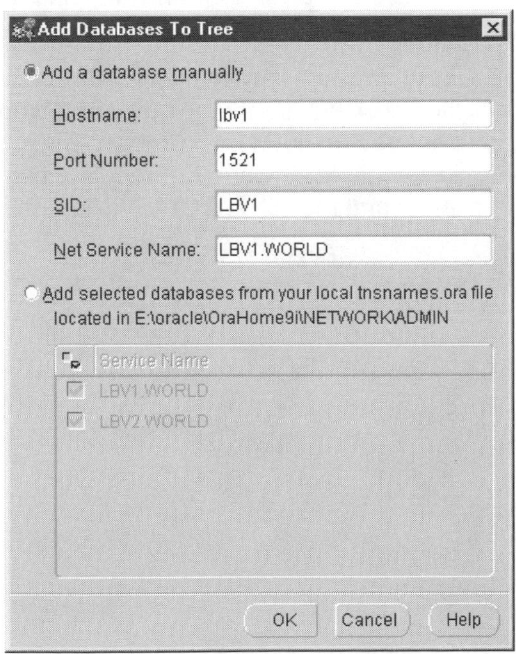

FIGURE 8-7. *Manually adding a database*

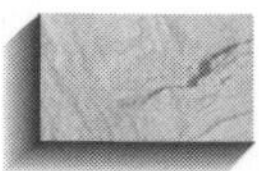

NOTE
The "Add a database manually" function will rearrange the `TNSNAMES.ORA` file after adding databases to the navigator tree. Trying to keep a well-structured `TNSNAMES.ORA` with the different database service names grouped or sorted and with comments is not possible because of this. You might want to back up your `TNSNAMES.ORA` file before invoking EM in standalone mode for the first time.

Importing Database Service Names from TNSNAMES.ORA

Before choosing this option, you must ensure that the `TNSNAMES.ORA` file is stored in the `TNS_ADMIN` location on the machine from where you invoke the EM Console in standalone mode. Then follow these steps:

1. Choose Navigator | Add Database To Tree. The Add Database To Tree screen is displayed.
2. Choose the "Add selected databases from your local tnsnames.ora file" check box.
3. You will see a list of database service names (TNS alias) all marked for import. Check the check box for those you want to import and uncheck the check box for those you do not want to import. Then click OK to store the information. An example is shown in Figure 8-8, where the LBV1.WORLD database is imported and the LBV2.WORLD database is not.

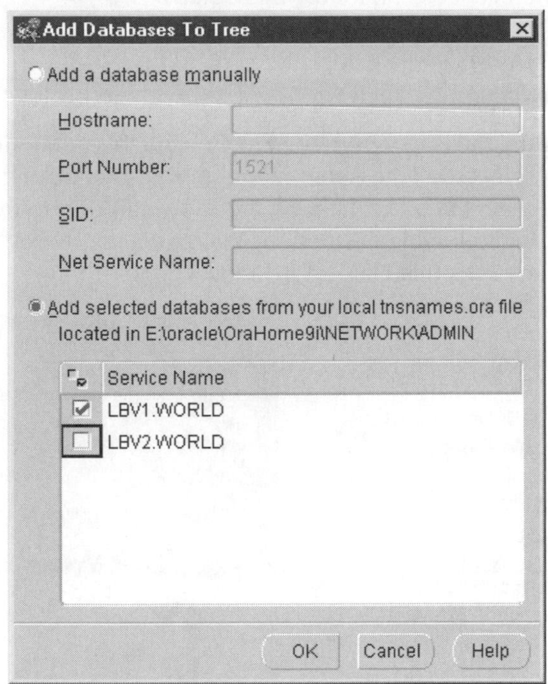

FIGURE 8-8. *Importing a database name*

Pinging an Agent

The Ping Agent function tests the availability of a selected target node by sending a ping message to the Intelligent Agent on that node and waiting for a response. This works much like the TCP/IP ping, or Oracle's TNSPING utilities for testing if a given host or TNS Listener can be contacted across the network.

To use the Ping Agent, you must be logged into your EM Console using the Management Server and not the standalone mode.

To ping the Intelligent Agent, follow these steps:

1. In the EM Console Navigator tree, expand the Nodes entry and click on the node where the Intelligent Agent to be pinged is located.
2. Start the Ping the Agent from the EM Console by right-clicking the selected node and select the Ping Agent menu item or by clicking the Ping Agent button beneath the traffic light on the EM detail part to the right. This is shown in the following illustration. You can also invoke the ping from the EM menu by selecting Navigator | Ping Agent.

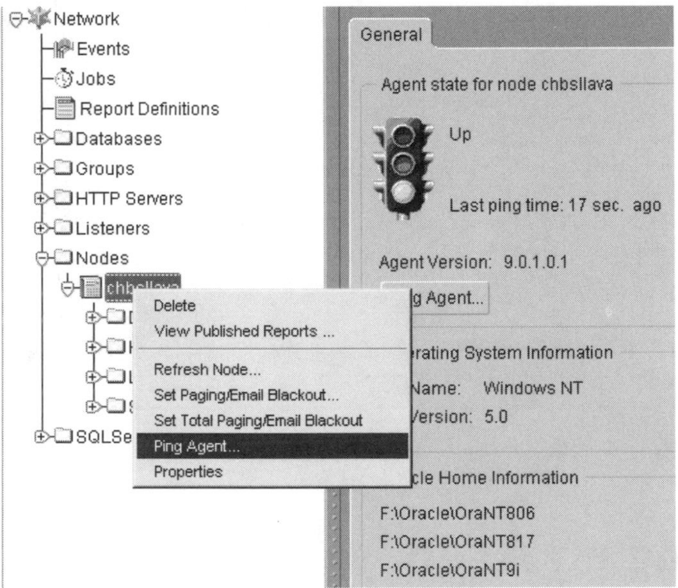

3. A dialog box appears, tracking the ping process.
4. If the Intelligent Agent on the node was pinged successfully, the dialog box will inform you of the success. Click Close to exit the dialog box. If the ping was not successful, an error message is displayed. Click Close to acknowledge the error.

If the ping was successful, the Intelligent Agent is running on the node, but not necessarily the services (database, TNS Listener, HTTP Server) on the node. If the ping was not successful, you know that either the node could not be contacted across the network, or the agent is not running. Ping does not tell anything about the state of the services on the node. For more about troubleshooting the Intelligent Agent, see Chapter 20.

Summary

In this chapter, you have learned how to populate the EM Navigator with the different target nodes and services available on the nodes. You know how to perform automatic discovery as well as how to manually add target nodes and databases, in case you cannot perform automatic discovery. In the section "Adding Database Service Names in Standalone Mode," we showed how to add databases to the navigator tree, when running the EM Console in standalone mode. We have also showed you how you can refresh already discovered target nodes, for example if you have added services (e.g., listener, database, or HTTP server) since the last discovery. As mentioned in the introduction to this chapter, we recommend that you complete some basic configuration within the EM Console before you begin working with your target nodes. In the next chapter, we will take a look at the configuration of EM and the different options available in the Configuration menu of the EM Console.

CHAPTER 9

Configuring Your EM Environment

This chapter describes the different areas of configuration within the EM environment. Some configurations you might want to do before discovering your target nodes (covered in Chapter 8). These include configuring paging and e-mail services, defining the super and regular administrators of EM, and defining Management Regions, if required. Other configurations are done after the target node and service discovery and throughout the life cycle of your EM environment. All configuration tasks are done from the Configuration menu of the EM Console. This menu is available when you are connected to the Management Server, and a couple of the settings are also available in standalone mode. This chapter focuses on the configurations available while connected to a Management Server, but the configurations available in standalone mode are covered where appropriate.

Managing Administrators

The first thing you probably want to configure in EM is to create the different EM administrators, for example, the DBAs who will be using EM to manage your environment. With EM version 2.*x* and higher, multiple EM administrators can log in to a single repository, thereby sharing the objects in the repository.

NOTE
When multiple administrators are logged into the OMS, remember that the last update performed to shared objects will be the one saved.

You can, of course, still choose to run with multiple EM repositories, if you need to keep certain areas of your environment separated, but then there can be no sharing of objects between these repositories.

Normal Administrators Versus Super Administrators

With EM9i, you can define two types of EM administrators:

- Super administrator
- Normal or regular administrator

Super administrators grant access to the target nodes and the managed services to the regular administrators. This is known as the *Customizable Console*, because each regular administrator's view is reflected by the access to specific targets.

NOTE
EM administrators are only administrators within the EM environment for managing EM jobs, events, groups, and the different services registered. These administrator accounts have nothing to do with database users. The only database user or schema involved is the one in which the EM repository is stored.

The following sections describe the difference between super and regular EM administrators. We will then show you how to maintain these two types of administrators within EM.

Super Administrator

The super administrator is the highest level of administrator within the EM environment. One super administrator account always exists by default in your EM environment: the SYSMAN account. This is pretty much like the SYS account, which always exists in an Oracle database, or the root account on your Unix/Linux system. The name of this administrator is fixed; only the password can be changed, and this user cannot be deleted. You must log in to the Management Server the first time using the SYSMAN account, but after you have created other super/regular administrators in EM, you might not want to use the SYSMAN account anymore, just as you normally would not connect to your database as SYS or to your UNIX system as root when doing your daily work.

NOTE
When logging in to the OMS using the Management Server for the first time, the password for SYSMAN is default set to OEM_TEMP (passwords are not case sensitive). You will be prompted to change this password at your first login to the EM Management Server, which we strongly recommend.

A super administrator has the following characteristics:

- Can start and stop the Management Server
- Can discover, refresh, and remove managed nodes and services
- Has full privileges for all objects
- Can manage other administrators (super and regular)
- Can modify all settings and configurations within EM

NOTE
In addition to the SYSMAN super administrator account, another super administrator is automatically created when the EM repository is created. This is the REPORTS_USER, which is used by the Enterprise Manager Reporting Website. This administrator also has the default password OEM_TEMP. We discuss the EM reports in detail in Chapter 13.

Normal Administrator

The normal or regular EM administrators are defined by EM super administrators and require specific access granted to the objects that they are allowed to manage. Further, they can be granted access to use the job and event system within EM, and they have limited access to the Configuration menu.

Managing Administrators

This section describes how to maintain the two types of EM administrators through the Manage Administrators menu item.

NOTE
The Manage Administrators menu item in the Configuration menu is only available for EM super administrators.

You can choose to add administrators reflecting your organization. For example, you could create personal EM administrator accounts, where your DBAs are super administrators and developers are regular administrators with access to relevant nodes, such as the job scheduling system. You can also choose to create two or more EM administrators per DBA, reflecting different work areas and tasks performed in the EM environment. Or, you can choose to define non personal administrator accounts for special areas or roles in the administration. For example, you could use the UNIXDBA, WINDBA, and WEBADMIN administrator accounts for DBAs on Unix and Windows and webmasters, respectively. Several administrators can log in to the OMS using the same EM account without any problems. In most cases, the personalized accounts should be preferred, enabling you to define responsibility and notification specifically for each person within your IT department.

Adding Administrators

To add an EM administrator, login to the OMS as an EM super administrator, and follow these steps:

1. Select Configuration | Manage Administrators, or press CTRL-M.
2. The Manage Administrator Accounts dialog appears, as shown in Figure 9-1. The existing administrator accounts are listed, and you can choose to add, modify, or delete an EM administrator. Because you want to add a new administrator, click Add.
3. The Create Administrator Account screen appears. Enter a unique EM administrator username and initial password, including password confirmation. Specify whether this EM administrator is a super administrator by checking the Super Administrator account check box. Access to job and event system can be granted through the check boxes Access to job system and Access to event system, respectively.

NOTE
Granting a regular administrator access to the EM event and job system does not automatically give access to all events and jobs. Access must be granted on these individually by the owner or by a super administrator.

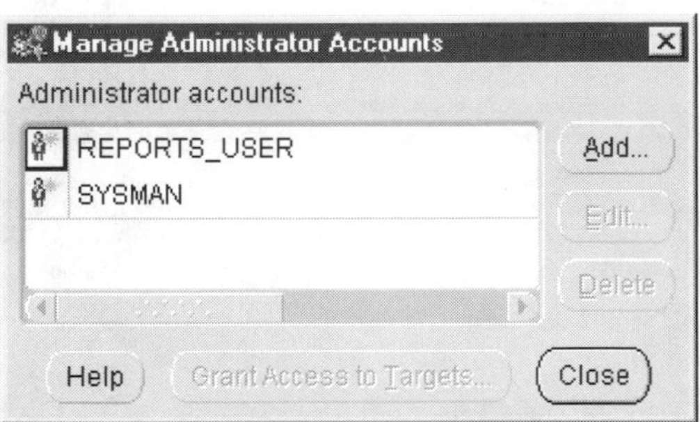

FIGURE 9-1. *Managing administrators from EM*

4. Click OK to complete EM administrator creation and to return to the Manage Administrator Accounts window.

NOTE
If you create an EM super administrator by checking the Super Administrator account check box, you cannot grant specific access to the job or event system. EM super administrators always have full access to the EM environment, meaning all targets and all jobs and events.

5. If you have created a regular EM administrator, you need to grant specific access to target nodes and discovered services. You can do this now or do it when you discover the target nodes (see Chapter 8). To grant access now, click the Grant Access to Targets button in the Manage Administrator Accounts dialog box. The Access to Targets screen is shown where you grant access to target nodes and services by checking the check box for each object (see also the section "Granting Access to Targets" later in this chapter). Enter the appropriate information and click OK. Figure 9-2 shows that access to the SUSE1 database has been granted to the regular administrator LBV.
6. You are now back in the Manage Administrator Accounts screen, where you can continue adding other EM administrators or click Close to exit and return to the EM Console.

If you now log into the OMS as the newly created regular EM administrator LBV, your EM navigator tree will look like the following illustration:

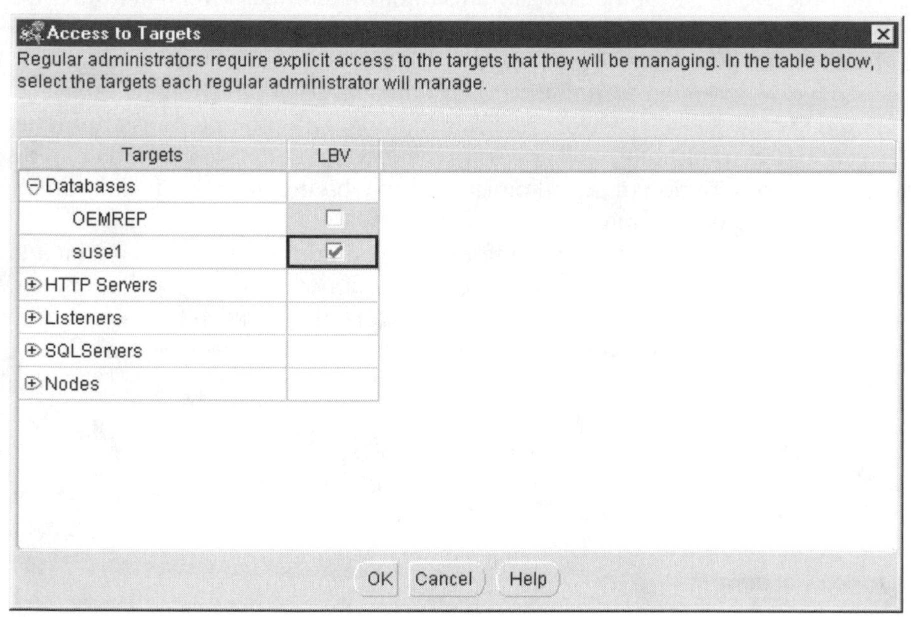

FIGURE 9-2. *Granting access to specific targets after adding a user*

After you have created EM administrators, you can log into the OMS and set up administrator preferences. This is done through the Edit feature of the Manage Administrator Accounts screen and is described next.

Modifying Administrator Preferences

Just as you can create new EM administrators, you can also modify the existing ones. You will find that there is much more information available for you to modify than you created. The following steps show you how to modify administrator preferences. You must be logged into the OMS as a super administrator.

1. Select Configuration | Manage Administrators, or press CTRL-M.
2. The Manage Administrator Accounts dialog box appears (see Figure 9-1). Because you want to modify an administrator, click the administrator you want to modify and then click Edit (or double-click the administrator you want to modify). The Edit Administrator preferences screen appears.

The different pages of the Edit Administrator preferences screen are described in the section "Modifying Your Preferences" later in this chapter.

There is one difference when modifying the preferences for another administrator. This concerns modifying the information on the first page, the General tab.

You can change the password, the status of the particular administrator (change to/from super administrator) and access to the job and event system. You can also add a textual description of the administrator, maybe including contact information such as a mobile phone number.

If you change a regular administrator to a super administrator by checking the "Super Administrator account" check box, you will not need to grant specific access to the job or event system. EM super administrators always have full access to the EM environment, meaning all targets and both the job and event system.

NOTE
You will not be able to change the SYSMAN built-in super administrator into a regular administrator, not even if you are logged in as SYSMAN. You can only change the password and the description for this account.

Deleting Administrators

Just as administrators can be created and modified, they can also be deleted. There is no other way to lock an administrator account, except by changing the password. If you delete an administrator who is the owner of any objects, you need to reassign object ownership to another EM administrator. Otherwise, you must delete all owned objects first.

To delete an EM administrator, log into the EM Console as a super administrator, and follow these steps:

1. Select Configuration | Manage Administrators, or press CTRL-M.
2. The Manage Administrator Accounts dialog appears (see Figure 9-1). Because you want to delete an administrator, click the administrator you want to delete, and then click Delete. Now an Administrator deletion dialog box appears, where you must confirm the deletion. Click Yes to continue with the deletion of the administrator.

If you delete an administrator, and the administrator owns any objects, such as jobs or events, a dialog box will show up enabling you to reassign the objects to another administrator. Even registered events and jobs can be reassigned. If you do not want to reassign the objects, you must delete them before deleting the administrator.

It is possible to change the ownership of EM objects in general, such as jobs, events, or groups. This is done for each single object, for jobs in the Job Library, and for events in the Event Library. You change the ownership in the object properties via the Owner drop-down list on the Access page.

NOTE

To change ownership of an EM object, you must be logged into the OMS as a super administrator or as the regular administrator who is the object owner.

Granting Access to Targets

EM super administrators control what the regular administrators see in the EM Console Navigator through the Access to Targets dialog box, thereby creating customized Navigators for these administrators. The super administrator accounts do not need specific access to targets and their services, because they always have full access to all EM objects.

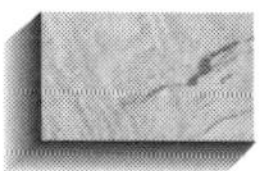

NOTE

You must be logged into the OMS as a super administrator in order to grant access. Granting access to objects does not apply when running the EM Console in standalone mode.

You can choose to grant access to targets and their services when these are discovered (see Chapter 8), or when creating regular administrators (see the "Adding Administrators" section earlier in this chapter). You can reach the Access to Targets screen in the following ways:

- Select Configuration | Grant Access to Targets.

- Select Configuration | Manage Administrators (or press CTRL-M) and then click the Grant Access to Targets button in the Manage Administrator Accounts dialog box.
- After having successfully discovered or refreshed targets.

All of these operations should result in the Access to Targets screen being displayed (it is not displayed if no targets have been discovered or refreshed). This dialog box contains a multi-column list. The first column shows all the different types of services that can be managed by EM. Clicking on the plus sign next to the name of the object type expands it (the Database service type is always expanded). There is one column for each regular EM administrator defined, and you grant access to a certain service by checking the appropriate check box. In the same way, you can revoke access by unchecking the check box for this particular service.

Enter the appropriate information for each administrator by expanding the different types of services and checking the check box for each object you want to grant access to. Then click OK to store the information. Figure 9-3 shows an example.

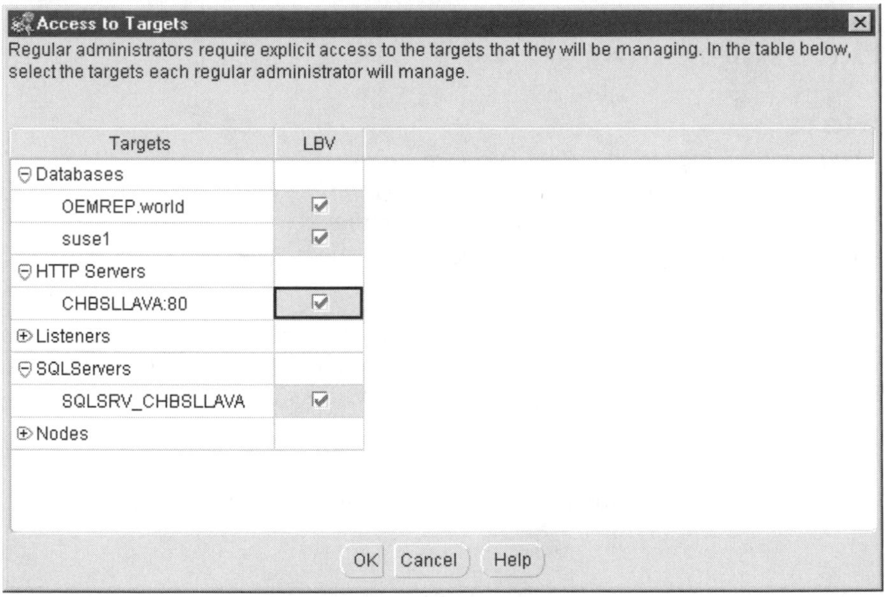

FIGURE 9-3. *Granting access to specific targets*

Modifying Your Preferences

Most programs contain an option for entering set up information, such as Settings, Options, or Preferences. In EM, this information is accessible through Configuration | Preferences. If you are a super administrator, you can also change the preferences of other EM administrators. This process is explained earlier in this chapter in the "Managing Administrators" section.

To modify your own Preferences, log into the OMS. Select Configuration | Preferences, or press CTRL-P. The Edit Administrator Preferences screen appears, as shown in Figure 9-4.

The Edit Administrator Preferences screen contains the following pages, which you can switch between by clicking on the respective tabs:

- General
- Notification

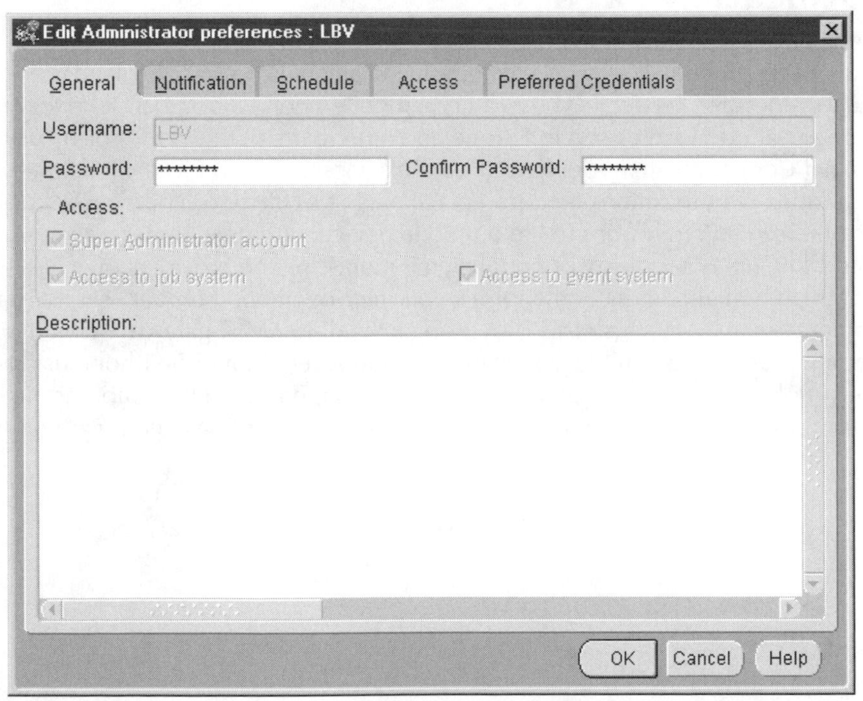

FIGURE 9-4. *Editing administrator preferences*

- Schedule
- Access
- Preferred Credentials

When you enter the Edit Administrator preferences screen, you are placed on the first page, the General page. The following sections take a closer look at each of these administrator configuration areas.

General Page

On the General page, you can change your password and the textual description of the administrator. You cannot change your own status as administrator or your access to the EM job and event systems (the Access area is ghosted out). Not even a super administrator can change his or her own status; this can only be done by another super administrator.

Notification Page

You can use the Notification page to send messages to each EM administrator, via e-mail, pager, or both, known as *enhanced* notifications. You can also send notifications via Short Message Service (SMS) to a GSM mobile phone (Global System for Mobile communication, widely used in Europe and other parts of the world) or by using Personal Communications Services (PCS) Text Messaging (in the United States). These kinds of notifications tend to replace paging notification, but you cannot send a text message directly from EM to a mobile device; you need a message forwarding service, known as a gateway or portal. Some mobile phone providers offer this service through an e-mail address of the form *<your mobile phone number>@<provider>*. Another way to accomplish this is by using a "mail-to-SMS" gateway, which polls a certain mail address and forwards messages to a certain mobile phone using SMS. An example of such a gateway is WWW.2SMS.CH, provided by Dolphins Network Systems. Remember that mobile phones have a maximum message length of 160 characters.

NOTE

To use enhanced notification via e-mail and/or pager, you should first complete the basic configuration by selecting Configuration | Configure Paging/Email. This is explained later in this chapter in the "Configuring E-mail and Paging" section. On the Notification tab, you can modify information about how and in which cases the administrator is to be notified about the status of submitted EM jobs and events. Through the filtering defined on this page, you ensure that only relevant information is sent to the administrator, and that it is sent in the desired way. In addition, you can define how the mail or pager message is composed (header and body message parts), and you can restrict the length of the message.

As shown in Figure 9-5, the left part of the Notification screen is a hierarchical navigator tree containing three parts: Filters, E-mail, and Paging. The right side changes according to your selection in the navigator tree.

NOTE

With the first release of EM9i (9.0.1.0.0), you can only enter one e-mail address per EM administrator. Workaround is to either create additional "dummy" EM administrator accounts only for notification purposes or to use an e-mail address, which will forward to several e-mail addresses. Also, a patch has been provided by Oracle Corporation (patch name EM_901_1847262, patch set 1847205), which enables you to enter multiple e-mail addresses.

E-mail and Pager Filtering

When you click the Notification tab, the Filters entry is selected by default. The right side of the screen shows the Notification Filters. The upper half of this page defines the notification for e-mail and pagers for EM events (Event Filters); the lower half defines the notification for EM jobs (Job Filters).

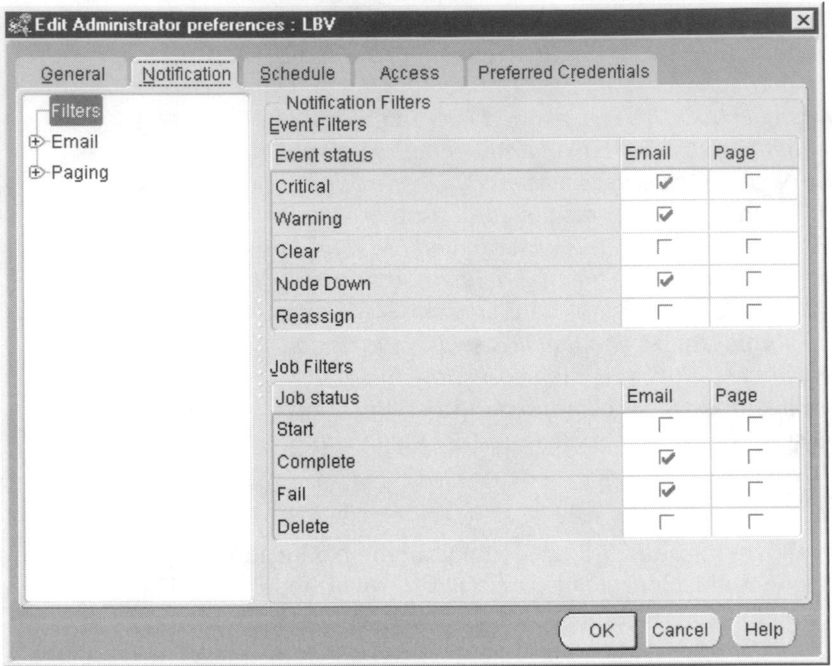

FIGURE 9-5. *Specifying notification preferences*

An EM event can have one of the following severity levels:

- **Critical** The event reached Critical threshold.
- **Warning** The event reached Warning threshold.
- **Clear** The event has been cleared (the problem is gone).
- **Node Down** The target node or the Intelligent Agent is down.
- **Reassign** The event has been reassigned (see the "Deleting Administrators" section earlier in this chapter).

An EM job can have the following status:

- **Start** The job has been started.
- **Complete** The job has completed successfully.

- **Fail** The job has failed.
- **Delete** The job was deleted.

You can set filtering at the user level by checking or unchecking the E-mail or Page check boxes for each desired severity level or status. In the example shown in Figure 9-5, the EM administrator LBV will be notified by e-mail if an event has reached the Critical, Warning, or Node Down severity level, or when a job has reached Complete or Fail status.

E-mail Preferences

The second part of the Notification screen is the E-mail Preferences page, which you access by selecting E-mail on the navigator tree. Here, you define how the administrator can be reached via e-mail. You must enter the e-mail address for the EM administrator. Optionally, you can enter a prefix used in the subject of the mail message, which can be useful for organizing your incoming messages. You can also restrict the length of the message to a specified number of characters; by default, the message length is unlimited. In the example shown in Figure 9-6, the administrator

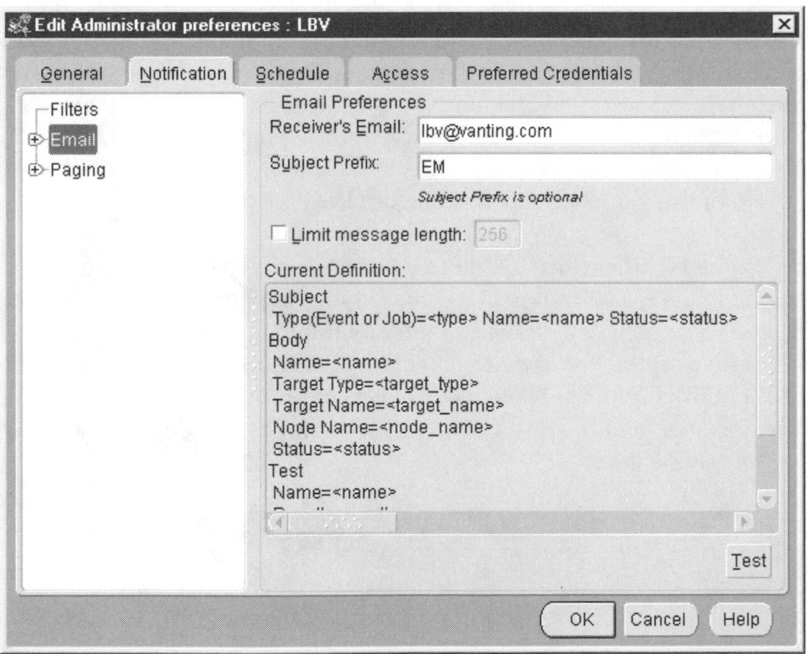

FIGURE 9-6. *Configuring e-mail preferences*

LBV is notified through the address lbv@vanting.com, and mail messages are prefixed with "EM."

Testing E-mail Notification You can test EM's e-mail configuration from this page by clicking the Test button at the bottom of the page.

During this test, the Management Server tries to send a message using the configurations and e-mail address you entered. A dialog box is displayed, showing the progress and the result of the test.

Viewing and Modifying the Composition of the E-mail Message The current format of the e-mail message is displayed in the Current Definition section. If you want to change this format, expand the E-mail object in the tree list and select the format and content options for either the Subject line or the Message Body. You can also specify options at a per-event test level (Name, Result, Status, and Timestamp) by expanding the Message Body object further.

Paging Preferences

The third part of the Notification screen is the Paging Preferences page, which you access by selecting Paging on the navigator tree. Here you define how to reach the administrator via pager. You must enter the name of the Paging Carrier and, if the recipient is using an alphanumeric pager, also the PIN. Optionally, you can restrict the length of the message to a specified number of characters. By default, the length is limited to 256 characters for pager messages. Pagers may have varying message lengths from 20 up to 400 characters, depending on the type. For pagers using TAP (Telocator Alphanumeric Protocol), the maximum length is 250 characters and for the FLEX-TD protocol it is 50 multi-byte characters or 100 single-byte characters. An example of this screen is shown in Figure 9-7.

Testing Pager Notification You can test EM's pager configuration from this page by clicking the Test button at the bottom of the page. For alphanumeric pagers, a popup is displayed where you enter the PIN number, then click Send.

When you start the test, the Management Server tries to send a paging message using the specified settings. The code 700 is sent for numeric pagers. A dialog box shows the progress and the result of the test. The following illustration shows a successful paging test:

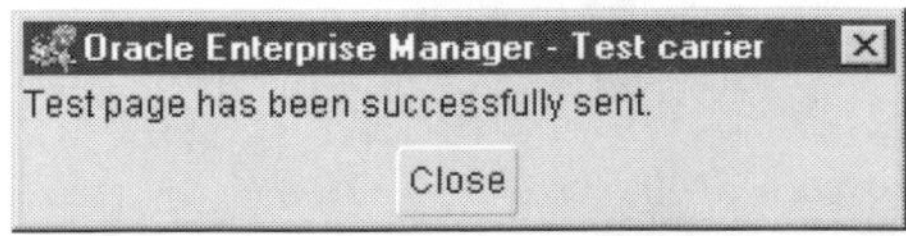

Viewing and Modifying the Composition of the Paging Message The current format of the message is displayed in the Current Definition section. If you want to

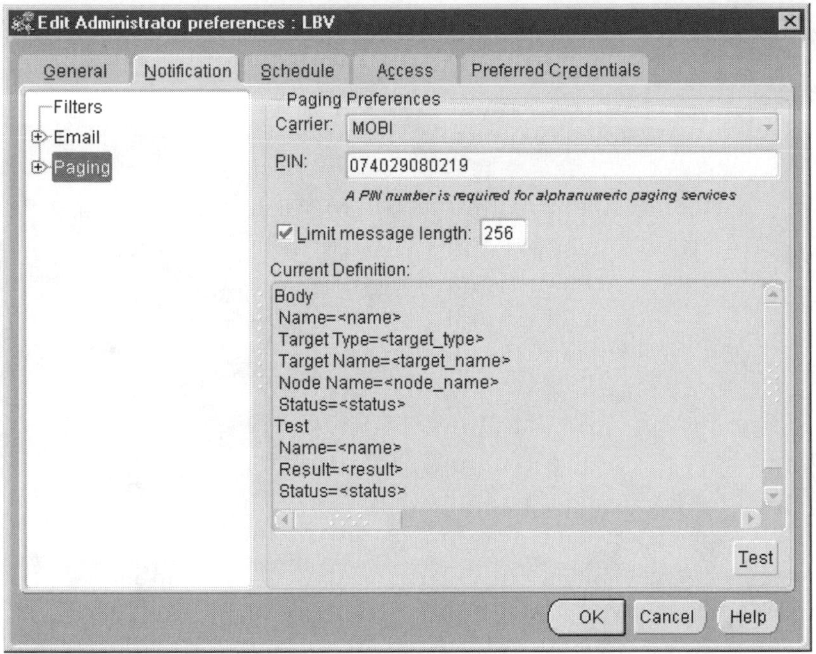

FIGURE 9-7. *Configuring pager preferences*

change this format, expand the Paging object in the tree list and select the format and content options for the Message Body. As with the e-mail message body, you can also specify options at a per-event test level.

Schedule Page

The third page of the Edit Administrator Preferences screen is the Schedule page. Each EM administrator can have his or her own schedule defined, which specifies when and how the administrator is to be notified as specified on the Notification tab. As you can see in Figure 9-8, you can specify the following settings:

- No notification (white)
- Notification via pager only (red)
- Notification via e-mail only (cyan)
- Notification via pager and e-mail (purple)

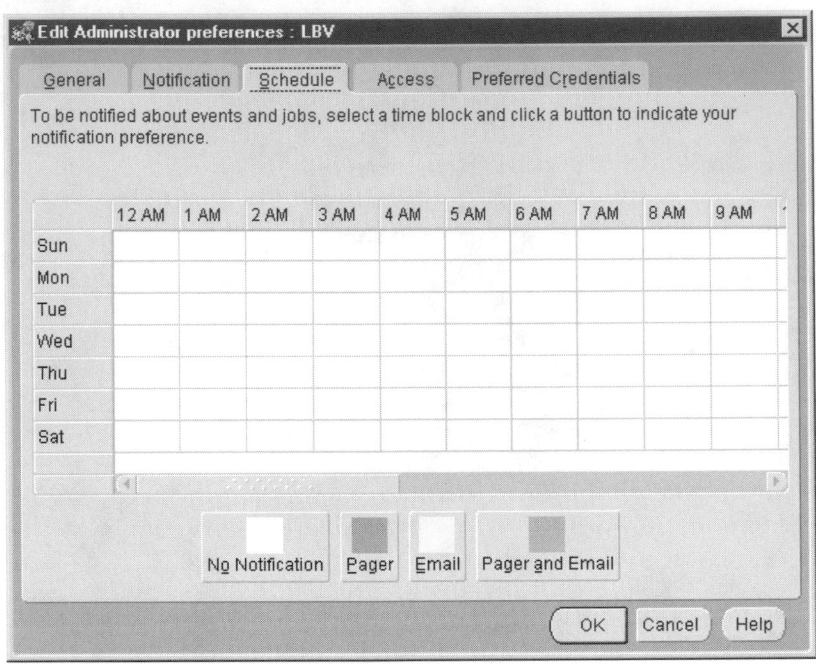

FIGURE 9-8. *Setting your notification schedule*

Paging is normally used for urgent events or critical systems. You can also switch between the two notification methods during the day or week. For example, you might use e-mail during office hours and paging when you are not in the office.

It is important to define a schedule for each EM administrator if you work in an environment with many managed and monitored nodes, and when many DBAs work in different teams and shifts. You must remember to specify a schedule, or you won't be notified at all via e-mail or pager. When you first access the schedule page, it is set to No Notification at all times by default.

To define the schedule for the administrator and indicate when to be notified per pager, e-mail, or both, you must first click one day-hour intersection block. Then click the method of notification (red, cyan, or purple) you want for the marked period of time. You can set the same notification for an entire day, or for the same hour every day, by clicking on the heading for that row or column. Only one row or column can be marked at a time. You can also mark several different blocks by keeping the CTRL key pressed while clicking the blocks. You can drag the cursor using the mouse (or use the keyboard by holding down the SHIFT key while using the arrow keys) to mark multiple blocks. Now notification in this time period will be enabled.

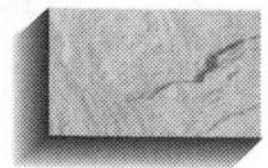

NOTE
You will only receive notifications for events and jobs occurring in the time interval specified, and only for the objects you have permission to access.

To disable notification, first mark the time period, and then click No Notification (white).

Access

Each EM administrator can define other regular administrators' default access privileges to objects (groups, jobs, and events) he or she creates. You can also indicate whether notification should be enabled per default for the objects created. You enter this information on the fourth page of the Edit Administrator Preferences screen, the Access page (see Figure 9-9).

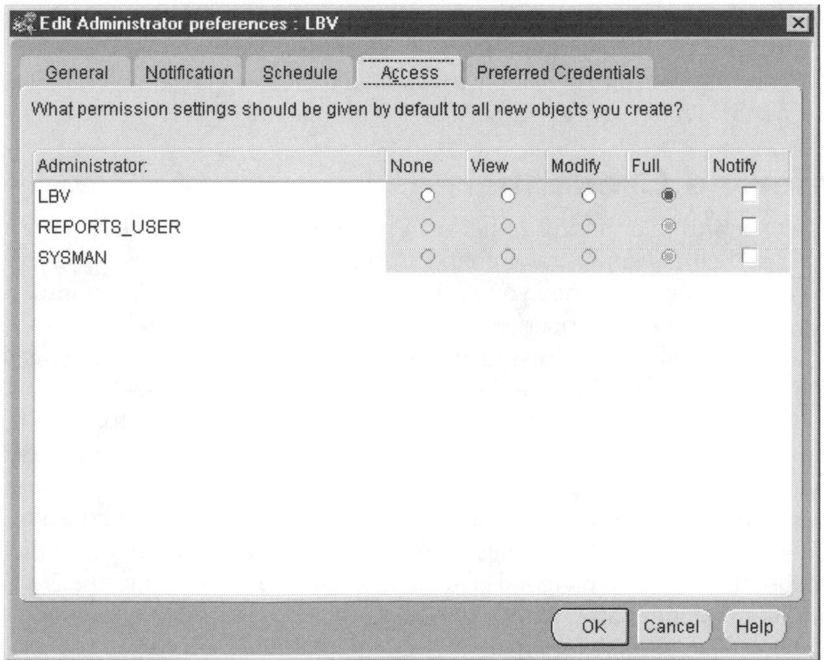

FIGURE 9-9. *Editing administrator preferences*

The different levels of permission that you can assign to administrators are

- **None** The administrator has no permission to view this object.
- **View** The administrator can view the object, view object properties, and receive notifications.
- **Modify** The administrator is allowed to edit the object's properties (except those for which you need full permission).
- **Full** The administrator has full access to the object, and can delete the object, modify permissions for other administrators, and change the ownership of the object.

You set the permission level for each regular administrator by clicking on the permission in the row for that particular administrator.

When an administrator creates an object, the creator automatically has full permission, as the object's owner, and these permissions cannot be modified. Super administrators always have full permissions.

Notification for newly created objects is enabled the same way. When you check the Notify check box, the administrator is allowed to receive notifications for the object. You cannot assign the Notify permission if the permission level is set to None for that administrator.

Preferred Credentials

Each EM administrator has his or her own set of preferred credentials, which define how this particular administrator connects to the different services managed by EM. The credentials are used when you access a service in the Navigator or from a group. If the credentials are set properly, an administrator only needs to log in once to the OMS, and then will have access to any service without having to log in again.

The last page of the Edit Administrator Preferences screen (see Figure 9-10) contains the preferred credentials for the particular EM administrator. This feature is available in both EM standalone and Management Server modes. Because there are many more types of services available when using a Management Server, the number of preferred credentials is much higher than for a standard console. You can define default login credentials for each type of managed service, which are used if the service has no preferred credentials entered. When running the EM Console in standalone mode, you can also store preferred credentials, but only for services of database type, and the information is stored in a file in encrypted format. Both types of credentials are described in the following sections.

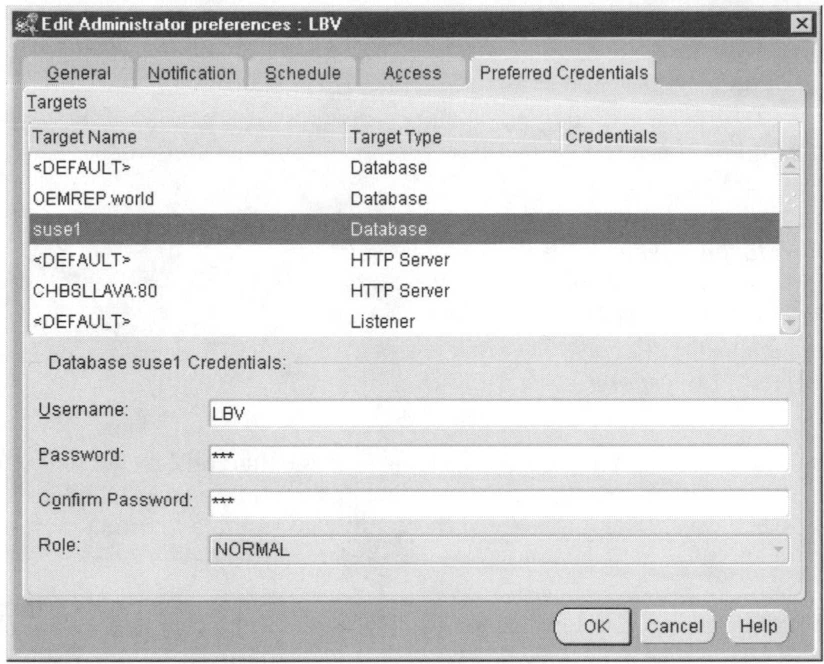

FIGURE 9-10. *Specifying preferred credentials*

Maintaining Preferred Credentials While Connected to the Management Server

Each row in the list shown in Figure 9-10 represents a single service of a given target type and includes the following attributes:

- **Target Name** The name of the target node or service.
- **Target Type** Can be one of the following: Database, HTTP Server, Listener, Node, Data Guard Configuration, Real Application Cluster, or SQL Server (specified by "oracle_sysman_sqlserver").
- **Credentials** A check mark in this column indicates that connection information has been specified.

You can click on a column heading to sort by that column. You cannot enter login credentials for services of type HTTP Server or SQL Server.

Entering Default Preferred Credentials If some services of a particular type require the same credentials, it is very useful to use the <DEFAULT> setting. This setting is available for each of the categories of services where credentials can be entered. If no login credentials are found for a particular service, the values of the <DEFAULT> entry are used. If no default credentials are found, or if the credentials are not valid for this target, you will be prompted for login credentials.

NOTE
Individual instances of a Real Application Cluster, formerly known as Oracle Parallel Server, are not listed. You should choose to use the same credentials for all individual instances as for the Real Application Cluster itself.

To enter the <DEFAULT> value, you can sort the target list by clicking on the Target Name column heading, thereby listing all available <DEFAULT> entries in the top. Click on a particular entry and enter the appropriate information for that <DEFAULT> value, which varies depending on the target type.

Entering Preferred Credentials for the Database Service Type The Database preferred credentials are used when you connect to a database in the EM Navigator (expanding the plus sign), when submitting EM jobs and events, or when you generate reports against a database through the EM Reporting Website. The preferred credentials for a Database service type (or the <DEFAULT> credentials for databases) consist of the following login information:

- **Username** The Oracle operating system usename for logging into this database
- **Password** The password for this Oracle user
- **Confirm Password** The password for this Oracle user again, for confirmation
- **Role** Choose the mode (NORMAL, SYSDBA, or SYSOPER)

Enter the appropriate login credentials and click OK to save the information. In Figure 9-10, the EM administrator LBV connects to the SUSE1 database using the Oracle user LBV in NORMAL mode:

NOTE
You must login with the SYSDBA or SYSOPER role to start up or shut down a database.

If you are connecting as the user SYS on an Oracle8, Oracle8i, or Oracle9i database, you must use the Role SYSDBA or SYSOPER if the database initialization parameter O7_DICTIONARY_ACCESSIBILITY is set to FALSE. This parameter was introduced in Oracle8 to be used when migrating from Oracle7. Many system or object privileges can be granted with maximum scope by adding the *any* keyword to the grant statement. For example, GRANT SELECT ANY TABLE TO LBV, instead of granting individual object privileges such as GRANT SELECT ON X.TABLE_A TO LBV; GRANT SELECT ON Y.TABLE_B TO LBV; If the parameter is set to TRUE (Oracle7 behavior and default in Oracle8 and 8i), access to objects in the data dictionary (SYS schema) is allowed. When set to FALSE (default in Oracle9i), access privileges do *not* allow access to objects in SYS schema, unless access to PUBLIC has been granted explicitly. It is recommended to keep this parameter set to FALSE and grant SELECT_CATALOG_ROLE, EXECUTE_CATALOG_ROLE or DELETE_CATALOG_ROLE to the accounts for which access to the data dictionary must be provided.

It is not possible to specify database login using *externally identified* Oracle user accounts by using the external authentication (OPS$) feature to provide single sign-on (by specifying a forward slash "/" as username). You must specify a username and password for each database login.

Entering Preferred Credentials for the Listener Service Type When you are entering preferred credentials for a particular Listener service type or the <DEFAULT> credentials, you can enter the following login information:

- **Password** The password for this Oracle user
- **Confirm Password** The password for this Oracle user for confirmation

These entries only apply if you have enabled a password for your TNS Listener. Enter the password and the confirmation, and click OK to save the information.

Entering Preferred Credentials for the Node Service Type When entering preferred credentials for a particular Target node or the <DEFAULT> credentials, you can enter the following login information:

- **Username** The username for logging in to the target node
- **Password** The password for this user
- **Confirm Password** The password for this user again, for confirmation

Enter the appropriate login credentials and click OK to save the information.

NOTE
It is possible to specify a network user account by including a domain when specifying the username for a Windows node, e.g., MYDOMAIN\LBV for the user LBV in the domain MYDOMAIN. Notice that if a local user with the same name exists (in this case, LBV), this local account will override the network account.The preferred credentials are required by the Intelligent Agent when submitting jobs and registering events. You must provide login credentials for the target node where you want to submit jobs and events. If you do not set the preferred credentials correctly, jobs and events will fail. We discuss EM jobs and events further in Chapters 11 and 12.

NOTE
Changes to the Preferred Credentials are not updated for already registered jobs and events. To update these jobs and events to reflect new preferred credentials, you must deregister and then re-register the jobs and events.

Maintaining Preferred Credentials in Standalone Mode

The preferred credentials in standalone mode are reduced to database connection information. You maintain them in the following way:

1. Start the EM Console in standalone mode.
2. Choose Configuration | Edit Local Preferred Credentials. Now the Edit Local Preferred Credentials screen appears, as shown in Figure 9-11.

The names of database services that have been added to the navigator are listed. For each database, you can enter the following login information:

- **Username** The Oracle username for logging into this database
- **Password** The password for this Oracle user
- **Confirm Password** The password for this Oracle user, for confirmation
- **Role** Choose the mode (NORMAL, SYSDBA, or SYSOPER)

Enter the appropriate login credentials, and click OK to save the information.

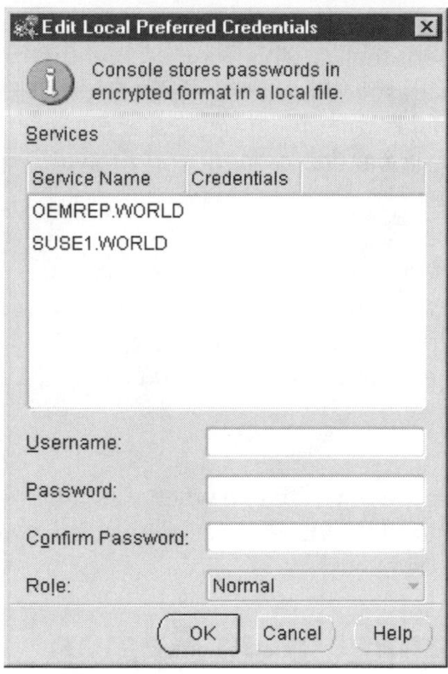

FIGURE 9-11. *Editing local preferred credentials in standalone mode*

In Standalone mode, it is possible to specify database login using *externally identified* Oracle user accounts, meaning you are using the external authentication (OPS$) feature to provide single sign-on. You do this by simply specifying a slash in the Username field and leaving the other fields empty. Other settings are required in your database and Oracle Net; refer to the Oracle documentation for more about how to configure the single sign-on feature.

Defining Management Regions

Some EM users maintaining environments in larger WANs, such as international companies with databases spread around the globe, have been noticing a high network traffic between the Management Server and Intelligent Agent components. With previous EM releases you could not reflect the network topology of the company in the configuration of the EM environment. Even having several local Management Servers would not guarantee that an Intelligent Agent did not communicate with a Management Server on the other side of the globe. This problem has been addressed in EM9i by defining *Management Regions* within EM, which are designations that reflect the network topology of your organization.

A Management Region is a subset of the managed nodes and the existing Management Servers. A particular node or management server is a member of one and only one management region. This way, the Intelligent Agents are instructed to communicate only with specific Management Server(s) and vice versa, thereby eliminating cross-regional communication. Advantages of having Management Regions are obvious for global deployment and firewall support.

NOTE
If no Management Server is available to service a particular Management Region, you can log on using a Management Server from a different region. You will be able to see all nodes in all Management Regions.

Management Regions are not available when running the EM Console in standalone mode. You must be logged into the OMS as a super administrator to maintain Management Regions.

Creating a Management Region

When you create the EM repository, the DEFAULT Management Region is defined. If you discover target nodes and services before creating additional Management Regions, all services are assigned to the DEFAULT region. To create additional Management Regions follow this step:

1. Select Configuration | Define Management Regions.
2. The Management Regions screen appears, as shown in Figure 9-12.
3. The existing Management Region names are listed, and the following attributes are displayed:
   - **Monitored** A check mark indicates that the management region is being monitored. If there is at least one active Management Server in the management region, it is considered to be monitored. This has nothing to do with the presence of EM events for monitoring purposes.
   - **Region Name** The name of the Management Region
   - **Total Management Servers** The total number of Management Servers in this region
   - **Active Management Servers** The number of currently active Management Servers within this region
   - **Nodes** The number of target nodes assigned to this region

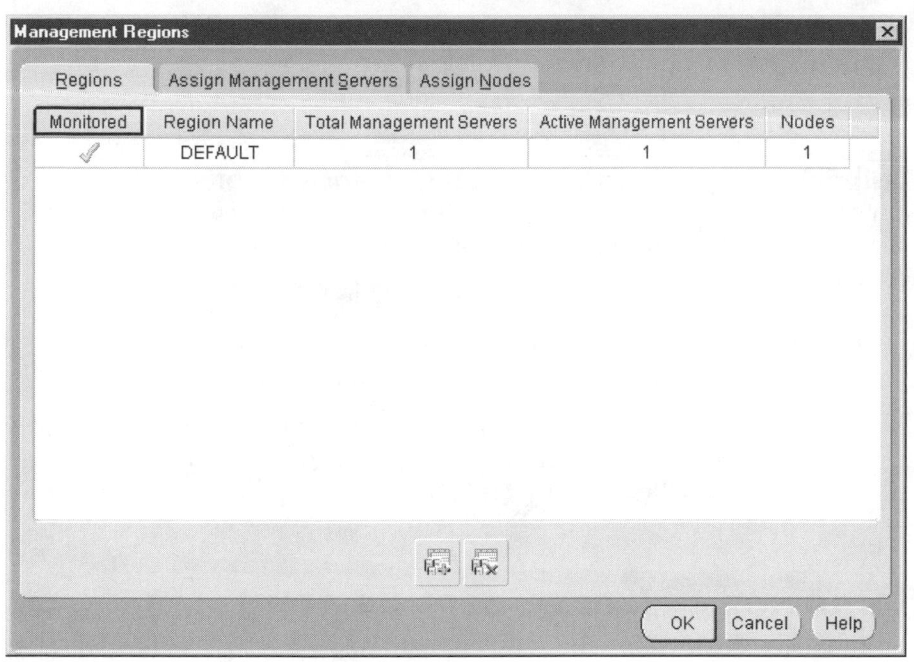

FIGURE 9-12. *Setting up Management Regions*

To add a new Management Region, click the Add Region button (the button with the green plus sign, at the bottom of the page). The Add Management Regions dialog appears. Enter a name for the new management region and click OK to save the new region.

Assigning Management Servers to Management Regions

Once you've created a new Management Region, you need to assign one or more Management Servers to it, if you want the region to be monitored. Follow these steps to add the servers:

1. Select Configuration | Define Management Regions. The Management Regions screen appears, as shown in Figure 9-12.
2. Select the Assign Management Servers tab on the Management Regions property sheet. The Assign Management Servers page is shown, where all the Management Servers and the Management Regions configured in that repository are listed. To associate a given Management Server to a Management Region, click the appropriate radio button.

NOTE
You cannot move the last Management Server from a Management Region, because doing so would leave the Management Region unmonitored.

Assigning Target Nodes to Management Regions

Now that you have a new Management Region with Management Servers, you can assign target nodes to the region for those servers to monitor. Follow these steps to add target nodes to the region:

1. Select Configuration | Define Management Regions. The Management Regions screen appears, as shown in Figure 9-12.
2. Select Assign Nodes from the Management Regions property sheet. The Assign Nodes page appears. To associate a given Target Node with a Management Region, click the appropriate radio button. Click OK to save the information.

Removing a Management Region

You can delete Management Regions, but only empty management regions; that is, regions with no configured Management Servers and no assigned nodes. To delete the management region, you must reassign or delete all the Management Servers and reassign all the nodes assigned to the region you want to delete. If you do not, an error message will appear telling you that you cannot remove the region.

To remove a Management Region, perform the following steps:

1. Select Configuration | Define Management Regions menu.The Management Regions screen appears, with the existing Management Region names listed.
2. To remove a Management Region, mark the region to be deleted and click the Delete Region button (the button with the red X at the bottom of the page). A confirmation dialog appears asking you if you want to delete the chosen region. Click Yes to delete the region and No to cancel.

Configuring E-mail and Paging

As stated earlier in the chapter, EM can notify administrators about the status of submitted jobs and the severity level of registered events in two ways:

- Notification message sent via E-mail
- Notification message sent via Pager

You should complete this configuration before defining the EM administrator notification preferences (described earlier in this chapter in the "Modifying Your Preferences" section). Only super administrators can configure these services, and the configuration is not available when running the EM Console in standalone mode.

Configuring E-mail

Before EM administrators can be notified through e-mail, you must complete the configuration of the e-mail services within EM. Configuring e-mail service within EM is quite simple. The only requirement is that you have access to a Simple Mail Transfer Protocol (SMTP) server for sending the messages.

NOTE
SMTP is a TCP/IP-based mail protocol, so TCP/IP services must be configured on the Management Server machine.

To configure the e-mail service, log into the OMS as a super administrator and follow these steps:

1. Select Configuration | Configure Paging/E-mail. The Configure Paging/E-mail screen is displayed, as shown in Figure 9-13.
2. This page allows you to specify the SMTP server and the sender's e-mail address. Both fields are required if you want to configure e-mail notification:
   - **SMTP Mail Gateway** Enter the node name or IP address of the SMTP mail gateway, such as mail.mycompany.com.
   - **Sender's SMTP Mail Address** Enter the name you want to use as the sender of the e-mail.

You can test the configuration from the notification settings of an EM administrator (see the "Modifying Your Preferences" section earlier in this chapter).

Configuring Paging

Notification through a pager from EM relies on the presence of a Paging Server. This component is installed with the Oracle Server or Oracle Management Server on Windows NT or 2000 only. You can use a Paging Server running on Windows from a Management Server running on Unix. Before configuring the paging service, you should verify that you have the Paging Server installed and running (identified by "Oracle<Oracle_home name>PagingServer" in the Windows NT/2000 services list).

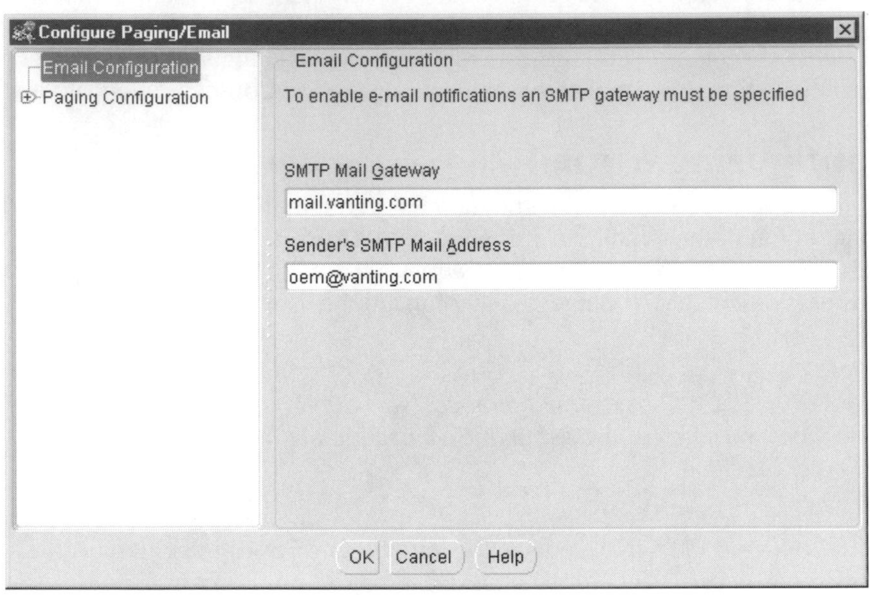

FIGURE 9-13. *Configuring paging and e-mail*

NOTE
To use Oracle Enterprise Manager paging functionality with pre-9i Oracle Intelligent Agents, install the Paging Service Agent Extensions in the Oracle Intelligent Agent ORACLE_HOME. The latest version 9i of the Intelligent Agent is recommended.

To start the Paging Server, use one of the following two options:

- Select Start | Settings | Control Panel, and open the Services screen.
  - **NT4:** Choose Services.
  - **Windows 2000:** Choose Administrative Tools | Services.
- Use the command line tool OEMCTL (see Chapter 19 for more details):

```
oemctl start paging
```

Also, the Management Server must be running before you can define the paging preferences.

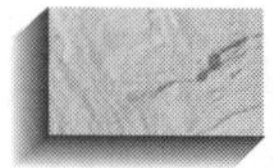

NOTE
Before configuring the paging service within EM, you need to configure your modem for your Windows NT/2000 system where the Paging Server is running.

To configure the paging service, log into the OMS as a super administrator, and follow these steps:

1. Select Configuration | Configure Paging/E-mail.
2. The Configure Paging/E-mail screen is displayed, as shown in Figure 9-13. Click the Paging Configuration object in the tree structure.
3. The Paging Servers page appears. This page allows you to add and remove paging servers. It is also possible to ping a specific paging server. To add a paging server, first ensure that the Oracle Paging Server is installed and running. Then click the Add Server button (the green plus sign at the bottom of the screen). Now the Add Paging Server dialog appears. Enter the host name or IP address of the server where the Paging Server is located and click OK.
4. Next, define one or more paging carriers. To do this, expand the Paging Configuration object in the tree structure to select the newly added paging server.
5. The Carriers page appears. To add a new paging carrier, click the Add Carrier button (the green plus sign at the bottom of the screen).
6. The Add Paging Carrier dialog box appears. You can choose between a *numeric* and an *alphanumeric* paging carrier type. For alphanumeric carriers, you have the choice of the TAP (Telocator Alphanumeric Protocol), FLEX-TD (used in Japan and based on the FLEX™ protocol developed by Motorola), and GSM (Global System for Mobile communication) protocols. Enter the appropriate information, as shown in Figure 9-14.

When using a numeric pager with job notifications, you will receive a three-digit number on your numeric pager indicating the status of the job:

100 Started

200 Completed

300 Failed

400 Deleted

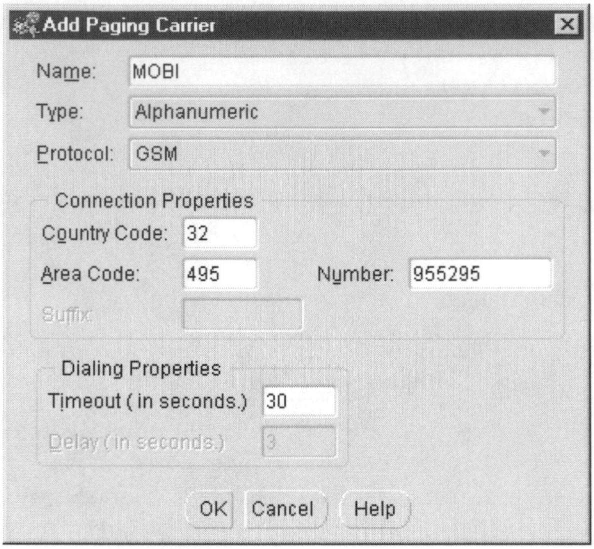

FIGURE 9-14. *Configuring a new paging carrier*

For event notifications, you will receive a three-or four-digit number on your numeric pager indicating the severity of the event:

500	Cleared
600	Warning
700	Critical
800	Node Down
900	Unknown
1000	Reassigned

You can test the configuration from the notification settings of an EM administrator (see the "Modifying Your Preferences" section earlier in this chapter).

Set Paging/E-mail Blackout

When monitoring your targets via EM events, you need to be able to turn off the monitoring temporarily for some or all of your managed services for a certain period of time. This is known as a *blackout* and is useful, for example, if you have implemented a maintenance window, where some administrative operations are performed on your targets. This could be rebooting the Windows servers or performing cold backups of your database instances. Through the Paging/E-mail Blackout feature in the Management Server, a super administrator can suspend paging and e-mail notifications for a specified target. You can also define the blackout as a recurring event or something that happens on certain days or maybe only once.

Enabling Paging and E-mail Blackouts

To enable Paging and E-mail Blackouts, follow these steps:

1. Click on the service for which you want to define a blackout in the EM Console Navigator tree. Select Configuration | Set Paging/E-mail Blackout, right-click on the service in the EM Console Navigator, and choose Set Paging/E-mail Blackout, or press CTRL-B.
2. The Paging/E-mail Blackout screen is displayed for the chosen service, as shown in Figure 9-15. To add a new blackout definition for this service (for example, the SUSE1 database service), click the Create button. If the service has existing blackouts, you can also click the Create Like button to create a similar blackout type. The screen changes, and you can enter a name, occurrence, and duration for the blackout. In Figure 9-15, the SUSE1 database is down due to migration for a duration of four hours. Click OK to save the information.

NOTE

When defining blackouts, remember that each day terminates at 12:00 A.M. When selecting the occurrences On Day(s) of Month and On Day(s) of Week, if the blackout period spans 12:00 A.M., you must define two blackout periods: The first period ends at 11:59 P.M., and a second begins at 12:00 A.M. and ends later.

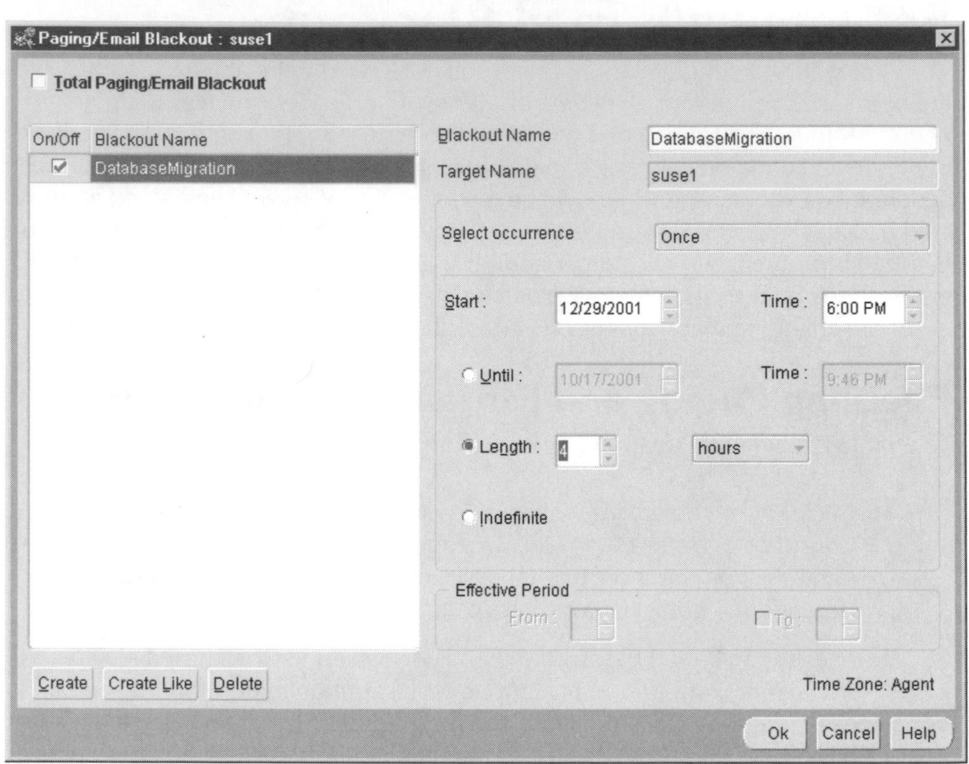

FIGURE 9-15. *The Paging/E-mail Blackout screen*

Paging and e-mail blackouts are set to ON by default, meaning they are enabled when created. It is possible to specify blackout periods for your targets through the "AGENTCTL" command-line utility. Refer to Chapter 19 for more details and examples of how to use this utility.

Modifying and Disabling Paging/E-mail Blackout

To modify or disable Paging or E-mail Blackout, click on the service for which to disable blackout in the EM Console Navigator tree. Select Configuration | Set Paging/E-mail Blackout, right-click on the service in the EM Console Navigator, and choose Set Paging/E-mail Blackout, or press CTRL-B. The Paging/E-mail Blackout screen is displayed for the chosen service.

You can edit the blackout information by simply clicking on the blackout listed to the left. All fields that were entered at the time of creation can be modified. Typically, you would reuse a blackout definition and simply change the occurrence information.

You can turn a paging or e-mail blackout on or off by checking the box located to the left of the individual blackout name. You can completely remove the blackout by clicking the Delete button.

Total Paging/E-mail Blackout

The Total Paging/E-mail Blackout setting specifies that a blackout should be started immediately with an indefinite duration. You might want to do this if you plan a major maintenance operation, such as a migration, and you do not want to be flooded by event notifications.

Enabling Total Paging/E-mail Blackout

You can enable Total Paging/E-mail Blackout either from the Configuration menu or by right-clicking on the target node or service and then choosing Set Total Paging/ E-mail Blackout.

NOTE
Setting a total paging/e-mail blackout overrides all individually defined blackouts for the service. The super administrator must disable the total blackout before any new blackout schedules can be defined and take effect, or before existing blackout schedules resume.

Disabling Total Paging/E-mail Blackout

You can disable Total Paging/E-mail Blackout either from the Configuration menu or by right-clicking on the target node or service and then choosing Unset Total Paging/ E-mail Blackout. You must be logged into the OMS as a super administrator to turn off the blackout. Both ways are described in the following sections.

Other Configuration Tools

So far in this chapter, we have been describing the core configurations within EM, many of which are crucial for you to use EM properly. There are also other configurations and features available in the Configuration menu of the EM Console, and these are described in the following sections.

SQL Logging

SQL Logging allows you to log execution of DML (Data Manipulation Language) and DDL (Data Definition Language) statements in EM. This feature is useful for keeping track of all changes performed to your managed services through the EM Console. In some businesses, such as the pharmaceutical industry, you might work with validated systems where logging and auditing is required. SQL Logging is available in both EM standalone and Management Server modes, but in two different ways:

- When you are connected to the Management Server, SQL statements are logged to a table.
- In standalone mode, SQL statements are logged to a file.

SQL Logging Connected to the Management Server

You must be logged in as super administrator to enable and disable SQL Logging, but SQL executed by all EM administrators is logged. If a super administrator enables SQL Logging, any user connecting to the Management Server will be able to view the SQL logged. Only super administrators can view all transactions; regular administrators will only be able to view their own transactions.

To enable SQL logging within the Management Server, follow these steps:

1. Select Configuration | SQL Logging. The SQL Logging dialog box is displayed, as shown in Figure 9-16.
2. To enable SQL Logging, first check the Enable SQL Logging check box. Now you can enter the following information:
   - **Maximum Number of Statements** Specifies the number of statements to log, which has an impact on the size of the log table.
   - **Data Definition Language (DDL)** Logs data definition language (DDL) commands, such as statements for creating or altering tables.
   - **Data Manipulation Language (DML)** Logs data manipulation language (DML) statements such as INSERT, UPDATE, or DELETE.
   - **Both DDL and DML** Logs both DDL and DML statements.
3. Click OK to activate the SQL Logging.

NOTE
The SQL statements are written to the table SMP_LOG_SQL in the EM repository.

To disable SQL Logging, uncheck the Enable SQL Logging check box.

SQL Logging in Standalone Mode

As mentioned earlier, you can also enable SQL logging from an EM Console running in standalone mode. This logging can only be done to a text file, and the logged SQL

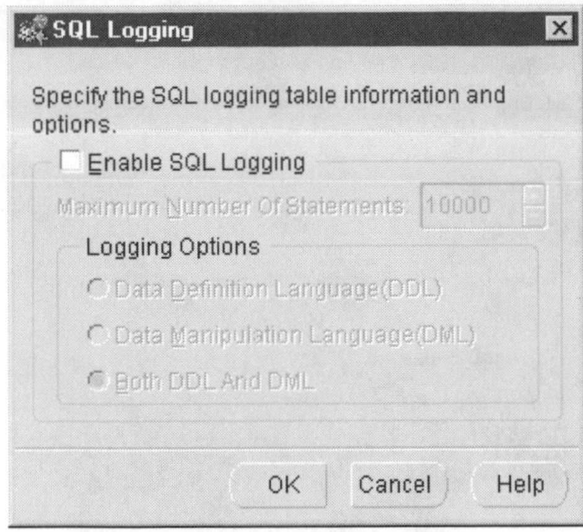

FIGURE 9-16. *Enabling SQL logging while connected to the Management Server*

statements can only be viewed by opening the file; no reporting function is available. To enable SQL Logging in standalone mode, follow these steps:

1. Start the EM Console in standalone mode. Select Configuration | SQL Logging. The SQL Logging dialog is displayed, as shown in figure 9-17.
2. To enable SQL logging, first check the Enable SQL Logging check box. Now you can enter the following information:
   - **File Name** Enter the name of the log file or browse to it by clicking on the Browse button. The default name for this file is oemsql.log, and the default location is ORACLE_HOME\sysman\log.
   - **File Size** Specify the maximum size of the log file in MB. You can let EM make a copy of the log file when it reaches the maximum file size. The name of the copy will be the name of the previous file with a timestamp.
   - **Data Definition Language (DDL)** Logs data definition language (DDL) statements such as CREATE TABLE or ALTER INDEX.
   - **Data Manipulation Language (DML)** Logs the data manipulation language (DML) statements, such as INSERT, UPDATE, and DELETE.
   - **Both DDL and DML** Logs both DDL and DML statements.
3. Click OK to activate the SQL Logging.
4. To disable SQL logging, uncheck the Enable SQL Logging check box.

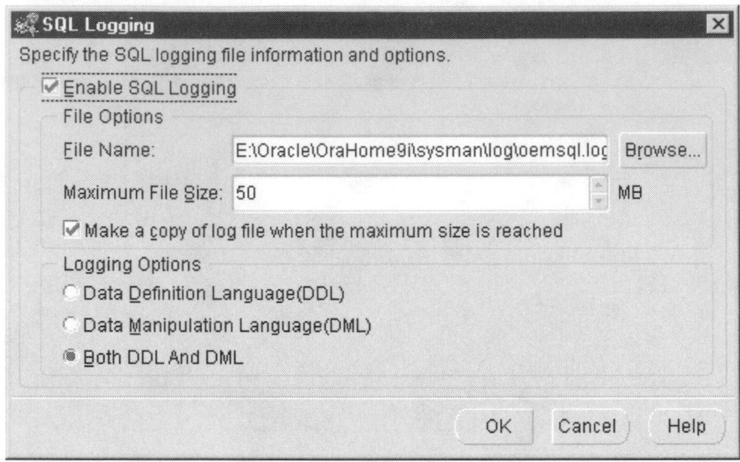

FIGURE 9-17. *Enabling SQL logging in standalone mode*

Viewing the SQL Log

The View SQL Logging menu item is only enabled when SQL Logging is enabled, and only when connected to a Management Server. If SQL Logging is disabled, the View SQL Logging menu item is ghosted out and not accessible. To view the SQL log, follow these steps:

1. Select Configuration | View SQL Log. The View SQL Log screen is displayed, as shown in figure 9-18.
2. Now you can browse all the logged SQL statements. Clicking on the column headings sorts that column in ascending or descending order. A filtering mechanism (Graphical Select Mode icon) and a reporting feature (Report icon) are also available from this screen. Click Close to exit the View SQL Log screen.

NOTE
If the number of rows returned from the SQL log table exceeds 500, a dialog box appears, prompting you to enter a filter for what you want to see.

The filtering mechanism, available through the Graphical Select Mode icon, is used to specify a filter in order to view certain log rows. On the Select From tab, you can choose the log information (columns from the SMP_LOG_SQL table) you

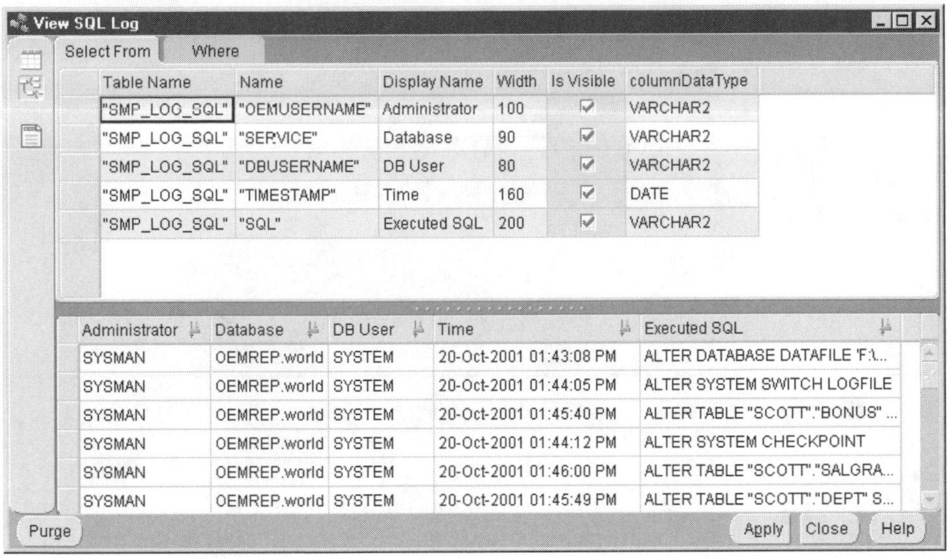

View SQL Log

Select From | Where

Table Name	Name	Display Name	Width	Is Visible	columnDataType
"SMP_LOG_SQL"	"OEMUSERNAME"	Administrator	100	☑	VARCHAR2
"SMP_LOG_SQL"	"SERVICE"	Database	90	☑	VARCHAR2
"SMP_LOG_SQL"	"DBUSERNAME"	DB User	80	☑	VARCHAR2
"SMP_LOG_SQL"	"TIMESTAMP"	Time	160	☑	DATE
"SMP_LOG_SQL"	"SQL"	Executed SQL	200	☑	VARCHAR2

Administrator	Database	DB User	Time	Executed SQL
SYSMAN	OEMREP.world	SYSTEM	20-Oct-2001 01:43:08 PM	ALTER DATABASE DATAFILE 'F:\...
SYSMAN	OEMREP.world	SYSTEM	20-Oct-2001 01:44:05 PM	ALTER SYSTEM SWITCH LOGFILE
SYSMAN	OEMREP.world	SYSTEM	20-Oct-2001 01:45:40 PM	ALTER TABLE "SCOTT"."BONUS" ...
SYSMAN	OEMREP.world	SYSTEM	20-Oct-2001 01:44:12 PM	ALTER SYSTEM CHECKPOINT
SYSMAN	OEMREP.world	SYSTEM	20-Oct-2001 01:46:00 PM	ALTER TABLE "SCOTT"."SALGRA...
SYSMAN	OEMREP.world	SYSTEM	20-Oct-2001 01:45:49 PM	ALTER TABLE "SCOTT"."DEPT" S...

Purge   Apply   Close   Help

FIGURE 9-18. *Viewing the SQL log*

want to see, such as Administrator, Database, DB User, Time, and Executed SQL. By default, all columns are shown. Uncheck the Is Visible check box to deselect a column. On the Where tab, you can define your filter by clicking NEW. Select the column and operator from the drop-down list box and enter the filter value. Click Apply to activate the filter.

You can create a report containing all logged SQL statements from within the View SQL Log screen. Follow these steps:

1. Click the Report icon on the left side of the screen. Now the Generate Report for SQL Log screen is displayed, as shown in Figure 9-19.
2. Now you can enter the following information:
   - **File Name** Enter the name of the log file, or browse to it by clicking the Browse button. The default name for this file is oemsql.html, and the default location is ORACLE_HOME\sysman\report.
   - **Format** Select the output format for the report: HTML (default), text, or comma-separate values.
   - **Rows** Choose between all rows (default) or only the selected ones.
3. Click OK to generate the report to the specified location.

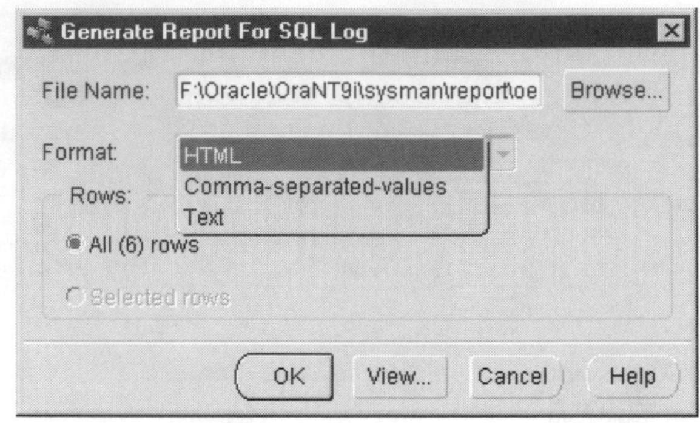

FIGURE 9-19. *Generating a SQL log report*

You can purge the SQL log table from the View SQL Log screen by clicking the Purge button at the bottom of the screen. A dialog box appears, prompting you to choose either to delete all rows of the SQL log table, or only to delete the selected ones if you have defined a filter.

Updating TNSNAMES.ORA

EM lets you update your local TNSNAMES.ORA Net8 configuration file with the database services that have been discovered in EM. This option is only available while connected to the Management Server.

NOTE
The TNSNAMES.ORA being updated is the one located on your EM Client, meaning locally on your PC, not on the Management Server.

To update your local TNSNAMES.ORA file, select Configuration | Add Services to tnsnames.ora. One of the two following things will happen, depending on whether a TNSNAMES.ORA file exists on your local system:

- If the TNSNAMES.ORA file does not already exist, it will be created.
- If the TNSNAMES.ORA already exists, EM appends to it and saves the previous version with an extension, for example, TNSNAMES.000.

Summary

In this chapter, we have covered most of the entries available in the Configuration menu including preferences for EM administrators, definition of Management Regions, and enhanced notification, as well as the SQL logging feature. Some of the settings you will perform right after you have installed and configured your Management Server, others you will do along the way. It is important that preferred credentials and notification schedules have been defined for all EM administrators before you begin to use the EM job and event systems.

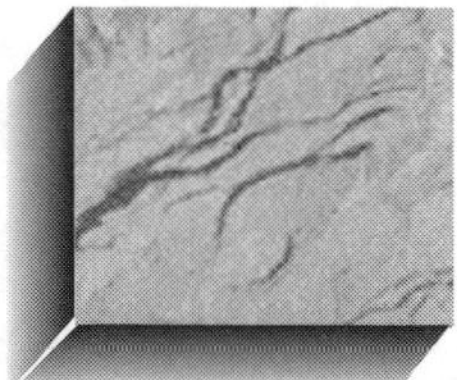

CHAPTER 10

Group Management

As discussed in Chapter 4, you can group your monitored and managed targets into logical groups. This is especially useful if you manage a large number of target nodes and services. With EM, you can organize targets such as nodes, databases, Real Application Clusters, listeners, HTTP servers, and MS SQL Servers into groups; you can even mix different types of objects in the same group. You can then manage the objects on a group basis, meaning you can submit jobs and events for whole groups. For example, you can submit a job that executes a SQL script on a group consisting of both databases and nodes. In this case, the job will only be applied to the services in the group of the database type. You cannot define groups with EM Console running in standalone mode.

NOTE
If a job or event is submitted for a group containing both manually configured and automatically discovered targets, the job or event will not be submitted for the manually added targets. There must be at least one automatically discovered target in the group, or the submitted job/event for that group will fail.

When monitoring objects using events on a group basis, remember that the group will inherit the worst state of any of its monitored members. If one object in the group is down, for example, a red flag will be shown on the group in the View pane. Other colors of the flag have different meanings, as discussed in more detail in Chapters 4 and 12, which cover the EM event system.

Planning Your Group Structure

You should carefully consider how to group your particular objects, and then decide on your grouping criteria. For example, you could group your objects according to the following standards:

- Target type (node, database, Real Application Cluster, SQL server)
- System type (Windows, Unix, Linux, VMS)
- Geographical location of the systems (city, region, state, country)
- Application on the system (E-Business Suite, PeopleSoft, SAP)
- Availability Level (office hours, always-on)
- Department in your organization (Sales, Shipping, Accounting, HR)
- Administrator (DBA) ownership/responsibility

With EM9i, you can include groups in other groups, thereby maintaining a hierarchical group structure. Having the group structure properly in place from the beginning makes a big difference for a productive usage of EM.

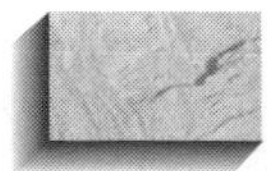

NOTE
Carefully consider how you name your groups. You will not be able to change the name of the group after creation, other than by deleting and re-creating the group.

Managing Groups in the EM Navigator

As mentioned in Chapter 4, groups appear in two places in the EM Console: in the Navigator and in the Group View pane (when you select an existing group that contains other groups in the Navigator). Each group is represented by an icon and a group name, and all groups are listed in the root level of the EM Navigator tree, even groups that are subgroups. If you did not create the group, the group name will be prefixed by the owner's name. To expand the group, double-click the icon or click the plus sign. You can also select the group by clicking on it once to display the Group View pane. The group view pane gives you a graphical view of the objects in the group and their individual status. You can also select the General and Access property pages; more about these later in the chapter. You can use a background image for each group, such as a map, a logo, or a graphical view of your network.

The following sections detail how to maintain your groups. They cover creating, modifying, and deleting groups, and defining your group hierarchy.

Creating a Group

Follow these steps to create a new group:

1. The most direct way is to right-click the Groups folder and choose the Create menu item from the pop-up menu, or choose Object | Create. If you want to create a new group similar to an existing one, right-click the existing group and choose Create Like from the pop-up menu. You can also select the existing group in the navigator tree or the group View pane and either select Object | Create Like or click the Create Like icon (the hollow green cube in the left toolbar). You can also press the Create icon (the green cube in the left toolbar) or press CTRL-N. All of these options result in the general Create dialog box being displayed. An example is shown in Figure 10-1. Choose the Group object and click Create.

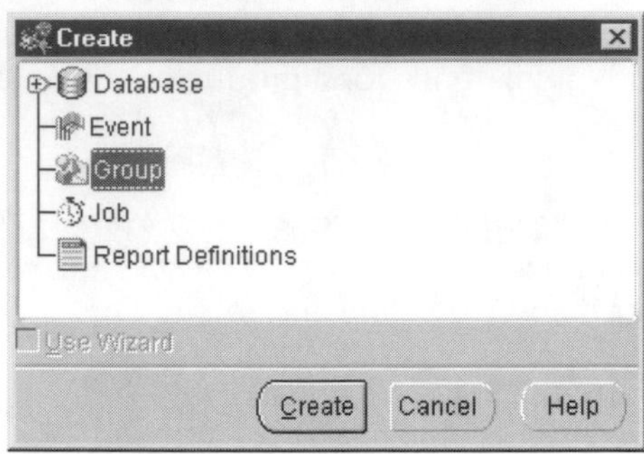

FIGURE 10-1. *Creating a new group object*

2. The Create Group screen appears, and you will be placed on the General property sheet. In the following sections, describe the different information that you can enter for a group. When all the appropriate information has been entered, click Create in order to save the new group.

Group General Property Sheet

On the General tab, you can enter information about the group and add objects to the group. The Group Name property is the only required property to create the group.

Group Name

Enter a name for the new group in the Group Name field. You can use upper-, lower-, or mixed case, and the case will be maintained. The group name cannot *begin* with numerical characters (0 through 9) and cannot *contain* any of the special characters ,) (% = ` ‘. You can enter up to 128 characters. Keep in mind that you cannot change the group name once it is created.

Description

Enter a description with a maximum of 1024 characters for the group and its contents in the Description field.

Use Background

Check the Use background check box if you want to display an image as the background of the group View pane. If you check the box, you can select the file name from the drop-down list box or enter the complete file name of the image in the field. When entering an image name, do not specify a directory, specify only the file name, such as europe.gif. The images are stored in the ORACLE_HOME\classes\oracle\sysman\resources\images directory on the machine where the Management Server is located. To use your own graphics, copy them to this directory; you can use GIF or JPG file formats. You do not need to restart the Management Server or the EM Console; just enter the file name on the line after you have copied it to the directory. Some sample images (asia.gif, europe.gif, japan.gif, usa.gif, and world.gif) are provided. Be aware that only these files are shown in the drop-down list box, not your own added files.

NOTE
If you are running the EM Console from a browser, you must also provide the files in ORACLE_ HOME\oem_webstage\oracle\sysman\resources\images.

Small/Large Icons

Choose whether you want to use small or large icons for the objects in this group. Small icons can be useful when a group contains a large number of objects.

Adding Objects to a Group

From the Available Targets list, expand the specific type tree list and select the target(s) you want to add to the group. This can also include other groups. You can select multiple objects by clicking them while holding down the CTRL key to add a specific object, or the SHIFT key to add a whole range of objects. Click Add to move the items to the Selected Targets list.

NOTE
An object can exist in different groups, but only one copy of the object can exist in one group at a time. Through the nesting of groups, an object can exist in several groups within the same super-group, however. Submitting an event or job for the super-group will result in only one event or job registration at the target object.

When you are finished entering the information, click Create to save the group definition. Figure 10-2 shows the General property page for creating of the LINUX-Oracle group containing the SUSE1 database.

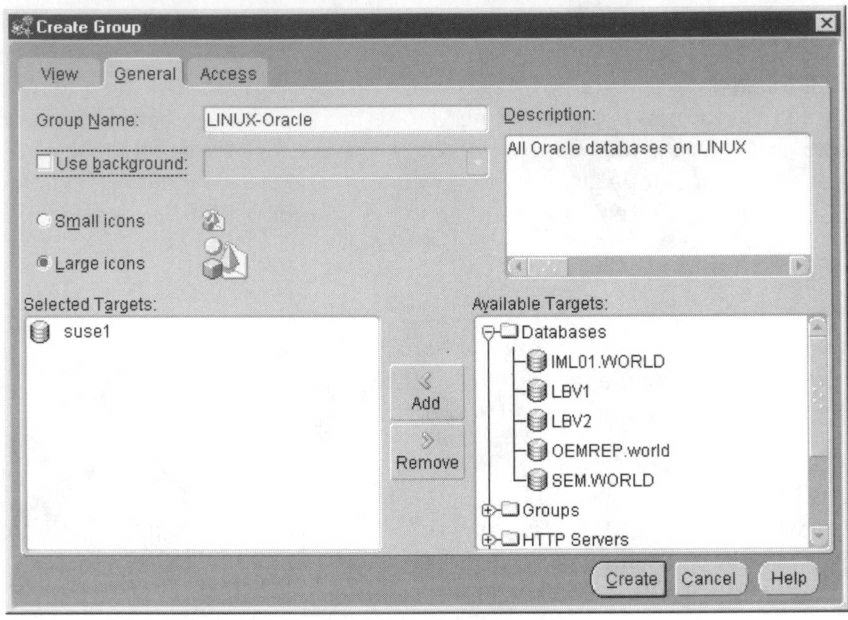

FIGURE 10-2. *Creating a new group*

Group Access Property Sheet

On the Access tab, you can grant access to the group to other administrators and also change the ownership of the group.

Modifying Administrator Access Permissions

You need to be either a super administrator or have been granted "Full" access to the group in order to be able to modify the information on this page. Any permission granted here supersedes the default permissions that might have been defined in Administrator Preferences (see Chapter 9). The levels of permission that you can assign to an EM administrator are as follows:

- **None** The administrator has no rights to this group at all.
- **View** The administrator can view the group and view group properties.
- **Modify** The administrator has permission to modify the group properties on the General page and on the View pane. You cannot delete the group

with this privilege. Access privileges on this page can only be modified when Full permission level has been granted.

- **Full** The administrator can modify all properties, including modifying permissions for other administrators, changing the ownership of the group, and deleting the group.

Super administrators always have full access, and this cannot be changed. For regular administrators, you assign the permission level by clicking the corresponding check box for the administrator. Figure 10-3 shows that regular administrator LBV has been granted Modify permission, and the administrator ADMIN1 has no permissions.

Modifying Group Ownership

To change the ownership of the group, choose the new administrator to be the new owner in the Owner drop-down list in the upper right corner of the Access property page. Click Apply to save the modification and Revert to undo the changes.

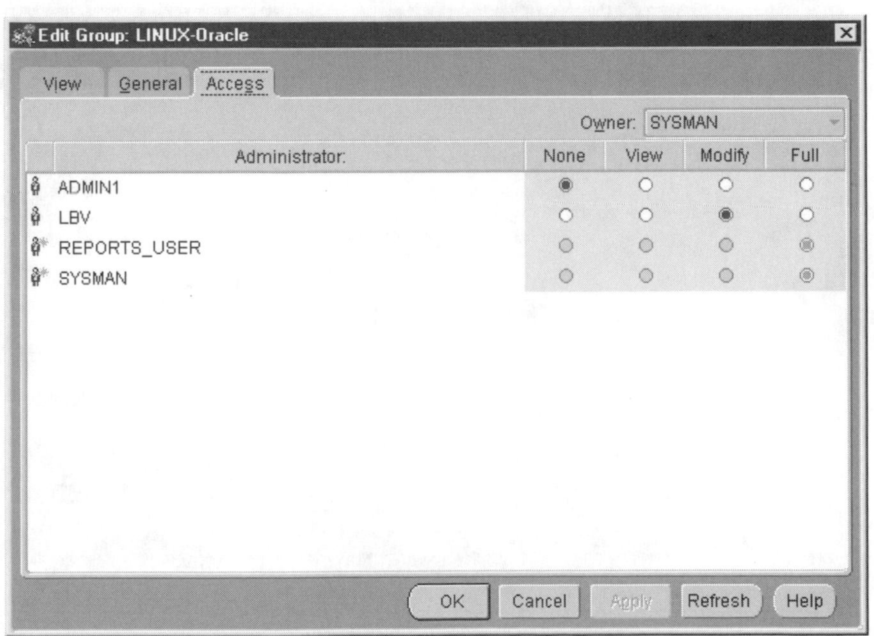

FIGURE 10-3. *Granting access permissions*

Group View Pane

Click on the View tab to display the View pane containing a graphical representation of the group. You can re-arrange the icons representing target objects and/or other groups on this page, as you like. Save this configuration by clicking Apply. An example is shown for the NT-Oracle group in Figure 10-4.

Normally, objects or groups are expanded within the Navigator. Some objects, such as database objects or subgroup objects, can also be expanded in the Group View pane by double-clicking the icon. Depending on the type of object you have selected, you can either expand it (if it is a group) or get to the property sheet for it (such as a database), allowing you to view or alter the properties of the object.

Also, you can launch a database application for a specific database. First select a database icon in the Group View pane. Then select a tool from the Tools menu or Tool drawers. You can also right-click on the database icon and select the tool from the Related Tools menu in the pop-up menu. You will now be connected to the database according to the user credentials defined in your preferred credentials. Refer to Chapter 9 for more information on user credentials.

FIGURE 10-4. *Rearranging the group view*

Defining a Hierarchical Structure

As mentioned earlier, you can nest groups within EM. You can do this nesting by either creating a new group explicitly as a subgroup to another group, or by assigning existing group(s) to another existing group.

Creating a Group as a Subgroup of Another Group

If you are creating a new group which is to be a member of another existing group, you can use one of the two following methods:

- Right-click the existing group, either in the Navigator tree or group View pane, and choose Create from the pop-up menu.
- Select the existing group in which to create the subgroup, either in the Navigator tree or group View pane, and choose Object | Create, or click the Create icon on the left toolbar.

Next, follow the steps outlined earlier in the "Creating a Group" section in this chapter. You must save the group assignment explicitly by clicking the Apply button when you are done.

Including Existing Groups in Another Existing Group

If you already have all the groups in place, there are two ways you can include groups in another group:

- Add the groups in the General property page of the group (see the "Adding Objects to a Group" section earlier in this chapter). You must save the group assignment explicitly by clicking the Apply button.
- Drag and drop groups into the group in the Navigator group tree list, either from other groups shown in the Navigator or from the Group View pane. You do not need to save explicitly, because the configuration is saved automatically when you drag and drop the objects.

Figure 10-5 shows an example of a hierarchical structure based on the operating system.

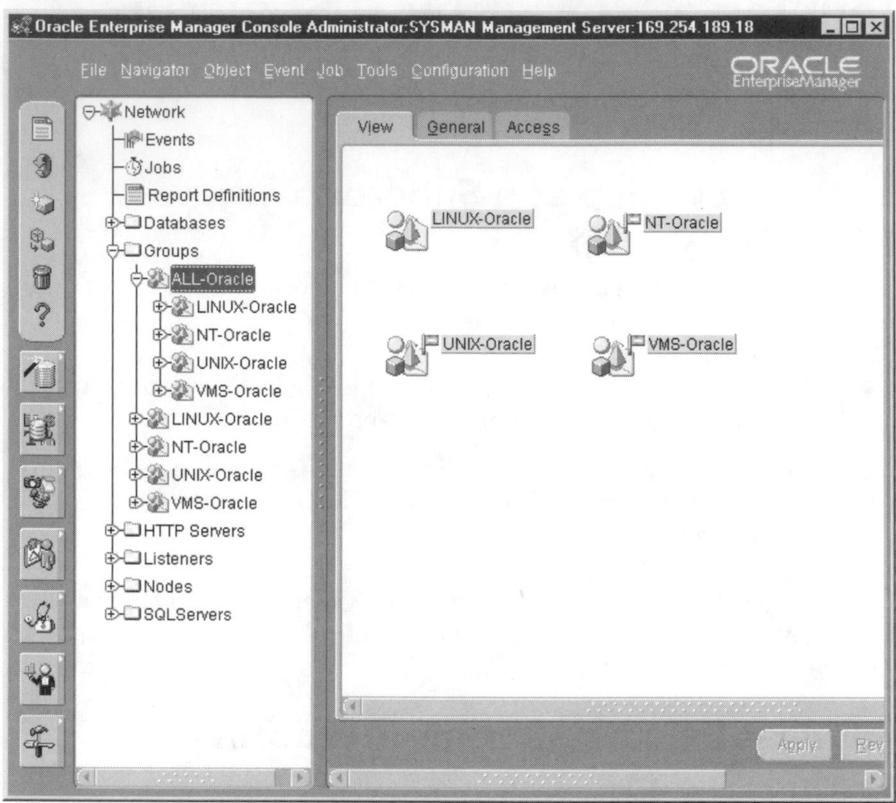

FIGURE 10-5. *A hierarchical example based on operating system*

Modifying a Group

To modify the properties of a group, you have two choices:

- Select the group in the Navigator by clicking it once and modify the information in the detail view on the right side of the EM Console.
- Right-click the group you want to modify in the Navigator and choose View/Edit Details from the pop-up menu or from the Object menu. Now the Edit Group screen appears.

Enter the information you want to edit just as if you were creating a group; see the "Creating a Group" section earlier in this chapter for details on the different property sheets and attributes. The only field you cannot modify is the group name. Click Apply (or OK in the View/Edit Group screen) to save the modified information.

Removing Objects From a Group

You can remove objects (including subgroups) from a group in the following three ways:

- Expand the group in the Navigator by clicking the plus sign. Select the object or group you want to remove from the group and press the DELETE key, or right-click the member object or group and choose Remove item from group in the pop-up menu or in the Object menu. When a confirmation dialog box appears, click Yes to confirm the deletion or No to continue without deleting the group.
- Open the group's View pane. Select the object or the group and press the DELETE key, or right-click on the object and choose Remove item from group from the pop-up menu or the Object menu. When the confirmation dialog box appears, click Yes to confirm the deletion or No to not delete the group. If you choose Yes to delete, then click Apply to save the change. Clicking the Revert button instead will continue without deleting.
- Go to the General properties page of the group, click on the object or group member to be removed in the Selected Targets area (you can mark several objects using the SHIFT or CTRL keys) and click the Remove button. Then click Apply to save the changes or Revert to continue without deleting.

An example of removing one group from another is shown in Figure 10-6.

When you remove an object (target or subgroup) from a group, you only remove the group assignment, not the object itself; it will remain in the EM Navigator tree. How to delete a group completely is discussed in the following section.

Deleting a Group

You encounter the option to delete a group at two places, each with a different scope:

- Delete a group which is a member of another group. Only the association to this particular group is deleted. The deleted group member remains in the EM Navigator tree or in any other group where it might be a member. This is covered in the previous section.
- Remove the group completely from EM. This removes the group from the EM Navigator tree and from every group where it is a member.

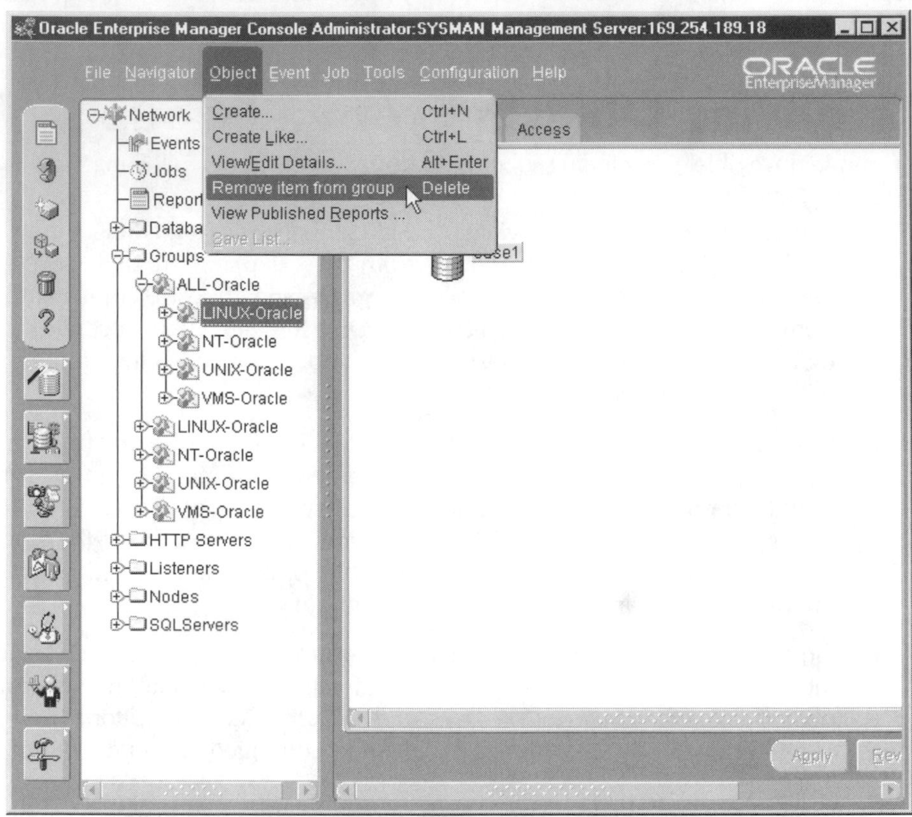

FIGURE 10-6. *Deleting a group from another group*

To delete a group completely from EM, you must expand the Groups item in the Navigator by clicking the plus sign in front of it. Select the group you want to remove from the highest level (that is not inside another group). Now you have multiple ways to delete the group:

- Right-click the group to delete and choose the Delete menu item from the pop-up menu. A dialog box will ask you to confirm the deletion; click Yes to delete the group or No to choose not to delete it.
- Select the group to delete, and either select Object | Delete, press the DELETE key, or click the Remove icon (the trash can in the left toolbar). In all cases, a dialog box will ask you to confirm the deletion; click Yes to delete the group or No to keep it.

Answering Yes in the confirmation dialog box means that the group is being deleted; no further apply or save action is required.

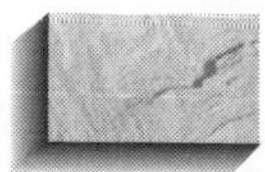

NOTE
If you are a regular administrator and do not have full permission for the group, you will be notified that you do not have sufficient permission, and the group will not be deleted.

Summary

In this chapter, you learned how to group your targets into groups and define a group hierarchy. This feature helps in providing a better overview and eases target management when dealing with larger amounts of targets. In the next two chapters, we will discuss the EM job and event system, including submitting jobs and events against groups of targets.

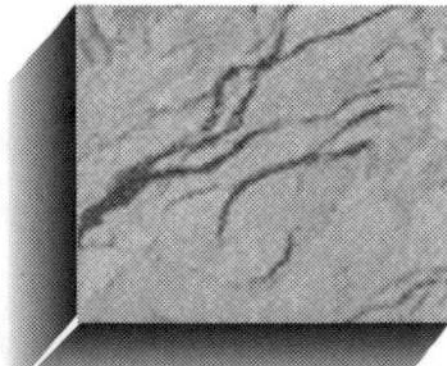

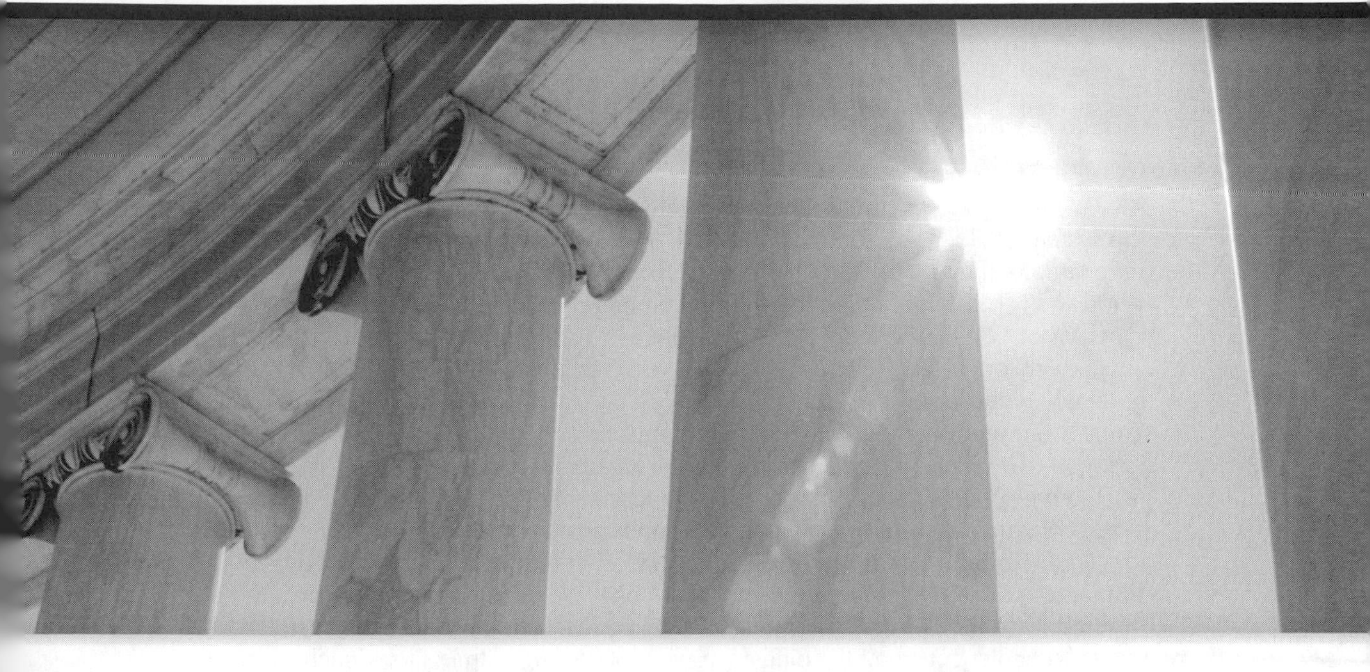

CHAPTER 11

Job System

As you saw in Chapter 4, one of the core functionalities of EM is its job scheduling system, which can schedule jobs of different kinds, such as running SQL scripts against one or more databases, starting and stopping Oracle Net Listeners and HTTP Servers, or executing operating system commands and batch scripts, including TCL scripts. The EM job system enables you to consolidate all of your current jobs scheduled through, for example, the Oracle PL/SQL built-in DBMS_JOB, cron on UNIX, at or winat on Windows NT/2000, or using the submit command and the batch queue on Alpha OpenVMS. You can schedule jobs on a single target, multiple individual targets, or against one or more EM groups. The only requirement for job submission is that the node where the target is present must have an Intelligent Agent installed and running. To be more precise, the Intelligent Agent must be running in order to execute the job, you can still submit the job, even if the agent is down.

From the EM Console you can create and manage the jobs, schedule their execution, and view information about defined and submitted jobs. You can store jobs in the job library for future use, or as a kind of template for creating other similar jobs. The EM job system is not available when running the EM Console in standalone mode.

This chapter covers all the different aspects of dealing with EM jobs, such as creating and submitting jobs against selected targets, storing jobs in the EM job library, modifying jobs, and deregistering jobs. We will not be able to cover all existing types of jobs (tasks) in this book, but we will provide examples of the most commonly used job types.

Setting up an Operating System Account

For the EM Console to submit jobs against a target (a database, Oracle Net Listener, HTTP Server or node), you must provide EM an operating system account in order to access the node and submit the job. You specify username and password for this OS account in the preferred credentials for the target node. Refer to the "Preferred Credentials" section in Chapter 9 for more details about how to specify the preferred credentials.

On Unix and Linux, the Intelligent Agent executable has the *setuid* flag set during installation (by the root.sh script), enabling the agent to run jobs as the user specified in the preferred credentials for the target node.

NOTE
On Unix/Linux, you can check if the `setuid` flag has been set for the agent executable by entering the command "ls –la $ORACLE_HOME/bin/dbsnmp". You should get an output like the following: rwsr-xr-x 1 root dba 1497980 Jan 12 21:04 dbsnmp. The "s" in the "rws" part means `setuid` has been set correctly.

The OS account must have its environment defined to be able to access the Oracle software and database(s) on the target node. To make sure that the OS account can perform a wide range of tasks through the EM job system (start/stop operations), you should make it a member of the "dba" group.

On Windows NT/2000 a special privilege is required, namely the "Log on as a batch job" privilege, but the user does *not* need to be able to logon interactively ("Log on locally"). The required privileges always depend on the tasks being performed by the job. If you, for example, only want to submit database jobs, the user does not require any other privileges, than the "Log on as a batch job" privilege in order for it to work (see below for details about how to grant this privilege). But if you want to start/stop databases and/or other services, such as Oracle Listeners or HTTP Servers, you need higher privileges on the node (e.g., member of the "Administrator" or "ORA_DBA" local group).

TIP
In an environment with many Windows NT/2000 nodes, consider creating a global NT user (in your account domain) and a local group on each node with the "Log on as a batch job" privilege granted. Then assign the global user to this local group. Please notice that a local user will override a global NT user if both accounts use the same name (e.g., local user "oia" overrides global user "YOURDOMAIN\oia"). If you are not familiar with issues such as local and global NT accounts and groups, ask your system administrator for assistance.

When you submit a job against a node and the job fails with an "Access denied" error in the job output, incorrect privileges are likely the problem. If you receive the "VNI-2015: Authentication error" error message, the user account is most likely lacking the "Log on as a batch job" privilege.

Assigning Logon as a Batch Job for Windows NT 4

To grant the "Log on as a batch job" privilege on a Windows NT 4 machine, you must be logged onto the Windows NT machine where the Intelligent Agent is running. Then perform the following steps:

1. Choose the User Manager (for Domains) program from Start | Programs | Administrative Tools.
2. Choose the User Rights entry in the Policies menu. The User Rights Policy screen appears.
3. Check the "Show Advanced User Rights" check box and choose the "Log on as a batch job" from the right drop-down list box.
4. Click Add to open the Add Users and Groups screen.
5. Locate the user or group and click the Add button, so the name appears in the Add Names field.
6. Click OK to return to the User Rights Policy screen.
7. Click OK to finish.

Assigning Logon as a Batch Job for Windows 2000

To grant the "Log on as a batch job" privilege on a Windows 2000 machine, you must be logged onto the Windows 2000 machine where the Intelligent Agent is running. Then perform the following steps:

1. Choose the Local Security Policy program from Start | Programs | Administrative Tools. The Local Security Settings screen appears.
2. Expand the Local Policies folder by clicking the plus sign, and select User Rights Assignment. All the privileges appear in the detail part of the screen. Figure 11-1 shows an example of the Local Security Settings screen.
3. Select the "Log on as a batch job" privilege. Right-click and choose Security from the pop-up menu, or simply double-click on the privilege to bring up the Local Security Policy Setting screen.
4. Click Add to open the Select Users or Groups screen.
5. Locate the user or group, select it, and click the Add button, so the name appears in the field below in the screen. You can also type the names of the users or groups directly in the field.
6. Click OK when finished to return to the Local Security Policy Setting screen.
7. Click OK to return to the Local Security Settings screen.

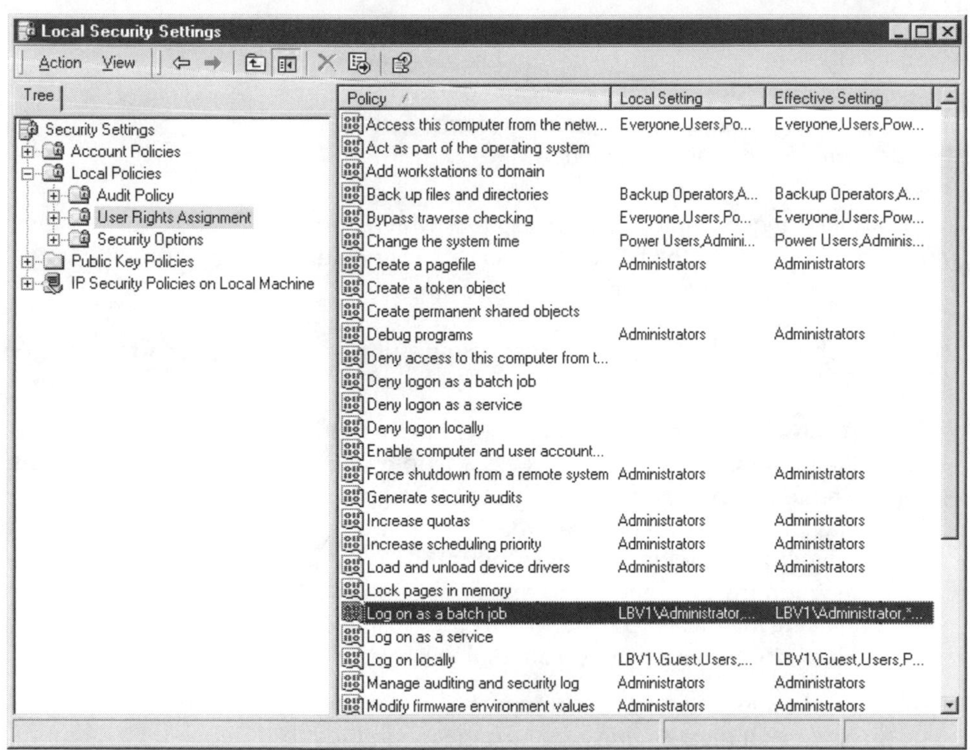

FIGURE 11-1. *Choosing the local security settings*

Creating Jobs

In this section, we take a detailed look at how to create a new job, which we will also submit and store in the job library. You will also see how to submit a job already existing in the job library, and create a similar job. Finally, you will learn about the special job type called the *fixit job*, which is used by EM events for proactive monitoring. Creating and submitting EM events is covered in more detail in Chapter 12.

Creating and Storing a New Job

This section explains how to create a new database job, submit it against one target database, and store it in the job library at the same time. This section will walk you through the most basic steps involved in EM job scheduling and explain the different settings and options.

NOTE
With the 9i version of EM, it is possible to submit an EM job using the command-line interface `oemutil` *together with the* `oemapp` *command. Refer to the "OEMUTIL" section in Chapter 19 for more details about this option.*

The following example is a database job, which consists of one SQL statement (coalesce free space in the USERS tablespace), scheduled once for a specific time. Follow these steps to create and submit the job:

1. Connect to the OMS as a super administrator, or as a regular administrator with access to the job system.
2. As always, when creating an object in EM, there are many ways to invoke the creation dialog. The quickest way to create a new job is to select Job | Create Job or press CTRL-J. You can also right-click the Jobs item in the Navigator tree and choose Create job from the pop-up menu, or select Object | Create Job from the Object menu. Finally, you can also create a new job from the general Create dialog either by choosing Object | Create, clicking the Create icon (the green cube) in the left toolbar, or pressing CTRL-N. Then choose Job in the Create dialog and click Create.
3. The Create Job property sheet appears, and you will be placed on the General page. You must enter a name for the job in the Job Name field; maximum length is 64 characters. Enter an optional description for the job in the Description field of up to 1024 characters. In the Target Type drop-down list box, leave the default Database target type selected. Select a target or group from the Available Targets list. You can mark individual targets, groups of targets, or a mix of individual targets and groups. Then click on the Add button (the < sign) to add the target to the Selected Targets list.

NOTE
Only targets on nodes that have been discovered correctly are included in the list of available targets. Manually added database targets do not appear.

   You can bypass the current preferred credentials defined for the targets and instead use a specified username and password for this job by selecting the check box labelled "Override Node Preferred Credentials for entire job." Notice these are the Node preferred credentials, which the EM job system must use to submit the job. If you are not overriding the credentials, make sure that the preferred credentials have been set up correctly for the target node(s). See the sections entitled "Modifying Your Preferences" and "Modifying Administrator Preferences" in Chapter 9 for more information about preferred credentials. Figure 11-2 shows a database job (a SQL command to coalesce the free space in a tablespace) being submitted against the OEMREP.WORLD database target.

NOTE

If a job is submitted against a group containing both manually configured and automatically discovered targets, the job will not be submitted against the manually added targets. There must be at least one automatically discovered target in the group, or the submitted job will fail.

4. In order to submit a job or to store it in the job library, in addition to entering a name for the job, you must specify at least one task. Click on the Task tab at the top of the job property sheet. You want to run a SQL statement against a database, so select Run SQL*Plus Script from the Available Tasks list by clicking it. Then click the Add button (the < sign) to add the task to the Job Tasks list.

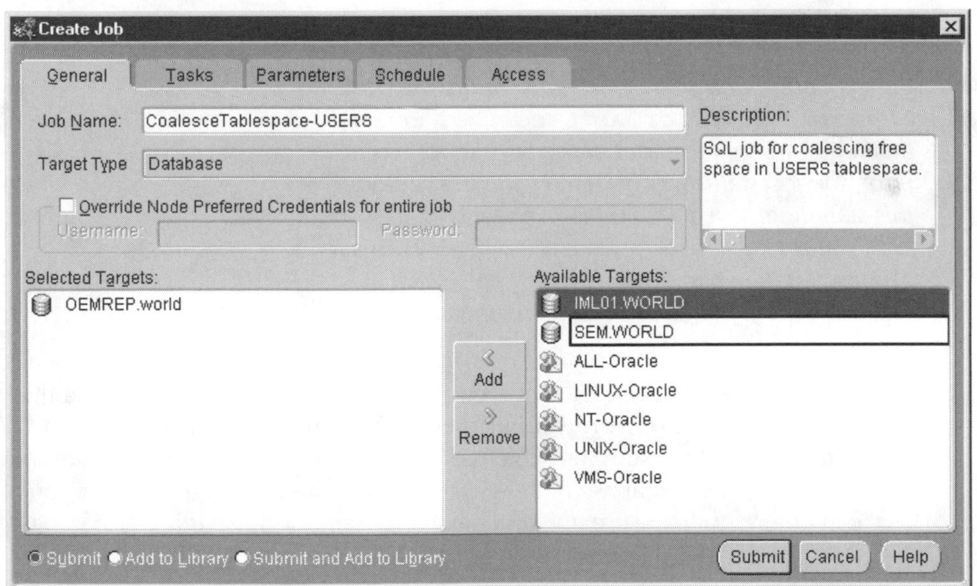

FIGURE 11-2. *Creating a new job*

NOTE
In this example, you will add only one task, but you can specify multiple tasks for a job and make the execution of a task conditional on a previous task having failed or successfully completed. See the section "Creating a Job With Task Dependencies" later in this chapter for an example.

5. Now you must enter the SQL statement for this task. Click on the Parameters tab in the top of the job property sheet. Enter **alter tablespace &1 coalesce;** (notice the &1 SQL*Plus parameter) in the Script Text field. If you leave out the semicolon, it will be added automatically. You can enter any legal SQL or PL/SQL statements, including all SQL*Plus formatting commands. You can also import existing SQL or PL/SQL scripts by clicking Import and then browsing to the script. You can only import one script per task. Another way is simply to copy and paste the script text directly into the Script Text field from your favorite editor. Now enter **users** in the Parameters field to parse this one parameter to the SQL command. You can enter more parameters separated with spaces and use these in the SQL script using &1, &2, and so forth. Notice that SQL*Plus must be installed on the target database to use this type of job task.

NOTE
To determine if an error has occurred during the execution of a SQL script, you should include `whenever sqlerror exit sql.sqlcode;` at the beginning of the script. If the SQL script has an error, the job status will be set to Failed. If you omit this statement, even a failed SQL script will appear with status Completed in the EM job history. This is also important when defining jobs with several tasks that are dependent on the results of previous tasks.

You can use the Override Preferred Credentials check box to override the username and password set in the preferred credentials for the target database(s). Make sure the Preferred Credentials for your chosen target have the appropriate database privileges to perform the SQL statement, or you can enter another username and password here for this particular database job. Figure 11-3 shows the task definition for coalescing the free space in the USERS tablespace.

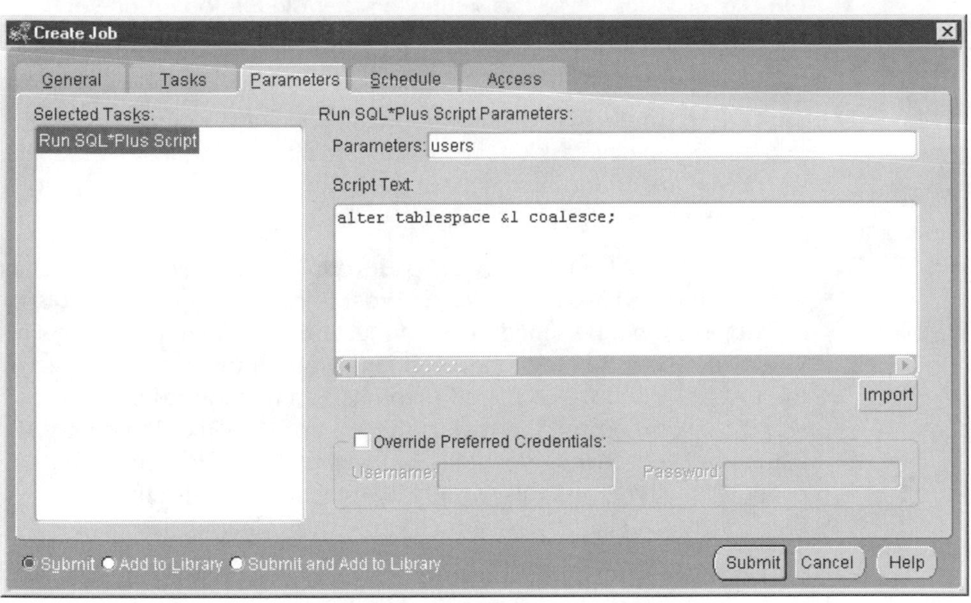

FIGURE 11-3. *Defining the task for the job*

6. You can now submit the job and add it to the job library by selecting the Submit and Add to Library radio button at the bottom of the job property sheet. You would then be using the default scheduling (immediately and only once) as well as default notification options. You want to schedule this job to be executed only once, and at a specific time. To do this, click the Schedule tab at the top of the job property screen. Select Once in the schedule interval type radio group on the left part of the screen. The following scheduling options are available:

   - **Immediately** Submits the job immediately and only executes it once. This is the default.
   - **Once** Executes the job once at a specific date and time you choose.
   - **On Interval** Enables you to schedule a specific time interval between task executions. The interval can either be a combination of hours and minutes, or be specified as a number of days. Select the value you want to change and click the up and down arrows. You can also select the value by clicking it once and typing in a new value.

- **On Day of Week** Use this setting to schedule the job on one or multiple days within one week. Check the check box(es) for the day(s) of the week for which you want to schedule the task.
- **On Day of Month** This setting works like On Day of Week, but allows you to schedule the task on one or multiple days within a month. Check the check box(es) for the date(s) of the month for which you want to schedule the task.
- **As a Fixit Job** Check this check box if you want to use this job together with a certain event as a *fixit job,* in order to correct a specific problem. A fixit job cannot be scheduled, but must be submitted to the target where the event is being monitored, and wait for the event to trigger the job's execution. Successfully submitting a fixit job results in a job status of Fixit. You can then select the job from the Fixit Job drop-down list in the Event Management Fixit Jobs page when you create an event. We will discuss this specific job type later in this chapter in the "Creating a Fixit Job" section, as well as in Chapter 12.

Set the Start Execution Date of the job by selecting the day, month, or year values, and then enter the correct value, or click the up and down arrows to change the value. In this example, you probably want to leave the default (current) date. Change the Start Execution Time to a value such as 10 minutes in the future. Use the same procedure that you used to set the date.

NOTE
The job will execute at the local time zone of the Intelligent Agent determined by the system time for each target node. This means that jobs do not necessarily run simultaneously. Keep this in mind when working with targets spread across time zones.

7. Click the Access tab of the job property sheet to assign permissions for this job to other (regular) administrators, and to define who will be notified about the progress and status of this job. For regular administrators, you can grant access to this job by checking the appropriate value (None, View, Modify, or Full). Notice that super administrators always have full privileges which cannot be changed. Check the Notify check box for the administrators you want to be notified about the status and result of this job. How and when an administrator is notified is defined in the administrator preferences on the Notification and Schedule pages. See Chapter 9 for more details about administrator notification settings. You cannot change the ownership

of the job at this point, but you can do that later. Figure 11-4 shows that the regular administrator LBV has been granted Full access to the job and is to be notified.

Each administrator can inspect his or her notification schedule by clicking the Show Notification Schedule button. This way you can check to see if there are holes in the notification, meaning a time when no administrator will be notified. A colored area means notification will take place during this time and white means no notification. You can add or remove notification for a specific administrator by right-clicking on a specific square, choosing Add Recipient or Remove Recipient in the pop-up menu, and then choosing the administrator.

8. Select the Submit and Add to Library radio button at the bottom of the Create Job screen. The button to the right of this radio group will change

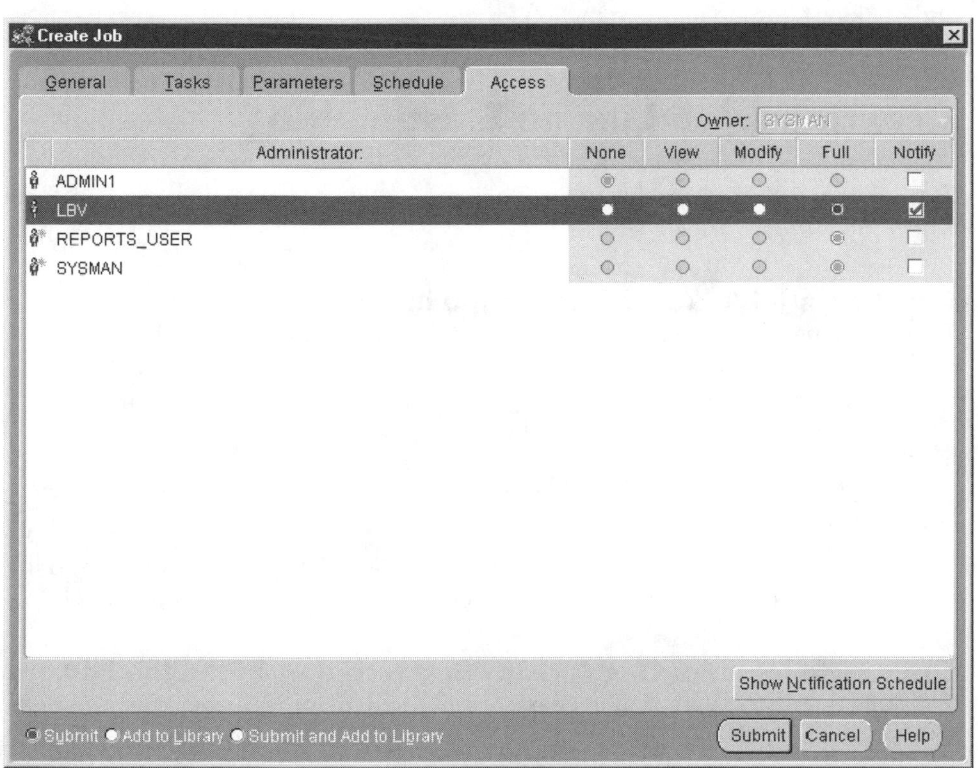

FIGURE 11-4. *Setting permissions and notifications*

its label, accordingly. Click Submit & Add. The job will be stored in the job library and submitted to the selected target(s).

A submitted job is sent to the Intelligent Agents at the selected targets. When the Intelligent Agent for a target begins processing the job, the job appears in the Active Jobs page in the Job window. If the job is processed successfully, the job will start executing on the specified time. If you want to modify this job before execution, select the job in the Active Jobs page and double-click the job to open the Edit Job screen. You cannot modify the job tasks or parameters, only General information, Access privileges, and notification settings. Modifying existing jobs is discussed in the "Modifying an Existing Job" section later in this chapter. You can view the progress of the job in the Active Jobs page, and check the Show targets check box to also include target information in the detail view. You can also follow the progress of the job and examine any output from the job in the Progress page of the Edit Job page. Click the Update Progress button to refresh the view. Examine the output by selecting the progress line with a Completed or Failed status, and then click Show Output. You can save the job output in a HTML or text file by clicking Save As in the Job Output screen, and clicking Close to return to the job Progress page. After a job has executed, it is moved to the job History page of the Job details window.

Creating a Job Like an Existing Job

You can use the "create like" feature for EM jobs, as you can for other EM objects. If you have existing jobs, either in the job library or already submitted, you can create a new job with the same characteristics.

Creating a Job Like an Existing Job in the Job Library

To create a new job based on an existing job in the job library, follow these steps:

1. Select Job | Job Library, or right-click the Jobs item in the Navigator tree and choose Job Library from the pop-up menu.
2. The Job Library screen appears. Click Create Like to open the Create Job property sheet.
3. Follow the steps explained in the "Creating a New Job and Storing it in the Job Library" section earlier in this chapter to create and submit the job.

Creating a Job Like One Already Submitted or in the Job History

To create a new job with similar characteristics to another job, select the Jobs entry in the Navigator tree. Click either the Active or History tab, depending on whether the job you want to use as a template is scheduled and still active or only in the job history. Right-click the job and choose Create Job Like from the pop-up menu, or choose Job | Create Job Like. You can also choose Object | Create Like, click the Create Like icon (the hollow green cube) in the left toolbar, or press CTRL-L.

Creating a Fixit Job

You can create jobs that are used specifically as fixit jobs, meaning they can be run automatically in response to an event occurrence, thereby trying to correct the problem. For example, you may want to run a job to restart the Oracle Net Listener or HTTP Server if it has stopped. You may want to extend a datafile or raise the max extents storage parameter for a table when these have reached their limit. You create fixit jobs with the Job system. These must be designated as fixit jobs, and are assigned to EM events. See Chapter 12 for more information on how to use fixit jobs with events.

The following example defines a fixit job that starts a Oracle Net Listener monitored by an EM event. To create this fixit job, follow these steps:

1. Select Job | Create Job, or press CTRL-J to get to the Create Job screen. You can also use the Create Like feature to create a job similar to another job in the job library or that has been submitted.
2. On the Create Job property sheet, enter a name for the job in the Job Name field. You may want to use a prefix to distinguish fixit jobs from other jobs. Enter a description for the job, and choose Listener in the Target Type drop-down list. Select the target listener (or target group) from the Available Targets list and click the Add button (the < sign) to add it to the Selected Targets list. If the user stored in the preferred credentials does not have appropriate privileges to start the Net Listener, check the Override Node Preferred Credentials for Entire Job check box, and specify the username and password of a user with these privileges for this fixit job.
3. Click the Task tab. Because you want to run a Listener task, expand the Listener entry in the Available Tasks list, and select Startup Listener. Then click the Add button (the < sign) to add the task to the Job Tasks list. Because there are no parameters for a Listener task, you can skip to the Schedule page.
4. Click the Schedule tab. Select the As a Fixit Job radio button on the left part of the screen.

5. Click the Access tab to assign permissions on the job to other (regular) administrators, and to define who is being notified about the progress and status of the fixit job.
6. Select the Submit and Add to Library radio button at the bottom of the Create Job screen, and then click Submit & Add.

The fixit job will now be submitted to the specified target, but not executed. Execution will occur when a registered event fires and the agent executes this particular fixit job to correct a detected problem. The fixit job has been successfully submitted when the job status reaches Fixit. Figure 11-5 shows a fixit job that has been successfully submitted.

The job can now be selected from the Fixit Job drop-down list in the Event Management Fixit Jobs page when you create an event. Events are discussed further in Chapter 12.

Creating a Job With Task Dependencies

As mentioned earlier, you can create a job that consists of several steps. These steps can be of different types (such as databases and nodes), and you can make the execution of a job depending on the success or failure of a previous job. The following example defines a job with several tasks that are dependent on of each other. This example only focuses on the Task page of the job property screen. Refer to the "Creating Jobs" section earlier in this chapter for details on the other pages of the Create Job property sheet. This example uses restarting (shuting down and starting up) a database to illustrate task dependencies in EM jobs. The job first shuts down the database; if this succeeds, the job starts the instance again. If the shutdown fails,

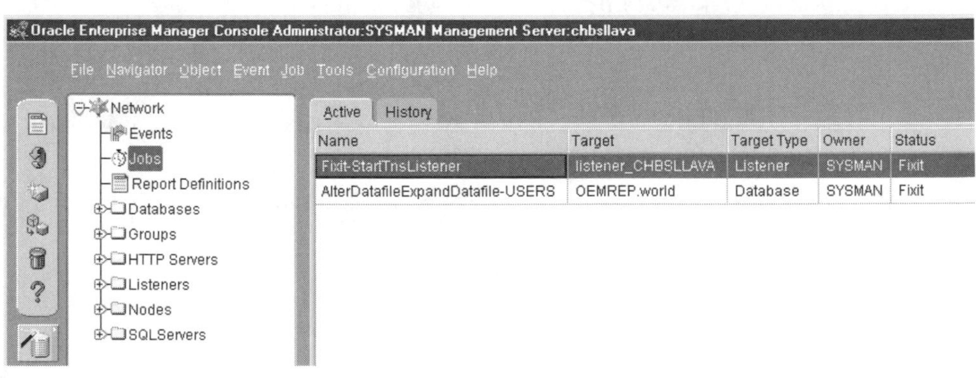

FIGURE 11-5. *A submitted fixit job*

the job sends a broadcast message to the node that the shutdown failed. Finally, the job sends a broadcast message to the node with the result of the instance startup.

1. Select Job | Create Job or press CTRL-J to get to the Create Job screen. You can also use the Create Like feature to create a job similar to another job present in the job library or already submitted.
2. On the Create Job property sheet, enter a name for the job in the Job Name field, such as **RestartDatabase**. Choose Database from the Target Type drop-down list box and add the target database you want to bounce to the Selected Targets list. Enter a description for the job.

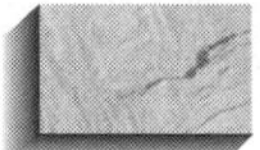

NOTE
For jobs with several mixed tasks, such as database and node tasks, you must select Database as the Target Type to be able to choose both database and node tasks. If you select Node as the Target Type (in this example, to perform the Broadcast Message), you will not be able to choose any database tasks. Node tasks are always available with other target type tasks.

3. Click the Task tab. The first task to be performed is the shutdown; expand the Database entry in the Available Tasks list and select Shutdown Database. Then click the Add button (the < sign) to add the task to the Job Tasks list. Now add the second task (Startup Database) in the same manner. Select the "Only on success of" radio button below the Job Tasks list. Now you must add the Broadcast Message, which is sent when the Shutdown Database task fails. Expand the Node entry in the Available Tasks lists and add Broadcast Message to the Job Tasks list. To specify that this task depends on the failure of the database shutdown, select the "Only on failure of" radio button, and choose Shutdown Database from the drop-down list box. Then add the two last Broadcast Message tasks, one for the success of the Database Startup task and one for the failure. Now the Create Job Tasks property page looks like Figure 11-6.
4. Click the Parameters tab to define the different tasks. For the Database Shutdown, choose Immediate in the Mode radio button group and SYSDBA in the Connect As radio button group. Then add the different messages to be broadcasted in the different cases.
5. Select the Submit and Add to Library radio button in the bottom of the Create Job screen and then click the Submit & Add button.

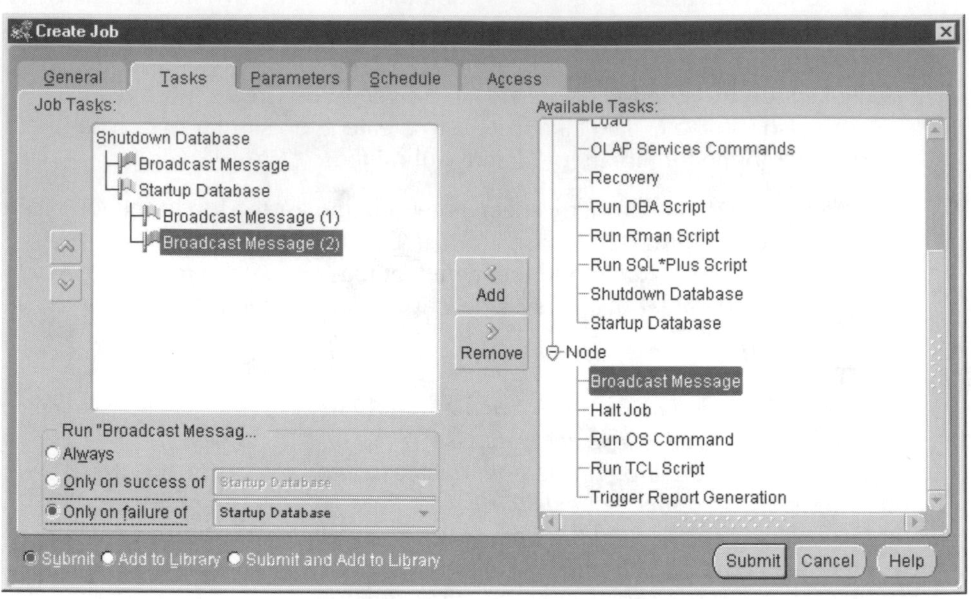

FIGURE 11-6. *Tasks with multiple dependencies*

The job will now be submitted and executed immediately, and the target database will be restarted.

Job History

When jobs have been executed, and have a Completed or Failed status, they are moved from the Active Jobs page to the Job History. The job history will grow more or less rapidly, depending on how much you use the EM job system.

To remove all jobs in the job history, select Jobs | Clear Job History. A confirmation dialog appears; click Yes to confirm the deletion of all jobs in the job history, or No to go back without clearing the job history.

You can generate a list of some or all of the jobs in the history by using the Save List feature. Follow these steps:

1. Mark the jobs (more than one) in the job history and choose Object | Save List.
2. Choose a format (HTML, text, or comma-separated) in the Format drop-down list box. HTML is the default format.

3. Enter a new filename, or accept the one suggested by default. You can use the Browse button to browse in the file system. The file will be stored on your EM Client machine, and in the ORACLE_HOME\sysman\report directory by default.

4. Click OK to generate the file and leave the Save List dialog. If you have chosen HTML as format, you can also click the View button to view the report in your browser.

Job Library

As you saw when creating a new job, you can choose to store your job definitions in the EM job library for later submission or as templates for creating other similar jobs. The Job Library dialog box is displayed when you select the Job Library menu option. The dialog box contains a list of the jobs that you have created and saved. In this dialog box, you can view summarized information about a job, such as the job's name and owner. You can submit these jobs to the job system, or you can use the Edit button to modify a job. To create a new job based on an existing job, select the desired job and click the Create Like button. The following sections provide a closer look at how the job library works.

Copying a Job to the Job Library

You can copy an already submitted job from the Active Jobs or job history to the job library. Select the job you want to copy in either the Active Jobs page or Jobs History page and right-click it. Choose Copy Job to Library from the pop-up menu. You can also choose Copy Job to Library from either the Job or Object menus. After the copy, the job will be available in the job library for submission or further modification.

Submitting a Job from the Job Library

When your jobs are stored in the job library, you can easily submit them again. Follow these steps:

1. Select Job | Job Library from the Job menu, or right-click the Jobs item in the Navigator tree and choose Job Library from the pop-up menu.

2. The Job Library screen appears, as shown in Figure 11-7.

3. To submit the job with its current definition as stored in the job library, click the Submit button. The job will be submitted.

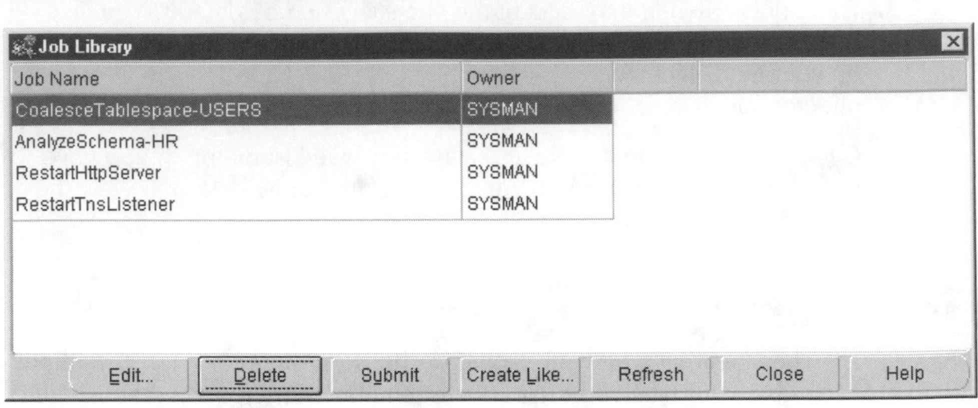

FIGURE 11-7. *The job library screen*

If you want to make changes to the job before submitting it, you must choose Edit instead and then modify the job definition. This is explained in detail in the following section.

Modifying a Job in the Job Library

When modifying a job in the job library, you can choose to make the change permanent, or only modify it for the new job submission and leave as is in the library. To modify a job in the job library, perform the following steps:

1. Select Job | Job Library, or right-click the Jobs item in the Navigator tree and choose Job Library from the pop-up menu.
2. The Job Library screen appears, as shown in Figure 11-7.
3. Select the job you want to modify and click Edit to open the Edit Job property sheet for the particular job. You can change any information, including the name of the job and the owner of the job on the Access page.
4. When you are finished with the changes, select either Submit, Save to Library, or Submit and Save to Library from the radio buttons at the bottom of the page, and click the button with the label Submit, Save, or Submit & Save. Notice that when modifying a job, the button label is Save instead of Add when creating the job. Click Close to exit the Job Library screen.

Deleting a Job from the Job Library

If you want to remove a job from the job library, follow these steps:

1. Select Job | Job Library or right-click the Jobs item in the Navigator tree and choose Job Library from the pop-up menu.
2. The Job Library screen appears, as shown in Figure 11-7.
3. Select the job you want to delete and click Delete. As soon as you press the Delete button, the job disappears. Be careful with this button, because there is no confirmation dialog box. Click Close to exit the Job Library screen.

Modifying an Existing Job

You can modify an EM job, either after it has been submitted against the target(s), or in the job library. You can change some of the job properties for an already-scheduled job. If you want to modify a scheduled job, select the job in the Active Jobs page and double-click the job to open the Edit Job screen. You cannot modify the job tasks or parameters, only the General information, Access privileges, and notification settings. To change the job schedule settings, you must first deregister the job from the affected targets, and then resubmit the job. See the "Deleting Jobs" section below for more about how to deregister (delete) EM jobs.

To modify a job stored in the job library, refer to the "Modifying a Job in the Job Library" section above.

Deleting Jobs

You can delete and thereby deregister scheduled job from the Active Jobs page, and you can delete the already-executed jobs from the job history. There is a special function available for deleting all jobs from the job history; refer to the "Job History" section earlier in this chapter. To delete individual jobs, either from the Active or History page, select the job you want to delete in either the Active Jobs page or the Jobs History page and right-click it. Choose Remove Job from the pop-up menu. You can also simply press the DELETE key, or choose Remove Job from either the Job or Object menus. You can also choose Object | Delete, or click on the Remove icon (the trashcan) in the left toolbar. A confirmation dialog box appears; click Yes to delete the job, or No to go back without deleting the job. Figure 11-8 shows how to remove a job through the pop-up menu.

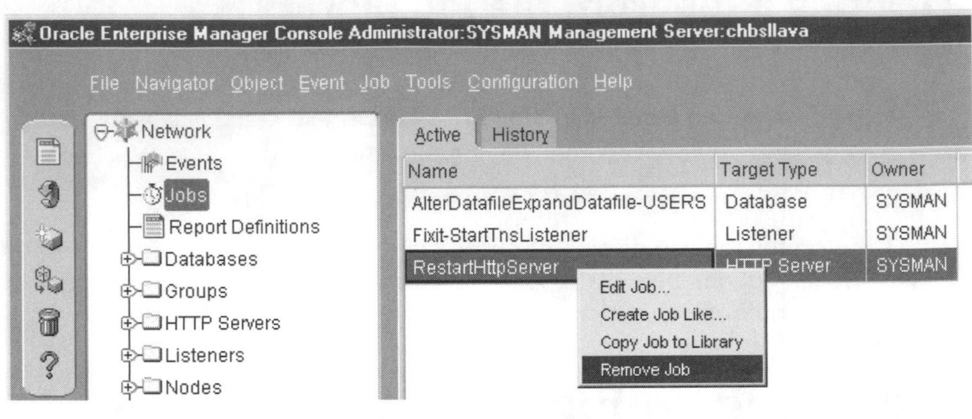

FIGURE 11-8. *Removing a job*

NOTE
Jobs that have been submitted against one or more EM groups must be deleted on each individual target.

Deleting a job from the job library is covered in the "Job Library" section earlier in this chapter.

EM Jobs and the Reporting Framework

You can create reports containing information about active jobs, failed or completed jobs, and jobs stored in the job library. You can also retrieve statistical information such as average execution time per job. This is accomplished through the EM Reporting Framework. Chapters 4 and 13 have more details about the reporting feature available with EM.

Summary

In this chapter, you have learned how to create and submit different type of jobs from the EM Console against one or more targets. You have seen how to store jobs in the job library and how to modify and resubmit them from here. You also learned about the special *fixit* job type, which is used together with EM events to proactively fix a particular problem causing an event to trigger. In the next chapter, we will take a closer look at the EM event system, which you use to monitor your target nodes and their different services such as databases, Listeners, and HTTP Servers.

CHAPTER 12

Event System

The EM event system is one of the key features of EM . Monitoring your enterprise is the key to reducing downtime and keeping your systems running smoothly. From the EM Console, you create and manage events, submit them, and view information about registered and triggered events. You can create and store events in the event library, either for later submission or as a template for creating other similar events. Note that the EM event system is not available when running the EM Console in standalone mode.

EM enables you to define events, which can consist of one or more event tests, and then submit these to monitor your different targets. The targets available with event tests are database, TNS Listener, node, and HTTP Server. The base event tests for these targets are the "UpDown" events. Additional event tests are provided with the optional Management Packs, such as the Diagnostic Pack. You can also define your own event tests through user-defined event tests. These event tests can be written in SQL or in any language you wish, provided the runtime environment is available on the target node.

Obviously, you can monitor more than database internal issues through EM events; you can also define tests for monitoring your applications. An example of defining an event using user-defined SQL is included in this chapter. You can also implement proactive monitoring, which means that EM can automatically attempt to fix problems it might detect on the monitored target. This is provided through the fixit job feature, which is discussed in more detail later in this chapter. As with jobs, you can submit events against a single target, multiple individual targets, or one or more EM groups. The only requirement is that an Intelligent Agent must be installed and running on the target node. You can even submit events if the agent is down. The Intelligent Agent component is responsible for detecting a specific event occurrence. When an event is triggered, the agent first notifies a Management Server, which in turn notifies the relevant administrators either through the EM Console as an alert or by using an e-mail or paging notification. We introduced the EM event system in Chapter 4 and demonstrated how the different components work. This chapter discusses how to work with EM events, including creating and submitting events, storing them in the EM event library, and modifying and deregistering events. We will focus on the event tests available with the core EM, not those available with the optional packs.

Defining an Oracle Account for Oracle Intelligent Agent

Events are registered and executed on a node using the permissions of the Intelligent Agent, through a special database user account (the DBSNMP database account, by default) to access the database. When you create events that require special privileges, you need to set up preferred credentials for the monitored database with a user account that has the appropriate system or object privileges, or you need to override the preferred credentials.

A default installation of the Intelligent Agent assumes that you will be using the DBSNMP database user with the default password "dbsnmp." An Oracle database creation normally also includes this user by executing the ORACLE_HOME\RDBMS\ADMIN\CATSNMP.SQL script. If you want to change the username, that is, replace the DBSNMP user with another account, you must tell the Intelligent Agent this through a parameter setting. You must do the same if you want to change the password for the DBSNMP user, which is highly recommended.

Editing the Intelligent Agent Configuration File

You configure the Intelligent Agent by editing the SNMP_RW.ORA file in the ORACLE_HOME\NETWORK\ADMIN directory for the Intelligent Agent software installation on the target. The parameters you must add to the SNMP_RW.ORA file (if they are not already present) are

```
SNMP.CONNECT.<database servicename>.NAME=<username>
SNMP.CONNECT.<database servicename>.PASSWORD=<password>
```

If the parameters are not present, the Intelligent Agent is using the default setting (username DBSNMP with password "DBSNMP"). For example, to change the password to "newpassword" for the database OEMREP.WORLD, change the parameters to look like the following (case is not important):

```
SNMP.CONNECT.OEMREP.WORLD.NAME=DBSNMP
SNMP.CONNECT.OEMREP.WORLD.PASSWORD=NEWPASSWORD
```

The Intelligent Agent must be restarted before the changes take effect.

Creating Your Own Intelligent Agent Database User

To create and grant the appropriate roles and privileges to your own agent user, run the SQL commands specified in catsnmp.sql, referring to your user account from SQL*Plus. Do not edit this script; instead, make a copy for your own use. The catsnmp.sql script creates a special role, OEM_MONITOR with appropriate privileges. You can use the OEM_MONITOR role to grant the minimum required privileges necessary to run database events (with earlier RDBMS releases, the SNMPAGENT role is used). In the release of Oracle9i, the DBSNMP user does not have the OEM_MONITOR role granted, but has the CONNECT role and the "SELECT ANY DICTIONARY" system privilege instead.

Creating Events

In the following sections, we will show how you create a new event, register it against a target and store it in the event library. We will also show how to submit an event already existing in the event library and also create a similar event. Finally, we will demonstrate how to define an event using a fixit job to proactively solve problem detected by the event. How to create and submit EM fixit jobs is covered in Chapter 11.

NOTE
With the 9i version of EM, it is possible to submit EM jobs and events using the command-line interface `oemutil` *which is part of the* `oemapp` *command. This way, you are not required to open the EM Console to submit a job or register an event. Refer to the OEMUTIL section in Chapter 20 for more details about this option.*

Creating a New Event and Storing It in the Event Library

This section describes how to create a new event. As an example, we will register an HTTP Server "UpDown" event test, submit it against one target (an HTTP server), and store it in the event library. This will walk you through the most basic steps involved in creating and registering EM events and explain the different settings and options. If you have read how to create and submit EM jobs in Chapter 11, you will see that creating events is very similar to creating jobs. Follow these steps to create and register the event:

1. Connect to the OMS either as a super administrator, or as a regular administrator with access to the event system.
2. There are many ways to get to the create event dialog, just like creating other objects in the EM Console. The quickest way to create a new event is to select Event | Create Event or press CTRL-E. You can also right-click on the Event item in the Navigator tree and choose Create Event from the pop-up menu, or choose Object | Create Event. Finally, you can also create a new event from the general Create dialog by choosing Object | Create, clicking

the Create icon (the green cube) in the left toolbar, or pressing CTRL-N. Then choose Event in the Create dialog box and click the Create.

3. The Create Event property sheet appears and you will be placed on the General page. Enter a name for the event in the Event Name field; the maximum length is 64 characters. Enter an optional description for the event in the Description field of up to 1024 characters. In the Target Type drop-down list box, select the HTTP Server target type (this is the default). Select a target HTTP server (or group) from the Available Targets list. You can mark individual targets, groups of targets, or a mix of individual targets and groups. Then click the Add button (the < sign) to add the target to the Selected Targets list. You can use the Remove button (the > sign) to remove one or more targets from the Selected Targets list.

NOTE
Only targets on nodes that have been discovered automatically are included in the list of available targets. Manually added database targets do not appear. If an event is submitted against a group containing both manually configured and automatically discovered targets, the event will not be submitted against the manually added targets. There must be at least one automatically discovered target in the group, or you will receive an error message when trying to register the event.

When you choose targets of the Node type, the OS drop-down list box appears. This box allows you to choose operating system-specific event tests. Choosing All (the default) from the list shows you event tests that work on all operating systems. Choosing a specific operating system, such as Windows NT, presents the event tests that are specific to the Windows NT operating system. Notice that the Available Targets list changes automatically, depending on your selection from the OS drop-down list box. The Intelligent Agent can only recognize these operating systems automatically if the version of the agent running on the target node is at least 8.1.7. Nodes running operating systems other than the OS selected or nodes that are running a pre-8.1.7 agent version are not displayed. These nodes are only available when you choose All.

4. To register an event or to store it in the event library, in addition to entering a name for the event, you must specify at least one event test. Click the Tests tab in the top of the event property sheet. You want to register an

HTTP Server event, which means you have to expand the HTTP Server item in the Available Tests tree by clicking the plus sign. The HTTP Server UpDown event is located in the Fault category, so expand this by clicking the plus sign, and select the HTTP Server UpDown event test by clicking it. Then click the Add button to add it to the Selected Tests list.

Figure 12-1 shows the event test definition for the event.

NOTE
This example uses only one event test, but you can specify multiple event tests for one event. Use this feature to add several related event tests in one single event definition, such as gathering database storage or performance related issues into one event.

You can now register the event and add it to the event library by selecting the Register and Add to Library radio button at the bottom of the event

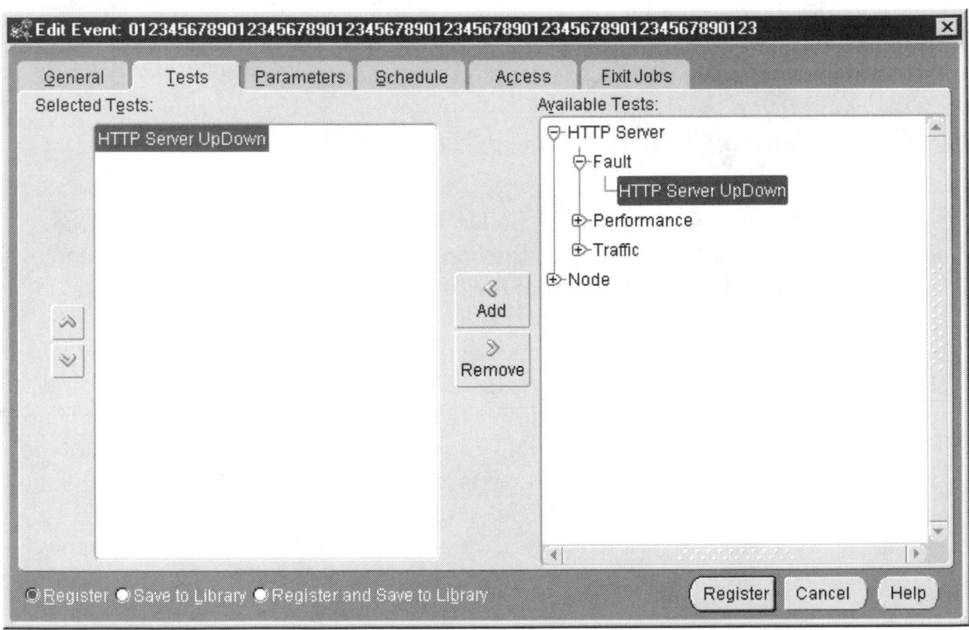

FIGURE 12-1. *Selecting an event test*

property sheet. This automatically selects the default scheduling (five minute intervals) with immediate registration, as well as the default notification options defined in your preferences. For the HTTP Server UpDown event test, there are no parameters available. Normally, the event test parameters define the threshold for warning and critical levels of the event. You can also override the preferred credentials on the parameters page, for example, if the event test requires higher system privileges.

5. Next, you need to provide the scheduling information for this event. Click the Schedule tab to get to the event test Schedule page. You define the scheduling of the event test through the radio button group in the left part of the screen. The default value is the On Interval setting, with five minute intervals and immediate registration. The following scheduling options are available:

    - **On Interval** This setting enables you to schedule a specific time interval between event tests. The interval can either be a combination of hours and minutes, or a specified number of days. Select the value you want to change and click the up or down arrow. You can also select the value by clicking it once and typing in a new value. You can additionally specify whether you want the event to be registered immediately after you register and store it (the default), or at a specific date and time. This can be useful if you know that the target currently is down due to maintenance, for example, but you expect it to be up and running at a later time.

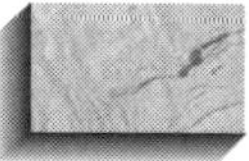

NOTE
The event executes at the local time zone of the Intelligent Agent (target node), which means that events are not necessarily tested simultaneously. Keep this in mind when you are monitoring targets spread across time zones and using a specific date and time for the event test.

- **On Day of Week** Use this setting to schedule the event on one or multiple days within one week. Check the check boxes for the days of the week for which you want the event to be tested. Then, specify the date and time for the event test to begin on these days by selecting the value you want to change and clicking the up or down arrows.
- **On Day of Month** This setting works like On Day of Week, but enables you to schedule the event to execute on one or multiple days within

a month. Check the check boxes for the dates of the month for which you want the task scheduled. You can now specify the date and time for the event test begin on these days by selecting the value you want to change and clicking the up or down arrows.

NOTE

Be aware that pre-9i Intelligent Agents do not support the On Day of the Week or On Day of the Month scheduling options. The event will result in the status "Registration Failed" and contain the error message "VNI-4022: Bad V1 schedule string." When you register an event against several targets, and one of the targets is running a pre-9i version, only the On Interval option is supported, although the other options are displayed as well.

6. Click the Access tab of the event property sheet to assign permissions on this event to other (regular) administrators, and to define who will be notified if the event triggers. For regular administrators, you can grant access to this event by checking the appropriate value (None, View, Modify, or Full). Remember that super administrators always have full privileges. Check the Notify check box for the administrators you want to be notified. You define how each administrator is notified, and when notification occurs through Preferences and Manage Administrators in the Configuration menu. See Chapter 9 for more details about notification settings. You check for "holes" in the notification schedule by clicking the Show Notification Schedule button. A white square means no notification, and a colored area means notification is set during the highlighted timeframe. You can add or remove notification for a specific administrator by right-clicking a specific square, choosing Add Recipient or Remove Recipient in the pop-up menu, and then choosing the administrator. You cannot change the ownership of the event at this point. Checking the Enable Notifications to External Services (SNMP Traps by Agent) check box in the bottom of the screen enforces that Simple Network Management Protocol (SNMP) traps are sent. These are used to notify third-party system management tools. The SNMP trap is picked up by a master agent at the target node and forwarded to the third-party management console. For more information about SNMP, please refer to *Oracle SNMP Support Reference Guide Release 9.0.1*.
7. Select the Register and Add to Library radio button at the bottom of the Create Event screen. The button to the right of this radio button group

changes its label accordingly. Click Register & Add. The event is stored in the event library and immediately registered on the selected target(s). See the "Monitoring the Registration of an Event" section later in this chapter for details about following the event registration procedure.

Creating an Event With User-Defined SQL

In addition to the predefined event tests available with the base EM, you can also define your own event tests using user-defined SQL. This way you can construct your own event tests using SQL and PL/SQL. For example, you can write a SELECT statement, which checks for a certain condition, such as counting the number of rows in a table. Or, you can call a PL/SQL function that does the checking from the SELECT statement. The only requirement is that the function must return a value that can be compared against the Warning and Critical thresholds. In this example, we will define an event that checks for the existence of database objects with the status INVALID in the DBA_OBJECTS data dictionary view.

1. Select Event | Create Event, press CTRL-E, or use the Create Like feature to get to the Create Event screen.
2. On the Create Event property sheet, enter a name for the event in the Event Name field. Enter a description for the event and choose Database in the Target Type drop-down list. Then select the target database (or target group) from the Available Targets list and click the Add button to add it to the Selected Targets list.
3. Click the Tests tab to go to the Tests page. Expand the Database entry in the Available Tests list and select User Defined SQL Test. Click the Add button to add the test to the Selected Tests list.
4. Click the Parameters tab in the top of the event property sheet. On the Parameters page, enter the SQL statement for your event test, for example, `select count(*) from dba_objects where status='INVALID'`. Choose your Critical and Warning thresholds. For example, if one occurrence is critical for you, choose >= as the Operator, enter **1** in the Critical field, and leave the Warning field empty. Figure 12-2 shows an example of such an event definition.
5. Click the Schedule tab and choose the scheduling for the event. Click the Access tab of the event property sheet to assign permissions for the event and define notification.
6. The last step is to select the Register and Save to Library radio button at the bottom of the Create Job screen and then click Register & Add. Now the event will be registered at the specified target.

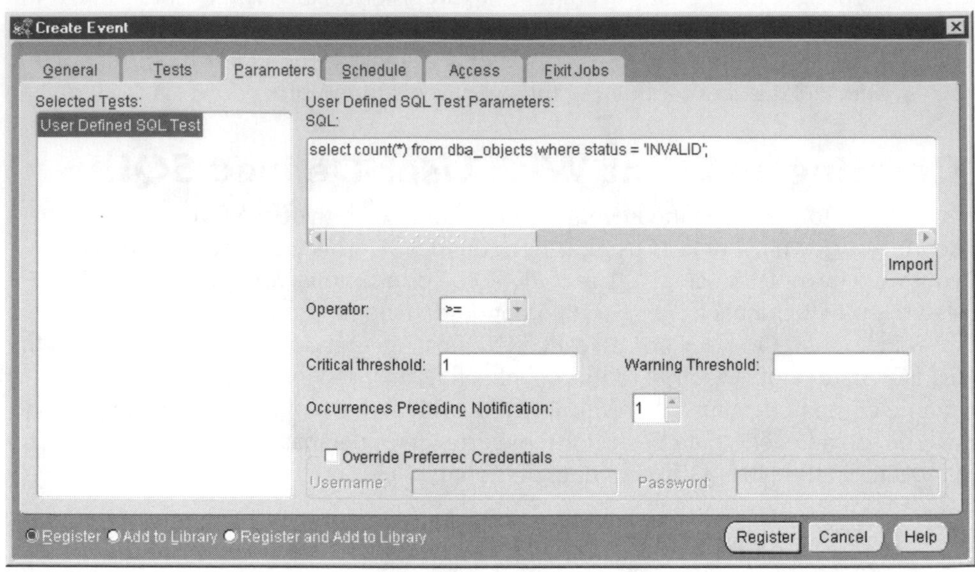

FIGURE 12-2. *Setting up a user-defined event*

Creating an Event with a Fixit Job

As mentioned in the introduction to this chapter, you can establish proactive monitoring with EM events. This is done using the special EM fixit job type, which you assign to the event so the Intelligent Agent will automatically attempt to correct the problem as it occurs. For example, you may want to run a job to attempt to restart the TNS Listener or HTTP Server if it has stopped. Fixit jobs are created with the EM Job system and must be designated as fixit jobs before you can associate them with an EM event. See Chapter 11 for more information on how to define fixit jobs using the EM Job system. In the following example, we will register an event to test for the TNS Listener UpDown event, and use a fixit job to try to restart the Listener. We assume the fixit job has been created and has the status Fixit on the target.

NOTE

You can create or edit fixit jobs in the Create Event property sheet, but for this example we will assume that the fixit job is already submitted and has the required Fixit status.

To create an event using an existing fixit job, follow these steps:

1. Select Event | Create Event, press CTRL-E, or use the Create Like feature to get to the Create Event Screen.
2. On the Create Event property sheet, enter a name for the event in the Event Name field. Enter a description for the event, and choose Listener in the Target Type drop-down list. Select the target listener (or target group) from the Available Targets list and click the Add button to add it to the Selected Targets list.
3. Then click on the Tests tab. Because you want to perform a Listener event test, expand the Listener entry in the Available Tests list and select Oracle Net UpDown. Then click the Add button to add the test to the Selected Tests list. Because there are no parameters for a Listener event test, you can skip to the Schedule page.
4. Click the Schedule tab in the top of the event property sheet. Accept the default schedule interval (On Interval) and change the interval from the default value of 5 minutes if you want. Click the Access tab of the event property sheet to assign permissions on the event to other (regular) administrators and to define who is being notified in case the event test will be triggered.
5. Click the Fixit Jobs tab of the event property sheet to assign the fixit job to the event. Check the "If ANY test triggers, run a fixit job" check box and choose the appropriate fixit job from the drop-down list box. As we already mentioned, you can also create new fixit jobs and modify existing ones from the Fixit Jobs page with the Create and Edit buttons, which open the Create Job and Edit Job screens, respectively. Figure 12-3 shows an example of a fixit job being assigned to an event.
6. Finally, select the Register and Save to Library radio button at the bottom of the Create Job screen and then click Register & Add. Now the event will be registered at the specified target. Execution of the fixit job will occur when the event detects a problem (when the TNS Listener is down). Administrators will be notified when the fixit job executes according to the notification settings of the fixit job.

Creating an Event Like an Existing Event

As with other EM objects, you can use the Create Like feature for EM events. If you have existing events, either stored in the event library or already registered, you can create a new event with same characteristics with the Create Like feature.

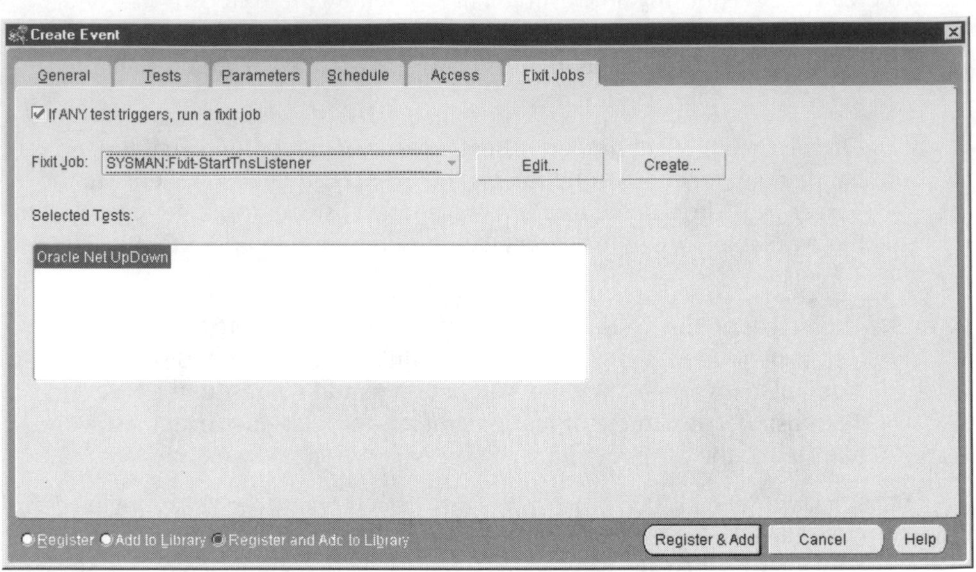

FIGURE 12-3. *Assigning a fix-it job to an event*

Creating an Event Like an Event Stored in the Event Library

To create a new event based on an existing event in the event library, follow these steps:

1. Select Event | Event Library or right-click the Events item in the Navigator tree and choose Event Library from the pop-up menu.
2. The Event Library screen appears. Click Create Like to open the Create Event property sheet.
3. Follow the steps explained in the "Creating a New Event and Storing It in the Event Library" section earlier in this chapter to complete event creation and registration.

Creating an Event Like an Event Registered or in the Event History

To create a new event with similar characteristics to another event not stored in the event library, but registered with an agent or located in the Event History, follow these steps:

1. Select the Events entry in the Navigator tree. Click either the Registered or History tab, depending on whether the event you want to use as a template is registered or only present in the event history. Right-click the event and choose Create Event Like from the pop-up menu, or choose Event | Create Event Like. You can also choose either Object | Create Like or Object | Create Event Like entry, click the Create Like icon (hollow green cube) in the left toolbar, or press CTRL-L.

2. The Create Event property sheet appears. Follow the steps explained in the "Create a New Event and Store It in the Event Library" section earlier in this chapter to complete event creation and registration.

Different States and Severity Levels of Events

When you register an event, it can take different states and severity levels. These states are indicated by the status field in the Registered Events page in the Events detail view window, or through the Severity field (a flag with different possible colors) in the Events Alerts and History pages. When an event occurrence takes place (an event test is triggered on the monitored target), it results in an outstanding alert on the Alerts page. If the target is a member of a group, the individual targets are also marked with a flag when you view them in the group view pane. In groups, no flag means that the target is not being monitored. See the "Monitoring Targets on a Group Basis" section later in this chapter for more about events and EM groups. The following are the colors an event flag can take:

- **Green** In the Alerts page you see a green flag when an event was returned back to a clear status from a warning or critical state. (For groups a clear flag is displayed when no error is detected.)
- **Yellow** An event test has reached the warning threshold.
- **Red** An event test has reached the critical threshold.
- **Gray** The status of the monitored target is unknown. This happens when an event has been registered against the target, but the Intelligent Agent cannot be contacted (possibly because of networking problems, or the target could be down). Because the Management Server relies on the Intelligent Agent when monitoring targets, it cannot tell anything about the state of the monitored target in this situation.

NOTE
A yellow hexagon with an exclamation point indicates an error state. This means there is a problem with the evaluation of the event condition and is more in relation to the event registration and test itself than to a warning or critical threshold being reached. This could happen if you register an Archive Full event against a database running in noarchivelog mode, or if there is a syntax error in the User Defined SQL Test event.

If an event triggers as an event test reaches warning or critical state, an alert will appear in the Events Alerts page. Additionally, notification of administrators through e-mail and pager will take place according to the notification settings of the event. See "Examining An Event Alert" later in this chapter for more about examining the details of an event alert.

Monitoring the Registration of an Event

When you register an event, it is sent to the Intelligent Agents at the selected target(s). If the Intelligent Agent is running, it registers the event and sends a confirmation back to the Management Server, which in turn sends the information to the EM Console. The event will appear in the Registered Events page in the Events detail view window. First, the event has the status Registration Pending; if the event is registered successfully, the status changes to Registered. Check the Show targets check box to also include target information in the detail view.

Monitoring Targets on a Group Basis

When you are monitoring targets by registering an event on a group basis, the group will inherit the worst state of any of its monitored members. For example, if one of the targets in the group has reached a critical state, a red flag will show on the group in the Group View pane, if the group is member of another group. No flag means that no targets are being monitored in the group. The EM group feature is covered in detail in Chapters 4 and 10.

Examining an Event Alert Using the Event Viewer

When an alert occurs for an event, it appears in the Events Alerts page. You can examine the alert from the Event Viewer, which you open by right-clicking the event and choosing Edit Event Occurrence from the pop-up menu, or by double-clicking the event with the alert. You will be placed on the first of three pages, the General page; the others are Log and Notification Details. On the General property page, you can assign this particular event alert to a specific EM administrator using the Assigned To drop-down list box. Each administrator can then view the alerts assigned to him or her in the Alerts page by sorting the list on the Assigned To column (click column header to sort the events). You can edit the event registration by clicking the Show Event Definition button on the General page. This opens the Edit Event screen; only the privilege and notification information on the Access page can be modified. The Log page displays an entry whenever an event changes state or is being assigned to another administrator. On the Log page, you can also enter comments, which is useful in an environment with many administrators. Regular administrators require explicit permission to the event to modify the event and enter comments. The Notification Details page lists notifications that have been sent to administrators.

You can save the event output, log, or notification details to a HTML or text file by clicking the Save List button available in all three pages of the Event Viewer. Click Apply to save changes and OK or Cancel to return to the EM Navigator.

Acknowledging an Event

Acknowledging an outstanding event (an event occurrence) in the Alerts page means that you as an administrator are aware of this problem and will take care of it. Or, maybe you know that the problem already has been solved, but the Intelligent Agent has not cleared the event yet. In the severity column, a pair of eyeglasses icon indicates that the alert has not yet been acknowledged. When you acknowledge an outstanding event, the eyeglasses disappear. In a multi-administrator environment, this feature is useful in order to inform your colleagues that this particular alert is being handled by someone. To acknowledge an event, right-click it and choose Acknowledge Event from the pop-up menu. You can also select the event and choose Event | Acknowledge or Object | Acknowledge Event.

Event History

When events have been cleared, they are automatically moved to the event history. You can also move an event from the Events Alerts page to the Event History by right-clicking the outstanding event and selecting Move to History from the pop-up menu. Depending on the number of event registrations, the event history will grow more or less rapidly.

To remove all events from the event history, select the Event | Clear Event History. A confirmation dialog appears; click Yes to confirm the deletion, or No to go back without clearing the event history.

You can generate a list of some or all of the events in the history through the Save List feature. Follow these steps:

1. Mark some or all of the events (you must select more than one) in the event history, and select Object | Save List.
2. Choose a format for the report, either HTML, text, or comma-separated, in the Format drop-down list box. HTML is chosen by default.
3. Enter a file name or leave the default. You can also use the Browse button to browse the file system and enter a file name. Notice that the file generated is stored on your EM Client machine by default in the ORACLE_ HOME\sysman\report directory.
4. Click OK to generate the file and exit the Save List dialog box. If you chose HTML as the format, you can click the View button to view the report in your browser immediately.

Event Library

The event library stores your defined events, which might already be registered or not. This enables you to easily resubmit events in the library or use them as templates for creating other similar events. The Event Library dialog box appears when you select the Event Library menu item. As shown in Figure 12-4, the dialog box contains a list of the events that you have created and saved in the event library. You can view summary information about an event, including the event name and owner. You can registe an event again using the Register button. You can modify an event by double-clicking it, or by using the Edit button. To create a new event based on an existing one, select the desired event and click the Create Like button. Click the Close button to exit the Event Library screen.

Copying a Registered Event to the Event Library

You can copy a registered event from the Registered Events page to the event library; for example, if you forgot to save the event to the library when you created it. Select the event you want to copy in the Registered Events page, right-click it, and choose Copy to Library from the pop-up menu. You can also choose Event | Copy Event to Library or Object | Copy to Library. After performing the copy, the event will be available in the event library for registration or further modification.

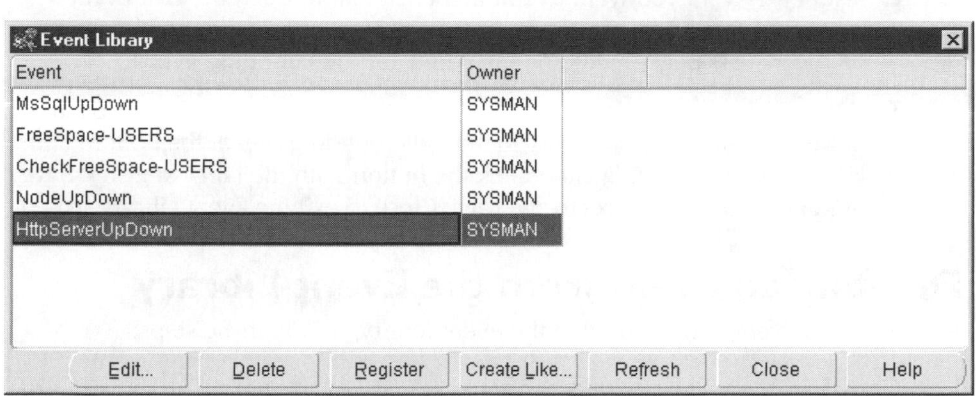

FIGURE 12-4. *The event library*

Registering an Event from the Event Library

When your events are stored in the event library, you can easily register them again. To do this, follow these steps:

1. Select Event | Event Library, or right-click the Events item in the Navigator tree and choose Event Library from the pop-up menu.
2. The Event Library screen appears as shown in Figure 12-4.
3. To register the event as it is stored in the event library, highlight the event you want to register and click the Register button. Now the event will be registered on the target(s) specified in the event definition.

Modifying an Event in the Event Library

If you want to make changes to the event before you register it, you must modify the event definition. You can choose to make the change permanent, or only modify it for a new event registration and leave as unchanged in the library. To modify an event in the event library, perform the following steps:

1. Select Event | Event Library or right-click the Events item in the Navigator tree and choose Event Library from the pop-up menu. The Event Library screen appears.

2. Select the event you want to edit and click Edit to open the Edit Event property sheet for the particular event. All information can be changed on the Access page, including the name and owner of the event.
3. When you are finished with the changes, either select Register, Save to Library, or Register and Save to Library in the radio button group at the bottom of the Edit Event property page and click the button with the label Register, Save, or Register & Save, respectively. Click Close to exit the Event Library screen.

Deleting an Event from the Event Library

To remove an event that is stored in the event library, follow these steps:

1. Select Event | Event Library or right-click the Events item in the Navigator tree and choose Event Library from the pop-up menu. The Event Library screen appears.
2. Select the event you want to delete and click Delete. As soon as you press the Delete button, the event disappears, without any confirmation dialog appearing. Be careful with this button! Click Close to exit the Event Library screen.

Modifying a Registered Event Dynamically

You can change some of the event properties for an event that you have already registered. If you want to modify a registered event, select the event in the Registered Events page and double-click it to open the Edit Event screen. You can modify some event properties when the Intelligent Agent on the target node is at least version 9i. Unlike the dialog box you saw when you created the event, you will see a different page as the first page, the Progress page. On this page, you can examine the status of the event (which should be Registered). Click Apply to save your changes or Cancel to exit without saving any changes.

To modify an event stored in the event library, refer to the "Modifying an Event in the Event Library" section earlier in this chapter.

Deregistering and Deleting Events

You can deregister (delete) registered events from their targets, and you can delete single or multiple events from the event history or the Event Library. Deleting an event from the Event Library is covered in the "Deleting an Event from the Event Library" section earlier in this chapter.

Deregistering Events

To deregister one or more events from the Registered Events page, select the event you want to deregister in the Registered Events page, right-click it, and choose Deregister from the pop-up menu. You can also simply press the DELETE key, choose Event | Deregister, Object | Deregister, or Object | Delete, or click the Remove icon (the trash can) in the left toolbar. A confirmation dialog appears; click Yes to deregister the event or No to go back without deregistering the event.

Removing an Event From the Event History

To delete one or more events from the History page, select the event(s) you want to delete in the Events History page, right-click it, and choose Delete Item(s) from the pop-up menu. You can also simply press the DELETE key, choose Event | Delete Item(s), Object | Delete Item(s), or Object | Delete, or click the Remove icon in the left toolbar. A confirmation dialog appears; click Yes to delete the event(s) or No to go back without deleting.

To remove all events from the event history, use the special Clear Event History function. See the "Event History" section earlier in this chapter.

Event Handler

As described in Chapter 4, the Event Handler has been available with EM since version 2.2. You can use this feature to customize actions or notifications triggered by an event. For example, you can create log entries in a log file or execute certain commands when certain events occur. You accomplish this with two components within the Event Handler: the Event Logger and the Command Executor. Before the Event Handler was included with EM, you had to use fixit jobs for handling such events. The Event Handler available with EM9i provides much more advanced features, such as taking action not only for one event but for a whole group of events. By default, the Event Handler is disabled in your EM environment, and you must enable it before you can configure and use it.

Enabling and Configuring the Event Handler

In this section, you will see how to enable and configure the Event Handler using the OEMCTL command on a Windows NT/2000 machine. The Management Server must be configured to use an EM repository before you run this configuration program. The OEMCTL utility connects to the EM repository using the same logon credentials that you specified in the Enterprise Manager Configuration Assistant (EMCA):

1. First, enable the Event Handler. You must perform this operation while the Management Server is stopped. Either stop the OMS from the Services program or open a command prompt and execute the following command to stop it:

   ```
   oemctl stop oms <oms super administrator>/<password>
   ```

   For example:

   ```
   C:\>oemctl stop oms sysman/sysman
   OEMCTL for Windows NT: Version 9.0.1.0.0
   Copyright (c) 1998, 1999, 2000, 2001 Oracle Corporation.  All rights reserved.
   Stopping the Oracle Management Server...
   ```

2. Now the Management Server is stopped, and you can enable the Event Handler. Enter the command:

   ```
   oemctl enable eventhandler
   ```

   For example:

   ```
   C:\>oemctl enable eventhandler
   Connecting to management server repository using credentials
   OEMREP_CHBSLLAVA/******@oemrep
   Event handler enabled.
   ```

3. Now you can configure the Event Handler. The parameters for the Event Handler are stored in the EM repository. The only way currently to change these parameters is to export the parameters to a file, edit the parameters in the file, and then import them back into the repository. To export the configuration file, enter the following command:

   ```
   oemctl export eventhandler <filename>
   ```

   For example, export to the file eventhandler_chbsllava.txt like this:

   ```
   C:\>oemctl export eventhandler eventhandler_chbsllava.txt
   Connecting to management server repository using credentials
   OEMREP_CHBSLLAVA/******@oemrep
   Event handler config dumped to file eventhandler_chbsllava.txt
   ```

NOTE

If an error occurs during the export operation stating `Could not open config file <filename>: File does not exist or you don't have permissions`*, simply create a text file first using your editor. The file will be overwritten each time you run the export command.*

4. You now must edit the Event Handler parameters in the above file. See the "Event Handler Parameters" section that follows for details on the event handler parameters. You might want to make a backup of the file generated by the export before applying your modifications. Then use your text editor to edit the file and save the modifications to it.

5. Import the modified parameters into the EM repository. To import the configuration file, enter the following command:

```
oemctl import eventhandler <filename>
```

For example:

```
C:\>oemctl import eventhandler eventhandler_chbsllava.txt
Connecting to management server repository using credentials
OEMREP_CHBSLLAVA/******@oemrep
Event handler configuration updated with contents of file
eventhandler_chbsllava.txt
```

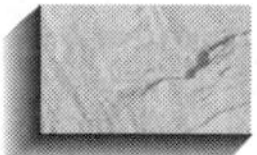

NOTE
Importing the parameter file overrides any previous Event Handler settings that were defined in the EM repository.

6. Now you can start the Management Server again using the Services program or the enter the following command in the command prompt:

```
oemctl start oms <oms super administrator>/<password>
```

For example:

```
C:\>oemctl start oms sysman/sysman
The OracleOraNT9iManagementServer service is
starting...............
The OracleOraNT9iManagementServer service was started
successfully.
```

You can verify the current Event Handler configuration using the dump option, by entering the command:

```
oemctl dump eventhandler
```

This prints out the current configuration. For more details about the OEMCTL command-line utility, refer to Chapter 19.

Event Handler Parameters

In this section, we will take a look on some of the Event Handler parameters. One of the central aspects of the Event Handler are the *template* parameters. You use templates for filtering events, thereby defining different logging or command execution for different groups of events occurring on certain targets. Each template must be identified by a unique name. We will look at an example of defining a template for recognizing the "HTTP-Server UpDown" event on a certain node and to send a message (a pop-up using NET SEND) to the target node in case this event is triggered. Refer to Chapter 6 in the *Enterprise Manager Administrator's Guide, Release 9.0.1* for more details on the available parameters.

The logfile Parameter

The logfile generated by the Event Logger is created when the first event test is triggered. The location of the Event Handler log file is specified through the parameter /com/oracle/sysman/em/eventlogger/templates/allevents/logfile. On Windows NT and 2000, the Event Handler logs information to the eventhandler.log file located in the ORACLE_HOME\sysman\log directory on the Management Server by default. The parameter will have the following value in the export of the parameters in the example above (step 3):

```
/com/oracle/sysman/em/eventlogger/templates/allevents/logfile=
F:\Oracle\OraNT9i/sysman/log/eventhandler.log
```

NOTE
Directory names that only use the backlash (\) as a delimiter do not work; use a forward slash (/) instead.

The respect_blackout Parameter

Use the respect blackout parameter to instruct the Event Handler that it must respect e-mail and paging blackouts when these have been activated. The parameter is set to false by default, meaning the Event Handler ignores any blackouts. To set it, use the following:

```
eventhandler.respect_blackouts=true
```

Event Logger Templates

The Event Logger can use the templates to recognize *which* events should be logged in the log file specified by the logfile parameter, and *how* the logging is to be done. You use the following format for entering Event Logger templates:

```
/com/oracle/sysman/em/eventlogger/templates/<template>/<property> =
<value>
```

Use the following for *<template>* and *<property>*—*<template>* must be the unique name for the template and *<property>* can be any of the following:

- *eventname* The name of the event being tracked
- *node* The node where the event is triggered
- *targettype* The type of target, which can be one of the following:
  - oracle_sysman_node
  - oracle_sysman_database
  - oracle_sysman_listener
  - oracle_sysman_cmanager
  - oracle_sysman_ops
  - oracle_sysman_webserver
  - oracle_sysman_hotstandby
- *targetname* The name of the target (of type *targettype*)
- *owner* The owner of the event
- *severity* The status of the event, which can be the following:
  - alert
  - error
  - warning
  - clear
  - nodedown

You can specify more than one event property by using multiple entries.

Command Executor Templates

Just as the Event Logger can use templates to make different log entries for different event occurrences, the Command Executor can execute a certain command, depending on which event(s) occurred. You use the following format for entering Command Executor templates:

```
/com/oracle/sysman/em/commandexecutor/templates/<template>/<property> = <value>
```

The same options are available for <*template*> and <*property*> as for the Event Logger template (see the previous section). The following is a simple example of parameter settings for sending a message to the target node, when the HTTP Server UpDown event is triggered (because the HTTP Server is down). The template defined is called HTTPServerChbsllava (it checks event occurrence on node CHBSLLAVA) and the NET SEND command is used to write a message to the console of the target node CHBSLLAVA:

```
/com/oracle/sysman/em/commandexecutor/templates/HTTPServerChbsllava/node = chbsllava
/com/oracle/sysman/em/commandexecutor/templates/HTTPServerChbsllava/target_type =
oracle_sysman_webserver
/com/oracle/sysman/em/commandexecutor/templates/HTTPServerChbsllava/severity = alert
/com/oracle/sysman/em/commandexecutor/templates/HTTPServerChbsllava/command = net send
chbsllava The HTTP-Server is down!
```

When you have imported these parameters into the EM repository, the Command Executor sends a message to the target node each time the HTTP server is detected to be down by an EM event.

Disabling the Event Handler

To disable the Event Handler, make sure the Management Server is stopped. Then open a command prompt and execute the following command:

```
oemctl disable eventhandler
```

For example:

```
C:\>oemctl disable eventhandler
Connecting to management server repository using credentials OEMREP_CHBSLLAVA/******@oemrep
Event handler disabled.
```

Now the Event Handler is disabled and you can start your Management Server again.

EM Events and the Reporting Framework

You can create reports containing information about items such as outstanding events, event history, and events stored in the event library. This is accomplished through the EM Reporting Framework. Refer to Chapters 4 and 13 for more details about the reporting feature available with EM.

Summary

In this chapter, you have learned about one of the key features of EM, the event system, which enables you to monitor your targets. You learned how to create and register events and store these in the event library, as well as to modify and register existing events from the event library. Additionally, you have learned how to make use of the Event Handler. In the next chapter, we will cover the EM reporting framework, which also can be used to provide information about EM events.

CHAPTER 13

Reporting Framework

ost DBAs have created their own collection of reports on issues such as tablespace usage, objects and their extents, number of users, and so on, created with SQL, PL/SQL, or Perl scripts. These reporting needs can now be fulfilled through the EM9i reporting framework, which has been greatly enhanced since version 2.2. There are numerous predefined reports available, and you can create your own custom reports as well. You can request the reports either from your Web browser or from the EM Console, and a publishing feature enables you to publish your reports to a central Website, such as your company intranet. You can either generate the reports on demand, or use the scheduling feature (based on EM jobs) to refresh the contents in regular intervals. This is also useful for scheduling resource-demanding reports to run overnight, for example. In Chapter 4, we discussed the reporting feature of EM9i. In this chapter, you dig into the configuration aspect as well as the use of reports. You will see how to view the output from the report, and how to create a custom report.

Note that the whole reporting framework (including publishing feature) is not available when running the EM Console in standalone mode. In standalone mode, you can also generate reports, but only locally on your EM console machine, either into a file (HTML, text, or comma-separated) or to your browser. This chapter mainly focuses on the reporting features available with the EM Console connected to a Management Server, but we also briefly explain the standalone reporting features in the "Reporting Features in Standalone Mode" section at the end of this chapter.

Configuring the EM Reporting Website

The EM Reporting Website is part of the core EM installation. The following required Reporting Website components are automatically installed when installing the Management Server software (see Chapter 2):

- Oracle HTTP Server to act as the reporting Web server. This is the same HTTP Server that is used by default for the browser-based Enterprise Manager.
- The Reporting Website (consisting of HTML files, images, Java classes, servlets, and more) must be installed in the ORACLE_HOME\oem_webstage directory.

Before you can use the reporting features, the reporting framework must be activated. Basically, you need to tell the Management Server where to find the Reporting Website, but also the Web server must know where to find the Management Server and EM repository, and the password of the REPORTS_USER administrator. If you choose View Published Reports from, for example, the Object menu in the EM Console before running the Management Server configuration, you will get an error.

The easiest way of running the Reporting Website is to use the Oracle HTTP Server supplied with your Oracle installation. You can also use the Microsoft IIS Web server, for example, but additional configuration is required, and it is not recommended by Oracle at the time of writing. Refer to Chapter 18 for more information about how to configure EM with the Oracle HTTP Server as well as the Apache and Microsoft IIS Web servers.

NOTE
There can only be one Web server configured for EM reports at a time. Configuring a new Web server disables previously configured Reporting Websites.

Configuring the Oracle HTTP Server for EM Reporting

In this section, you will take a closer look at how to configure the EM Reporting Website using the Oracle HTTP Server. Follow these configuration steps on a Windows NT or 2000 machine:

1. There is a built-in, dedicated super administrator account for the reporting part of EM, the REPORTS_USER. The default password is OEM_TEMP (case insensitive), just like for SYSMAN. Log onto the EM Console through the Management Server using *another* super administrator account, such as SYSMAN, and change the password for REPORTS_USER. See Chapter 9 for details about how to edit the EM administrator preferences.
2. On the node running your Management Server, you must configure the EM Reporting Website. Ensure that the Management Server you want to configure for the EM Reporting Website is running. You need to use the OEMCTL command included with your Management Server installation. For more about this utility, see Chapter 19. Open a command-line prompt and enter the command **oemctl configure rws**. You will be prompted for the following information:
   - Web server name where your HTTP Server runs
   - Port number to use for EM Reporting Website (the default is 3339)
   - Hostname where your Oracle Management Server runs
   - Password for the REPORTS_USER EM administrator account

   The following is an example where the HTTP Server on the Windows 2000 host CHBSLLAVA pointing to the Management Server and EM repository on the same host is configured to run on the default port 3339:

```
C:\>oemctl configure rws
Configuring the reporting web server...

This command line utility configures a web server on this machine so that
it can be used for Enterprise Manager reporting.  Answer each prompt and
hit return. After you answer each prompt, you will be asked for
confirmation before the web server is configured.
```

```
To quit this utility, hit CTRL-C.
For Help, see EM_ReportingConfig.HTML.

Webserver Name [default is CHBSLLAVA]:
Port number [default is 3339]:
Oracle Management Server [default is CHBSLLAVA]:
Password for the REPORTS_USER Administrator : reports_user

You have provided all of the information required to configure the web
server.
Configure the web server now? [Y/N, default is Y]:

CONFIGURATION COMPLETED: The webserver has been successfully configured.
You can now access the Enterprise Manager Reporting Home Page using the
URL http://CHBSLLAVA:3339/em/OEMNavigationServlet.
You can also access the Reporting Home page using the View Published
Reports menu command in the Enterprise Manager Console.
C:\>
```

NOTE
If you did not change the default password for REPORTS_USER, the above configuration will fail with an error message.

3. You can access the EM Reporting Website by entering the URL http://<*hostname*> :3339, for example, http://chbsllava:3339, and clicking Access Reports at the bottom of the screen. You can also enter the complete URL as http://<*hostname*>:3339/em/OEMNavigationServlet. Figure 13-1 shows an example of the EM Reporting Website Home Page running on the CHBSLLAVA host.

NOTE
If you cannot access this URL, check that the Web server is running. You can also try to restart the HTTP Server, either from the Services menu or by choosing the Stop HTTP Server powered by Apache and Start HTTP Server powered by Apache items in the HTTP Server program group (Start | Programs | Oracle - <Oracle Home> | Oracle HTTP Server). Also, Oracle states that the OMS and the Web server must reside on the same server. We have been able to complete the configuration with OMS and the Web server on two different nodes though, but recommend that you keep both components on the same server as Oracle specifies. Check also the Oracle Enterprise Manager Readme for the latest issues.

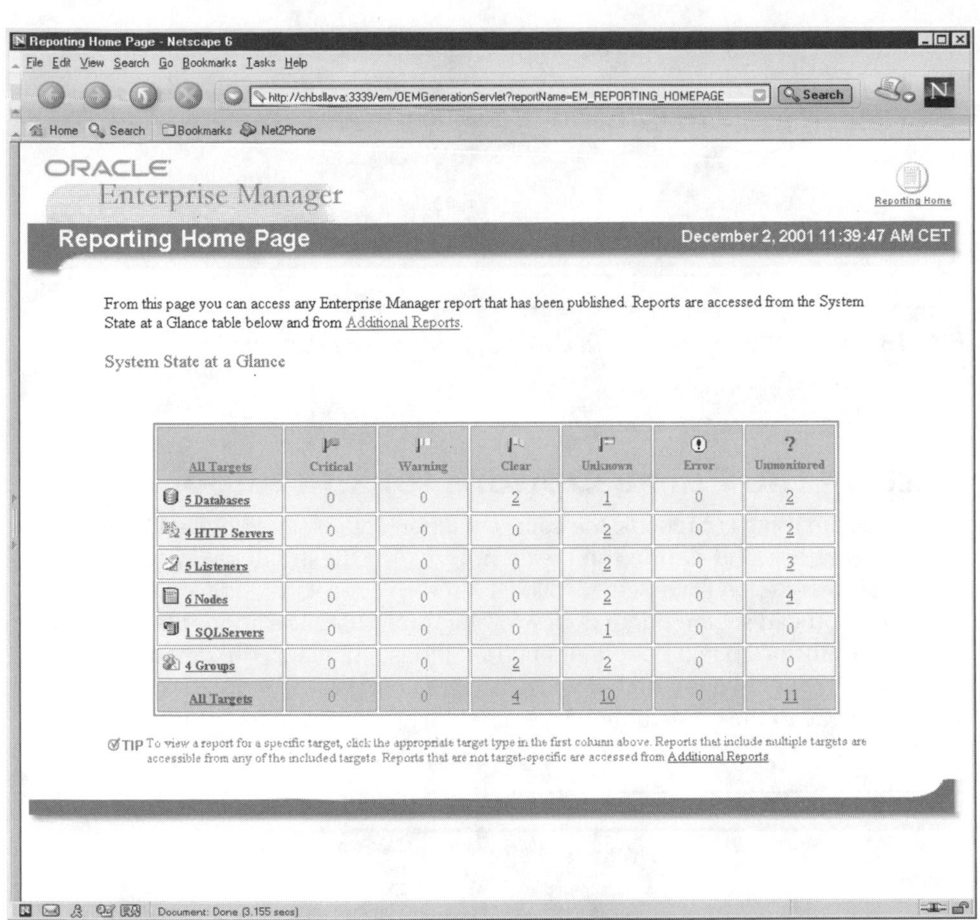

FIGURE 13-1. *The EM Reporting Home Page*

Checking the EM Website Configuration

You can verify the EM Reporting Website configuration by checking the settings through the EM Console Configuration menu. Select View Reporting Website Configuration. The dialog box shown in Figure 13-2 appears.

Click OK to exit the dialog box.

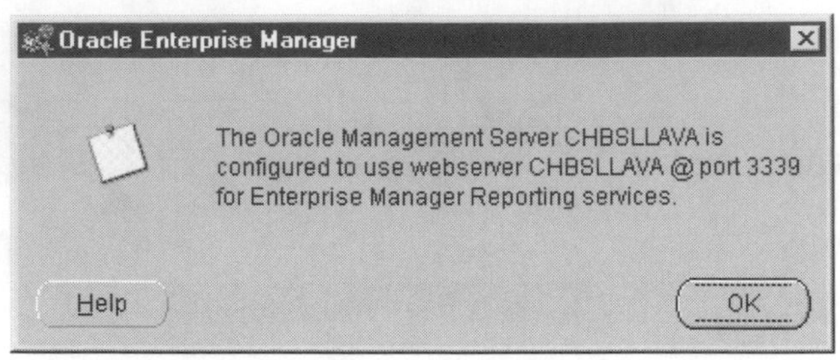

FIGURE 13-2. *Checking the Reporting Website configuration*

Setting the Purge Options for EM Reports

When you are using EM reports, the collected report data is stored in the EM repository tables. To check and define the purge options for these tables, choose the Configuration | Report Data Purge Options. A screen appears, as shown in Figure 13-3.

Here, you can set the purge policy for the report data log as an interval in days, weeks, months or up to a couple of hundred thousand years. The default is three years, which might be too high if you are generating a lot of reports. Any change that you make to the purge policy takes effect when the next report is generated.

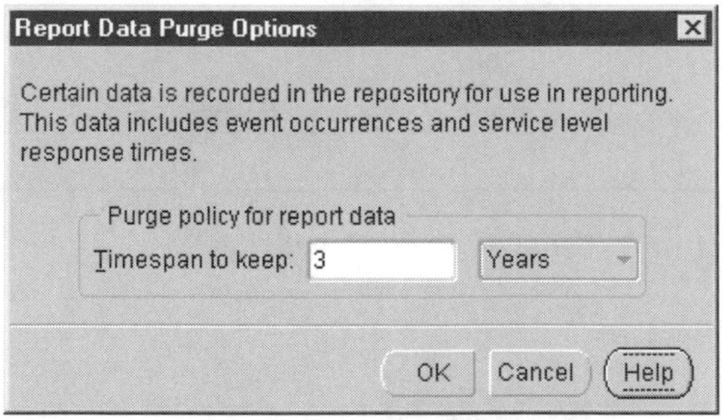

Report Data Purge Options

Certain data is recorded in the repository for use in reporting. This data includes event occurrences and service level response times.

Purge policy for report data

Timespan to keep: 3 Years

OK Cancel Help

FIGURE 13-3. *Defining purge options*

Viewing Output from an Existing Report

As mentioned earlier, a lot of predefined reports are available with EM, in addition to the ones you define yourself. To run these reports and view the output while connected to the Management Server, there are basically two options:

- **View Report** Request report generation on demand and get the output displayed from within the EM Console.
- **View Published Reports** View the published report output, which is either generated at certain intervals automatically or on demand when you access the report. You can do this either directly from your Web browser (the EM Reporting Website) or from within the EM Console.

You must consider which reports you (or other users) will access from the EM Reporting Website. All these reports are the published ones. The rest are the reports requested by the EM administrators from the EM Console on an as-needed basis; these are unpublished. All reports produce their output in HTML, whether they are published or unpublished.

Remember to set the Preferred Credentials for each database (or use the <DEFAULT> connection) for the REPORTS_USER. Otherwise, the report generation will fail with an error for those targets for which the REPORTS_USER user has no credentials defined, such as

```
Processing of report element # 2 failed:
oracle.sysman.vt.reporting.ReportGenerationException: Could not get
session for the target database.
```

Accessing the Report Definitions in the EM Navigator

You access the reports by selecting the Report Definitions entry in the EM Navigator. All available reports appear in the detail view. You can sort the list by clicking on a column heading. Definitions with a blue plus sign included in the icon left of the Report Title column are PUBLISHED, and those where a clock is also displayed are scheduled for publishing. Report definitions with a red X are not published (UNPUBLISHED). In Figure 13-4, you see an example of the Report Definitions detail view.

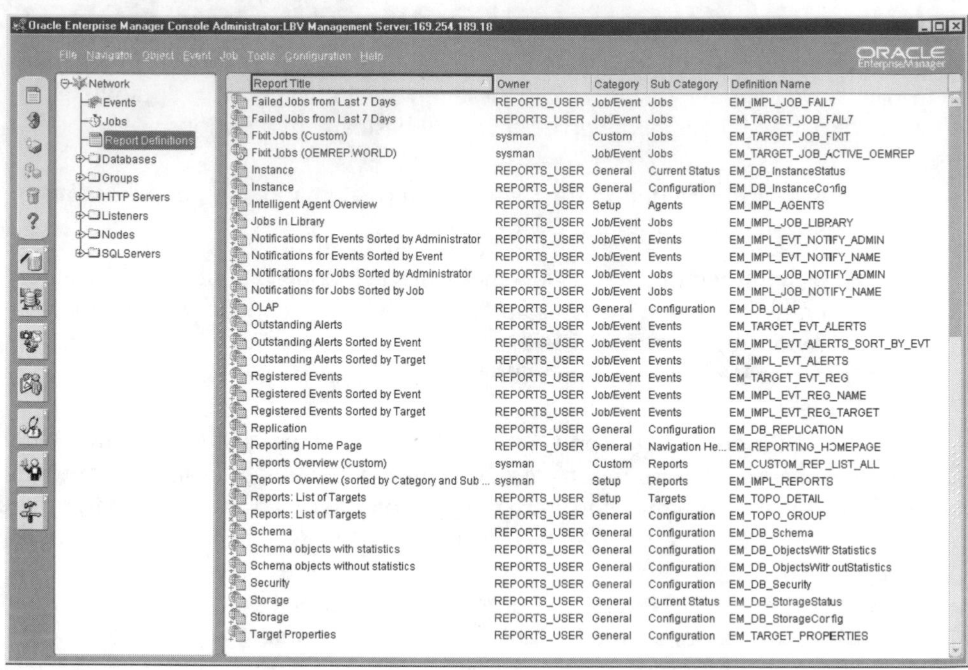

FIGURE 13-4. *Accessing Predefined Reports Through the Report Definitions Detail View*

Viewing Reports

As mentioned before, you can request generation of any report (published or unpublished) on demand and display the result while connected to the EM Console. When you select the Report Definitions entry in the EM Navigator, you can request generation of a single report and view the output. Simply right-click the report in the detail view and choose View Report from the pop-up menu. If you have chosen a report that is target-specific, and no target has been specified in the report definition, the Target Selection dialog box appears, as shown in Figure 13-5.

Select the target you want to create the report for and click OK to begin generating the report. You can select multiple targets in this dialog box by keeping the CTRL key pressed, or you select a range of targets by using the SHIFT key. The report output is generated and presented in your Web browser.

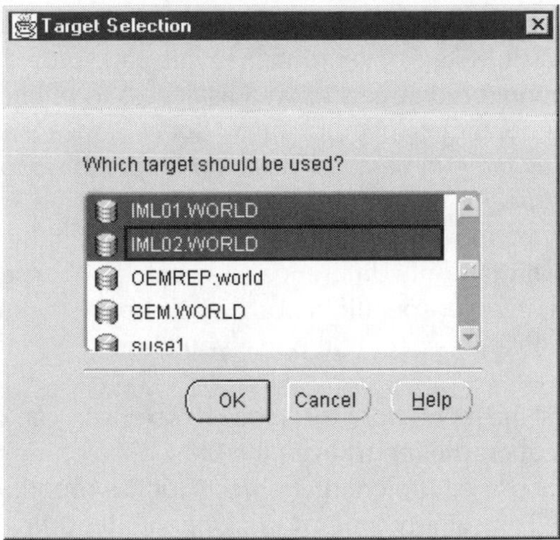

FIGURE 13-5. *Selecting a target to generate a report*

Viewing Published Reports

To view the published reports, you have two options:

- From your Web browser through the EM Reporting Website
- From the EM Console, which launches the EM Reporting Website in your Web browser

To generate and view published reports, the report definition must be set to publish to the EM Reporting Website. For more details about the report definition properties, see the "Creating Your Own Reports" section later in this chapter.

Accessing Published Reports From Your Web Browser

You can view the output from the published reports at the EM Reporting Website, which you can access directly from the Web browser. Either enter the URL http://<*hostname*>:3339 in your browser and then click Access Reports in the bottom of the screen, or enter the complete path for the EM Reporting Home Page, for example, http://chbsllava:3339/em/OEMNavigationServlet.

The EM Reporting Home Page appears (see Figure 13-1). This page shows the System State at a Glance and consists of a table containing all available target types (vertically) and all possible states (horizontally). This page provides a quick overview of the state of your monitored targets as well as access to published reports, which are target-specific or nontarget-specific. *Target-specific* means that the report is chosen after a specific target object such as a node, database, or listener has been selected. *Nontarget-specific* reports are accessed through the Additional Reports link, located at both the top and bottom of the screen. Actually, you access the same report definitions, the only difference is *when* you choose the target for which you run the report. For target-specific reports, you choose the target object *before* the report, and for nontarget-specific reports, you choose the target object *after* the report has been chosen.

When you request the report from the Web browser, you can only select *one* target object. When you request the report from the EM Console using the View Report function, you can choose multiple target objects for the report. You can return to the EM Reporting Home Page at any time by clicking the Reporting Home hyperlink in the upper right corner.

Accessing Target-Specific Reports When you are on the EM Reporting Home Page, you access the target-specific reports by clicking the link you want in the All Targets column in the System State at a Glance part of the screen (see Figure 13-1). For instance, if you want to view the database report "Schema objects with statistics" (definition name EM_DB_ObjectsWithStatistics), follow these steps:

1. Click the Database link in the All Targets column.
2. Your browser lists all database targets, including those not discovered automatically, but added manually. You select the database you want to view the report for by clicking the link (the database name).
3. All available database reports of type General appear in a screen. The other report categories (Job/Event, Service Levels, Performance, and Trending) are available through links (displayed as tabs) at the top and bottom of the screen.

NOTE
The Performance and Trending pages only appear if the optional EM Diagnostics Pack is installed. Further, to access the reports in the Trending category, you must have historical data collected by the Capacity Planner tool.

4. You can choose the report "Schema objects with statistics" by clicking the report title (link), and the report output will be generated and displayed. Depending on how much work the report is doing, the generation may take from a few seconds to several minutes.

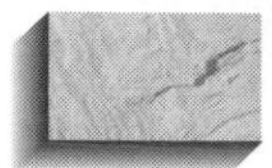

NOTE
If you selected a specific target object in the EM Console, say a database, when choosing "View Published Reports," you are taken directly to the available reports page for this particular target object. Remember that the REPORTS_USER must have preferred credentials for the target.

Accessing NonTarget-Specific Reports Nontarget-specific reports are accessed from the Additional Reports link, located at the top and bottom of the Reporting Home Page (Figure 13-1). Click one of the Additional Reports links and choose the report you want to run by clicking the link (report title) for it. A screen appears where you choose the target object for which the report is generated by clicking the name of the object. The report is generated and the output is displayed in the Web browser.

Accessing Published Reports from the EM Console

You can also access the published reports from the EM Console in many ways. You can click the View Published Reports icon in the left toolbar or choose View Published Reports from the Object menu or the pop-up menu for a certain target object. You can also go to the Report Definitions detail view by selecting Report Definitions in the EM Navigator tree. Right-click any report in the page and choose View Published Reports from the pop-up menu. Finally, you can launch the EM Reporting Home Page by right-clicking the report definition Reporting Home Page and choosing View Report. In any case, the EM Reporting Home Page is in your Web browser, and you can navigate through it as described in the previous sections.

Web Browser Does Not Launch from the EM Console

Sometimes, when you choose View Report or View Published Reports from the EM Console, your Web browser may not launch. Either the screen flickers, nothing happens at all, or the EM built-in IceBrowser browser appears instead, which is used by the EM Quick Tour. The reasons and solutions for this behavior vary, depending on the operating system you're using (see Chapter 20 for more issues on troubleshooting your EM environment).

On Unix Platforms You must add a parameter to the EM Console client configuration file clientconfig.properties located in $ORACLE_HOME/sysman/config directory. With Windows, you normally do not need to do this, just be sure that your browser launches automatically when you open an HTML document by double-clicking on it. On Unix platforms, you must add a line with the user.browser parameter, which must point to the executable (not a shell script) for the browser, such as:

```
user.browser=/usr/netscape/netscape
```

On Windows Platforms Although the EM thin client browser requirements say either Microsoft Internet Explorer version 5.0 or higher or Netscape Navigator version 4.7 or higher, we have experienced problems when using IE version 6 on Windows 2000 and Windows 98: The browser would not launch correctly from within the EM Console. After we applied a patch from Oracle (EM_9.0.1_1856434 for Windows 98 or 2000), the problem disappeared.

Creating Your Own Reports

You can create your own customized reports, store them together with the predefined report definitions, and publish them to the EM Reporting Home Page. You can create a report completely from scratch, but the easiest method is to use the Create Like feature on an existing report and then modify the report definition. To create EM reports from scratch, you should be familiar with basic HTML coding and JavaScript, but when you use an existing report as a template, it is actually not so complicated. Just be sure you know what you want your report to show and choose an existing report similar to the one you want. You can also choose to use your favorite text editor to write the report source, and then copy and paste the text into the EM report definition. In the sections that follow, we will show you how to create a new report definition (like an existing one) and how to schedule the publishing of the report to the EM Reporting Home Page. Oracle provides several views in the EM repository (with the "SMP_VIEW_" prefix) which can be useful when creating your custom repository reports. We recommend that you use these views when possible, instead of accessing the repository tables directly. Refer to Appendix C in the Oracle9i Enterprise Manager Administrator's Guide for more information about the content of these views.

Creating a New Report Definition

This section will walk you through an example of creating a new report definition which lists all existing reports in the EM repository. We will use the report definition Administrator Overview as a template:

1. Go to the Report Definitions in the EM Navigator and select the Administrator Overview report by clicking it once.
2. Right-click the report and choose Create Like from the pop-up menu. The Create Report screen appears, as shown in Figure 13-6.
3. You are placed on the General page.
   A. Enter a new Definition Name, such as **EM_CUSTOM_REP_LIST_ALL**, and be sure the name is unique (you will be told if it is not). No blanks are allowed in the name; use underscores (_) instead. This name is used internally by EM.

B. Enter a new Report Title and Report Description and choose the Custom value from the Category drop-down list box.

C. Select a value from the Subcategory list, or define your own subcategory, by entering the name you choose in the field. For this example, leave the value Repository in the Report Type drop-down list box. Because the report type is Repository, you cannot select any targets, and this part of the screen is grayed out.

D. Because we do not want to publish this report, uncheck the "Publish to Enterprise Manager Reporting Website" check box. Next, click the Elements tab at the top of the Create Report screen.

4. On the Elements page, you see the different parts of the report and its structure. Leave the Report Elements as is and click the Parameters tab at the top of the Create Report screen.

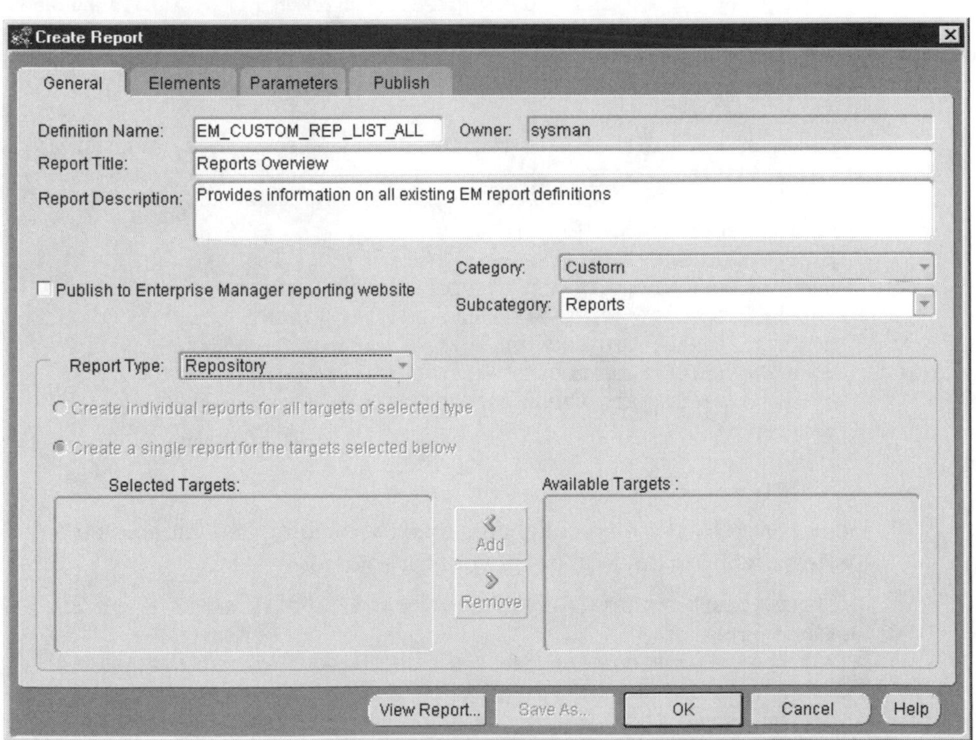

FIGURE 13-6. *Creating a new report*

5. On the Parameters page, you must edit all the report elements individually. Begin with the "For each row" element (report body) and enter the following query:

```
  SELECT  report_name   report_name
         ,upper(owner)  report_owner
         ,report_title  report_title
         ,description   report_desc
    FROM smp_vbo_reports
ORDER BY category,sub_category
```

6. Select the HTML element in the Selected Elements list and modify the HTML and JavaScript source in the Specify HTML text field. Change the variable names and the parameters for the ProcessRecord function, for example like this:

```
<SCRIPT LANGUAGE="JavaScript">
<!--
var tot_report   = 0;
var check_str    = "<IMG SRC=\""+GIFdir+"checked.gif\" ALT=\"checked\"
 WIDTH=16 HEIGHT=16>";
var uncheck_str = "<IMG SRC=\""+GIFdir+"space.gif\" ALT=\"unchecked\"
 WIDTH=16 HEIGHT=16>";
function PrintTotals () {
  document.writeln("<TR><TD BGCOLOR=#cccc99><FONT FACE=\"SANSSERIF\"
COLOR=\"#336699\" SIZE=2><B>Total: "+tot_report+"</B></FONT></TD>");
}
function ProcessRecord(report_name,
report_owner,report_title,report_desc) {
  document.writeln("<TR><TD BGCOLOR=#f7f7e7 VALIGN=\"top\"><FONT
 FACE=\"SANSSERIF\" SIZE=2>"+report_title+"</FONT></TD>");
  document.write("<TD BGCOLOR=#f7f7e7>"+report_owner+"</TD>");
  document.write("<TD BGCOLOR=#f7f7e7>"+report_name+"</TD>");
  document.write("<TD BGCOLOR=#f7f7e7>"+report_desc+"</TD>");
  tot_report   += 1;
}// Hide -->
</SCRIPT>
```

7. Select the HTML(1) element and change the heading and variable names corresponding to the SQL query you just entered.

```
<CENTER><TABLE BORDER cellPadding=3 summary="This table lists all the
defined reports.">
<TH scope="col" BGCOLOR=#cccc99 WIDTH=50><FONT FACE="SANSSERIF"
 COLOR="#336699" SIZE=2><B>Report Title</B></FONT></TH>
<TH scope="col" BGCOLOR=#cccc99 WIDTH=50><FONT FACE="SANSSERIF"
 COLOR="#336699" SIZE=2><B>Owner</B></FONT></TH>
<TH scope="col" BGCOLOR=#cccc99 WIDTH=50><FONT FACE="SANSSERIF"
 COLOR="#336699" SIZE=2><B>Report Name</B></FONT></TH>
<TH scope="col" BGCOLOR=#cccc99 WIDTH=50><FONT FACE="SANSSERIF"
 COLOR="#336699" SIZE=2><B>Description</B></FONT></TH>
```

8. You can leave the HTML(2) element as is and test the report by clicking View Report. The report will be generated and the progress is shown in a pop-up window before the output is displayed in your Web browser. You will not be able to enter any information on the Publish page, because you have chosen not to publish this report. All fields on this page are grayed out.

9. When you are satisfied with the report, store it by clicking the OK button. Your custom report appears together with all the other predefined ones in the Report Definitions detail view.

Creating a New Report Definition and Scheduling Publishing

In this section, you will see an example of creating a new report definition, which will be scheduled for publishing on the EM Reporting Home Page using the schedule feature. You will create a report that lists all registered fixit jobs on a selected target database, using the Active Jobs report definition as template. Follow these steps:

1. Go to the Report Definitions in the EM Navigator and select the Active Jobs report by clicking it once.

2. Right-click the report and choose Create Like from the pop-up menu. The Create Report screen appears, as shown in Figure 13-6.

3. Enter a new Definition Name, such as **EM_TARGET_JOB_FIXIT**, and be sure the name is unique. Enter a new Report Title and Report Description and choose the Custom value from the Category drop-down list box. Now select the Jobs value from the Subcategory list or define your own subcategory, by entering the name. Leave the value All Managed Targets in the Report Type drop-down list box. Also, leave the "Create individual reports for all targets of selected type" check box checked unless you want to specify specific target objects to be included in the report. Because you want to publish this report, be sure the "Publish to Enterprise Manager Reporting Website" check box is checked.

4. Select the HTML(3) element and click the Remove (>) button to delete this report element. Then click the Parameters tab at the top of the Create Report screen.

5. On the Parameters page, edit all the report elements individually. Begin with the "For each row" element (report body) and modify the query. Remove the js.status BETWEEN 1 AND 2 AND part, and modify the j.fixit_job = 0 line to read j.fixit_job = 1. Click the Publish tab at the top of the screen to enter the publishing information.

6. On the Publish page, you should be able to choose between two values, "Whenever the report Web page is viewed" or "Only when scheduled," because you checked the "Publish to Enterprise Manager Reporting Website" check box earlier on the General page. Select the "Only when scheduled" value and click the Schedule button, which now appears beside this field. A dialog box appears with some additional information; click OK to continue.
7. The Create Job dialog box appears. The report generation job will be scheduled on the node running the Web server by default if it has an Oracle9i Intelligent Agent installed. Click on the Schedule tab to specify the schedule for the report generation.
8. On the Schedule page, now select the scheduling, such as On Interval, with a 15 minute interval.
9. You are ready to store and submit the job. Choose Submit and Add to Library in the radio button group at the bottom of the screen and click the Submit & Add button. The job will be stored in the job library and submitted. Click OK to store your report definition and exit the Create Report screen.

You can monitor the progress of the report generation job by selecting Jobs in the EM Navigator tree. For more information about how to manage and monitor the submission of EM jobs, refer to Chapter 11.

Modifying a Report

You modify a report definition by selecting it in the Report Definitions detail view and choosing Edit from either the pop-up menu or the Object menu. You can also press ALT-ENTER or double-click the report definition. The Edit Report screen appears, which is the same as the Create Report screen shown in Figure 13-6. You can change all the properties of the report except the report definition name in the Definition Name field, and the owner of the report definition. You can use the View Report button to test the report and save the report definition under a different name with the Save As button. When you are finished with your modifications, click OK, or click Cancel to exit without saving your changes.

Deleting a Report

You delete a report definition by selecting it in the Report Definitions detail view. You can either press the DELETE key or choose Delete from the Object or pop-up menu. A confirmation dialog appears; click Yes to confirm the deletion, or No to continue without deleting the report definition.

When you delete a report definition, there might be a job scheduled for publishing the report to the EM Reporting Home Page. This job is not deleted when you delete the report definition. Follow the steps outlined in Chapter 11 to delete a job.

Security Aspects of the EM Reporting Website

As described earlier in this chapter, the EM Reporting Website is reachable via the URL http://<*hostname*>:3339. This is the default without any kind of security, such as a password. Using the Apache Web server in your Oracle distribution and installation, Oracle HTTP Server, you can restrict access to this URL. You restrict access to the startup page and *all* reports within the EM Reporting Website, allowing access only to authenticated user(s). We will now take a closer look at the steps involved for this configuration.

To restrict general access to the EM Reporting Website and grant access to special users only, perform the steps outlined below. In this case, we create a special account to be used for accessing the whole EM Reporting Website, called emrws:

1. Log on to the machine where the Oracle HTTP Server is running.
2. To enable password checking in Apache, you must first create a password file. Go to the directory ORACLE_HOME\Apache\Apache\bin and execute the following command, which creates the user emrws with the password *welcome* (Windows specific):

   ```
   htpasswd -bc ..\conf\emrws.pw emrws welcome
   ```

3. Edit the Apache configuration file httpd.conf in the directory ORACLE_HOME\Apache\Apache\conf (make a backup copy first). Add the following lines (Windows specific)) to only allow access to EM reporting to user emrws (substitute the ORACLE_HOME with your own):

   ```
   <Location /em>
         AuthName "EM Reporting Website"
         AuthType Basic
         AuthUserFile "E:\Oracle\OraHome9i\Apache\Apache\conf\emrws.pw"
         Require user emrws
   </Location>after the section
   <Directory />
       Options FollowSymLinks
       AllowOverride None
   </Directory>
   ```

4. On Unix you use forward slash when running the htpasswd command and editing the httpd.conf file, for example:

```
<Location /em>
      AuthName "EM Reporting Website"
      AuthType Basic
      AuthUserFile "/opt/oracle/9.0.1/Apache/Apache/conf/emrws.pw"
      Require user emrws
</Location>
```

Restart the HTTP Server, either from the Services menu or by choosing Stop HTTP Server powered by Apache and then Start HTTP Server powered by Apache in the HTTP Server program group. The HTTP Server asks for username and password, and only allows access to the EM Reporting Website for the user emrws. When you access the EM Reporting Website URL, a dialog appears like the one shown in Figure 13-7, where authorization of the connection to the LBV1 Web server is requested.

NOTE
Both usernames and passwords are case sensitive with the Apache Web server.

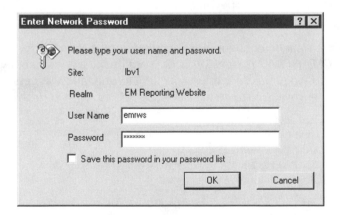

FIGURE 13-7. *Logging into the Reporting Website*

Reporting Features in Standalone Mode

When you run the EM Console in standalone mode, you can still generate reports, but the number of reports is limited compared to when the Console is connected to a Management Server. The complete reporting framework is not available in standalone mode. Obviously, all reports related to the EM repository, jobs, and events, as well as those available for target types other than databases, are not available in standalone mode. Instead, various static object (database) reports are available. You can extract all kinds of information from a database, e.g. configuration and status, and present it in useful reports. You can also customize the report to fit your needs. To generate a report in standalone mode, follow these steps:

1. Select a database target in the Navigator tree and connect to it. Then choose Create Report from the Object menu or from the pop-up menu for the selected database. The Generate Report dialog box appears, as shown in Figure 13-8.

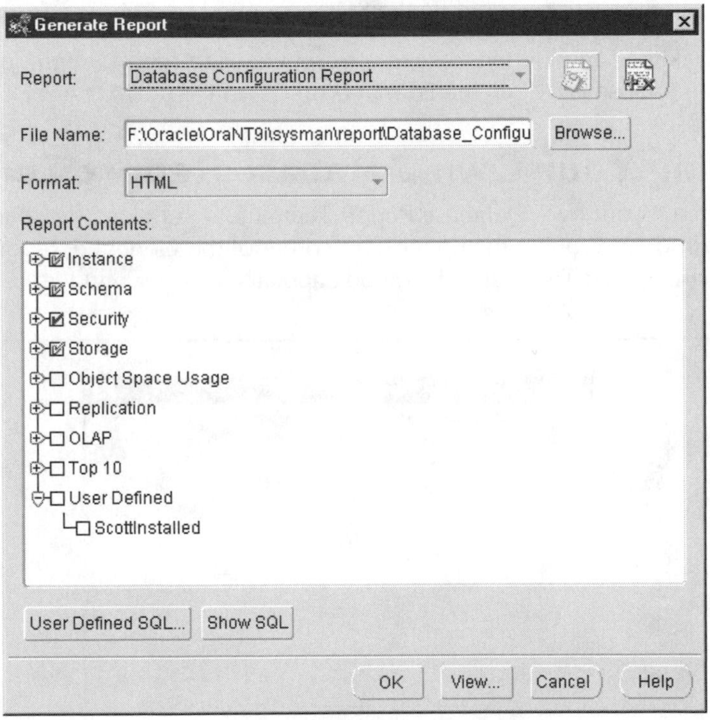

FIGURE 13-8. *The Generate Report dialog box in standalone mode*

2. Choose a Database Report Template in the Report drop-down list box. You can also create your own template, as described in the following section. Depending on which template you choose, the selection in the Report Contents tree changes.
3. Enter the filename for the report output in the File Name field by entering the filename, or browse to it using the Browse button.
4. Select the format of the output from the Format drop-down list box. Possible values are HTML, text, or comma-separated.
5. In the Report Contents tree, you can select the information you want included in the report. Expand the top-level items by clicking the plus sign, and select or deselect the appropriate values. You can define your own user-defined SQL statements and include them in your report (or Database Report Template). See the "Generating a Report With User-Defined SQL" section later in this chapter. The Show SQL button toggles between displaying all the SQL statements included in the report (those selected in the Report Contents section) or hiding the SQL generated by EM.
6. Click the View button to generate and view the report output, but only if you choose HTML in the Format drop-down list box.

Creating Your Own Database Report Template

You can create your own Database Report Template by clicking the icon with the green plus and red cross in the upper right corner of the Generate Report dialog. The Database Report Templates dialog box appears, as shown in Figure 13-9.

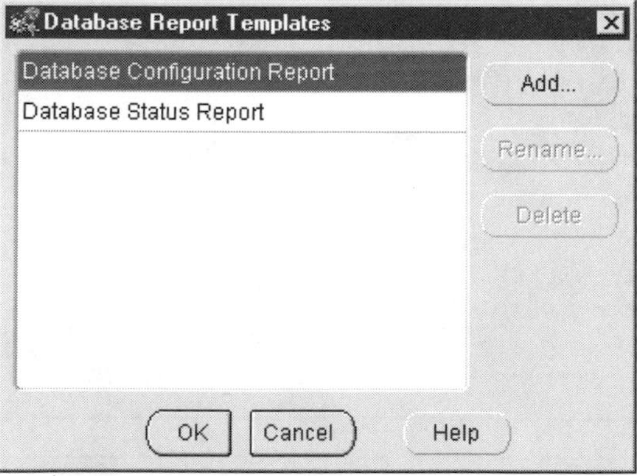

FIGURE 13-9. *Working with database report templates*

Here you can add, rename, or delete your templates, which are stored locally on your EM Client machine. To add a new template with your own definition, click the Add button in the Database Report Templates dialog box (see Figure 13-9). Now the Add Report Name dialog box appears. Enter a name for the template and click OK. Now click OK to get back to the Generate Report dialog, where your added template will be chosen in the Report drop-down list box.

Now define the report content for the new template in the Report Contents part of the screen by expanding the navigator tree and selecting contents by checking the corresponding check boxes. Choose the format of the report from the Format drop-down list box (HTML, comma-separated, or Text). The report template will by default be stored in the directory ORACLE_HOME\sysman\report. To save the template, you must click the icon with the floppy disk in the upper right part of the Generate Report dialog. Finally, you can click OK to generate the report in the specified file and close the dialog box or you can click View to generate and view the report in your Web browser.

To modify one of your existing templates, choose it from the Report drop-down list box in the Generate Report dialog box (Figure 13-8) and change information as required. The template can be renamed by clicking the icon with the green plus and red cross in the upper right corner of the Generate Report dialog. Now the Database Report Templates dialog box appears. Highlight the template in the list and click Rename; now the Edit Domain dialog box appears. Enter the new name for your template and click OK. To save your modifications to the template, click the icon with the floppy disk in the upper right part of the Generate Report dialog. You cannot modify the predefined templates, and the Rename button is grayed out until you have added your own templates.

To delete an existing template, click the icon with the green plus and red cross in the upper right corner of the Generate Report dialog (Figure 13-8). Now the Database Report Templates dialog box appears. Highlight the template you want to delete in the list and click Delete. Now click OK to confirn the deletion or Cancel to interrupt and continue without deleting the template. You cannot delete any of the predefined templates, and the Delete button is grayed out until you have added your own templates.

Generating a Report With User-Defined SQL

You can include your own SQL statements in the reports or templates by clicking on the User-Defined SQL button in the Generate Report dialog box. The User-Defined SQL dialog appears. Here you can add or remove your user-defined SQL statements, which are stored locally on your EM Client machine. Enter a name for the SQL statement and the SQL statement itself, and click OK to store it. Your user-defined SQL statements appears in the Report Contents tree under User- Defined SQL. Figure 13-10 shows a SQL statement that checks to see if the SCOTT schema is installed on the database.

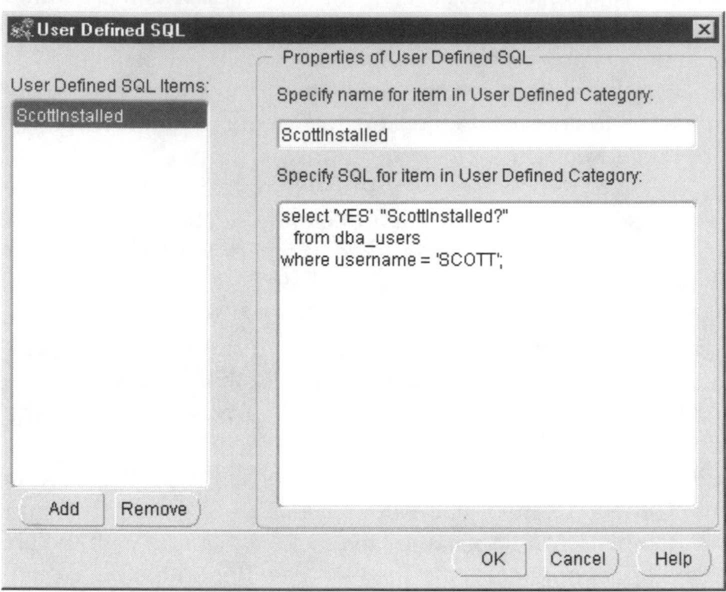

FIGURE 13-10. *Adding user-defined SQL*

Summary

In this chapter, you have learned about the reporting functionality available with the 9i version of EM. The configuration of the Oracle HTTP Server to run the EM Reporting Website has been discussed together with security aspects of this special Website. You have seen how to generate reports based on the predefined report definitions from the EM Console connected to an OMS and to view the output in your web browser. You have also seen examples of creating and publishing your own report definitions. The report feature available when running the EM Console in standalone mode has also been covered, and you have seen how to maintain your own report templates.

CHAPTER 14

Database Management

In addition to the job and event systems and the reporting framework, EM contains a lot of tools for database administration, which can be divided into two groups: tools and wizards. Some tools, and the wizards, are available from the Tools menu, and other tools are available when you are connected to a database instance in the Navigator tree. In this chapter, we will take a look at all the tools available in the EM Navigator for database administration. In Chapter 15, we will look more closely at the wizards and other database applications available with EM. The following eight database administration tools are included in the EM Navigator, both when connected to a Management Server and when running in standalone mode:

- Instance
- Schema
- Security
- Storage
- Replication
- OLAP (On-Line Analytical Processing)
- JVM (Java Virtual Machine)
- Workspace

NOTE
The last four tools are not shown for a database when the database instance is not in Open mode or when for the option is not available for this particular instance. For example, if the JVM is not configured for the instance, JVM will not be available in the Navigator tree.

We assume that you are familiar with general database administrative issues such as initialization parameters, INIT.ORA, System Global Area (SGA), users, roles, tablespaces, datafiles, etc. We will try to explain as many details as possible, but this chapter is focused on the EM functionalities rather than core RDBMS issues. Chapter 6 also provided an overview of the tools which are covered in this chapter. But in the following, we will go more into details and provide examples for most of the eight tools. For more details about managing the Oracle RDBMS, refer to *Oracle9i Database Concepts* and the *Oracle9i Database Administrator's Guide*.

Accessing the Database Administration Tools

To access the database administration tools, you must connect to the database and expand it in the Navigator tree by clicking the plus sign (see Figure 14-1).

The following sections will take you on a tour through these eight tools while connected to the Management Server. Because of the immense number of features available in these tools, we will focus on those that you need to be most familiar with.

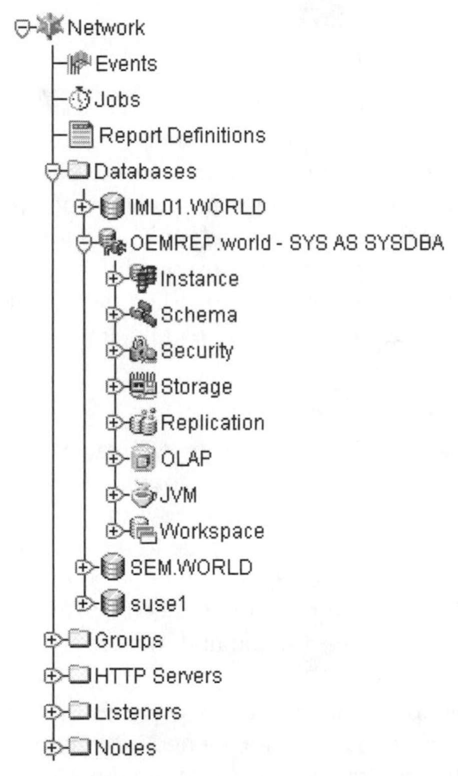

FIGURE 14-1. *Database management tools available in EM Navigator*

One important and useful thing to notice is that when you are performing changes through the EM GUI interface, you can track exactly which SQL statements have been executed against the target database. You can do this in three ways:

- Click the Show SQL button in the detail view pane *before* applying your changes using the Apply button. A field appears displaying the actual SQL statement for the modification. You can copy the SQL statement using CTRL-C.
- View the last 100 SQL statements in the Application SQL Log Window, which is launched from the Navigator menu.
- View the SQL statements in the SQL log through the SQL Logging function in the Tools menu (different functionality for OMS and standalone mode). You must enable the SQL logging feature before your changes will be logged. See Chapter 9 for more details about the SQL Logging feature within EM.

Instance

The Instance Management tool is used primarily for starting and stopping the database instance, managing recovery and undo, and examining and modifying instance parameters, including the dynamic memory parameters available with Oracle9i RDBMS. In addition, it includes an overview of current database sessions and locks, in-doubt transactions (distributed/replicated transactions), and features regarding resource consumer groups and resource plans defined for your instance. You enter the Instance Management by expanding the Instance tree item, the icon with the two traffic lights (see Figure 14-1), by clicking the plus ("+") sign.

Configuration

When you expand the Instance item, the first entry is called Configuration. This is where you perform operations such as starting and stopping the database instance, as well as examining and modifying instance parameters and resource monitors. For Oracle9i instances, you can also manage the mean time to recover and undo retention time.

When right-clicking on the Configuration entry, you have access to various database instance related functions in the context-sensitive menu. These are the same as you will find in the Object menu and include:

- **View/Edit Details** Launches a window with the same contents as the Detail View pane containing the General, Memory, Recovery, Resource Monitors, and Undo pages (see the respective sections below).
- **Startup** Will appear if the database instance is not started and is used for starting the instance. See the "Starting a Database Instance" section later in this chapter for more information.

- **Shutdown** Appears if the database instance is started and is used for shutting down the database instance. See the "Stopping a Database Instance" section later in this chapter for more details.
- **Automatic Archival** This function will only be available if the database runs in ARCHIVELOG mode, and it is used to toggle automatic archiving of the online redo log files on and off. Notice that changes made through this menu entry will only affect the running instance. To make changes permanent, you must modify the instance initialization parameters. See the "Recovery Property Page" and "Initialization Parameters" sections later in this chapter. If you choose not to use automatic archiving, you must manually archive the logs. See Manually Archive below.
- **Manually Archive** Use this function to manually archive online redo log files when automatic archival has been disabled (see Automatic Archival above). The Manually Archive function is only available when the database is running in ARCHIVELOG mode. You can choose between archiving the *current* or *next* log or *all* log files and choose another destination folder for the archive logs. Choosing Current will force a log switch and archive the current online redo log file group. Choosing Next will archive the next redo log file group that is full but has not yet been archived. The All entry will archive all redo log file groups that are full but have not yet been archived. See the "Recovery Property Page" section later in this chapter for more details.
- **Restrict** This function is used to enable and disable *restricted session* for the instance. In restricted mode, database connections are only allowed for users having the RESTRICTED SESSION system privilege. See also the "Restricted Mode" section below.
- **Save** Choose this menu item to launch the Save Initialization Parameter dialog, where you can choose to store the current active initialization parameters into a file on your EM client machine. See also the "Storing Initialization Parameters in a Stored Configuration" section later in this chapter.
- **Create spfile** The SPFILE (Server Parameter File) is available with Oracle9i and makes it easier to start up a database remotely. This menu item, therefore, is only available for Oracle9i instances and will launch the "Create an spfile from a pfile" dialog. Here you can choose an existing PFILE (INIT.ORA file) on your local EM client machine as source and specify an SPFILE to be generated, also on your local EM client machine.
- **Create pfile** Like Create spfile, this feature is only available in Oracle9i. It will launch the "Create a pfile from an spfile" dialog. You choose an existing SPFILE on your local EM client machine as source and can specify a PFILE to be generated also on your local EM client machine.

In the following, we will take a closer look at the different property pages available for the database instance. Select the Configuration item by clicking it, and you will be placed on the General property page, which is one of five pages (when you are connected to an Oracle9i instance). This page is shown in Figure 14-2.

General Property Page

On the General page, you get a quick overview about the instance, including hostname, database and instance names, database version, installed options, instance startup

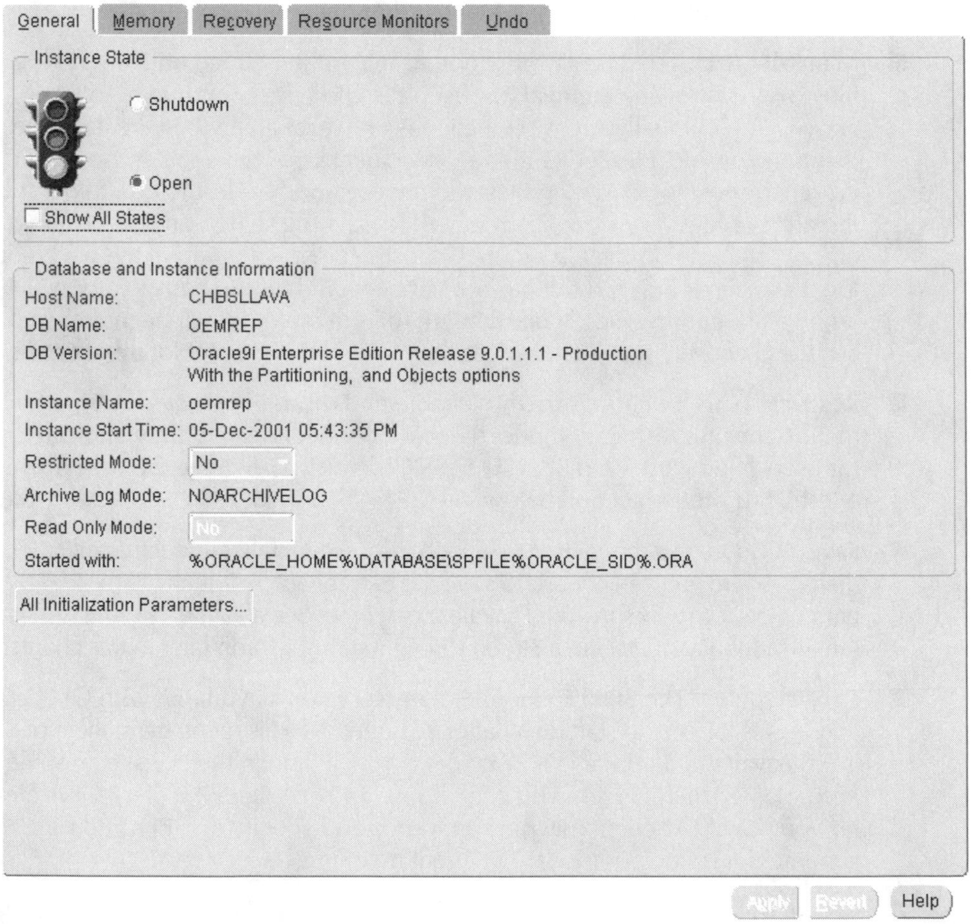

FIGURE 14-2. *The database configuration general property page*

time, archive log mode, and the current state of the instance. For Oracle9i instances, the parameter file used for startup is also displayed. A traffic light indicates the current state of the database instance; only two of four possible states are shown by default:

- **Green light** The database is running and open
- **Red light** The database is shut down and closed

To show all four states including the Started (NOMOUNT) and Mounted states, you must check the "Show All States" check box. This box is used when you are performing operations that require the database to be in the NOMOUNT or MOUNT state, such as re-creating the control file, switching archivelog mode, or performing recovery operations. In the Started and Mounted states, the traffic light is yellow.

NOTE
For the traffic light operations to be enabled, and to start up and shut down the instance, you must be connected with the SYSDBA privilege.

Restricted Mode You can use the Restricted Mode drop-down list box to toggle running the database in restricted mode when opening it. In restricted mode, only users with the RESTRICTED SESSION system privilege can access the database. Users already connected are not affected by the change, only future connections. You use this setting when you want to perform administrative operations and keep out normal database users.

Read-Only Mode You can use the Read Only Mode drop-down list box to toggle read-only mode. When the database is in the Mounted state and you choose to open it, you can choose to open it read-only. You can also choose this option when starting the database instance in different modes, as described in the "Starting a Database Instance" section later in this chapter. The read-only mode is often used in database standby configurations, where the hot standby instance can be used for reporting and query purposes.

Initialization Parameters

If you want to examine or modify the database instance initialization parameters, or save them to a stored configuration, click the All Initialization Parameters button. The All Parameters page appears, where you can edit the initialization parameters, as shown in Figure 14-3.

For each parameter, the parameter name, its value, and the category are shown. The Default column indicates whether the parameter has been assigned its default

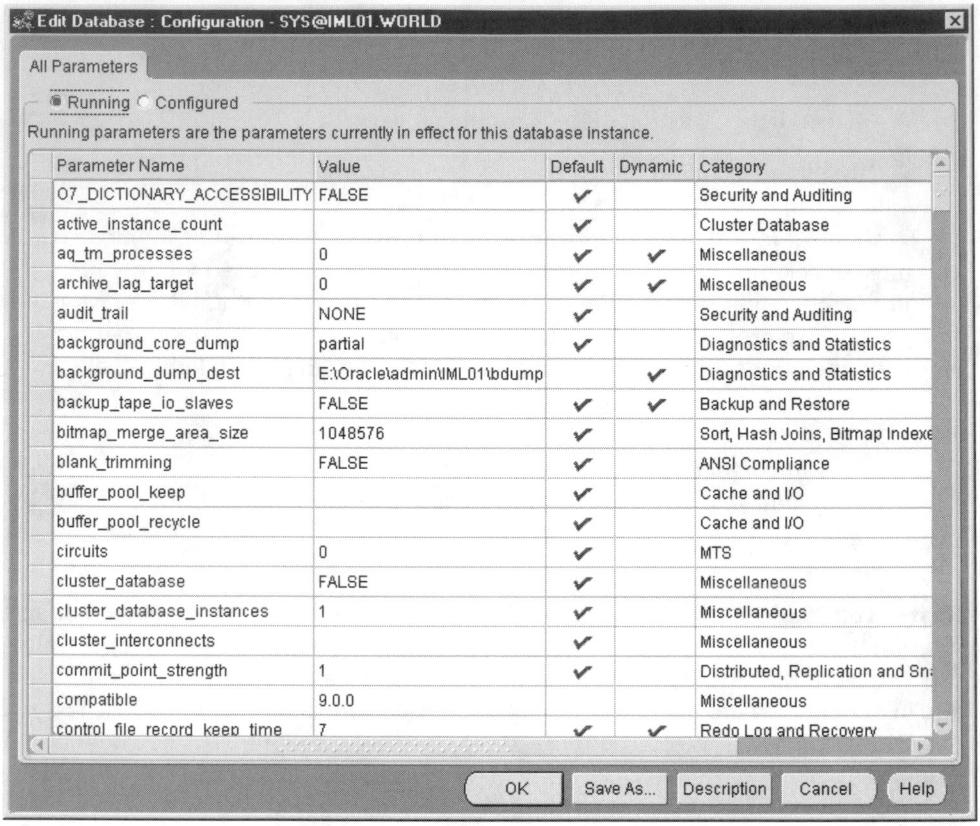

Edit Database : Configuration - SYS@IML01.WORLD

All Parameters

Running / Configured

Running parameters are the parameters currently in effect for this database instance.

Parameter Name	Value	Default	Dynamic	Category
O7_DICTIONARY_ACCESSIBILITY	FALSE	✔		Security and Auditing
active_instance_count		✔		Cluster Database
aq_tm_processes	0	✔	✔	Miscellaneous
archive_lag_target	0	✔	✔	Miscellaneous
audit_trail	NONE	✔		Security and Auditing
background_core_dump	partial	✔		Diagnostics and Statistics
background_dump_dest	E:\Oracle\admin\IML01\bdump		✔	Diagnostics and Statistics
backup_tape_io_slaves	FALSE	✔	✔	Backup and Restore
bitmap_merge_area_size	1048576	✔		Sort, Hash Joins, Bitmap Indexe
blank_trimming	FALSE	✔		ANSI Compliance
buffer_pool_keep		✔		Cache and I/O
buffer_pool_recycle		✔		Cache and I/O
circuits	0	✔		MTS
cluster_database	FALSE	✔		Miscellaneous
cluster_database_instances	1	✔		Miscellaneous
cluster_interconnects		✔		Miscellaneous
commit_point_strength	1	✔		Distributed, Replication and Sn
compatible	9.0.0			Miscellaneous
control_file_record_keep_time	7	✔	✔	Redo Log and Recovery

OK | Save As... | Description | Cancel | Help

FIGURE 14-3. *Editing initialization parameters*

value, and the Dynamic column indicates if it can be changed dynamically. For your convenience, you can sort on each of these columns by clicking the column heading. Optionally, you can get a description at the bottom of the screen for the currently selected parameter by clicking the Description button. As the Dynamic column indicates, there are two types of parameters:

- **Static** Cannot be modified without restarting the instance
- **Dynamic** Can be modified without restarting the instance

With Oracle9i, more parameters have become dynamic, including the System Global Area (SGA) parameter SHARED_POOL_SIZE, which can now be modified without restarting the instance. The data cache (buffer pool) can also be resized dynamically in Oracle9i through the new parameter DB_CACHE_SIZE.

Modifying Initialization Parameters You change a parameter by clicking in the Value field for the particular parameter and either entering the new value or, for some parameters, selecting it from a drop-down list box. Then click OK to leave the All Parameters page, and click Apply in order for your changes to take effect. Clicking the Revert button will undo changes made since you last clicked Apply. Depending on whether you changed a static or dynamic parameter, you will be asked if you want to restart the instance.

NOTE
To modify a static initialization parameter in an Oracle9i database instance, you must be connected to the database with the SYSDBA privilege. The SYSDBA privilege is not required for you to edit a dynamic parameter, but you still need appropriate system privileges to change dynamic parameters. You can see and edit the dynamic parameters, but you will receive an ORA-01031 "insufficient privileges" error when you try to apply the changes. For pre-9i databases, you must be connected as SYSDBA to be able to edit initialization parameters at all.

If you change a static parameter, you will be asked if you want to restart the instance (shut down and restart) to activate the new parameter value. In addition, you will be asked if you want to save the new instance parameters in a stored configuration. Stored configurations are discussed later in this chapter. If you used an INIT.ORA file to start the instance, the changes will not be written into this file, but you can export the stored configuration to a file. If you changed a dynamic parameter when the instance has not been started using an SPFILE, a pop-up window will notify you that the change will affect future sessions only. If the instance is an Oracle9i instance and has been started using an SPFILE, the behavior is different, because you can then modify either the currently active parameters or only those configured in the SPFILE. What this means and how it affects modification of parameters is explained in the following section.

Running and Configured Parameters If you are connected to an Oracle9i instance, the top of the All Parameters screen also contains a radio button group with two different values:

- **Running** Currently active parameters for the instance
- **Configured** Parameters as they are stored in the SPFILE

This is related to the SPFILE functionality available from Oracle9i, and only appears if the instance was started using the SPFILE. This section outlines the differences between these two modes, which are important for you to understand when modifying the initialization parameters.

If you select the *Running* radio button, the page shows the parameters that are currently active as you would see them in V$PARAMETER. When you modify a dynamic parameter in this mode, the change takes effect immediately (without restarting the instance), but if you restart the database after the modification, it will start up with the original parameter value. This occurs because the change has not yet been saved to the SPFILE. If you change a static parameter in the Running mode and apply the change, the SPFILE will be updated, and you will be asked if you want to bounce (shut down and restart) the instance to activate the parameter. For more about restarting an Oracle instance, see the "Starting and Stopping the Database Instance" section later in this chapter.

If you select the *Configured* radio button, the page will show the parameters as they are stored in the SPFILE and as seen in V$SPPARAMETER. When you change a *dynamic* parameter in this mode, the modification is written to the SPFILE when you apply the change. You will also be asked through a dialog box whether you want to activate the new parameter value for the instance. Click Yes to activate immediately, or No to wait for next instance startup using the SPFILE.

When you modify a *static* parameter in the Configured parameters mode, the SPFILE is updated, and a dialog box appears asking if you want to restart the instance for parameter activation when applying your change. This is just as you may remember from pre-9i versions, or when using an INIT.ORA file; the good old way of editing your parameter file and then restarting the instance to activate the changes. If you click No, the instance will not be restarted; clicking Yes brings up a dialog box with options for shutting down the instance. For more information about restarting an Oracle instance, see the "Starting and Stopping the Database Instance" section later in this chapter.

Storing Initialization Parameters in a Stored Configuration You can choose to store the initialization parameters as they are currently defined for the instance. In this way, you can easily start the instance with different configurations from the EM Console without having many different INIT.ORA files. If the instance has been started using an SPFILE, you can only store the parameters shown on the Running parameters page in a Stored Configuration. For Configured parameters, the Save As button is grayed out. See the "Stored Configurations" section later in this chapter for more about maintaining stored configurations in EM.

Initialization Parameters with Resource Limit Statistics Some of the parameters have a red plus sign left of the parameter name. This indicates that resource statistics are available for the parameter, which is the same information as you can view in V$RESOURCE_LIMIT. To access this information, right-click the red plus sign and choose Resource Limit from the pop-up menu. The Resource Utilization dialog box appears, displaying the Current, Max, and Initial Utilization values, which you cannot edit. The Limit field specifies the current limit as specified in your parameter file (INIT.ORA or SPFILE), and this field can be modified. Enter the new value for the limit and click OK. You are returned to the All Parameters page, and can continue working. If you want to store and activate the change, click OK in the All Parameters page, and then click Apply in the Configuration General page. Because all parameters with resource limit statistics are static, you will be asked to store the configuration and restart the instance for activation.

Starting and Stopping the Database Instance

One of the most important features of the Instance management tool is the ability to remotely shut down and start up database instances. You can store different INIT.ORA configurations in Stored Configurations, and use these when starting the instance. With Oracle9i, this has been made even easier using the server side parameter file (SPFILE), which eliminates the need for you to store INIT.ORA files outside the database server.

NOTE

Be sure you are not connected to the database that you want to start up or shut down through a MultiThreaded Server (MTS, also known as Shared Server) connection. You must be connected through a dedicated server process, or you will receive the ORA-00106 "cannot startup/shutdown database when connected to a dispatcher" error. You can enforce connection through a dedicated server by setting a parameter in your TNSNAMES.ORA (SERVER=DEDICATED) or SQLNET.ORA (USE_DEDICATED_SERVER=ON) net client configuration file.

Starting a Database Instance You start a database and bring it to the normal Open state by selecting the Open value in the radio button group beside the traffic light in the General page. If you do not want to bring the database into Open mode, but instead bring it up in either NOMOUNT or MOUNT state, you must check the

Show All States check box and then select the Started or Mounted values, respectively. Then click Apply. The Startup Options dialog box appears, where you specify which parameter file to use for starting the instance. You can also specify whether you want to open the database in restricted mode, read-only mode, or both (these modes are explained in the "General Property Page" section earlier in the chapter), by checking the Restrict access to database and Read-Only Mode check boxes, respectively. These are shown in Figure 14-4.

With an Oracle9i database instance, you will have three options; only the second and third are available for pre-9i releases:

- Use the SPFILE (always stored on the database server)
- Use an EM Stored Configuration (see the "Storing Initialization Parameters in a Stored Configuration" section earlier in the chapter)
- Use an INIT.ORA file stored in the file system, either on your EM client machine or on the Management Server to which you are currently connected

If you want to use an SPFILE, check the Use Configured Parameters check box (checked by default for Oracle9i). To use either a specific EM stored configuration or an INIT.ORA file, uncheck this check box and check the appropriate value. In the Stored configuration drop-down list box, you can select among your Stored

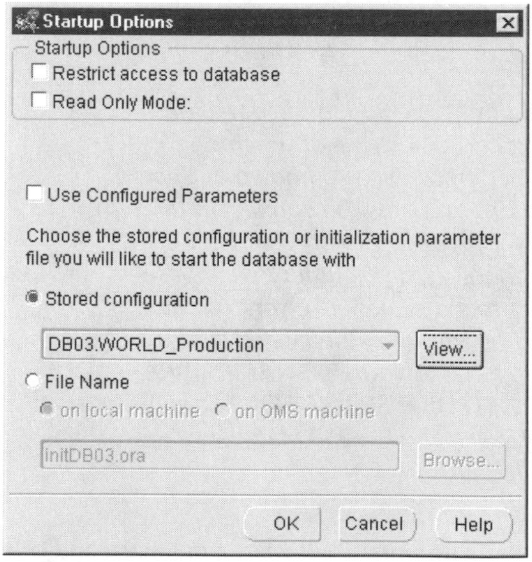

FIGURE 14-4. *Setting the startup options*

Configurations. There is a default generated configuration containing the non default instance specific parameter values. You can examine the stored configuration using it for starting the instance by clicking the View button. If you check the File Name value, you can choose to either enter a file name or browse for it. You cannot browse in the file system of the Management Server. If you only specify the file name, such as initprod.ora, it must be stored in the ORACLE_HOME\sysman\ifiles directory of the Management Server. Otherwise, you can use a fully qualified file name to specify the location, such as d:\dba\initprod.ora. Select the desired parameter file and click OK. A Starting up database progress screen appears. When the startup has completed, click Close.

Stopping a Database Instance You stop a database by selecting the Shutdown radio button next to the traffic light and clicking Apply. A dialog box with the four shutdown options (normal, immediate, abort, or transactional) appears, including an explanation of each option, as shown in Figure 14-5. The immediate option is suggested by default and is also normally recommended.

Choose the option you want to use for this shutdown and click OK, or click Cancel to go back to the Instance Manager without shutting down. A Shutting down database progress window is displayed. The duration of the shutdown depends on the option you chose. Click Close to close the window when finished.

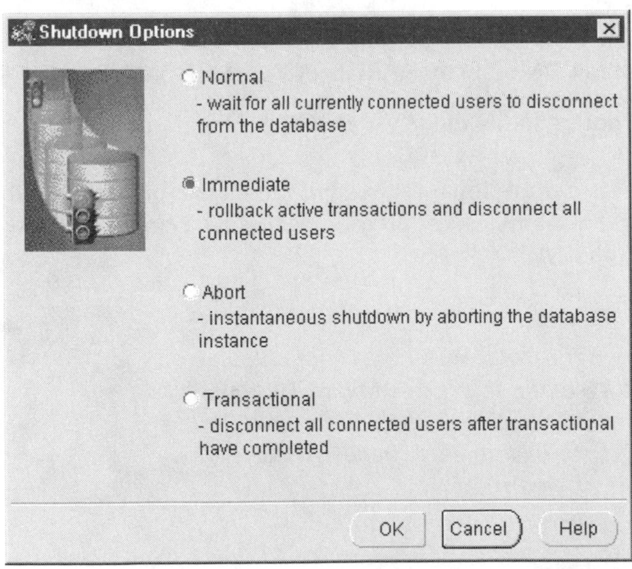

FIGURE 14-5. *Selecting a shutdown option*

NOTE
If you stop the EM repository database from the EM Console while connected to the Management Server, the console-OMS connection will be cancelled. You get a dialog box asking if you want to close the console or reconnect to another (or the same) OMS. This has been improved in 9i compared to earlier releases, where the OMS simply crashed or went into zombie-mode. The EM Console just showed an error and had to be cancelled and restarted.

Memory Property Page

On the Memory page of the Instance Manager, you will find information about the sizes of the different components of the System Global Area (SGA) including a pie chart for a quick overview. The whole pie represents the total SGA size, excluding the log buffer. Figure 14-6 shows an example of the Memory property page.

SGA Parameters The upper part of the page has four fields where you can change the value of the different SGA components:

- **Shared Pool** Modify the SHARED_POOL_SIZE parameter
- **Buffer Cache** Modify the DB_CACHE_SIZE (Oracle9i only) or DB_BLOCK_BUFFERS parameter
- **Large Pool** Modify the LARGE_POOL_SIZE parameter
- **Java Pool** Modify the JAVA_POOL_SIZE parameter

Each field has a drop-down list box with the available units for the parameter (B for bytes, KB for kilobytes, or MB for megabytes). Choose the new value for the parameter and click Apply.

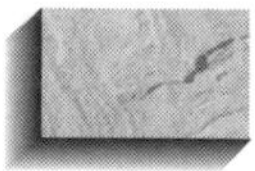

NOTE
If the value in the Total SGA field is not calculated correctly (too small), this is due to bug 1909393. Workaround is to click in Buffer Cache field and exit the field, for example using the TAB key. Now the value will be correct.

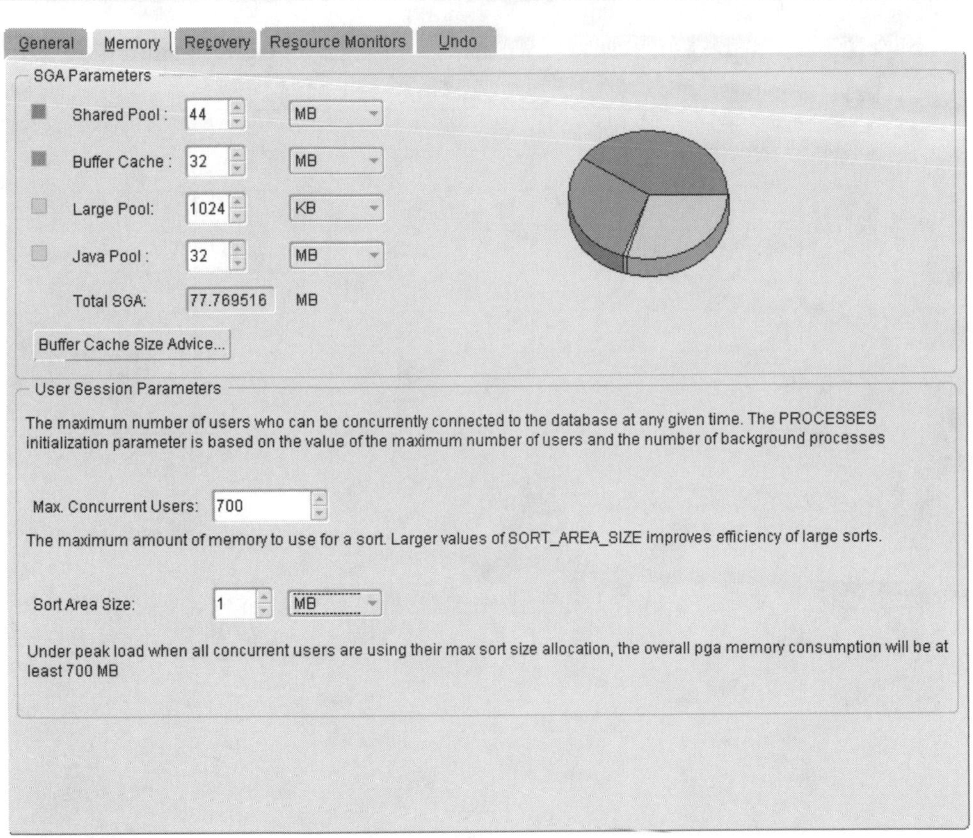

FIGURE 14-6. *The Instance Manager memory property page*

Buffer Cache Size Advice Click the Buffer Cache Size Advice button to launch the advice feature for choosing the appropriate size of the buffer cache. This feature is only available when you are connected to an Oracle9i database. The INIT.ORA parameter DB_CACHE_ADVICE must be set to ON to enable statistics gathering. If this initialization parameter has not been set to ON, a dialog box appears, asking if you want to change the parameter. Click Yes to change the DB_CACHE_ADVICE parameter value to ON. The Buffer Cache Advice Size screen appears, as shown in Figure 14-7.

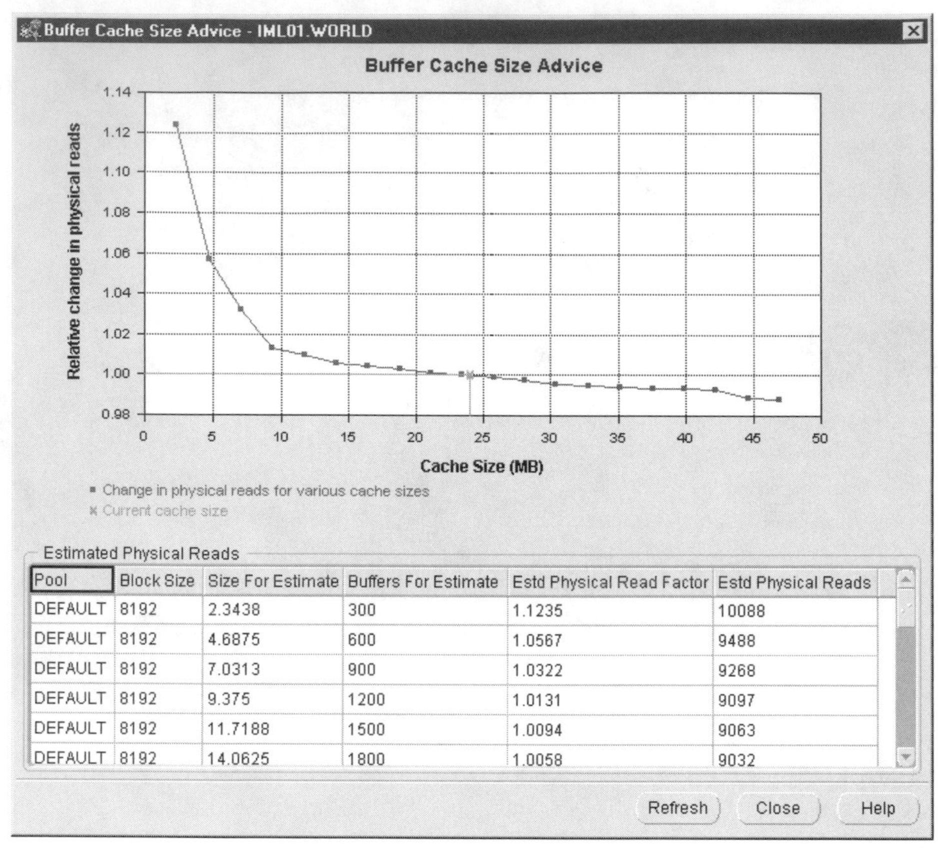

Pool	Block Size	Size For Estimate	Buffers For Estimate	Estd Physical Read Factor	Estd Physical Reads
DEFAULT	8192	2.3438	300	1.1235	10088
DEFAULT	8192	4.6875	600	1.0567	9488
DEFAULT	8192	7.0313	900	1.0322	9268
DEFAULT	8192	9.375	1200	1.0131	9097
DEFAULT	8192	11.7188	1500	1.0094	9063
DEFAULT	8192	14.0625	1800	1.0058	9032

FIGURE 14-7. *The Buffer Cache Size Advice screen*

The Buffer Cache Size Advice screen tells you the impact on physical reads when decreasing (to the left on X-axis) or increasing (to the right on X-axis) your data cache. Point with your mouse on the curve to get the impact shown (appears in a balloon help text box). The advice is based on the I/O activity since the advice feature was enabled through setting the DB_CACHE_ADVICE parameter to ON.

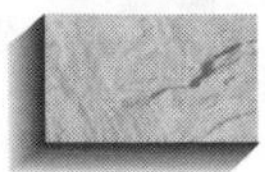

NOTE
Information is collected in V$DB_CACHE_ADVICE, and values for cache size advice numbers are stored in megabytes in the SIZE_FOR_ESTIMATE column. If you have incorrect values on the X-axis (such as zeros), it is because EM assumes these numbers are in kilobytes and thereby divides the numbers by 1024 to convert to MB. You need to apply an EM patch to correct this (for Windows NT or 2000, the patch name is EM_901_1801602).

Max Concurrent Users The Max Concurrent Users field shows the number of users who will be concurrently connected to the database, including the background processes. If you set this value to 150, for example, the instance parameter PROCESSES will be set to 150–10 = 140, thereby making room for 10 background processes in addition to the 140 OS users. When you have configured your database to allow connections through Shared Server (formerly known as MTS), the value of the Max Concurrent Users field will include the maximum number of Shared Server connections as well. You can enter a value for maximum number of users or use the arrow keys to increase or decrease the value. When using the Shared Server option, you might want to modify the initialization parameters to control the maximum concurrent users instead of changing the value here.

Sort Area Size In the Sort Area Size field, you can change the dynamic instance parameter SORT_AREA_SIZE to specify the amount of memory to use for a sort in memory per database session. The change is valid for future sessions only. Enter a new value in this field or use the arrow keys to increase or decrease the value, and then choose a unit of measure (B for bytes, KB for kilobytes, and MB for megabytes). Click Apply to store the new setting. A pop-up window appears to inform you that the change is valid for new database sessions.

Recovery Property Page

The Recovery page of Instance Manager contains information about which archive mode the instance is currently in, and how fast recovery is to be completed. The Control instance crash recovery time check box controls the instance parameter

FAST_START_MTTR_TARGET, which specifies the (estimated) amount of time a media recovery requires. Check this check box to enable this feature and specify the amount of time it may take to complete in the "Desired mean time to recover" field. The unit is either seconds or minutes, and is chosen in the drop-down list box beside the field. The Archive Log Mode check box specifies whether the database is running in ARCHIVELOG (checked) or NOARCHIVELOG mode (unchecked). If you are not connected as SYSDBA, this box is grayed out and cannot be changed. Changing this value requires you to connect as SYSDBA, and you must restart the database and bring it to the mount state to either enable or disable archive logging before opening it again. This is handled by EM automatically; you only have to choose the shutdown option (Normal, Immediate, Abort, or Transactional) when prompted.

The Automatic archival check box enables you to specify that redo log files are archived automatically when the database is running in ARCHIVELOG mode. If this box is not checked, and the instance is running in ARCHIVELOG mode, you must manually archive the redo log files using the ALTER SYSTEM ARCHIVE LOG command.

The Log Archive Filename Format field specifies how the archived log files are named. The default format is ARC%S.%T, where %s or %S indicates the log sequence number, and %t or %T indicates the instance thread number.

For example, you can use LOG%t_%s.ARC as the format. When several instances are running on the same server, you can also include the System Identifier (SID), for example LOG%t _%%ORACLE_SID%%_%s.ARC to avoid mixing up your archive files. Using the uppercase version results in a fixed file length and the numbers are left-padded with zeroes. For example, on the Windows NT/2000 platform, the log sequence number is a maximum of five digits long. For instances that generate a lot of archive log files, it is recommended to not use the %S to avoid wrapping the log sequence id. Check your OS specific documentation for the maximum value of the %S value.

Finally, the Archive Log Destination(s) list is used to specify the destination(s) where the archive log files are written. Each line represents one destination. Figure 14-8 shows an example of the Recovery property page for the OEMREP.WORLD database instance.

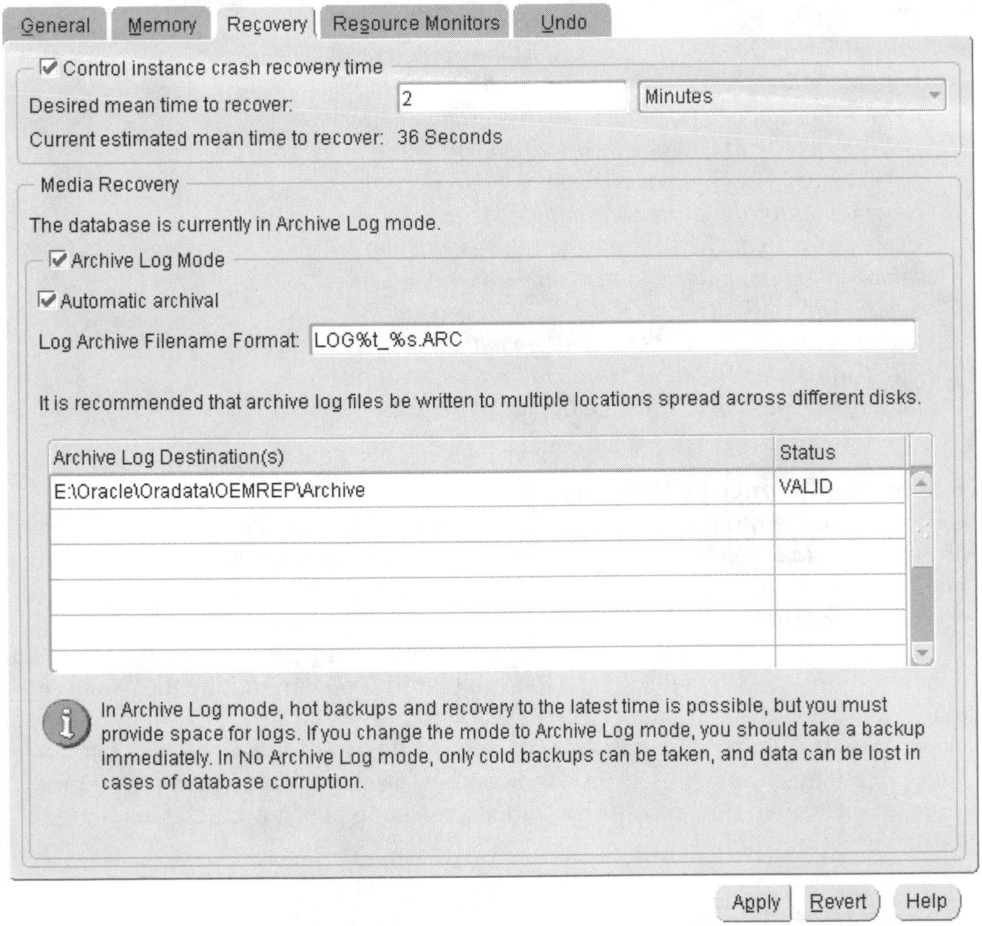

General | Memory | Recovery | Resource Monitors | Undo

☑ Control instance crash recovery time

Desired mean time to recover: 2 Minutes

Current estimated mean time to recover: 36 Seconds

Media Recovery

The database is currently in Archive Log mode.

☑ Archive Log Mode

☑ Automatic archival

Log Archive Filename Format: LOG%t_%s.ARC

It is recommended that archive log files be written to multiple locations spread across different disks.

Archive Log Destination(s)	Status
E:\Oracle\Oradata\OEMREP\Archive	VALID

In Archive Log mode, hot backups and recovery to the latest time is possible, but you must provide space for logs. If you change the mode to Archive Log mode, you should take a backup immediately. In No Archive Log mode, only cold backups can be taken, and data can be lost in cases of database corruption.

Apply | Revert | Help

FIGURE 14-8. *The Recovery Property Page for the OEMREP.WORLD Instance*

NOTE
The database instance needs to be restarted when changing the value of Archive Log Mode (switching between ARCHIVELOG and NOARCHIVELOG modes requires instance to be mounted). The instance restart is suggested by EM automatically when you apply the changes. Other changes made on this page only have effect for the current running instance. To make permanent changes to these settings, edit the initialization parameters instead on the General page. Set the FAST_START_MTTR_TARGET parameter and set the LOG_ARCHIVE_START parameter to TRUE, and specify one or more archive destinations (LOG_ARCHIVE_DEST and LOG_ARCHIVE_DEST_n).

Resource Monitors Property Page

On the Resource Monitors page, you can get a view of how the different resource groups are using the available resources within the instance. If no resource plan has been activated, this page will show nothing. Figure 14-9 shows how the Resource Monitor property page can look with an activated resource plan.

This page shows the CPU usage and wait information per consumer group. You can refresh the view by clicking the Refresh button. You can modify the resource plan by clicking the Edit button. The Reset button resets all CPU statistics and the view shows the usage from that point on. Refer to the "Resource Consumer Groups," "Resource Plans," and "Resource Plan Schedule" sections later in this chapter for more about how to define consumer groups, resource plans, and schedule these for different time frames.

Undo Property Page

The Undo page is used to configure the automatic UNDO management feature available with Oracle9i. Therefore, it is only available for Oracle9i and later database versions. The Current Undo Tablespace drop-down list box lets you choose between available UNDO tablespaces (these must be created with the UNDO option), and select the one to use. The Undo Retention field lets you specify the retention time of committed undo information as a number in seconds, minutes, or hours. Enter a new value and choose the unit of measure (Seconds, Minutes, or Hours) in the drop-down list box beside the field and click Apply. Based on the activity in the database, you will now be able to read the required amount of UNDO space for the chosen

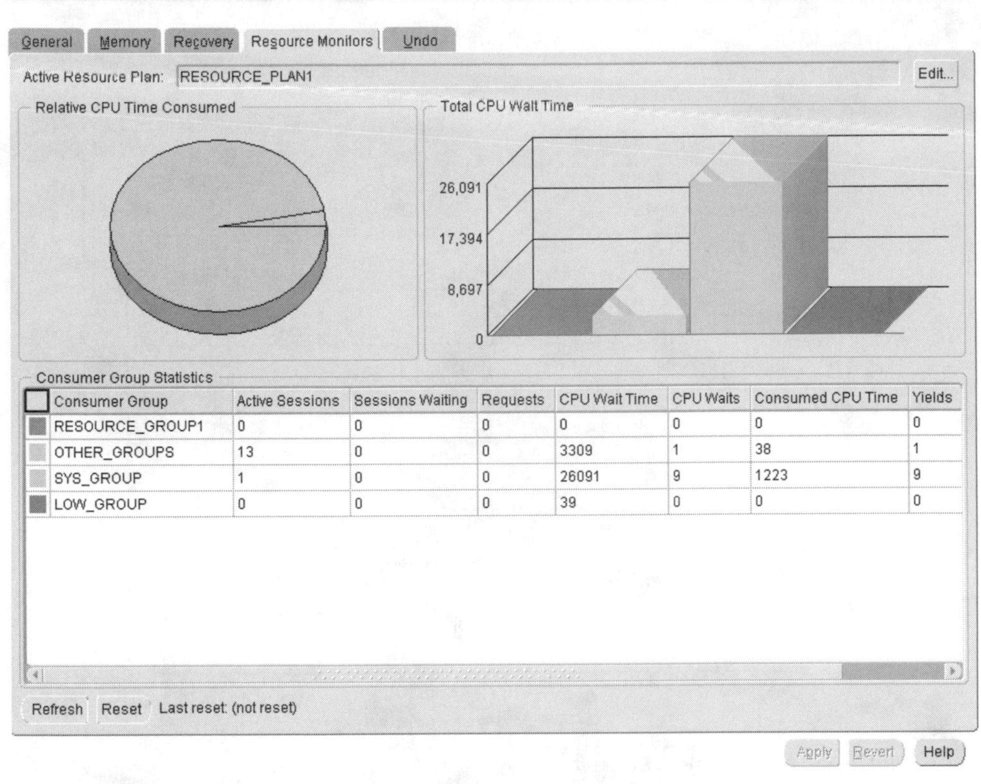

FIGURE 14-9. *The Resource Monitors property page*

retention time. Figure 14-10 shows an example of the Undo property page, where the undo retention time has been set to 45 minutes. The upper curve reflects the maximum undo generation rate and the lower curve the average undo generation rate.

Stored Configurations

The Stored Configurations entry in the Instance Manager contains all stored initialization parameter configurations. How to store the initialization parameters in a stored configuration is described in the "Storing Initialization Parameters in a Stored Configuration" section earlier in the chapter. To access the configurations, expand the Stored Configurations entry in the Navigator tree. By default, there will

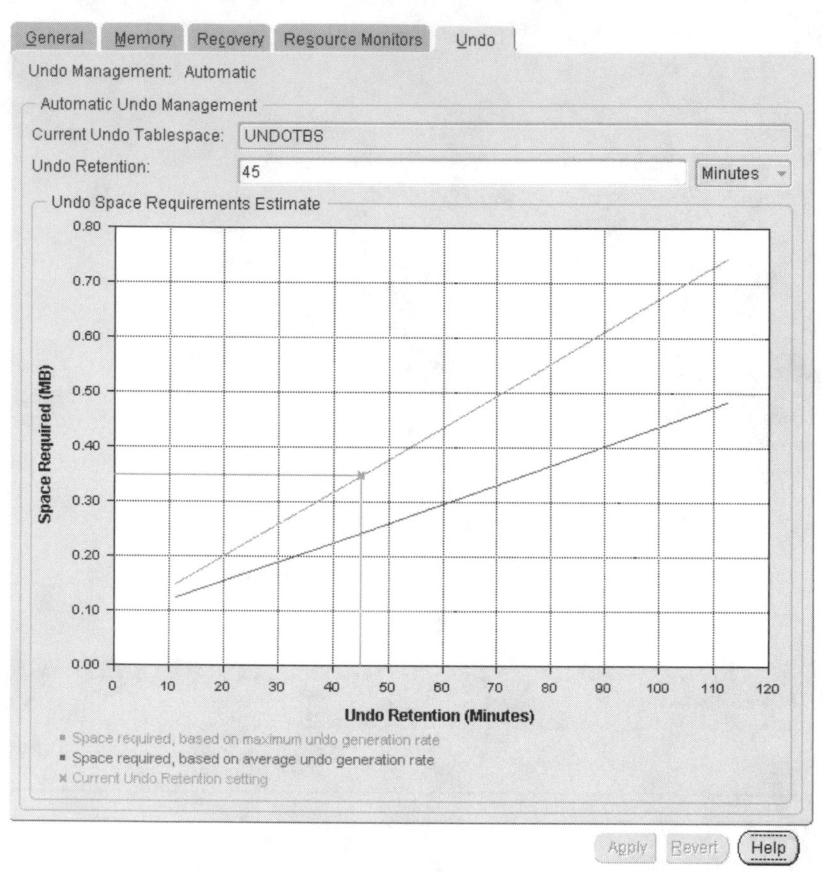

FIGURE 14-10. *The Undo Property Page For an Oracle9i Instance*

be a defaultStoredConfig configuration, generated by EM, even if the database was added manually. You can modify the stored configurations here, and also save them to a stored configuration under a new name using the Save As button. You can export parameters in a stored configuration into an INIT.ORA file, either locally on your EM Client, or on the Management Server machine. You do this by expanding the Stored Configurations item in the Instance tool (just below the Configuration entry) and selecting the stored configuration you want to export. Now right-click the configuration and choose Export to File from the pop-up menu. The Export Stored Configuration dialog box appears, as shown in Figure 14-11.

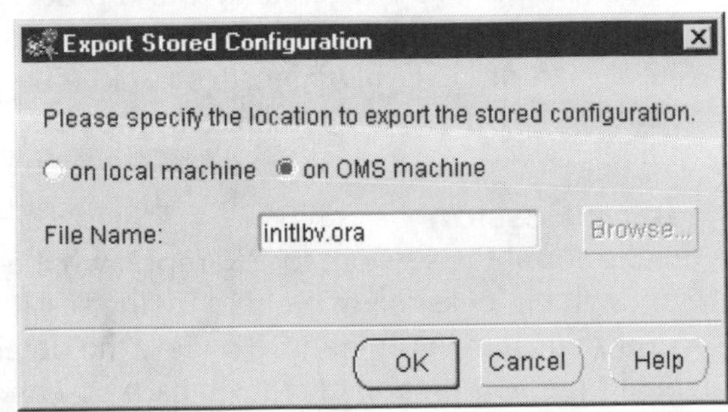

FIGURE 14-11. *Exporting a stored configuration*

You choose between storing the INIT.ORA file either on the local machine (EM Client) by selecting the "on local machine" radio button, or on the Management Server (OMS) to which you are currently connected by selecting the "on OMS machine" radio button. In the File Name field, you can enter a file name for the INIT.ORA file, or click the Browse button to browse for the location. You cannot browse in the file system of the node running the Management Server. If you choose "on OMS machine" and only specify a file name, such as initLBV.ora, the file will be stored in the ORACLE_HOME\sysman\ifiles directory of the Management Server. If you choose "on local machine" and do not enter a fully qualified file name, it will be stored in the ORACLE_HOME\bin directory (or where EM was started from). Otherwise, you can use a fully qualified file name to specify the location, such as f:\oracle\admin\lbv\pfile\initlbv.ora.

Sessions

When you select the Sessions item in the Navigator, you see a list of the current database sessions in the detail view. You can sort the list by clicking on a column header; each click toggles between ascending and descending order. You can also use the Top sessions drop-down list box to choose to sort by CPU, Memory, or I/O. You can define your own customized view by clicking the Customize button and then selecting the Statistic Category and Sort Statistic from the two drop-down list boxes. You can also specify if you want all sessions, or only the top sessions to be listed in the Show Top field. Either choose All or 10 (the default), or simply enter your own preferred number. Refresh the view manually by clicking the Refresh button (arrow) in the bottom of the screen. You can also refresh by choosing

Navigator | Refresh or by pressing CTRL-R. The background processes are the ones with an empty Username field. This is pretty much the same functionality provided with the Top Sessions tool (part of the EM Diagnostics Pack). The following sections will take a closer look at which features are available in the Sessions item.

Showing Details for a Session

You can get a lot of details about the session, for example, what SQL statement is being executed currently, which locks might be held by the session, the progress of long running queries, and statistical information. To view the details for a specific session, you must highlight the session and click Details. You can also right-click the session and choose View/Edit Details from the pop-up menu, or select Object | View/Edit Details, or press ALT-ENTER. The Edit Session screen is displayed with the following pages:

- **General** This page contains general session information such as session id, user and schema name, logon time, and program, as shown in V$SESSION. You can also kill the session by clicking the Kill Session button in the bottom of the page. See the "Killing a Session" section later in this chapter for more information about killing a session.
- **Long Operations** This page is only displayed if the session is a long running query. See the "Long Running Queries" section for more details.
- **SQL** This page shows the SQL statement currently being executed or the last one that was executed by the session.
- **Statistics** This page shows the session statistics, which are available from V$SESSTAT and V$STATNAME.
- **Locks** If the session maintains any database locks, these will be listed here. For more details, see the "Locks" section that follows.

Show SQL Statement and Explain Plan The SQL tab provides information about the SQL statement currently being executed, or the last one that was executed. By default, the SQL statement is shown using the classic EXPLAIN PLAN view (Tabular Display). You can switch to the tree structure shown in Figure 14-12 with the Graphical Display button in the toolbar on the right side of the screen.

You can step through the query plan by using the First Step, Next Step, and Previous Step buttons in the toolbar on the right. You can also get detailed information about a certain step (if available) by clicking the View Details button in the toolbar. Each step is described at the bottom of the screen.

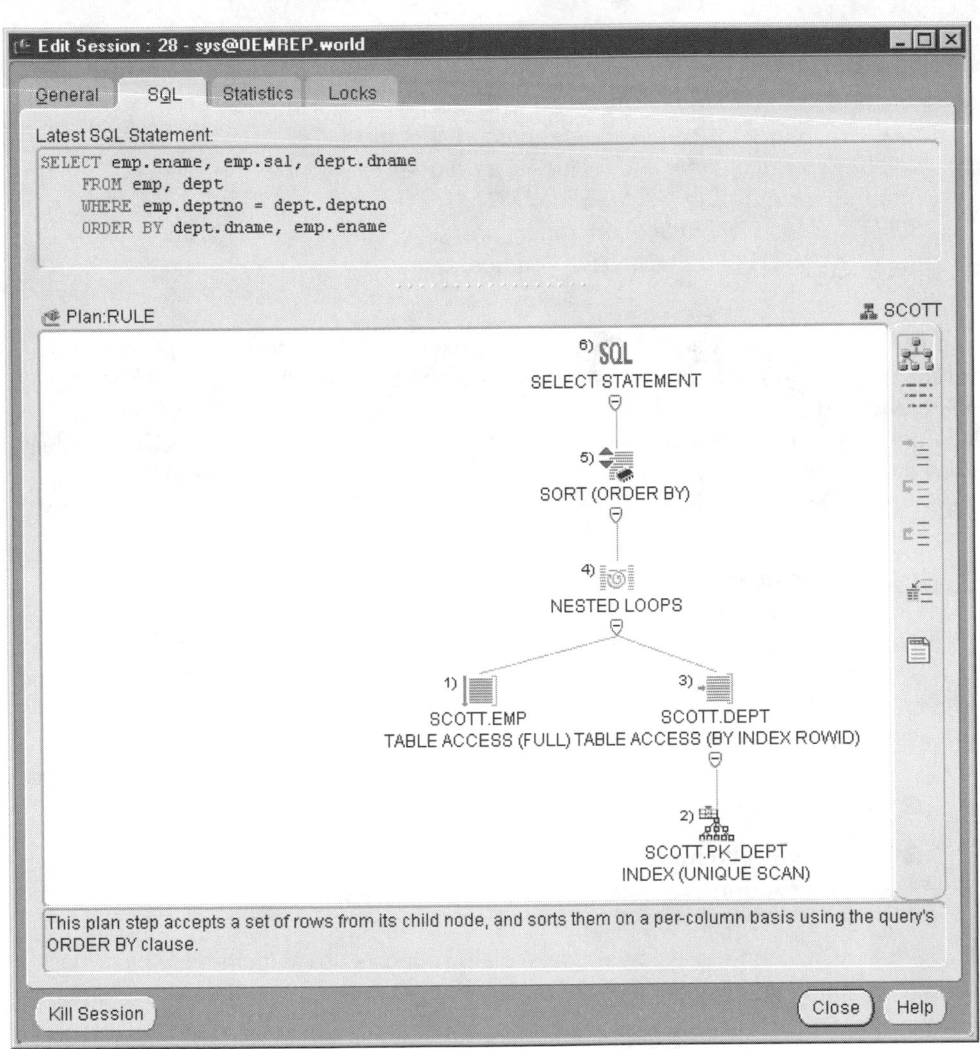

FIGURE 14-12. *Viewing the SQL statement in graphical format*

You can generate a SQL Explain Plan report in HTML format (one index.html file and several GIF files) through the Report button in the right toolbar. By default, the report should be located in the ORACLE_HOME\sysman\report\ExplainPlans directory.

NOTE
In our version of EM, the report was not generated into the ORACLE_HOME\sysman\report\ExplainPlans directory, but into the ORACLE_HOME\sysman\report directory instead in a folder named after the database service name and including a unique number, for example "OEMREP.WORLD_SELECT_3412579" for a query run against the OEMREP.WORLD database instance.

Long-Running Queries If the session is executing *long-running operations*, a clock displays in the icon (the power plug) in the Sessions detail view. The Long Operations page is available in the Edit Session dialog box. This is a very useful feature, which enables you to follow the progress of such sessions and get an idea about when the query will be finished. Figure 14-13 shows an example of a long running operation that is 71 percent through.

Killing a Session

If you want to kill a session, perhaps because the user is hogging the system, highlight the session and click Kill Session. You can also right-click on the session and choose Kill Session from the pop-up. Finally, you can also kill a session from the Edit Session screen (see the "Showing Details For a Session" above). In all cases, you must choose between two options for killing the session:

- **Immediate** Kill the session immediately and roll back the transaction
- **Post Transactional** Wait for the user to finish the current transaction with either commit or rollback, and then kill the session.

When using the Kill Session button, a dialog appears box with these two options; select the option you want and click OK. No further confirmation dialog boxes appear.

Switching the Consumer Group for a Session

You can switch a session from the user's current consumer group to another. To do this, highlight the session and either choose Object | Switch Consumer Group, or right-click the session and choose Switch Consumer Group from the pop-up menu. When the Switch Consumer Group dialog appears, choose the new consumer group from the Group drop-down list box. You can move all the user's sessions to the consumer group by checking the "Switch all sessions belonging to the user" check box (checked by default). Click OK to close the dialog box and store the change. Notice that this does not affect future sessions for the user; the user's default consumer group is used for new sessions.

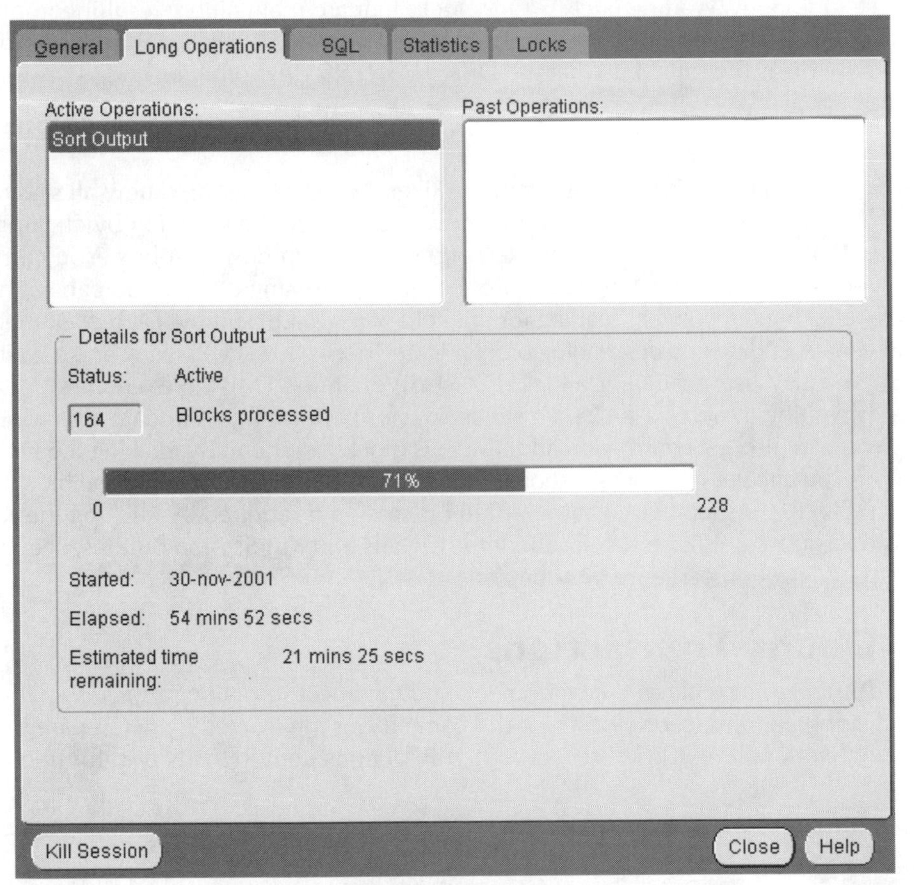

FIGURE 14-13. *Monitoring a long-running query*

Locks

On the Locks page, you can view all database locks that are currently maintained across database sessions. Select the Locks item in the Navigator tree, and all locks are listed in the detail view. The screen looks similar to that of Sessions, described earlier in this chapter. Instead of choosing between all or the top sessions, you choose from the following:

- **User Type Locks** Locks from user processes (default); the background processes are excluded.

- **Blocking/Waiting Locks** Only locks that are maintained, resulting in other sessions waiting for them to be released, as well as those waiting are shown (this is the same info that the DBA_WAITERS view provides).
- **All Locks** All locks are displayed, including those from background processes.

Select the criteria for the view from the Filter drop-down list box; now all sessions fulfilling the criteria are listed. You might want to refresh the selection by clicking on the Refresh button (arrow) to the left of the Filter drop-down list box. You can also refresh by choosing Navigator | Refresh, or by pressing CTRL-R. You can sort the list by clicking the column heading for the field you want to sort by. Each click toggles between ascending and descending order. Figure 14-14 shows a blocking and a waiting lock. The LBV user maintains a lock (EXCLUSIVE) on the EMP table, and the SCOTT user is waiting to apply a lock on a single row for performing an update operation.

You can also get information about who is blocking whom. By clicking the Details button, you can get more details about the session. You can either contact the blocking user (LBV) for further investigation, or kill his session if required by clicking the Kill Session button. For more details about the Details and Kill Session buttons, see the "Sessions" section earlier in this chapter.

In-Doubt Transactions

In a distributed or replicated environment, you might get *in-doubt transactions*. These are distributed transactions for which the commit was interrupted in the prepare state by a network failure. Click the In-Doubt Transactions item in the Navigator tree to

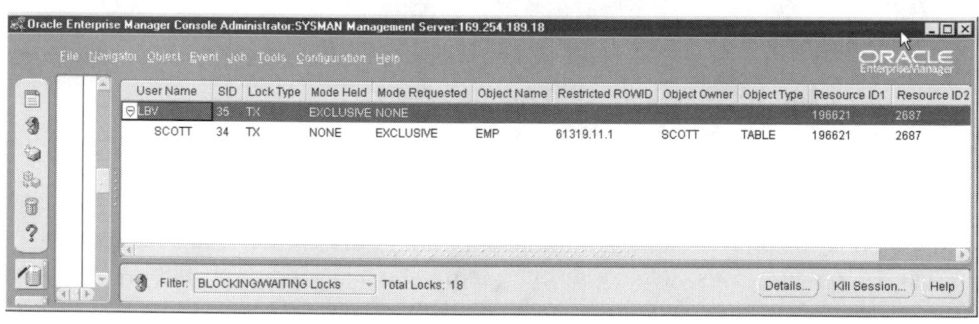

FIGURE 14-14. *Viewing the locks*

access the detail view. The following information is displayed for each in-doubt transaction (this is the same information as provided in the DBA_2PC_PENDING view):

- **Local ID** The node where the transaction is to be completed.
- **Global ID** The node where the distributed transaction originates.
- **State** The in-doubt transaction can be in one of the following states: COLLECTING, PREPARED, COMMITTED, FORCED COMMIT or FORCED ROLLBACK.
- **Advice** The suggested resolution method: C for Commit, R for Rollback, or NULL, which indicates that the state needs no immediate action.
- **Commit Comment** If the transaction was committed using the COMMENT option, this text is displayed.

These in-doubt transactions must be resolved manually by you through a COMMIT or ROLLBACK FORCE, if they are not handled automatically by the RECO (recover) background process. From within the EM Console, you do this by selecting the in-doubt transaction and choosing either Transaction | Force Commit or Transaction | Force Rollback in the pop-up menu. Manually resolving distributed transactions can be complicated; refer to the chapter "Distributed Transactions Concepts" in the *Oracle9i Database Administrator's Guide* for more details.

Database Resource Management Features

Database resource management was introduced in Oracle8i, and enables you to prioritize certain user sessions when the node the database runs on has a CPU utilization of 100 percent. This way you can:

- Ensure that selected users are prioritized in the processing of their transactions.
- Distinguish between daytime and nighttime resource allocation methods, and switch between them without having to restart the instance. These methods are implemented as Resource Plans, and the switching is accomplished through the Resource Plan Schedule. For example, you could choose to give OLTP (On-Line Transaction Processing) users 20 percent and batch-oriented users 80 percent CPU resource in your night plan, and the other way around in your day plan.

- Provide different (more or less) CPU resources for different types of users.
- Limit the degree of parallelism per user or group of users.
- If one user is hogging the system with a long-running query, you can move this user to a resource consumer group with lower resources, instead of just killing the session. See the "Switching the Consumer Group for a Session" part in the "Sessions" section earlier in this chapter.

Although there are three entries in the Instance Manager Navigator tree concerning resource management, we will cover these as a whole, because they are closely related and depend on each other. The "Resource Monitors Property Page" section earlier in this chapter described how to monitor the resource plan usage when a resource plan schedule has been established. The following sections take a closer look at the three different components of database resource management and how they relate to each other.

Resource Consumer Groups

The first and lowest-level component of the database resource management is the definition of resource consumer groups. These provide a way of grouping your different types of users who have similar processing and resource usage requirements (OLTP, DSS, DBA, and so on). Users can be members of multiple consumer groups, but only one group is active at a time for a session. A default group is assigned to each user at login. The consumer groups are then assigned to one or more resource plans, which are scheduled using the resource plan schedule.

Creating a New Resource Consumer Group To create a new resource consumer group, do the following:

1. Right-click the Resource Consumer Group tree item and choose the Create menu item from the pop-up or from the Object menu. You can also click the Create icon (the green cube in the left toolbar) or press CTRL-N. which in either case displays the general Create dialog box. If you want to create a new consumer group similar to an existing one, right-click the existing group and choose Create Like from the pop-up menu (or from the Object menu) or click the Create Like icon (the hollow green cube in the left toolbar).
2. The Create Resource Consumer Group dialog appears, and you will be placed on the General page. Enter a name for the consumer group and optionally enter a description.

3. Click the Users tab. On this page, you choose the users who are to be members of this consumer group. Highlight the users in the Available Users list and click the arrow pointing down to add these to the group. You can also double-click a user to include him or her in the consumer group. Checking the Admin Option column enables the user to grant the switch privilege to other users. By checking the Initial Group, you specify that the consumer group created is the initial consumer group for the user.

4. Click the Roles tab. Here you can assign database roles to the consumer group in the same fashion as you did for users. When you have entered all appropriate information, click Create to save the new resource consumer group.

Modifying an Existing Resource Consumer Group To modify the properties of an existing resource consumer group, you have two choices:

- Select the consumer group in the Navigator by clicking it once, and modify the information in the detail view in the right side of the EM Console.
- Right-click the consumer group you want to modify either in the Navigator or in the detail view and choose View/Edit Details from the pop-up menu or the Object menu. The Edit Resource Consumer Group screen appears.

The information is entered just as when creating a new resource consumer group. You cannot change the name of the consumer group. Click Apply (or OK in the Edit Resource Consumer Group screen) to save the modified information.

Resource Plans

A resource plan defines *how* the CPU time and parallel query resources are allocated among the different consumer groups. You can define several resource plans within an instance, but only one can be used at a time. You can nest resource plans so that one resource plan may be part of another plan, or a subplan. The SYSTEM_PLAN is created by default at the time of database creation.

Creating a New Resource Plan After you have created your resource consumer groups, you have two options for creating a new resource plan:

- Use the Create dialog box (like creating a new Resource Consumer Group)
- Use the Resource Plan Wizard

You create a new resource plan by performing the following steps:

1. Right-click the Resource Plan item in the Navigator tree and choose Create from the pop-up menu, or use the other ways to create a new object, including the Create Like feature.
2. The Create Resource Plan dialog box appears, and you are placed on the General page. First, enter a name for the resource plan, and then add the resource consumer groups to the plan individually by double-clicking them in the Available Groups/Subplans list. You can also highlight one or more consumer groups and click the down-arrow to include these. Next, define the resource plan directives. For each included consumer group in the "Items in this plan" list, you now can specify up to eight levels of CPU usage, each level specifying how the CPU usage is partitioned using percentages. Consumer groups at a level with a lower level number get first priority to override consumer groups having a higher level number. If there are CPU resources remaining after all consumer groups have been run at a given level, these are assigned to the next higher level. Each resource plan must have a directive for the OTHER_GROUPS consumer group. You can activate the new plan and deactivate the currently active plan through the check box in the bottom of the page. Finally, you can enter a description for the resource plan.
3. Click the Parallelism tab. Here you specify the maximum parallel degree for each consumer group.
4. Click Create to store the new resource plan.

To create a new resource plan using the wizard, follow these steps:

1. Right-click the Resource Plan item in the Navigator tree and choose the Create Using Wizard menu item from the pop-up menu or from the Object menu. The Resource Plan Wizard launches.
2. Walk through the different steps of the wizard, which enables you to create a new consumer group on the fly. You can choose between Basic and Advanced CPU resource allocation methods. With the Basic method, all percentages assigned to each consumer group will only be for one level (level 2). With the Advanced method, you specify the percentage of CPU resources using the levels 1 to 8, as if you were using the Create Resource Plan dialog box. The wizard also enables you to activate the new resource plan.

Resource Plan Schedule

The final step in resource management is to define the schedule for the different resource plans. You can choose an automatic schedule, or you can switch between the resource plans manually by using the Activate check box on the General property page for the resource plan you want to activate.

To define and enable a resource plan schedule, choose the Resource Plan Schedule item in the Navigator tree. Enter a new time for switching resource plans by clicking the green plus sign in the bottom of the screen. Enter the time when the resource plan is to be activated, either by entering the number or by using the up/down arrows to change the hour and minute values. Then choose the resource plan from the Resource Plan drop-down list box. Repeat this step to add other resource plans to the schedule. Choose the Enable radio button, and click Apply to store the resource plan schedule.

NOTE
To change the resource plan schedule, you must login as SYS.

Schema

Schema Management allows you to administer database objects of all kinds. You can create, alter, and delete database objects, as well as view information about object dependencies. For tables, you can even view and modify the contents through the Table Data Editor. To access the Schema Management, click the plus sign next to the Schema entry in the EM Navigator tree when you are connected to the database you want to manage. The structure and handling in Schema Management are more or less the same for all these different types of objects. To access an existing object of a certain kind, you have two options:

- Click the entry in the tree for whatever object type you want to access. All objects are listed in the detail view. You can sort the list by clicking once on the column heading. You can access the object properties by selecting the particular object in the detail view and choosing Edit/View Details from the Object or pop-up menus, or simply by double-clicking the object.
- Expand the tree by clicking the plus sign to the left of the object type. You must know in which database schema the object resides, and expand the schema entry of that name, again by clicking the plus sign. All the objects of this particular type existing in this schema are listed in the Navigator tree, where you select an object by clicking it once. The object properties are displayed in the detail view.

Depending on the type of object, the object properties will look different and have a different number of property pages which can be accessed by tabs at the top of the detail view.

Changing the Navigator Tree View

As described in the previous section, the Navigator tree lists all different object types as the first level and the schemas as the second level, which contain objects of the particular type. You change this view to the opposite, however, so the first level shows all database schemas, and the second level shows all object types.

- **View by Object** This is the default view when entering Schema Manager. You choose this view by checking the View By Object check box in the Navigator menu. This view lists all object types, and for each entry, the schemas where objects of this particular type exist.
- **View by Schema** This view lists all existing database schemas in the Navigator tree, and for each entry, all object types, even if the schema does not contain any objects of this type. You choose this view by checking the View By Schema check box in the Navigator menu.

Creating a Database Object

You can either create a new object through the Create feature or create one similar to an existing object by using the Create Like feature. You access the Create and Create Like features either from the Object Menu or the pop-up menu by pressing CTRL-N (Create) or CTRL-L (Create Like), or by clicking the Create or Create Like icon in the left toolbar. You can also make a copy of an object, as described in the next section.

For some types of database objects (dimensions, tables, and views), the Create Using Wizard entry appears in the Object menu, meaning a wizard is available for creating a new object. Let the wizard guide you through creation of the object.

Copying a Database Object

You can copy a database object between schemas and databases. This is handled by the Oracle DB Propagate function, which is part of the optional Change Management Pack. You activate this function using the Drag and Drop feature: Select and drag the object you want to copy, and drop it into the target schema in the Navigator tree. After dropping the object on the target schema, a confirmation dialog box appears. Click OK to launch Oracle DB Propagate and Cancel to stop. The first step is generating an Impact Report, which checks to see if copying this particular object is valid. See the Most Serious Message Level field; if it says NO ERRORS, you can continue, otherwise, browse the Impact Report text to get more details about the error. A TCL script is generated for performing the copy operation. The Script Summary shows which steps are performed by the propagate function. You can modify the script by clicking Edit script.

NOTE

The method used in the generated script for copying a table including data is a PL/SQL CURSOR FOR-LOOP. Be aware that this is not the most efficient way of copying large amounts of data compared to using Export/Import or the COPY command.

Click Next to get to the last step (executing the script) of Oracle DB Propagate. Here you can execute the script immediately by clicking Execute, or choose to submit an EM job for scheduled execution by clicking Submit As Job. When you choose to execute immediately, the copy process begins and the progress is displayed in the Execution Log field. You can interrupt the process by clicking Interrupt. When finished, click Keep to make the changes permanent, or click Undo to undo the copy operation. When you choose to submit a job, a dialog box for submitting the job will be launched. Enter the job name and description, and specify a date/time for execution.

NOTE

When you submit the copy operation as a job, you will not be able to undo the operation. You must manually undo the changes by dropping the copied object.

Click Finish to exit Oracle DB Propagate.

Viewing and Modifying Data

The Table Data Editor function lets you view and modify the actual table data stored in a particular table. To access the Table Data Editor, select the object, either in the detail view or Navigator tree, and choose the Table Data Editor entry from the Object or pop-up menus. If the table contains more than 500 rows, you can choose between showing all rows or refining the query in a dialog box. You can now insert, modify, and delete data. To modify a row, simply click in the row and change the data. To insert a new row, or to delete an existing row, right-click the area just to the left of

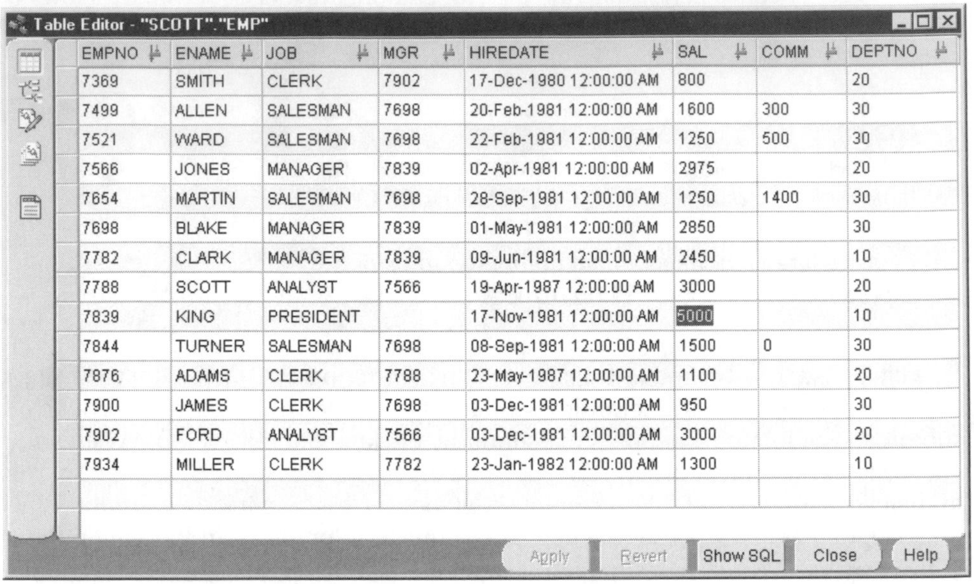

Table Editor - "SCOTT"."EMP"

EMPNO	ENAME	JOB	MGR	HIREDATE	SAL	COMM	DEPTNO
7369	SMITH	CLERK	7902	17-Dec-1980 12:00:00 AM	800		20
7499	ALLEN	SALESMAN	7698	20-Feb-1981 12:00:00 AM	1600	300	30
7521	WARD	SALESMAN	7698	22-Feb-1981 12:00:00 AM	1250	500	30
7566	JONES	MANAGER	7839	02-Apr-1981 12:00:00 AM	2975		20
7654	MARTIN	SALESMAN	7698	28-Sep-1981 12:00:00 AM	1250	1400	30
7698	BLAKE	MANAGER	7839	01-May-1981 12:00:00 AM	2850		30
7782	CLARK	MANAGER	7839	09-Jun-1981 12:00:00 AM	2450		10
7788	SCOTT	ANALYST	7566	19-Apr-1987 12:00:00 AM	3000		20
7839	KING	PRESIDENT		17-Nov-1981 12:00:00 AM	5000		10
7844	TURNER	SALESMAN	7698	08-Sep-1981 12:00:00 AM	1500	0	30
7876	ADAMS	CLERK	7788	23-May-1987 12:00:00 AM	1100		20
7900	JAMES	CLERK	7698	03-Dec-1981 12:00:00 AM	950		30
7902	FORD	ANALYST	7566	03-Dec-1981 12:00:00 AM	3000		20
7934	MILLER	CLERK	7782	23-Jan-1982 12:00:00 AM	1300		10

Apply | Revert | Show SQL | Close | Help

FIGURE 14-15. *Editing a table in the Table Editor*

the first column and choose Add Row or Delete from the pop-up menu. Figure 14-15 shows an example of the EMP table being loaded in the Table Editor.

The icons on the left side activate the Update Table Mode, Graphical Select Mode, Free SQL Mode, and Free SQL History. The left toolbar also has a Report icon that activates a Report feature. The function Display Contents is available for views and synonyms (on tables and views).

Security

Security Management helps you maintain database security issues; more precisely, users, roles, and profiles. The Users part is used to grant object and system privileges to users, or revoke them, as well as grant or revoke access on Workspaces (see the "Workspaces" section later in this chapter). You can also change the password, lock or unlock the account, and administer tablespace quotas. Finally, you can assign users and roles to Consumer Groups and grant privileges for each consumer group. See the "Resource Consumer Groups" section earlier in this chapter for more details.

Storage

Storage Management allows you to administrate your tablespaces, datafiles, rollback and undo segments, as well as online redo log groups and files. It also enables you to view control file information and to view the archive logs that have been created. When you expand the Storage item in the Navigator tree, you see the following items:

- **Controlfile** Shows database control file information; you cannot make changes here.
- **Tablespaces** Contains all tablespaces defined in the database. You can create, drop, and modify tablespaces. For example, you can modify default storage parameters, add datafiles, or take tablespaces offline and online. The Tablespace Map (part of the optional Tuning Pack) is a very useful feature for examining the single extents stored in the tablespace.
- **Datafiles** Lists all datafiles in the database. You can create and drop datafiles, as well as extend and shrink them.
- **Rollback Segments** Lists the rollback segments defined for the database if you are using the conventional pre-9i method. If you are using the automatic undo management 9i feature, only the SYSTEM rollback segment will be listed.
- **Redo Log Groups** Contains the online redo log groups and their members, which you can create and drop. You can also initiate a checkpoint operation or a log switch from here.
- **Archive Logs** Lists all archived redo log files registered in the database (the same as V$ARCHIVED_LOG shows). You cannot make changes in this part.

Figure 14-16 shows a list of the Tablespaces, which is a very useful overview of the space usage in the database.

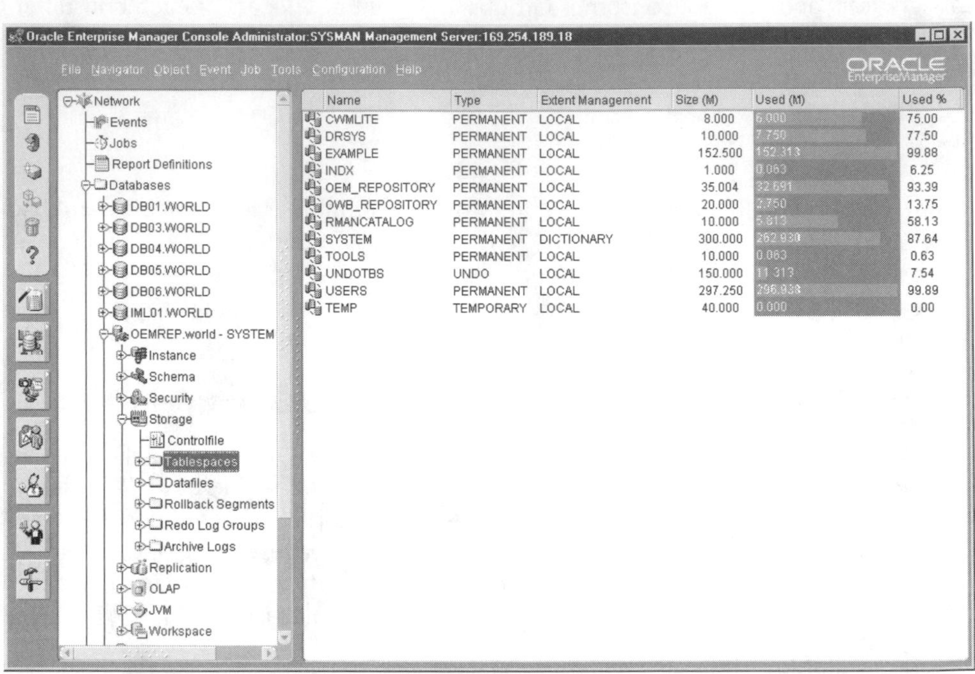

FIGURE 14-16. *Viewing the tablespace list*

Replication

With earlier releases of EM, the Replication Manager was a separate tool; now it is an integrated part of the EM Navigator, and has matured into a very useful tool. Using this tool, you can easily set up, administer, and monitor your replicated environment. A comprehensive wizard is available for preparing your databases for supporting both multimaster and materialized view (snapshot) replication, and assisting in replicating schema objects. In Chapter 6, we provided an overview of the Replication management within EM; in the following, we will walk you through the steps performed in EM to successfully set up master sites as well as materialized view sites. Refer to *Oracle9i Replication* for more information about Oracle Replication.

Setting up a Master Site

Creating a master site is the prerequisite for replicating information, either for *multimaster* or *materialized view* (snapshot) replication. This involves creating a replication administrator (REPADMIN) and a propagator/receiver, as well as a default link and purge job schedules. All is accomplished through a setup wizard, but you can generate a PL/SQL script containing all commands required for the configuration. The wizard is launched through the Setup Master Sites entry from the Object or pop-up menus when either the Multimaster Replication or Master Site (Materialized View Replication) entry in the Navigator tree is selected. You can set up multiple master sites at the same time.

Setup Master Sites Wizard

Before you start the Setup Master Sites Wizard, make sure that you are logged in using either SYS or SYSTEM to successfully set up replication. The setup wizard goes through the steps of selecting one or more target databases as master sites, creating replication user accounts in these databases and replicated schemas. It helps you schedule the propagation of data, and also provides purging mechanisms for the deferred transactions queue containing the successfully propagated transactions. It also allows you to customize master sites individually when single sites should receive attributes different from the rest. According to your specifications, the wizard will create replication administrator accounts, which also serve as data propagator and receiver accounts. The default name for such an account is usually REPADMIN, and is automatically granted all necessary privileges. Once the initial setup is done, you need to use this account for further activities. Finally, the wizard schedules propagation and purging for all master sites. After this is done, you can start creating master groups, which we explain in the following section "Create Master Group Wizard."

Create Master Group Wizard

When the master site has been prepared, you can create the master groups that are to be replicated. This must be performed while you are connected to the master site as the replication administrator (REPADMIN). To create a new Master Group, you select the Master Groups entry in the Navigator tree, either from the Multimaster Replication or Master Site (Materialized View Replication) entry. Then, choose Object | Create or click the Create icon in the left toolbar to initiate the general Create dialog box. Here you choose Master Group and click Create. You can also right-click the Master Groups entry, or an existing Master Group, and choose Create from the pop-up menu. The wizard guides you through the creation of a master group.

The master group is basically a group of objects to be replicated between your sites, these being other master sites or materialized view sites. First, specify a name for the new master group. Specify a connection qualifier if you use different database links to the same databases. You then add objects to the master group and select the master sites between which these objects should be replicated. Once the group is created, it will appear in the navigator tree, including its objects. Using the detail pages of the master group, you can start and stop the replication activity, and view and manage administrative requests, including sending custom DDL statements to a list of master sites. You can also add more objects later if you discover you missed some during the initial setup, or even add more master sites later. Adding more master sites requires that replication communication (refresh activity) is temporarily paused, which is often called *quiesce*.

NOTE

To replicate the master group to other master sites, database links must have been created, and the databases must be able to connect to each other through Oracle Net. If you configure a materialized view site, this site must be able to communicate with the master via a database link through Oracle Net. In this case, the master site does not need to have database links created against the materialized view site.

From the Administration entry in the Navigator tree, you can monitor and administer your replicated environment. In the detail view pane, a page appears with the following tabs:

- **Topology** A graphical map of your replicated environment. Through the Refresh button, you can refresh the map. By clicking the Statistics button, you can get information about the activity between the sites on a per database link level. You can examine various statistics about the deferred transactions being propagated between the sites. These figures are based on the V$REPLQUEUE dynamic view.
- **Errors** If the deferred transactions are not able to be applied on a master site, they will appear in the Errors page. By clicking on the Details button, you can get more information about a particular transaction. You can retry applying a deferred transaction by highlighting it and clicking the Retry button. Or, you can delete the deferred transaction by clicking Remove.
- **Transactions** This page lists all the deferred transactions in the queue on this master site. You can get detailed information about a single transaction by clicking the Details button. By clicking the Push Transactions button, you can request a push of deferred transactions; for example, if you have disabled automatic push or do not want to wait for the next push to take place (see Schedule below). Through the Remove button, you can delete a deferred transaction.

- **Schedule** On this page, you can manage your scheduling for *push* and for *purge* operations for the site. You need to schedule a purge job in order to periodically empty the deferred transaction queue table. If you generate a lot of transactions, be sure that this interval is not too long. If there are a lot of transactions to be purged, this takes a longer time, and transactions will not be pushed during this purge operation.
- **Configuration** On this page, you can change the setting for the GLOBAL_NAMES, JOB_QUEUE_PROCESSES, and JOB_QUEUE_INTERVAL initialization parameters as well as view the status of administrative requests for the site.
- **DBMS Job** This page shows all existing database jobs which have been scheduled to support replication operations, such as refresh, push, and purge. These jobs have nothing to do with the EM job system, which we discuss in Chapter 11. It is possible to modify existing jobs using the Edit button, delete jobs using the Delete button, and create new jobs by clicking the New button. You can also execute an existing job by clicking on the Run button.

Figure 14-17 shows an example of a Topology view showing a multimaster setup with DB01.WORLD as the Master Definition Site and DB03.WORLD as another master site.

Setting up a Materialized View Site

Much like setting up master sites and master groups, you will have to set up materialized view sites and create materialized view groups. Optionally, you can create Refresh Groups for grouping your materialized views, typically to secure consistency during a refresh operation. Three different refresh options are available to you: *fast, complete,* and *force*. The fast refresh updates only the rows that have changed since the last refresh, whereas the complete refresh always updates the entire materialized view. The force refresh option tries a fast refresh first, and switches to complete refresh in case of problems. In order to use fast refreshes, you need to set up materialized view logs, which record all changes to the master tables or master materialized view. To create such a log, you can use the dialog box accessed through right-clicking Materialized View Logs in the Navigator tree and selecting Create.

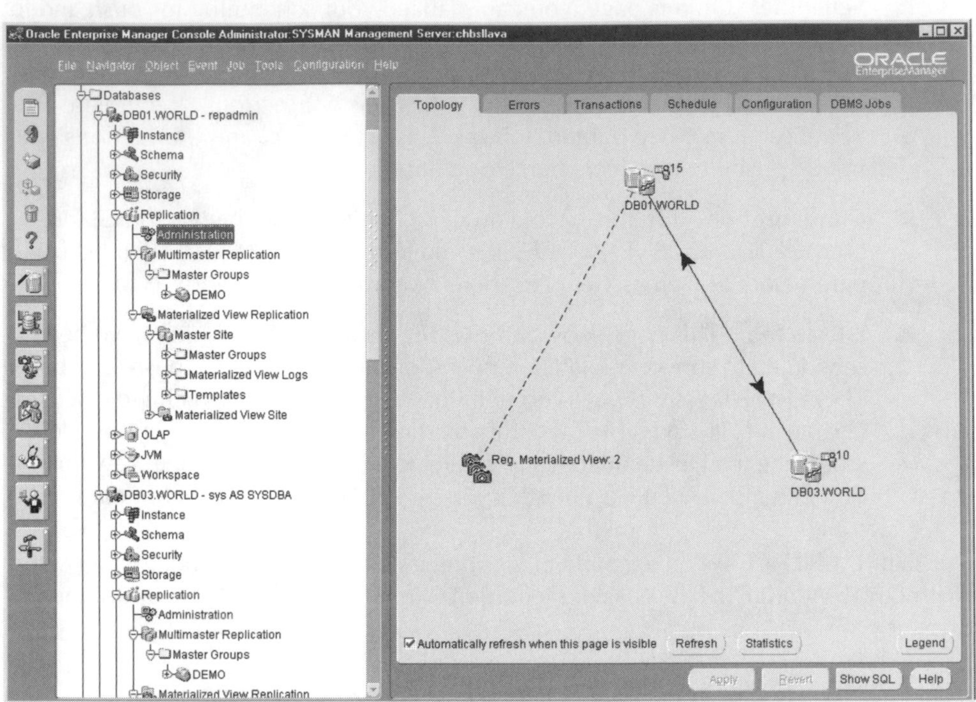

FIGURE 14-17. *Monitoring the replicated environment*

In the following, we will describe the two wizards available to set up a materialized view site: the Setup Materialized View Sites Wizard and the Create Materialized View Groups Wizard.

Setup Materialized View Sites Wizard

You launch the wizard through the menu entry Setup Materialized View Sites from either the Object or pop-up menus, when the Materialized View Site (Materialized View Replication) item in the Navigator tree is selected. You will need to specify the master site, the materialized view sites, an administrator account to be created at each materialized view site, and optionally, a different data propagator and receiver account. Typically, this account is called MVADMIN. You then select the schemas to be created at the materialized view sites, and specify the refresh attributes as well as the purge options. Optionally, you can customize settings for individual sites before the activity is submitted.

Create Materialized View Groups Wizard

Before you can create a materialized view group, you need to connect to the materialized view site as either the materialized view administrator, which is typically MVADMIN, or the replication administrator, which is typically REPADMIN. You can then access the wizard by selecting Create Using Wizard in the right-click menu of the Materialized View Groups item in the navigator tree. The wizard offers all available database links to master target databases, after which you will see existing target master groups. You have to select the link you would like to use for your new materialized view, and whether the propagation should be synchronous or asynchronous using a deferred transaction queue. Select relevant objects from the master group and create a refresh group, or add them to an existing refresh group. You will also have to specify whether the materialized view will be updateable, which refresh method should be used, and optional storage settings for the materialized view. Before the group is created, you can again modify the settings for individual groups that should be different from the rest.

Depending on the individual needs of the different groups of users, you might need a number of different materialized views containing different data. As a DBA, you can prepare the definition of such available materialized views in the form of *templates* without actually creating them. The user then browses through the available templates and instantiates a template, which then causes the materialized view to be created. This can be done online or offline. To create such a template, EM offers the Deployment Template Wizard.

Deployment Template Wizard

The Deployment Template Wizard can be accessed by right-clicking the Templates folder and selecting Create Using Wizard. You have to name the template and specify the schema that owns it. When you add tables to the template, you can specify if the corresponding materialized view data will be updateable or not. This can only be selected when the master table is part of a master group and has a primary key.

You can further determine the row and column subsetting, if the view should not contain all rows and all columns of the master table. In addition, you can select objects other than materialized views, such as indexes or procedures, to be deployed at the materialized view's site, or create new objects on the spot. You then see an overview of your planned activity; you can view the SQL generated and optionally save it as script. The option to save it as a script is important when you want the template to be instantiated offline, which means that the remote site has to be set up without being connected to the master site. This can be done through a script, which you can generate with help of the Template Script Generation Wizard. Once the template is created, it appears in the navigator tree, and can be managed through its detail pages. You can also compare two templates easily by selecting Compare in the right-click menu of one of the templates.

Template Script Generation Wizard

You can access this wizard in a number of places; one is by right-clicking an existing template and selecting Template Script Generation. You first select the template you would like to generate a script for and specify the proxy user. The proxy user is the user at the master site through which the users at the materialized view site will connect to the master site. If no proxy user exists, you will be able to create one. You also specify for which individual users you want to create an instantiation script. The wizard generates a separate script for each individual user. After entering the refresh parameters, you can select the schemas that will be generated at the materialized view site. The wizard then generates the scripts needed for instantiation: one setup script preparing the materialized view site for replication, one template script for each user creating and populating objects at the materialized view site, and a refresh script, which can be used by all users to refresh the data in the materialized views.

OLAP

New with Oracle9i and EM9i is the integration of On-Line Analytical Processing (OLAP) features, which enables users to selectively extract and view data from different points-of-view (also called "slice-and-dice"). These features are known as Oracle OLAP Services, and consist of the following components:

- Oracle's Java API for OLAP
- One or more OLAP services
- An OLAP metadata repository in each database instance
- Tools within EM for creating OLAP metadata and managing OLAP services

The OLAP feature is available on several platforms, including Windows NT/2000 and Unix. The implementation will be different, but the management within EM will be the same. From the OLAP management in the EM Navigator, you can maintain your cubes, dimensions, and measures. You can create new cubes and dimensions through the Cube Wizard and the Dimension Wizard, respectively. Refer to the OLAP section in Chapter 6 for more information about cubes and dimensions.

OLAP Services run as child processes within the database instance and are managed using the OLAP Services Instance Manager (OSIM). OSIM is a Java-based tool that communicates via CORBA. Using OSIM, you can configure and manage OLAP services and sessions. In particular, you can perform the following:

- Change configuration parameters for an OLAP service
- Start, stop, and pause OLAP services
- Create new Oracle OLAP services and remove existing services
- View system log files where status messages from OLAP services are recorded
- View module information for an OLAP service
- Monitor client sessions

When you choose to install the OLAP option, for example during Oracle software installation or through the Database Configuration Assistant (DBCA), you will find a tablespace called CWMLITE in your database. This tablespace holds the OLAP repository, also known as Common Warehouse Metadata (CWM), meaning all the database objects used by OLAP Services. Additionally, the following database users are created:

- OLAPDBA with default password OLAPDBA. This user is used by the OLAP Services and you should use it as an administrator account when managing OLAP in your database. When you change the database password for the OLAPDBA user, you must make the same change to the UserPassword parameter setting for OLAP Services through OSIM (Parameters | Security | DBA).
- OLAPSVR with default password INSTANCE. Used as proxy identification by all OLAP Services connections. If you change the database password for the OLAPSVR user, you must make the same change to the OlapProxyPwd parameter setting for the OLAP Service through OSIM (Parameters | Security | Security).
- OLAPSYS with default password MANAGER. This user holds all the OLAP repository objects.

Please check if these accounts are locked before using the OLAP feature. In case they are locked, you should unlock them. You should change their default passwords too, but you can choose to do this after you have configured the OLAP Services required in your environment from within the OLAP Service Instance Manager (OSIM). All three OLAP database accounts are granted the OLAP_DBA role, which is the highest level of privilege for administering OLAP Services. This role is managed by database security. The OLAP_DBA role is granted automatically to the DBA role, and can be granted to other users, for example through the Security database administration tool within EM. Other types of administration privileges for OLAP Services are managed through OSIM under the Instance Security navigator tree entry. You can choose between two privileges from the Privilege Type drop-down list box:

- Instance Administration Privilege. Can manage a particular OLAP service such as start and stop the service, change configuration settings, and terminate sessions.
- OLAP Service Administration Privilege. Includes the Instance Administration Privilege, plus the ability to create new OLAP services, remove existing services, and grant the OLAP Service Administration Privilege to other users.

A user with the OLAP_DBA role in the database automatically has the OLAP Services Administration Privilege in Instance Manager.

NOTE
Changes made through OSIM on a Windows NT/2000 machine will modify the Registry, for example in the OLAP\ExpressServer\OLAPServer\Security key located under HKEY_LOCAL_MACHINE\SOFTWARE\ORACLE. On Unix systems the olap.key configuration file located in $Oracle_HOME/olap.

On Windows NT/2000, you will find the following two services:

- Oracle OLAP Agent. This service is the backend for OLAP Instance Manager and has to be started in order for OSIM to work. It performs the tasks specified in OSIM, such as creating a new OLAP service, starting and stopping an OLAP service, or changing its configuration settings.

- Oracle OLAP 9.0.1.0.1. The default OLAP service created when installing the OLAP option, and through OSIM you can create additional such services. This service is the core of the OLAP Services and performs complex statistical, mathematical, and financial calculations along with predictive analysis functions such as forecasting, modeling, consolidations, allocations, and scenario management.

In the following, we will take a look at the OLAP Services Instances Manager and manage OLAP Services running on the Windows 2000 machine CHBSLLAVA. Before you start OSIM, be sure the three OLAP database accounts mentioned above have been unlocked and that the Oracle OLAP Agent service is running. To launch OSIM, first connect to the EM Console, either in standalone mode or connected to an OMS. Click the database whose OLAP services you want to manage, and supply valid login credentials for a DBA account; for example, use the OLAPDBA account. Right-click the OLAP entry in the EM Navigator and choose OLAP Services Instance Manager.

NOTE

If the OLAP entry is not shown in the EM Navigator, notice the following. In order to decide whether OLAP is installed or not, EM will check for the existence of the function GET_VERSION in the OLAPSYS.CWM$UTILITY package. The PUBLIC synonym CWM_UTILITY points to this package. If this function is not found or if the OLAPSYS.CWM$UTILITY package is invalid, OLAP will not appear in the EM Navigator tree.

Now OSIM will launch and you should see the default OLAP Server; for example, CHBSLLAVA.OLAPServer for the OLAP service running on the host CHBSLLAVA. You can change the logon credentials for your connection to the OLAP Service from within OSIM by choosing Logout from the Service menu or by clicking the Logout icon (power plug) in the left toolbar. Now the Database Authenticate dialog appears where you specify the new logon credentials.

To check the status of the OLAP service, expand the entry for it and click on the Instance entry in the Navigator tree. As you know it from the database instance management described earlier in the Instance section of this chapter, a traffic light will indicate the status of the OLAP service. If the service is not running (traffic light is red), you can start it by choosing the Service Start value right to the traffic light and click Apply. Now the OLAP service will be started. In Figure 14-18, you see an example of the OLAP service running on the host CHBSLLAVA being started.

NOTE
On Windows NT/2000, you can additionally start and stop the OLAP services from the services control panel. On Unix, the OLAP Service Manager command-line utility can be used. This is called through the executable xscosvc, which can also be invoked from the cosvc script.

You can create a new OLAP Service from within OSIM by choosing Create from the Service menu or by clicking the Create Service icon in the left toolbar. Now you will be guided through OLAP service creation by the Create New Service Wizard. Specify a name and description for the OLAP service as well as the DB Proxy Service

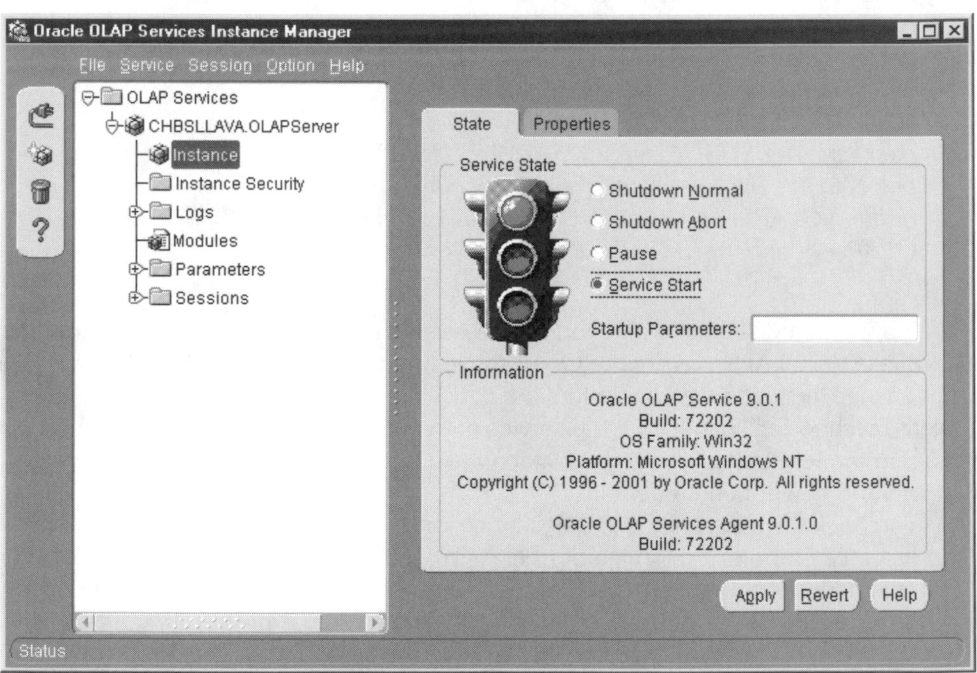

FIGURE 14-18. *Starting an OLAP Service from within OSIM*

(database in which the OLAP Server runs) and DB Proxy User Id and Password (OLAPSVR account).

For more information about the OLAP feature, please refer to the *Oracle9i OLAP Services Concepts and Administration Guide.*

JVM

The Oracle9*i* JVM (previously known as JServer) is a Java Virtual Engine embedded in the database. It enables you to store and execute Java classes in the database as well as write Java Stored Procedures, which can interact with your stored PL/SQL components. You can define EJBs (Enterprise Java Beans) and CORBA (Common Object Request Broker Architecture) components. You use the JVM entry in the EM Navigator to:

- Manage contexts, also known as *namespaces,* which separate your Java components
- Browse the Java components in the contexts
- Change permissions for the published components in the contexts
- Execute stored Java classes and view the output

NOTE
If the JVM is not configured for the instance, JVM will not be available in the Navigator tree.

Connecting to a Java-Enabled Database

You can change the login credentials for your JVM connection. When you expand the JVM entry, you are connected to JVM using the same credentials as for your database connection. To change the connection, choose Connect to JVM from either the Object menu or the pop-up menu for the JVM Navigator tree entry. The JVM Connect Information dialog appears, where you can enter the login credentials, as well as choose the URL for the JVM server. Figure 14-19 shows an example.

The connection established to JVM goes via GIOP (General Inter-ORB Protocol), which was originally designed to describe message formats and data representations for communication between Object Request Brokers (ORBs). GIOP provides ORB-to-ORB communication across any connection-oriented network transport protocol; to secure message exchange over TCP/IP, a special protocol is used, the Internet Inter-Orb Protocol (IIOP). Notice that the GIOP port number used by default is 2481. To change this or other connection properties, click the button to the right of the URL field (three dots) to access the JVM URL Configuration dialog box.

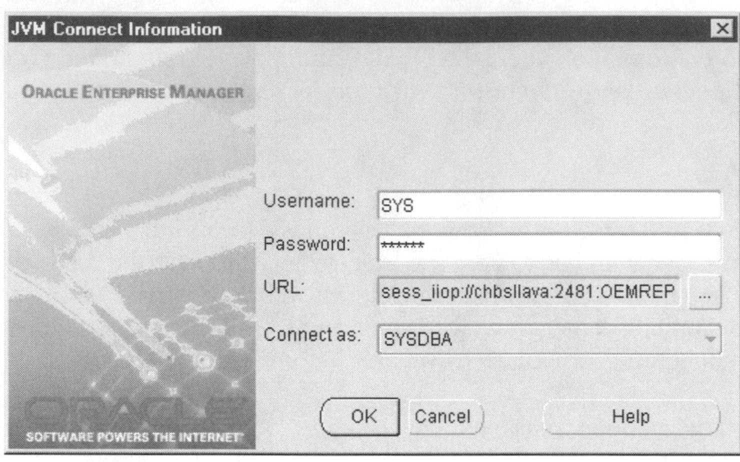

FIGURE 14-19. *Connecting to the JVM*

Executing Java Classes Using Java Worksheet

You can execute a Java class and view the output from the Java Worksheet. Select Show Java Worksheet either from the Object menu or the pop-up menu. The Java Worksheet dialog box appears. Enter the name in the Class Name field or use the browse button (the coffee cup with the magnifying glass) to get a tree list of all Java classes in the database. Notice that in order to execute a Java class, a main() method is required in the class.

Workspace

The workspace feature is available with Oracle9i, and can be managed from EM using the Workspace Manager. Workspaces are areas containing different versions of data. This enables users to create new versions of data to work on, while maintaining a copy of the old data. For example, you might want such a copy for testing purposes when a new version of an application is being put into production. Workspaces can be contained in other workspaces, enabling you to define a hierarchical structure. You should carefully plan your workspace structure before you begin to create your own workspaces.

Version-Enabling Tables

Before creating a workspace, you must version-enable the tables that are to be included in the workspace. This is done through the Version Enabled Tables entry in the Workspace Navigator tree.

NOTE
To version-enable a table, you must define a primary key constraint for it. Also, if a table is referenced by another table, this other table must be version-enabled, too. For example, in the SCOTT schema you cannot version-enable the DEPT table without version-enabling EMP first.

Select the tables from the Available Tables list and add them to the Version-Enabled Tables list by clicking the > button, and then click Apply to store the changes.

When you are version-enabling a table, Oracle will *rename* the original table (with the name <*tablename*>_LT) and create a view with the original table name. Also, an auxiliary table (<*tablename*>_AUX) will be created along with other views (with the postfixes _BASE, _CONF, _BPKC, and so on). Version-enabling SCOTT.EMP results in EMP being renamed to EMP_LT, and creates a view EMP and a table EMP_AUX. Also, Workspace Manager-specific columns are added to the original table (VERSION, NEXTVER, DELSTATUS, and LTLOCK), and the VERSION column is added to the primary-key constraint. Do not change any of these added columns in any way.

Managing Workspaces

To access the workspaces, select the Workspaces entry in the Workspace Navigator tree. The existing workspaces are listed in the detail view. The LIVE worksheet is created by default and is the parent of all workspaces.

Creating a New Workspace

To create a new workspace, you can either select the Workspaces entry in the Navigator tree and choose Object | Create from the Object menu, or click the Create icon in the left toolbar to initiate the general Create dialog box. Here you choose Workspace and click Create. Another more direct way is to expand the Workspaces entry by clicking the plus sign, right-click on an existing workspace (such as LIVE), and choose Create from the pop-up menu. You cannot use the Create Like feature for workspaces. Next, enter a name for the new workspace.

Granting Users Access to a Workspace

When you have created your workspace, you must add users to it. Workspaces have their own set of system privileges that are different from the normal Oracle database privileges. You grant these privileges to users using Security Manager. On the Object Privileges page, a Workspaces entry appears in the Object tree list on the left side. Expand the Workspaces entry by clicking the plus sign and select the workspace for which you will grant access. The privileges ACCESS_WORKSPACE, CREATE_WORKSPACE, ROLLBACK_WORKSPACE, REMOVE_WORKSPACE, and MERGE_WORKSPACE appear in the Available Privileges list. Grant the privileges to the user (or role) and click Apply. Figure 14-20 shows an example.

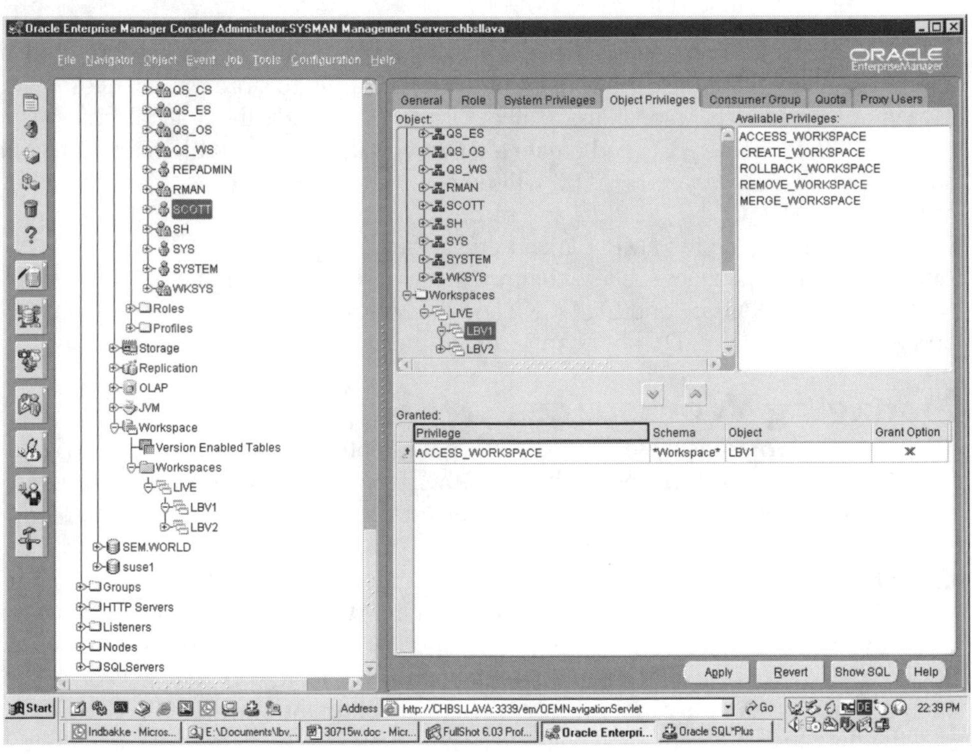

FIGURE 14-20. *Granting access to a workspace*

Other Workspace Features

You can compare two workspaces through the Show Differences entry in the Object or pop-up menu. The Show Differences dialog appears, where you can specify two workspaces to compare; one in the Top part of the dialog and the other in the Bottom part. An example is shown in the illustration below, where the workspace LBV1 is compared to the LBV2 workspace as it looked at the save point ICP-3:

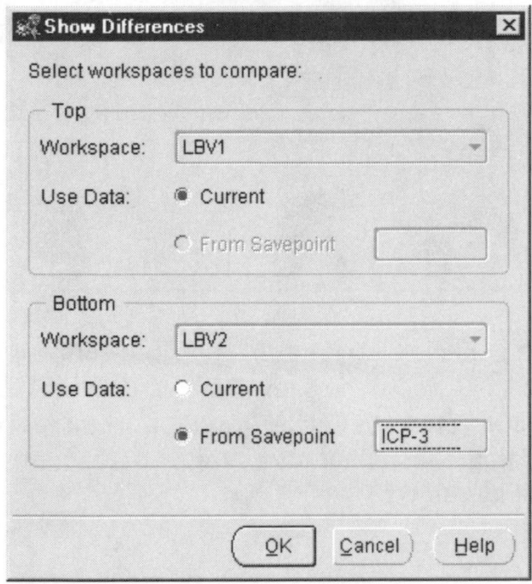

When you have defined workspaces as members of other workspaces, you can merge the contents of one workspace into its parent workspace. This is accomplished by selecting the Merge into parent entry in the Object or pop-up menus for the workspace to be merged. The Merge Workspace Into Parent dialog box appears, where you can choose to either merge the complete workspace or only a selected table with the contents of the parent workspace of a specified workspace. In case you choose to merge only a selected table, you can specify a WHERE clause limiting the number of rows to be included in the merge operation. Notice that the WHERE clause can only involve primary key columns. If you select complete, you can also specify that the workspace is to be deleted after the successful merge operation. In the illustration below, you see an example of a workspace merge operation:

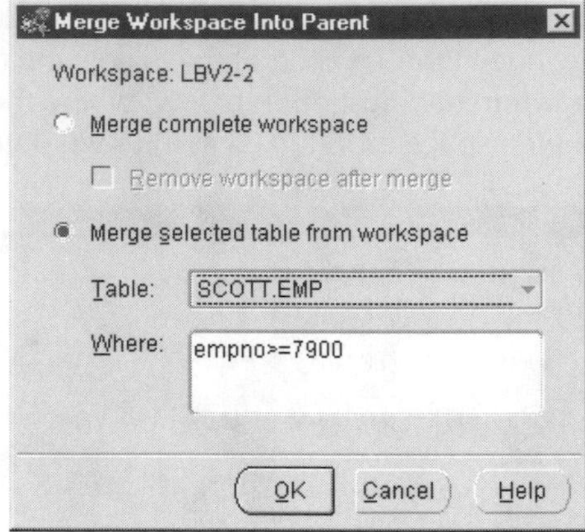

It is also possible to check for and resolve possible conflicts between a workspace and its parent workspace. Choose the Show/Resolve Conflicts in the Object or pop-up menu for the workspace you want to check. After a while (depending of the size of the workspaces), a dialog will appear informing you about any conflicts or tell you that no conflicts were identified.

Summary

In this chapter, you have been presented with the eight database administration tools available in the EM Navigator. These are used for instance, schema, security, storage, and workspace management as well as managing the Replication, OLAP, and JVM database options. In the next chapter, we will discuss the wizards and other database management applications available with EM.

CHAPTER 15

Database Applications and Wizards

any of the tools for database administration are available as wizards. The wizards available with Oracle9i and EM9i have never been better; they do their job for you in a quick and easy way. In Chapter 14, we covered the database administration tools available in the EM Navigator when connected to a database. In this chapter, we will take a look at all the wizards and other tools available for database administration. The tools and wizards covered are those in the Tools menu or from the Database Wizards and Database Applications icons in the left toolbar in the EM Console. All tools from the optional Diagnostic, Tuning, and Change Management Packs are excluded.

NOTE

Although they appear in the Tools menu and the left toolbar, you cannot run all of the wizards from the standalone console. Only the Analyze and Summary Advisor Wizards will launch in standalone mode. In addition, Data Guard Manager and LogMiner Viewer are not available in the Database Applications menu in standalone mode.

Data Guard Manager

Oracle Data Guard works with an Oracle standby database, which is used to maintain a consistent copy of another Oracle database (called the primary database). In case of a failure on the primary database, the standby database can be used instead. The standby database can also be used as a query and reporting database (read only), while modifications take place on the primary one. The state of the standby database is maintained by copying the archived redo log files from the primary database and applying these to the standby database. The Oracle9i Data Guard assists the DBA in copying and applying the archived redo logs from the primary database to the standby database. The Data Guard Manager helps you complete the tasks involved in configuring and managing your standby database environment, which includes defining archive completion requirements and archive destinations, I/O failure handling, and automated transmission restart capability. You launch the Data Guard Manager by choosing Tools | Database Applications | Data Guard Manager. Data Guard Manager will open in a new window, and existing configurations are listed in the Data Guard Configurations Navigator tree when you expand it.

Creating a New Data Guard Configuration

To use the wizard to create a new Data Guard configuration, follow these steps:

1. Either click the Create Configuration Wizard icon (the green cube) in the left tool bar or select Object | Create Configuration Wizard. You can also right-click the Data Guard Configurations tree entry and choose Create Configuration Wizard from the pop-up menu. The Create Configuration Wizard launches, and you are placed on the Welcome screen. Here you can examine information about important prerequisites for configuring the Data Guard standby database by clicking the Details button. Click Next to continue.
2. Enter a name for your standby configuration in the Configuration Name field. This must be a valid Oracle identifier, a maximum of 30 characters long, containing alphanumeric characters and the characters _, $, or #. Click Next.
3. A list of available (discovered) database targets appears. Choose the one you want to use as *primary* site and enter a name in the Primary Site Name field. Some of the prerequisites for a primary site are
   - The database must be at least Oracle9i Enterprise Edition database, pre-9i versions are not supported by Data Guard.
   - The database instance must be a primary database, meaning the value of the CONTROLFILE_TYPE column in V$DATABASE is CURRENT.
   - The database must be running in ARCHIVELOG mode.
   - Oracle Net must be configured and TNS listener must be running and listening on a TCP/IP port.
   - The initialization parameter SHARED_POOL_SIZE should be at least 160 megabytes.

   Click Next to continue.

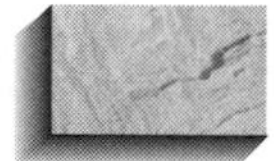

NOTE
If you have not set the preferred credentials for the database chosen as primary site, you will be prompted for login credentials as SYSDBA.

4. Now you have two options:

- Create a *new* standby site from within the wizard.
- Choose a standby site you already have prepared. Note that this site must have been prepared according to the *Oracle9i Data Guard Concepts and Administration*, and the Oracle MetaLink Note 154489.1.

The following two sections explain how to continue the setup with each of these two options.

Create a New Standby Database

Choose Create a new standby database and click Next. When you create a new database, you are presented with a list of Oracle Homes on discovered nodes, 9i and pre-9i installations. Choose an Oracle Home on the node where you want the Data Guard wizard to create the standby database, and then click Next. Now you must choose how to copy the database files from the primary site to the standby site. Two options are available:

- Use Oracle Recovery Manager (RMAN); this is the default method and is available on all supported Oracle platforms.
- Use operating system copy (not available on all Oracle platforms, in which case it will be grayed out).

Choose the method you want to use and click Next. If you are using the RMAN copy method, you must specify a network drive directory on the primary host that corresponds to the destination directory on the standby host. This is specified as an NFS (Network File System) mount point on Unix, or a UNC (Universal Naming Convention) pathname for a network share on Windows, such as \\chbsllava\db05data. You can also choose to map each file by choosing the "Copy files to different directories" value. If you are using OS copy, you only need to specify the destination directory. The Standby archived log file directory used for the log shipping will be set to be the same as the destination directory by default; change it if required. Click Next. Finally, you can enter a name for the standby configuration (or accept the default), and provide a new password for connecting using the SYS account as SYSDBA. You can check the "Shutdown primary database prior to datafile copy" check box to shut down the primary database (with the immediate option) and bring it into the MOUNT state before copying the datafiles. If the primary database is not currently open, this check box will be grayed out. You can examine and modify the initialization and TNS listener parameters with the View/Edit initialization file and View/Edit listener.ora buttons, respectively. Click Next to get to the Summary screen, and then click Finish to begin creation of the standby database and Data Guard configuration.

Choose an Already Existing Standby Database

Choose Add an existing standby database and click Next. You are presented with a list of discovered databases, again including pre-9i instances. Select your prepared 9i standby database and click Next.

NOTE
If you have not fulfilled the prerequisites for the primary site or standby, an error will occur. In this case, the wizard cannot continue. You should exit the wizard, resolve the problem, and then restart the Data Guard Wizard. Also, if the preferred credentials for the database chosen as standby site have not been set, you will be prompted for login credentials as SYSDBA.

If no errors are found, a summary screen will be displayed with the Data Guard configuration information. Click Finish. The Data Guard Wizard creates the Data Guard configuration for your primary and standby sites. If it is not already set, the DRS_START initialization parameter is set to TRUE to enable the Disaster Recovery Monitor (DRMON) process, also known as the Data Guard Broker. Further, the parameters FAL_CLIENT and FAL_SERVER are set to the respective TNS connection strings for primary and standby sites.

When the wizard has successfully finished the configuration, you can locate the new Data Guard configuration in the Navigation tree within the Data Guard Manager. It will be in disabled mode at first; right-click the Data Guard configuration name and choose Enable/Disable from the pop-up menu. In the dialog box that appears, click OK to enable the configuration. The detail view pane shows the status of the two participating instances in your standby configuration. Figure 15-1 shows an example of an enabled Data Guard configuration.

LogMiner Viewer

The LogMiner has been available since Oracle8i, but has been greatly simplified and improved in Oracle9i. With the LogMiner Viewer you can examine the redo log files generated by Oracle, both online and archived. You can also build a LogMiner dictionary, either in the redo logs or in an external flat file. You launch the LogMiner Viewer by selecting Tools | Database Applications | LogMiner Viewer, or from the Related Tools submenu in the pop-up menu for a particular database. You can also launch it from the Database Applications icon group in the left toolbar. The LogMiner Viewer launches in new window. If no existing queries have been found for the chosen database, a dialog box appears informing you of this. Click OK.

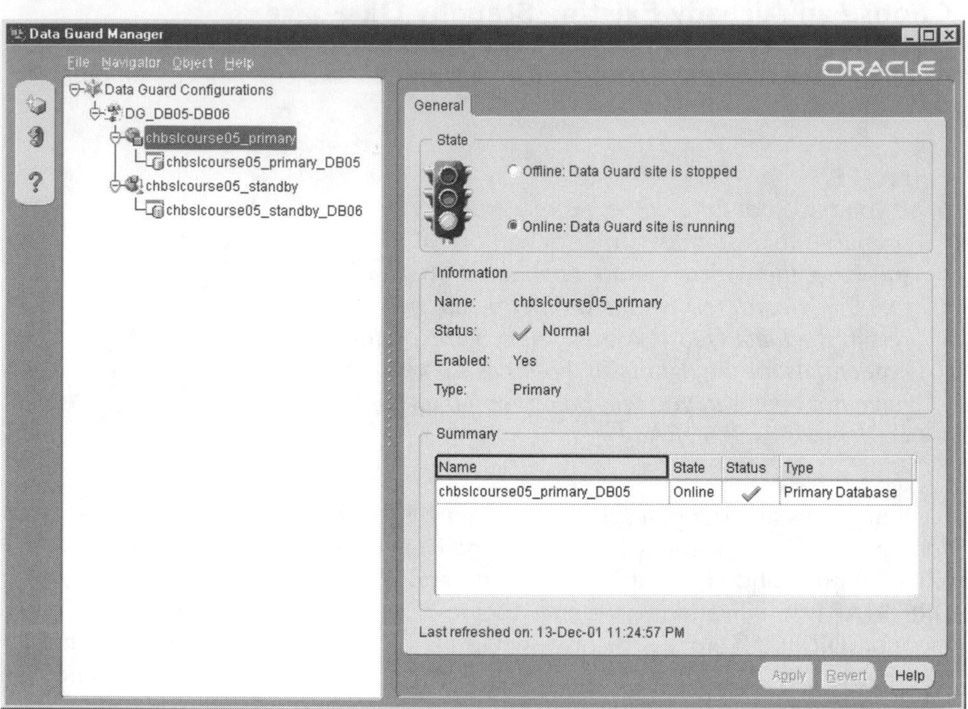

FIGURE 15-1. *A completed Data Guard configuration*

Creating Queries and Examining Redo Log Files

Using LogMiner Viewer to examine the redo log files is called *creating a query*. When you create a query, you define search criteria, either by entering the WHERE clause as text or through a graphical query-builder. To create a query for a particular database, which you can analyze through the LogMiner Viewer, follow these steps:

1. Select the database in the LogMiner Viewer Navigator tree, and either click the Create Query icon (the green cube) in the left toolbar or select Create Query from either the Object menu or the pop-up menu. If there are existing LogMiner queries for the database, you can also use the Create Like feature.

NOTE
You cannot use the Create Like feature to create a similar query for a database other than the one it is created for. For example, if a query exists for database DB05.WORLD, you cannot use it to create a similar query for database DB06.WORLD.

2. The Create Query dialog appears. You must enter the criteria for your query defining what information you are searching in the logs. You can choose between entering the query text manually as a WHERE clause, or through a graphical query-builder. When you have entered your query, click Find Now to start the search. Figure 15-2 shows an example of a search for all statements affecting segments owned by SCOTT. By checking the check box "Show committed transactions only," you can exclude all *uncommitted* transactions from the query.

   You can choose to save your query in the repository for later use by clicking Save Query and entering a name in the Save Query dialog box. You can choose between saving the query only (the default), the results only, or both the query and the results. Click OK to store the query, which now will appear in the Navigator under the database for which it was created.

Including Other Redo Log Files in the Query

When you define a new LogMiner query, only the online redo log files are inspected, by default. You can include other log files that fulfill the following conditions:

- The file must be from an Oracle database, release 8.0 or later.
- The file can be either from the analyzed database or from another database instance. All included log files must be from the same database and from the same database version. If the log files are from a database other than the one you are analyzing, the same hardware platform and the same database character set must be used.
- If the redo log files are from a database on another node, you must copy them to the same node as the analyzed database.

To change the log files being included in the query, click the Redo Log Files tab. You will see a list of redo log files that are included in your query. Click the Change Redo Log Files button. The Change Redo Log Files dialog box appears, as shown in Figure 15-3.

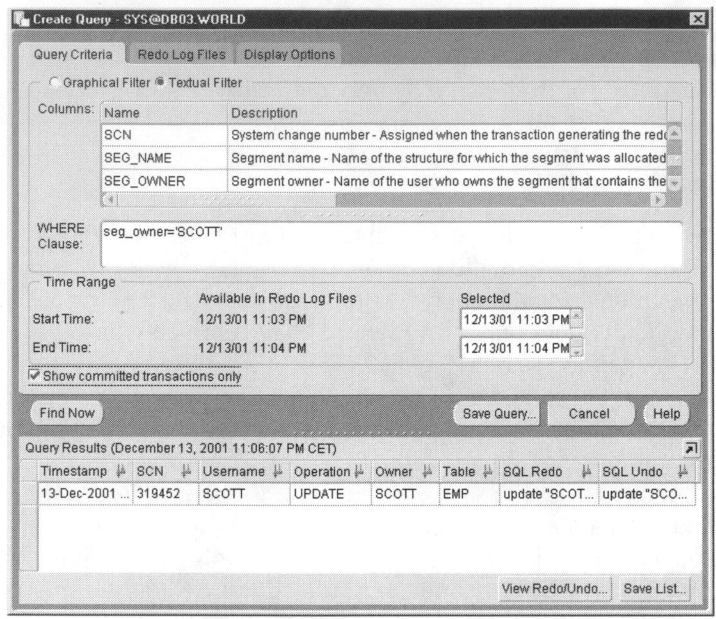

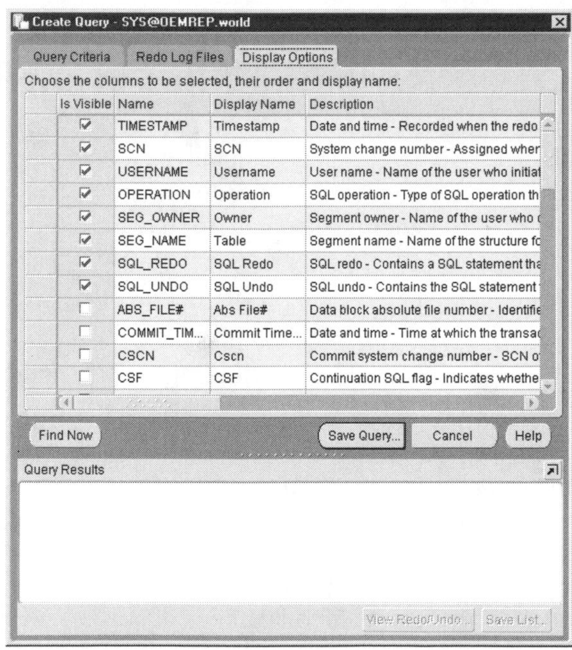

FIGURE 15-2. *Searching for all statements that affect segments owned by SCOTT*

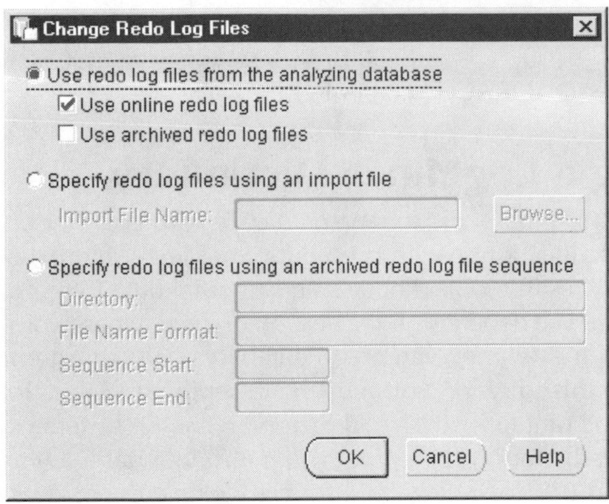

FIGURE 15-3. *Changing the redo log files*

In this dialog, only the "Use online redo log files" box is checked by default, indicating that only online redo log files are to be included. Choose one of the following three options and click OK:

- **Use archived redo log files** If you want to include the archived redo log files from their archive destination, check this check box.
- **Specify redo log files using an import file** If you check this box you can enter a name of a text file containing the redo log files to be included in the query. You can also browse to this file. Notice that the browse location is on your client machine where the EM Console is running. The file specification in the file must conform to the platform being used by the analyzed database, such as D:\BACKUP\ARCHIVE\DB05\ LOG001_00123.ARC.
- **Specify redo log files using an archived redo log file sequence** This option uses archived redo log files within a certain directory, matching a certain file pattern, and within a specified sequence range. In the Directory field, you specify the directory where the archived redo log files are stored. In the File Name Format, you specify a format string for the file name, for example LOG001_%S.ARC. Be aware that LogMiner Viewer does not support specifying the thread number using the %T parameter, so you must specify the thread number explicitly (001 in the example). In the Sequence Start and Sequence End fields, you specify the start and end sequences (the %S

parameter) to be included in the query. Figure 15-4 shows an example. The criteria provided in the figure includes the files LOG001_00005.ARC, LOG001_00006.ARC, LOG001_00007.ARC, and LOG001_00008.ARC from the folder D:\ORACLE\LOGMINER.

Specifying a LogMiner Dictionary

You can change the type of dictionary to analyze with LogMiner. A *dictionary* is a LogMiner-specific location, which is used for translating internal object identifiers (OIDs) and datatypes into object names and external data formats. The type of dictionary you can use depends on the version of the database you want to analyze with LogMiner. For example, with pre-9i databases only an external dictionary is available. For this to work, you must have set the initialization parameter UTL_FILE_DIR to point to a physical directory in the file system on the database server. Without a dictionary, LogMiner will return internal OIDs and present the data in hex format. The following list describes the different options available when choosing a dictionary. Click the Set Dictionary button to open the Set Dictionary dialog box, as shown in Figure 15-5.

- **Use the dictionary that is contained in the redo log files** This option uses a LogMiner dictionary contained in the online redo log files, and is only

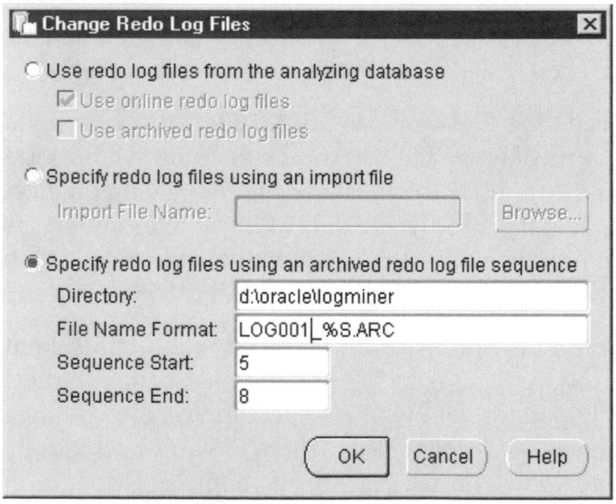

FIGURE 15-4. *Specifying the redo log files*

available for Oracle9i databases. When you use this option, LogMiner automatically stays synchronized with DDL changes in the database. Extracting the dictionary to the redo log files is faster than extracting it to a flat file, but it does consume database resources.

- **Use an existing dictionary file** This option is valid only if the redo log files are from a version 8.0 or later Oracle database. You must enter a fully qualified name for an existing dictionary file in the File Name field. The directory specified must be on the database server that you are currently analyzing. When the dictionary is in a database external flat file, fewer database resources are required than when it is contained in the redo log files. The tradeoff is that it will take longer to extract the dictionary to a flat file than to the redo log files.

NOTE
To build the dictionary to an external text file, you must have set the initialization parameter UTL_FILE_DIR to a directory on the database server where the file is to be generated, such as D:\ORACLE\LOGMINER. Remember that UTL_FILE_DIR is a static parameter, so you must restart the database instance before the new value is activated.

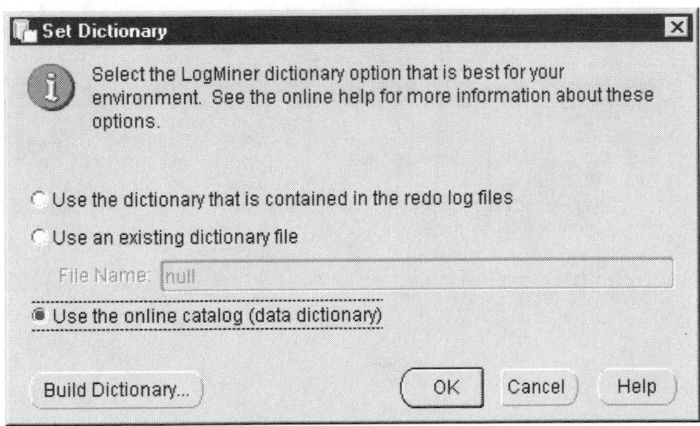

FIGURE 15-5. *Setting the dictionary*

- **Use the online catalog (data dictionary)** This option uses the database data dictionary, is only available for Oracle9i log files, and is chosen by default for 9i instances. This option is faster than the other options, because the data already resides in the dictionary.

NOTE
The database must be mounted and open to use the online catalog option.

You can build a LogMiner dictionary from within the Set Directory dialog box, which we describe in the following section.

If you click the Build Dictionary button in the Set Dictionary screen (see Figure 15-5), the Build Dictionary dialog box appears. The dialog box looks different depending on your database version. Figure 15-6 shows an example from an Oracle9i database.

For an Oracle9i instance, you can choose between building the dictionary in the online redo log files (which is checked by default) or to an external text file. To build the external dictionary file, check the "Create a separate dictionary file" check box and enter the full file specification, such as d:\oracle\logminer\LogMinerDictionary.ora in the File Name field. Click OK.

Figure 15-7 shows an example from a pre-9i instance. For pre-9i instances, you can only choose to build an external flat file. To build the external dictionary file, enter a fully qualified file name, such as d:\oracle\logminer\ LogMinerDictionary.ora and click OK. A confirmation dialog box appears

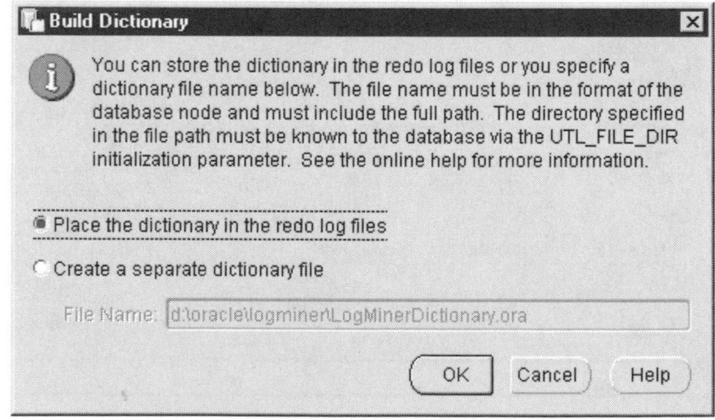

FIGURE 15-6. *Building a dictionary in a 9i database*

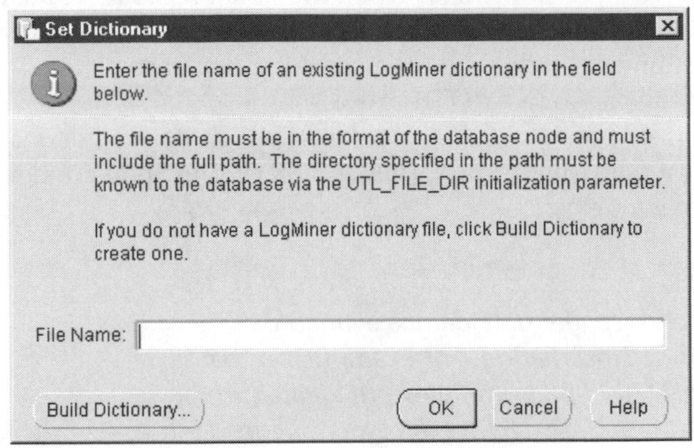

FIGURE 15-7. *Building a dictionary in a pre-9i database*

informing you that the dictionary generation can take a while; click Yes to begin the dictionary generation or click No to cancel.

Display Options

You can choose which columns are shown in the result set of the LogMiner query. Click the Display Options tab on the Create Query page shown in Figure 15-2 and check or uncheck the check box in the Is Visible column corresponding to the columns you want to include or exclude, respectively.

Spatial Index Advisor

The Spatial Index Advisor is an aid that helps DBAs to analyze and optimize Oracle spatial indexes in order to improve query response time for spatial queries. You can analyze layers of spatial data, which is of the type SDO_GEOMETRY (owned by the MDSYS schema). You can associate a spatial index with the spatial data, which contains a set of *tiles*. The DBA controls the size and number of these tiles. You must be familiar with spatial data within the Oracle RDBMS to use the Spatial Index Advisor. For more information about spatial data in Oracle, refer to the online help in EM and the *Oracle Spatial User's Guide and Reference*.

Launching the Spatial Index Advisor

You can launch the Spatial Index Advisor from the EM Console either when connected to an OMS or in standalone mode. Choose Tools | Database Applications |

Spatial Index Advisor, or in the icon group in the left toolbar. You cannot launch it for a particular database, but you can launch the Spatial Index Advisor from the Related Tools submenu in the pop-up menu for a database target. The Add Layer dialog box appears, as shown in Figure 15-8.

Now you must choose a spatial data layer, which basically consists of a table and a column (of type MDSYS.SDO_GEOMETRY). The Spatial Index Advisor checks to see if such objects exist.

NOTE
There are some spatial data demos available with the Oracle installation. For example, on the Windows NT/2000 platform, they are located in the ORACLE_HOME\MD\DEMO directory. Figure 15-8 shows the NH_COMPUTER_STORES object, which has been created in the SCOTT schema through the four SQL scripts in the geocoder subdirectory.

You can choose the spatial object by expanding the database tree entry and then the schema containing spatial objects, by clicking on the plus sign. Optionally, you can enter an alias for the selected layer, which you can use later to reference the

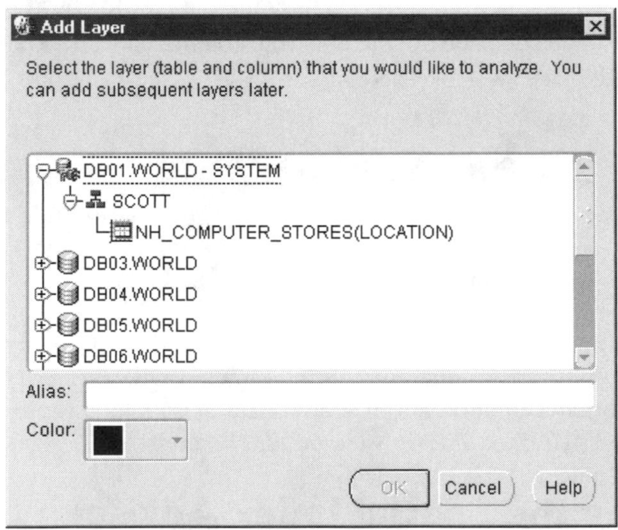

FIGURE 15-8. *Adding a layer*

layer. This alias is shown at the bottom of the Spatial Index Advisor screen. If you enter an alias that is already in use, a number is added to the string. Also, you can choose a color for the layer from the Color drop-down list box, which is used in the drawing area. Click OK in the Add Layer dialog to continue. The Spatial Index Advisor screen appears with the chosen layer as the active layer, as shown in Figure 15-9.

You can add other layers by selecting Layer | Add Layer, or by clicking the Add Layer icon in the left toolbar. You can switch between layers through the Current

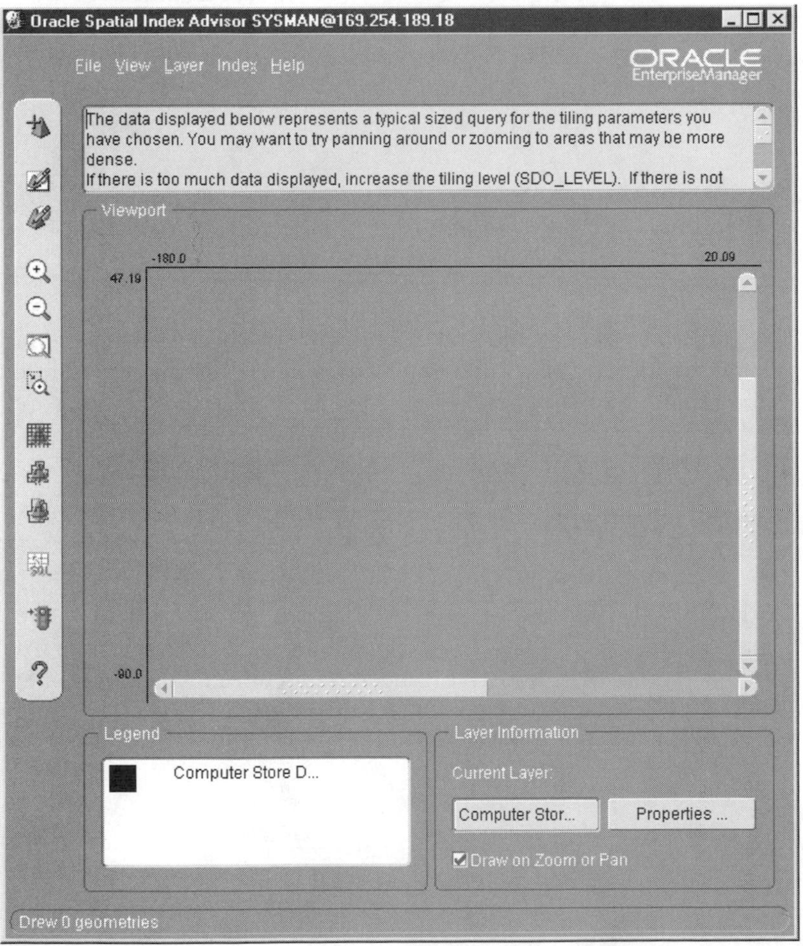

FIGURE 15-9. *The Spatial Index Advisor screen*

Layer drop-down list box at the bottom of the screen. You can remove a single layer with Layer | Remove Layer, or remove all layers with Layer | Remove All Layers. In the upper part of the screen, you will be presented with informative text and tips along the way.

Modifying Spatial Indexes

The main purpose of the Spatial Index Advisor is to modify, and if necessary, rebuild the spatial indexes found in your application. Select Index | Modify Index to open the Edit Index dialog box, where you can modify the storage parameters for the spatial index. You can also view the current computed statistics (on the Statistics page), as well as define the type of index (R-Tree or Quad-Tree) and rebuild it (on the Spatial page) by clicking the Submit Job button.

NOTE
To rebuild the index, you must be connected to an OMS, because the EM job system is used to schedule the index rebuild (immediately or at a specified time).

The R-Tree index type is simpler to create and administer than the Quad-Tree index, which provides means for the more experienced spatial data administrator to perform fine-tuning. Click OK to save your changes to the spatial index and to close the Edit Index dialog.

SQL*Plus Worksheet

The SQL*Plus Worksheet is basically a GUI version of the SQL*Plus executable (ORACLE_HOME\bin\sqlplus.exe) with some improved and added features such as statement history. This implies that the SQL*Plus executable must be installed on your client machine for SQL*Plus Worksheet to function. If you can start SQL*Plus from outside EM Console, the executable has been installed correctly, and you will be able to launch it via SQL*Plus Worksheet.

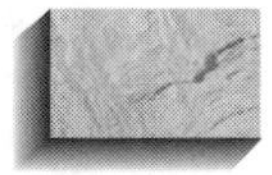

NOTE
On UNIX and Linux clients, you must have set the environment variable SQLPLUS_LD_LIBRARY_PATH to point to the shared library folder in your ORACLE_HOME, for example /oracle/admin/product/9.0.1/lib.

Launching the SQL*Plus Worksheet

You can use the SQL*Plus Worksheet from the EM Console either when connected to an OMS or in standalone mode. You can launch SQL*Plus Worksheet for a particular database, which you select in the EM Navigator prior to launching, or without any database selected (NOLOG mode). The preferred credentials are used for the database connection. You can launch SQL*Plus Worksheet in the following ways:

- Select Tools | Database Applications SQL*Plus Worksheet.
- Select Related Tools | SQL*Plus Worksheet in either the pop-up or Object menus when you have selected a database in the EM Navigator tree.
- Expand the Database Applications icon group in the left toolbar, and click the SQL*Plus Worksheet icon.

The SQL*Plus Worksheet launches in new window, as shown in Figure 15-10. In order to change the language in the SQL*Plus Worksheet, you can specify the SQLPLUS_NLS_LANG parameter in the SQL*Plus Worksheet configuration file.

NOTE
*When connecting to a database in SQL*Plus Worksheet through the OMS, note that the SQL*Plus executable as well as the Net configuration files on the Management Server are used.*

Working With the SQL*Plus Worksheet

The SQL*Plus Worksheet screen is divided into two parts; an input part (the upper half) and an output part (the lower half). You enter SQL and PL/SQL statements or load scripts into the input field and execute them. The result of your statement is displayed in the output part of the screen.

Entering and Executing SQL and PL/SQL Statements

You can enter SQL and PL/SQL commands directly into the input field or read statements from a script stored in a text file. You can edit the text in the input pane using the mouse, keyboard functions, and the Edit menu. You can also copy text from the output pane and paste it into the input pane.

To execute the command you have entered in the input field, you can click the Execute icon (the yellow lightning bold) in the left toolbar, select Worksheet | Execute, or press F5.

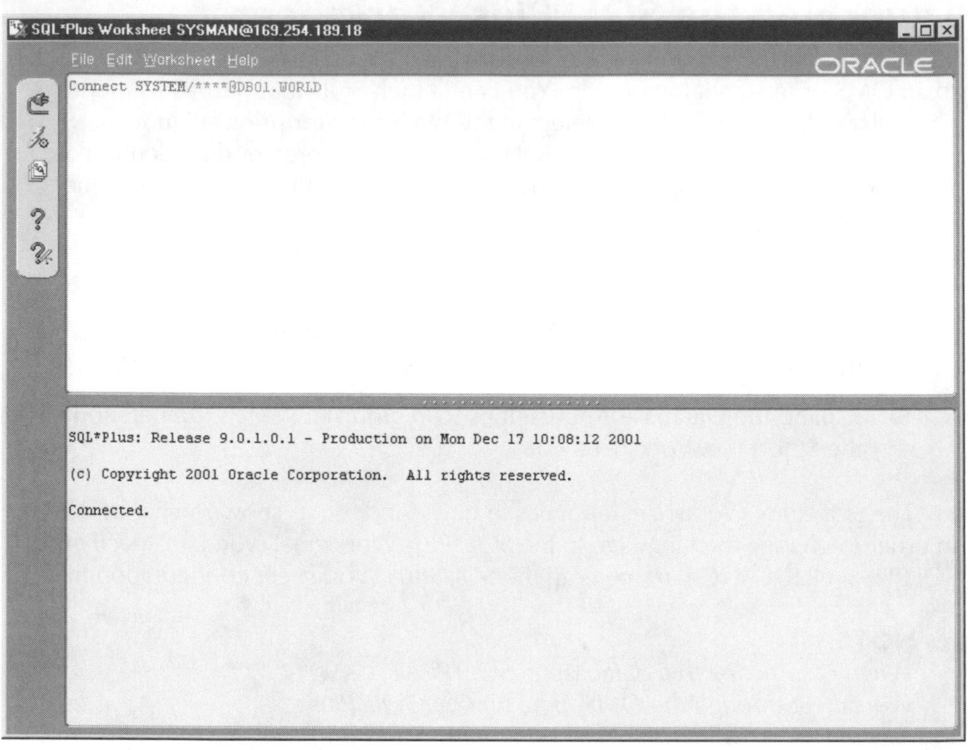

FIGURE 15-10. *The SQL*Plus Worksheet connected to the DB01.WORLD database*

After you execute a command, it remains in the input field and is added to the command history.

NOTE

*Because of limitations on the middle-tier component, not all SQL*Plus commands are supported, and will return the SP2-0738 Restricted command error message. Examples of unsupported commands are @, @@, and START, as well as HOST, EXIT, and WHENEVER OSERROR/SQLERROR. These restrictions especially apply when working with your own scripts. For more details, see the online help in SQL*Plus Worksheet.*

Storing Your Statements in Scripts You can store your command(s) in the input pane in SQL*Plus Worksheet by selecting File | Save Input As.

Loading and Executing Scripts You can load and execute scripts containing SQL and PL/SQL statements in SQL*Plus Worksheet. Choose File | Open, and enter the filename for your stored script or browse to it. This loads the content of the script into the input field where you can continue editing it or execute it right away.

You can also load and execute a stored script in one operation by choosing Worksheet | Run Local Script. You can enter or browse to a filename, which will be executed immediately.

Command History The command history is maintained automatically and stores the last 50 commands you have executed. You can access the history by selecting Worksheet | Command History, by clicking the Command History icon in the left toolbar, or by pressing CTRL-H. The Command History dialog box appears, as shown in Figure 15-11.

Highlight the statement you want to retrieve and click the Get button. The statement is copied to the input field for further modification or execution. You can also retrieve a statement by pressing CTRL-P or by choosing Worksheet |

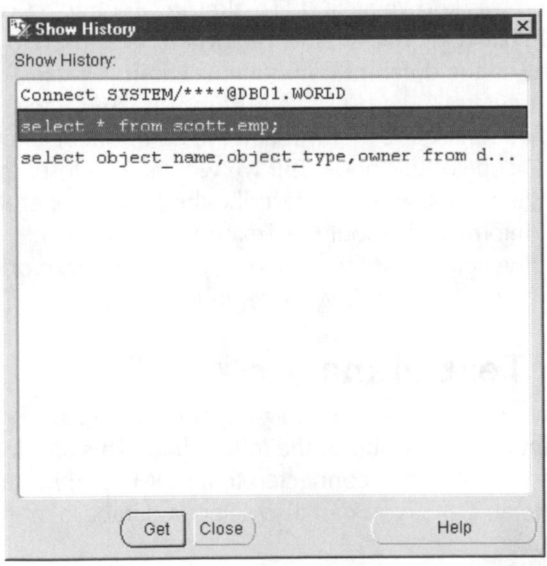

FIGURE 15-11. *Viewing the command history*

Previous Command from the Worksheet menu. In the same way, you can choose the next statement in the history (if any) by pressing CTRL-N or choosing Worksheet | Next Command.

Changing the Database Connection

You can change your database connection in different ways:

- Click the connection icon (the power plug) in the left toolbar or choose File | Change Database Connection. A database login dialog box appears, where you can enter username and password as well as database name. Then click OK to perform the connect.
- Enter the CONNECT (or CONN) statement in the input field and execute it.

Text Manager

The Oracle9i database server includes the Oracle Text component, which is a text management system including content-management and text-search capabilities. It enables you to search and manage text just as you would any data, such as scalar data types. Through the document routing and filtering features you can set up rules for classifying an incoming stream of documents based on their content. In pre-9i releases, this option was known as SQL*TextRetrieval, Oracle ConText Cartridge, and Oracle interMedia Text. The Oracle Text Manager is used to manage (create, modify, and delete) all the different components within Oracle Text, such as text indexes, libraries, operators, word-lists, and stop-lists. All Oracle Text objects are stored in the CTXSYS schema. Describing all the components included with Oracle Text is beyond the scope of this book, but we will take a closer look at how the Oracle Text Manager works, and also describe the process of creating new text indexes. For more information about the Text option and Oracle Text Manager, refer to the EM online help, the *Oracle Text Application Developer's Guide, Release 9.0.1*, or the *Oracle Text Reference, Release 9.0.1*.

Launching Text Manager

You launch Oracle Text Manager by choosing Tools | Database Applications | Text Manager, or in the icon group in the left toolbar. This application is available from the EM Console both when connected to an OMS and in standalone mode. When connected to an OMS, you can also select a database in the EM Navigator tree before starting Text Manager. In this case, you can also choose Related Tools | Text Manager in the pop-up menu. You will be connected to this particular instance in Text Manager, as shown in Figure 15-12.

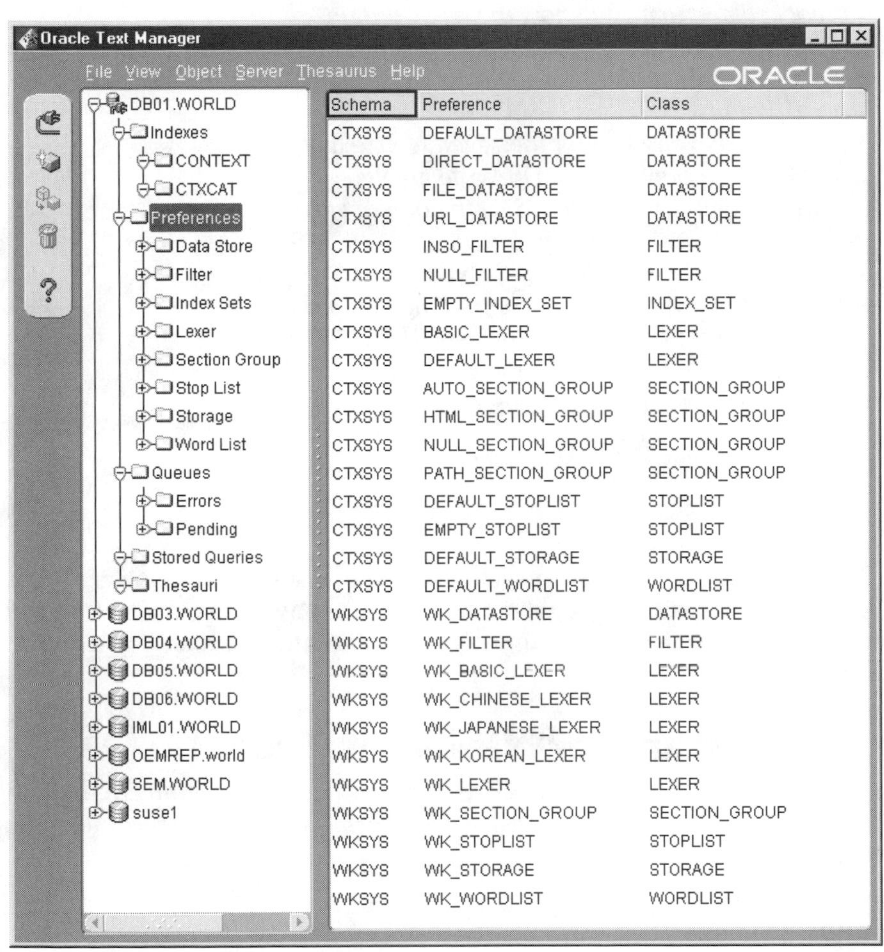

FIGURE 15-12. *The Oracle Text Manager Navigator tree*

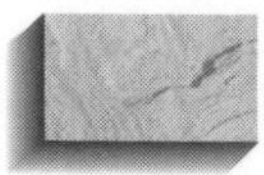

NOTE
Because all Oracle Text objects are stored in the CTXSYS schema, you should log in using the CTXSYS account when using Text Manager. Generally, this account is installed with an Oracle9i instance, but it is locked. Be sure that the CTXSYS account is unlocked and that you know the password. In Oracle9i, after unlocking the account, you will have to set a new password, because the password has been expired (you will get the "ORA-28001: the password has expired" error message). Notice that the CTXSYS account has the DBA role granted. If you are going to use the Ultra Search component of Oracle Text, you should be sure that the WKSYS user exists and the account is unlocked, too. Ultra Search is used for indexing and searching Websites, database tables, files, and mailing lists. The WKSYS user holds all the Ultra Search dictionaries and PL/SQL packages. The WKSYS user has also been granted the DBA role besides the roles CONNECT, CTXAPP, JAVASYSPRIV, JAVAUSERPRIV, and RESOURCE.

In the standalone mode, a connection dialog box appears for the first database in the Navigator tree, which might not be the one you want to connect to. Click Cancel and choose the database you want to connect to by expanding it in the Text Manager Navigator tree.

The Text Manager Navigator Tree

The Navigator tree contains all database instances registered within EM, both those automatically discovered and manually added ones. Figure 15-12 shows an example of the Text Manager Navigator tree.

Indexes

The Indexes item is used for maintaining the Oracle Text indexes, whose main purpose is to speed up text searches. There are three types of text indexes:

- **CONTEXT** The "normal" type of Oracle Text indexes are used for indexing text columns of type CHAR, CLOB, BLOB, BFILE, VARCHAR2, or XMLType, containing, for example, plain text or text formatted in Microsoft Word, Microsoft Excel, HTML, or XML.

- **CTXCAT** A catalog index type introduced with Oracle8i Release 3 (8.1.7), which improves mixed query performance, particularly when querying smaller text fragments together with other columns.
- **CTXRULE** This index type is used for building document classification applications.

NOTE
The CTXRULE index type is not supported by EM9i, and therefore does not appear in the Indexes entry. Use the CREATE INDEX statement with the INDEXTYPE IS CTXRULE option to create a text index on a VARCHAR2 or CLOB table column. Only these two data types are supported for CTXRULE indexes. For more details, see the Oracle Text Reference, Release 9.0.1.

Because documents can be stored in many different schemes, formats, and languages, each Oracle Text index has many options that need to be set to configure it for a particular situation. We will take a more detailed look at some of these in the section "Creating Oracle Text Indexes" later in this chapter.

Preferences

In the Preferences item, you will find the following Oracle Text preference sets:

- **Data Store** The storage definition for the text data, for example, in one or more columns, external file (FILE_DATASTORE), or URL (URL_DATASTORE).
- **Filter** The definition of how the documents can be converted to plain text. Documents are stored in their proprietary format, but converted to plain text using a filter definition. The plain (ASCII) text filter is used by default.
- **Index Sets** An Index Set is a collection of one or more indexes (not text indexes) on nontext columns, which you also include in your queries. Index sets are used when creating text indexes of type CTXCAT to link the text index with the nontext indexes.
- **Lexer** Describes the language and its different components (tokens) that are indexed. The default lexer is for English or other Western European languages.

- **Section Group** A section group specifies a group of document sections. This is required if you want to be able to query within the sections using the WITHIN operator.
- **Stop List** Contains all words, themes, and classes that are not to be included in the text index generation, such as the words "if," "as," "but," "the," and so on.
- **Storage** Defines where the text index data is to be stored physically (tablespace and other storage parameters).
- **Word List** Defines how the "stem" and "fuzzy" queries are to be expanded. The "fuzzy" operator is used to expand a query so it includes words that are spelled similarly to those in a specified term. The "stem" ($) operator will expand a query to include all terms having the same stem or root word as the specified term. For example, specifying "$write" would expand the query to include the words "write," "writing," and "wrote."

Because of the complexity of text indexes, most situations require users to configure the indexes by specifying the exact preferences. The preference sets discussed here are used when creating text indexes, and act as default preferences. You can override these default preferences by creating your own customized ones.

Queues

The Queues item lists the DML queue and the pending requests (text index synchronization), as well as those requests where an error has occurred.

Stored Queries

Query expressions are used to create criteria for organizing and categorizing documents. Also, stored queries can be used when performing iterative queries, where an initial query is refined using one or more additional queries.

Thesauri

The Thesauri item contains terms and information about relationships (such as synonyms and related terms) for each term and based on the ISO-2788 and ANSI Z39.19 standards. Two functions are available in the Thesaurus menu:

- **Extend/Revert Knowledge Base** This function lets you add phrases to the Oracle Text knowledge base, or revert to the default installation state.
- **Import/Export Thesaurus** This function lets you export a thesaurus to a file, or import one from a file.

NOTE
These functions are only available when the EM Console is connected to a Management Server, not in standalone mode. This is because you reference a certain database instance on a certain node, and this information is taken from the EM repository.

Creating Oracle Text Indexes

You can create text indexes of type CONTEXT and CTXCAT from the Create Index dialog. If you are creating an index of type CTXCAT, you should define an index set first; see the discussion of Index Set in the "Preferences" section earlier. You can launch the Create Index dialog from Text Manager by clicking the Create icon in the left toolbar, choosing Object | Create, or pressing CTRL-N. The Create Text Object dialog box appears, as shown in Figure 15-13.

Choose either CONTEXT or CTXCAT, depending on which index type you want to create, and click Create.

You can also right-click the Indexes tree entry and choose either Create CONTEXT Index or Create CTXCAT Index from the pop-up menu. Or, right-click either the CONTEXT or CTXCAT entry under Indexes and choose Create from the pop-up menu. You cannot use the Create Like feature, but you can also right-click on an existing index and select Create CONTEXT Index or Create CTXCAT Index from the pop-up menu. In all cases, the Create Index dialog box appears, where you enter the index properties.

- Enter a name for the index, and choose the schema to be owner of the index.
- Choose the table column you want to create an index on by selecting the owner, table name, and column from the drop-down list boxes.

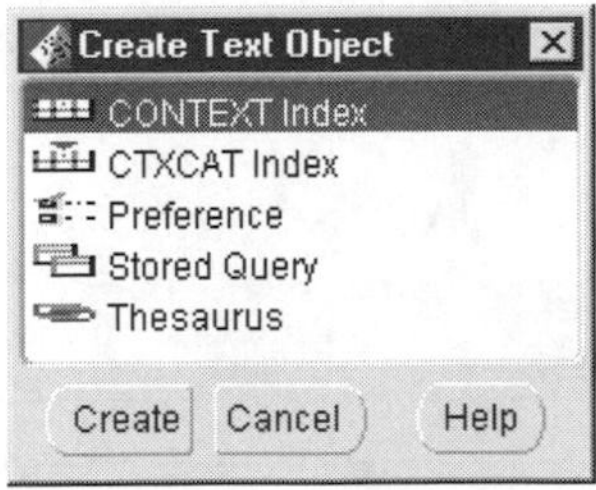

FIGURE 15-13. *Selecting the type for a new text index*

- You can change the memory allocation for index creation and synchronization from the default (12MB) by selecting the Set Memory Use value and enter a number. The value can be in either MB or GB, which you choose from the drop-down list box.
- The Populate check box indicates whether the index should be populated with table data. If you do not check the Populate check box, the index is created empty.
- Click the Create button to create the text index, using the default preferences. If you want to specify you own preferences for the index, skip to the Preferences and Preference Columns pages before clicking Create.

Figure 15-14 shows an example of a text index of type CONTEXT created on the column TTEXT in the table SCOTT.LBV_TEXT.

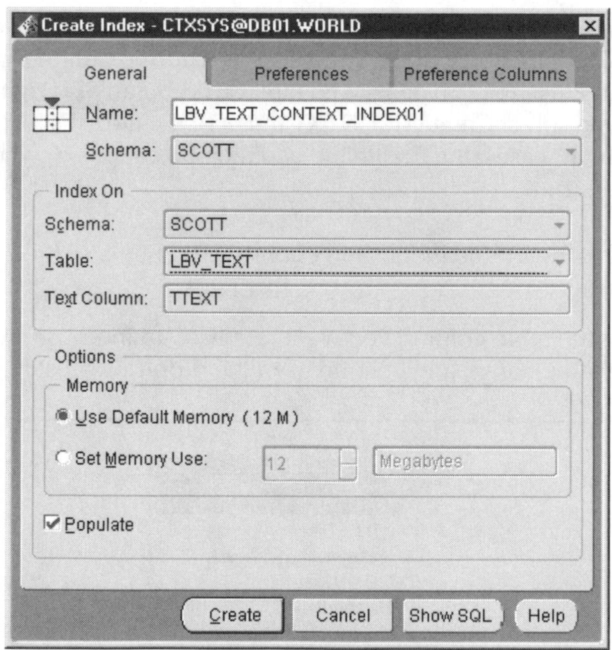

FIGURE 15-14. *Creating a new text index*

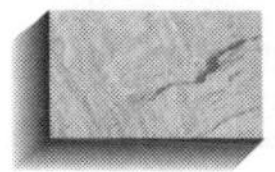

NOTE
You can view errors that occurred during the index creation or synchronizing process by querying the DR$INDEX_ERROR table owned by CTXSYS.

Synchronizing Text Indexes

The process of keeping a text index up to date with the content of its base table is known as *synchronizing* the index. You can do this either manually or automatically through the CTXSRV process. From within Text Manager, you can initiate an index synchronization for text indexes of type CONTEXT. Select the index (of type CONTEXT) to be synchronized in the Indexes entry in the Navigator tree and select Synchronize from the Object menu or the pop-up menu. The Edit Synchronize Operation dialog appears. You can change the memory allocation for the synchronization process, if required, through the Set Memory Use field. Click OK to start the synchronization.

NOTE
The process of synchronizing a text index can place a heavy load on the database. You might want to use the EM job system to schedule this operation for a specific time, such as overnight, using the PL/SQL built-in CTX_DDL.SYNC_INDEX. Refer o the Oracle Text Reference for more details.

Backup Management

The Backup Management wizards are based on the Recovery Manager (RMAN) backup system provided by Oracle. Using RMAN, you can back up your databases, either through cold (offline) or hot (online) backups. To perform a hot backup, the database must be running in ARCHIVELOG mode. You can choose to use RMAN together with a special RMAN catalog, which is a repository that keeps track of all your databases and their backup status. You can also run RMAN without this catalog and instead use the information stored in the control file of the databases to back up. Note that if you run without a catalog, the available backup features are limited. To write the backup to a physical media other than disk, such as a tape station, RMAN uses *channels* as an interface against different vendors' backup solutions and storage systems. The first thing to do when you use RMAN is to create a Backup Configuration defining the defaults for your RMAN backups, including specifying such a channel. We will describe this in the following sections. Note that none of the Backup Management features are available when running the EM Console in standalone mode.

Managing Backup Configurations

If you try to launch Catalog Maintenance without first defining at least one backup configuration, you will receive an error message stating that you must first create a backup configuration. A default configuration is available (named "DefaultConfiguration") using a channel for backing up to disk. It uses the same directory for the backup files as where the first datafile (typically for the SYSTEM tablespace) is stored.

Creating a Backup Configuration

To create a backup configuration, follow these steps:

1. Choose a database in the EM Navigator. If you are creating a specific configuration for a certain database, select this particular database, otherwise, choose any database.
2. Select Tools | Backup Management | Create Backup Configuration or select Database Wizards | Create Backup Configuration in the pop-up menu.
3. Enter a name and a description for the backup configuration and click the Channels tab.
4. On the Channels page, you must choose between two options:
   - **Backup Set** This option creates RMAN-specific files for the backup (the default option). Specify whether the channel is of type disk or tape, and enter a name for the channel. Then, enter the directory name and the format for the backup set, such as b_%u_%s_%p, which is the default format (*b* is the prefix for backup, *u* is the unique name, *s* is the backup set number, and *p* is the backup piece). The t parameter can be used to specify a timestamp. If the channel is of type Tape, you can also enter device-specific parameters in the Parameters field. If you click the Channel limits button, you can modify the Maximum Capacity, Maximum Read Rate, and Maximum Open Files channel parameters. You can create several channels per configuration. Click the Insert button to enter a new channel and the Remove button to delete a channel in the Channels defined list.
   - **Image Copy** This option works only on disk, and works like an OS copy. Choose the number of channels used by the copy and enter a directory name in Base Location. The value entered in Base Location must end with the appropriate directory separator; for example, on Windows, it must be a backslash (\). The Channel limits button is not relevant for backups using Image Copy.

The screen looks different depending on which option you choose. Figure 15-15 shows an example of a definition of a backup set. When you have entered the information, click the Recovery Catalog tab to continue.

5. On the Recovery Catalog page, you can choose between using the target database control file or an RMAN catalog. If you choose the RMAN catalog, you must provide the login credentials (Username, Password, and Service Name) for this. Then click the Backup Parameters tab.

6. The Backup parameters are used to optionally override RMAN settings for the backup set and will only be available if the Backup Set method has been chosen on the Channels page (see step 4). Check the Override Recovery Manager defaults check box to modify the parameters Maximum files at a time in a backup set, Maximum size of a backup set, and

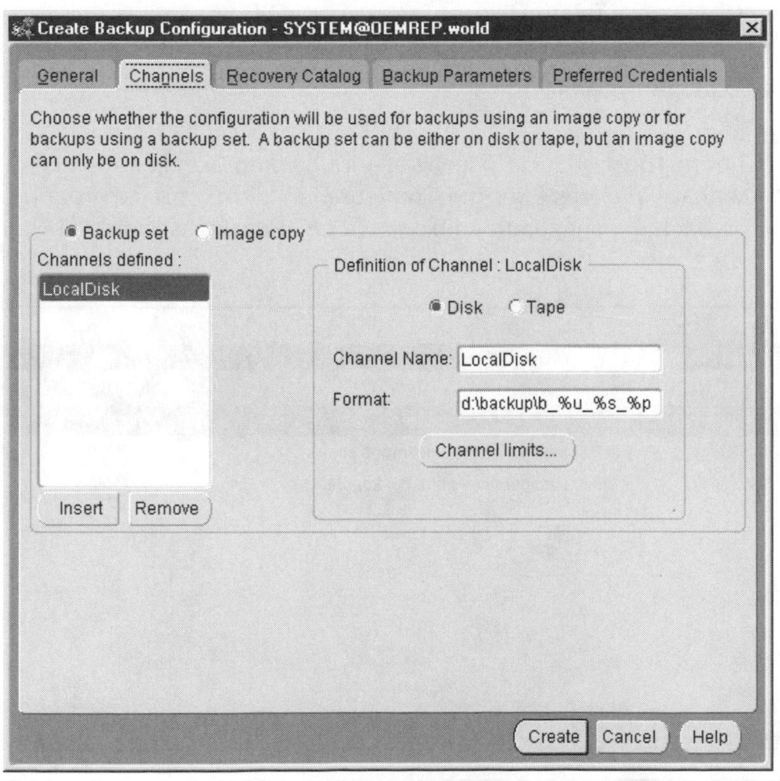

FIGURE 15-15. *Defining a backup set*

Maximum size of a backup set for archivelogs for data files and archive logs. Then click Preferred Credentials.

7. On the Preferred Credentials page, you can choose between using the preferred credentials stored within EM for the database that you want to back up, or to override the login credentials.
8. Finally, click Create to store the backup configuration in the library, where you will be able to further modify it.

You can also create a new backup configuration similar to an existing one. This is performed through the Backup Configuration Library, which is described in the next section.

The Backup Configuration Library

All defined backup configurations, including the DefaultConfiguration, are stored in the Backup Configuration Library. To access the library, follow these steps:

1. Select a database in the EM Navigator tree; for example, the one where the RMAN catalog is installed.
2. Choose Tools | Backup Management | Backup Configuration Library or Database Wizards | Backup Configuration Library from the pop-up menu. The Backup configuration library screen appears, as shown in Figure 15-16.

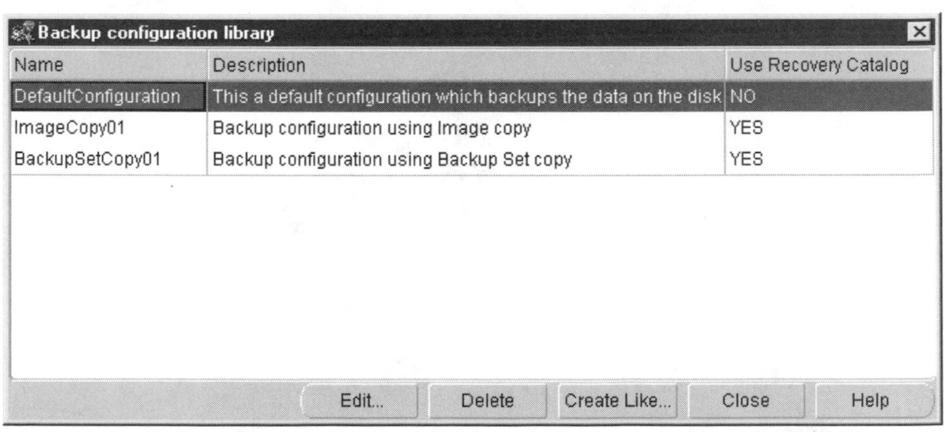

FIGURE 15-16. *The backup configuration library*

The screen shows the name and description for each backup configuration and indicates whether it uses an RMAN catalog or not in the Use Recovery Catalog column. You can sort the list by clicking the column headings once. To modify an existing backup configuration, you can click Edit, and modify all the fields except the Name.

You can also create a new backup configuration similar to an existing one. Highlight the backup configuration you want to use as the template, and click Create Like to open the Create Backup Configuration dialog. Follow the steps described in the previous section, "Creating a Backup Configuration."

Catalog Maintenance

Before you can maintain a Recovery Manager catalog, you must create one. In an Oracle9i default (that is, General Purpose) database created through the Database Configuration Assistant, you will normally already have a RMAN account in place. This account is locked by default; you must unlock the account on the database you want to use as the Recovery Manager catalog, using Security Manager for example, and change the password. If you have no RMAN account, create a new user to hold the RMAN catalog. Then create the RMAN catalog using the rman executable to create one in the OEMREP.WORLD database:

```
C:\>rman catalog rman/rman@oemrep.world
Recovery Manager: Release 9.0.1.1.1 - Production
(c) Copyright 2001 Oracle Corporation.  All rights reserved.
connected to recovery catalog database
recovery catalog is not installed
RMAN> create catalog;
recovery catalog created
RMAN>
```

For further details about RMAN, refer to the *Oracle Recovery Manager User's Guide*. You will not be able to launch Catalog Maintenance from EM before at least one backup configuration is using the RMAN catalog. When you have the RMAN catalog in place, and you have defined your backup configuration to use it, you can perform catalog maintenance operations from within EM. You launch Catalog Maintenance in the following way:

1. Select a database in the EM Navigator tree, such as the one where the RMAN catalog is installed.
2. Choose Tools | Backup Management | Catalog Maintenance, or choose Database Wizards | Catalog Maintenance from the pop-up menu.

3. Now you can choose among the following RMAN catalog operations:
   - **Register database** Register a new target database to back up using the catalog.
   - **Resynchronize catalog** Resynchronize existing catalog info with current database information.
   - **Reset database** Reset the database to a previous or new incarnation (the state in the RMAN catalog).

Registering a Database

Use the Register database feature to register databases that you want to back up using the RMAN catalog. You must do this before submitting backup jobs against the database using the RMAN catalog feature. To register a new database, follow these steps:

1. Select the database you want to register in the EM Navigator. Choose the Register database option and click Next.
2. On the next page, you can select the backup configuration containing the Recovery Manager catalog information, that is, the catalog you want to register the database with. Click Next to continue.
3. Select the database(s) to register in the Available targets list and click the add button (>). Click Finish when all targets have been selected for registration.
4. A summary screen appears. Click OK to begin target registration. An EM job is submitted with the name "RegisterCatalog<sequence number>" and immediate execution. A confirmation dialog is displayed informing you of successful submission; click OK to exit the dialog box. Check the status of this job in the EM job detail view pane.

Resynchronizing a Catalog

You use the Resynchronize catalog feature to initiate a synchronization between the information already stored in the RMAN catalog and the current status of the database. Follow these steps to resynchronize catalog information:

1. Select the catalog you want to resynchronize in the EM Navigator. Choose Resynchronize catalog and click Next.
2. On the Configuration page, you can select the backup configuration containing the Recovery Manager catalog information, that is, the catalog you want to resynchronize. Click Next to continue to the Schedule page.

3. On the schedule page, you can schedule the resynchronization job using the normal EM job scheduling options (see Chapter 11 for more details about EM jobs).

4. Click Next to select the targets for resynchronization. Click Finish when all targets have been selected. A summary is shown; click OK to submit the job. A confirmation dialog box appears informing you about the job submission of the job. Monitor the status of this job via the EM job detail view pane.

NOTE
You can also click Finish on the Configuration page to accept the default schedule (On Interval, every 1 day).

Resetting a Database

You use the Reset Database option to inform RMAN that a new incarnation of the database has been created (a database has been opened with the RESETLOGS option), or if you want to go to a previous incarnation for a point-in-time recovery operation. To reset a database, do the following:

1. Select the database you want to reset the RMAN catalog information for in the EM Navigator. Choose the Reset database option and click Next.

2. Select the backup configuration containing the Recovery Manager catalog information, that is, the catalog you want to reset the database information in. Click Finish to continue.

3. A summary screen appears; click OK to begin the reset operation. An EM job is submitted immediately with the name "ResetCatalog<sequence number>." A confirmation dialog box is displayed informing you of successful submission; click OK to exit. You can monitor the status of the reset job in the EM job detail view pane.

Backup Wizard

If you launch the Backup Wizard without first having created a new backup configuration, you will be using the Default Configuration. You launch the Backup Wizard in the following way:

1. Select the target database for the backup in the EM Navigator tree. Note that this must be an automatically discovered target database, not a manually added one.

2. Choose Tools | Backup Management | Backup, or Database Wizards | Backup from the pop-up menu. The Backup Wizard Welcome screen appears. Click Next.

3. You can choose between these two options:

   - **Predefined backup strategy** You can choose from between three different backup strategies: Full backup once a week, Full backup every day, or Full backup once a week and incremental backup every day.

   - **Customize backup strategy** You define the backup yourself, and you can choose between Full or Incremental backup. You must choose this option if you want to perform Image Copy backups.

   Choose either the predefined or customized option and click Next. The following sections explain the steps within each of these two options.

Predefined Backup Strategy

Choose from the following values in the radio button group:

1. The "My database is not frequently updated (DSS)" option performs a full backup once a week.

2. The "My database is moderately updated (OLTP) and is not very large" option performs a full backup every day.

3. The "My database is frequently updated and is large or medium" option performs a full backup once a week and an incremental backup every day.

For options 1 and 3, you can choose the weekday for the weekly backup, in a drop-down list box; the default is Sunday. Click Next.

On the Backup Time page, enter information about what time of day the backup job is to be executed. Then click Next.

On the Configuration page, you can choose the Backup Configuration to use for this backup, or create a new configuration by clicking the Launch Wizard button.

Then, click Next to choose the databases to be included in the backup; select these by highlighting the database in the Available Targets list and clicking the > button.

NOTE

Only automatically discovered target databases are selectable in the Available Targets list.

Click Finish. A confirmation dialog appears displaying information about the backup job. Click OK to submit the backup schedule or Cancel to stop. After submission, you can follow the EM job status in the Active Jobs view pane.

Customized Backup Strategy

Choose between Full or Incremental backup. For incremental backups, you can specify the level (0 to 4) and whether the backup is cumulative or not. Note that if your database is running in NOARCHIVELOG mode, you can only perform a full backup (a dialog box will appear informing you about this). Click Next.

On the Configuration page, you can choose the Backup Configuration to use for this backup, or create a new configuration by clicking the Launch Wizard button. Then click Next to enter scheduling information for the backup.

The Backup Wizard uses the EM job feature to perform the backup. On the Schedule page, you can schedule the backup job using the normal EM job scheduling options. Refer to Chapter 11 for more information about EM jobs. Click Next.

You can enter the name for the job and choose to submit it immediately or schedule it for later (regular) execution. Also, you can choose to only submit the job, store it in the job library, or both. Click Finish to continue. A confirmation dialog box appears displaying information about the backup job. Click OK to submit the backup job, or Cancel to stop. After submitting the job, you can check the status of this job in the EM job detail view pane.

Recovery Wizard

When you need to recover a database, you launch the Recovery Wizard in the following way:

1. Select the target database for the recovery operation in the EM Navigator tree.
2. If you are performing a complete database recovery, be sure the database is in the MOUNT state; otherwise, recovery is not possible. If the database is in the OPEN state, you will only be able to recover tablespaces and datafiles.
3. Choose Tools | Backup Management | Recovery from the Backup Management, or Database Wizards | Recovery from the pop-up menu. The Recovery Wizard Welcome screen appears; click Next. Now you have to choose to recover the entire database, tablespaces, or datafiles, as shown in Figure 15-17.

You can check the "Perform recovery without restoring the datafiles" check box if the datafile already exists, and you only need to perform a recover operation.

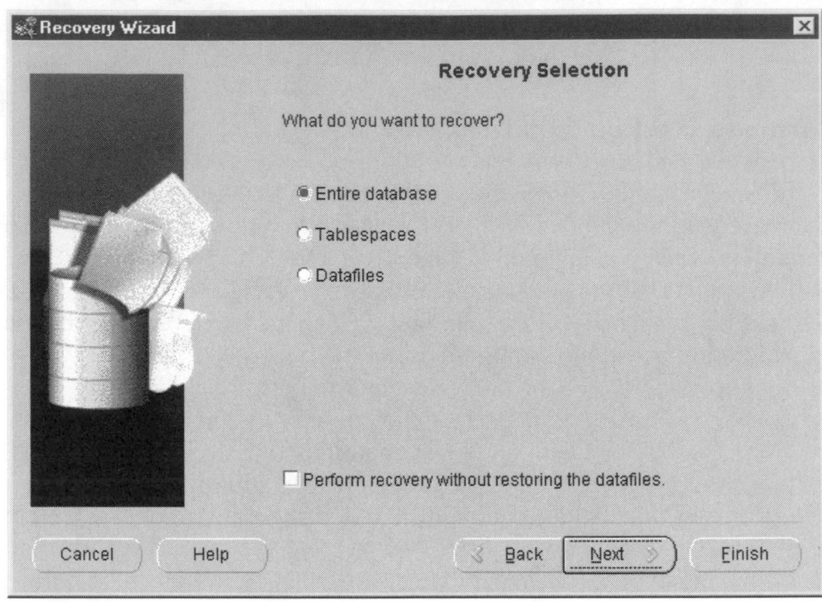

FIGURE 15-17. *Selecting items to recover*

Recovering a Tablespace or Datafile

You can choose to recover an entire tablespace or a single datafile. This can be performed while the database is open.

1. Choose tablespace or datafile and click Next.
2. Select the tablespace(s) or datafile(s) to be recovered and click Next.
3. On the Rename page, you can specify a new location for the recovered datafile(s) in the New Name column. Click Next.
4. The Configuration page allows you to choose the backup configuration used for the backup, and shows information about the recovery operation. Click Finish to continue.
5. A confirmation dialog box appears showing the recovery information. Click OK to begin the recovery or Cancel to stop.

The Restore Wizard uses the EM job feature to perform the recovery, and submits the job immediately after the wizard completes. A dialog box appears informing you that the job has successfully been submitted; click OK. You can check the status of the recovery job in the EM job detail view pane.

Recovering a Complete Database

To recover a complete database, you must first bring the instance into MOUNT mount state. You can use either EM Instance Manager or SQL*Plus by first shutting down the instance and then mounting it. Then, launch the Recovery Wizard as described previously and skip to the Recovery Selection screen (see Figure 15-17):

1. Choose Entire Database and click Next.
2. You can choose to perform point-in-time recovery for the database by checking the Until check box and entering the date and time you want to recover to. If you leave the Until check box unchecked, the database will be recovered to the most recent time possible. Click Next.
3. Optionally, specify a new location for the recovered datafile(s) on the Rename page, and then click Next.
4. On the Configuration page, choose the appropriate backup configuration and click Finish.
5. A confirmation dialog box appears, showing the recovery information. Click OK to begin the recovery or Cancel to stop.

The Restore Wizard uses the EM job feature to perform the recovery, and submits the job immediately after the wizard completes. A dialog box appears informing you that the job has successfully been submitted; click OK. You can check the status of the recovery job in the EM job detail view pane.

Data Management Wizard

You are probably familiar with the three Oracle data unload and load tools, Export, Import, and SQL*Loader, in their command-line versions. These are all available in GUI- and wizard-based versions in EM through the Tools | Database Wizards | Data Management Menu. You can either execute the operations immediately through the wizard, or schedule them for later execution through the EM job feature. Note that all three tools in the Data Management menu only run from the EM Console when you are connected to a Management Server. This is because they rely on the EM job system for scheduling their respective jobs.

Export

The Export Wizard exports (dumps) data into a binary file, which can be imported by the Import utility. You launch the Export Wizard in the following way:

1. Select the database that you want to export in the EM Navigator tree.
2. Choose Tools | Data Management | Export, or choose Database Wizards | Export from the pop-up menu. You can also click the Export icon in the Database Wizards icon group in the left toolbar. The Export Wizard launches, and you will be placed on the Introduction screen. Click Next.
3. Specify the dump file that will be generated by the export. This file will be written on the database server for which you perform the export. Enter the path and filename and click Next.

NOTE
For databases of release 8i and later, you can specify several export files and the file size (default 2GB) to use for all the export files.

4. Select the type of export to perform: Database (full), User (one or more selected schemas), or Table (one or more selected tables), by choosing the appropriate value in the radio button group. Click Next. If you chose either the User or Table option, you will have to select users or tables for the export. Be aware that besides the SYS schema, the ORDSYS, CTXSYS, MDSYS, ORDPLUGINS, and LBACSYS schemas will not be exported if you select them. Add the users or tables in the Available Users/Tables list to the Selected Users/Tables list by clicking the > button, and then click Next. When the Database option has been chosen, you will be taken to the Associated Objects page.

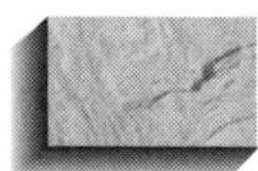

NOTE
To export a complete database, or tables owned by another user, you must have the EXP_FULL_DATABASE role granted and enabled. This role is granted to the DBA role. For more information about exporting data, refer to Oracle9i Database Utilities.

5. On the Associated Objects page, specify all the options for the export operation, which you might know from the command-line version `exp`. Use either the four check boxes or click the Advanced button, which opens a dialog like the one shown in Figure 15-18. You can change parameter values on the General and Tuning pages. When you are finished with the parameter modification, click OK to return to the Export Wizard. Check the "Fail jobs only on errors (not on warnings)" check box if you do not want your EM job to get the Failed status when only warnings occur during the export. Even with warnings, the export is normally fine, but the export utility can encounter one or more problems during the export. Click Next to schedule the export operation.

6. The Export Wizard uses the EM job system to submit the export job. On the Schedule page, you can change the scheduling from the default (execute immediately). Then click Next.

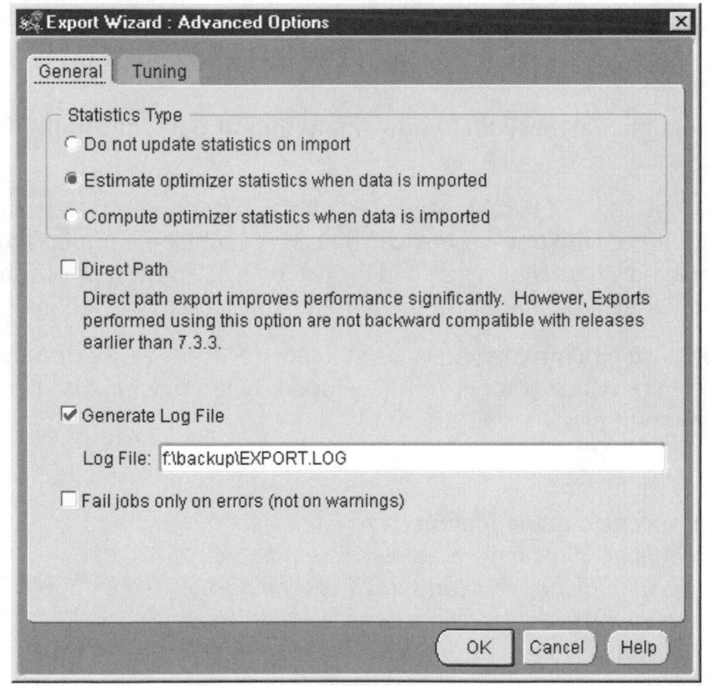

FIGURE 15-18. *Selecting advanced export options*

7. On the Job Information page, you can enter a name and description for the export job. The default name for the job is "Export<sequence number>." You can choose to submit the job immediately, store it in the job library, or both, and you can override the preferred credentials for the job. Click Finish to submit the job.

8. A Summary page appears, and you can examine the contents of the job. Click OK to begin job submission or Cancel to quit.

9. When the export job has been submitted, a dialog box informs you of the job submission. Click OK to exit the dialog box, and follow the progress of the export job in the EM job detail view pane.

Import

With the Import Wizard, you can import dump files created by the Export utility. This is useful for transferring data between databases, and across hardware platforms. One thing to be aware of is that the character set used by the database *exporting* the data must be compatible with the database character set for the importing database instance. For more details about the import utility, refer to Chapter 2 in *Oracle9i Database Utilities*. You launch the Import Wizard in the following way:

1. Select the database that you want to import data into in the EM Navigator tree.

2. Choose Tools | Data Management | Import, or choose Database Wizards | Import from the pop-up menu. You can also click the Import icon in the Database Wizards icon group in the left toolbar. The Import Wizard launches, and you will be placed on the Introduction screen. Click Next.

3. Specify the dump file you want to import. This file resides on the database server for which you perform the import. Enter the path and filename for the import file.

NOTE
The user specified in the preferred credentials for node credentials must have read permission to the import file. In addition, you can specify several dump files for the import, if the target database is of version 8i or later. The Import Wizard processes the specified files in the order they are listed. Be sure to specify the correct sequence of import filenames (the same order in which they were exported). You can change the position of a selected filename with the up and down buttons.

You have two options now for continuing the import:

- If you do not know the contents of the import file, you can retrieve information about the contents and view this in the Import Wizard. You can do this by choosing the value "Read import file(s) and select what objects you want to import" and clicking Next. An EM job will be submitted with the name "Internal<sequence number>," which will read the contents of the specified import file and present the result in the Import Wizard. During the process, the Progress page appears, informing you about the status and progress of the job. If you want to stop the job, click Stop. When the job has finished successfully, the Import Type page appears automatically with the options available (Database, User, and Table) for importing the file. Choose the option you want and click Next. Now you must select the Users/Tables to import on the Selection screen and click Next.
- If you know the contents of the import file, accept the default value, which is "Manually specify what you want to import," and click Next. Select the type of import to perform: Entire files(s), User (one or more selected schemas), or Table (one or more selected tables), by choosing the appropriate value in the radio button group. You specify multiple users or multiple tables using a comma as a separator. Click Next.

NOTE
To perform a full import, or import into tables owned by another user, you must have the IMP_FULL_DATABASE role granted and enabled. This role is granted to the DBA role. For more information about importing data, refer to Oracle9i Database Utilities.

4. On the User Mapping page, you have the option to map the users in the import file to users in the target database (fromuser/touser import parameters). If you want to map, choose the "Yes, import into different users' schemas as shown below" value in the radio button group. Choose the username in the Destination Name drop-down list box and click Next.
5. On the Associated Objects page, specify all the options for the import operation, either through the four check boxes, or by clicking the Advanced button, which opens the Advanced Options dialog box, containing the General, Tuning, and Statistics pages. Click OK to leave the dialog box and then click Next.

6. On the Schedule page, you can change the scheduling for the import job from the default (execute immediately). Then click Next.
7. On the Job Information page, you can enter a name and description for the import job. The default name for the job is "Import<sequence number>." You can choose to submit the job immediately, store it in the job library, or both, and you can override the preferred credentials for the job. Click Finish to submit the job.
8. A Summary page appears, and you can examine the contents of the job. Click OK to begin job submission or Cancel to quit.
9. If you choose to submit the job, a dialog box informs you of the job submission. Click OK to exit the dialog box, and monitor the status of the import job in the EM job detail view pane.

Load

With the Load Wizard, you can load data into the database from a flat file, where data can be in comma-separated format, or structured using either fixed- or variable-length records. For more details about the import utility, refer to Part II in *Oracle9i Database Utilities*. You launch the Load Wizard from the EM Console in the following way:

1. Select the database that you want to load data into in the Navigator tree.
2. Choose Tools | Data Management | Load, or choose Database Wizards | Load in the pop-up menu. You can also click the Load icon in the Database Wizards icon group in the left toolbar. The Load Wizard launches, and you will be placed on the Introduction screen. Click Next.
3. Specify the SQL*Loader control file that you want to use for the load operation. This has nothing to do with database control files. The file must reside on the database server where you want to perform the load operation. Enter the path and filename for the load control file and click Next.
4. On the Data File page, you must specify where the data for the load is located; either stored in the control file, or in a data file (normally with a .DAT extension). Enter the appropriate information and click Next.
5. On the Load Method page, you must choose the method to use for the load. There are three methods for loading data:
   - **Conventional Path** The default method, which uses the standard SQL interface (INSERT statement) and therefore can become a bottleneck when loading large amounts of data.

- **Direct Path** Bypasses the standard SQL interface and writes the data directly into the database's datafiles.
- **Parallel Direct Path** Like Direct Path, but performed in parallel.

By clicking the Advanced button, you can access the Advanced Options dialog box, which enables you to modify the SQL*Loader parameters on the General, Tuning, and Optional Files pages. Click OK to accept the parameter changes and return to the Load Wizard. Click Next to advance to the Schedule page.

6. On the Schedule page, you can change the scheduling for the load job from the default (execute immediately). Then click Next.
7. On the Job Information page, you can enter a name and description for the load job. The default name is "Load<sequence number>." You can choose either to submit the job immediately, store it in the job library, or both. You can also override the preferred credentials for the job. Click Finish to submit the load job.
8. A Summary page appears, and you can examine the contents of the job. Click OK to begin job submission or Cancel to quit.
9. If you choose to submit the job, a dialog box informs you of the job submission. Click OK to exit the dialog box. You can monitor the status of the load job in the EM job detail view pane.

Analyze Wizard

The Analyze Wizard helps you to generate statistics for the Cost Based Optimizer (CBO) for database objects of your choice. You have the option of using either the classic ANALYZE statement or the DBMS_STATS package, which were introduced with Oracle8i. You launch the Analyze Wizard in the following way, either connected to an OMS or in standalone mode:

1. Select the target database for the analyze operation in the EM Navigator tree.
2. Choose Tools | Database Wizards | Analyze, choose Database Wizards | Analyze in the pop-up menu for the database, or click Analyze in the Database Wizards icon group in the left toolbar. The Analyze Wizard Welcome screen appears; click Next.
3. You must choose the method for generating the statistics (Compute or Estimate), or to delete the statistics. With the check box in the bottom of the Default Options page, you can specify that the PL/SQL built-in package

DBMS_STATS is used for the statistics operation. This option is supported for 8i Rel 2 (8.1.6) and higher databases. Click Next.

NOTE
If you select the "Use latest 8i analyze method (dbms_stats package)" option, you will not be able to validate the structure of the objects (option Validate structure of the objects is ghosted) or identify migrated and continued rows for tables or clusters (option List migrated and continued rows are ghosted). Also, notice that before validating structures or listing migrated and continued rows, the SQL scripts utlvalid.sql and utlchain.sql (located in ORACLE_HOME\rdbms\admin) must be executed to create objects used by these two options.

4. Select the whole schemas or individual schema objects (tables, indexes, or both) from the Available objects list. Then click Next.

NOTE
The objects you choose to analyze must either be owned by you or you must have been granted the ANALYZE ANY system privilege.

5. You can override the analyze options for selected objects or schemas. Highlight the object or schema in the "Object list to be analyzed" section and choose Compute, Delete, or Estimate statistics. Then click Next.
6. The Analyze Wizard will use the EM job feature to perform the analysis operation. On the Job Information page, you can enter a name and description for the job. You can also choose to submit it immediately, store it in the job library, or both. You can override the preferred credentials for this particular job. Click Next to enter schedule information for the job, or click Finish to submit the job.
7. The Summary page appears, and you can examine the contents of the job. Click Finish to begin job submission, or Cancel to exit the Analyze Wizard.

You can monitor the job progress in the EM job detail view pane. Further, when the job is being executed and you use the DBMS_STATS option, you can follow the progress of each of the statements in V$SESSION_LONGOPS, either from SQL*Plus, SQL*Plus Worksheet, or EM Instance Manager Sessions view pane.

Summary Advisor Wizard

Summaries are typically used in data warehouse environments for defining static totals, thereby speeding up the performance for queries dramatically. They are implemented as materialized views (snapshots) and the "query rewrite" feature is used by the Cost Based Optimizer (CBO) to utilize the summaries. The goal is to identify the optimal balance for your environment regarding the number of summaries. The Summary Advisor Wizard assists you through recommendations for creating, dropping, or keeping materialized views. It also helps you with the implementation of the materialized views.

The Summary Advisor Wizard performs its analysis in two different ways:

- Use hypothetical workload statistics, meaning analyze existing star schemas instead of using workload statistics.
- Use workload statistics gathered before using Summary Advisor, or from the SQL Cache. This provides a more accurate recommendation.

The workload statistics are the basis for the analysis performed by the Summary Advisor Wizard. The workload is a collection of queries that is included in the analysis. These queries can be identified either from the SQL cache in the SGA, an Oracle Trace collection using the Oracle Expert facility (part of the optional EM Tuning Pack), or stored in a database table.

To use the Summary Advisor properly, you need to be familiar with issues such as dimensions, fact tables, and the concept of materialized views (snapshots). The Summary Advisor Wizard only works with database releases 8i and later; some features are only available for Oracle9i.

Requirements if not Using a Workload

If you choose to not use real workload statistics, the Summary Advisor Wizard searches for star schema definitions (one larger *fact* table surrounded by several *dimension* tables). The Summary Advisor Wizard uses the hierarchy metadata provided by the dimensions to determine which summaries should be created. All fact and dimension tables, as well as the possibly existing materialized views must have been analyzed (table- and column-level statistics) before launching the Summary Advisor. How to analyze database objects is described earlier in this chapter in the "Analyze Wizard" section. For more details about replication and materialized views, refer to *Oracle9i Replication*. For more information about fact tables and dimensions, refer to *Oracle9i OLAP Services Concepts and Administration Guide.*

Requirements When Using a Workload (only Oracle9i)

If you choose to use workload statistics based on Oracle Trace, either stored in a schema or in a table, the trace must be available. Also, all existing materialized views must have been analyzed. No star schema definitions are required for this option to work.

Launching the Summary Advisor Wizard

The Summary Advisor Wizard can be launched from the EM Console, either when connected to an OMS or in standalone mode. To launch Summary Advisor, follow these steps:

1. Select the target database for the Summary Advisor Wizard to run on in the EM Navigator tree. Choose Tools | Database Wizards | Summary Advisor, choose Database Wizards | Summary Advisor from the pop-up menu for the particular database, or select Summary Advisor from the icon group in the left toolbar. The Summary Advisor Wizard Welcome screen appears with information about the advisory process. Click Next.
2. If the database is a pre-9i version, the Workload Statistics page appears, and you are presented with two options: "Use hypothetical workload statistics" or "Use real workload statistics." For the latter option, you are again presented with three choices of using the real workload statistics in a radio button group:
   - Collect workload statistics from SQL cache
   - Use workload statistics that you have collected
   - Use workload statistics collected by Oracle Trace in schema

   Select the method you want to use. If you choose option 2, you must specify the name of a table where the workload statistics are stored. You can click Select Table to open the Select a workload table dialog box. Highlight the table and click OK to return to the Summary Advisor Wizard. If you choose option 3, you must specify an Oracle Trace schema by selecting the trace schema from the drop-down list box.

3. Check the check box "Use workload filter to limit the workload scope" to refine the set of SQL statements being analyzed. Click the Specify Filter button to initiate the Workload Filter dialog. If you do not specify a filter, all target SQL statements will be collected. Click Next to initiate the workload analysis.
4. The Summary Advisor Wizard begins its analysis, and a progress bar appears. When the process is finished, you are presented with the Select Fact Tables screen, where you must choose the fact tables to be handled by the Summary Advisor. Select the table(s) in the Available Tables list and add them to the Selected Tables list by clicking the > button. Then click Next.
5. If any existing summaries (materialized views) are found, you are presented with the Retain Summaries page, where you must tell the Summary Advisor which summaries you are sure you want to keep. Select the summaries by checking the check box left to the Schema column, or click Select All to retain them all, and click Next.
6. The recommendations are generated, this may take a while. You are then presented with the recommendations on the Recommendations screen. If no recommendations have been made, a dialog box appears; click OK to acknowledge.

Summary

In this chapter, we have taken a tour through the wizards and other tools that assist you with your database administration tasks within EM. The database administration tools and wizards covered are those in the Tools menu, located in the Database Wizards and Database Applications submenus. In the next two chapters, we will describe services other than databases that can be managed using EM, such as Nodes, HTTP Servers, Oracle Net, Oracle Internet Directories, and Real Application Clusters.

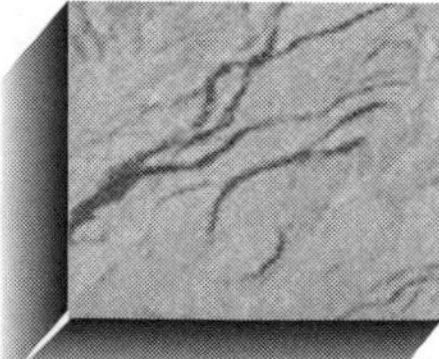

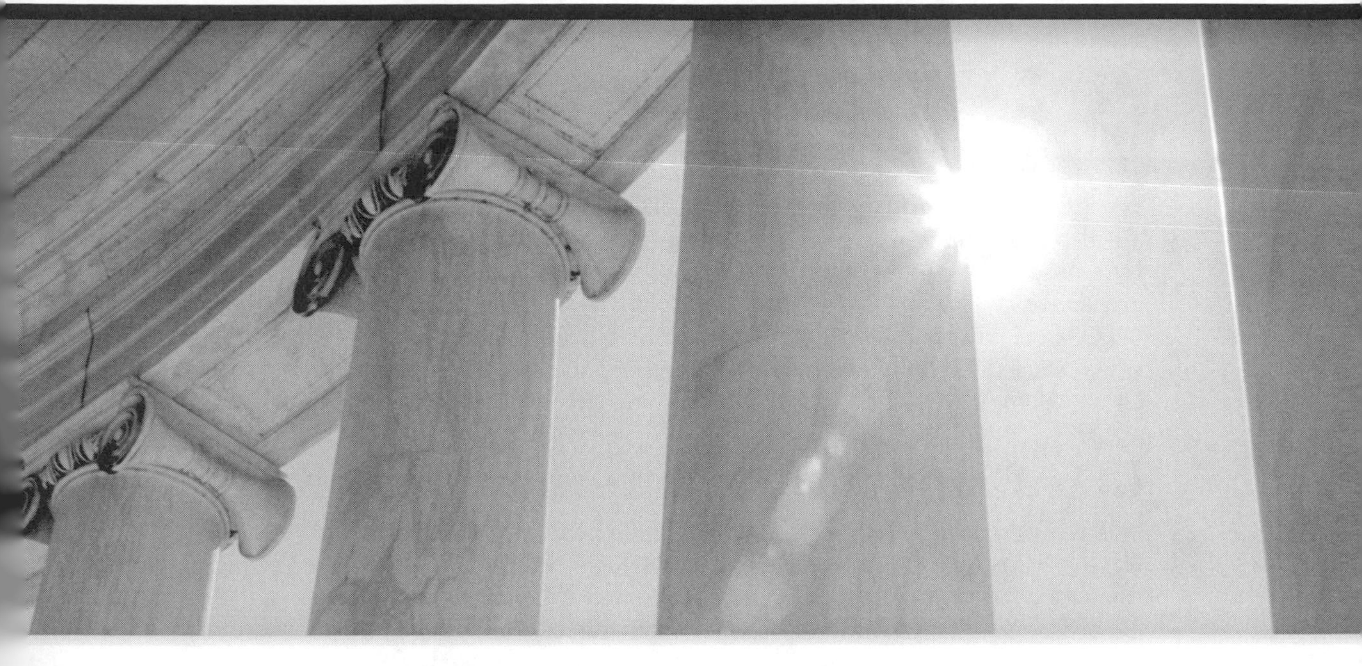

CHAPTER 16

Managing Directory Services and Oracle Net

In Chapters 6, 14, and 15, we covered the database administration tools and wizards available within the core EM framework. In this chapter and in Chapter 17, we will switch focus and take a look at the administration tools available for nondatabase services. In this chapter, we will explain how to use the tools in the Tools | Service Management menu, which are also available from the Service Management tool drawer on the left side of the EM Console. One of these tools is the Oracle Internet Directory Manager. It is used to manage an Oracle Internet Directory (OID), which is Oracle's implementation of LDAP (Lightweight Directory Access Protocol). The other tool is Net Manager, which is used to configure Oracle Net components, including Internet Directory, Oracle Names, Net Listener, and local naming (TNSNAMES.ORA).

LDAP and Oracle Internet Directory

In a network, a *directory* tells you where in the network something is located, just like the index in this book directs you to the page for a certain subject. For networks using the TCP/IP protocol (including the Internet), the domain name system (DNS) is the directory system used to resolve a domain name to a specific network address (a unique location on the network, specified by an IP address). However, you may not know the domain name. LDAP (Lightweight Directory Access Protocol), also known as X.500 Lite, enables you to search for individuals or user-specified resources, without knowing where they are located. It is a *lightweight* (meaning it uses less code) version of Directory Access Protocol (DAP), which is part of the X.500 ISO standard for directory services. LDAP originated at the University of Michigan and has since been adapted by many companies besides Oracle, such as Netscape, Microsoft (as part of its Active Directory product), Novell, and Cisco. The LDAP specifications are managed by the Internet Engineering Task Force (IETF), who have also standardized HTTP and TCP/IP.

An LDAP directory is organized in a simple tree hierarchy known as a Directory Information Tree (DIT), which consists of the following levels (also called the X.500 model):

1. The *root directory* is the starting point of the tree.
2. Below the root node, *country* information appears, followed by entries for national *organizations,* companies, or states.
3. At the next level are entries for *organizational units,* such as branch offices and departments.
4. Last are *common names,* such as Oracle databases and users.

The single entries in the directory are identified using an entry called a *distinguished name* (DN). An entry of the *country* type is specified by c=<*country name*>, an *organization* by o=<*organization name*>, an *organizational unit* by ou=<*org. unit name*>, and a common name by cn=<*common name*>. For example, if you wanted to refer to the individual "Lars Bo Vanting," you would use c=usa, o=McGraw-Hill,ou=Osborne,ou=authors,cn=Lars Bo Vanting. Another tree structure is also available, called the *Domain Component* model, where you define entries using the dc (Domain Component) and cn (Common Name) notation.

An LDAP server is called a *Directory System Agent* (DSA). An LDAP server that receives a request from a user takes responsibility for the request, passing it to other DSAs as necessary, but ensuring a single coordinated response to the user.

You can use the Oracle Internet Directory (OID) to provide central administration for connect identifiers (TNS aliases), as well as for user authentication through the Oracle Advanced Security component, which is part of Oracle's Enterprise User Security.

Components of the Oracle Internet Directory

Oracle implements LDAP through an Oracle Internet Directory (OID) server and the directory itself, which consists of twelve tablespaces and two schemas (ODS and ODSCOMMON) in an Oracle database. By default, the password for these two database users is the same as the username. You can change the password for the database user ODS with the command-line utility `oidpasswd.exe` and for OSDCOMMON using the Security Manager in EM, or the ALTER USER SQL statement. OID is the successor of Oracle Names, in terms of the Oracle Net naming resolution mechanism, and has been bundled with the Oracle software since Oracle8i Release 2. Figure 16-1 shows an overview of the different OID components.

You administer the OID with a GUI administration tool called the Oracle Internet Directory Manager (sometimes only Oracle Directory Manager), which we will describe in the following section. To export (back up) the content of an Oracle Internet Directory, use the command-line tool ldifwrite.exe. Several standard LDAP command-line tools are available, such as ldapsearch, ldapadd, ldapmodify, and ldapdelete. Finally, some shell scripts are available (located in ORACLE_HOME\ldap\bin), such as bulkload.sh and bulkappend.sh. To execute these on Windows NT or 2000, you need either the MKS Toolkit (commercial, http://www.mks.com) or Cygwin (open source, http://www.cygwin.com) software installed. For more details about OID, refer to the *Oracle Internet Directory Administrator's Guide*.

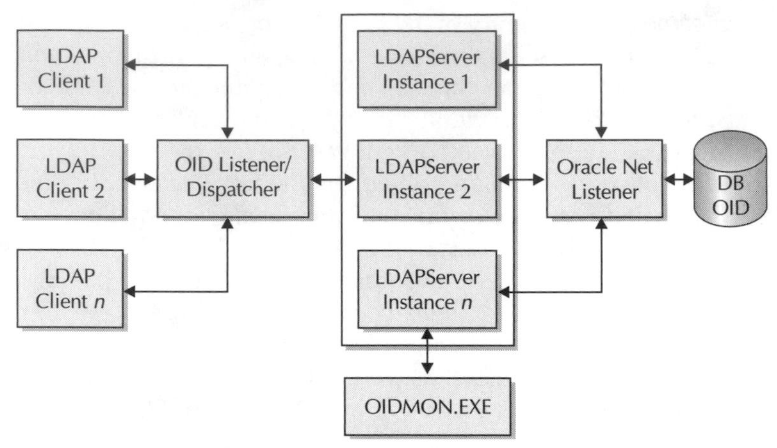

FIGURE 16-1. *Oracle Internet Directory architecture*

Installing and Configuring Oracle Internet Directory

Before looking into the Oracle Internet Directory Manager, we will look at the steps required to install the OID software and install the directory on a Windows NT or 2000 machine. You must install the OID software separately, because it is not automatically included when you install the RDBMS or OMS software as described in Chapter 2.

First you must install the OID software component; refer to Chapter 2 in the section "Installing the Management Server Only" for the following steps.

1. In the Available Products screen (see Figure 2-3), you must select the "Oracle9i Management and Integration 9.0.1.0.0" option. Then click Next.
2. On the Installation Types screen (see Figure 2-11), choose "Oracle Internet Directory" and click Next.
3. You are asked if you want to create a *new* database instance (choose No) for the OID or use an *existing* one (choose Yes). Make your choice and click Next. If you answer No, you must specify the global database name and SID for the new instance to be created as well as the location for the datafiles. If you answer Yes, you must provide the SID of the existing database instance and the path for the directory to hold the OID datafiles. Be sure the existing database is up and running. Notice that in both cases, the database instance and file location is on the server where you are currently installing OID.

NOTE
The OID follows the LDAP version 3 internationalization standard (I18N). When creating a database for the OID, you must use UTF-8 (Unicode Transformation Format 8-bit) as the database character set to provide storage of characters supported by Oracle Globalization Support in the directory. Set the environment variable NLS_LANG to the corresponding language. For example, use AMERICAN_AMERICA.UTF8 for American English, and GERMAN_GERMANY.UTF8 for German. For Windows NT/2000 client and server machines, this is set in the Registry for each Oracle Home (HOME0, HOME1, and so on).

4. A summary of the installation is displayed; click Install to begin the software installation and Oracle Internet Directory creation. After a short software installation, the OID Configuration Assistant is automatically started to create the OID database objects.

You will find a new Windows NT/2000 service called OracleDirectoryService_<*SID*>, where *SID* is the SID of your OID database. This service is called the Oracle Internet Directory Monitor, and is responsible for starting and shutting down all OID servers (oidldapd, oidrepld, and oidmetad). When started, this service monitors the OID servers and restarts them if they die. You can start it from the service panel, but after a successful OID installation and configuration, it should already be running.

NOTE
*The OID Configuration Assistant uses the SQL script newldap.sql, located in the ORACLE_HOME\ldap\admin directory on the server where you installed the OID software, to create the OID users and tablespaces. If something goes wrong during the OID creation, you can run this script manually from SQL*Plus. Notice that it connects to the database using the /as sysdba and system/manager connect strings, as well as fixed paths for the tablespaces created. You may want to review and change the SQL scripts before running them. Before doing this, please check that the OracleDirectoryService_<SID> service has been created (SID is the SID of your OID instance). If it has not, then you should retry the OID installation.*

You can uninstall OID by removing the OID software (through the Oracle Universal Installer), and by dropping the two users ODS and OSDCOMMON as well as the 12 OID tablespaces.

You can start an instance of the Oracle Internet Directory Server using the command-line utility `oidctl.exe`, to start a second (SSL) enabled OID server, for example. To start one instance (number 1) of the OID server on database OEMREP .WORLD, execute the following from a command prompt:

```
oidctl connect=oemrep.world server=oidldapd instance=1 start
```

This command requires a valid and functioning Oracle Net connection to the database specified in the connect parameter and will also make use of the NLS_LANG environment variable.

NOTE
*If starting the OID server using oidctl.exe fails, and you receive the error "Instance number already in use," this indicates that a previous OID server instance with that number was not cleanly shut down. If the table ODS .ODS_ PROCESS still contains entries, check this in SQL*Plus as the ODS user with the select statement SELECT * FROM ODS.ODS_ PROCESS. If it returns a row for the instance (check the value of the INSTANCE column), you can delete the row using the statement DELETE FROM ODS.ODS_PROCESS WHERE INSTANCE = <instance number>. Then try to start the OID server with that instance number again. In addition, a command-line utility is available to manage the Oracle Internet Directory Monitor called oidmon.exe. To start the OID Monitor on OEMREP.WORLD with ten seconds (default if omitted) between the probes, execute the following command from the command line:*

```
oidmon connect=oemrep.world sleep=10 start
```

NOTE
Starting the Oracle Internet Directory Monitor also starts an OID server with instance number 1, meaning you only need to start the Oracle Directory Service_<SID> on Windows NT/2000.

Configuring Your OID Using Network Configuration Assistant

You can configure your OID schemas and contexts within the OID with the Network Configuration Assistant. This is a part of the preparation for using your OID for directory naming. Follow these steps the first time you configure your OID. In Windows NT or 2000, you launch the Network Configuration Assistant from Start | Programs | Oracle - <*Oracle Home Name*> | Configuration and Migration Tools. The Welcome screen appears; choose Directory Usage Configuration and click Next. On the next page, called Directory Usage Configuration, you are presented with four options:

- Select the directory server you want to use. The directory server must already be configured for Oracle usage. This option enables your client computer to use a specific directory server that you have configured for directory usage (for example, using option 2). It creates or updates the LDAP.ORA configuration file located in the ORACLE_HOME\network\admin directory.
- Select the directory server you want to use, and configure the directory server for Oracle usage. (Create or upgrade Oracle schema and Oracle Context as necessary.) This option is used to configure your OID for directory naming and enterprise user security features. It allows you to create a schema and a context, if these have not yet been created. Once you have completed this step, this option enables this computer to look up entries in the directory (as option 1 does).
- Create additional or upgrade the existing Oracle Context (Advanced). This option can create an additional Oracle context in an already configured directory. If no Oracle schema exists (option 4), you cannot create an Oracle context.
- Create or upgrade the Oracle Schema (Advanced). This option creates (or upgrades) the Oracle schema in the directory. The Oracle schema contains OID metadata and defines the Oracle entries and their attributes.

NOTE
You must have the appropriate directory permissions to create the Oracle context and schema. For instance, you can use the built-in OID administrator cn= orcladmin with the default password welcome.

Choose the second option and click Next. Now you must choose the Oracle Internet Directory (chosen by default) or Microsoft Active Directory value to specify the type of directory. Accept the default value from the Directory Type drop-down list box and click Next.

Now you must provide information about your OID server (Hostname, Port, and SSL Port). Enter the hostname, accept the default port numbers, and click Next.

If no Oracle context exists, you are prompted to create one. You can accept the default (Root entry) or enter another context name. In addition, if no Oracle schema exists, you are prompted to create it. Accept the default (cn=OracleContext) and click Next. After a successful OID installation and configuration, you will have both an Oracle schema and a context and you will therefore not be prompted.

Registering a Database in OID Using the Database Configuration Assistant

When your OID is configured and ready for directory naming, you can register your database instances in the OID through the Database Configuration Assistant (DBCA). In Windows NT or 2000, launch the DBCA from Start | Programs | Oracle - <*Oracle Home Name*> | Configuration and Migration Tools. First, click Next on the Welcome page, then choose "Configure database options in a database," and click Next. Now you are presented with a list of available database instances on the machine where you run the DBCA. Choose the database instance you want to register and click Next. On the next page, you are asked if you want to register the database with OID. Choose Yes, enter the OID administrator user's distinguished name (DN) and password, and click Finish. Now the selected database will be registered with the OID. You can also use the Net Manager to enter your database service names into your OID, either manually or as an export from existing TNSNAMES.ORA entries. This is described later in this chapter in the "Directory" section.

Launching Oracle Internet Directory Manager

You launch the Oracle Internet Directory Manager from the EM Console when you are connected to an OMS. Choose either Tools | Service Management | Oracle Internet Directory Manager, click the Oracle Internet Directory Manager icon in the Service Management icon group in the left toolbar. You can also start Oracle Internet Directory Manager for Windows NT or 2000 by clicking Start | Programs | Oracle - <*Oracle Home Name*> | Integrated Management Tools | Oracle Directory manager. The Oracle Internet Directory Manager Connect dialog appears. The first time you connect, you must add a server in the Select Directory Server dialog box. Click Add and enter the server name and port number (the default is 389) for the OID server you are using. The Available column indicates whether the server is available (Yes) or not (No). Choose a server and click Select. Now you can choose to log on either as a super administrator (the username is cn=orcladmin and the default password is *welcome*), or as an anonymous user (the username is cn=orcladmin and leave the password blank) to the Directory Manager. Enter the user name and password and click Login. Figure 16-2 shows an example of the login dialog box.

Logging on Using SSL

To log on using SSL (Secure Socket Layer) security, you must check the check box SSL Enabled and provide information about your wallet location and password on the SSL tab. Depending on the SSL authorization level, a wallet is required either on the server, the client, or both. Before you can log on using SSL, you must configure

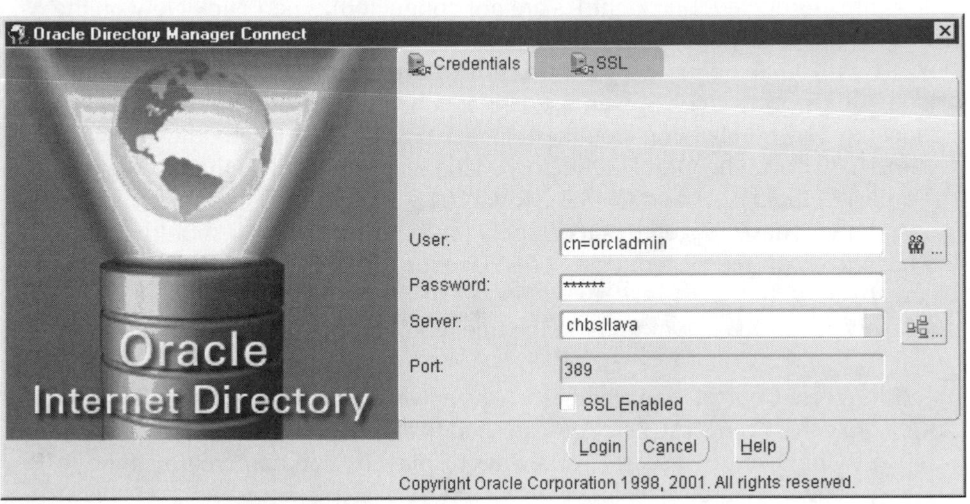

FIGURE 16-2. *Logging into Oracle Internet Directory*

the OID server to use SSL, which you do from the Oracle Internet Directory Manager. Expand the Navigator tree and choose Server Management | Directory Server | Default Configuration Set and click the SSL Settings tab. If you choose to configure SSL for your OID, you should start a separate OID server to handle SSL connections only. The default port number used for SSL is 636. Discussing SSL and wallets is beyond the scope of this book, but for more information about enabling the OID to use SSL, refer to the chapter "Managing Secure Sockets Layer (SSL)" in the *Oracle Internet Directory Administrator's Guide.*

NOTE
You can create a wallet in Windows NT or 2000 using the Wallet Manager in Start | Programs | Oracle - <Oracle Home Name> | Integrated Management Tools | Wallet Manager.

Overview of Oracle Internet Directory Manager Components

When the Oracle Internet Manager has launched, you will be presented with a Navigator tree and detail view pane just as you know it from the EM Console. The top level in the tree structure is the Oracle Internet Directory Servers entry, below which all available OID servers are listed. To connect to a new OID server, select the Oracle Internet Directory Servers item to display the detail view pane (blue entries are connected, black entries are not connected). Then click New on the Connected Servers pane to launch the Oracle Directory Manager Connect dialog box, where you can choose an existing OID server entry or add one. You can also add an OID server on the Server List pane by clicking the Add button, and then connect to it by highlighting it on the Connected Servers pane and clicking Connect. Figure 16-3 shows the Oracle Directory Manager connected to the OID servers on the nodes CHBSLLAVA and CHBSLORACLE01.

When you have logged in successfully for the first time, you should change the passwords on the System Passwords page for the OID server connection (see Figure 16-3).

Below each OID server entry in the tree, you find the following five main areas:

- **Access Control Management** Lets you view, add, modify, and delete Access Control Points (ACPs). You can specify that ACPs are to be displayed only as the result of a search, or always displayed. You can create a new ACP using a wizard.

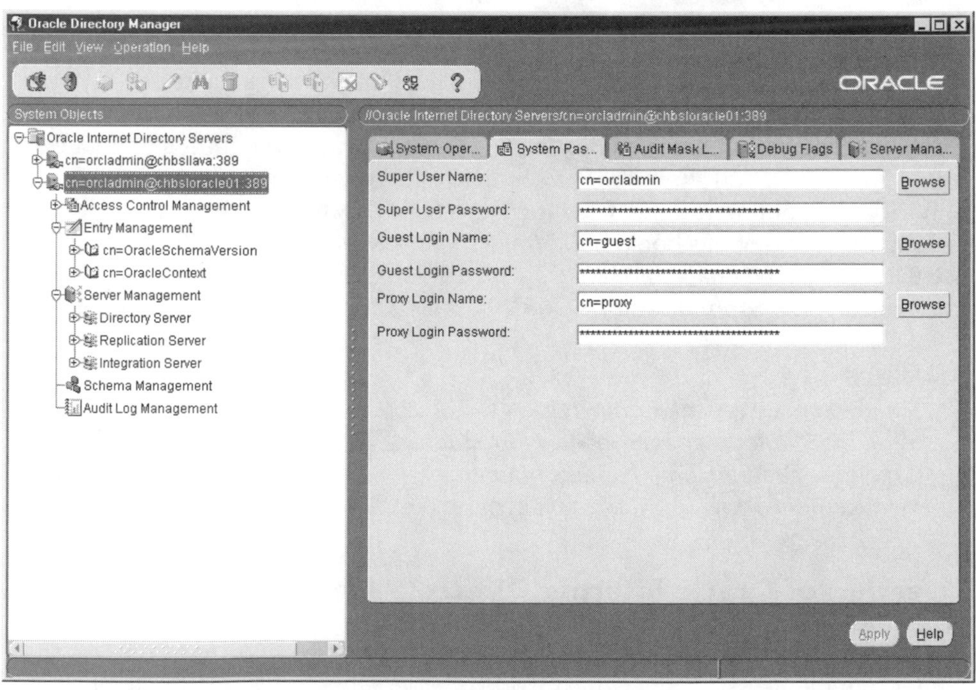

FIGURE 16-3. *The Oracle Directory Manager*

- **Entry Management** Lets you manage (add, modify, and delete) the entries in your Directory Information Tree.
- **Server Management** Lets you manage Oracle Directory Servers, OID Replication Servers, and OID Integration Servers. An LDAP directory can be distributed among many servers. Each Replication server can have a replicated version of the total directory, which is synchronized periodically. Most of the steps to set up replication are done outside of the Oracle Directory Manager. This replication has nothing to do with the Oracle Replication option we described in Chapters 6 and 14.
- **Schema Management** This entry contains metadata information about the DIT, such as object classes, attributes, matching rules, and syntaxes. This information is stored in a special subentry class. The OID holds schema definitions in the subentry called subSchemaSubentry.
- **Audit Log Management** You can search and view the OID audit log, which logs successful and failed binds to the OID server. You can modify the audit level on the Audit Mask Levels property page for a selected OID server connection.

The following sections take a look at how you design your DIT, and manage the entries from within Oracle Internet Directory Manager. We cannot cover all the features within Oracle Internet Directory Manager in this book, so we will focus on the creation of entries in your OID (Entry Management). As mentioned earlier, the Network Configuration Assistant can help you in maintaining your schemas and contexts within OID. Later in this chapter, we will show how you can easily create entries into your OID as well as export existing TNSNAMES.ORA entries directly into OID.

Managing Entries in the Oracle Internet Directory

You start managing OID by defining your Directory Information Tree (DIT) and begin with the definition of the naming context. For example, for the company "mycompany" operating in different countries, you could define the tree structure as shown in Figure 16-4 using the X.500 DIT model (for Switzerland, c=ch). Or, you could use the Domain Component model, as shown in Figure 16-5.

Using the Domain Component notation, for example, you can connect to user SCOTT on the database hrdb. You have defined this user in your OID like this (using SQL*Plus):

```
sqlplus scott/tiger@hrdb.ch.mycompany.com
```

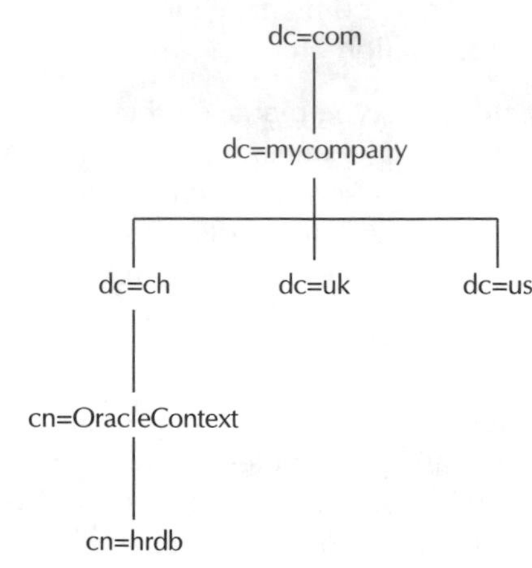

FIGURE 16-4. *Defining a tree structure using the X.500 model*

When you enter the Oracle Internet Directory Manager for the first time, you will find two root-level entries under the Entry Management item: cn=OracleSchemaVersion and cn=OracleContext. The Oracle Context is

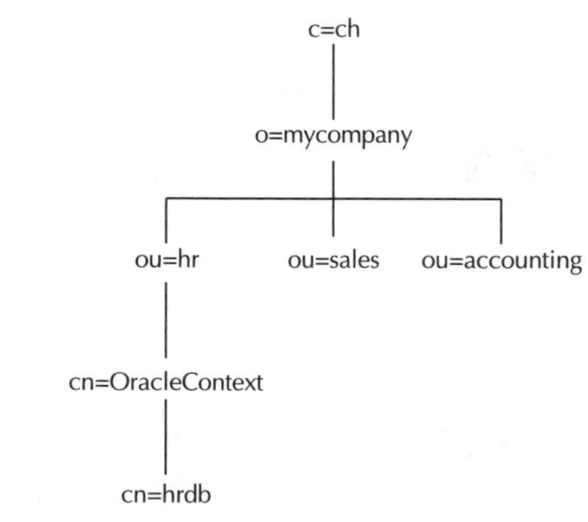

FIGURE 16-5. *Defining a tree structure using the Domain Component model*

a special entry in the Directory that contains Oracle subentries to implement your security concept, such as OracleNetAdmins (whose members manage Oracle Net objects) and OracleDBCreators (whose members manage Oracle databases). There can be several OracleContext entries in one DIT at each branch/level, for example, below each country in Figure 16-5.

The Oracle Context is included in the administrative context, also known as the *directory naming context.* The naming context is a subtree that resides entirely on one server and can range in size from a single entry to the entire DIT. It must be contiguous, meaning it must begin with an entry that acts as the top and extends downward to either leaf entries or references to subordinate naming contexts. Oracle Net clients use the administrative context as the default entry in the directory when it performs naming resolution through LDAP. For example, your administrative context for the example in Figure 16-5 would be dc=ch,dc=mycompany,dc=com. Part of your OID *client* configuration is the LDAP.ORA configuration file, in which you define your default administrative context using the DEFAULT_ADMIN_CONTEXT parameter. For example, using Figure 16-5 and the OID server CHBSLORACLE01 (using the default port number 389):

```
DEFAULT_ADMIN_CONTEXT = "dc=ch,dc=mycompany,dc=com"
DIRECTORY_SERVERS = (chbsloracle01:389)
DIRECTORY_SERVER_TYPE = OID
```

The LDAP.ORA file is created automatically during the installation of the OID software and configuration of the OID database (see the "Installing and Configuring Oracle Internet Directory" section earlier in this chapter). To create and configure LDAP.ORA, you can also use the Net Configuration Assistant as described earlier in this chapter in the section entitled "Configuring Your OID Using Network Configuration Assistant".

Besides the LDAP.ORA, you must also have set the following parameter in the client-side SQLNET.ORA Oracle Net configuration file:

```
NAMES.DIRECTORY_PATH = (LDAP)
```

Or, if LDAP is used together with local naming (TNSNAMES.ORA) so that TNSNAMES.ORA will be used in case an LDAP (OID) lookup does not return anything:

```
NAMES.DIRECTORY_PATH = (LDAP, TNSNAMES)
```

NOTE
The Oracle Net client software must be at least version 8i Release 2 (8.1.6) to work with OID.

For more information about how to modify the Oracle Net configuration files, refer to the "Net Manager" section later in this chapter.

Creating an Entry Using Oracle Internet Directory Manager

To create a new entry in your Oracle Internet Directory, perform the following:

Choose Operation | Create Entry. You can also select the "Entry Management" entry in the tree and choose Create from the pop-up menu, or click the Create icon in the toolbar (the green cube). The New Entry dialog appears.

NOTE
Many of the dialog boxes open minimized. You will have to resize the dialog boxes yourself in order to work with them properly .

Enter a distinguished name for the new entry in the Distinguished Name field. For example, for the hrdb database in Figure 16-5, this would be cn= hrdb,dc=ch,dc=mycompany,dc=com. Choose the object class for your entry by clicking the Add button. The Super Class Selector dialog box appears; highlight the object class you want to use (such as orclNetService) and click Select. Finally, enter the common name for the entry in the cn field, such as hrdb, and click OK to save the entry. Figure 16-6 shows an example of the hrdb entry.

TIP
Use the Create Like feature when creating subentries to spare yourself from entering long values in the Distinguished Name field. You can simply add to or change the first part of the DN.

Use the Refresh SubTree Entries function located in the pop-up menu for a given entry to refresh the view and display the newly added subentries.

For more information about the Oracle-specific object classes, refer to Appendix A in the *Oracle9i Net Services Reference Guide.*

Create OID Entries Using Net Manager

A much easier way to enter your net service names into the OID is through the Oracle Net Manager, which creates all required subentries for the database service automatically. You can also migrate existing net service names entries from a TNSNAMES.ORA file into OID with Net Manager. Both tasks can be accomplished

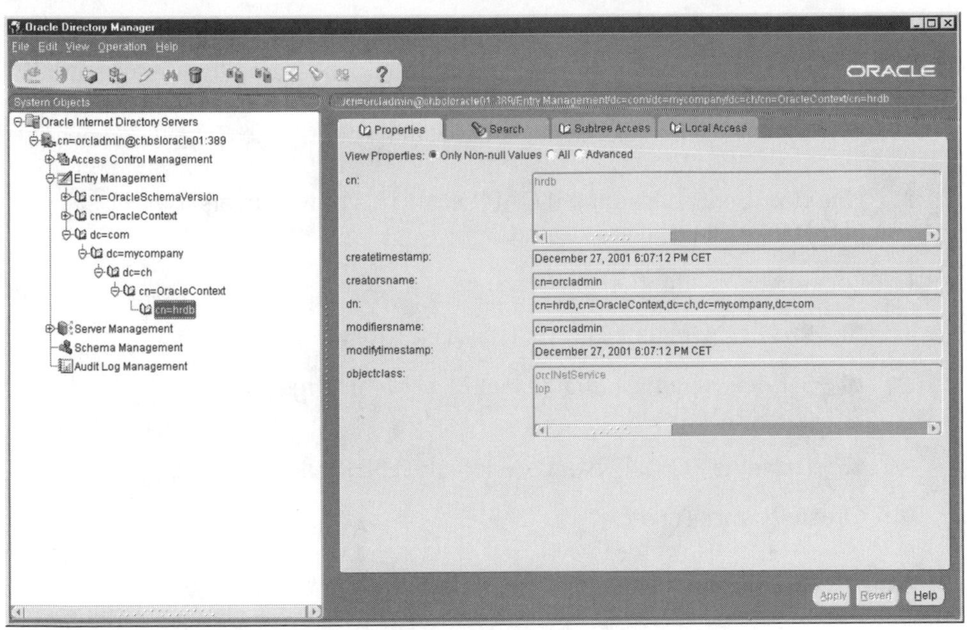

FIGURE 16-6. *Creating a new OID entry*

through the Directory Service Naming feature within Net Manager. For more information about Net Manager, please refer to the next section of this chapter.

Bulk-Loading Existing LDAP Entries into OID

When you initially create your Oracle Internet Directory, you might want to load existing LDAP information instead of typing in all these entries. Besides the migration feature provided for database service names through Oracle Net Manager (see the previous section), you can do this through the bulkload.sh shell script. You also use this script when replicating OIDs. See the "Components in Oracle Internet Directory" section earlier in this chapter for more about the command-line utilities and shell scripts.

For more details about managing OID entries, refer to the "Managing Directory Entries" chapter in the *Oracle Internet Directory Administrator's Guide* and Chapter 11 and Appendix A in the *Oracle9i Net Services Reference Guide*. For more information about how to configure your Oracle Net environment to use LDAP, please refer to Chapters 3, 8, 9, and 10 of the *Oracle9i Net Services Administrator's Guide*.

Net Manager

In addition to the Net Configuration Assistant, which you normally use for initial installation and configuration, Oracle provides you with the Oracle Net Manager. It enables you to configure the following areas within your Oracle Net environment:

- Directory Service Naming (LDAP.ORA). This only appears if the LDAP.ORA file has been found.
- Local net configuration and naming:
  - **Profile** Oracle Net profile (SQLNET.ORA)
  - **Service Naming** Oracle Net local naming resolution (TNSNAMES.ORA)
  - **Listeners** Oracle Net Listener (LISTENER.ORA)
- Oracle Names Server

With Net Manager, you can perform almost any changes without having to manually edit the Oracle Net configuration files. You can also configure Oracle Names Servers using Net Manager. In the following sections, we will concentrate on the Local configuration part as well as the Directory Service Naming within Net Manager. The role of the Oracle Names component is slowly being taken over by the Oracle Internet Directory for centralized security and naming. For more details about Oracle Net configuration, refer to the *Oracle9i Net Services Administrator's Guide* and *Oracle9i Net Services Reference Guide*.

The Net Manager is available from the EM Console, both when connected to an OMS and in standalone mode. To launch Net Manager, choose Tools | Service Management | Oracle Net Manager, or click the Net Manager icon in the Service Management icon group in the left toolbar. In Windows NT or 2000, you can also start Net Manager by selecting Start | Programs | Oracle - *<Oracle Home Name>* | Configuration and Migration Tools | Net Manager. The Oracle Net Manager screen appears with the Directory Service Naming, Local, and Oracle Names Servers entries displayed in the tree. To access the local Oracle Net configuration files, expand the Local entry by clicking the plus sign. Now you have access to the Profile, Service Naming, and Listeners entries, as shown in Figure 16-7.

If the files SQLNET.ORA, TNSNAMES.ORA, and LISTENER.ORA have been located in ORACLE_HOME\network\admin or in the directory specified by the TNS-ADMIN environment variable on your EM client machine. If you want to load configuration files from another location, you can do this by selecting File | Open Network Configuration. The Open Network Configuration dialog box appears, where you can browse to the directory, as shown in Figure 16-8. If you

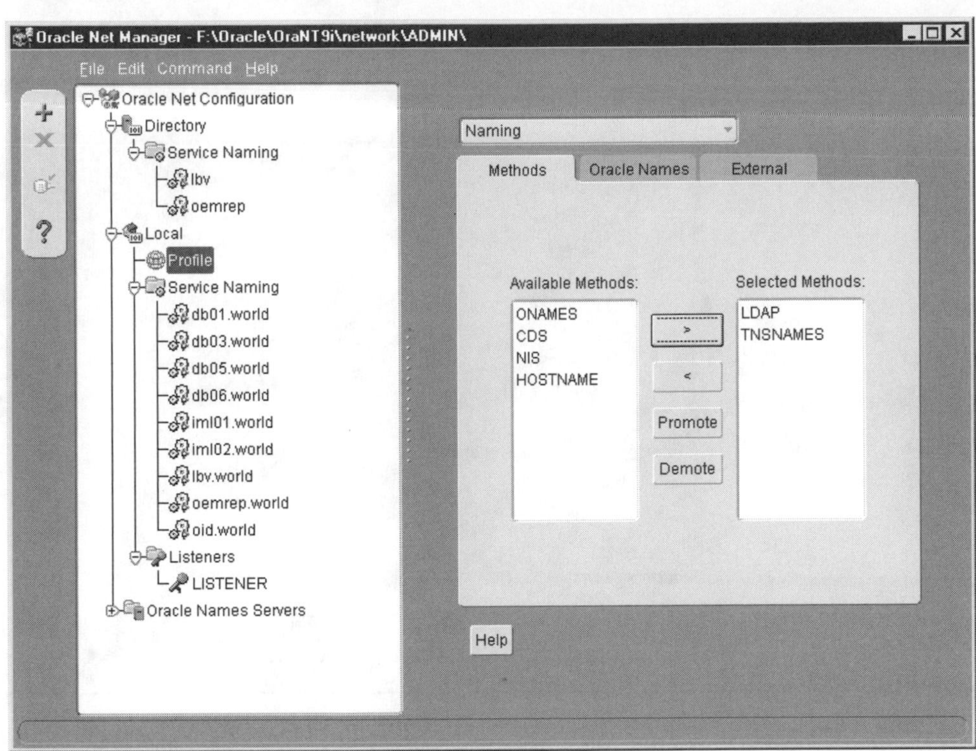

FIGURE 16-7. *The Oracle Net Manager Local configuration entries*

want to browse to a directory on another disk drive, enter the drive letter or path name in the Directory field.

When you modify information through Net Manager, there is no Apply or Save button to press to save your changes. Instead, you must choose File | Save Network Configuration to write the changes to the currently opened configuration files. You can also use File | Save As to store the modified files in another directory. If you have unsaved changes and, for example, you choose to open a new set of configuration files, the Changed Configuration Confirmation dialog box appears to warn you that your changes have not been saved yet. Click Save to save the changes before continuing, Discard to continue without saving your changes, or Cancel to cancel the operation and go back to your current configuration. If you have made changes to your configuration that have not been saved yet, and you want to revert to the state of the last save (or open) operation, you can select File | Revert to Saved Configuration. A confirmation dialog box appears; click Yes to discard any unsaved changes and revert to the latest saved configuration, or click No to cancel the operation and go back to Net Manager.

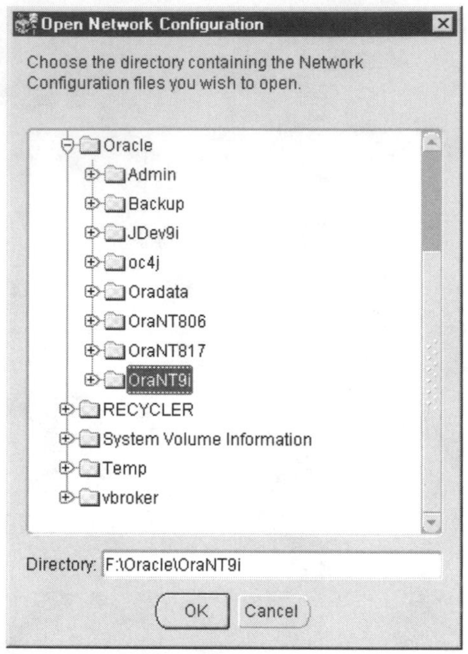

FIGURE 16-8. *Browsing for the network configuration files*

Directory

The Directory entry corresponds to the LDAP.ORA client configuration file used for accessing an Oracle Internet Directory. From here, you can create new entries in your Oracle Internet Directory for your databases, modify them, or delete them. This is much easier than manually entering these entries in Oracle Internet Directory Manager, as explained earlier in this chapter. To access the OID service names, expand the Directory entry in the tree by clicking the plus sign. Then expand the Service Naming entry. The Directory Server Authentication dialog box appears, as shown Figure 16-9.

Enter the distinguished name and password for a user with administrative privileges, such as cn=orcladmin, if you have not yet created other users in your OID. The default password for the orcladmin user is *welcome*. Click OK to log in. You can change your OID login at a later time by choosing Command | Directory | Set Authentication. You can choose an administrative context other than the default one specified in the LDAP.ORA file using the DEFAULT_ADMIN_CONTEXT parameter. You do this by selecting Command | Directory | Change Current Context. For more

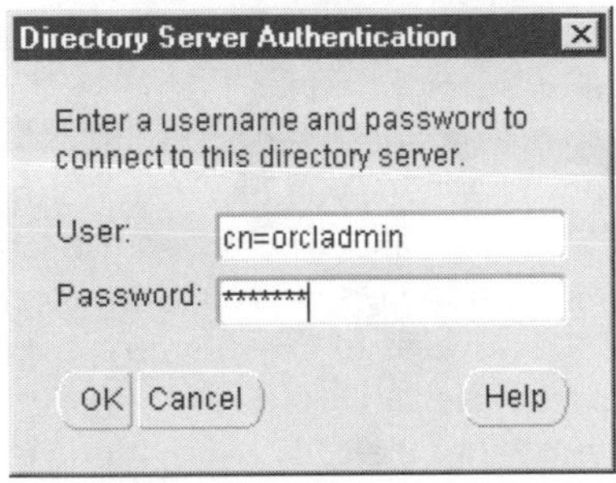

FIGURE 16-9. *Entering a name and password for the server*

information about OID, see the "Launching Oracle Internet Directory Manager" section at the beginning of this chapter.

Creating a New Database Net Service Name Entry

To enter a new net service name in your currently connected OID, select the Service Naming item. Then, either click the Create icon (the green plus sign) in the toolbar or choose Edit | Create. The Net Service Name Wizard is launched and you are placed on the Welcome page. Enter a name to be used for the net service (database) you are adding, such as DB01, and click Next.

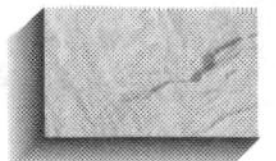

NOTE
You cannot include the domain for the net service name, such as DB01.WORLD, when creating OID entries as you can for normal (local) service names, as described later in this chapter in the "Service Naming" section.

On the Protocol page, you must choose the network protocol you want to use when connecting to the database. For example, choose TCP/IP and click Next. The Protocol Settings page appears. Depending on which protocol you choose, the Protocol Settings page will look different. For TCP/IP connections, you must provide the hostname of the database server as well as the listener port (1521 by default). Then click Next.

On the Service page, you must choose between using the SID or the service name in the connect descriptor for the database service. The "service name" method has been available since Oracle8*i*; use SID if the database is a pre-8*i* version. Also, you must choose whether to force the connection through either a dedicated or shared server process, or to use the default configured for the database and Net Listener. Choose the value from the Connection Type drop-down list box and click Next.

You reach the last page of the Net Service Name Wizard, the Test page. You can perform a test connection to the database service with the Test button. The result is displayed in a separate window, where you also can change the login credentials for the test from the default (SCOTT/TIGER) through the Change Login button. Click Close when you are finished with the test. If you want to change anything, you can use the Back button to step backwards in the different pages of the wizard. Click Finish to store the new entry in the OID. Figure 16-10 shows an example of the DB01 database service entered into the OID using Net Manager and displayed from Oracle Internet Directory Manager.

Exporting Database Net Service Names from TNSNAMES.ORA into OID

You can easily export your existing net service names from a TNSNAMES.ORA file (see the "Service Naming" section later in this chapter) into an OID. To export one or multiple entries from the TNSNAMES.ORA into your currently connected OID, select the Service Naming entry in the Navigator tree. Then choose Command | Directory | Export Net Service Names. The Directory Server Migration Wizard is

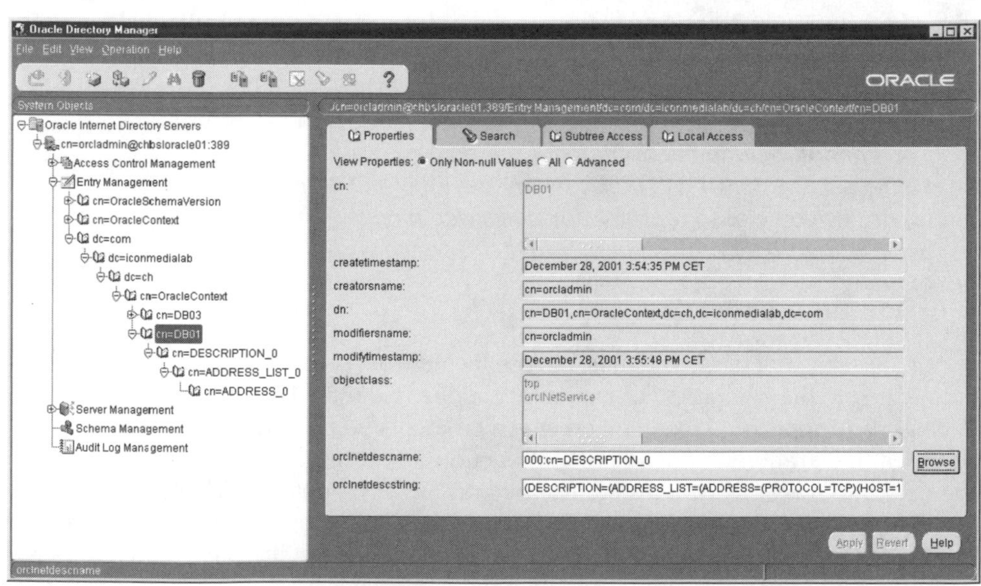

FIGURE 16-10. *The DB01 database entry in Oracle Internet Directory Manager*

launched and you are placed on the Introduction page. Click Next to get to the Select Net Service Names screen. Highlight the net services (databases) you want to export to OID, such as DB05 and DB06, and click Next.

NOTE
Only one domain can be exported at a time, so if your TNSNAMES.ORA file contains net service names with different domains (such as WORLD and YOURCOMPANY.COM), you must repeat the export for each domain.

Next, you are placed on the Select Destination Context page. Select a value from the Directory Naming Context drop-down list, if any are available; otherwise, leave it as is. Then select the administrative context from the Oracle Context drop-down list box, where the exported entries should be stored. An example is shown in Figure 16-11, where the context cn=OracleContext,dc=ch,dc=iconmedialab,dc=com is chosen.

Click Next to begin the Directory Server Update process. When it is finished, a summary screen is displayed, as shown in Figure 16-12.

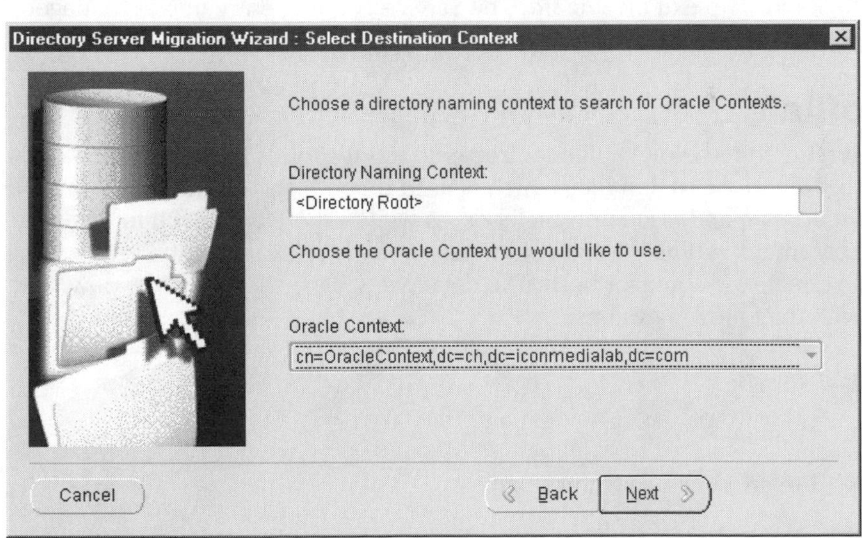

FIGURE 16-11. *Selecting a context for the destination*

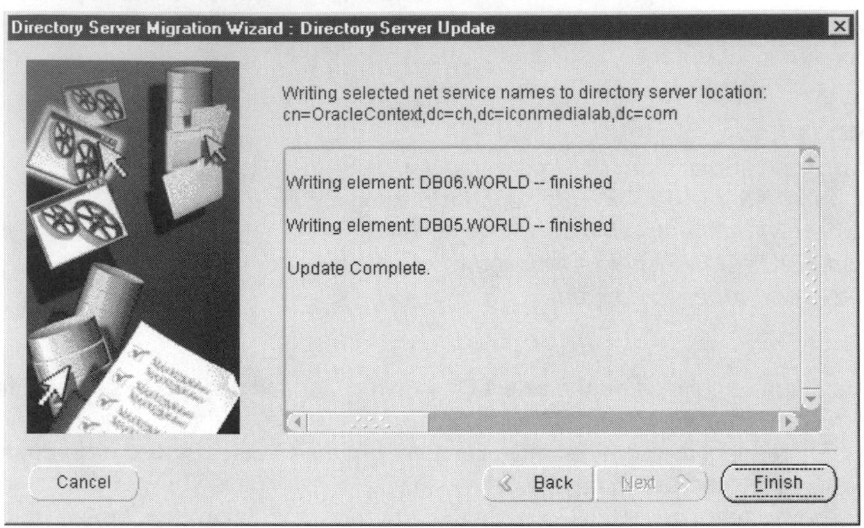

FIGURE 16-12. *Summary for the exported entries*

Click Finish to exit the wizard. The Service Naming entry in Net Manager is refreshed to display the exported entries.

Profile

The Profile entry below the Local tree entry corresponds to the SQLNET.ORA Oracle Net configuration file, which is used on both server and client to define default domain and resolution methods, as well as more advanced tuning and trace parameter settings. Some parameters are only relevant for the server, others for the client, and some for both. The detail view pane shows a drop-down list box with the following values:

- Naming
- General
- Preferred Oracle Names Servers
- Oracle Advanced Security

When you choose a value from the drop-down list box, the detail view pane changes accordingly.

Naming

On the Naming properties page, you find the three tabs and the parameter settings described in the following sections.

Methods Choose this tab to specify which naming methods this client should use, as well as the order of priority when you combine several methods. For example, you can choose to use TNSNAMES as the primary naming resolution method and HOSTNAME as the secondary resolution method (if no entry is found in TNSNAMES.ORA). The parameter that you set through this operation is SQLNET.AUTHENTIFICATION_SERVICES. The following naming methods are available in Net Manager:

- Local naming using a TNSNAMES.ORA file (TNSNAMES).
- Internet Directory naming (LDAP) This is name resolution using an Oracle Internet Directory (OID). See the section about OID earlier in this chapter.
- Oracle Names (ONAMES). This is name resolution through an Oracle Names Server.
- Naming resolution through the hostname adapter (HOSTNAME) On a TCP/IP network, a local hosts file or DNS server (Domain Name Service) is used to resolve the connection descriptor. The host and global database names must be equal and must use default port 1521. In this configuration, the TNSNAMES.ORA file is not used.
- Network Information Service (NIS) NIS is external naming and is Sun Microsystem's own implementation of the *Yellow Pages* (yp) client-server protocol used for distribution of host and usernames between computers in a network.
- Cell Directory Service (CDS) This is external naming and part of Oracle Advanced Security. CDS is the directory service component within the DCE (Distributed Computing Environment) middleware from the Open Group, formerly known as the Open Software Foundation. Refer to the *Oracle9i Advanced Security Administrator's Guide* for more information about configuring CDS in Oracle Net. For more information about DCE and CDS refer to the Open Group Website http://www.opengroup.org/dce.

Oracle Names In addition to the definition of the default domain, the Oracle Names page contains various parameters for configuring Oracle Names.

- **Default Domain (NAMES.DEFAULT_DOMAIN)** This parameter defines the domain from which the client most often looks up name resolution requests. The default domain name specified here is automatically appended to any unqualified database service name.
- **Maximum Wait Each Attempt (NAMES.INITIAL_RETRY_TIMEOUT)** This parameter is used to configure Oracle Names, and determines how much time (in seconds) a client will wait for a response from an Oracle Names server before trying the next server in the preferred servers list (NAMES.PREFERRED_SERVERS).
- **Attempts Per Names Server (NAMES.REQUEST_RETRIES)** This parameter defines the number of retries per Names server in the preferred servers list (NAMES.PREFERRED_SERVERS).
- **Maximum Open Connections (NAMES.MAX_OPEN_CONNECTIONS)** This parameter specifies the maximum number of connections that can be open at the same time.
- **Initial Preallocated Requests (NAMES.MESSAGE_POOL_START_SIZE)** This parameter determines the number of messages initially allocated in the message pool on the client side for message requests.

External On the External page, you configure special parameters used for third-party external naming resolution methods, including the CDS/DCE (Cell Directory Services/Distributed Computing Environment) and NIS (Network Information Service) authentication methods.

- **Cell Name (NAMES.DCE.PREFIX)** This parameter specifies the prefix for the Distributed Computing Environment (DCE) cell name, which is used for name lookups.
- **Meta Map (NAMES.NIS.META_MAP)** This parameter specifies the map file to be used for mapping Network Information Service (NIS) attributes to an NIS map name (the default is sqlnet.maps).

General

The General properties page contains five tabs, which are described in the following sections.

Tracing The Tracing page contains parameters to enable/disable tracing of connections through Oracle Net. The parameters are grouped into two areas of the page:

- **Client Information** Defines trace parameters on the client side of the Oracle Net communication. The parameters are TRACE_LEVEL_CLIENT, TRACE_DIRECTORY_CLIENT, TRACE_FILE_CLIENT, and TRACE_UNIQUE_CLIENT.
- **Server Information** Defines trace parameters on the server side, including TRACE_LEVEL_SERVER, TRACE_DIRECTORY_SERVER, and TRACE_FILE_SERVER.

Logging The Logging page contains parameters for enabling or disabling logging of Oracle Net connections, and the parameters are grouped into two areas of the page:

- **Client Information** Defines the two logging parameters LOG_DIRECTORY_CLIENT and LOG_FILE_CLIENT for logging on the client side of the Oracle Net communication.
- **Server Information** Defines the LOG_DIRECTORY_SERVER server-side logging parameter.

Routing On the Routing page, you can define whether you want to force Oracle Net connections to be dedicated, and if a particular Connection Manager should be used:

- **Always Use Dedicated Server (USE_DEDICATED_SERVER)** When this option is set to ON, connections from this client are forced to use a *dedicated* server process, even if a *shared* server, formerly known as MultiThreaded Server (MTS), has been configured for the server. When using a dedicated server for the connection, each client process is served by one server process in a one-to-one mapping. A shared server is a pool of server processes that serve a large number of users, thereby enabling you to provide database access for thousands or even ten thousands of users. The (SERVER=DEDICATED) instruction is appended automatically to the connect descriptor used for the Oracle Net connection.
- **Prefer Connection Manager Routing (USE_CMAN)** When TRUE, this parameter routes the client to a protocol address for an Oracle Connection Manager.

Access Rights The Access Rights page lets you specify which client machines are explicitly excluded or allowed to perform Oracle Net connections. The following parameters are available:

- **Check TCP/IP client access rights (TCP.VALIDNODE_CHECKING)** Check this check box to enable access control for specified client machines via the two following parameters.
- **Clients excluded from access (TCP.EXCLUDED_NODES)** Enter the hostnames or IP addresses for the clients to be excluded explicitly. You can enter several entries separated with a comma, space, tab, or new line.
- **Clients allowed to access (TCP.INVITED_NODES)** Enter the hostnames or IP addresses for the clients to be granted explicit access. You can enter several entries separated with a comma, space, tab, or new line.

These parameters are relevant for the server-side configuration only.

Advanced On the Advanced page, the following parameters are available:

- **TNS Timeout Value (SQLNET.EXPIRE_TIME)** This is a server-side specific parameter. If it is set to a value other than zero, the *dead connection detection* mechanism is enabled. The value of this parameter determines the time interval (in minutes) between sending a probe to verify that the session is active. Connections that do not respond to this probe signal are automatically disconnected, locks, which might be held are released, and uncommitted transactions are rolled back.
- **Client Registration ID (SQLNET.CLIENT_REGISTRATION)** Set this parameter on the client side to a unique identifier (an alphanumeric string up to 128 characters) for this client. This identifier is passed to the listener with the connection requests and is included in the Audit Trail.
- **Turn Off UNIX Signal Handling (BEQUEATH_DETACH)** Set this parameter to YES to turn on signal handling for Unix systems. On Unix platforms, the Bequeath (BEQ) protocol adapter is the default Oracle Net driver. Setting this parameter to YES will cause the BEQ driver to perform a "double fork" in order to avoid potential problems with signal handling (SIGCHLD) and "wait" code in the client process. What happens is that a process is spawned, which again spawns another process. The "middle" process is terminated and the Oracle shadow process (server-side process for the client connection) becomes "orphaned" and the parent process becomes the "init" process. In the process listing, the Oracle shadow process will be listed with 1 as parent process id (PPID column).

- **Disable Out-of-Band Break (DISABLE_OOB)** This parameter enables Oracle Net to send and receive break messages through the underlying protocol, such as TCP/IP. It is set to YES by default.

Service Naming

The Service Naming entry, found in the Net Manager Navigator tree underneath the Local entry, maintains your local naming definition (TNSNAMES.ORA file), used both on the server and client side. Here you define the net service names, also known as TNS aliases, for all the databases you want to be able to connect to. You can create, modify, and delete net service names from within Net Manager. To access the net service names, expand the Service Naming entry by clicking the plus sign. The existing net service names will be listed in the tree. You can test a certain net service by selecting it in the tree and choose Command | Test Service.

A wizard is available to create a new net service name. Select the Service Naming entry in the tree and either click the Create icon (the green plus sign) in the toolbar or choose Edit | Create from the Edit menu. The Net Service Name Wizard launches and you will be placed on the Welcome screen.

Enter a name for the new net service in the Net Service Name field, such as PROD.WORLD. It can be any name you choose to identify the database service, which allows you to use meaningful names such as SALES, HR, or ACCOUNTING instead of abstract names like such as DB01 and P127. Click Next.

NOTE
Oracle Net Manager does not support the creation of multiple connect descriptors for a net service name.

Continue entering information as described earlier in this chapter in the "Creating a New Database Net Service Name Entry" section.

Listeners

The Listeners entry, found in the Net Manager Navigator tree underneath the Local entry, is used for maintaining your Net Listener configuration (the LISTENER.ORA file) on the server. You can add, modify, and remove listener definitions using Net Manager. The parameters you can modify through Net Manager include:

- General Parameters
- Listening Locations
- Database Services
- Other Services

To create a new listener, select the Listeners entry in the tree and either click the Create icon in the toolbar or choose Edit | Create. The Choose Listener Name dialog box appears. Enter a name for the listener and click OK. Next, add a listener address using the Add Address button. Then continue to modify the listener properties in the detail view pane by choosing the different areas from the drop-down list box. In the following sections, we will take a look at the parameters available when configuring a Net Listener.

General Parameters

The General Parameters page has three tabs (General, Logging, and Tracing and Authentication).

General On the General page, the following parameters are available:

- **Startup Wait Time (STARTUP_WAIT_TIME_<*listener_name*>)** This parameter specifies the number of seconds that the listener will wait before responding to a "start" command issued from the Oracle Net Listener control utility (lsnrctl). In Oracle9i, this parameter has been deprecated. If you enter a value, a dialog box appears with a warning. You can still use this parameter if you need it by clicking Yes.
- **Save Configuration on Shutdown (SAVE_CONFIG_ON_STOP_ <*listener_name*>)** If this parameter is set to TRUE, any changes made by the SET command from the Listener Control utility (LSNRCTL.EXE) are automatically saved upon shutting down the Listener.
- **SNMP Contact Information (SNMP.CONTACT.<*listener_name*> in the SNMP_RW.ORA Intelligent Agent configuration file)** This parameter provides contact information for the specified Listener (*listener_name*); for example, the name, phone, and e-mail address of the responsible DBA or system administrator.

Logging and Tracing The Logging and Tracing page contains the following parameters:

- **Logging Disabled/Enabled (LOGGING_LISTENER)** To enable Listener logging, choose the Tracing Enabled radio button, and enter the path (LOG_DIRECTORY_<listener-name>) and file name (LOG_FILE_<listener-name>) in the Log File field, or use the Browse button to browse to a log file.

- **Tracing Disabled/Enabled (TRACE_LEVEL_<listener-name>)** To enable Listener tracing, choose the Tracing Enabled radio button. Choose the trace level (User, Administrator, or Support) from the Trace Level drop-down list box. Enter the path (TRACE_DIRECTORY_<listener-name>) and file name (TRACE_FILE_<listener-names>) in the Trace File field, or browse to a file using the Browse button.

Authentication On the Authentication page, you can set one parameter:

- **Require a Password for Listener Operations PASSWORDS_ <listener-names>)** Choose this value from the radio-button group and click Change Password to enter the new password to use for the Listener in the Change Password dialog box. The first time you enable a password for a Listener, this dialog box appears automatically. Enter the new password and confirmation and click OK.

Listening Locations

The Listening Locations page contains the protocol and port number that the Listener is supposed to listen on. You add a new address by clicking the Add Address button. Then choose the protocol from the drop-down list box. Depending on which protocol you choose (TCP/IP, TCP/IP with SSL, IPC, or NMP), you may need to enter other parameters. For example, for TCP/IP you must enter the hostname (or IP address) in the Host field, and the port number to listen on (1521 is the default) in the Port field.

The "Statically dedicate this address for JServer connections" check box is used for backward compatibility with version 8.1 to enable GIOP (General Inter-Orb Protocol) endpoints used by the Oracle JVM option. For Oracle9i databases and listeners, endpoints are dynamically configured during service registration and static configuration is therefore not necessary.

You can enter several addresses per Listener. These are then each presented on their own tab (Address1, Address2, and so on). You can remove the currently selected Listener address by clicking the Remove Address button.

Database Services

On the Database Services page, you specify the database service(s) for which the Listener is to handle connect requests using *static* service configuration. As in Oracle8i, *dynamic* service registration is performed to automatically inform the listener about the database service. Pre-8i databases require static service configuration using the SID (System Identifier). In addition, the Intelligent Agent requires static service configuration to automatically discover the databases served by the Listener.

If you are using dynamic service configuration, you do not enter any information on this page.

Click Add Database to add a database service to be handled by the Listener. Next, enter the database name and domain name of the database in the Global Database Name field. This is the same as the value of the SERVICE_NAMES database instance initialization parameter (or DB_NAME and DB_DOMAIN together), such as OEMREP.WORLD. In the Oracle Home Directory field, you can enter the Oracle Home for the database, for example /opt/oracle/ora9i. This is not necessary for databases running Windows NT or 2000. Finally, enter the System Identifier in the SID field, such as OEMREP.

Several entries can exist for one Listener; each is represented by its own tab (Database1, Database2, and so on). Click the Remove Database button to delete the selected Database Service.

Other Services

The Other Services page configures the Listener to handle services other than databases, for example, External Procedure Calls or ODBC data sources via the Heterogeneous Services (HS) feature.

Example of External Procedure Configuration Figure 16-13 shows an example of the external procedure call feature configured in the Listener.

The TNSNAMES.ORA file must contain a corresponding entry, such as:

```
EXTPROC_CONNECTION_DATA.WORLD =
  (DESCRIPTION =
    (ADDRESS_LIST =
      (ADDRESS = (PROTOCOL = IPC)(KEY = EXTPROC))
    )
    (CONNECT_DATA = (SID = PLSExtProc)(PRESENTATION = RO))
  )
```

This enables you to perform callouts from PL/SQL to Dynamic Link Libraries (.DLL) on Windows NT or 2000 and shared libraries (.so) on UNIX.

Example of ODBC Data Source Configuration Figure 16-14 shows an example of the ODBC data source hsodbc configured in the Listener.

The program name entered in the Program Name field (hsodbc) must exist in your ORACLE_HOME\bin directory, for example, HSODBC.EXE. For the ODBC data source to work, you must also configure a TNSNAMES.ORA entry, like this:

```
HSODBC.WORLD =
  (DESCRIPTION=
    (ADDRESS=(PROTOCOL=tcp)(HOST=CHBSLLAVA)(PORT=1521))
    (CONNECT_DATA=(SID=hsodbc))
    (HS=OK)
  )
```

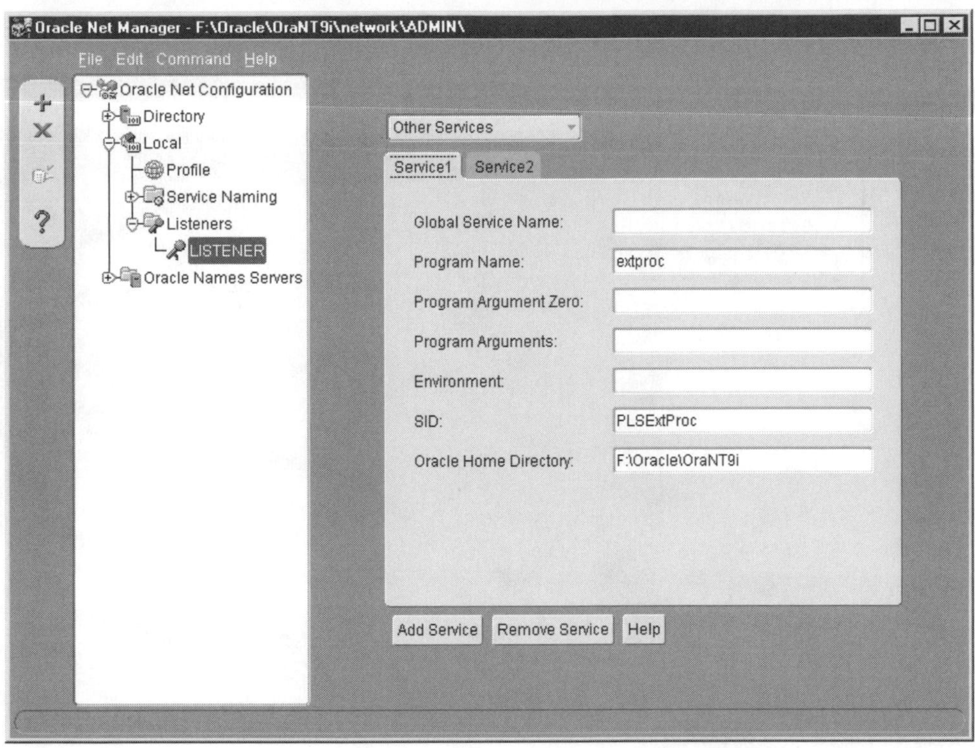

FIGURE 16-13. *Configuring an external procedure call in the Listener*

An ODBC data source of type System DSN must be created to point to the ODBC data source (Microsoft Access or SQL Server database), for example, called HSODBC_SQLSERVER. Edit the configuration file INITHSODBC.ORA located in ORACLE_HOME\HS\ADMIN (notice the name syntax: init<*TNS alias*>.ora) to match the ODBC Data source type, for example:

```
HS_FDS_CONNECT_INFO = HSODBC_SQLSERVER
```

Now you can create a database link in your Oracle database to point to the ODBC data source (SQL Server) like this:

```
create database link hsodbc connect to guest identified by hello using
'hsodbc.world';
```

Now you can select data from the ODBC source through the database link.

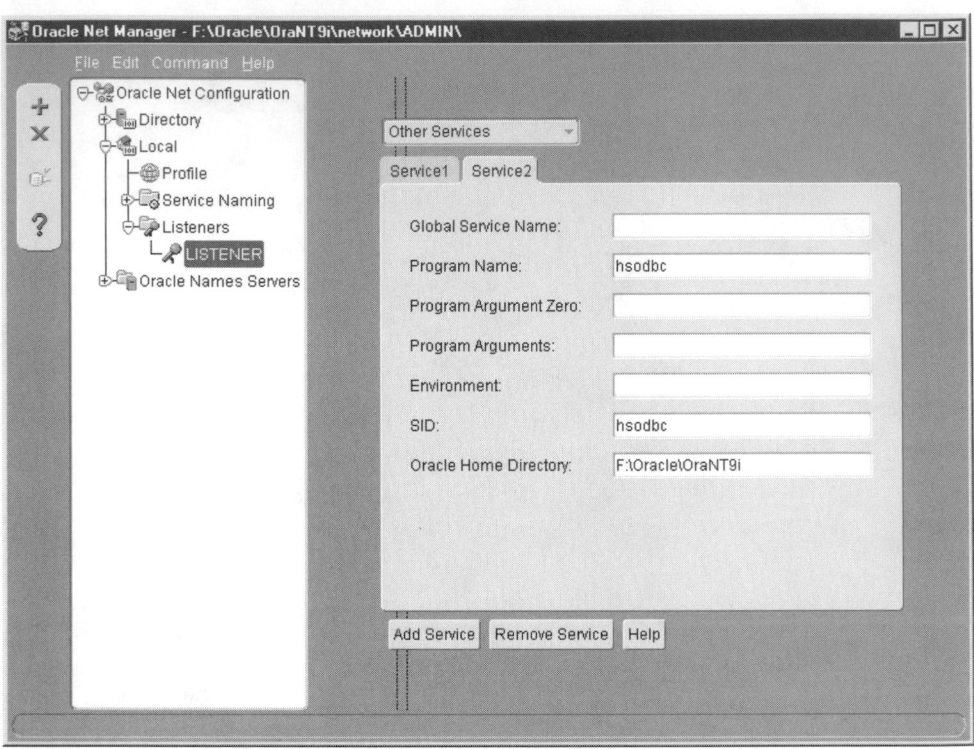

FIGURE 16-14. *Configuring an ODBC data source in the Listener*

Summary

In this chapter, you have been introduced to LDAP and Oracle's implementation of it, called Oracle Internet Directory (OID). You have seen how to install and configure OID, as well as manage its entries through Internet Directory Manager and the Network Configuration Assistant. You have also been introduced to the Net Manager network administration utility, which manages your Oracle Net configuration files, Oracle Names servers, and Oracle Internet Directory servers. In the next chapter, we will take a look at some other nondatabase administrative areas, namely, managing Listeners, Nodes, HTTP Servers, and Real Application Clusters (RAC).

CHAPTER 17

Managing Other Services

In addition to managing and monitoring Oracle databases, you can manage and monitor a range of other target types using EM, as discussed in Chapter 3. In this chapter, we will take a look at some of these other services, including Listeners, HTTP Servers, Nodes, and Real Application Clusters (RAC). Your EM Console must be connected to an OMS to manage these services.

Listeners

The Oracle Net Listener component is required on the Oracle database server to provide remote database connections. Therefore, the availability of this component is crucial for your application to work properly; it can become a single point of failure when running your application or Web server on a node other than the database. You can monitor the Listener process with EM, and try to restart it in case of failure using the EM fix it job feature. The EM job feature, including fix it jobs, is described in Chapter 11, and the EM event system is described in Chapter 12.

To access the discovered listeners, expand the Listeners entry in the Navigator tree view by clicking the plus sign. You can select a particular listener and view its details in the detail view pane (see Figure 17-1).

In the detail view pane, you see the properties for the listener, such as the database(s) being served by this listener, and the listening address information. Click the Listener Status button to request status information about the listener. Figure 17-2 shows the status for the listener named LISTENER running on the Windows 2000 host CHBSLLAVA. Click Close to exit the Listener Status screen.

As you can see in Figure 17-1, the following functions are available for a particular listener, either in the context-sensitive menu or the Object menu:

- **Delete** Removes the listener from the EM repository. This function is also available by pressing the DELETE key. A confirmation dialog box appears; click Yes to delete the listener or No to continue without deleting it. If you choose to delete the listener, and any events or jobs are registered, you will be notified about this and deletion cannot be completed. Deregister all registered events and remove all active jobs for the listener first. See Chapters 11 and 12 for more details about EM Jobs and Events.
- **View Published Reports** Launches the EM Reporting Website and displays the published reports relevant for the listener. For more information about publishing EM reports, refer to Chapter 13.

- **Set Paging/E-mail Blackout** Launches the Paging/E-mail Blackout dialog box. This function is also available by pressing CTRL-B. See Chapter 9 for more details about paging and e-mail blackouts, and how to define them.
- **Set/Unset Total Paging/E-mail Blackout** Enables (Set) or disables (Unset) total paging/e-mail blackout for this particular listener. See Chapter 9 for more information about total paging and e-mail blackouts.
- **Ping Agent** Contacts the Intelligent Agent on the node where the listener is located. See Chapter 8 for more details.
- **Listener Status** Provides status information for the particular listener (the same as executing the STATUS command through the LSNRCTL utility). See Figure 17-2 for an example of output from the listener status request.

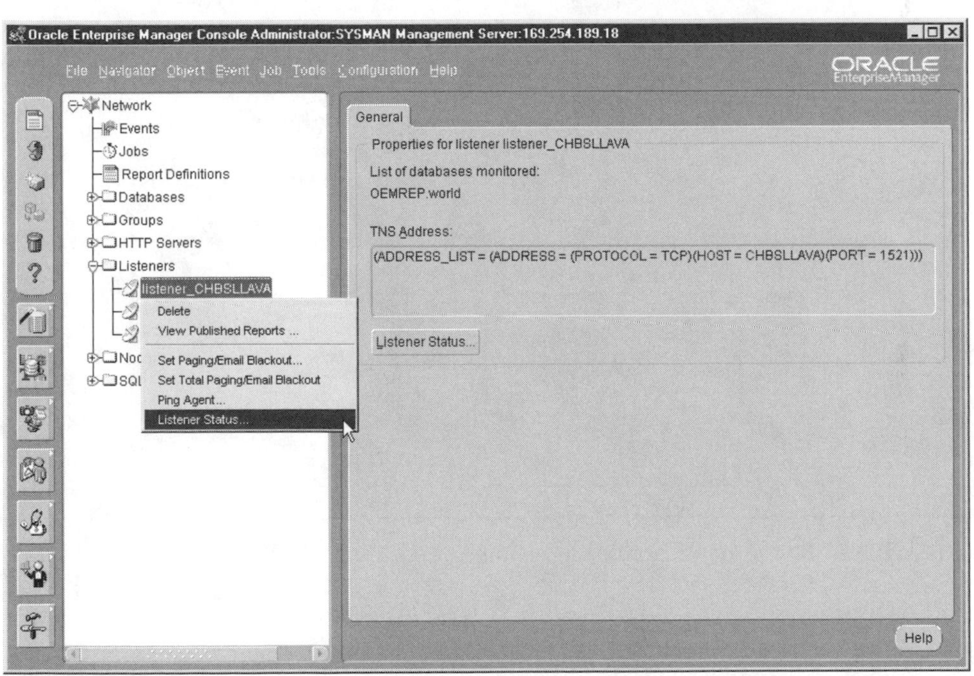

FIGURE 17-1. *The detail view pane for the listener on node CHBSLLAVA*

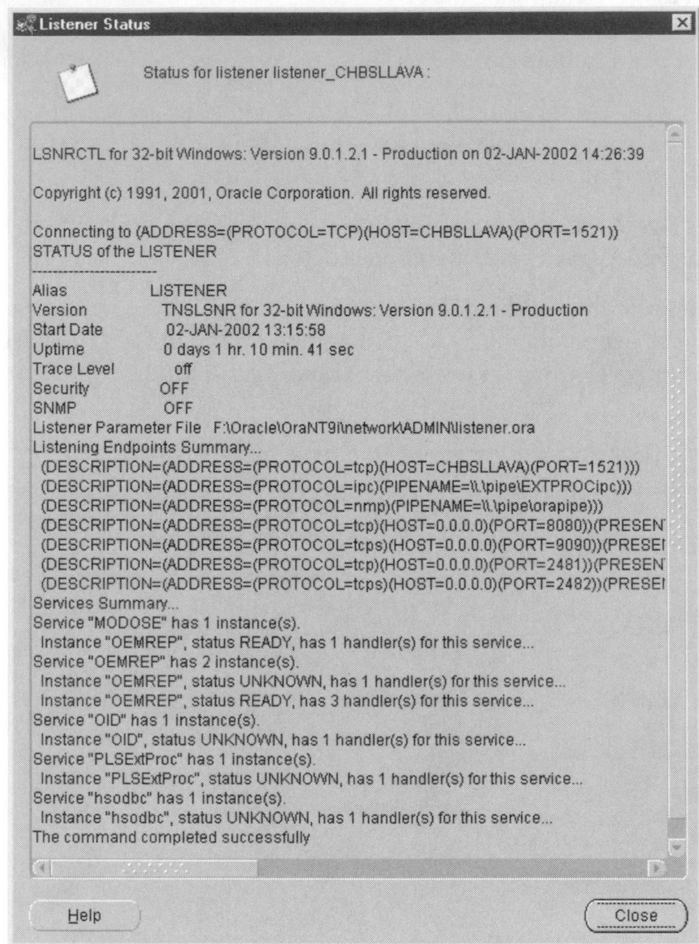

FIGURE 17-2. *Output of the listener status request*

NOTE
If the Listener Status feature does not work (if it returns an error message) when connected to an OMS running on Windows NT or 2000, this might be due to a bug. Try to apply the patch EM_9.0.1_1815492 on the OMS machine to resolve the problem.

HTTP Servers

The HTTP Server is Oracle's Web server, which is based on the Apache Web Server. In addition to serving your Web applications, the HTTP Server can also be used to Web-enable the EM Console and host the EM Reporting Website. In Chapter 18, we describe how to configure the EM Thin Client, and in Chapter 13 we describe the configuration of the EM Reporting Website using an HTTP Server.

You can monitor the HTTP Server in a proactive way and restart it in case of failure using the EM fix-it job feature. The EM job feature is described in Chapter 11 and the EM event feature in Chapter 12.

To access the discovered HTTP Servers in the EM Navigator tree, expand the HTTP Servers entry by clicking the plus sign. You can select a particular HTTP Server and view its status and details in the detail view pane (see Figure 17-3).

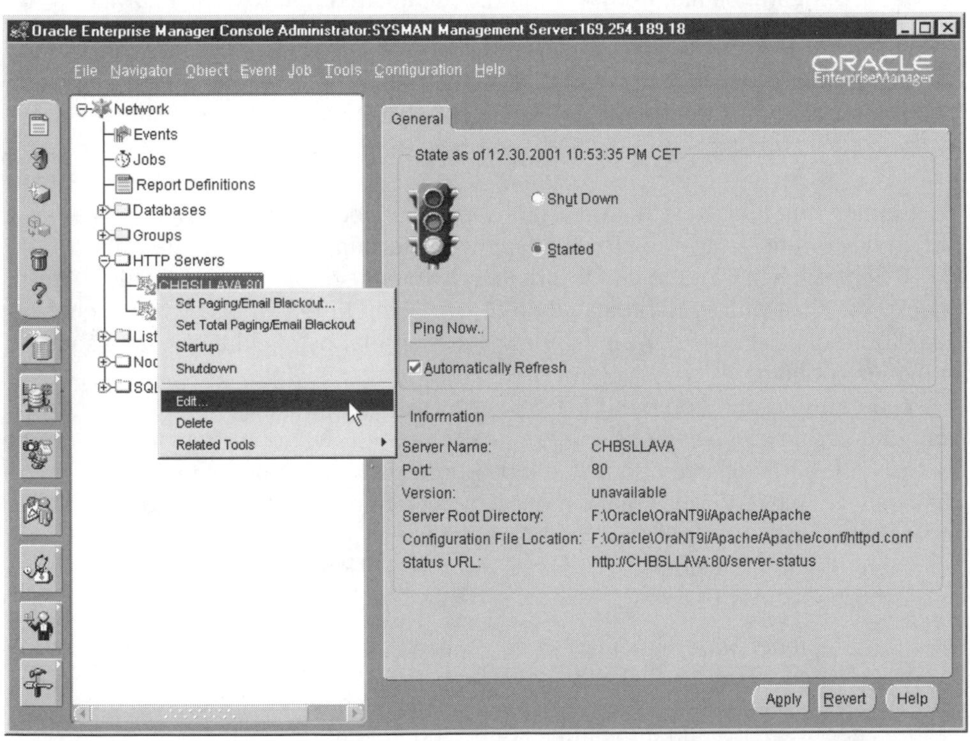

FIGURE 17-3. *The detail view pane for the HTTP Server on node CHBSLLAVA*

On the General page in the detail view pane, you see the status for the HTTP Server illustrated by a traffic light, similar to a database instance. Green means the HTTP Server is running, and red that it is not running. In the bottom of the General page, you see the following HTTP Server details:

- **Server Name** The hostname for the Web server (or the IP address if the server does not have a registered DNS name).
- **Port** The network port on which the HTTP Server is listening (the default is 80).
- **Version** The version number of the HTTP Server.
- **Server Root Directory** The top-level directory for the HTTP Server where configuration, error, and log files are stored.
- **Configuration File Location** The name and path of the HTTP Server configuration file, normally httpd.conf, located in ORACLE_HOME\apache\apache\conf.
- **Status URL** Specification of the URL providing HTTP server statistics, for example, for the HTTP Server on CHBSLLAVA, http:// chbsllava:80/server-status.

Clicking the Ping Now button establishes a connection to the HTTP Server to obtain its current status. A dialog box appears informing you about the status of the HTTP Server; click Close to exit this dialog. If you check the Automatically Refresh check box, the status is automatically refreshed each time you access the General page (but not when you refresh the view, for example, by clicking the Refresh Icon in the left toolbar).

You can start and stop the HTTP Server by selecting the appropriate value in the radio button group and clicking Apply. EM uses its own job system to perform the startup and shutdown operations. A dialog box appears informing you that an EM job has been submitted to perform the requested operation; click OK. You can follow the progress and status of the job in the Jobs detail view pane.

The following functions are available for the HTTP Server from the Object menu or the context-sensitive menu:

- **Set Paging/Email Blackout** Launches the Paging/E-mail Blackout dialog box (also available by pressing CTRL-B). See Chapter 9 for more details about paging and e-mail blackouts, and how to define them.

- **Set/Unset Total Paging/E-mail Blackout** Enables (Set) or disables (Unset) total paging/e-mail blackout for this particular HTTP Server. See Chapter 9 for more information about total paging and e-mail blackouts .
- **Startup** Attempts to start the HTTP Server through an EM job submission.
- **Shutdown** Shuts down the HTTP Server by submitting an EM job. Note that no confirmation dialog appears; the EM job is submitted immediately.
- **Edit** Opens the Edit HTTP Server dialog box, which is the same as the General page in the detail view pane. Click OK or Cancel to exit the dialog box.
- **Delete** Removes the HTTP Server from the EM repository and Navigator tree (also available by pressing the DELETE key). A confirmation dialog box appears. Click Yes to remove the HTTP Server, or No to continue without deleting it. If you choose to delete the HTTP Server, and any events or jobs are registered against it, you will be notified about this and deletion cannot complete. You must deregister all registered events and remove all active jobs for the HTTP Server first. See Chapters 11 and 12 for more details about EM Jobs and Events.
- **Related Tools** This submenu contains the tool: Capacity Planner and Performance Manager, which are part of the EM Diagnostics Pack. See Chapter 7 for more information about the optional EM Management Packs.

Nodes

To access the discovered nodes, expand the Nodes entry in the EM Navigator by clicking the plus sign. Now you can select a particular node and view detailed information about it in the detail view pane (see Figure 17-4).

On the General page, you see the status for the Intelligent Agent on the node illustrated by a traffic light. Green means the Intelligent Agent is running (also indicated by "Up"); red means it is not running (indicated by "Agent Down"). The time of the last agent contact (ping) is also displayed, as well as the version of the Intelligent Agent. Click the Ping Agent button to request a ping of the Intelligent Agent, which contacts the Agent to request current status information. See Chapter 8 for more details about this feature. In the Operating System Information part of the page, the name and version of the OS running on the node are displayed. In the Oracle Home Information part, all Oracle Homes are listed.

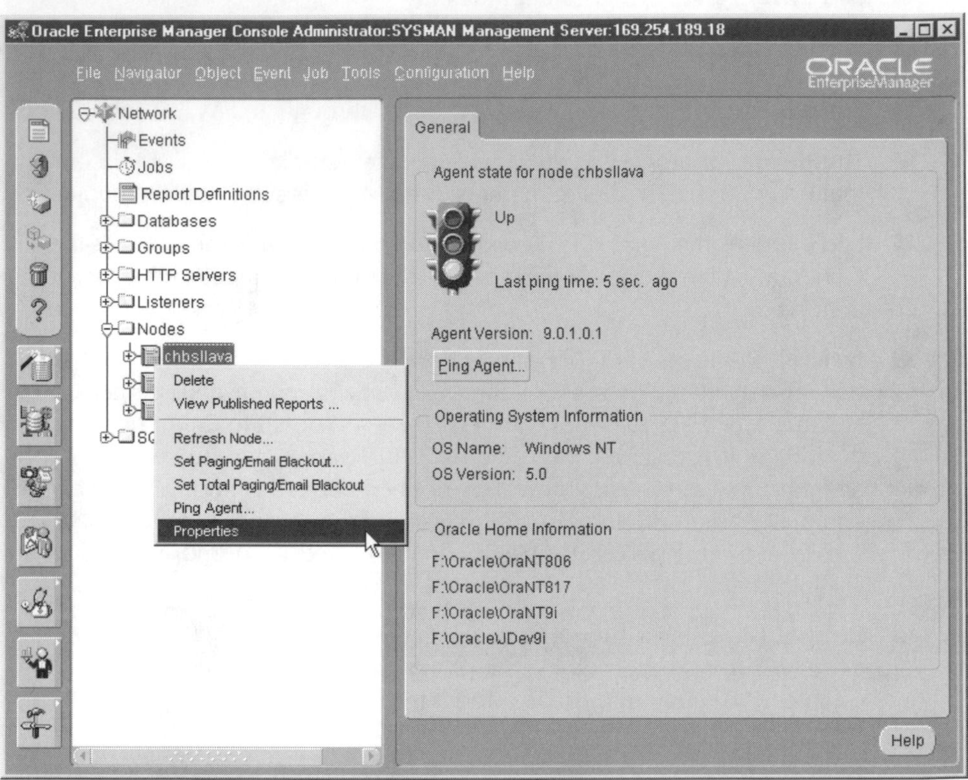

FIGURE 17-4. *The detail view pane for the node CHBSLLAVA*

NOTE
The amount of information displayed on the General page depends on the version of the Intelligent Agent. To provide information about the Oracle Homes on the node, the Intelligent Agent must be of version 9i or later.

As you can see in Figure 17-4, the following functions are available for a particular node from the context-sensitive menu or the Object menu:

- **Delete** Removes the node (and its associated targets) from the EM repository. This function is also available by pressing the DELETE key.

A confirmation dialog box appears; click Yes to continue with deletion, or No to cancel the deletion. If you click Yes, another confirmation dialog appears; click Yes to delete the node or No to continue without deleting it. If any events or jobs are registered for the node or any targets on it, you will be notified about this through the Network Target Removal dialog box, which lists all events and jobs registered against the node. Deletion of the node cannot complete until you have deregistered all registered events and removed all active jobs listed in the Network Target Removal dialog box. See Chapters 11 and 12 for more details about EM Jobs and Events.

NOTE

If the Intelligent Agent cannot be contacted when you have chosen to delete the node from the EM repository, a dialog box appears. It lists the events and jobs registered against the node (or its targets), and provides you with the opportunity to force node deletion by clicking OK. If you choose to do so, and the Intelligent Agent is a pre-9i version, you risk inconsistency between the EM repository and the information on the Intelligent Agent side (jobs/events removed from EM repository, but still present in agent files).

- **View Published Reports** Launches the EM Reporting Website and displays the reports published for the node. See Chapter 13 for more information about publishing EM reports.
- **Refresh Node** Launches the Refresh Wizard, which performs a refresh operation for the node, thereby discovering (new) targets on that node. This is normally used when you have installed or configured additional targets on the node, for example, if you have added a database instance. You can also use this feature if you accidentally deleted one or more targets on the node. See Chapter 8 for more details about the Refresh Wizard.
- **Set Paging/E-mail Blackout** Launches the Paging/E-mail Blackout dialog box. This function is also available by pressing CTRL-B. See Chapter 9 for more details about defining paging and e-mail blackouts.
- **Set/Unset Total Paging/E-mail Blackout** Enables (Set) or disables (Unset) total paging/e-mail blackout for this particular node. See Chapter 9 for more details about total paging and e-mail blackouts.

- **Ping Agent** Contacts the Intelligent Agent on the node to get its current status, which is the same as clicking the Ping Agent button described earlier in this section.
- **Properties** Opens a dialog box displaying the node name, OS type, and version and the Intelligent Agent version. Click OK to close the dialog.

For each node in the Navigator tree, the different target types registered on the node will be listed if they exist on the node. This way you can conveniently work with all targets for a particular node. Figure 17-5 shows an example of the objects available on the node CHBSLLAVA (database, listener, HTTP Server, and SQL Server).

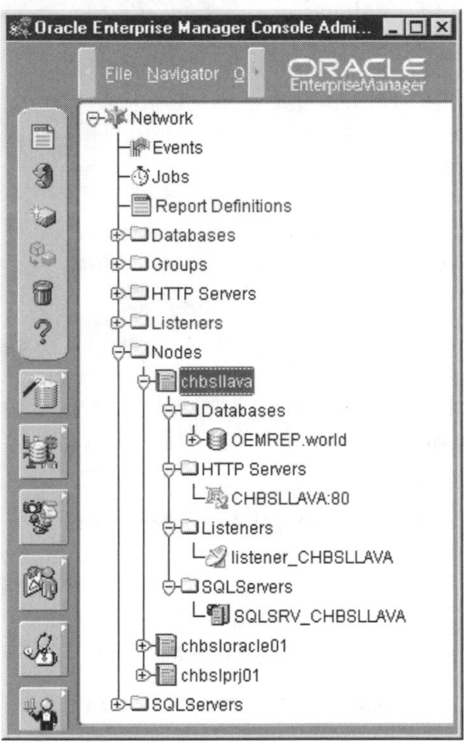

FIGURE 17-5. *Viewing target types on the node CHBSLLAVA*

Real Application Clusters

Oracle Real Application Cluster (RAC), formerly known as Oracle Parallel Server (OPS), is Oracle's database clustering solution. RAC is not just a new 9i marketing name for OPS, but a completely new architecture for handling multiple database instances. The Oracle8i OPS remaining lock contention and pinging for "write-write" situations have been eliminated, so that all operations can be performed through the special Cache Fusion RAC component. Nearly 100 percent scalability can now be accomplished for any application, including legacy applications and enterprise resource planning (ERP) solutions such as SAP, PeopleSoft, and Oracle E-Business Suite, without the need for any data or user partitioning between the instances.

You can manage your RAC clusters through EM, including performing tasks such as starting and stopping the whole cluster, or single instances within the cluster. In addition, you can monitor the cluster and submit jobs against it using EM. In Oracle9i, the OPSCTL command-line utility does not exist any more; it has been replaced by SRVCTL (Server Control Utility), which is used for the following:

- Starting or stopping the whole cluster database
- Starting or stopping individual cluster database instances
- Starting or stopping the listener(s) associated with the cluster database
- Providing status information for cluster databases, instances, and listeners

The SRVCTL process delivers information about the RAC instances to EM and serves as a single point of control between the Intelligent Agent and the cluster nodes. Only one Intelligent Agent communicates with SRVCTL, which in turn communicates with the SRVCTL processes on the other cluster nodes through Oracle Net. Before you can use SRVCTL, the Global Services Daemon (GSD) must be configured and running. Start *one* GSD process on each of the cluster nodes, regardless of how many RAC databases exist on these nodes. For more information about GSD, refer to the *Oracle9i Real Application Clusters Installation and Configuration Guide.*

For a RAC, you will find two different target types in the Create Event and Create Job dialog boxes: Cluster Database (the whole cluster) and Cluster Database Instance (individual cluster instances). Figure 17-6 shows an example of the Create Event dialog box for a cluster target type.

The discovered cluster and its instances appear in the console under the Databases entry, together with the single-instance databases. Expand the Databases entry in the

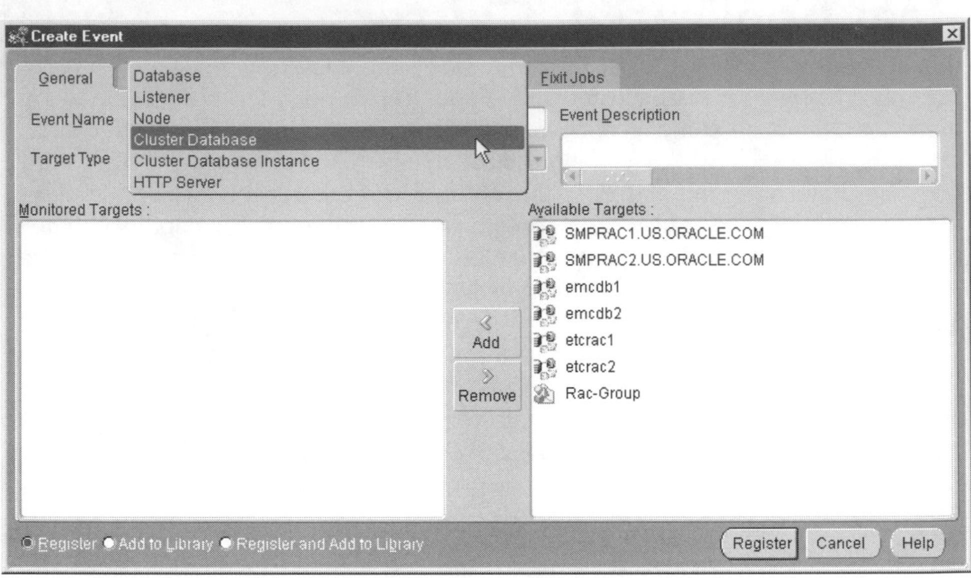

FIGURE 17-6. *Creating an event for a cluster database*

Navigator tree view by clicking the plus sign. You can select a particular cluster (identified by a special icon with a database and three monitors) and view its details in the detail view pane (see Figure 17-7).

For the cluster as a whole, the General page in the detail view pane displays Connection Information and Operating System Information, but no Setup Information (Oracle Home and Listeners) like it does for single instances. In addition, a list of the database instances in the cluster is shown in the bottom of the screen.

Another difference compared to the EM Navigator tree structure for a single instance is that within the Instance entry, the subfolders are split into two functional groups for a cluster:

- **Database-specific information** The entries In-Doubt Transactions and Resource Consumer Groups are for the cluster database as a whole across all participating instances.
- **Instance-specific information** for each single cluster instance is listed under the Cluster Database Instances entry.

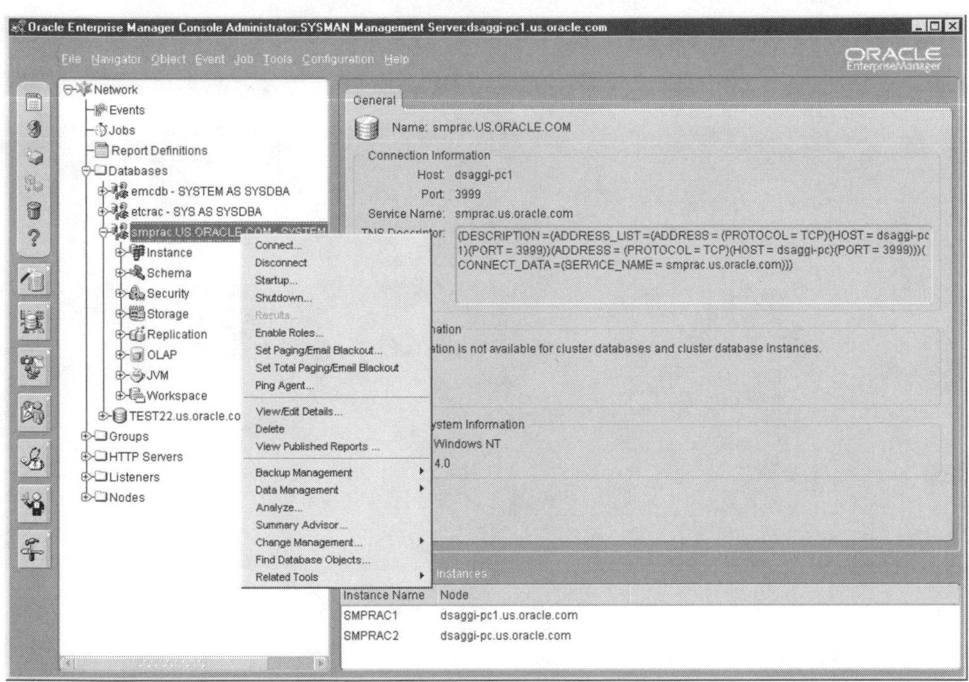

FIGURE 17-7. *An Oracle cluster selected in the EM Navigator*

You can select a particular instance within the cluster and view its details by expanding first the Instance and then the Cluster Database Instances entries below the cluster. The details for a given cluster instance are the same as for other single instances, and the functions available in the pop-up or Object menus are the same. An example of the details for a single cluster instance is shown in Figure 17-8.

From within the EM Console, you can perform various operations on the cluster or individual instances within the cluster. In the pop-up or Object menus for a cluster as a whole, the following functions are available (see Figure 17-7):

- **Connect** Opens the Database Connect Information dialog box. Enter login credentials and click OK to connect to the cluster database.
- **Disconnect** Disconnects from the cluster database.
- **Startup** Starts up the entire cluster database (all involved database instances) or selected instances within the cluster. As with the Shutdown

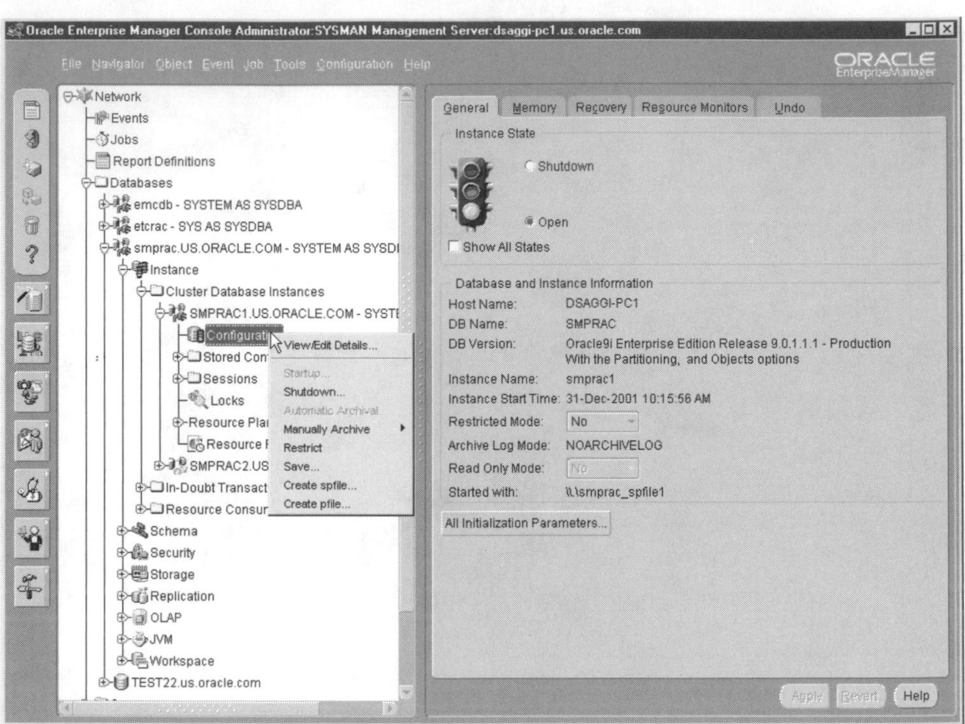

FIGURE 17-8. *Detail view for a cluster database instance*

operation, you can click Select Instances to select particular instances to start. If you do not select particular instances, the instances and the related services (listeners) are started on all of the cluster nodes. Click Startup to initiate the startup operation; the Startup Progress dialog box appears. This dialog box has two available views:

- **Status Details** Displays a table showing the state of the startup operation for selected instances and listeners. Each cell represents the state of a particular cluster database component (Instance or Listener) on a specific cluster node. A blank cell indicates that the component is not configured on the node. A green flag (Up) indicates that the component is running. A red flag (Down) indicates that the component is not running. A timer icon (In Progress) indicates that EM cannot determine the state of the cluster component, which is typically the case when the startup operation has not yet completed.

- **Output** Displays the command executed at the managed cluster node and any other messages during execution of the startup operation.
  You can click Cancel to interrupt the startup operation. Clicking the Hide button removes the Startup Progress dialog box, but does not actually stop the startup operation.

NOTE
After hiding the Startup Progress dialog box, you can view it again by highlighting the cluster database name in the Navigator tree and choosing Progress from the Object or pop-up menus.

- **Shutdown** Shuts down the entire cluster database (all involved instances) or selected instances within the cluster, optionally including all other associated services. The following options are available for the cluster shutdown operation:
  - **Shut Down Database Only** Shuts down the cluster database as a whole (all participating instances), but does not shut down other services, such as listeners.
  - **Shut Down Database And Other Services** Shuts down all the cluster instances as well as the related services (such as listeners).
  - **Select Instances** Use this button to select particular cluster instances to be shut down. If you do not select any particular instances, the entire cluster database is shut down by default. Click Shutdown to begin the shutdown operation. The Shutdown Progress dialog box appears, which is similar to the Startup Progress dialog box described previously. You can click Cancel to cancel the shutdown operation. Clicking the Hide button removes the Shutdown Progress dialog box, but does not stop the shutdown operation.

NOTE
After hiding the Shutdown Progress dialog box, you can view it again by highlighting the cluster database name in the Navigator tree and choosing Progress from the Object or pop-up menus.

- **Results** Displays information about the progress of the instance startup or shutdown operation you have performed. The results are presented in two views: Status Details and Output, as described previously.

- **Enable Roles** Launches the Enable Roles dialog box, which is used to enable roles for the administrator's session. Select the role(s) to enable and click OK. The selected roles are enabled, and the dialog box closes automatically.
- **Set Paging/E-mail Blackout** Launches the Paging/E-mail Blackout dialog. This function is also available by pressing CTRL-B. See Chapter 9 for details about paging and e-mail blackouts, and how to define them.
- **Set/Unset Total Paging/E-mail Blackout** Enables (Set) or disables (Unset) total paging/e-mail blackout for this cluster. See Chapter 9 for more information about total paging and e-mail blackouts.
- **Ping Agent** Contacts the Intelligent Agents on the cluster nodes. See Chapter 8 for more details about pinging the Intelligent Agent.
- **View/Edit Details** Provides information about available database instances within the cluster as well as other associated services (listeners). There are two pages available:
  - **General** Displays the version of the Oracle RDBMS and information about the currently running instances, such as instance number and name, and, if applicable, an indication whether the instance is the Primary or Secondary configuration.
  - **Status Details** Displays the status of instances and listeners for all the nodes configured within the cluster. Notice that this information is only available if all the Intelligent Agents are started on the respective cluster nodes. See Figure 17-9 for an example of the Status Details screen.

  Click Refresh to update the status details. Click Close to close the View/Edit Details dialog.
- **Delete** Removes the cluster from the EM repository. This function is also available by pressing the DELETE key. A confirmation dialog box appears; click Yes to delete or No to continue without deleting. If you choose to delete the cluster, and any events or jobs are registered against it, a dialog box will notify you about this and deletion cannot complete. Deregister all registered events and remove all active jobs for the cluster and/or its individual instances first.
- **View Published Reports** Launches the EM Reporting Website and displays the published reports relevant for the cluster. For more information about publishing EM reports, refer to Chapter 13.

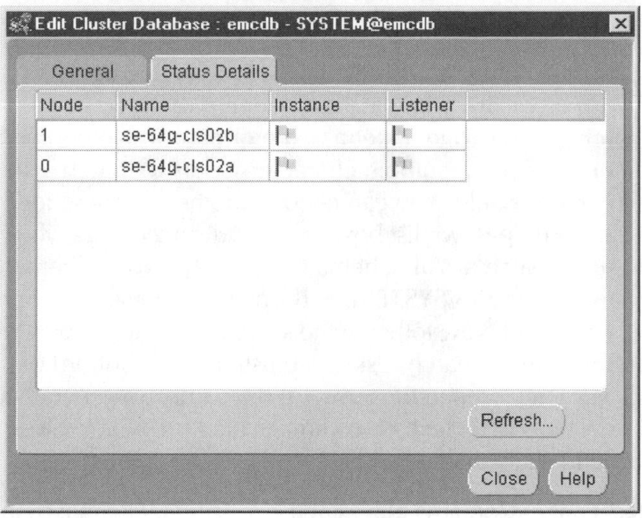

FIGURE 17-9. *Viewing the status details*

- **Backup Management** Provides access to the backup and recovery features available through EM. These include the Backup and Recovery wizards, Catalog Maintenance, Create Backup Configuration, and Backup Configuration Library. Refer to the "Backup Management" section in Chapter 15 for more details about these features.
- **Data Management** This entry contains the three data management features available with EM; Export, Import, and Load (SQL*Loader). Refer to the "Data Management" section in Chapter 15 for more information.
- **Analyze** Launches the Analyze Wizard, which is used to generate statistics for the Cost Based Optimizer (CBO). See the "Analyze Wizard" section in Chapter 15 for more details about this wizard.
- **Summary Advisor** Launches the Summary Advisor Wizard, which can provide recommendations for creating, dropping, or keeping summaries (materialized views), used, for example, in your data warehouse environment. The "Summary Advisor Wizard" section in Chapter 15 describes this wizard in more detail.
- **Change Management** Provides access to the Compare Database Objects and Capture Database Objects functions available with the optional

Change Management Pack. For more details about the Management Packs available with EM, see Chapter 7.

- **Find Database Objects** Launches the Find Database Objects dialog box, where you can search the database for certain objects. You are placed on the Search Criteria page. Enter a name or part of name (use the wild card character * to match multiple characters and ? to match a single character) in the Search For field. You can choose another database for the search from the Database drop-down list box. On the Advanced page, you can set options for the search such as All Schema Objects, All Non-Schema Objects, Any Schema, Exclude SYS/SYSTEM, and Any Object Name or Specified Object Name. Click Find Now to begin the search operation. You can click Interrupt to stop the search. Search results are listed in the bottom of the screen. You can click Report to open the Save List dialog box to generate a list containing the results (in HTML, text, or comma-separated). Click Close to exit the Find Database Objects dialog box.
- **Related Tools** Contains all Database Wizards, Database Applications, and optional Management Packs tools as they also appear in the Tools menu. See Chapter 15 for more information about Database Wizards and Database Applications. For more details about the optional Management Packs, refer to Chapter 7.

As you can see in Figure 17-6, the same functions are available for a single instance within the cluster as for a single instance. See Chapter 14 for more information about instance details and administrative features. For more details about managing a Real Application Cluster, refer to "Administering Real Application Clusters Databases with Oracle Enterprise Manager" in chapter 5 of *Oracle9i Real Application Clusters Administration*.

Summary

This chapter described how to manage some of the other target types which can be managed through EM in addition to Oracle databases. The previous chapter covered managing Oracle Internet Directory and Oracle Net configuration. In this chapter, you have seen how to manage target types such as Oracle Net Listeners, Oracle HTTP Servers, Nodes, and Real Application Clusters (RAC) from the EM Console. The next chapter shows how to run the EM Console from a Web browser, including how to configure your Web server for running the EM Website.

CHAPTER 18

Running EM from a Web Browser

ou can run the EM Console as a thin client from your Web browser. The EM Console is a Java applet, which is a piece of Java code that is downloaded to the client and then executed in a Java Virtual Machine (JVM). The original promise of Java applets was that any applet would run on any browser; unfortunately, reality falls somewhat short of this promise: Some browsers support only an old version of the Java language, and the latest Microsoft browser (version 6.0 at the time of this writing) does not have a JVM included; you must download this as a plug-in.

Oracle has solved this problem by making the EM Console ask for a specific JVM to run in. The EM Console applet thus does not use any available Java support in your browser, but instead checks to see if you have the JInitiator Java plug-in installed.

The EM Console can only run on browsers and platforms where JInitiator is available—currently, this means MS Internet Explorer or Netscape Navigator, but only on Windows platforms (Windows NT, 2000, and 98) because JInitiator is only available on these platforms. JInitiator is described later in this chapter.

The Web browser versions supported are Netscape Navigator 4.7 and later and Microsoft Internet Explorer (IE) 5.0 and later. Running IE from an Active Desktop is not supported for the EM Console. You can also configure the Web server on Unix to provide the EM Website, but you can't run the client on this OMS .

Confirm that the Enterprise Manager Website has been installed on the Management Server machine. By default, it is installed during the Management Server (OMS) installation in the same directory as the OMS. Refer to Chapter 2 for more information about installing the OMS component.

Restrictions for the EM Thin Client

The following EM applications are not Web-enabled and cannot be used with the EM thin client:

- Oracle Diagnostics Pack
  - Oracle Capacity Planner
  - Oracle Trace Data Viewer
- Oracle Tuning Pack
  - Oracle Expert
  - Oracle Index Tuning Wizard
  - Oracle SQL Analyze

- Integrated Applications
  - Oracle Directory Manager
  - Oracle Net Manager

These tools do not appear in the icon tool drawers or the Tools, Objects, or pop-up menus, as they do for the fat-client version of the EM Console.

Configuring Your Web Server for EM

To Web-enable your EM Console, you first need a Web server. You can configure the following Web servers to run the EM Website:

- Oracle Internet Application Server (9iAS) HTTP Server, release 1.0 and higher on Intel Solaris, Sun SPARC Solaris, HP-UX, IBM AIX, Compaq Tru64, Linux, and Windows NT or 2000
- Apache Web Server, release 1.3.9 and higher on Sun SPARC Solaris and Windows NT or 2000
- Microsoft Internet Information Server (IIS), release 4.0 and higher, on Windows NT or 2000

A preconfigured Oracle HTTP Server is included with the EM Website installation to act as its Web server. Configuring Web servers other than the HTTP Server requires additional manual configuration. Further, the EM Reporting Website is not supported on Web servers other than the Oracle HTTP Server. We recommend using the HTTP Server, which is delivered out of the box and ready to use. In the following sections, we describe how to configure all three different Web servers to run the EM thin client. The EM Reporting Website is not described, because it is only supported with the Oracle HTTP Server, as you'll see in Chapter 13.

Configuring Oracle HTTP Server

As mentioned before, using the HTTP Server with the EM Website is easy and recommended. The Oracle HTTP Server is based on the Apache Web server (see later in this chapter). No special configuration is required to configure the HTTP Server to launch the EM Website. When installing the Oracle Management Server component, both the EM Website and the HTTP Server are installed and configured automatically, by default.

The EM Web server configuration script is located in the directory on the Management Server machine. This file is included in the file located in the directory, using the include statement. For example, for the Oracle Home F:\Oracle\OraNT9i, use the following:

```
include "F:\Oracle\OraNT9i/oem_webstage/oem.conf"
```

The oracle_apache.conf file is then included in the httpd.conf HTTP Server (Apache) configuration file located in the same directory. You can also include the "oem.conf" file directly in the "httpd.conf" file, but be sure not to include it twice.

Verify that this configuration has been performed and that the HTTP Server is running. You can start it either from the service control panel, or by selecting Start | Programs | Oracle - <Your Oracle Home> | Oracle HTTP Server | Start HTTP Server powered by Apache. On Unix, use the command-line interface apachectl start | stop, located in $ORACLE_HOME/Apache/Apache/bin. To stop the server, use:

```
apachectl stop
```

To start the HTTP Server, use:

```
apachectl start
```

Launch the EM Website by following the instructions provided in the "Launching the EM Website" section at the end of this chapter.

Configuring Microsoft Internet Information Server

To configure Microsoft Internet Information Server (IIS) to run the EM Website, either install the EM Website without the Oracle HTTP Server, or be sure the Oracle HTTP Server service is stopped in order to avoid any port conflicts. Install IIS, at least version 4.0. Consult your Windows and IIS-specific configuration documentation for more detailed installation and configuration information.

The following steps show how to configure IIS version 5.0 installed on a Windows 2000 Professional machine. To use EM with IIS, you will need to create three virtual directories pointing to the oem_webstage directory and two subdirectories inside of that directory.

1. Select Start | Programs | Administrative Tools | Internet Services Manager. The Microsoft Internet Service Manager screen is displayed, as shown in Figure 18-1.

2. Expand the navigator tree for the host name (in Figure 18-1, it is CHBSLLAVA) entry by clicking the plus sign. Select the Default Web Site item and choose Action | Properties. You can also right-click on Default

Web Site to display the pop-up menu, and choose Properties. The Properties sheet of the IIS Default Web Site appears. Verify that the IP address for the Web server is correctly defined in the IP Address field, which it normally should be after the IIS installation. Then click OK.

3. Define a virtual directory below the Default Web Site entry by selecting New | Virtual Directory from the pop-up menu or from the Action menu.

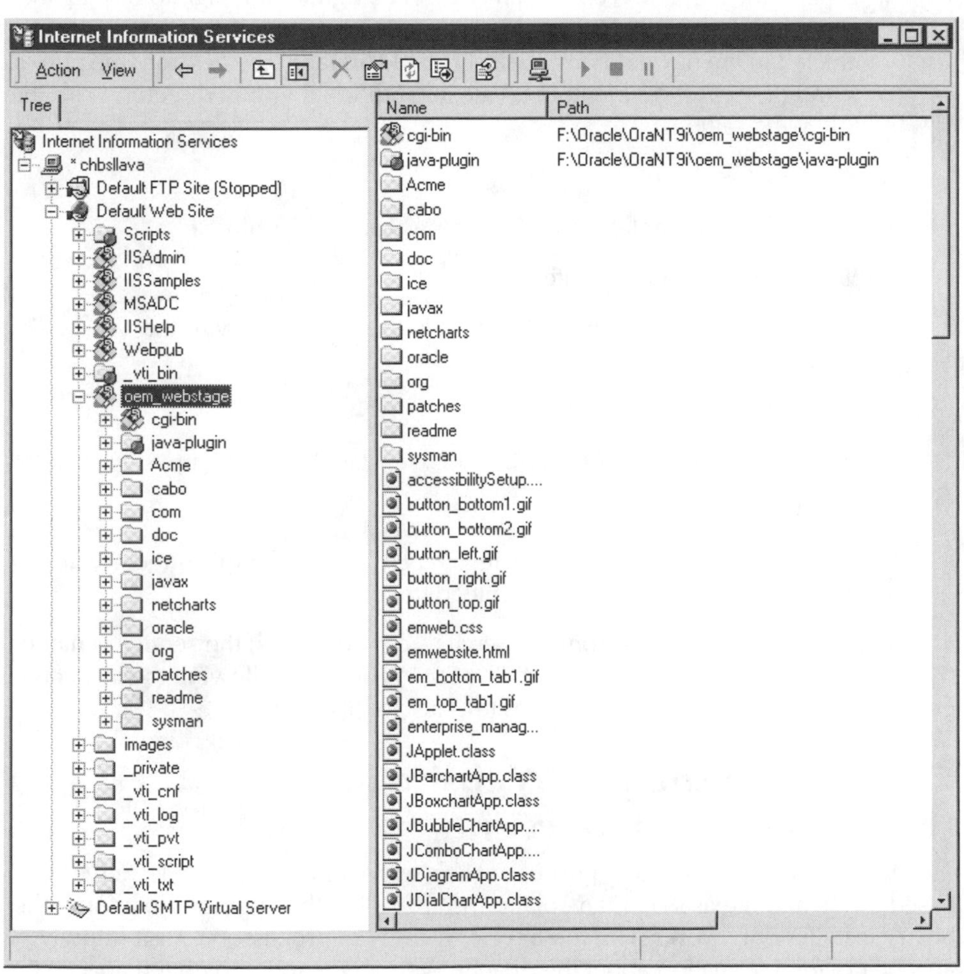

FIGURE 18-1. *EM Virtual Directories in MS Internet Service Manager*

The Virtual Directory Creation Wizard launches. Specify the following settings (Note: This example is for the F:\Oracle\OraNT9i Oracle Home; replace this path with your own Oracle Home):

- **Alias** oem_webstage
- **Path** F:\Oracle\OraNT9i\oem_webstage
- **Access** Read, Execute

4. Expand the Default Web Site entry by clicking the plus sign to display the new virtual directory. Select the oem_webstage virtual directory you just created in the navigator tree. Select New | Virtual Directory from the pop-up menu or the Action menu to create an additional virtual directory with the following settings:

   - **Alias** cgi-bin
   - **Path** F:\Oracle\OraNT9i\oem_webstage\cgi-bin
   - **Access** Read, Execute

5. Create an additional virtual directory in the same way with the following settings:

   - **Alias** java-plugin
   - **Path** F:\Oracle\OraNT9i\oem_webstage\java-plugin
   - **Access** Read-only

   Make sure you do not enable execute permissions for this directory; if you do, you will not be able to download the plug-in.

Restart the IIS Web server from the Services control panel; the service is named IIS Admin Service. Now you can launch the EM Website by following the instructions in the section "Launching the EM Website" later in this chapter.

Configuring the EM Website for the Apache Web Server

The Apache Web server is the most used Web server (the Oracle HTTP Server is based on it), and it exists on many platforms, including the Windows platform (the binary installer only works with the Intel *x*86 family of processors). Visit http://www.apache.org for information about the Apache Web server and http://httpd.apache.org to download the latest version.

The following steps show you how to configure Apache on Windows 2000, but the configuration on Unix is similar. To install Apache on Windows, download the apache_1.3.22-win32-x86.exe file. Execute the file and follow the installation instructions (supply domain name, Web server name, and contact info).

NOTE
When you are using Windows NT 4.0, either service pack 3 or 6 is recommended. Service pack 4 introduced known issues with TCP/IP and winsock integrity that were resolved in SP 5 and later. Also, you need the Microsoft Installer version 1.10 installed (which already exists on Windows 2000), before you can install the Apache runtime distributions. For more information about Apache on Windows platforms, see http://httpd.apache .org/docs/ windows.html.

After the installation on Windows, you should have a service called Apache, which should be running. You can test your installation by entering http://*<Web server name>* in your Web browser, which should launch the Test Page for Apache Installation. You can also test the syntax of the Apache configuration file httpd.conf by using the Apache Test Configuration program, located at Start | Programs | Apache HTTP Server | Configure Apache Server | Test Configuration. This test should respond with a Syntax OK message.

Be sure you have installed the EM Website on the OMS machine (located in the ORACLE_HOME\oem_webstage directory). To install it, follow the steps described in the "Installing the Management Server Only" section in Chapter 2. If the Oracle HTTP Server is installed, you should make sure it is stopped before configuring another Web server.

To configure the Apache Web server to access the EM Website, follow these steps:

1. Edit the httpd.conf file located in the conf directory of your Apache installation, such as C:\PROGRAM FILES\APACHE GROUP\APACHE\CONF, by performing the following changes (our ORACLE_HOME is F:\Oracle\OraNT9i, replace it with your Oracle Home):

   - Add a ScriptAlias entry to control which directories contain server scripts. Note that the forward slash character is used also for path specifications on Windows.

     ```
     ScriptAlias /oem_webstage/cgi-bin/
     "F:\Oracle\OraNT9i/oem_webstage/cgi-bin/"
     ```

- Add the following alias to point to the oem_webstage directory:

```
Alias /oem_webstage/ "F:\Oracle\OraNT9i/oem_webstage/"
```

NOTE
You can add as many aliases as you want. The format is alias <aliasname> <actualname>. *If you add a trailing forward slash character (/) for* aliasname, *the Web server requires it to be present in the URL. For example, /oem_webstage is not aliased; /oem_webstage/ is aliased. The ScriptAliases are similar to Aliases, except that documents in the* actualname *directory are treated as applications and run by the Web server, instead of being sent to the client as a document.*

- Change the entry <Directory "C:/Program Files/Apache Group/Apache/cgi-bin"> to the following:

```
<Directory "F:\Oracle\OraNT9i/oem_webstage/cgi-bin">
    AllowOverride all
    Allow from all
</Directory>
```

- The EM Web server configuration script oem.conf is located in the ORACLE_HOME\OEM_WEBSTAGE directory on the Management Server machine. Include the oem.conf file in the httpd.conf file using the include statement:

```
include "F:\Oracle\OraNT9i/oem_webstage/oem.conf"
```

2. Edit the oem.conf file located in the ORACLE_HOME\OEM_WEBSTAGE directory on the Management Server machine:

   - Change the line "ApJServMount /em /oemreporting" to the following:

```
<IfModule mod_jserv.c>
ApJServMount /em /oemreporting
</IfModule>
```

3. Restart the Apache Web server. You can start it either from the service control panel or using the Stop and Start commands from Start | Programs | Apache HTTP Server | Control Apache Server | Stop or Start. On Unix platforms, use the APACHECTL command-line utility (apachectl stop and apachectl start).

Verify that the Apache Web server is running. You can now launch the EM Website by following the instructions in the following section.

Launching the EM Website

The EM Website is the main page for the EM thin client. When you are using the Oracle HTTP or Apache server, you start your Web browser and enter the following URL to access the EM Website:

```
http://<Web server hostname>:<port number>
```

Or when using IIS, you enter this URL:

```
http://<Web server hostname>/oem_webstage/emwebsite.html
```

Web server hostname is the name (or IP address) of the Web server and *port number* is the port number configured for EM (the default is 3339 for a preconfigured HTTP Server). For example, to access the EM Website on the host CHBSLLAVA, using the default port number 3339, you enter http://chbsllava:3339

The EM Website appears, presenting you with the following options:

- Launch the Oracle Enterprise Manager Console
- Access Oracle Enterprise Manager Reports
- Information (Documentation, Release Notes, and Quick Tour)
- Useful Links (Web resources, Download Plug-in, and Accessibility Setup)

Figure 18-2 shows an example of the EM Website main page.

To launch the EM Reporting Website from the EM Website, enter the hostname (or IP address) for the Web server configured to handle the EM Reporting Home Page in the Reporting Web Server field and the port number (if different from the default 3339) in the Port field. The EM Reporting Home Page launches in a new browser window. You can also launch the EM Reporting Website from the EM Console while connected to an OMS. For more about configuring and using the EM reporting framework, refer to Chapter 13.

The JInitiator Plug-in

As mentioned earlier, the EM thin client is only available on Windows platforms through the required JInitiator Java plug-in. A *plug-in* is a piece of code that works together with your browser to offer additional capabilities. For example, you might

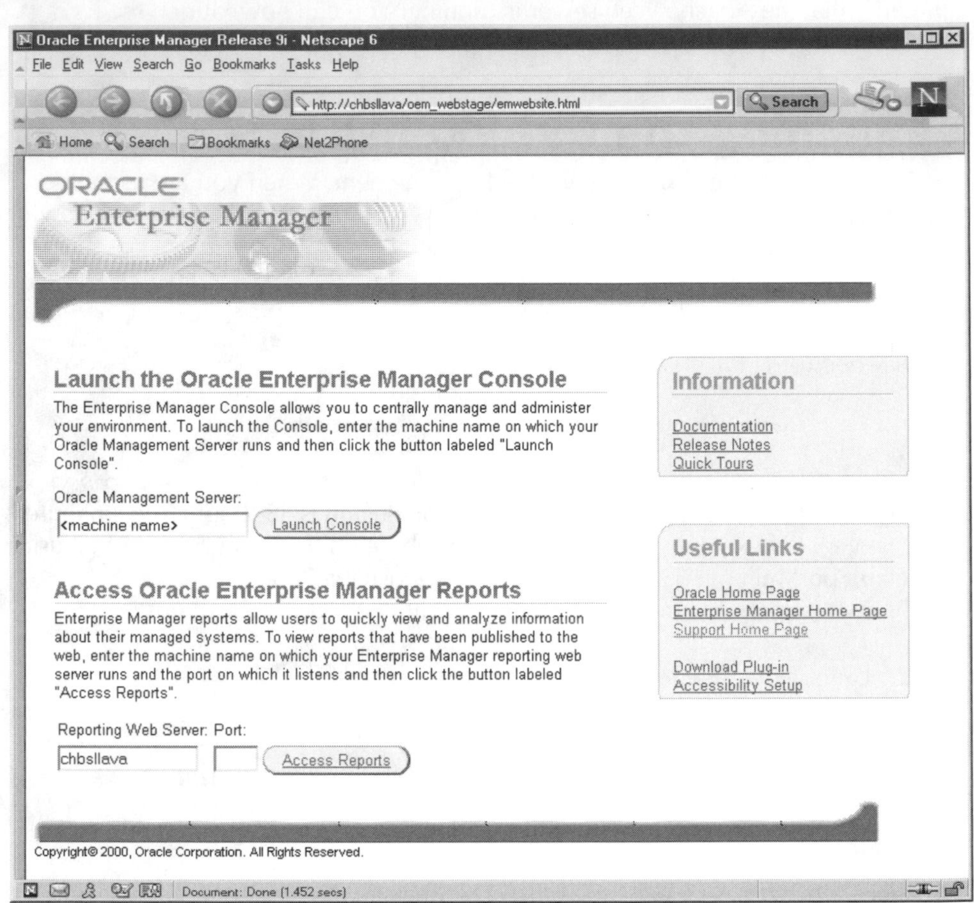

FIGURE 18-2. *The EM Website main page on the host CHBSLLAVA*

download and install the Flash Player plug-in to be able to see animations on some Web sites.

Oracle JInitiator is a Java Virtual Machine as a browser plug-in (Oracle's own version of JavaSoft's Java plug-in). Through JInitiator, you can specify the use of a specific JVM on Web clients, rather than using the Web browser's default, JVM. Oracle JInitiator is implemented for the Netscape Navigator browser as a plug-in, and for Internet Explorer as an ActiveX component.

You must install the JInitiator plug-in on the client PC before you can launch the thin client version of the EM Console. Oracle supplies the JInitiator plug-in free of charge with base EM. If you have disabled execution of ActiveX components in your IE browser, the plug-in cannot install automatically. When using Netscape Navigator, a prompt appears enabling you to perform the plug-in installation.

Click the Get the Plug-in button. You will be placed on the Download and Install Oracle JInitiator page. Click the Download Plug-in hyperlink to install the JInitiator plug-in.

NOTE
If you choose exit or cancel in Netscape Navigator browser from the plug-in installation dialog box, the prompt does not reappear. To obtain the plug-in again, go to the URL specified in the following list.

You can also perform the plug-installation manually in the following ways:

- Click the Download Plug-in hyperlink in the EM Website (see Figure 18-2). The Download and Install Oracle JInitiator page appears. Click the Download Plug-in hyperlink and choose either to execute (Open) the executable or Save it on another location on your disk, from which you run it.
- Enter the URL http://<*Web server hostname*>/oem_webstage/java-plugin/install_win32.html and click the Download Plug-in hyperlink on the Download and Install Oracle JInitiator page.
- Execute the jinit11810.exe executable in the ORACLE_HOME\ oem_webstage\java-plugin directory.

Launching the EM Console in Your Web Browser

To launch the EM Console for a certain Management Server from the EM Website (Figure 18-2), enter the hostname of the Management Server machine in the Oracle Management Server field and click Launch Console. If you are launching the EM Console from your Web browser for the first time after having downloaded and installed the JInitiator plug-in, a pop-up appears. This pop-up shows the progress of the applet download. This applet is cached by your browser and is not downloaded again the next time you launch the EM thin client.

1. The Console applet is opened in a separate (normally small) browser window.

2. The EM Console Login dialog box appears, where you can enter your EM administrator credentials.

3. Click OK to log in, and the EM Console appears.

NOTE
Do not close the Console applet window. If you do, the EM Console will be closed, too.

Launching the EM Console Thin Client Directly Against a Specific OMS

You can also launch the EM Console directly by providing the URL http://<*Web server*>/oem_webstage/cgi-bin/oemapp_cgi.exe?console@<*oms host name*>, where <*Web server*> is the hostname (or IP address) of the machine running the Web server and <*oms host name*> is the hostname (or IP address) of the machine running the Management Server you want to connect to.

For more information about the EM thin client, refer to "Running Enterprise Manager from a Web Browser" in Chapter 5 of the *Oracle Enterprise Manager Configuration Guide*. For information about how to troubleshoot the EM Website, refer to Chapter 20.

Summary

In this chapter, you learned how to configure the EM Website for the Apache Web server, the Oracle HTTP Server (Apache-based), and the MS Internet Information Server (IIS). We recommend using the preconfigured Oracle HTTP Server for the EM Website, but we have included the two other Web servers, if you have special reasons for using these. You also learned how to configure the EM thin client, which enables you to run the EM Console from your Web browser. Further, you learned which restrictions exist for the EM thin client compared to the fat client version of the EM Console. This chapter is the last chapter in Part III providing you with hands-on information for EM. The next part contains information concerning configuration files and command-line utilities as well as how to troubleshoot your EM environment.

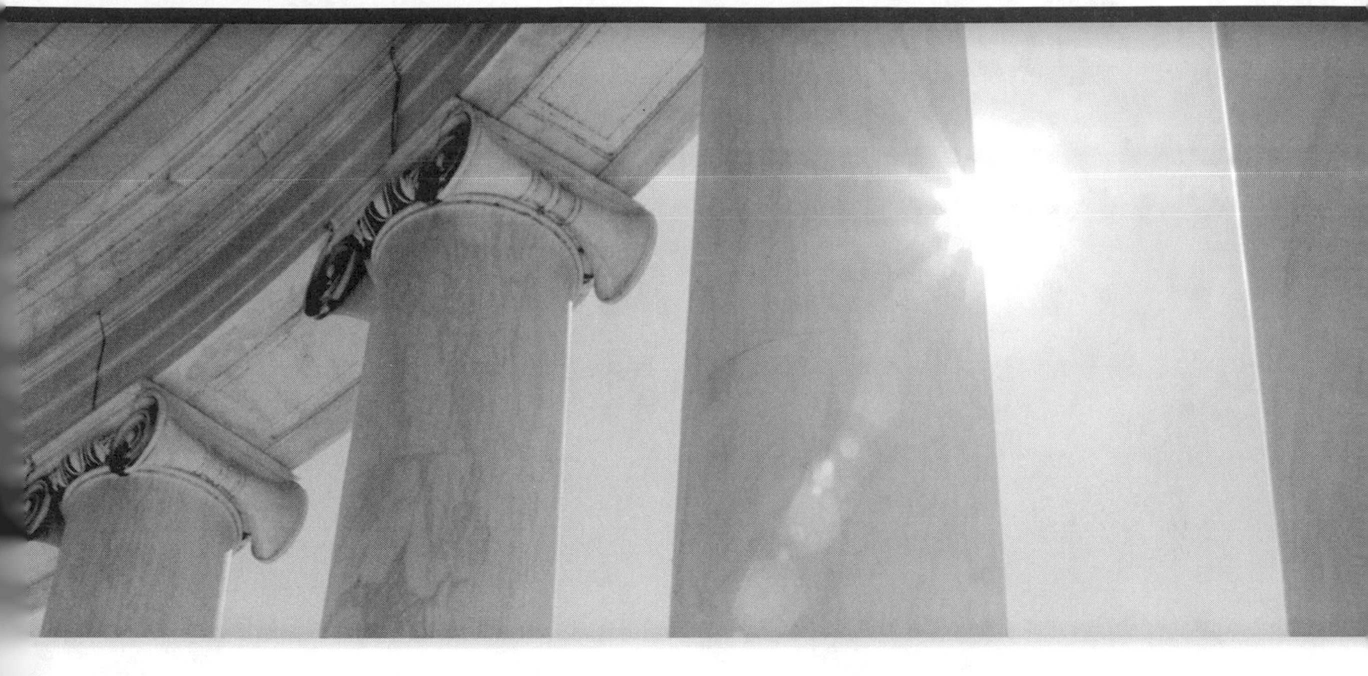

PART IV

Other Useful Information

CHAPTER 19

Command-Line Utilities

This chapter gives an overview of important command line interfaces and utilities available for EM. Most have been mentioned in context throughout this book; this chapter is intended to provide complete information with exact syntaxes and options. We cover in alphabetical order agentctl, nmumigr8, oemapp, oemctl, oemevent, oemutil, ocm, and omsntsrv.

agentctl

Agentctl is used to manage the Agent process and Agent-based blackout functionality. It is new with version 9i and is now used instead of the previous interface lsnrctl (which has been changed to lsnrctl in 9i) through which pre-9i Agents are started, stopped, and checked. You can type agentctl at a command prompt to display the options.

The syntax for the agentctl command is:

```
agentctl start|stop|status|restart [agent]
agentctl start|stop|status  blackout [<target>] [-d/uration <timefmt>]
[-s/ubsystem <subsystems>]
```

The parameters for the agentctl command are

- **start** This parameter starts the Intelligent Agent process called DBSNMP, including the watchdog, a thread that checks if the agent is running and restarts it when necessary. Watchdog has some configuration options, which can be found in Chapter 2 of the *Intelligent Agent User's Guide.* You can optionally add the word `agent` after the command.

NOTE
On Windows-based platforms, you might encounter problems with this command when you enter multiple `agentctl` commands within a short time period. The reason is, that the prompt is returned faster than the actual background operation is completed. You can avoid this by waiting a bit after issuing a command or use NET START Oracle<HomeName>Agent instead to manage the Agent, in which <HomeName> is the name of your Oracle Home directory. You can see the exact name of your Agent service in the services panel of your Windows system.

- **stop** This parameter stops the Agent process. Note that you have to wait until the Agent process is really stopped before issuing more `agentctl` commands or use NET STOP Oracle<*OracleHome*>Agent on Windows-based systems.
- **status** Returns status information on the Agent running on this node. The following example displays version, Oracle Home, and User information in addition to reporting when the Agent process has been started.

```
DBSNMP for 32-bit Windows: Version 9.0.1.0.1 - Production on 04-JAN-2002 09:50:11
Copyright (c) 2001 Oracle Corporation.  All rights reserved.
Version              : DBSNMP for 32-bit Windows: Version 9.0.1.0.1 - Production
Oracle Home          : D:\oracle\v901
Started by user      : SYSTEM
Agent is running since 01/04/02 09:46:41
```

- **restart** This option causes the Agent process to shut down and start back up using one command. Because the Agent discovers its environment only during startup, this command is very useful if you have added services or changed parameters in your environment, and would like the Agent to reflect these changes. After a restart, you can refresh information from this Agent to the console.
- **start blackout** This command starts an Agent-based blackout that can suspend event, job, and historical data collection activities. This makes maintenance or emergency activities easier to perform, because no events are evaluated or triggered. There can only be one active blackout per target at a time. If you need to change blackout parameters, you need to stop an existing blackout and start a new one with modified parameters. Refer to Chapter 2 of the *Intelligent Agent User's Guide* for more information. If you do not use any of the following parameters, all node-related activities are blacked out for an indefinite time:

```
C:\>agentctl start blackout
DBSNMP for 32-bit Windows: Version 9.0.1.0.1 - Production on 04-JAN-2002 10:22:24
Copyright (c) 2001 Oracle Corporation.  All rights reserved.
Blackout started on dschepan-LAP.de.oracle.com, ORACLE_NODE
```

The following parameters are available to start blackouts only for certain targets for a limited time period:

- **[<*target*>]** Specifies the name of the target on the node for which notification shall be suspended, such as v901.de.oracle.com for a database. Defaults to ORACLE_NODE if not provided.
- **[-d <*timefmt*>]** Specifies the duration of the blackout in the format [dd] hh:mm. For example, agentctl start blackout –d 02 01:07 starts a total blackout for the next two days, one hour, and seven minutes.

- **[-s <*subsystem*>]** Restricts the blackout only to a subystem on the target, in which <*subsystem*> can be jobs, events, or collections. For example, agentctl start blackout -d 00:30 -s events starts a blackout on all events on the node for the next 30 minutes.
- **stop blackout** Stops individual blackouts when used with the parameters listed for start blackout. For example, agentctl stop blackout stops all node blackouts; blackouts for the target type database remain intact. Note that a blackout can only be stopped by the user who originally started it.
- **status blackout** This command gives a list of all currently active blackouts. The following example shows three blackouts: Database and Listener have one blackout each for all subsystems, and there is a blackout active on the overall node for the event system only.

```
C:\>agentctl status blackout
DBSNMP for 32-bit Windows: Version 9.0.1.0.1 - Production on 04-JAN-2002 10:52:37
Copyright (c) 2001 Oracle Corporation.  All rights reserved.
Target=v901.de.oracle.com,ORACLE_DATABASE  Subsystem=All Endtime=01/06/02 11:43:39
Target=listener_dschepan-lap.de.oracle.com,ORACLE_LISTENER  Subsystem=All
Endtime=01/04/02 11:39:13
Target=dschepan-LAP.de.oracle.com,ORACLE_NODE  Subsystem=EVENTS Endtime=
01/04/02 11:22:23
```

nmumigr8

Throughout this book, we recommended that you upgrade to the latest version of the Agent to have the most features and functionality available. To do this, you need to install the Agent in a new Oracle Home, switch off the old Agent, and start the new one. If you have events, jobs, and collections active with the old Agent, however, you need to migrate them to the new one. The command-line utility to do this migration for you is called nmumigr8, pronounced "nmumigrate." It can upgrade necessary files from Agent of versions 8.0.6, 8.1.6, or 8.1.7 to Agent version 9.0.1. You can get usage information by entering `nmumigr8 ?` at a command prompt. You must set the ORACLE_HOME environment variable to point to the 9.0.1 Agent's ORACLE_HOME before using nmumigr8. A logfile called nmumigr8.log is generated in the ORACLE_HOME/network/log/ directory. You need to stop the old Agent before migrating.

The syntax for the nmumigr8 command is

```
nmumigr8 [-source_home <source ORACLE_HOME>] [-source_agent_name
<source Agent name>] [-destination_agent_name <destination Agent name>]
[-password <password>] [-verbose]
```

The parameters for the nmumigr8 command are

- **-source_home** Defines the source Oracle Home directory, which contains the .q files of the old Agent and Data Gatherer's data collection files. If you do not supply source_home, the value defaults to the destination Oracle Home, which is set in the *ORACLE_HOME* environment variable.
- **-source_agent_name** This parameter is provided for Windows NT FailSafe configuration and defines the NT service name of which created the source agent state files. It defaults to -destination_agent_name, if not provided.
- **-destination_agent_name** Provides the agent service name of the agent that will use the NT FailSafe state files. It defaults to source_agent_name, if not provided.
- **-password** You can define a custom password used by the Agent to encrypt its queue files. If not supplied, the default encryption password is used.
- **-verbose** Using this option causes detailed migration information to be written to a trace file called nmumigr8.trc located in the ORACLE_HOME/network/trace directory. If you do not use this option, only summary information is written. The trace file is overwritten each time nmumigr8 is run. For example:

```
SET ORACLE_HOME = D:\oracle\v901
nmumigr8 -source_home D:\oracle\v817 -verbose
```

oemapp

The oemapp command is a batch file that allows you to start many of EM's components. If you are mostly using Windows systems, you might not use this command often, because you can start almost everything from the Windows Start menu. Most components are also available on Unix-based platforms, on which you need to use oemapp to start EM. The command is version-specific, which means that it can only start tools in its own Oracle Home directory. If you have multiple homes on your node, you need to make sure to use the correct oemapp.bat.

The syntax for the oemapp command is

```
oemapp <application_name>
```

The syntax of the command is very simple, and the number of parameters and options is limited according to the usage given from the command itself. However, you have a huge number of options to use with this command. Starting tools is just one of them. Table 19-1 lists the possible oemapp.bat parameters with EM9i. Note that some of the listed tools might not be available on all platforms EM is available on. A special command is oemapp oemutil, which is discussed separately later in this chapter.

Parameter	**Description**
capacityplanner (cp on Unix)	Capacity Planner
console or dbastudio	Enterprise Manager Console
cpta	Concurrent Processing Tuning Assistant
dataguard	Data Guard Manager
esm	Enterprise Security Manager
ifsmgr	Internet File System Manager
lmviewer	LogMiner Viewer
oam	Oracle Applications Manager
ocm (ocmcli on Unix)	Oracle Change Manager
performancemanager (pm on Unix)	Performance Manager
opm	Oracle Policy Manager
sdoadvisor	Spatial Index Advisor
security	Security Manager
topsess	Top Sessions
txtmgr	Text Manager
worksheet	SQL*Plus Worksheet

TABLE 19-1. *Parameters for Use with* **`oemapp`**

NOTE
If you do not type any parameter, or if you type a nonexistent parameter or a tool that is not installed, the command simply does nothing on Windows-based platforms. That has been fixed in release 9.2 of EM.

For example, to start the console on any platform, type:

```
oemapp console
```

On Unix platforms, you can also start the console directly in a specified mode:

```
oemapp console oem.loginmode=standalone
oemapp console oem.loginmode=oms oem.credential= username/password@oms
```

oemctl

The oemctl utility is used for a number of administrative commands regarding the OMS. It also affects the event handler, which is part of the OMS, the paging server, and the repository credentials settings. It is also needed to configure the reporting framework. You can get usage instructions by typing oemctl at a command prompt. Note that starting with EM9i, the command changed from oemctrl to oemctl to make it more consistent with other Oracle commands.

The syntax for the oemctl command is

```
OEMCTL START OMS
OEMCTL STOP OMS <EM Username>/<EM Password>
OEMCTL STATUS OMS <EM Username>/<EM Password>[@<OMS-HostName>]
OEMCTL PING OMS
OEMCTL START PAGING [BootHost Name]
OEMCTL STOP PAGING [BootHost Name]
OEMCTL ENABLE EVENTHANDLER
OEMCTL DISABLE EVENTHANDLER
OEMCTL EXPORT EVENTHANDLER <filename>
OEMCTL IMPORT EVENTHANDLER <filename>
OEMCTL DUMP EVENTHANDLER
OEMCTL IMPORT REGISTRY <filename> <Rep Username>/<Rep Password>@<RepAlias>
OEMCTL EXPORT REGISTRY <Rep Username>/<Rep Password>@<RepAlias>
OEMCTL CONFIGURE RWS
```

The parameters for the oemctl command are

- **START OMS** Starts the OMS on the node on which the command is executed.
- **STOP OMS <*EM Username*>/<*EM Password*>** Stops the OMS process on the node on which it is running. You need to provide a valid username and password of an EM super administrator account.
- **STATUS OMS <*EM Username*>/<*EMPassword*>[@<*OMS-HostName*>]** Checks the status of an OMS on a specified node. You must provide valid credentials of an EM administrator account. This does not need to be a super DBA account. The returned information is quite extensive; for example:

```
C:\>oemctl status oms sysman/secret
OEMCTL for Windows NT: Version 9.0.1.0.0
Copyright (c) 1998, 1999, 2000, 2001 Oracle Corporation.  All rights reserved.
The Oracle Management Server on host [ds-lap.us.oracle.com] is functioning properly.
The server has been up for 0 06:47:44.318
Target database session count: 0 (session sharing is off)
Operations queued for processing: 1
Number of OMS systems in domain: 1 (ds-lap.us.oracle.com)
Number of administrators logged in: 2
Repository session pool depth: 15
Repository session count: 7 in-use and 3 available, pool efficiency: 99%
```

- **PING OMS** Checks whether a local OMS is running and responsive.
- **START PAGING [*BootHost Name*]** This option starts the paging server on your Windows-based node, which presents an alternative to starting a paging server through the services panels. You can optionally specify the BootHost parameter, which is used when the machine is equipped with multiple network cards and you want to select the name assigned to a specific network card.
- **STOP PAGING [*BootHost Name*]** Stops the paging server.
- **ENABLE EVENTHANDLER** Activates the event handler feature of the OMS. Note that you need to stop the OMS before you can enable the event handler. Refer to Chapter 6 of the *Oracle Enterprise Manager Administrator's Guide* for more information on the event handler.
- **DISABLE EVENTHANDLER** Deactivates the event handler functionality.
- **EXPORT EVENTHANDLER <*filename*>** Writes the current event handler configuration parameters to a file with the specified path and name.

- **IMPORT EVENTHANDLER <*filename*>** Reads the specified event handler parameter file.
- **DUMP EVENTHANDLER** Displays the current event handler settings.
- **EXPORT REGISTRY <*Rep Username*>/<*Rep Password*>@<*RepAlias*>** Exports OMS repository connection information from the registry to standard output. You can divert the output to a file, for example, by appending >><*filename*> to this command in a DOS box of a Windows-based computer. The output contains a number of internal OMS parameter settings, including the event handler parameters, and should not be manipulated without deeper OMS internal background knowledge.
- **IMPORT REGISTRY <*filename*> <*Rep Username*>/<*Rep Password*>@ <*RepAlias*>** Imports a specified registry parameter file back to the registry.
- **CONFIGURE RWS** This command must be used to configure your reporting framework. It gives verbose instructions, and asks for a number of parameters. It writes the configuration for your Web server, and provides a URL through which you can access EM Reporting. The following is an example:

```
C:\>oemctl configure rws
Configuring the reporting web server...
This command line utility configures a web server on this machine so
that it can be used for Enterprise Manager reporting.  Answer each
prompt and hit return.  After you answer each prompt, you will be
asked for confirmation before the web server is configured.
To quit this utility, hit CTRL-C.
For Help, see EM_ReportingConfig.HTML.

Webserver Name [default is DS-LAP]: DS-LAP
Port number [default is 3339]:3339
Oracle Management Server [default is DS-LAP]:DS-LAP
Password for the REPORTS_USER Administrator : sysman

You have provided all of the information required to configure the
web server. Configure the web server now? [Y/N, default is Y]:Y

CONFIGURATION COMPLETED: The webserver has been successfully
configured. You can now access the Enterprise Manager Reporting Home
Page using the URL http://DS-LAP:3339/ em/OEMNavigationServlet. You
can also access the Reporting
Home page using the View Published Reports menu command in
the Enterprise Manager Console.
```

oemevent

The oemevent utility is an executable that is used in the context of unsolicited events. These are events monitored and raised by EM external or third-party software, and need to be communicated to EM's event system. This way they can use EM's notification system. It needs to be executed by an external mechanism, along with parameters, and is the equivalent to the orareportevent Tcl-verb. The oemevent utility does not offer any usage help.

The syntax for the oemevent command is

```
oemevent <eventname> <object> <severity> <message>
```

The parameters for the oemevent command are

- **<eventname>** This parameter specifies the name of the event, and always needs to be a string of the format /a/b/c/d to reflect an event hierarchy for the event you developed, such as /oracle/rdbms/fault/updown.
- **<object>** Specifies the name of the service for which the event is to be raised.
- **<severity>** Specifies the event severity, and can be a string containing alert, warning, or clear.
- **<message>** Specifies the message to be displayed in the EM console.

NOTE
You need to create and register an unsolicited event of the specified name in the console beforehand. Afterwards, you tell the Agent to raise this event by executing oemevent.

oemutil

The oemutil command is a utility that performs various job-related and event-related tasks. It provides a command-line alternative to performing the same functions from the EM Console for registering and deregistering events or jobs, and changing database passwords stored in the repository. This tool is actually accessible via the oemapp command mentioned previously, but because it contains important functionality unrelated to starting EM tools, and is usually referred to as if it were a separate command, it is mentioned here separately as well. As with oemapp, there is no usage help available with oemutil.

The syntax for the oemutil command is

```
oemapp oemutil <username>/<password>@<oms> <command> <parameters>
```

The parameters for the oemutil command are

- ***<username>*** This parameter specifies a valid EM administrator account. It is the same account used to log into the EM console.
- ***<password>*** The password for the EM administrator account.
- ***<oms>*** The name of the machine running the OMS.
- ***<command><parameters>*** A command to be performed by oemutil with corresponding parameters. The available commands are discussed in the following sections.

omsCredentials

The omsCredentials command logs into an OMS using the username and password for an existing EM administrator account. You mainly need this command before you execute a number of other commands in a batch file using the -cmdfile option, explained later in this chapter. The parameters are the same as described in the previous section.

The syntax of the omsCredentials command is

```
omsCredentials <username>/<password>@<oms>
```

submitJob

The submitJob command allows you to submit an OS job to one or multiple Agents. A successful execution means that the data has been successfully transferred to the OMS. Whether the actual job has been executed successfully needs to be tracked in the console.

The syntax of the submitJob command is

```
submitJob <jobName> <nodeName> <osCommand> <parameters>
```

The parameters for the submitJob command are

- ***<jobName>*** Specifies a name to assign to the job
- ***<nodeName>*** Specifies the name of the node you want the job to be executed on, which must be exactly as displayed in the EM console. The OMS contacts the Agent running on that node and submits the job. Because the Agent is used, all targets specified to be used through oemutil must have been discovered automatically.

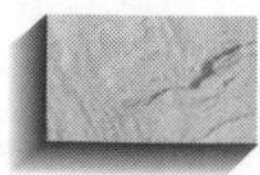

NOTE
You can also specify a group name if you want to submit the job to multiple nodes. You need to submit <groupowner:groupname| oracle_sysman_group>; for example, SYSMAN:allmynodes|oracle_sysman_group. If you use this command directly with the oemutil command and not in a batch file, you must enclose the parameter in double quotes.

- ***<osCommand><parameters>*** Specifies which OS job you want to run with which parameters.

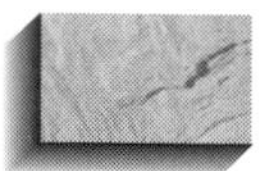

NOTE
This command only submits OS jobs against nodes that are scheduled to be executed right away. To submit new jobs that have a more complex execution schedule or contain targets other than nodes, such as databases, you need to define the job in EM first, save it to the job library and execute a job from the library with the oemutil command submitJobFromLibrary, which is described in the next section.

submitJobFromLibrary

This command enables you to execute a job that has been previously defined in the job library of the EM repository.

The syntax of the submitJobFromLibrary command is

```
submitJobFromLibrary <jobName> <ownerName> <targetName> [<admin to be notified>]
```

The parameters for the submitJobFromLibrary command are

- ***<jobName>*** Specifies the job name exactly as it is defined in the library. If the name has special characters or spaces, you need to use a command file and enclose the name in quotes; for example, "Shutdown Warning Message."
- ***<ownerName>*** Specifies the EM administrator account that owns the job.
- ***<targetName>*** You need to specify a target for the job to be submitted. Targets defined with the job in the library are ignored. You can also submit the job against a group of services the same way as noted in the previous section.

- **[<*admin to be notified*>]** This is an optional parameter, which specifies the EM administrator account who will get the Notify privilege for this job. This admin must at least have the View privilege.

registerEventFromLibrary

The registerEventFromLibrary command allows you to register an event to targets that already exists in the event library of the EM repository. The saved event must at least have one valid target, although the target provided as a parameter will be used.

The syntax of the registerEventFromLibrary command is

```
registerEventFromLibrary  <eventName> <ownerName> <targetName> [<admin to be notified>]
```

The parameters for the registerEventFromLibrary command are

- **<*eventName*>** The name of the event exactly as assigned in the repository.
- **<*ownerName*>** The EM administrator account that owns the event.
- **<*targetName*>** Target name against which the event should be registered. If the event name contains spaces or other special characters, you need to enclose the name in quotes and use the command file option. You can again use a group name instead as outlined previously.
- **[<*admin to be notified*>]** This is an optional parameter, which specifies the EM administrator account who will get the Notify privilege for this job. This admin must at least have the View privilege.

deregisterEvent

The deregisterEvent command allows you to deregister a previously registered event from targets.

The syntax of the deregisterEvent command is

```
deregisterEvent <eventName> <owner> <targetName> <targettype>
```

The parameters for the deregisterEvent command are

- **<*eventName*>** The exact name of the event to be deregistered. Use quotes and the command file option as outlined previously if the name contains spaces or other special characters.
- **<*owner*>** Specifies the EM administrator who owns the event.
- **<*targetName*>** The name of the target as displayed in the EM console.
- **<*targettype*>** Specifies the type of target against which the event is to be deregistered. Table 19-2 lists the valid target types.

Target Type	Parameter
Database	oracle_sysman_database
Node	oracle_sysman_node
Listener	oracle_sysman_listener
Concurrent Manager	oracle_sysman_cmanager
Parallel Server Node	oracle_sysman_ops
Apache Webserver	oracle_sysman_webserver
Standby Database	oracle_sysman_hotstandby

TABLE 19-2. *Valid Parameters for <targettype>*

changeCredentials

The changeCredentials command allows you to change *database* credentials, which are stored as preferred credentials in the repository for specific users.

The syntax of the changeCredentials command is

```
changeCredentials <EM username> <targetName> <user> <password> <role>
```

The parameters for the changeCredentials command are

- ***<EM username>*** Specifies the EM administrator account you want to change preferred credentials for.

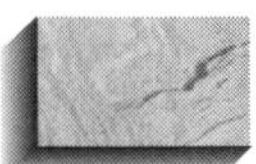

NOTE
You can only change other administrators' credentials if you logged in via omsCredentials using a super DBA account. If you used a normal DBA account, you can only specify your own new credentials.

- ***<targetName>*** Specifies the name of the database you want to change credentials for. If you want to change the default credentials, which are applied by EM for all targets with no specific credentials, use <default> as the target name.
- ***<user>*** Specifies the new database user name in the target database.

- ***<password>*** Specifies the password of the database user in the target database.
- ***<role>*** Specifies the role associated with the database user, and must be NORMAL, SYSDBA, or SYSOPER.

NOTE
We recommend that you apply patch number 1967876, available on MetaLink, to fix bugs number 1967876 (password is displayed in console after changing it via oemutil) and 1891330 (oemutil does not update SYSDBA credentials).

-cmdfile

Use the -cmdfile command if you want to perform several commands in a row. You need to provide the path and filename containing the commands in text format, with each command on one line with its corresponding arguments. Arguments may be quoted if they contain white spaces or other special characters, such as job or event names. You can also use the backslash character (\), such as \" for a literal quote. The commands are executed in the order they are listed, similar to a batch file. Each execution result is displayed to standard output and does not impact the execution of the succeeding commands. That means if one execution fails, the failure is displayed, and the next command in sequence is executed.

The syntax of the -cmdfile command is

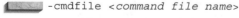

```
-cmdfile <command file name>
```

A sample command file might look like this

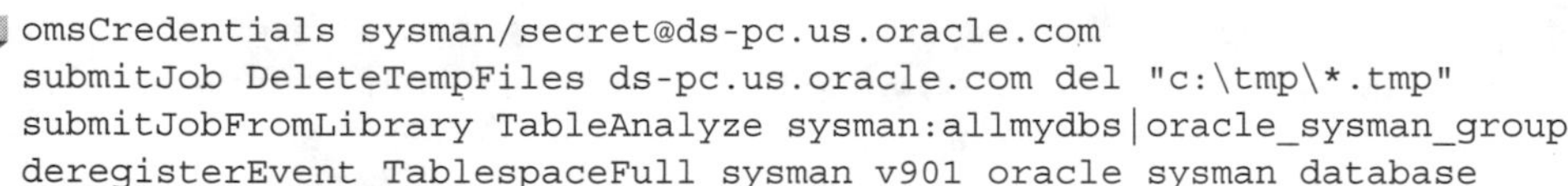

```
omsCredentials sysman/secret@ds-pc.us.oracle.com
submitJob DeleteTempFiles ds-pc.us.oracle.com del "c:\tmp\*.tmp"
submitJobFromLibrary TableAnalyze sysman:allmydbs|oracle_sysman_group
deregisterEvent TablespaceFull sysman v901 oracle_sysman_database
```

ocm

OCM is a command-line interface to be used in conjunction with the Change Management Pack, which is introduced in Chapter 7. It enables you to trigger captures, comparisons, and so on from a command-line interface. You can get usage help by entering ocm at a command prompt.

The syntax for the ocm command is

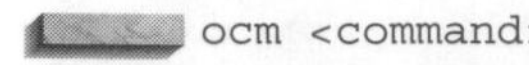

```
ocm <command>
```

The parameters for the ocm command are

- **ocm login <*identity*>** This command prompts you to choose between logging into an OMS or to a standalone Change Manager repository. You need to provide valid credentials for the option you choose. <*identity*> is -idsysman if you want to login as sysman.

NOTE
There is no space between -id and the user name. When <identity> is used in the following command options, it always refers to -id<name>. <identity> is case sensitive.

NOTE
The logon command always asks for credentials interactively. If you combine some of the following commands in a script, you need to logon before you can run the script.

- **ocm logout <*identity*>** Logs the session out of the OMS or the standalone Change Manager repository.
- **ocm capture [<*flags*>] *baseline-spec-name* <*identity*>** This command causes an existing baseline in the repository to be recaptured and stored under the administrator you used in the login command. <*flags*> can be set to -l (for logging) if you want to see the messages that displayed during a baseline creation operation while the capture command is running. If the name of your baseline contains a space or other problematic characters, you must enclose them in quotes. For example:

  ```
  ocm capture -l "my initial dev baseline" -idsysman
  ```

- **ocm compare <*flags*> *comparison-spec-name* <*identity*>** This command enables you to rerun an existing comparison with the same options as mentioned previously.

- **ocm generate <*flags*> *planName databaseName* <*identity*>** This command allows you to generate a script, script summary, and impact report on an existing change plan named *planName*. You need to specify against which database the script, script summary, and impact report should be generated through the *databaseName* parameter. The script will only be generated, not executed. Execution can be managed through the execute command mentioned next. For example:

  ```
  ocm -l "Change Plan 21" v901 -idsysman
  ```

- **ocm execute <*flags*> *planName databaseName* <*options*> <*identity*>** This command allows you to execute an existing script for the change plan *planName* that was generated for the database *databaseName*. You have the following additional options for <*options*>:

  - **-d{forward | backward | cleanup}** The forward option executes the script. The backward option is equivalent to the Undo button, which reverses executed changes. The cleanup option deletes temporary objects that are generated to make an undo possible. This command is the equivalent to the Keep button in the GUI of Change Manager.

  - **-s{cleanup | exit}** This option allows you to specify an action if the script executes successfully. The cleanup option removes temporary objects, equivalent to the Keep button. The cleanup option only makes sense when the script is executed in the forward direction with the -dforward option. When you select exit, the changes made by the script are neither kept nor undone, which means that the script execution stays in a pending status. You need to specify later whether you want to keep or undo the changes to complete the task.

  - **-e{undo | exit}** This option takes action if the script does not execute successfully. You can select undo to undo the changes or exit to leave the script in a pending status. For example:

    ```
    ocm execute "Plan 21" v901 -dforward -scleanup -eundo -idsysman.
    ```

This command executes an existing script in a change plan called "Plan 21," keeps the changes if the script finishes successfully, and undoes the changes if the script returns with an error, all running as user sysman.

omsntsrv

The omsntsrv executable offers some options to control the OMS that are especially useful on Windows platforms. It not only offers an alternative to NET START OMS or OEMCTL START OMS, but also offers commands to manipulate the service definition itself. Use omsntsrv only when the other options (OEMCTL and NET START <*service*>) do not work. You can see the usage options by typing omsntsrv -? at a command prompt.

The syntax for the omsntsrv command is

```
omsntsrv <command>
```

The parameters for the omsntsrv command are

- **-?** Displays command options.
- **-i [*ORACLE_HOME_NAME*] [AUTO | DEMAND]** Installs the OMS service with automatic or manual startup.
- **-u** Uninstalls the OMS service.
- **-s** Starts the OMS service. Forms an alternative to net start <*servicename*>.
- **-x** Stops the OMS service. There is no option to enter super DBA credentials after the command, which are required to stop the OMS. You must enter credentials in the window that opens up, or you must use oemctrl stop oms *admin_user/password*.
- **-d [*ORACLE_SID*] [*ORACLE_VERSION*]** Sets a dependency for the service.
- **-q** Reports if the OMS service is STOPPED or RUNNING.
- **-c [AUTO | DEMAND]** Changes the service to auto or manual startup.

Summary

This chapter explained the most important command-line interfaces and utilities available for EM. We described the syntaxes, options, and parameters for each of them. The next chapter provides information about troubleshooting for EM.

CHAPTER 20

Troubleshooting

In this chapter, we provide some information used for troubleshooting the Management Server (OMS), the EM Client, and the Intelligent Agent components. We do not cover all possible error situations, which might arise from special conditions in your particular environment, such as your OS, network, firewall, or product version dependencies. We do list some of the most common problems that you might encounter when working with EM. These issues are grouped into three areas:

- Troubleshooting the OMS
- Troubleshooting the EM Client
- Troubleshooting the Intelligent Agent

In some situations, it will be difficult for you to place a problem in its correct context, and problems experienced in one area can arise because of problems in one of the other two areas. Because several components are working together and special conditions and privileges must be fulfilled, it can be difficult to narrow down the origin of a particular problem. We recommend that you enable logging and tracing of the different EM components to provide you with as much information as possible about the problem you encounter.

Troubleshooting the OMS

Besides the Intelligent Agent, the OMS plays a central role in your EM environment. In the following sections, we list typical problems as well as explain the reason for each problem and suggest one or more solutions or workarounds. When configuring the Management Server through EMCA (see Chapter 2), problems are typically related to lack of privileges (an account with DBA privileges must be provided) or problems with the access to the EM repository database. When you investigate problems while connected to the OMS, you should enable logging and tracing of the OMS through the parameters specified in the `omsconfig.properties` configuration file. In this way, you (and if necessary, Oracle Support) will get detailed information and error messages.

- **Problem The Management Server does not start.** When you issue a start request for the OMS, either through the oemctl start oms command or on Windows NT or 2000 using the Service panel, the Management Server does not start. On Windows NT or 2000, the errors 2140 and 1067 are typically displayed on the screen. Examine the Eventlog in Windows NT/2000 (Start | Administrative Tools | Eventlog) and look for returned error messages and warnings. Also, check the log files (oms.nohup and oms.log), which by default are located in ORACLE_HOME\sysman\log, for more information.

- **Reason** There can be many different reasons for this problem; check the error message returned in the OMS log file. The obvious reason (if it has been working before) is that the OMS is not able to connect to the EM repository, for example, because the database is down or not reachable through Oracle Net. Another reason could be that the password you entered is invalid. When starting OMS, the bug 1784544 causes the OMS to hang (start takes more than 10 minutes). It will not start at all if your EM repository is stored in an Oracle9i database, which is configured for Shared Server mode (MTS) and the Resource Manager option is enabled.
- **Resolution** Check that you can establish a database connection to the EM repository database as the EM repository owner; for example, using SQL*Plus. If this works, try to start the OMS again. Also, you can repeat the OMS configuration using the "Configure local Oracle Management Server" option in the Enterprise Manager Configuration Assistant (EMCA) as explained in Chapter 2. If you are hitting bug 1784544, the only workaround (at the time of this writing no patch exists) is to disable the Shared Server mode and disable resource management through the database initialization parameter resource_manager_plan.

- **Problem You want to reset the password for SYSMAN.** You have forgotten the password for the OMS super administrator account SYSMAN and want to reset it to the default password again (OEM_TEMP).

  - **Resolution** You have two options for resetting the SYSMAN password. After you have performed one of these options, you will be prompted to change the SYSMAN password at the next logon to the EM Console through OMS. Below the two options are described and examples provided for both:

    1. Run the script vduResetSysman.sql located on the OMS machine in the ORACLE_HOME\sysman\admin directory as the EM repository owner account from SQL*Plus. For example, for the EM repository in the schema OEMREP_CHBSLLAVA in the OEMREP.WORLD database:

```
SQL> connect oemrep_chbsllava@oemrep.world
Enter password: ****************
Connected.
SQL> @F:\Oracle\OraNT9i\sysman\admin\vduResetSysman.sql
1 row updated.
Commit complete.
```

    2. Log on to the EM repository database as the EM repository owner account using SQL*Plus and run the PL/SQL procedure smp_maintenance.reset_sysman. For the EM repository stored in the

schema OEMREP_CHBSLLAVA in the OEMREP.WORLD database, this would look like the following:

```
SQL> connect oemrep_chbsllava@oemrep.world
Enter password: ****************
Connected.
SQL> execute smp_maintenance.reset_sysman();
PL/SQL procedure successfully completed.
SQL> commit;
Commit complete.
```

Troubleshooting the EM Client

When you investigate problems with the functionality of your EM Client (EM Console and management applications), we recommend that you enable logging and tracing of the EM Client as well as the Management Server, when connected to an OMS.

- **Problem EM Console does not appear after you enter your OMS credentials.** You want to launch the EM Console, and choose to connect to an OMS by entering the EM administrator credentials and clicking OK. Nothing happens; the EM Console does not appear, but you do find a jrew.exe process in your task list.
  - **Reason** The reason for this phenomenon is unknown.
  - **Resolution** Resolution on Windows platform (where we have experienced it) is to locate the jrew.exe process (the jre.exe process is the OMS), terminate (kill) it, and then restart the EM Console. The console should now launch correctly after you have provided the credentials.

Problems When Discovering Target Nodes

In this section, we look at two problems related to the automatic discovery process, which you can perform from the EM Console while connected to an OMS.

- **Problem No Targets are discovered when performing automatic discovery in EM.** You discover the target node successfully, but none of its targets are shown in the EM Navigator as you would expect them to be.
  - **Reason** The first step of the automatic target discovery is performed by the Intelligent Agent on the node, when it is started. If the agent does not discover anything on the node, you won't be able see the targets in the EM Console.

- **Resolution** Check that the Intelligent Agent has actually discovered all services located on the target node. See the "Troubleshooting the Intelligent Agent" section later in this chapter for more information.

- **Problem Cannot discover a target node through the EM Console automatic discovery.** It is not possible to discover a target node from the EM Console using the automatic discovery feature (see Chapter 8). You receive the "Cannot resolve name <*hostname*>" (either VD-4065 or VD-4564) error message.
  - **Reason** The OMS cannot resolve the hostname provided for the target.
  - **Resolution** Be sure that the hostname can be resolved; for example, issue a ping <*Hostname*> command from the OMS machine. If it fails, either a DNS modification is required or you can add an entry in the host's file on the OMS machine. Another solution is to use the IP address instead. Ask your network administrator for assistance if you are not comfortable with issues such as DNS and IP addresses.

Job and Event Submission Errors

In this section, we take a look at several problems that occur when you submit EM jobs and events against your targets.

- **Problem You get "VNI-4048: Agent internal error" when submitting an event or job.** When you register an EM event, it gets the Registration Failed status, and displays the output "VNI-4048: Agent internal error (e.g., Out of memory, Operating system error)." EM jobs also get status Failed, and the job displays the same.
  - **Reason** The Oracle Intelligent Agent cannot contact the OMS via ports 7772 and 7773, probably because a firewall is between the Intelligent Agent and the OMS blocking the ports. This can be tested either using the telnet (telnet <Hostname or IP address> <Port>) or tnsping command from the node where the Intelligent Agent resides against the Management Server node. From a command-line prompt on the agent node, use the tnsping command to check the port using tnsping (address=(protocol=tcp)(host=<*Hostname* or *IP Address*>) (port=<*Port*>)). For example, if the OMS resides on the node CHBSLLAVA, you see the following:

```
C:\> tnsping (address=(protocol=tcp)(host=chbsllava)(port=7772))
TNS Ping Utility for 32-bit Windows: Version 9.0.1.2.1 - Production
Copyright (c) 1997 Oracle Corporation.  All rights reserved.
Attempting to contact (address=(protocol=tcp)(host=chbsllava)(port=7772))
OK (740 msec)
```

If you get an error message like "TNS-12541: TNS:no listener," the Intelligent Agent is unable to communicate with the OMS in order to update the job or event status information in the EM Console. Two-way communication between the OMS and the Intelligent Agent must be possible in order for the jobs and events to work. Also, the OMS must be able to contact the Intelligent Agent through the ports 1748 and 1754.

- **Resolution** Open the ports 1748, 1754, 7772, and 7773 on the firewall or place the OMS on the same side of the firewall as the Intelligent Agent.

- **Problem You get a "VNI-2015: Authentication error" when submitting a job.** When you submit an EM job, it gets Failed status and displays the output "VNI-2015: Authentication error."
  - **Reason** In general, this error occurs when the OS account used for the job to log on to the target node does not have the appropriate privileges. On Windows NT or 2000 nodes, this might happen when the OS account is lacking the "Log on as a batch job" privilege. For Windows target nodes, verify that the "Deny logon as a batch job" privilege has not been granted to the OS account as this will override the "Logon as a Batch Job" privilege. Another reason is that the account does not exist or the password is wrong.
  - **Resolution** In general, ensure that the OS account has appropriate privileges on the ORACLE_HOME\network directory. On Windows NT or 2000 platforms, be sure to grant the "Log on as a batch job" privilege to the OS account and be sure the "Deny logon as a batch job" privilege is not granted.
- **Problem You get the "VNI-4022: Bad V1 schedule string" error when submitting an event.** When you register an EM event, it gets Registration Failed status, and the output "VNI-4022: Bad V1 schedule string" is displayed.
  - **Reason** Pre-9i Intelligent Agents do not support the On Day of the Week or On Day of the Month scheduling options.
  - **Resolution** Use a different scheduling option, such as On Interval, or upgrade the Intelligent Agent to 9i.
- **Problem The job stays in Submitted status after having been submitted.** When you submit an EM job, it gets Submitted status and stays in the Active Jobs pane.
  - **Reason** Either the Intelligent Agent on the target node is not running, or it is not able to provide a feedback to the OMS about the job status.

- **Resolution** Check that the Intelligent Agent is running on the target node by pinging it from the EM Console Node properties, for example. It the agent is running, verify that the target node is able to reach the OMS machine through the network and resolve the hostname via DNS.

Issues Concerning the EM Reporting Website

When you work with the EM Reporting Website, there are various errors you might encounter. In this section, we take a look at some of the most frequent ones.

- **Problem Configuring the EM Reporting Website using OEMCTL fails.** When you configure the EM Reporting Website using the oemctl configure rws command (see Chapter 13), the configuration fails with the "CONFIGURATION FAILED" error message.
  - **Reason** As OEMCTL suggests in the error message, the EM administrator used for the EM Reporting Website (REPORTS_USER) still has the default password (oem_temp). Another reason could be that the password you entered is invalid.
  - **Resolution** Repeat the configuration, and be sure to enter the correct password for REPORTS_USER. If it is still the default (because you never changed it), or you are not sure what it is, change the password for the EM administrator REPORTS_USER through the EM Console. Log on to the EM Console as another EM administrator, such as SYSMAN (see Chapter 9). Repeat the configuration of the EM Reporting Website using OEMCTL.
- **Problem The browser does not launch when you choose to view a published report in EM.** When choosing to view a published report from the EM Console, the Web browser does not launch. Either the screen flickers briefly or nothing at all happens.
  - **Reason** This can either be because the parameter user.browser has not been set (especially relevant on Unix and Linux). Another reason, when running on a Windows 2000 or 98 machine can be the 1856434 bug, for which a patch is available (EM_9.0.1_1856434).
  - **Resolution** Sometimes the browser launches when you close the EM Console window. On Unix or Linux platforms, you must add the user.browser parameter to the clientconfig.properties file to point to the Web browser executable (see Chapter 19). If you are running on Windows 2000 or 98, apply the EM_9.0.1_1856434 patch to your client machine.

- **Problem An error is returned when you launch the EM Reporting Website.** When launching the EM Reporting Website to access the (published) Web reports, you get an error message in the Web browser. You either receive the "page cannot be displayed" error, or you get the following error, when accessing the Web server CHBSLLAVA, which you have configured for the EM Reporting Website:

  ```
  "The management server Chbsllava is using a different webserver
  Chbsllava for Enterprise Manager reporting services. This
  webserver CHBSLLAVA will be deconfigured and will no longer
  support Enterprise Manager Reporting. To access Enterprise Manager
  Reports in the future, please use the webserver Chbsllava".
  ```

  - **Reason** If you get the "page cannot be displayed" error, either the Web server used for the EM Website has not been started or it has not been properly configured to run the EM Reporting Website, as described in Chapter 13. The other error message is a result of incorrect capitalization of the server name between the Apache configuration file and what the oemctl configure rws command offers per default as server name. For example, the server name will be written as Chbsllava in the Apache configuration, but the oemctl dialog offers CHBSLLAVA. That causes your reports to fail, because Chbsllava is a different machine than CHBSLLAVA to Apache.

  - **Resolution** If you have configured everything, first check that the Web server and Management Server are running and available. Also, you can search for the ServerName parameter in the Apache configuration file httpd.conf and read its value. This file is typically located in ORACLE_HOME\Apache\Apache\conf if you are using the Oracle HTTP Server. Then, repeat the configuration of the EM Reporting Website to use a specific Web and Management Server (see Chapter 13). Now, specify the hostname as you read it in the httpd.conf file, maintaining the case, instead of accepting the default value provided.

- **Problem An error when accessing the Performance chart in the EM Reporting Website.** This problem is related to the optional Diagnostics Pack, and occurs when you choose to view a chart in the Performance feature for a particular database. The Web browser either hangs or it returns one of the following error messages:

  ```
  DBA-01200: Error: Oracle LOGON failed ORA-01017: invalid
  username/password; logon denied SQL: OCISessionBegin ODG-05271:
  Error: message decode: VP_INITIALIZE_REQ: vppcallbb failed
  ```

```
Internal Server Error The server encountered an internal error
or misconfiguration and was unable to complete your request...
```

- **Reason** The first error typically is because the preferred credentials are not correctly defined for the target database for the REPORTS_USER. The second error can be the result of a bug, where EM cannot connect to the target database with the selected connection options. These options are Direct Connection or Connect through Intelligent Agent.
- **Resolution** Ensure that the credentials for the REPORTS_USER administrator have been defined for all targets accessed through the EM Reporting Website. When you connect to a database, you can specify whether to make a direct database connection from the client or to connect through the Intelligent Agent. Open Performance Manager and choose Set Connection Details from the pop-up menu for the target database. The Database Logon dialog box appears; click the Connection Details button. If the Connection Details button is grayed out, it is because a connection is established. In this case, disconnect first by choosing Service | Disconnect in the pop-up menu for the database. In the Connection Details dialog box, choose the Connect through Intelligent Agent option and click OK. Relaunch the EM Reporting Website and try to access the Performance information for the database.

Troubleshooting the Intelligent Agent

On each target node there must be at least one Intelligent Agent installed and running in order for you to monitor and manage the targets through OMS. An important new feature concerning the Intelligent Agent provided with the 9i release is the Watchdog component. This component monitors the Intelligent Agent process and tries to restart it if it fails for some reason.

In this section, we cover some of the Intelligent Agent issues concerning the operation (starting and stopping) of the agent and target discovery performed by the agent. You should enable logging and tracing of the Intelligent Agent through the parameters specified in the SNMP_RW.ORA file described in the "Intelligent Agent Configuration Files" section in Chapter 19. For more information about how to troubleshoot the Intelligent Agent, refer to Appendix B in *Oracle9i Intelligent Agent User's Guide*.

Intelligent Agent Operational Issues

You might encounter the following problem when starting and stopping the Intelligent Agent process using the agentctl utility.

- **Problem The Intelligent Agent does not respond to the agentctl utility.** When starting the Intelligent Agent using the agentctl command-line interface on Windows NT or 2000, you might experience the error message "Starting Oracle Intelligent Agent... Agent already running."
    - **Reason** Typically, this occurs when you try to restart the Intelligent Agent by issuing the `stop` and `start` commands after each other. The agentctl utility returns the prompt to you before the operation has actually completed.
    - **Resolution** Wait for the agent to stop completely before you issue the start command.

Intelligent Agent Discovery Issues

The Intelligent Agent has the responsibility of discovering all available target types (listener, database, HTTP Server, and so on) on the node where it is running. It relies upon TCP/IP being used as network protocol, and on the existence of Oracle Net configuration files. The discovery is performed *each* time the Intelligent Agent starts, and the information is stored in the Intelligent Agent configuration files (see Chapter 19). For more information about the Intelligent Agent, also refer to the "Intelligent Agent" section in Chapter 1. In the following, we discuss a problem related to agent discovery.

- **Problem Target Databases are not Discovered by the Intelligent Agent.** When you start the Intelligent Agent, it performs target discovery on the node and registers all discovered targets in the services.ora file located in the ORACLE_HOME\network\agent directory and the snmp_ro.ora and snmp_rw.ora files in ORACLE_HOME\network\admin. If these files are empty after the Intelligent Agent has started, it means that no targets were discovered at all.
    - **Reason** There can be several reasons for this. The obvious reason is that you have created one or more services on the node, since the Intelligent Agent was started. The Intelligent Agent utilizes various TCL scripts to perform the discovery when it starts up. It examines the Oracle Net configuration files (listener.ora and tnsnames.ora), in general as well as the oratab file on Unix and Linux and the Registry on Windows NT and 2000. One typical reason for databases not being

discovered is that the Oracle Listener on the target node does not specify the SID in the sid_list_listener section (for the default Listener named LISTENER). From version 8i, this is not required (but still allowed), because the database instance can register itself with the listener. If the sid_list part of the listener.ora file looks like the following (only extproc is included to handle external procedure calls), you are using the automatic instance registration, and the Intelligent Agent will not be able to discover the database instances:

```
SID_LIST_LISTENER =
  (SID_LIST =
    (SID_DESC =
      (SID_NAME = PLSExtProc)
      (ORACLE_HOME = F:\Oracle\OraNT9i)
      (PROGRAM = extproc)
    )
  )
```

- **Resolution** Add a SID_DESC entry to the listener.ora file for each database, like the following for the LBV and OEMREP instances on the CHBSLLAVA node:

```
SID_LIST_LISTENER =
  (SID_LIST =
    (SID_DESC =
      (SID_NAME = PLSExtProc)
      (ORACLE_HOME = F:\Oracle\OraNT9i)
      (PROGRAM = extproc)
    )
    (SID_DESC =
      (GLOBAL_DBNAME = OEMREP)
      (ORACLE_HOME = F:\Oracle\OraNT9i)
      (SID_NAME = OEMREP)
    )
    (SID_DESC =
      (GLOBAL_DBNAME = LBV)
      (ORACLE_HOME = F:\Oracle\OraNT9i)
      (SID_NAME = LBV)
    )
  )
```

You do not need to restart the Oracle Listener for the Intelligent Agent to discover the database, because the Agent will examine the istener.ora file.

Summary

In this chapter, you have been presented with different explanations and solutions to some problems you might experience when working with the Management Server, EM Client, and Intelligent Agent. Besides the Oracle documentation, you will be able to find more information about troubleshooting and tracing the EM components in miscellaneous Oracle Web support sites and newsgroups. This chapter also ends Part IV of this book and is the last practical information you need to assist you in your work with EM.

Glossary

administrator An account that provides access to the EM framework. The account can be either a regular or a super administrator account. Regular EM administrators cannot drop or discover nodes, and may have restricted access to discovered targets or the job and event system. All that can be done by super administrators who create accounts for regular administrators and provide them with access to the individual targets. Having an EM administrator account does not automatically provide access to databases or other targets and should not be confused with a database account.

Advanced Events A set of additional events that are part of the Oracle Diagnostics Pack, Oracle Management Pack for Oracle Applications, and Oracle Management Pack for SAP R/3. These events extend the Event System with specialized monitoring features.

Apache The Web server process used for establishing the Oracle HTTP Server, which is used for the EM Website. The Apache Group is an organization of developers and users that controls development of various open-source products. One of its first products is the Apache Web server, initiated in 1995. Today, the Apache Web server is one of the most used Web servers on the Internet. More information is available at http://www.apache.org.

blackout A setting that disables notification for events for scheduled maintenance and deactivates enhanced notification (paging and e-mail) while the target is down. A blackout can be set up on the Agent level with the agentctl command, or on the OMS level.

Capacity Planner Part of Oracle Diagnostics Pack used for collecting, storing, and analyzing historical data collected from managed databases, nodes, or other targets. It can be extended by the Management Pack for Oracle Applications and the Management Pack for SAP R/3.

Change Management Pack An optional extension to EM to manage changes to database objects. It allows you to compare database objects, create baselines, search for objects, identify differences, synchronize them, and propagate changes across multiple targets. These features can be accessed through Change Manager.

Concurrent Processing Tuning Assistant (CPTA) A component of the Management Pack for Oracle Applications, which is analyzing the information in the FND tables of an Applications Schema.

console The main client user interface of EM which is the first tier in the three-tier architecture. The console can be started as installed application, or run in a Windows-based browser as Java applet. The console can also be run in standalone mode, in which it connects directly to the databases. The standalone console allows a single person to use some of EM's more basic administration tools without requiring an OMS or Intelligent Agent.

Cube Viewer A component in OLAP Management enabling you to browse the data associated with OLAP metadata. A cube is a logical organization of multidimensional data.

Data Definition Language (DDL) SQL statements that define, maintain, or drop objects. DDL statements also include statements that permit a user to grant other users special privileges or rights within the database.

data dictionary A read-only set of tables maintained by the database. It provides extensive information about the associated database.

Data Manipulation Language (DML) SQL statements that manipulate the data inside database objects, such as INSERT, UPDATE, or DELETE statements. Locking a table or view and examining the execution plan of an SQL statement are also DML operations.

Data Guard Manager A component that helps to manage a Data Guard configuration, including the primary and standby databases, including the log transport and log apply services.

Database Configuration Assistant (DBCA) A component that helps to create a database with parameters according to your individual requirements.

DBSNMP The Intelligent Agent executable, and also the default database user account used for the Intelligent Agent to access the database.

Diagnostics Pack An optional extension to EM that monitors databases and other targets, including detecting and diagnosing problems and capacity planning. It includes Advanced Events, Performance Manager, Capacity Planner, and Trace Data Viewer.

discovery Discovery can be split in two phases: *Automatic discovery* done by the Agent during each startup to define a list of all services it can manage, and *target discovery* performed from the console to transfer the list of targets from the Agent to the EM framework so that they are displayed in the Navigator tree of the console.

Directory Manager An integrated tool in EM used for administering most areas of Oracle Internet Directory and its related processes.

Enterprise Manager Configuration Assistant (EMCA) A component that helps in creating a repository to be used by Oracle Management Servers.

Enterprise Security Manager An integrated tool in EM for administering the data inside an LDAP-compliant directory server, such as the Oracle Internet Directory.

Event A notification by the Agent, when the Agent detects a change of status in one or more events the agent is instructed to perform. Such events are usually communicated to DBAs by showing a flag in the console, or via an e-mail or paging message.

Event Handler A component that was introduced with EM version 2.2, and is used to define an EM external activity triggered by the OMS as response to certain event occurrences. It can be used to create trouble tickets automatically, or to propagate event notifications to other management frameworks like Tivoli, HP OpenView, or CA Unicenter.

Event System The system in EM through which events are registered to agents from the EM Console. It is used for proactive monitoring, and gives system administrators time to correct the problem before they affect system performance.

Expert A component of the Tuning Pack that helps with tuning initialization parameters, applications, and database structures.

Explain Plan An access path determined by the query optimizer. It is often used synonymously with Execution Plan.

Export Wizard A wizard that helps export data from a database to a file.

fixit job A job that can be scheduled to run as a response to an event occurrence.

group A logical collection of targets that can be used as a virtual target for more efficient management and administration by addressing group members simultaneously.

Health Overview Chart A chart in Performance Manager of the Diagnostics Pack displaying key metrics of a database and underlying node in real time. The chart offers drill-down capabilities and advice on almost all metrics.

hints Instructions in SQL statements that cause the optimizer to use specific methods when creating an explain plan.

Import Wizard A wizard that helps transfer data from an exported binary file to a database.

Index Tuning Wizard Part of the Tuning Pack that helps to identify and correct index problems.

Intelligent Agent A separate process on a managed node, that communicates with the OMS and is responsible for discovery of targets, running jobs, events, and monitoring.

job A set of administrative tasks run by the Agent on managed nodes.

Job System The system in EM through which jobs are defined and scheduled to be run by the agent.

Lightweight Directory Access Protocol (LDAP) A protocol used with directory services. It enables you to locate organizations, individuals, and other resources such as databases and devices on the Internet or a corporate intranet. Oracle implements LDAP through the Oracle Internet Directory (OID), which replaces Oracle Names.

Load Wizard A wizard that helps transfer data from text files or other formats to an Oracle database.

LogMiner Viewer A tool that helps to analyze online or archived log files.

Management Pack for Oracle Applications An optional extension of EM designed for monitoring and diagnosing the Oracle Applications environment. It extends the Event System, Performance Manager, and Capacity Planner, and contains the Concurrent Processing Tuning Assistant.

Management Pack for SAP R/3 An optional extension of EM designed for monitoring and diagnosing SAP R/3 middle tiers. It extends the Event System, Performance Manager, and Capacity Planner.

notification EM administrators can be notified of the status of jobs and the occurrence of events. The console allows you to define notification options.

Online Analytical Processing (OLAP) A feature that enables you to easily and selectively extract and view data from different points of view. To facilitate this kind of analysis, OLAP data is stored in a multidimensional way. Typically, OLAP is used in the field of data warehousing.

Online Transaction Processing (OLTP) OLTP applications are usually high-throughput, insert/update intensive systems, which can be characterized by constantly growing large volumes of data that several hundred users access concurrently.

optimizer A component in the database that determines the execution path of a SQL statement. There are four modes of optimization available: Rule, Cost-based optimization for response time, Cost-based optimization for throughput, and Choose. For more information, refer to the *Oracle9i Database Performance Guide and Reference.*

Oracle Internet Directory (OID) Oracle's implementation of LDAP, implemented as a set of tablespaces and schemas in an Oracle database, and the Oracle Internet Directory service.

Oracle Management Server (OMS) The OMS is the middle tier of the EM framework. It provides DBA accounts, access to the job and event systems, and manages the flow of information between consoles and agents. You can add additional OMSs to balance workload and use failover mechanisms. All OMSs share a *repository,* which stores all information about your environment.

Outline Editor, Outline Management A component of Tuning Pack that controls the optimizer behavior by modifying and saving the optimizer mode, join order, or index usage to outlines without having to change the statement in the application code.

Performance Manager A component of the Diagnostics Pack for real-time monitoring through graphical charts. Provides advice, drilldowns, and overview charts for various targets.

Policy Manager Manages policies, along with their labels, authorizations, and protected objects for Oracle Label Security.

Program Global Area (PGA) A memory region that contains data and control information for a single process (server or background).

Reorg Wizard Part of Tuning Pack that helps to correct space usage problems by reorganizing database objects.

REPORTS_USER A super administrator account that is used by the EM Reporting framework. Its initial password is set to OEM_TEMP, and has to be changed before it can be used by the reporting framework. It should not be used for common administrator activities.

repository A schema used by the OMS, which can be located in any Oracle database. The name of the schema is the name of this repository, and this name is used throughout the network to identify objects in the repository. The name of the repository must be a unique schema name across the entire managed network.

Simple Network Management Protocol (SNMP) A network protocol that manipulates OIDs. Oracle supports two primitive SNMP operations: get oid, which fetches the value of oid, and getnext oid, which gets the value of the next OID after oid.

SQL Analyze A component of the Tuning Pack that analyzes and tunes problematic SQL statements and generates index recommendations. It also contains the Virtual Index Wizard.

Standard Management Pack An optional extension to EM for users of the Standard edition of the database. It combines several components of the Diagnostics, Tuning, and Change Management packs.

super administrator EM is set up with a default super administrator account called SYSMAN, which can be used for the initial login. The super administrator account is similar to root on Unix or Administrator on Windows NT, and is a user that cannot be deleted or renamed. A super administrator account is used to create other accounts, discover or drop nodes, and grant access to targets for regular administrators.

SYSMAN The initial Super Administrator after creating a repository. Its initial default username is SYSMAN, and its default password is OEM_TEMP.

System Global Area (SGA) A shared memory region that contains data and control information for a database instance. An SGA and the Oracle background processes constitute an Oracle instance. Oracle allocates the system global area when an instance starts, and deallocates it when the instance shuts down. Each instance has its own SGA. Connected users share the data in the SGA. The information stored within the SGA is divided into several types of memory structures, including the database buffers, redo log buffer, and the shared pool. These areas have fixed sizes and are created during instance startup. The appropriate setting of SGA parameters affects efficient utilization of memory. Examples of these parameters include the db_block_buffers and shared_pool_reserved_size parameters.

Tablespace Map A component of the Tuning Pack for analyzing tablespace usage.

target A managed process or system in the EM framework that can be selected as the object for administrative activities such as jobs or events. Examples for targets are nodes, databases, and listeners.

TopSessions A chart in Diagnostics Pack to identify the database sessions causing the biggest impact on performance.

Trace Data Viewer A component of the Diagnostics Pack used for formatting, viewing, and analyzing database trace data.

Transparent Network Substrate (TNS) A foundation technology that works with any standard network transport protocol. It is built into the Oracle Net foundation layer, which is a networking communication layer responsible for establishing and maintaining the connection between the client application and server, as well as exchanging messages between them. Although TNS is a concept introduced with SQL*Net V2, it has survived several Oracle Net versions and is still used in connection with the Oracle Net Listener (TNS Listener) or Net Service Name (TNS alias).

Tuning Pack An optional extension to EM used to optimize database performance. Components of the Tuning Pack are SQL Analyze with Virtual Index Wizard, Expert, Tablespace Map, Reorg Wizard, Index Tuning Wizard, and Outline Management.

unsolicited events Events that are not monitored and triggered by EM, but from another monitoring mechanism, but propagated to EM's event system. The Agent needs to be instructed to listen for unsolicited events, and the external mechanism needs to use the oemevent command.

Virtual Index Wizard Part of the Tuning Pack in SQL Analyze that helps you estimate the usefulness of a new index without actually creating it.

watchdog A new process with 9i that monitors the Intelligent Agent and tries to restart it in case of an error.

Workspace Management A component in the console to version-enable tables and create, modify, refresh, and merge workspaces. It is an area in which multiple data versions are stored in the database as different workspaces. Users can create new versions of data while maintaining a copy of the original data.

Index

A

B

C

D

E

F

G

J

L

M

N

O

P

Q

R

T

U

V

INTERNATIONAL CONTACT INFORMATION

AUSTRALIA
McGraw-Hill Book Company Australia Pty. Ltd.
TEL +61-2-9417-9899
FAX +61-2-9417-5687
http://www.mcgraw-hill.com.au
books-it_sydney@mcgraw-hill.com

CANADA
McGraw-Hill Ryerson Ltd.
TEL +905-430-5000
FAX +905-430-5020
http://www.mcgrawhill.ca

GREECE, MIDDLE EAST, NORTHERN AFRICA
McGraw-Hill Hellas
TEL +30-1-656-0990-3-4
FAX +30-1-654-5525

MEXICO (Also serving Latin America)
McGraw-Hill Interamericana Editores S.A. de C.V.
TEL +525-117-1583
FAX +525-117-1589
http://www.mcgraw-hill.com.mx
fernando_castellanos@mcgraw-hill.com

SINGAPORE (Serving Asia)
McGraw-Hill Book Company
TEL +65-863-1580
FAX +65-862-3354
http://www.mcgraw-hill.com.sg
mghasia@mcgraw-hill.com

SOUTH AFRICA
McGraw-Hill South Africa
TEL +27-11-622-7512
FAX +27-11-622-9045
robyn_swanepoel@mcgraw-hill.com

UNITED KINGDOM & EUROPE (Excluding Southern Europe)
McGraw-Hill Education Europe
TEL +44-1-628-502500
FAX +44-1-628-770224
http://www.mcgraw-hill.co.uk
computing_neurope@mcgraw-hill.com

ALL OTHER INQUIRIES Contact:
Osborne/McGraw-Hill
TEL +1-510-549-6600
FAX +1-510-883-7600
http://www.osborne.com
omg_international@mcgraw-hill.com

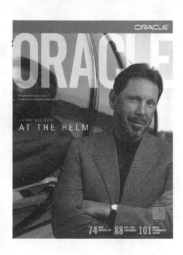